The Canadian Kennel Club

BOOK *of* DOGS

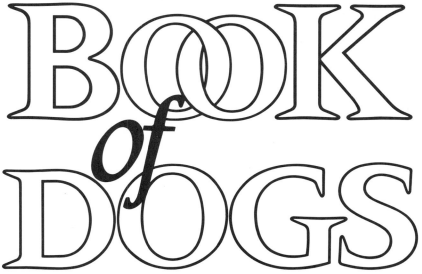

The Canadian Kennel Club

BOOK *of* DOGS

THE OFFICIAL PUBLICATION OF THE CANADIAN KENNEL CLUB

General/*Toronto*

First published in 1982 by
General Publishing Co. Limited,
30 Lesmill Road,
Toronto, Canada
M3B 2T6

Second printing

DESIGN: Brant Cowie/Artplus Ltd.

CANADIAN CATALOGUING IN PUBLICATION DATA

Canadian Kennel Club.
Canadian Kennel Club book of dogs

Includes index.
ISBN 0-7736-0104-X

1. Dogs—Standards—Canada.   2. Dog Breeds—Canada.
I. Title.

SF426.C36   636.7'1'0971   C82-094178-6

Printed and bound in Canada

G. Ellwood Smith
1929 — 1981

This First Edition of *The Canadian Kennel Club Book of Dogs* is dedicated to Mr. G. Ellwood Smith in recognition of the effort he put into the realization of this book, an undertaking he piloted almost to completion.

Mr. Smith was a breeder, judge, and CKC Director for Manitoba at the time of his death, and his work towards the betterment of the CKC and pure-bred dogs in Canada left a lasting impression on all who met him.

Contents

The Breeds   *50-750*
  Breed Histories
  BY JOAN K. MORDEN

FOREWORD

In this book, The Canadian Kennel Club has produced a definitive, readily accessible reference text which will be read and appreciated for many years to come by all who have an interest in purebred dogs in Canada.

Publication of The Canadian Book of Dogs fills a long felt need for information concerning all aspects of the Canadian purebred dog fancy, particularly activities falling under the jurisdiction of The Canadian Kennel Club. Before now, copies of the Canadian breed standards have been available to a rather limited public of breeders and judges with a specialized interest in dogs and dog breeding. Kennel Clubs in other parts of the world have produced volumes catering to a more general interest in dogs, but until now no Canadian source of similar information has existed.

The Book of Dogs includes not only the complete breed standards for all breeds currently recognized by The Canadian Kennel Club, but visual presentations of the ideal in each breed, by noted Canadian artist Gertrude Stenhouse, and colour photographs of many outstanding Canadian dogs. As well, an extensive activities section provides a wealth of information concerning the multi-faceted world of purebred dogs.

The Canadian Kennel Club is to be congratulated on the preparation and publication of this informative, comprehensive, and highly enjoyable book. Its contribution to the knowledge, understanding and appreciation of purebred dogs must not be underestimated. Today, and in the future, The Canadian Book of Dogs will be valued by everyone with an interest in purebred dogs, not only in Canada but around the world.

Governor General of Canada

Acknowledgements

The Canadian Kennel Club gratefully acknowledges the assistance and efforts of:

Patricia H. Allinson, Co-ordinating Editor
E. D. Bonnyman
Monica J. Briggs
Sandy Briggs
Norman F. Brown
Dorothea Daniell-Jenkins
Paula B. Ewles
Leah Harrington, Editor of Breed Standards
Lorna Jackson
Betty McHugh
William Moore
Joan K. Morden, Author of Breed Histories
Roberta Pattison, Editor of Glossary
David E. Ring, Editor
John C. Ross, Editor of Glossary
Gertrude Stenhouse, Illustrator
Margaret Thomas
S. M. Weir and C. Gardiner, Poodle anatomical sketch
Committee for the Publication of a Breed Standards Book:
   John C. Ross, Chairman
   Sandy Briggs
   Evelyn Kenny
   Flora Mackenzie
   Marian Wait
All persons who served on committees to review sketches
All clubs and members who assisted with sketches
CKC staff.

The CKC wishes to thank the owners of the colour photographs contained in this book, who have contributed to the success and appeal of this publication through their paid displays.

The Canadian Kennel Club

*T*HE **CANADIAN KENNEL CLUB** (CKC) is a membership organization, and is incorporated under the Livestock Pedigree Act as the sole registry body for pure-bred dogs in Canada, as well as having jurisdiction over all official dog show and trial events held in Canada.

The CKC operates under its By-Laws and amendments to these By-Laws can only come about by Referendum voted in by the cross-Canada membership, and by obtaining final approval from the Minister of Agriculture.

In accordance with the By-Laws, the CKC encourages the development of pure-bred dogs by:

—keeping records and issuing certificates of pedigree registration of all recognized breeds of pure-bred dogs
—collecting, preserving and publishing data, information, and documents relating to pure-bred dogs
—carrying out a system of registration as may be found satisfactory to the members and in accordance with the By-Laws
—establishing standards of breeds
—adopting and enforcing rules and regulations governing dog shows, racing, coursing, obedience trials and field trials for pure-bred dogs where the clubs or associations staging such events desire to hold same under said rules and regulations of the Club
—adopting means to encourage and assist persons engaged in activities referred to in these objects
—compiling statistics and furnishing official and authentic information in respect to pure-bred dogs
—assisting, in all ways possible, any activity involving dogs intended to further and/or protect the property and interests of the country and its inhabitants
—assisting any activity where those interested in pure-bred dogs desire to associate with those interested in other pure-bred livestock for the purpose of furthering the interests of their respective breeds or species

—and in such other ways permitted by the Livestock Pedigree Act, and as it may seem fit, encourage, guide, and advance the welfare of pure-bred dogs and their owners.

The Official Organ of the CKC is published monthly and forwarded to every member as part of the magazine *Dogs in Canada*. Members thereby receive a top-quality magazine, in addition to the CKC information on upcoming events, show and trial results, amendments to rules, etc.

It has long been felt that the CKC was overdue in publishing a quality book that would appeal to breeders, exhibitors, and the general public alike. *The Canadian Kennel Club Book of Dogs* is not just a book of breed standards. Many articles have been prepared especially for this book, including histories of the CKC, the breeds, the magazine, and dogs as companion to man in Canada. Two Canadian veterinarians have prepared a comprehensive and valuable section on the proper care for, and management of, your dog. In the coming pages we have set out procedures for buying and registering pure-bred dogs, as well as outlines of each show and trial activity.

We hope you find this, the First Edition of *The Canadian Kennel Club Book of Dogs*, to be both informative and enjoyable.

Organization of The Canadian Kennel Club

Patron: His Excellency
The Right Honourable
Edward Schreyer, CC, CMM, CD,
GOVERNOR GENERAL OF CANADA

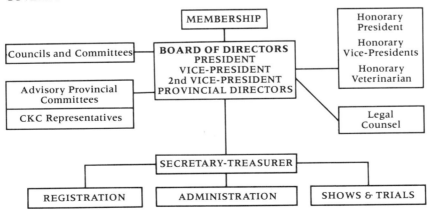

A History of
The Canadian Kennel Club

Beginnings

By the 1880s, firm interest in pure-bred dogs in Canada was indicated by a proliferation of dog shows held in Saint John, Montreal, Toronto, and London, and in Manitoba. With the formation of the American Kennel Club in 1884, these shows were held under AKC rules, and pure-bred dogs were registered with that club. By 1887 it seemed obvious that a national Canadian club was needed and the following year, at a general meeting held at Tecumseh House in London, Ontario, The Canadian Kennel Club was formed. The purposes of the Club were to promote the breeding and exhibiting of "thoroughbred" dogs in Canada, to formulate rules for the governing of dog shows, to recommend suitable judges, and to open a registry for pure-bred dogs. Most of the officers elected were from Ontario. Richard Gibson of Delaware, Ontario was the President and C.A. Stone of London was the Secretary. Two of the Vice-Presidents came from Quebec and one from Winnipeg. By 1889, the fledgling Club had its own official publication, *The Kennel Gazette*, which was printed as a supplement to *The Canadian Poultry Review*.

A close relationship developed between the AKC and CKC. The American Kennel Club agreed to allow dogs to be exhibited on both sides of the border without requiring registration in both national stud books. Both clubs would uphold suspensions and expulsions of members. The AKC cancelled the first part of this arrangement in 1894, but continued to recognize CKC suspensions and expulsions.

In the first year, membership rose from fourteen to seventy, and registrations reached 350. Registrations were free to members, and only members could register dogs with the Club. The first dog registered was the Club Secretary's winning English Setter, Leicester. By 1891 there were 847 registrations. That same year, five new clubs were formed and held shows at Montreal, Kingston, Ottawa, Toronto, and Hamilton. Entries at

4 HISTORY OF THE CKC

these shows were large, 733* at Toronto in 1892, and individual kennels entered quite a number of dogs (for example, twenty-four came from one breeder in Boston).

Quite early in the CKC's existence, financial crisis, caused by a sudden drop in membership, put the Club in the red, and a decision was made to return to the AKC, which assumed responsibility for registrations and holding dog shows. At the same time, the CKC President was charged with misdemeanour and in turn laid counter-charges of libel. Six months later things seem to have been straightened out and the membership requested the cancellation of the agreement with the AKC. The running of the Club was not the only point of conflict, for the choice of judges at the shows provoked criticism. By 1896, the By-Laws, Constitution, and Dog Show Rules had been revised. At this time numbered armbands for exhibitors were introduced to identify dogs to the judges. Championships were awarded somewhat differently from today. A dog had to win four Winners classes, two of which were at shows having 400 or more entries, or failing that, had to have won $500 in cash prizes. The regions of British Columbia and Manitoba were allowed lower limits of 200 entries or $300 in prizes. The previous system had been modelled on the Challenge Certificate system, which was then in use in the States. Provisions were made for those dogs which had already acquired certificates to be credited towards their championship.

A number of "firsts" occurred around the turn of the century. The first Field Trial under CKC rules was held near Chatham in 1889 with a total of twenty-three entries, six coming from Michigan. Listing fees for shows were adopted, and the members were to receive the *Gazette* and Stud Book as part of their membership fee. Women members were allowed to speak at meetings in 1903. That same year saw the first dog show with 1000 entries held at Toronto. At that time, major entries came from St. Bernards, Bloodhounds, Great Danes, Russian Wolfhounds, English Pointers, English Setters, Cocker Spaniels, Poodles, Bulldogs, and Bull Terriers. The largest entries came from Boston Terriers, Fox Terriers, and Irish Terriers. Toy Spaniels were right up at the top as well.

---

*It should be remembered that a single dog entered in three classes at a show would count as three "entries." This practice was similar in England where a dog could be entered several times; the prize money did often pay for the dog's expenses.

The revisions to the organization of the Club in 1906 brought it closer to what we know. There was a President, First and Second Vice-President, and one Vice-President from each province. In the same year, the revision of the Dog Show Rules introduced the "10 points under the two judges system" for awarding championships. At the same time, Canada was divided into two regions at Port Arthur, with the number of dogs needed for point wins fewer in the west. Points were decided on the total number of dogs benched in the show rather than entered in the breed. It is interesting to note that the breeds recognized included Chinese Crested and the Russian Owtchar (Sheep Dog).

It would seem that by the time the name of the official publication was changed to *Kennel and Bench* in 1912, the CKC was well established as the national club for Canada. However, western dissatisfaction with the eastern "establishment" in power at the CKC was partly responsible for the formation of the Dominion Kennel Club in Winnipeg in 1913. Despite efforts to bring the two clubs together, the CKC formulated a rule which forbade members to officiate at a show not held under CKC rules. As many as thirty-five members, some of long standing, were disqualified.

Nevertheless, the CKC was not in a good position financially, and had failed to publish its Stud Book for 1892–1896. Between 1913 and 1915 a state of war existed between the two clubs, and records indicate that the CKC was on the losing side. In 1914 the Dominion Kennel Club made application for incorporation under the Live Stock Pedigree Act to the federal Department of Agriculture, and in 1915, the CKC followed suit. It was left to that body to decide which club would represent dogs in Canada, and, in April 1915, the CKC was incorporated under the Act. So ended the first years of the Club. Incorporation under the Live Stock Pedigree Act ensured that The Canadian Kennel Club would survive and prosper.

The Middle Years

With the incorporation of The Canadian Kennel Club under the Live Stock Pedigree Act, the registration office was moved to Ottawa where, in common with most other pure-bred livestock clubs, registrations were recorded at the National Livestock Records Office. Success against the Dominion Kennel Club came at a time when war was disrupting the normal life of the times. While Canada was not affected too badly, English shows were cancelled, and many good dogs found their way to North America. A number of the working breeds were imported at this time, including Alsatians, later known as German Shepherds.

When the First World War ended, dog show activities resumed their growth. The familiar ribbon colours were established, although a white ribbon was awarded for Reserve Winners, and no fourth placing existed. The next major change in the dog show system saw the introduction of the Group level. Previously, all Best of Breed winners could enter the Best in Show class. The Groups proposed were five: Sporting, Working, Terrier, Toy, and Non-Sporting; Best of Breed winners could be entered into competition at the Group level for a higher fee, should the show-giving club choose to charge one. Confusion invariably erupted as the following account of show activities in 1929 describes:

At shows where ring space is invariably small, the existing arrangement is provocative in the extreme. The procession moves on. A Shepherd Dog takes a snap at a Peke, or vice versa. Nose to tail they go, and if anyone stops, the others seem to pile up, and there is trouble from the start. In the ring there may be a score or more that have no earthly chance to be placed ... twenty-seven dogs would be the most that could come together to have their ''Best'' selected ... With these groups coming together in this impressive grouping, there would be impressive interest sustained as the show was nearing its close. Then as the five animals selected from the Groups came together for the Best Dog in Show, all breeds, there would be sensible ring room. The judges would have at least a chance to see the virtues of the selected five, and to rate their qualities conveniently and accurately. The interest would be sustained until the very last moment of judging, and much of the unrest so noticeable at most shows amongst the exhibitors would disappear.

With the exception of the limit of twenty-seven on the number of breeds represented in the largest group, the suggestions made in 1929 seemed quite sensible. By 1931, regulations were established for the licensing of judges, although handlers were not yet to be licensed. Ear-cropping, too, was accepted. Amendments were made much more rapidly than in later years. All that was required was a Notice of Motion to the Secretary before the Annual General Meeting. The proposer would find a seconder at the meeting, the item would be discussed by those present, and be either passed or rejected. However, during the discussions, the original motion might be amended so many times as to become unrecognizable, and often the parties with the greatest stamina saw their wishes prevail.

The first Field (Obedience) Trial held under CKC rules was in 1932. The tests that were run were the forerunners of what we know today as Obedience Trials. Evidently the basics of the sport were not well established, and considering the rapid way in which rules could be changed at the Annual General Meetings, sometimes even the judges were confused. However, progress was made in 1933 with the division of the Puppy class at dog shows into Junior and Senior, and the addition of the Best of Winners class.

Although pure-bred dogs had been registered under the Live Stock Pedigree Act for twenty-one years, no attempt had been made to enforce the provisions in the Act for the identification of the individuals registered. The matter was brought up in 1938, and not since the early years of the Club had an issue provoked such dissension. Club members had a choice of charting (identifying by colour markings), noseprinting, tattooing, or writing a detailed description of colour and markings. During World War II, nickel requirements for the war effort were such that tattooing equipment could not be manufactured and in the emergency, the CKC reverted to the practice of simply describing colours of a dog. Identification was reinstated in 1948 with two acceptable methods—tattooing and noseprinting. It is interesting to note that one of the great advantages accorded Canadian breeders today in contrast to breeders in other lands is the fact that individual identification makes it very difficult to switch papers or even to steal tattooed dogs. Perhaps ease of identification is the reason tattooing has recently become more popular than noseprinting.

At the turn of the decade, *Kennel and Bench* became *Dogs in Canada*. Also by this time Sporting (Hounds) had been inserted as Group 2 at the dog shows, and several breeds had changed groups—for instance, Standard Poodles left the Working Group and were added to the Non-Sporting Group. As well, Cockers were separated into English and American and interbreeding was prohibited. The Second World War brought rationing to Canada, and those wishing to show their dogs had to plan their outings very carefully. It was especially frustrating to travel by rail, for military personnel had priority, and exhibitors could find themselves stranded, sometimes for days.

At the end of the war, the Board decided not to publish the Club minutes in *Dogs in Canada*, thus making it very difficult for readers today to follow what was happening. Publication of the minutes resumed in 1948. Professional handlers also were licensed by the CKC and had to pay a fee after 1948. Immediate post-war dog show activity increased so rapidly that the Board felt it necessary to have a representative whose duties were to attend dog shows and field trials, to give assistance to the officials in the running of the events according to CKC rules, as well as to observe and report infractions of those rules to the Board. The representative was also to assist in forming new clubs.

One change to the Dog Show Rules, which specified that a dog show must not last more than one day, resulted in the loss of some of the most prestigious shows such as at the Royal Winter Fair in Toronto. The multiple show was later reintroduced for a few years, but the association with the great Agricultural Fairs had been weakened. Eventually, dog shows reached such a size that very few venues could be found which could house both a dog show and a fair. Those exhibitors who remember moving into the horse stalls immediately after the horses moved out seldom regret the change.

By the early 1950s, another financial crisis, accompanied by a major redraughting of the Constitution (which was not accepted by the Minister of Agriculture), resulted in the raising of most fees, the imposition of the recording fee, and the postponement of the Stud Books for 1948–1951. The redraughted Constitution allowed the club to apply for bank loans, and introduced voting by referendum ballot. However, no one was willing to run for President in 1952, and the Vice-President had to run the Club until he was appointed President at the Annual General Meeting of that year. From that point on, the Club's fortunes improved, and the late fifties saw the start of a sustained rise in membership and registrations.

The Recent Decades

Expansion, crisis, and reorganization have been the concerns of the CKC in the last two decades. An increasingly urban population in Canada, with money to spend, especially in the sixties, saw interest in dogs spreading to all sorts of people from all social classes. Just as Canada became a multicultural country, so the dog world saw an increase of fanciers of varying ethnic backgrounds.

The increase in members and registrations brought about certain changes. Not the least of these changes was the attempt by the CKC, with the encouragement of Canada's Commissioner of Languages, to ensure that all regulations, By-Laws, and Breed Standards were available in French. The whole aspect and character of dog shows changed as the unbenched show superseded the benched show. The exhibitors at benched shows had to be prepared to come early and stay late. They made many friends, often discovered an interest in other breeds and groups, and occasionally sold a puppy or two to spectators. At the same time, by bench displays, they promoted their breeds. However, benching required a large investment from the show-giving club. Staying all day at the show meant an investment in time which many exhibitors were not prepared to make. The increasing size of the shows meant that fewer and fewer buildings could be found to house the show. As a result of all these factors, and considering the trend in the States, the unbenched show became the norm. Exhibitors no longer had to line up to "go through the vet." They needed arrive only fifteen minutes before the scheduled ring time, and could depart immediately afterwards if not needed for further judging. While most of the problems of overcrowding were relieved, the unbenched show has resulted in a much more fragmented dog show fancy. Relatively few exhibitors stayed to engage in those long, satisfying talks about dogs in general which were the start of so many of our all-round judges and knowledgeable breeders. While the dog show fancy increased in numbers, some quality was lost, and novices had to find other routes to experience. Gone also was the casual attitude towards running the show. At the start of the sixties, many of the larger shows ran overtime, with some of the Best in Show judging lasting until the small hours of the morning. However, because exhibitors depended upon a judging schedule to know when to arrive, this situation could not be allowed to continue. Increasingly, the shows saw professionals—superintendents, show secretaries, stewards, handlers, and even judges—and the CKC had to regulate all aspects of show procedure.

One of the changes most effective in keeping the shows on schedule was to limit the judges to 175 dogs per day. A Dog Show Council was set up along the lines of the Obedience and Field Trial Councils. Attempts were made to bring uniformity to the measuring of height and weight of dogs. The first *Book of Breed Standards* was published in 1962. A standard form for premium lists was set up. Finally, after a great deal of discussion, new Dog Show Rules appeared in 1971. Some of the major changes made to these rules restricted the Specials Only class to Champions of record; eliminated the separate Best of Winners class, and introduced the awards of Best Puppy in Breed, Group, and Show. A show-giving club had the option of awarding Best Canadian Bred Puppy or Best Puppy. Best Canadian Bred in Breed, Group, and Show also became optional. One might argue that making the Canadian Bred Awards optional was the result of the coming of age of Canadian dog breeding, for we no longer needed the protection of a special award to distinguish our dogs from the American competition. Americans could no longer count on coming over the border and picking up a Canadian championship in a weekend or two.

A further change in the sixties was the addition of the Miscellaneous Class for rare breeds. The object of this class was to allow the promotion of a rare breed within the dog show. To offer this class was an option for the show-giving club, and in some areas it never became popular. Nevertheless, a steady stream of new breeds was accepted, such as the Akita, Tibetan Terrier, Finnish Spitz, Bernese Mountain Dog, and Pharaoh Hound, to name only a few.

As well as new breeds, new aspects of dog sports were accepted. Junior Kennel Clubs and the regulation of the Junior Handling Competition at dog shows were started. The purpose of the Junior Kennel Club was to serve as a training ground for the future leaders in the dog world. They were to promote training in dog show handling, obedience and field trial training, and education in the care of the dog. The sport of lure coursing was accepted under the CKC umbrella in 1982.

The expansion of the sixties also brought problems. The membership had increased from 529 in 1915, to 2610 in 1946 and 6588 by 1968. In turn, registrations had increased over the same period to 48,910 individual dogs registered in 1968. By 1967, the increasing number of registrations had led to a very slow turnaround. Where registering a dog normally took less than a month with the AKC, delays of two or three months were not unusual with the Canadian National Livestock Records Office. In addition, members were concerned that the Stud Book records at the Livestock Records building in Ottawa were in danger of destruction by fire.

A committee was formed to look into data processing for registrations, and by 1969, Project Candor was approved. The decision was made to remove the responsibility for registering pure-bred dogs from the Livestock Records Office and to consolidate all operations at the CKC head office in Toronto. The CKC was not the first organization to be driven to the verge of bankruptcy by the attempt to automate its record keeping. Unfortunately for the CKC, Project Candor coincided with the start of the inflationary spiral in Canada's economy. Expenses rapidly outstripped income, and the membership turned down a fee increase. Many economies had to be instituted, among them the reduction of the CKC minutes published in *Dogs in Canada*. That magazine went to tabloid format. The Club could no longer publish an annual Stud Book, and the information given on registration papers was reduced. As had been traditional in the history of the CKC, a hard core of members rallied around the President, the Secretary-Treasurer and the Registrar, and worked feverishly to put the Club back on a financial even keel. During the crisis, of course, registrations fell way behind, and the CKC gained a reputation in the public's mind which it has not yet entirely lived down. There were several changes in the system before the most efficient means to register dogs was found, and all concerned felt an immense sense of accomplishment and, may we say, relief, when the Registrar was able to report registrations current in 1976.

Even before the registration crisis, the expansion in membership and workload prompted the Board in 1965 to hire outside consultants to do a management study. *Their* conclusion was that CKC operations had grown to the extent that "staff operations frequently get out-of-hand, with a serious lack of cost consciousness and a lack of proper systems and work flow." Diligent efforts on the part of the office staff were no longer sufficient. The report also stated, "many decisions are being made by routine personnel, which should probably be referred to higher authority, because they are exceptional items, while at the same time, the Secretary-Treasurer is being loaded with a mass of detail, much of which could be passed on as routine functions to others." They commented not only on the organizational structure of the main office, but also on the "image" of the CKC— not just on efficiency, but also on the good of dogs—since "the Canadian Kennel Club *is* dogdom in Canada." Major recommendations were that the CKC automate as many systems as possible; that the Secretary-Treasurer be freed for long-range planning, and that much of the detailed work go to an Assistant Manager; that specialized areas such as Shows and Trials or Public Relations be separated out into their own departments; and that many of the nitty-gritty details which were taking up the time of the Board be given over to an Executive Committee. The difficulties encountered with Project Candor interfered with the carrying out of these recommendations in the short run. Fifteen years later, however, both automated registrations and the streamlining of office systems are in evidence.

Despite the observations on the part of the management consultants, it is clear from the published financial statements that a few positive steps were taken during this period. With the exception of a minor change in the membership fee when provision was made for Associate Members, no other fees were increased between the years 1953 and 1970. The Club's net worth increased from $15,000 in 1952 to $136,000 at the end of 1964. The Club published Stud Books for the years 1949–54, filling gaps during the time the books were not published. In 1962 the Club provided every Ordinary Member with a free copy of the CKC's first *Book of Breed Standards*.

One referendum vote produced a crisis for the Board itself. Since dog shows rely on judges, and conformation judges make their decisions without scoring as is the case in Obedience, ringside spectators can often be heard questioning both the judge's knowledge and honesty. Regulations in these years gradually isolated the judges from even the appearance of outside influence, and separated the running of the show from the judging of it. Nevertheless, Board members were often active at shows, and in keeping with the trend to separate those with the authority to decide from those affected by their decisions, a referendum ballot was proposed which would prevent any Board member (President, Vice-President, and Director), from judging, handling, or officiating at a show run under the Board's jurisdiction. The referendum passed in 1974 and left many Board members in an either/or situation. Some Board members chose to resign, while others gave up their judging assignments in Canada. While theoretically this separation was to remove the Board from undue influence or conflict of interest, it soon became evident that our best people were those actively involved in the shows, and that in giving up "influence" the Club was also giving up experience. The next referendum rescinded this rule.

One of the acute concerns of Canadian dog breeders has always been the downgrading of dogs which occurs when pet stock is bred, often against the explicit arrangements made during the sale of a pet. The only solution was spaying or neutering, an operation which increased the expense of keeping the pet, and which was not really a valid solution in the case of puppies which could be late developers. The introduction of the Non-Breeding contract and the Non-Breeding registry was a well-received solution to this perennial problem. The Non-Breeding contract form, originated by the CKC and enforceable in civil courts, allowed breeders to sell their stock without worrying whether the individual animal would turn up in the pedigrees of "puppy farm" pets, and yet, because the arrangement could be cancelled with the breeder's permission, those specimens which were worth showing and breeding could be salvaged later. An added bonus from the breeder's point of view was that the contract provided an opportunity to give advice to the dog's owner about prospective breedings. Despite the decision of the AKC not to accept these dogs for registration, Canadian breeders have been thankful for their "third option."

Besides the new Dog Show Rules, this period has seen a consolidation of the By-Laws, the issuance of rules for Sanctioned Matches, a standard format for breed standards, provision for National Clubs and Parent Clubs, an attempt to standardize colour terminology on registration applications (which proved unsuccessful), and many other efforts to eliminate the problems posed by growth. The introduction of a permit system for approving judges was designed to allow more judges to qualify, but put them on probation rather than give them outright approval at the start of their careers. One disruptive outside influence has been frequent mail strikes. The CKC has even developed procedures to get around that obstruction, including the long-banned telephone entry to dog shows. Undoubtedly, more regulation is unavoidable in the future, even though it seems now that there is a rule for everything. No solution, however, has been found to the difficulty of ensuring that members read the minutes and notices of the Club as published in *Dogs in Canada*. Concerned members must take comfort from the fact that all democratic systems face the same kind of voter apathy.

The CKC Board has made efforts to break new ground in the recent decades, especially in the area of public issues which affect its members. Problems of pet overpopulation, especially in urban areas, have caused local municipal councils to attempt to regulate the number of dogs per household, to ban dogs from parks, to deny kennel licences, to regulate or license the sale of puppies, and in general to punish responsible dog breeders as well as irresponsible dog owners. In several specific cases, the Board has made representations to provincial and municipal levels of government on behalf of the dog fancy with considerable success. The Board has also cooperated with Humane Societies in the matter of kennel inspection programmes. Besides its efforts on behalf of breeders with the government, the CKC has supported research programmes into hereditary defects such as hip dysplasia and has indicated a continuing interest in such methods of breed improvement as artificial insemination. One thorny problem over which the CKC has had limited success is the importation of puppies in lots from England and the United States for the pet market in Canada. Despite representation to the Minister of Agriculture, the Board found little could be done other than requiring the individual puppies to be tattooed before entry into Canada so that registration papers would not be confused. One unusual step which the CKC took was to assist in the setting up of the Bermuda Kennel Club. For a number of years, the CKC handled registrations and dog show and obedience trial records for that country until, in 1968, Bermuda went on its own.

Conclusions

What will be the future direction of The Canadian Kennel Club? Judging by past history, the Club is guaranteed a major policy crisis every fifteen years, and a severe financial crisis every thirty years. In the immediate future, there may be an abrupt change from the steady growth of entries at competitive dog events. So many CKC functions depend on access by cheap, flexible transportation. When the price of gasoline rose drastically in England a few years ago, exhibitors turned to co-operative transportation—chartering busses or trains to take groups of them to dog shows. As well, efforts were made to establish one or two central venues which would be available to all clubs. These solutions are possible in a country with a small geographic area and a large population. In Canada, where there is a large geographic area and a small population, exhibitors may have to curtail their activities.

The areas of public relations and education seem to need considerable attention in the future. Many instances of "anti-dog" attitudes have surfaced in the recent past, and if the dog fancy is to avoid punitive legislation, some form of internal regulation may be necessary. Again, the English experience may be instructive, for universal licensing of dog "breeders" is a fact in that country. The relationship of the sport of dogs to the business of dogs is another area of concern. If the CKC is to remain "dogdom in Canada," it must face and solve these issues.

Whatever happens, The Canadian Kennel Club, more than most national clubs, depends on its members. Membership apathy can be a deathblow because it is a democratically run organization. Commitment to the good of dogs in Canada means participation in the intense discussions which occur over policy decisions, and because of the organization of the CKC, policy decisions often require political action. The fact that the CKC is membership-run may mean abrupt changes in direction after Board elections. Often, in the past, the Secretary-Treasurer has had to hold the Club together while such policy changes were being worked out. This process is not unique to the CKC—an examination of Canada's recent constitutional debate will show a similar situation. Many of the forces which disrupt the Canadian union also affect the CKC. Regionalism in a wide geographic area, feelings of isolation from the power structure, and the example and influence of the United States all have their effect in dividing the Club membership. In the final analysis, it all depends on the willingness of the Club members, first of all to participate in policy decisions, and secondly, to accept those decisions when they are made. While, in the thick of debate, it may seem that destruction of the Club is imminent, a look at this short history indicates that the CKC will survive, or be resurrected, to carry on.

Notes on Buying a Pure-bred Puppy

*A*S WITH ANY EXPENSIVE PURCHASE, buying a pure-bred puppy requires as much consideration as possible. You must consider the care, attention, exercise required, and the costs of feeding and medical care. Shop around at different kennels before you decide on a puppy; try to gird your heart against the first pair of appealing brown eyes.

The condition of the dogs in the kennel (and the kennel itself) will be an indication of the quality of the breeder. If the sire and dam are on the premises, ask to see them and their registration certificates. Make sure they are registered, and ask for their litter registration number. It is an offence under the Livestock Pedigree Act for any dog to be sold as pure-bred without the furnishing of a certificate of registration. It is also an offence to sell as pure-bred a dog not eligible for registration. The *breeder* of the dog is fully responsible for its registration, "with no extra cost" to the purchaser. There have been cases of as much as $250 added to the purchase price for a registration fee. Any extra charge is illegal.

If buying a pure-bred dog, insist on its papers. You will need them for showing, breeding, or selling the dog. These papers are also your guarantee that the animal is pure-bred. However, you should allow the breeder a reasonable time to obtain the papers for you.

The dog must be identified by tattoo or noseprint.

One should be aware of any hereditary defects which may take some time to surface in some breeds. A reputable breeder will give a guarantee against such an occurrence. Some defects cannot be spotted at an early age; therefore a replacement should be guaranteed. Whether or not you receive such a guarantee may enter into your decision about buying a particular puppy. Enquire whether the sire or dam has exhibited any hereditary defects. This is the best way of avoiding the heartbreak of having a dog that has been with a family for some time develop unanticipated and serious health problems.

Regarding the transaction, you should obtain a written receipt (even if payment is made by cheque) and a copy of any agreement entered into signed at the time of sale. You should also have a copy of the litter registration, or at very least, the litter registration number.

Registration of a Pure-bred Dog

WHEN BUYING A DOG represented as pure-bred, you are entitled to receive a certificate of registration. To protect your rights, you should ensure that the contract of sale states the breed of dog, and that it is pure-bred and eligible for registration with The Canadian Kennel Club. With such a sales contract (or bill of sale) in hand, your right to a certificate of registration is protected by federal legislation—the Livestock Pedigree Act. Every person who sells a dog as pure-bred which is eligible for registration must identify the dog for registration purposes, and so register it in the records of The Canadian Kennel Club, and provide the buyer, at no additional cost, with the CKC certificate of registration upon which is recorded the transfer of ownership. If such certificate of registration is not provided by the seller within a reasonable period of time, the buyer can lay an Information Charge against the seller for violation of the Livestock Pedigree Act, Article 17(E). The penalty for violation of the Act is a fine not exceeding $500.00 and not less than $50.00, or imprisonment for a term not exceeding two months. *Before* purchasing your dog, you should establish certain criteria which are prerequisite to a pure-bred dog's eligibility for CKC registration. If such criteria are not confirmed by the seller, *you should not buy the dog*.

Canadian Born Dog

If the dog has been born in Canada, ask to see its litter certificate issued by the CKC. The certificate will indicate the breed of the litter, the date of birth, the registered names and numbers of the litter sire and dam, number of males and females in the litter, the litter registration number, and the name and address of the person who owned the litter at birth. You should take note of the litter registration number and the name and address of the owner at birth as it is this person who is responsible for identifying the dog before you purchase it and also must register the dog with the CKC. If a litter certificate is not available, ask to see the CKC certificates of registration pertaining to the dog's dam and sire. It is important to establish that the litter or dam of the dog are CKC registered in the name of the litter owner, as both registrations are prerequisites for registration of the dog you may purchase. The sire of a litter may be a foreign-born stud dog which is not owned by a resident of Canada, in which case the owner of the litter should have a foreign certified three-generation pedigree for the sire for presentation to the CKC in support of the litter registration.

Identification

A pure-bred dog born in Canada and eligible for CKC registration must be identified by one of two methods so that the certificate of registration issued for the dog will make it possible to distinguish it from any other dog of the same sex and breed. It is the responsibility of the owner (at birth) to identify the dog before ownership passes to another person. A breeder of pure-bred dogs may choose either noseprints or tattoo letters to identify dogs which he owns at birth; if tattoo letters are his chosen method, only those tattoo letters assigned to him by the CKC may be used for identification purposes.

Before you buy your pure-bred dog, ensure that the owner has either noseprinted or tattooed the dog. Do not accept responsibility for identifying the dog yourself, for both methods require the hand of an experienced person to be acceptable to the CKC. If the seller of a Canadian-born pure-bred dog can satisfy these requirements, you should not encounter difficulty in acquiring from the seller the dog's CKC certificate of registration within a reasonable period of time (approximately three months).

Imported Dog

If the dog you wish to purchase is represented as a pure-bred imported to Canada, and it is your wish to be provided with a CKC certificate of registration, extra care must be taken to protect your interests. Unless the contract of sale specifies that CKC registration forms part of the sale, the seller is not obligated to provide CKC registration, but may instead provide you with the dog's foreign registration certificate or require you to apply to the foreign registry association for the dog's certificate at your own expense. Bear in mind that if the dog is to be used in Canada for breeding purposes, or competition in CKC-licensed events, it must be CKC registered. If CKC registration is to be provided, the responsibility for acquiring it rests entirely with the person who imported the dog to Canada. The CKC will not entertain an application for registration of an imported dog if the application is completed and presented by anyone other than the importer. The importer must identify the dog in the manner described above *before* the dog is transferred to another resident of Canada. He must also provide the CKC with the duly completed application for registration, the foreign certificate of registration (which shall reflect the registered ownership of the Canadian importer), a certified three-generation pedigree of the dog, and the appropriate registration fee. If the dog is to be transferred to another resident of Canada, the importer must also provide the CKC with an application to transfer ownership and the transfer fee. When the CKC certificate is issued to the importer, he must then send it to the new owner.

Application for Registration of Canadian Born Litter

Section A of the litter application must be completed and signed by the CKC-registered owner(s) or lessee(s) of the dam at birth of the litter.

Section B of the litter application is to be completed only if the breeder is *not* the owner of the dam on date of litter whelping.

Section C of the litter application must be completed and signed by the registered owner(s) of the sire at time of service to the dam.

The completed litter application, with CKC registration fee, shall be submitted to the CKC by the owner(s) at birth of the litter. Complete regulations governing CKC registration of Canadian-born litters are printed on the litter application form, available from the CKC upon request.

THE CANADIAN KENNEL CLUB

PLEASE PRINT

INCORPORATED UNDER THE LIVE STOCK PEDIGREE ACT AT THE DEPARTMENT OF AGRICULTURE OTTAWA CANADA

APPLICATION FOR REGISTRATION OF <u>LITTER BORN IN CANADA</u>

COMPLETE SECTIONS A & C. SECTION B TO BE COMPLETED IF REQUIRED

FOR OFFICE USE ONLY

SECTION A

BREED ___POODLE___

DAM NAME ___LITTLE MISS MUFFET___ LW12345 REGISTRATION NUMBER

SIRE NAME ___LITTLE BOY BLUE___ LC9999 REGISTRATION NUMBER

DATE OF MATING — DAY 30 MONTH 10 YEAR 80

NUMBER OF PUPS IN LITTER — MALES 1 | FEMALES 1

DATE OF BIRTH OF LITTER — DAY 01 MONTH 01 YEAR 81

WAS DAM IMPORTED IN WHELP? ☐ YES ☒ NO — IF ANSWER IS YES GIVE NAME OF IMPORTER AND COUNTRY FROM WHICH DAM WAS IMPORTED

WAS THIS LITTER CONCEIVED BY USE OF IMPORTED SEMEN? ☐ YES ☒ NO — IF ANSWER IS YES REFER TO SECTION 3e OF INSTRUCTIONS BELOW

CKC REGISTERED OWNER(S) OR LESSEE(S) OF DAM AT BIRTH OF LITTER

NAME JOHN DOE

ADDRESS 100 SMITH AVENUE

TORONTO — TOWN | ONTARIO — PROVINCE | M6S 4V7 — POSTAL CODE

I WAS THE OWNER OF THE ABOVE NAMED DAM AT THE TIME SHE WAS SERVED BY THE ABOVE NAMED SIRE
☒ YES ☐ NO — IF NO PLEASE COMPLETE SECTION B BELOW

I HEREBY DECLARE THAT I WAS THE OWNER OF THE ABOVE NAMED DAM AT THE TIME OF THE BIRTH OF THIS LITTER AND THAT ALL OF THE FOREGOING INFORMATION IS IN ACCORDANCE WITH MY PRIVATE RECORDS AND IS CORRECT TO THE BEST OF MY KNOWLEDGE

John Doe — SIGNATURE OF OWNER(S) OR LESSEE(S) OF DAM

DATE OF APPLICATION — DAY 15 MONTH 01 YEAR 81

SIGNATURE OF CO-OWNER(S)

SECTION B

This Section to be completed ONLY if breeder is NOT the owner of the dam at the time of birth of this litter

I HEREBY DECLARE THAT I WAS THE OWNER OR LESSEE OF THE ABOVE NAMED DAM AT THE TIME SHE WAS SERVED BY THE ABOVE NAMED SIRE

SIGNATURE

SIGNATURE OF CO-OWNER(S)

SECTION C

REGISTERED OWNER(S) OR LESSEE(S) OF SIRE

NAME JOHN DOE

ADDRESS 100 SMITH AVENUE

TORONTO — TOWN | ONTARIO — PROVINCE | M6S 4V7 — POSTAL CODE

I HEREBY DECLARE THAT ACCORDING TO MY PRIVATE RECORD THE ABOVE NAMED DAM WAS SERVED BY THE ABOVE NAMED SIRE ON THE DATE AND UNDER THE CONDITIONS INDICATED ABOVE

ACCORDING TO THE RECORDS OF THE AMERICAN KENNEL CLUB, THE ABOVE NAMED SIRE WAS OWNED, ON THE DATE OF MATING SHOWN ON THIS APPLICATION, BY THE PERSON SIGNING THIS DECLARATION AS THE OWNER OF THE SIRE.

John Doe. — SIGNATURE OF OWNER(S) OR LESSEE(S) OF SIRE

Certification Signature — To be signed by A.K.C. Official

SIGNATURE OF CO-OWNER(S)

INSTRUCTIONS:

1. **APPLICATION FOR REGISTRATION.** — The owner at the time of the birth may make application for registration of a litter born in Canada.

2. **DAM OF THE LITTER.** — The dam must be registered with The Canadian Kennel Club in the name of the person(s) signing the application for registration as owner(s) or lessee(s) at the time of the birth of the litter.

3. **SIRE OF THE LITTER.** — (a) If owned or leased by a resident of Canada, the sire must be registered with The Canadian Kennel Club in the name of the person certifying the service.
   (b) If owned by a resident of the United States the sire must be registered with The American Kennel Club in the name of the person certifying the service. In such cases, the above certification must be completed by The American Kennel Club and this application must be accompanied by a three-generation pedigree for the sire, available from The American Kennel Club.
   (c) If owned by a resident of a country other than Canada or the United States, a certificate of service issued by the recognized British or Foreign Stud Book shall be required as well as a certified copy of the known pedigree of the sire to the minimum of three generations.
   (d) If the owner or lessee of the sire of a litter shall refuse, fail or neglect to sign where required, an application for registration of a litter when requested to do so by the owner of the dam at time of birth of the litter, the Board of Directors shall have the power to authorize registration of the litter, through the Registration Committee if it is satisfied that the owner of the sire has no justifiable reason for withholding his signature.
   (e) If the litter was conceived from artificial insemination using semen imported to Canada, registration of such litter is subject to special regulations available upon request from the CKC.

4. **SIGNATURES.** — (a) If owned or leased by resident(s) of Canada or the United States the signature(s) in ink of the owner(s) or lessee(s) of the sire will be required certifying as to the date(s) of service.
   (b) The signature(s) in ink of the owner(s) or lessee(s) of the dam at the time of the service will be required certifying as to the service of the dam to the sire named on the application on the date(s) set forth on the application.
   (c) The signature(s) in ink of the owner(s) or lessee(s) of the dam at the time of birth of the litter will be required certifying the date of birth of the litter and the number of males and females alive at the time of the application for registration of the litter.

5. **BREEDER.** — The breeder of a litter is the owner or lessee of the dam at the time of service. The first owner is the owner or lessee of the dam at the time the litter was born.

6. **AGE.** — No litter out of a dam under six months or over twelve years of age at the time of mating, or by a sire under six months or over twelve years of age at the time of mating will be registered unless the application for registration is accompanied by an affidavit or evidence which shall prove the facts, set out in the application for registration of a litter, to the satisfaction of the recording office.

7. **ARTIFICIAL INSEMINATION.** — A litter born in Canada as a result of artificial insemination, the progeny of a sire and dam registered in the records of the Club may be registered under the regulations approved by the Club and the Department of Agriculture for Canada.

8. **MATINGS.** — Notwithstanding any other provisions of these By-laws no litter is eligible for registration if the dam of the litter was mated to two or more stud dogs during the period of three months immediately preceding the birth of the litter.

REMIT TO: **THE CANADIAN KENNEL CLUB, 2150 BLOOR ST. W., TORONTO, ONTARIO M6S 4V7** R.D. 108 (REV. APRIL 1980)

CKC Litter Certificate

This certificate is issued by the CKC to the person who owned the litter at birth. With the certificate, the owner at birth receives the appropriate number of application forms each of which he must complete and submit with registration fees to the CKC to acquire individual registration of each litter member.

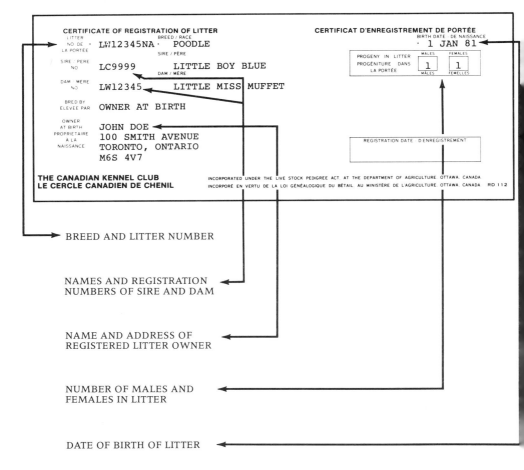

BREED AND LITTER NUMBER

NAMES AND REGISTRATION NUMBERS OF SIRE AND DAM

NAME AND ADDRESS OF REGISTERED LITTER OWNER

NUMBER OF MALES AND FEMALES IN LITTER

DATE OF BIRTH OF LITTER

Application for Individual Registration of a Canadian Born Dog

THE CANADIAN KENNEL CLUB
INCORPORATED UNDER THE LIVE STOCK PEDIGREE ACT
AT THE DEPARTMENT OF AGRICULTURE OTTAWA CANADA

APPLICATION FOR REGISTRATION OF AN
INDIVIDUAL DOG BORN IN CANADA

IMPORTANT NOTICE:
THIS FORM IS NOT A CERTIFICATE OF REGISTRATION AND MUST NOT BE REPRESENTED AS SUCH. It is the responsibility of the owner at birth to ensure the dog is identified by noseprint or tattoo BEFORE it is transferred to a new owner and also submit this application to the CKC with the registration and transfer fees. The owner at birth must provide to the buyer of the dog, AT NO CHARGE, a CKC certificate of registration reflecting the buyer's recorded ownership. Where errors or omissions are noted, this application will be returned by the club to the owner at birth for correction.

BIRTH DATE

		BREED	
LITTER REG NO *	LW12345NA	POODLE	1 JAN 81
SIRE REG. NO	LC9999	SIRE LITTLE BOY BLUE	1 1
DAM REG. NO	LW12345	DAM LITTLE MISS MUFFET	

BREEDER   OWNER AT BIRTH

OWNER AT BIRTH   JOHN DOE
100 SMITH AVENUE
TORONTO, ONTARIO
M6S 4V7

FOR OFFICE USE ONLY

READ REVERSE SIDE CAREFULLY BEFORE COMPLETING THIS APPLICATION. PLEASE PRINT

NAME   LITTLE RED RIDING HOOD
FIRST CHOICE

SEX   FEMALE

SWEET MISSY RED
SECOND CHOICE

RED HONEY
THIRD CHOICE

COLOUR   WHITE

IDENTIFICATION SECTION
COMPLETE **ONE** SECTION ONLY (NOSE-PRINT OR TATTOO) BUT **NOT BOTH**

NOSE-PRINT
IF THIS DOG HAS BEEN NOSE PRINTED, INDICATE NUMBERS APPEARING ON OFFICIAL NOSE-PRINT FORMS ACCOMPANYING THIS APPLICATION. ONLY CLEAR AND DISTINCT PRINTS, FREE FROM SMUDGES OR BLOTS, WILL BE ACCEPTED

INSERT NUMBER HERE   INSERT NUMBER HERE

TATTOO
THE DOG FOR WHICH THIS APPLICATION IS SUBMITTED HAS BEEN CLEARLY AND LEGIBLY TATTOO MARKED AS FOLLOWS

I HEREBY CERTIFY THAT ON   28/2   81
I PLACED ON THE DOG COVERED BY THIS APPLICATION THE TATTOO MARKINGS STATED AT LEFT AND SAID MARKINGS ARE CLEARLY LEGIBLE

| TATTOO COMBINATION | A | B | C | RE ☐ RF ☒ LE ☐ LF ☐ |
| TATTOO NO & YEAR LETTER | 2 | N | | RE ☐ RF ☒ LE ☐ LF ☐ |

SIGN HERE   John Doe

RE-RIGHT EAR RF-RIGHT FLANK LE-LEFT EAR LF-LEFT FLANK

SIGNATURE OF PERSON WHO ACTUALLY TATTOO MARKED THE DOG

IF SOLD OR OTHERWISE DISPOSED OF, THIS TRANSFER SECTION MUST BE COMPLETED

NOTE: IF THIS SECTION IS COMPLETED, TRANSFER FEE MUST BE REMITTED IN ADDITION TO REGISTRATION FEE.

NAME (INCLUDING INITIALS) OF NEW OWNER   HARRY SMITH

FULL ADDRESS   283 RIVERSIDE DRIVE
TORONTO, ONTARIO M6S 4B1

DAY	MTH	YEAR
0 1	0 3	8 1

DATE OF TRANSFER OF OWNERSHIP

IN CASE OF ERRORS OR OMISSIONS, THIS APPLICATION WILL BE RETURNED TO THE OWNER AT BIRTH FOR CORRECTION

THE CERTIFICATE, WHEN ISSUED, SHALL BE FORWARDED TO THE OWNER AT BIRTH FOR ONWARD TRANSMISSION WHERE APPLICABLE

I HEREBY CERTIFY THAT

(1) THE INFORMATION SHOWN ON THIS APPLICATION IS CORRECT AND IS IN ACCORDANCE WITH MY PRIVATE BREEDING RECORDS

(2) THE DOG HAS BEEN IDENTIFIED AS INDICATED IN THE IDENTIFICATION SECTION OF THIS APPLICATION

(3) I TRANSFERRED OWNERSHIP OF THE ABOVE NAMED DOG AS INDICATED (IF APPLICABLE)

SIGN HERE   John Doe
SIGNATURE OF OWNER OF DOG AT TIME OF BIRTH

CALCULATION OF FEE ENCLOSED

SIGN HERE
SIGNATURES OF ALL CO-OWNERS AT BIRTH ARE REQUIRED

REGISTRATION FEE	
TRANSFER FEE	
TOTAL AMOUNT ENCLOSED	

DATE _____ 19___

RD106-REV 7-80   INDICATE IF CERTIFICATE IS TO BE ISSUED IN ENGLISH ☐   or FRENCH ☐

(Litter Registered by the CKC)

This section of application is completed by the CKC before the application is provided to the owner at birth.

The balance of the application must be completed by the person who owned the dog at birth:

1. Colour(s) and sex of dog

2. 3 unique name choices for the dog.

3. Identification of the dog—if tattooed, the letters used, the location of tattoo and the date upon which the dog was tattoo marked. If noseprinted, attach 2 or 3 clear noseprints taken from the dog and insert the noseprint numbers in the boxes provided.

4. If dog disposed of prior to application for registration, complete date of sale, name and address of new owner(s) are required.

NOTE: If owner at birth has registered his kennel name with the CKC, this kennel name may be used as a prefix or suffix to the three dog name choices.

Only those tattoo letters registered by the CKC for the owner(s) at birth (or the person(s) named in the transfer of ownership section of application) may be used to tattoo mark the dog. Registration application and required fees must be submitted to the CKC by the owner at birth.

CKC Certificate of Registration for Canadian Born Dog

This is a sample of the CKC certificate you are entitled to receive when you have purchased a pure-bred dog eligible for registration in Canada. In some instances, a breeder will offer a dog for sale on the understanding that the dog must not be used for breeding purposes. Such agreement will have no force or effect unless, *at the time of sale,* the vendor and purchaser sign the non-breeding agreement form provided by the CKC and the form is submitted to the CKC with the application for registration and/or transfer of ownership of the dog. Under such circumstances, the CKC will issue a certificate of registration which clearly identifies the dog as one which must not be used for breeding purposes. Any person who sells as pure-bred the progeny of a dog covered by such an agreement shall be deemed to have violated the provisions of the Livestock Pedigree Act, Section 17, and is subject to its penalties. Full particulars concerning non-breeding agreements and their cancellation can be obtained from the CKC.

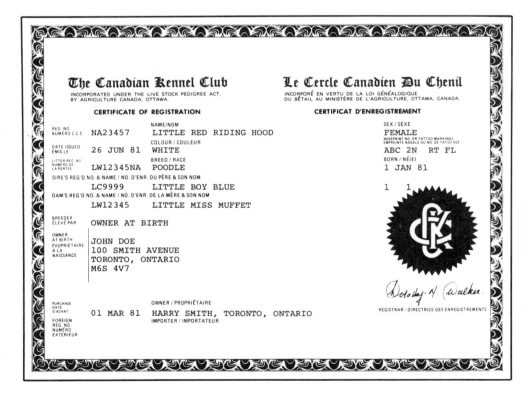

Transfer of Ownership–CKC Registered Dog

On the reverse side of any CKC certificate of registration can be found an application for ownership transfer of a registered dog. When a dog is disposed of for a consideration (monetary or otherwise), the registered owner must sign the transfer application and provide the complete name and address of the person to whom the dog was sold, the date of sale, and name and registration number of the dog. The person disposing of the dog must then submit the certificate with completed transfer application to the CKC together with the transfer fee.

Unless otherwise specified by the vendor, the certificate of registration reflecting the names of the new owners shall be returned to the vendor by the CKC for onward referral to the new owners. Transfers of ownership of a dog which is registered as a non-breeding animal will not be considered by the CKC unless the vendor and new owner of the dog complete and sign a new non-breeding agreement for submission to the CKC with the transfer of ownership application. A non-breeding agreement can be cancelled by mutual consent of the parties who originally entered into the agreement providing the CKC is notified by submission of the signed "Cancellation of Agreement" form and the appropriate fee.

For a fee, the CKC will also issue certified pedigrees for any CKC-registered dog, to the extent of three (3) or four (4) generations. It should be noted, however, that the seller of a pure-bred dog is not obligated to provide a certified pedigree to the buyer, though he must provide a certificate of registration. Any person may acquire a certified pedigree by writing the CKC and providing the registered name and number of the dog and submitting the pedigree fee. Any inquiries regarding registration or transfer of ownership of a pure-bred dog should be directed to The Canadian Kennel Club, 2150 Bloor Street West, Toronto, Ontario, M6S 4V7 or by telephoning (416) 763-4391.

———— APPLICATION FOR TRANSFER OF OWNERSHIP ————

I/we hereby certify that I/we sold the animal named on the accompanying Registration Certificate

TO _____
(Name of Purchaser)

ADDRESS _____ PROV. _____ POSTAL CODE _____
(Full Address of New Owner)

DATE OF SALE _____ DAY OF _____ 19 _____

DOG NAME _____ REGISTRATION NO. _____

SIGN HERE _____
Registered Owner Sign here, if Co-owned, Signatures of all Co-owners are required.

ADDRESS _____ PROV. _____ POSTAL CODE _____

I/WE HEREBY REQUEST THAT THE CERTIFICATE
SHOWING TRANSFER TO THE NEW OWNER BE
FORWARDED BY THE CLUB TO THE NEW OWNER.

VENDOR(S) SIGN HERE _____

TRANSFER FEE	
ORDINARY C.K.C. MEMBERS	$5.00
OTHERS:	$7.50
FEE SUBJECT TO CHANGE.	

R.D. 110 REV. 7-80

Indicate if certificate to be issued in ENGLISH ☐   or FRENCH ☐

Show and Trial Activities

*O*VER 1000 OFFICIAL SHOW AND TRIAL EVENTS are held each year under the auspices of the CKC. Each *type* of activity has its own set of rules, which can be obtained directly from the offices of the CKC. A brief history and outline of each activity follows.

Dog Shows

The first known dog show was held at Newcastle-on-Tyne, England in 1859, and in the years which followed dog shows gained in popularity. Before long it became obvious that if the sport were to become one in which people would wish to participate, it would be essential to found an organization to enact and enforce rules to govern the sport. Thus it was that The Kennel Club in Britain was founded in 1873. Shows are reported to have been held in Canada (in the Maritimes and Montreal) as early as 1881. In 1884 the American Kennel Club was founded, and for a while a few clubs in Canada held their shows under American Kennel Club rules. As the sport became better established in Canada, a feeling grew that a national organization should be formed and interested fanciers met in London, Ontario in September 1888 and founded The Canadian Kennel Club.

Each year, more than 1000 competitive events for dogs are held under Canadian Kennel Club rules, and almost half of these are championship shows. Championship shows (where points are awarded towards a Championship) are divided into two types: Specialty and All-Breed. Specialty shows are limited to dogs of specific breed or grouping of breeds; for example, the Afghan Hound Club of Canada Specialty is for Afghan Hounds only, the Dachshund Club of Canada Specialty is for all Dachshunds, and the Group VI Specialty is for all breeds in Group 6. All-Breed shows, naturally, are open to all breeds. These shows are organized by clubs and associations officially recognized by The Canadian Kennel Club.

Shows: An overview of one of Canada's largest dog shows with judging taking place in several rings.

Judging: Judging at a championship or conformation show is a process of elimination. At a show there are five official classes in which a dog may be entered to obtain points. These classes are:

Junior Puppy —for dogs six months of age but less than nine months on the day of the show;

Senior Puppy —for dogs nine months of age but less than twelve months on the day of the show;

Canadian Bred —for dogs born in Canada, Champions in any country excluded;

Bred by Exhibitor— for dogs owned and handled in the ring by the breeder;

Open Class —for all dogs.

All official classes are divided by sex, and males compete against males, females compete against females; there is no intersex competition at this point.

The judge begins with the Junior Puppy Male class, and evaluates each dog, finally placing them first, second, third, and fourth, depending on the entries in the class. The judge then proceeds through the remainder of the male classes. After all classes have been judged, the dogs placing first from each class are brought back into the ring to compete against each other for the Winners award. This is called WINNERS MALE. After the Winners Male is selected, the dog that placed second to it in the regular class competition is brought into the ring and competes against the other class winners for RESERVE WINNERS MALE. This dog will be awarded the points if, for any reason, the win is disallowed by the CKC. The process is repeated for females, with one dog being selected for WINNERS FEMALE, and one for RESERVE WINNERS FEMALE. Specials Only dogs are all finished champions of record. All dogs entered for Specials Only are brought into the ring, along with the Winners Male and Winners Female. The judge goes over all dogs and selects one for BEST OF BREED. He then selects the BEST OF OPPOSITE SEX TO BEST OF BREED. From the Winners Male and Winners Female he selects the BEST OF WINNERS. If the Winners Male or Female has been awarded Best of Breed, they are automatically awarded Best of Winners. Additional points may be won here as the larger the number of entries, the more points available to a limit of five.

After the selection of Best of Winners award, the judge selects one puppy as BEST PUPPY IN BREED from all undefeated puppies in competition. At an All-Breed show, all Best of Breed dogs in each group are brought together, and the judge selects first, second, third, and fourth in group. All first-placing group dogs are then brought together and one is selected BEST IN SHOW. The best puppy in each breed competes for Best Puppy In Group, and similarly for Best Puppy in Show.

At the largest shows, almost 1300 competitors are narrowed down to the BEST IN SHOW WINNER for the day.

In order to become a Champion, a dog must earn at least ten Championship points under at least three different judges, and either must defeat another dog in its own breed, or place in a Group where five or more breeds are competing, and must be individually registered in the records of the Canadian Kennel Club. Points may be won at the Winners level, or by placing in a group, or both. Points are given to the dog awarded Winners and are based on the number of dogs defeated. A dog may earn from one to five points at each show (where a club holds two or more

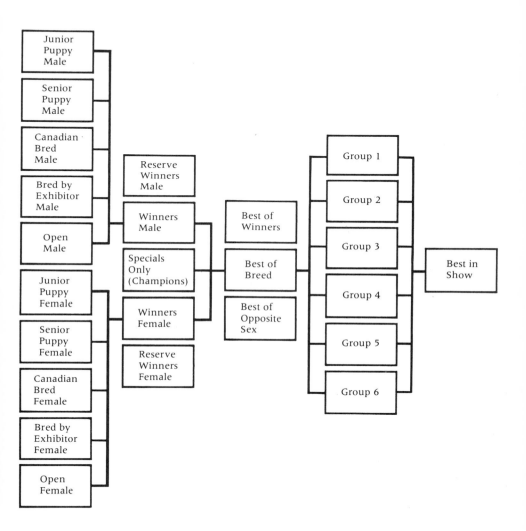

NOTE: The judging procedure for Best Puppy in Breed, Group, and Show is explained in the attached information.

shows at the same location, each show is considered separate), but may not be credited with more than five points for each show, regardless of the wins made by the dog.

Sanction Matches: Sanction Matches are informal events held by clubs at which dogs are judged as closely as possible to the rules of a regular Championship show, but no championship points are awarded. Judges are not necessarily on The Canadian Kennel Club list of approved judges, but must be knowledgeable in the breeds they are adjudicating. Ribbons are given out, and trophies are usually presented. These events are excellent training grounds not only for dogs and aspiring judges, but also for exhibitors and show personnel. Rules are laid down by The Canadian Kennel Club and are very close to official Show Rules; the major exception is that dogs from three to six months of age may compete. A complete range of awards, including Groups, and Best in Match, is usually made.

Miscellaneous Class: A club wishing to hold a Miscellaneous Class at their show must designate it in their premium list. The breeds may be paraded in the ring, and a short history of the breed read out, but they may not be judged in any way. Regulations for entry into the Miscellaneous Class are as set by the Board of Directors. Usually, breeds are placed in the Miscellaneous Class while working towards meeting Canadian Kennel Club requirements for total recognition of a *new* breed. Those breeds in the Miscellaneous Class as of 31 December 1981 are:

> Australian Kelpies
> Border Collies
> Canaan Dogs
> Miniature Bull Terriers
> Spinoni Italiani
> Tahltan Bear Dogs.

Obedience

In Canada, the title conferred upon a dog who has completed the requirements for his first obedience degree is "Companion Dog." The title is descriptive, for the aim of basic obedience training is

Obedience: A Saluki performing the High Jump, one of the exercises required during Open Obedience competition.

to turn untrained dogs into better, more pleasant, and more useful companions. Obedience training develops a unique rapport between dog and handler; the time, patience and hard work involved in training a dog are amply rewarded when a handler discovers this acute new sense of communication between himself and his dog. A trained dog is, by and large, a happy, contented pet, having acquired a discipline which enables him to cope with the many stresses of modern, urban life—stresses with which dogs must cope if they are to survive as man's companion in an increasingly crowded world.

Obedience training—to use the term in its broadest sense—probably dates back to the time dogs were first domesticated by man. But organized obedience, licensed trials offering competition for obedience titles and degrees, is a relatively new phenomenon. The first official Canadian Kennel Club obedience trials were held in 1944, although for many years before this the German Shepherd Dog Club of Canada conducted "Field Trials" for German Shepherd Dogs, conferring titles which were recognized by The Canadian Kennel Club. In those first 1944 obedience trials, the only class to have entries was Novice, but by 1945 the first Open classes were held.

The sport grew throughout the '50s as obedience clubs were formed and all-breed clubs began to offer training classes and hold obedience trials along with their annual all-breed shows. Obedience first gained a foothold in central Canada, but interest soon spread from coast to coast. Obedience clinics sponsored by breed and training clubs provided an opportunity for obedience enthusiasts to learn more about this fledgling sport. Information-hungry participants travelled hundreds, even thousands, of miles to attend clinics conducted by Canadian obedience pioneers such as Mrs. Alex Casgrain of Montreal, and such well-known American authorities as Blanche Saunders. Today, obedience clinics are even more widely held and are always well attended, as obedience instructors and students alike strive to learn more about training dogs and about training people to train dogs.

From small beginnings, the obedience sport has grown until, in 1980, 348 licensed trials were held in Canada, attracting total entries of 19,593 dogs. The largest trial attracted entries of over 200 dogs, while entries at many trials were over 100. Dogs of 118 different breeds, representing all six groups, earned obedience degrees in 1980.

Obedience is for all dogs. Even at the most advanced levels, the exercises can be mastered by dogs of all shapes and sizes, from Chihuahuas to Irish Wolfhounds. Any dog may be trained, but only pure-bred dogs (including the Miscellaneous breeds as recognized by the CKC) may compete in licensed obedience trials, to obtain degrees at any one of three levels: Novice, Open, and Utility. In Novice, dog and handler complete a series of exercises, some on lead, some off lead, including heeling, stand for examination, recall, and sit and down stays. A good Novice dog is trained well enough to be an enjoyable, well-behaved pet, but many handlers are bitten by the obedience bug, and may train their dogs for the more advanced classes, which offer great challenges and an undeniable sense of achievement when successfully completed. In Open, all exercises are done off lead, and more difficult variations of the basic Novice exercises are joined by retrieving and jumping. Utility is by far the most demanding class, usually attempted only by the most keen handlers with the most talented dogs, although today the Utility class at trials across Canada is attracting larger and larger entries. As in Open, all work is off lead, and includes such difficult exercises as scent discrimination, response to hand signals, and directed jumping. At obedience trials, the Utility ring attracts many spectators who are inevitably impressed by the high degree of skill which dogs and handlers can demonstrate.

Obedience trials are often held in conjunction with all-breed or specialty dog shows, but they differ from dog shows in that at trials, competition against other dogs is not necessarily a major concern for participants. Certainly, trophies and rosettes are awarded for high scores, and top obedience dogs are often campaigned at trials throughout the year, to become recognized as the best of their breed or group. But the first, basic, goal of trial entrants is a qualifying score, and any or all dogs entered at any given trial may achieve that goal. For all classes, a perfect score is 200. To gain a qualifying score at any level from Novice through Utility, a dog must earn at least fifty per cent of the marks available for each exercise, and at least 170 marks out of the total 200 over-all. Three qualifying scores must be obtained at each level before the dog may proceed to the next. A dog gaining three qualifying scores in the Novice class earns his Companion Dog (CD) degree; three qualifying scores in Open earns him his Companion Dog Excellent (CDX); he earns his Utility Dog (UD) degree when he qualifies three times in the Utility class. A dog who has completed his UD is designated "Obedience Trial Champion," a title to be accepted with pride. Once a dog has earned his CD, he may no longer compete in the Novice class, but dogs may compete in Open and Utility classes as often as their handlers wish to enter them. Trial competition is an enjoyable sport, and need not end for a handler just because his dog has obtained the necessary three "legs" for his CDX or UD.

Today, obedience training classes led by qualified instructors are readily available in most larger centres across Canada. These classes serve a dual purpose. They help pet owners turn un-trained puppies and boisterous older dogs into well-mannered, lovable canine citizens; and they provide handlers who want to proceed into competitive obedience with the information and skills necessary to do so. In fact, many a successful trial participant began as a frustrated pet owner.

Obedience is fun, for both dog and handler. It is a useful endeavour, an enjoyable pastime, and a relatively inexpensive year-round sport for which the basic equipment is simply a dog, a collar, and a six-foot lead. It is no wonder that obedience classes across the country are filled to capacity, and that entries at trials are increasing every year. For as long as there is a man and his dog—or a woman and her dog—obedience will be around too.

Field Trials for Basset Hounds

Basset Hound Field Trials were not officially recognized by The Canadian Kennel Club but, in January 1980, the Basset Hound Club of Canada approached the CKC. At the Annual Meeting of 1980, a special committee was formed to consider field trials for Basset Hounds. The committee met with and discussed the requirements of the Basset Hound people, and a set of rules, based primarily on the Field Trial Rules for Beagles, was prepared and published for comment in *Dogs In Canada*.

Subsequently, the rules as proposed by the Basset Hound Club of Canada and the special committee have been approved by the Board of Directors, and a separate Field Trial Council for Basset Hounds has been established. The first licensed Basset Hound Trials were held in 1982, using approved Beagle Field Trial judges.

Field Trials for Beagles

Beagles originated in the British Isles and are the "scent" hound branch of sporting dogs, and one of the oldest breeds in history, derived from the Bloodhound.

The Beagle was developed to hunt rabbits and he does it better than any other creature on four legs. This is not to say that every Beagle, by instinct, is a top rabbit hound. At one time, with a little familiarization, Beagles could perform equally well on both cottontail and hare, and Dual Champions (Show and Field) were not uncommon. However, the vagaries of breeding strictly for beauty and the sacrifice of all-round ability for so-called "style" have led to the deterioration of the breed into three distinct and separate types: the show hound, the cottontail hound, and the hare hound. Of these, only the hare hound retains the four hunting qualities of nose, brains, desire, and stamina, and is still a superb gun dog; but even the hare hound can no longer meet the show standard.

The first importers of Beagles to North America were General Richard Rowett of Carlinville, Illinois in the early 1870s, and Mr. Norman Elmore of Newark, New Jersey. A few years later, Mr. Hiram Card of Elora, Ontario became a serious breeder and had a great influence on the American Beagle. One of his first stud dogs was Card's Blue Cap by Imp. Blue Cap and Imp. Blue Bell imported to North America by Mr. William Asheton of Virginia. Card's Blue Cap sired many of Mr. Card's hounds and he developed the strain known as the "Blue Cap" family which is still bred today.

Beagles are small hounds, standing no more than fifteen inches at the withers. They are a trailing hound, whose only contact with the quarry is the scent left on the ground by the rabbit in passing. The hound gives tongue continually while it has scent and it may be because of this that the rabbit shows an astonishing lack of concern during the hunt. At any given time it knows exactly how close, and exactly where, the Beagle is, and its natural enemies tend to move out of any area where the hounds are running. As well, the rabbit is in its natural element and has an adequate bag of tricks to throw the hound off its trail. No firearms are used in field trials, and the hounds are judged on their ability to find wild game and trail it in the prescribed manner.

The first Beagle Field Trial in Canada was held at Objibway, Ontario near Windsor, approximately 1915–1918. Currently, twenty-two Beagle Clubs operate in Atlantic Canada, Quebec, and Ontario. Activity is now commencing in Manitoba.

Beagle Field Trials may be run in two ways—Brace (two hounds) or Pack (Small Pack and Large Pack). Three Small Pack Trials and four Brace Trials are held each year in Ontario. Slightly under thirty Pack Trials are held each year in New Brunswick, Newfoundland, Nova Scotia, Ontario, P.E.I. and Quebec.

Entries in Canada last year ranged from 31–115 per trial with an average entry of sixty-four. The entries at a Field Trial are divided into four classes by sex and size (thirteen inches and under Bitch, thirteen inches and under Dog; over thirteen but not exceeding fifteen inches Bitch, over thirteen but not exceeding fifteen inches Dog). Prior to the running of each class, every entry must have an Official Measurement Certificate, or be measured. A number, corresponding to that allotted on its entry form by the Field Trial Secretary, is painted on both sides of each hound, and from this time on the hounds lose their identity.

Brace Trial: In Brace Trials the hounds entered in each Class are cast, by draw, two by two. The judges order the first brace cast to search for game and the gallery moves along behind the hounds to help find game. When the dogs or gallery jump a rabbit, the hounds are put on the line and the gallery stands still. The judges follow the hounds and assess each dog's ability to follow scent. When the judges are satisfied, they return to the gallery and the next brace commences. This process continues until all dogs entered have their run. The top hound in each brace is brought back to compete in subsequent series until the five placing hounds have defeated each hound placed beneath them. Brace Trials are always run on cottontail.

Pack Trials: In Small Pack Trials the entries in each class are divided by draw into packs not exceeding seven hounds. They compete as one pack, with the meritorious hounds being brought back to compete in subsequent packs. Small Packs may be run on either cottontail or hare.

Large Pack Trials are always run on hare and all the entries in each Class, be they two or twenty, are cast as one pack and so compete, barring elimination for faults, until that Class is completed.

Field Trials for Foxhounds

The first Foxhound Field Trials in Canada were held in 1946 in Ontario, and were run under the International Fox Hunters Association U.S.A. (known as the Chase Registry). In 1947, what was known as the "All-Canadian Fox Hunters Association" came into existence, and leading Foxhounds competed for all-Canadian honours. This hunt eventually ran under CKC rules and eight clubs participated in the National CKC Championship.

An outbreak of rabies resulted in a decimated supply of foxes, and this, combined with dissatisfaction amongst some clubs with the Canadian registry and eligibility system, brought about the demise of the "All-Canadian" in 1961.

Since that time, active Foxhound Clubs have run their trials quite successfully under the Chase Registry. Currently there are approximately five clubs in Ontario and two clubs in Quebec holding annual fox hunts averaging 125 to 140 entries each. In addition, one-day fun trials are held by two or three clubs in these same provinces.

The CKC Council for Foxhounds is conferring with the clubs to determine whether a Canadian registry system could be established, and domestic foxhunting become "All-Canadian" once again.

Field Trials for Pointing Breeds

Point, judge—the two dynamic, spine-tingling words that proclaim to all, and in particular to those honoured to evaluate pointing dog performance, what pointing dog sport is all about. It is an activity for sportsmen who, possessing dogs of the pointing breeds and not being content with abbreviated hunting seasons, vanishing hunting terrain, diminishing game species, and the multitude of pressures of an urbanized society, can play at the sport of hunting.

The future of the pointing breeds depends on the breeders interested in competitive events. These breeders stress function, as opposed to form and fancy, and continually strive to improve the hunting qualities of their breeds. As in any genuine competition, it is quality and excellence of performance that count. These characteristics can best be measured by competitions conducted under actual or simulated hunting conditions.

The various types of field trials and tests are formal means of evaluating pointing dog performance and potential. Each has a set of formal rules which lends order and substance to the competition. Each has a set of standards of performance which experienced judges use as their guide to evaluation. But there are subtle differences of quality in performance, way of going, manner of searching, style and intensity of pointing, honouring of bracemates, and use of wind and terrain, which only the truly knowledgeable judge is capable of evaluating.

Pointing dog competitions within the Canadian Kennel Club are the field trials, Field Dog and Field Dog Excellent (FD and FDX) events. Field trials have been a feature of CKC activity for many years, though varying in frequency and interest across Canada. The Continental breeds have been the principal motivators of

Pointing: German Shorthaired Pointer holding point — dog remains on point until handler goes in to flush the bird.

interest in each province, with a sprinkling of Pointers and Setters in most trials. Traditionally, the four most active areas have been Ontario, Manitoba, Alberta, and British Columbia. An examination of the book *Field Trial Record of Dogs in America,* by Major J.M. Taylor, indicates that field trials for pointing breeds were held in Canada prior to the formation of The Canadian Kennel Club in 1888: the Manitoba Field Trial Club held its inaugural trial at Morris, Manitoba in September 1886 and continued to hold trials in succeeding years. There is a record of a trial held in the name of The Canadian Kennel Club at Chatham, Ontario in November 1889 and the Calgary Rod and Gun Club held its first trial in September 1890.

A revival of interest in the past decade has seen a broadening of club-sponsored trials to include All-Breed, German Short-haired Pointer, Brittany, Vizsla, and Irish Setter clubs. At the same time there continues to be a steady, though modest, level of participation in the CKC-licensed FD and FDX tests. Again, these are club-sponsored events with the German Shorthaired

Pointer, Vizsla, and Brittany clubs being the most active. These events serve an extremely useful function by testing a dog's ability, and keeping pointing dog field performance at a high level among the less competitive, but still highly motivated, owners.

Within the CKC, renewed emphasis and interest in the field activities of the pointing breeds has been promoted through its Field Trial Council for Pointing Breeds. The Council has been rebuilt and revitalized by the appointment of experienced field dog people involved in the many facets of pointing dog activity. Procedures are being streamlined; advice, co-operation, and support from the breeders are sought and encouraged.

Field Trials for Retrievers

Man and his dog, companions depending on each other for mutual well being, have played a large part in the settlement and development of many countries. This was certainly true in Canada and it was only natural that the success of many hunting outings depended on the capabilities of the dogs, to find and to bring back the game that had been shot. Natural too, that whenever men gathered to talk of their hunting experiences, the abilities of their dogs would be discussed, and perhaps boasted about. The retrieving of game was of paramount importance, whether from land or water. Not only were various Retriever breeds more highly favoured than others for specific conditions, but the virtues of individual dogs brought about competitive events where these abilities could be demonstrated and assessed. As early as 1900, retriever breeds were participating in conformation shows. However, it was not until the mid-1930s that the first official events were organized, although training and non-official trials preceded these by several years.

July 16, 1938 was the date the Manitoba Gun Dog Club held the first Canadian Kennel Club Licensed Retriever Trial, followed by one hosted by The British Columbia Gun Dog Club on October 2nd. In 1939 only one licensed trial was held, and that was by the Manitoba Gun Dog Club. During the Second World War, trials lapsed in Manitoba. However, the B.C. Gun Dog Club carried on with Spring and Fall trials through 1941 to 1945. In addition, the lower Mainland of B.C. Gun Association held trials in 1944 and 1945 and the Pacific Coast Retriever Association hosted licensed trials in the Spring and Fall of 1945. The Alberta

Retriever being lined up for a blind retrieve. Note dog's attention focused on bird.

Field Trials Club was also active hosting trials in the years 1943 through 1945.

The first known licensed trials in the east were held in Ontario in 1949 and 1950 by the York Retriever Field Trial Club, followed by one staged by The Labrador Retriever Association of Ontario, now known as The Labrador Retriever Club of Ontario, in 1950. In May 1960 the Montreal Gun Dog Club was the first Quebec (and bilingual club) to hold a licensed trial. In the Maritimes, The Moncton Gun Dog Club and The Tantramar Kennel Club of Nova Scotia were the first clubs to hold licensed trials.

The complexity of the tests has increased over the years. In the 1938 B.C. Gun Dog Trial, dead pigeons were tossed into the Fraser River with lacrosse sticks and those few dogs that completed the single retrieve from the water were considered top Retrievers of the day. In 1939, a dead mallard was dragged through the bush to simulate a wounded bird escaping; a shot was fired, and the dog ordered to retrieve. The 1940s saw the introduction of double-marked retrieves and simple blinds. Junior or derby dogs were often required to honour. Often dog and handler ran from within a plywood blind, the dog peering through an opening to mark the falls. It was in 1950 that live, shackled ducks were used at a trial and the majority of novice dogs were afraid to pick them up, indicating the desirability of training with live birds if retrievers were to preserve live, shot cripples.

Field trials should simulate, as nearly as possible, the conditions met in an ordinary day's shoot. The function of a non-slip retriever is to seek and retrieve "fallen" game when ordered to do so. The dogs are judged on natural abilities including memory, sagacity, intelligence, attention, nose, courage, perseverance, and style, and abilities acquired through training: steadiness, control, response to direction, and delivery.

Licensed trials today, normally held over a two-day weekend, have two All-Age Stakes, one Qualifying Stake, one Junior Stake, and most likely one Puppy Stake. In addition to the licensed trials held from March to November each year across Canada, many clubs hold training or picnic trials during other months. The type of test a dog will encounter depends on the age and ability of the dog. A Puppy Stake, for dogs six months to one year old, will consist of several single marks on land and water. A mark constitutes a dog seeing a bird in the air and, as it falls, marking the fall. A Junior Stake, for dogs one to two years of age, will normally consist of single and double marks on land and water. Unlike a puppy, a Junior dog must be steady on line and not leave until the handler has told him to retrieve. A Qualifying Stake will consist of several marks, normally three at one time, followed by a blind on land and then repeated on water. In a blind a dog does not see the bird placed and is initially lined by the handler to that bird, and if necessary, handled by whistle and hand signals. An All-Age Stake will consist of several marks, normally three at one time (with one or two blinds at the same time or following) on land and repeated on water. In both Qualifying and All-Age Stakes a dog will be required to honour the work of another dog.

The idea of holding a Canadian Retriever Championship Stake for dogs which qualify each year by their placements in an Open, Limited, Special, or Amateur All-Age Stake became a reality in 1949 when the National Retriever Club (Canada) Ltd. was incorporated under the laws of the Province of British

Columbia. The first Championship Stake was held in Vancouver on November 3, 4, and 5, 1950 with twelve dogs competing. On August 25, 1958, The National Retriever Club of Canada was incorporated under Federal Charter to succeed the previous club, thus giving the Club a truly "National" character. National Championships have been held annually since 1950, rotating across Canada in three-year cycles with the country being divided into three areas—west, central, and east.

The number of competing dogs has increased gradually over the years. Following the war, the growth of Retriever Trials has been one of the remarkable developments in the history of pure-bred dogs. Today, there are more than fifty Retriever field trial clubs located across Canada, holding at least one licensed trial each year. In 1966, thirty-one clubs hosted fifty-four licensed stakes; in 1980, forty-five clubs held one hundred and eighteen, representing over 4300 entries, an increase of more than 800 over the 1978 entries.

The need for conservation, the popularity of the Retriever breeds and the enjoyment field trialing offers as a sport all indicate that Retrievers and trials will continue to interest dog owners and will encourage increased participation in the future.

Field Trials for Spaniels

It has been said that the real history of the English Springer Spaniel in Canada began with Mr. Eudore Chevrier, whose Avandale Kennels were located at Winnipeg, Manitoba. Field Trial Rules for Spaniel Trials were written by Mr. William H. Pym of Vancouver in 1934. The first record of a licensed trial in the last fifty years was one held by the English Springer Spaniel Club of B.C. in 1936. At that trial two Avandale Springers figured prominently in the awards. The same club held trials in 1937. In 1938 the Manitoba Gun Dog Club ran licensed trials as it did in 1939. In 1939 the Sporting Dog Club of Western Canada also held trials for Cockers and Springers. The Standard Procedure for Spaniel Field Trials in the Field Trial Rules and Regulations was adopted from the American Kennel Club in the mid-'50s. An ardent group of Canadians, in competition in the United States, banded together to formulate regulations for trialing in Canada. While the sport of spaniel trialing has roots as far back as Mr. Chevrier in Manitoba, it was in essence adopted from the Americans.

The Field Trial Rules and Standard Procedure for Spaniel Trials have, from the beginning, insisted that the purpose of a Spaniel Field Trial is to demonstrate the performance of a perfectly trained spaniel in the field; his performance should not differ from that in an ordinary day's shooting, except that in the trials he should work in a nearly perfect way.

In the mid-1950s, there were five clubs in Ontario holding licensed events. The records show a stormy period of organization. There were several major issues of concern: the holding of a national championship, proper care and handling of birds, use of points posted to judge a performance, and a Standard Procedure for the water test.

The first National Championship was held in 1960 by the Western Ontario Spaniel Club. The second-place dog was a Cocker Spaniel. In those days the springers and cockers could and did compete on equal terms. Today, there are few cockers of field trial quality. The demise of the cocker as a competitive dog is a major concern of ardent spaniel trialers. In the early days, the performance of the dogs was more akin to the typical style of the cocker—close-working and very animated. The expectation changed in the mid-'60s and '70s to a big, hard-running dog that covered much ground quickly. The short-legged cocker just couldn't meet this expectation. The '60s and '70s brought the advent of the big white and liver spaniel, fine of bone and angulation and of great speed. These dogs flew over the ground in great casts, abandoning the flat, windshield wiper pattern or figure-eight pattern so frequently associated with typical spaniel work. They found birds quickly and were a thrill to handle and judge.

The National Championship ceased after 1964 and was not revived until 1972 by the Western Ontario Spaniel Club. The major issue to fracture the sport was a Standard Procedure for a water test. The Criminal Code of Canada prohibits the release of a bird from hand for the expressed purpose of shooting it. There was considerable discussion of the letter of this law and its intent as it applied to having full flying birds at a spaniel trial. There were guidelines presented for care and humane treatment of the birds. There were several suggestions tendered to bring greater consistency into the sport. The water test procedures parted the many viewpoints. It wasn't until the late '70s that a procedure was finalized and entered in the revised rules and regulations along with a series of Standard Procedures.

In the early '70s the Canadian Spaniel Field Trial Association was formed with representation from all the major clubs in Canada. The purpose of the Association was to co-ordinate trialing, bring needed revisions to the regulations, and provide a forum at each National Championship for discussion.

The CSFTA is only a focal point for yearly discussion at the National and holds its main priority as finding a host club for the ensuing National Championship Stake. The big-running, long-legged, white dogs of the early '70s are waning in popularity in contrast to the closer working, animated spaniels (probably far more atypical of the spaniel in the field). The influence of the west and east will continue to enrich the game. Entries at spaniel trialing events are greater than ever before, more good dogs are available, and there is a larger brain trust for training and advice. The trials themselves are very cordial; fierceness of competition is evident, but sportsmanship prevails.

Tracking in Canada

In the very late 1940s and early '50s, Tracking was in its infancy in Canada. There had been Tracking Tests held in the provinces of Quebec and British Columbia only. At the time, there was only a single test, the TD (Tracking Dog). This test was identical to the one approved by the American Kennel Club. In the very early '60s our Tracking Test Regulations were rewritten, and changes were made in the TD Test, and a new and more difficult Test proposed and accepted. At the same time all mention of Tracking was removed from the Obedience Trial Standards and Regulations where they had been included and a new booklet on Tracking came into being.

Tracking has come a long way since the '50s, with some provinces having several TD and TDX (Tracking Dog Excellent) tests held within their boundaries each year. From Quebec to British Columbia one will find at least one Tracking Test annually.

There are now numerous knowledgeable persons approved as Tracking Test judges. This is a far cry from 1951 when there was only one approved judge in Canada west of Ontario, a resident of British Columbia. It is somewhat unfortunate that Tracking activities are not widely promoted. Many persons are totally unaware of the ability of even the smallest of breeds to follow a certain "human scent" over a prescribed course of varying

Tracking: Dog on track during a test. The dog must discern a pre-laid track by nose only.

terrain. The general public should be offered an opportunity to observe dogs proving their ability to do "scent work" under diverse weather and ground conditions.

Lure Coursing

One might suspect that folk who spend entire weekends outdoors encouraging their dogs to chase a white plastic garbage bag are beyond recall. Consider, however, that the dogs are sighthounds; that is, those breeds stimulated by sight to hunt game using their remarkable athletic talents. Consider further that today it is neither necessary nor morally acceptable for sighthounds to chase live game for sport or sustenance of hound and master. That is why owners of Afghans, Borzoi, Scottish Deerhounds, Greyhounds, Irish Wolfhounds, Whippets, Salukis, Pharaoh Hounds, Ibizans, and Basenjis are releasing their dogs on a merry chase after simulated prey (the white garbage bag) in the exciting new sport of lure coursing.

Although organized lure coursing began in the United States in 1972, the first Canadian lure coursing club was founded in Victoria, B.C. in 1976 and became the founding club of the Canadian Sighthound Field Association. The Canadian Sighthound Field Association has the goals of preserving and further developing the natural beauty, grace, speed, and coursing skill of the sighthound through a system of lure field trials.

The Vancouver Island Sighthound Association hosted the first Canadian lure field trials in 1976 with entries of over forty

Lure Coursing: During a lure coursing meet, the dogs chase a white lure operated on a continuous loop pulley system, which simulates the movement of a rabbit in the field.

hounds. The following year, eight more trials in Vancouver and on the Island attracted one hundred and forty-four entries; thirteen of them earned Canadian field championships. In June 1978, the first trials outside the West Coast were held in Ottawa by the Capital Area Sighthound Association. In 1981, there were thirty-three trials run in British Columbia, Alberta, Manitoba, Quebec, and Ontario. Over one hundred hounds had been awarded field championships and many had completed the requirements for the field champion excellent certificate. In January 1982, The Canadian Kennel Club officially recognized the sport.

The lure is the key element of the lure coursing system. It is attached to a line which is reeled in around special pulleys set in the ground by a special electric machine. The pulleys permit the lure to change direction thereby simulating turns made by live prey. The course may be from five to one thousand yards in length and the terrain may add additional challenge.

To be eligible to compete in a Canadian lure field trial a registered sighthound must be at least one year old; it may be spayed, neutered, or monorchid but may not exhibit any breed disqualification. Bitches in season and those dogs judged to be unsound prior to or during competition may not compete. Courses of up to three dogs of the same breed are determined by a random draw. Released by special slip-leads to the sound of a huntmaster yelling "Tally-ho!", the hounds are distinguished by coursing blankets of bright yellow, pink, or blue. Two judges score each dog on the basis of speed (25), agility (25), endurance

(20), enthusiasm (15), and follow (15) for a total of 100 points. At a trial each hound has the opportunity to run a preliminary course and a reversed final course. Thus, for each course, there is a possible combined score of 200. The first one over the finish line is not necessarily the winner. The dog with the highest score of the two courses is the winner with his competitors ranked accordingly.

Lure coursing is a rare opportunity to observe the sighthound in its working gait; the double suspension gallop. Whippets and Afghans are notorious for vocalizing their enthusiasm. The larger breeds are almost uncontrollable once sighted on the lure and require substantial handlers to anchor them at the start. Salukis and Greyhounds are spectacular coursers displaying great speed and power. Watching the hounds doing what comes naturally is an exciting experience.

Scent Hurdle Racing

The whole idea of scent hurdle racing is that a team of four dogs, one at a time, runs a course of four jumps, retrieves one of four dumbbells by scent discrimination, and carries it back over the four jumps to the finish line. The first team with all four dogs back with all the correct dumbbells wins. The course is forty-six feet long, and a winning time for *all four dogs* is around twenty-eight seconds.

Jumps are painted in team colours, and are set between ten and eighteen inches (at the shoulder height of the smallest dog on the team). The course consists of a start/finish line, four feet to the first jump, ten feet between jumps, and twelve feet to the dumbbell platform. The platform has four numbered sections on which the dogs' dumbbells are placed. Each dog wears a team jacket with his number; his dumbbells also bear this number. At the starting judge's whistle, the first dog on each team starts out on his course, chooses his own dumbbell, and returns to the finish line. As he crosses the line, the next dog on his team starts and so on until all four dogs have brought back the correct dumbbell. As each dog leaves the platform, the team's steward replaces his dumbbell with a spare so that all dogs have four dumbbells to choose from. If a dog returns with the wrong dumbbell or misses a jump, he must run again after the rest of his team has completed the course. Time penalties are assessed for propelling a dog over the starting line and for a dog

Scent Hurdling: Dog returning to handler after retrieving dumbbell during scent hurdling race.

entering the course before the previous dog has left it. A dog interfering with an opposing dog, or crossing the centre line between courses, dogs retrieving two incorrect dumbbells, the team steward encouraging or correcting a dog, or a handler stepping over the starting line onto the course will automatically lose the heat for that team. A race consists of three heats.

The first Scent Hurdle Racing Team ever to demonstrate at a dog show in Canada was put together in Regina during the spring of 1974. This combined team later ran against a team from Saskatoon's German Shepherd Dog Club. Later that year two Regina clubs each formed their own teams, and the Belvedere Tobacco Company donated a trophy for the best team in the country each year. The Belvedere Cup became the symbol of the annual National Scent Hurdle Racing finals. Yet another Saskatoon team was formed in 1975, the Hub City Racing Team, and this was also the year in which Regina teams were invited to the Calgary Stampede. A Winnipeg team and the Saskatchewan teams soon split further to produce more teams and better competition.

Today, scent hurdle races are run at nearly all point shows in Manitoba and Saskatchewan, as well as many sanctioned and fun matches. The many teams with their uniforms, dumbbells, jumps and dog jackets all done in club or team colours add a cheery note to the Best in Show festivities. The dogs' obvious enjoyment and their intense competitiveness draw hundreds of spectators to the shows, and the training that the dogs receive has propelled many of them into the Open and Utility rings.

CKC Events Statistics

Year	No. of Championship Shows	No. of Field Trials	No. of Obedience Trials & Tracking	No. of Entries in these Events
1915	14	—	—	1,400 (est)
1938	52	12	—	8,000 (est)
1958	114	67	91	25,597
1968	213	117	141	62,601
1978	453	189	317	189,903
1981	504	202	389	194,403

THE BREEDS

Histories, Sketches and Official Breed Standards

A COMPLETE HISTORY, breed standard, and sketch for each breed currently recognized by the CKC appears on the following pages. At present, pure-bred dogs are divided into six Groups for show purposes, and are presented alphabetically within their group.

For the benefit of the novice dog fancier, it must be explained that the breed standard is a description of the "ideal" for that breed and sets a goal towards which a breeder can work. Breed standards are also the "ideal" from which a judge will select his winners. Metric figures are shown in brackets in the breed standards. When metric measurement is implemented these figures will become effective.

The CKC is very proud of the sketches of the breeds. Commissioned by the CKC, the artist, Gertrude Stenhouse, worked closely with breeders and breed clubs across Canada and attempted at all times to draw what would be considered close to the "ideal" as described in the breed standards. We feel Miss Stenhouse has performed her duty admirably, and is to be congratulated on her 139 pages of sketches.

Colour photographs have been submitted and paid for by dog fanciers across the country. Photographs were reviewed and selected on the basis of colour clarity and quality of the breeds, with the ultimate goal of representing as many breeds as possible. The colour sections are meant to be entertaining, as well as informative, and should be viewed as such.

Certain breed standards contain "Disqualifications" which result in elimination for show purposes. All "Disqualifications" sections are found at the end of the breed standard and are in italics for ease of reference. In addition, the following disqualifications apply to all breeds:

The judge shall disqualify a dog, if in his opinion it is blind in one or both eyes, is a castrated male or spayed female.

A judge shall excuse a male dog which does not have two testicles located in the scrotum.

The Dog's Anatomy

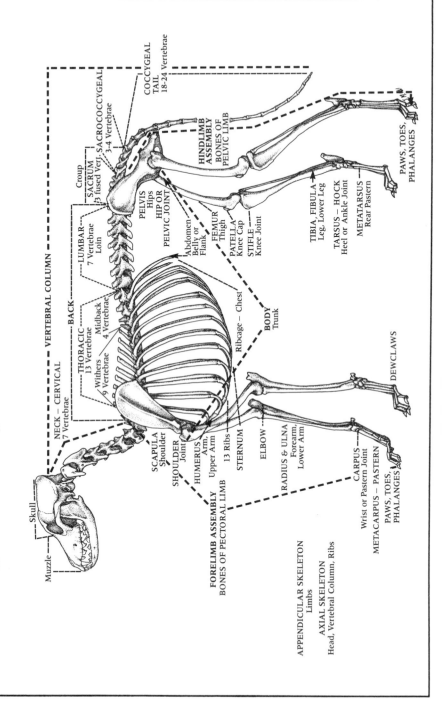

COCCYGEAL
TAIL
18-24 Vertebrae

Croup

SACRUM
3 fused Vert, SACROCOCCYGEAL
3-4 Vertebrae

HINDLIMB
ASSEMBLY
BONES OF
PELVIC LIMB

LUMBAR
7 Vertebrae
Loin

PELVIS
Hips
HIP OR
PELVIC JOINT

Abdomen
Belly or
Flank

FEMUR
Thigh

PATELLA
Knee Cap

STIFLE
Knee Joint

PAWS, TOES,
PHALANGES

TIBIA, FIBULA
Leg, Lower Leg

TARSUS — HOCK
Heel or Ankle Joint

METATARSUS
Rear Pastern

THORACIC
13 Vertebrae
Midback
4 Vertebrae

Withers
9 Vertebrae

BODY
Trunk

Ribcage — Chest

DEWCLAWS

NECK — CERVICAL
7 Vertebrae

VERTEBRAL COLUMN

BACK

SCAPULA
Shoulder

SHOULDER
Joint

HUMERUS
Arm,
Upper Arm

13 Ribs

STERNUM

ELBOW

RADIUS & ULNA
Forearm,
Lower Arm

CARPUS
Wrist or Pastern Joint

METACARPUS — PASTERN
PAWS, TOES,
PHALANGES

FORELIMB ASSEMBLY
BONES OF PECTORAL LIMB

Skull

Muzzle

APPENDICULAR SKELETON
Limbs

AXIAL SKELETON
Head, Vertebral Column, Ribs

GROUP I: SPORTING DOGS

Griffon
(Wire-Haired Pointing)

*T*HIS ROUGH-COATED SPORTING DOG was first known as the Korthals Griffon, so named for the man who standardized the breed, Eduard Korthals, a Dutchman. Born in Amsterdam, Korthals moved to Germany where he worked to perfect the breed between 1865 and 1885. At one time the breed was also known as the Griffon d'Arrêt à Poil Dûr.

Most authorities seem to agree that the breeds used in the development of the Wire-Haired Pointing Griffon were the French Pointer (Braque Français), a medium sized, energetic sporting dog and the French Barbet, an intelligent, obedient, water retriever. From the Braque the Wire-Haired Pointing Griffon is said to have inherited his keen nose and field ability; from the Barbet, his superior intelligence, his aptitude for working marshland, and his bristly, water-repellant coat. It is reported that it was the purity of its breeding that persuaded the Federation Cynologique Internationale (FCI) to classify the Wire-Haired Pointing Griffon as French. However, other writers claim that the bloods of the Otterhound, setter and spaniel were also used. But this opinion seems to be in the minority.

The breed was shown first in Britain in the late nineteenth century and came to this continent in 1901 where it was registered under its present name.

In addition to his harsh coat, which has been described as being "as rough as boar bristle," his colouring is distinctive: chestnut markings against a grey or "dirty white" background.

The breed is highly regarded as a sporting dog, being classified with the versatile gun-dog group—those that work equally well on land or over water. And because of his biddable, affectionate nature he can double as a house pet and companion for the weekend nimrod. Only occasionally does the Wire-Haired Pointing Griffon make an appearance in the show ring in Canada. It would be rare indeed to hear of one earning a group placing.

Griffon (Wire-Haired Pointing)

Official Breed Standard for the Griffon (Wire-Haired Pointing)

General Appearance: The Wire-Haired Griffon is a dog of medium size, fairly short-backed, rather a little low on his legs; he is strongly limbed, everything about him indicating strength and vigour.

His coat is harsh like the bristles of a wild boar and his appearance, notwithstanding his short coat, is as unkempt as that of the Long-Haired Griffon, but on the other hand he has a very intelligent air.

Size: Height—21½–23½ in. (55–60 cm) for males, and 19½–21½ in. (50–55 cm) for females.

Coat and Colour: Hard, dry, stiff coat, never curly, the undercoat downy. Steel grey with chestnut splashes, grey white with chestnut splashes, chestnut, dirty white mixed with chestnut, never black.

Head: Long, furnished with a harsh coat, forming a moustache and eyebrows; *skull* long and narrow; *muzzle* square. *Nose* always brown. *Eyes* large, open, full of expression, iris yellow or light brown. *Ears* of medium size, flat or sometimes slightly curled, set rather high, very lightly furnished with hair.

Neck: Rather long, no dewlap.

Forequarters: Shoulders long, sloping. Forelegs very straight, muscular, furnished with rather short wire hair.

Body: Ribs slightly rounded.

Hindquarters: Hind legs furnished with rather short stiff hair, the thighs long and well developed. Feet round, firm, and well formed.

Tail: Carried straight or gaily, furnished with a hard coat without plume, generally cut to a third of its length.

Pointer

THE POINTER HAS BEEN CALLED "the gun dog par excellence," and was named for the work he does— pointing game for the huntsman. At first called "the pointing dog," his lineage traces to sporting breeds imported into England from various continental countries, among them France, Italy, Germany, and Spain. But it is acknowledged that the chief country of development of the modern Pointer was England.

Towards the end of the 17th century a dog known as the double-nosed Spanish Pointer was used by huntsmen to locate game. This breed, it is reported, was both slow and cautious—too slow to keep pace with the advance in firearms—so a cross to the Foxhound produced a dog with the necessary speed. It has also been suggested that various other crosses were employed, namely setter, bloodhound, and greyhound. While some are said to have been disastrous, British breeders persisted until they had developed a dog that had a keen nose, intense concentration, pace, stamina, and nerve, while at the same time being amenable to discipline.

The first dog show held was in Newcastle-on-Tyne, Northumberland, in 1859. The purpose of the show was to prove that a working field dog could also be a beautiful animal. While this event was exclusively a competition for pointers and setters, it is historically important because it was the forerunner of the all-breed championship show.

A breeder from the north of England, William Arkwright, is credited with improving and stabilizing the breed. Old prints dating to Arkwright's time show little change from the good dogs of his day to the modern Pointer. The head is carried high, the tail extended straight behind him as his upturned nose with wide open nostrils searches the air for scents of game. When he locates it, the dog freezes "on point." Many are the tales told of dogs so well trained they held this statue-like pose for several hours.

White with liver, black, orange, or lemon markings are the usual coat colours, although self-coloured is also acceptable and at one time there was a strain of solid blacks.

Pointer

The Westminster Kennel Club show catalogue (1877) lists more than 100 Pointers in competition. Classes were divided "under and over fifty pounds." Winner of the Open Male class was listed for sale at $100. In 1889 there were fifty-four Pointers registered with The Canadian Kennel Club.

Official Breed Standard for the Pointer

General Appearance: The Pointer is bred primarily for sport afield; he should unmistakably look and act the part. The ideal specimen gives the immediate impression of compact power and agile grace; the head noble, proudly carried; the expression intelligent and alert; the muscular body bespeaking both staying power and dash. Here is an animal whose every movement shows him to be a wide awake, hard-driving hunting dog possessing stamina, courage, and the desire to go. And in his expression are the loyalty and devotion of a true friend of man.

Temperament: The Pointer's even temperament and alert good sense make him a congenial companion both in the field and in the home. He should be dignified, yet show a responsive attitude at all times.

Balance and Size: Balance—over-all symmetry—is much more important in the Pointer than size. It is just as vital in a dog bred for field work as it is in an athlete or a racehorse, and for the same reasons: it indicates muscular co-ordination, endurance, and an equilibrium of power. Whether large or small, a well put-together Pointer, "smooth all over," is to be preferred to an uneven one with contrasting good and bad points. Provided there is balance, considerable variation in size and weight is permissible.

Coat and Colour: Coat short, dense, smooth with a sheen. Liver, lemon, black, orange; either in combination with white or solid-coloured. A good Pointer cannot be a bad colour. In the darker colours, the nose should be black or brown; in the lighter shades it may be lighter or flesh-coloured.

Head: *Skull* long and proportionately wide, but indicating length rather than width. Slight furrow between the eyes, cheeks cleanly chiselled. A pronounced stop midway between nostrils and occiput. *Muzzle* long, in the same plane as the skull. Nostrils large, spongy, widely open. *Jaws* ending level and square, with scissors or even bite, the flews clean. *Eyes* of medium size, rounded, pleasant in expression and the darker the better. *Ears* set on at eye level. When hanging naturally, they should be somewhat pointed at the tip—never round—and soft and thin in leather. They should reach below the lower jaw, close to the head, with little or no folding.

Neck: Long, dry, muscular and slightly arched, springing cleanly from the shoulders.

Forequarters: Shoulders long, thin, and sloping. The top of blades close together. Elbows well down, directly under the withers and truly parallel, so as to work just clear of the body. Forelegs straight and with oval bone. Knee joint never to knuckle over. Pasterns of moderate length, perceptibly finer in bone than the leg, and slightly slanting.

Body: Back strong and solid, with only a slight rise from croup to top of shoulders. Chest, deep rather than wide, must not hinder free action of the forelegs. The breastbone bold without being unduly prominent. The ribs well sprung, descending as low as the elbow-point. Loin of moderate length, powerful and slightly arched. Croup falling only slightly to base of tail. Tuck-up should be apparent, but not exaggerated.

Hindquarters: Muscular and powerful, with great propelling leverage. Thighs long and well developed. The hocks clean and parallel. Stifles wide and well bent. Decided angulation is the mark of power and endurance. Feet oval, with long, closely-set arched toes, well padded, and deep.

Tail: Heavier at the root, gradually tapering to a fine point. Length no greater than to reach to the hock joint. Carried straight, ideally on a level with the back.

Gait: Smooth and frictionless, with a powerful hindquarters' drive. The head should be carried high, the nostrils wide, the tail moving from side to side rhythmically with the pace, giving the impression of a well-balanced, strongly-built hunting dog capable of top speed combined with great stamina.

Faults:

1. General Appearance—Lack of true Pointer type, hound or terrier characteristics.

2. Temperament—timid, unruly.

3. Head—Blocky or apple head. Short or snipey muzzle or frog face. Bulging cheeks or pendulous flews. Lack of stop, down-faced, Roman nose. Undershot or overshot. Small or dry nostrils.

4. Ears—Low set, round, heavy, folded, leathery or hound ears.

5. Eyes—Light, hard, almond, or staring eyes.

6. Neck—Ewe neck. Throatiness. Short, thick neck.

7. Shoulders—Loaded or bossy shoulders. Set wide apart at top. Straight shoulder, no slope.

8. Front—Elbows turned either in or out. Forelegs knuckled over. Straight pasterns, terrier-front. Bone of forelegs coarse, fine, or round. Narrow chested, shallow, shelly, pigeon-breasted. Chest too wide, resulting in elbows out. Ribs too flat or too barrelled.

9. Back—Roach or sway back. Unbalanced length of body. Cobbiness. Steep rise, or none at all, in topline. Sagging or long, thin loin. Croup falling away too sharply.

10. Tail—Rat tail. Set on too high or too low. Carried between the legs, or carried high, flag-pole tail.

11. Hindquarters—Straight or narrow stifles. Cowhocks. Lack of angulation or straight in stifle. Any suggestion of weakness in hindquarters.

12. Feet—Cat-foot. Thin or soft pads. Splayed feet. Flat toes.

13. Coat—Long hair or curl. Soft or silky coat.

14. Colour—Weak or washed-out colours. Light or flesh-coloured nose in a dark-coloured dog. Butterfly nose.

15. Gait—Crossing-over, sprawling or side-tracking. Stepping too high in front—the hackney gait.

(Breed Standard continued)

Scale of Points:

Head	10
Ears	3
Eyes	4
Neck	5
Shoulders	8
Front	6
Back	4
Tail	5
Hindquarters	15
Feet	9
Coat and colour	5
Gait	6
Balance and true Pointer type	20
TOTAL	100

Pointer
(German Long-Haired)

RAREST OF THE German pointers, the German Long-Haired, is closely related to three other long-coated sporting breeds of German origin: the Large Munster-lander, the Small Munsterlander, and the Wachtelhund, the latter being the German equivalent to the English Spaniel. Of these, only the German Long-Haired Pointer is officially recognized by The Canadian Kennel Club.

Tallest of the four breeds, the German Long-Haired stands 25 to 27½ in. (63 to 70 cm) at the shoulder. The breed has a long, soft coat in solid liver, liver with white markings, or white with liver markings. The tail is long and feathered and there is feathering on the legs.

In outline the breed resembles a rather heavily made setter, which probably gives rise to the assumption, held by some writers, that the German Long-Haired Pointer represents a cross between the old-fashioned Gordon Setter and the French Spaniel. Those who hold this view state that the breed appeared on the scene no earlier than 1860.

However, noted canine authority, writer, and international all-breed judge Ivan Swedrup, writes that the breed traces back at least to mediaeval times. Breeds similar to this have been known for several centuries in northern Germany where they were valued as farm and hunting dogs.

On the continent the German Long-Haired seems to have reached its peak of popularity at the turn of the century. But there are still a few kennels breeding Long-Haireds in Germany, where it is highly regarded as a versatile gun dog and family companion.

A few specimens have been imported to Canada and have made rare appearances at dog shows. When they do sporting dog enthusiasts invariably ask: "What breed is that?" because the general appearance is totally different from that of the other two breeds of German Pointer—the Shorthaired and the Wire-Haired. The Long-Haired is not officially recognized by the American Kennel Club.

Pointer (German Long-Haired)

Official Breed Standard for the Pointer (German Long-Haired)

General Appearance: Strong muscular build, streamlined appearance. Massive and bear-like look is to be avoided. With lightweight dogs strong muscles are essential. Intelligent expression, noble and clean-cut outlines. Dogs under 22 in. (56 cm) and those with poor bone structure should not be used for breeding purposes.

Coat and Colour: Great importance to be given to coat. The coat should not be excessive nor too short; on the back and the side of the body approximately 1–2 in. (3–5 cm) long. Underneath the neck, the chest, and belly, the hair can be somewhat longer. On the ears the hair is wavy and overhanging. Tail with good feathering. Backs of the front and hind legs are feathered, shorter on the lower running parts of the leg. Spaces between toes have dense hair growth for protection against rough ground. Protruding hair between the toes is not desired. On the head, hair is considerably shorter, but nevertheless longer than on a short-haired dog. Over-all, the coat should be smooth and slightly waved so that the dog is able to shake off water easily. The hair may be shiny, but not silky, and should be firm to the touch. The complete coat only develops fully after the first year of life, often still later. During summer the dog loses more than half of its winter coat. Colour brown, brown with light spot on chest, white with patches and small brown spots.

Head: Long, equally divided between skull and jaw. Slightly curved crown. Stop rising gradually, not abruptly cut in. Bridge of *nose* only slightly arched and not too narrow. Depending on the colour of the dog, the nose should be more or less brown. Nose not split. Lips not overhanging too much. Over- and under-biters should not be used for breeding purposes. *Eyes* brown, no light hawk's eye. Eyes well closed, without visible red eyelid. Dogs with open eyes should not be used for breeding purposes. The eyes should be neither too deep in the skull nor protruding. *Ears* lying close to skull, broad at the skull, rounded at the bottom, inner edges covered with hair. Hairs on the ears slightly waved and overhanging at end of ear.

Neck: Strong and noble. Without loose skin, joining the chest in a pleasing line.

Forequarters: The shoulder blade, the upper arm, the forearm and pastern should, when viewed from the front, be vertical when the dog is standing. Shoulders should lie flat against the body. The elbows pointing directly to the rear or at the most slightly outwards. When the dog is motionless and seen from the side, shoulder blade and forearm should form a 90-degree angle, but the forearm with the lower arm a flat angle (about 135 degrees). No steep pastern, joint only very slightly bent, yet not entirely straight.

Body: Back has to be straight and strong, not overbuilt in front or back. Back should be strongly developed without sag. Chest should give the appearance of depth in comparison to width, no barrel-shaped appearance. Has to be deeper than the elbow joint, accordingly the abdomen must be correspondingly tucked up to give the hind legs sufficient room when running. Loins especially muscular. Croup should not be straight, but slightly sloped. Downwards hanging skinfolds on the flanks are to be avoided. The back determines the right proportions of the length to the height of the dog.

Hindquarters: Seen from the back, the hip bone, the thigh bone, the shank bone and the metatarsus should form a vertical line. Well-angled hocks. Dewclaws are to be removed. Toes well closed. Pads firm and strong.

Tail: High set, either almost straight or slightly bent upwards. Should not be carried too high, but at least in the front part, almost horizontal. The tail tip should not hang forward. Good feathers, longest at the middle of the tail.

Faults:
Bushy eyebrows and long beard.
Curly hair and curls.
Red or black nose.
Open eyes.
Ears too long or too big. Leathery ends on ears.
Cowhocks. Bowed legs.
Cat- or long hare-paws.
Curled tail.

Disqualifications: *Black, red, and pure white with only little markings.*

Pointer
(German Shorthaired)

BY THE 19TH CENTURY the right to hunt game in Germany was no longer restricted to the nobility. And while there were still those who maintained kennels of specialist sporting dogs for hunting fur or feather, on land or over water, maintaining dogs in variety was beyond the means of the average sportsman. The need for an all-purpose gun dog was obvious and breeders rose to the challenge. Perhaps the most significant contribution to the group of dogs now known as the "versatile gun dogs" was the German Shorthaired Pointer whose development began in Germany between 1870 and 1880.

Based mainly on dogs of Spanish Pointer origin, crosses to various breeds were tried—with mixed results. The most successful breeders are said to have followed the advice of Prince Albrecht zu Solms-Brauenfels, which was to forget how the dog looked. The breeders' first consideration should be how the dog worked. Once the desired working ability had been achieved, he claimed, good conformation would follow as a natural result. The most significant advance in achieving the goal of the all-purpose dog was the introduction of English Pointer blood, which added dash and superior scenting ability.

For a time this also added the Pointer's upturned nose, as evidenced by early photographs. But by the 1880s two outstanding specimens had been bred: Nero v Hoppenrade and Treff, who were to become the pillars of the emerging "Kurzhaar" or the German Shorthaired Pointer, as it is known in this country. By 1911 type had been standardized and the new breed did everything that was expected of it. News of the Kurzhaar spread and in 1925 the first imports began arriving in the United States. By 1928 there was sufficient interest in the breed to warrant its official recognition by the American Kennel Club. Three years later the breed was also registered in Canada.

Since its introduction the German Shorthaired Pointer has accounted for a growing number of Dual Champions—dogs that have qualified in Field Trials as well as in the show ring. The breed continues to give the lie to those who claim that brains

Pointer (German Shorthaired)

and beauty can't be found in the same dog. This breed states loud and clear—"yes, they can."

Official Breed Standard for the Pointer (German Shorthaired)

General Appearance: The over-all picture which is created in the observer's eye should be that of an aristocratic, well-balanced, symmetrical animal with conformation indicating power, endurance, agility, and a look of intelligence and animation.

The dog should be neither unduly small nor conspicuously large. It should rather give the impression of medium size, but be like the proper hunter, "with a short back, but standing over plenty of ground." Tall, leggy individuals seldom possess endurance or sound movement.

Dogs which are ponderous or unbalanced because of excess substance should be definitely rejected. The first impression should be that of a keenness which denotes full enthusiasm for work without indication of nervous or flighty character. Movement should be alertly co-ordinated without waste motion.

Grace of outline, clean-cut head, sloping shoulders, deep breast, powerful back, strong quarters, good bone composition, adequate muscle, well-carried tail and taut coat all of which should combine to produce a look of nobility and an indication of anatomical structure essential to correct gait which must indicate a heritage of purposefully conducted breeding.

Size: Weight—dogs, 55−70 lb. (25−32 kg); bitches, 45−60 lb. (20−27 kg)
Height—dogs, 23−25 in. (58−64 cm); bitches, 21−23 in. (53−58 cm)

Coat and Skin: The skin should look close and tight. The hair should be short and thick and feel tough and hard to the hand; it is somewhat longer on the underside of the tail and the back edge of the haunches. It is softer, thinner, and shorter on the ears and the head.

Colour: Solid liver, liver and white spotted, liver and white spotted and ticked, liver and white ticked, liver roan. Any colours other than liver and white (grey white) are not permitted.

Head: Clean-cut, neither too light nor too heavy, in proper proportion to the body. **Skull** should be reasonably broad, arched on side and slightly round on top. Scissura (median line between the eyes at the forehead) not too deep, occipital bone not as conspicuous as in the case of the Pointer.

The *foreface* should rise gradually from nose to forehead—not resembling the Roman nose. This is more strongly pronounced in the dog than in the bitch, as befitting his sex. The chops should fall away from the somewhat projecting nose. Lips should be full and deep, never flewy. The chops should not fall over too much, but form a proper fold in the angle. The jaw should be powerful and the muscles well developed.

The line to the forehead should rise gradually and should never possess a definite stop as in the case of the Pointer, but rather a stop-effect when viewed from the side, due to the position of the eyebrows.

The *muzzle* should be sufficiently long to enable the dog to seize properly and to facilitate his carrying game a long time. A pointed muzzle is not desirable. The entire head should never give the impression of tapering to a point. The depth should be in the right proportion to the length, both in the muzzle and in the skull proper. **Nose** brown, the larger the better; nostrils well opened and broad. Flesh-coloured and spotted noses are not desirable. The **teeth** should be strong and healthy. The molars should intermesh properly. Incisors should fit close in a true scissors bite. Jaws should be neither overshot nor undershot. The *eyes* should be of medium size, full of intelligence, and expressive, good-humoured, and yet radiating energy, neither protruding nor sunk. The eyelids should close well. The best colour is a dark shade of brown. Light yellow, china, or wall (bird of prey) eyes are not desirable. **Ears** should be broad and set fairly high, lie flat and never hang away from the head. Placement should be above eye level. The ears, when laid in front without being pulled, should about meet the lip angle. In the case of heavier dogs, they should be correspondingly longer.

Neck: Of adequate length to permit the jaws reaching game to be retrieved, sloping downwards on beautifully curving lines. The nape should be rather muscular, becoming gradually larger towards the shoulders. Moderate hound-like throatiness permitted.

Forequarters: The shoulders should be sloping, movable, well covered with muscle. The shoulder blades should lie flat. The upper arm (also called the cross bar, *i.e.*, the bones between the shoulder and elbow joints) should be as long as possible, standing away somewhat from the trunk so that the straight and closely muscled legs, when viewed from in front, should appear to be parallel. Elbows which stand away from the body or are pressed right into same indicate toes turning inwards or outwards, which should be regarded as faults. Pasterns should be strong, short, and nearly vertical.

Body: Back should be short, strong, and straight with a slight rise from root of tail to withers. The breast in general should give the impression of depth rather than breadth; for all that, it should be in correct proportion to the other parts of the body with fair depth of chest.

The ribs forming the thorax should be well curved and not flat; they should not be absolutely round or barrel-shaped. Ribs that are entirely round prevent the necessary expansion of the chest when taking breath. The back ribs should reach well down.

The circumference of the breast immediately behind the elbows should be smaller than that of the breast about a hand's-breadth behind elbows, so that the upper arm has room for movement.

Excessively long or hog-backed should be penalized. Loins strong, of moderate length and slightly arched. Tuck-up should be apparent.

Hindquarters: The hips should be broad with hip sockets wide apart and fall slightly toward the tail in a graceful curve. Thighs strong and well muscled. Stifles well bent. Hock joints should be well angulated with strong, straight bone structure from hock to pad. Angulation of both stifle and hock joints should be such as to combine maximum combination of both drive and traction. Hocks should turn neither in nor out. Feet should be compact, close-knit and round to spoon-shaped, the toes sufficiently arched and heavily nailed. The pad should be strong and hard.

Bones: Thin and fine bones are by no means desirable in a dog which should be able to work over any and every country and should possess strength. The main importance accordingly is laid not so much on the size as being in proper proportion to the body. Dogs with coarse bones are handicapped in agility of movement and speed.

Tail: Is set high and firm, and must be docked, leaving approximately two-fifths of length.
   The tail hangs down when the dog is quiet, is held horizontally when he is walking, never turned over the back or considerably bent but violently wagged when he is on the search.

Gait: A smooth, lithe gait is most desirable.

Symmetry and field quality are most essential. A dog well balanced in all points is preferable to one with outstanding good qualities and defects.

Faults: Bone structure too clumsy or too light; head too large; too many wrinkles in forehead; dish-faced, snipey muzzle; ears too long, pointy or fleshy; flesh-coloured nose; eyes too light, too round or too closely set together; excessive throatiness; cowhocks; feet or elbows turned inward or outward; down on pasterns; loose shoulders; sway back; black coat or tricoloured; any colours except liver or some combination of liver and white.

Pointer
(German Wire-Haired)

THERE IS NO DOUBT that the German Wire-Haired Pointer is a "man-made" breed. But just how this was accomplished seems to be a moot point. Most authorities claim the breed represents a cross between the German Shorthaired Pointer and the Airedale. Other researchers claim that the breed descends from the ancient Sheep- or Hunting-Poodles, and that at one time it was divided into four breeds now classified as one under the name "Deutsche Drahthaar" in Germany, its country of origin. Yet another school of thought has it that the Wire-Haired also carries the blood of the Griffon and the Bloodhound.

Whichever, the breed was developed and stabilized by a group of German sportsmen at the turn of the century. Their aim was to produce a gun dog with the versatility of the Shorthair but aggressive enough to be used in hunting dangerous quarry. What they arrived at was a dog along classic pointer lines, possessing more nerve but slightly less speed than the Shorthair, with a tough, weather-resistant coat that would protect him in the densest cover. In Germany the breed gained quite a reputation as a versatile gun dog and its popularity rose, but it was some years before the Wire-Haired became known outside its home borders.

On two occasions, in 1910 and again in 1920, efforts were made to introduce the Wire-Haired in the United States, but these met with small success. However, after World War II, interest on this continent was again revived and this time the breed caught on. In 1959 the breed was officially recognized by the American Kennel Club and the standard as adopted then is still in use in both Canada and the United States.

Pointer (German Wire-Haired)

Official Breed Standard for the Pointer (German Wire-Haired)

General Appearance: The German Wire-Haired Pointer is a dog that is essentially Pointer in type, of sturdy build, and lively manner, having an intelligent, determined expression.

Temperament: In disposition the dog has been described as energetic, rather aloof but not unfriendly.

Size: Height of males should be from 24–26 in. (61–66 cm) at the withers, bitches smaller but not under 22 in. (56 cm).

Coat and Colour: The coat is weather resisting and to some extent water repellent. The undercoat is dense enough in winter to insulate against the cold but so thin in summer as to be almost invisible. The distinctive outer coat is straight, harsh, wiry and rather flat-lying, from 1½–2 in. (4–5 cm) in length, it is long enough to protect against the punishment of rough cover but not so long as to hide the outline. On the lower legs it is shorter and between the toes of softer texture. On the skull it is naturally short and close fitting, while over the shoulders and around the tail it is very dense and heavy. The tail is nicely coated particularly on the underside, but devoid of feather. These dogs have bushy eyebrows of strong, straight hair and beards and whiskers of medium length.

The coat is liver and white, usually either liver and white spotted, liver roan, liver and white spotted with ticking and roaning or sometimes solid liver. The nose is dark brown. The head is brown, sometimes with a white blaze, the ears brown.

Head: The head is moderately long, the *skull* broad, the occipital bone not too prominent. The stop is medium, the *muzzle* fairly long with nasal bone straight and broad, the lips a trifle pendulous but close and bearded. The *nose* is dark brown with nostrils wide open, and the teeth are strong with scissors bite. *Eyes* are brown, medium in size, oval in contour, bright and clear and overhung with bushy eyebrows. Yellow eyes are not desirable. The *ears,* rounded but not too broad, and close to sides of the head.

Neck: The neck is of medium length, slightly arched and devoid of dewlap; in fact, the skin throughout is notably tight to the body.

Forequarters: Forelegs are straight, with shoulders obliquely set and elbows close. Leg bones are flat rather than round, and strong, but not so heavy or coarse as to militate against the dog's natural agility.

Body: The body is a little longer than it is high, as ten is to nine, with the back short, straight and strong, the entire back line showing a perceptible slope down from withers to croup. The chest is deep and capacious, the ribs well sprung, loins taut and slender. Hips are broad, with croup nicely rounded. The tuck-up is apparent.

Hindquarters: The thighs are strong and muscular. The hind legs are moderately angulated at stifle and hock and as viewed from behind, parallel to each other. Round in outline, the feet are webbed, high arched with toes close, their pads thick and hard, and their nails strong and quite heavy.

Tail: The tail is docked, approximately two-fifths of original length.

Faults: A short smooth coat, a soft woolly coat, or an excessively long coat is to be severely penalized. Any black in the coat is to be severely penalized. Spotted and flesh-coloured noses are undesirable and are to be penalized.

Pudelpointer

TOWARDS THE LATTER PART of the 19th century, German sportsmen set themselves the task of breeding the ideal versatile gun dog. This "dream dog" would have the keen, game-finding nose of the pointer, the toughness to work over rugged terrain, and a coat that would defy the weather and protect the dog in dense, thorny cover. In addition it would be soft-mouthed and willingly retrieve both upland game and waterfowl. To this end, many sporting breeds were developed and if they did not quite measure up to the ideal of the "dream dog," some came very close. All enjoyed a share of popularity among sportsmen in their own country. A few, like the German Shorthaired and Wire-Haired Pointers and the Weimaraner, were well received in Canada and the United States. Others were not. One of these was the Pudelpointer or Poodlepointer as he is also known.

The breed is not, as the name suggests, a simple cross between the poodle and the pointer, although some writers would have it so. Instead, the breed is said to represent a cross between the Barbet Pointer (a woolly-coated French breed that figures importantly in the ancestry of many European sporting breeds) and various short-haired gun dogs. In turn, dogs from this cross were bred to the English Pointer. The leader in the Pudelpointer's development was Baron von Zedlitz.

The result of all this crossbreeding is a dog that stands about twenty-four inches at the shoulder and weighs from fifty-five to sixty pounds. The dog is said to be elegant in appearance with a head resembling that of the Drahthaar. It is active and eager to work, easily trained and well suited to water work. His fanciers claim he has no equal.

Nevertheless, his numbers seem to be declining in all countries annually. In Canada, the centre of greatest breed activity was in the Trenton, Ontario area with a scattering of enthusiasts elsewhere in the province. In Canada interest in the breed peaked during the early 1960s when it was officially recognized by The Canadian Kennel Club. One Pudelpointer was benched

Pudelpointer

in 1961 at the Burlington Kennel and Obedience Club show where it was part of a rare breeds exhibit. None have ever been shown in conformation, therefore there are no Pudelpointer champions of record in Canada. The breed is not recognized in the United States.

Official Breed Standard for the Pudelpointer

General Appearance: The over-all picture should be that of an agile, versatile hunting dog with sufficient height, standing over plenty of ground. The dog should look powerful, taut with grace and nobility.

Temperament: His character should indicate enthusiasm for work, keenness, spark, and strong nerves.

Coat and Colour: Coat dense and hard, rather tight to the body with fine woolly undercoat. Medium long. Dark liver to autumn leaves. Black only where dogs carry concentrated Pointer blood. Inconspicuous small white marks (chest and paws) are permitted.

Head: Long and wide, harmonically balanced muzzle and forehead. Well-developed beard and eyebrows. *Eyes* rather large, agile, dark amber, well-closed eyelids. Open eyelids disqualify dogs for breeding purposes. *Ears* medium size, close to head, slightly turned forward, not fleshy or houndy, rather pointed than round, and well covered with protecting hair.

Neck: Medium long, well muscled and arched.

Forequarters: Shoulder close to the body, well covered with muscles. Shoulder and upper arm with plenty of angulation creating a long stride. Elbow located well back off brisket neither turned in nor outwards. Forearm straight; dry, clear lines and bones; well covered with hard protecting hair.

Body: Chest wide, very deep, ribs rather barrel round. Short, strong loins and croup wide with well-developed muscles. Tail in line with croup, not carried upwards.

Hindquarters: Upper and lower thigh well angulated, lower thigh long with backward slope towards hock joint. Bone from hock to pad absolutely straight. Paws round, closed, with hard pad. Hairs on and between paws not long.

Tail: Rather thin, carried level, no feathering but covered with hard dense hair, docked like other versatile gun dog breeds.

Faults: Long, soft, open hair that does not fit close to the body, as well as short, mousy hair without beard.

▲**Pointer (German Shorthaired)**
Ch. Jontue of Abingdon
Breeders:
David & Anne-Louise King

ABINGDON KENNELS REG.
David & Anne-Louise King
35 High Point Rd.,
Don Mills, Ont. M3C 2R2

◄**Pointer (German Shorthaired)**
Ch. Crannaford Brightstar
Ch. Glenmajors Erin
Owner: Anne-Louise King

▲Retriever (Curly-Coated)
Ch. Windpatch Kyne Black
Pearl and puppies
Owner: Sandy Briggs

WIMBERWAY KENNELS (PERM.)
Sandy Briggs
RR 2, Claremont, Ont. L0H 1E0

▼Retriever (Labrador)
Can. Bda. Am. Ch.
Wimberway's Elosca Excole,
C.D.
Breeder/Owner: Sandy Briggs

◄Retriever (Labrador)
Can. Am. Ch. Proud Chico
von Schwarzenberg
(Sweden)
Breeder: Sven Eric Deler
Owners:
Mr. & Mrs. Dieter Dohmen
Box 4,
Crawford Bay, B.C. V0B 1E0
SHWARZENBERG KENNELS
REG.

◄Retriever (Flat-Coated)
Can. Ch., Am. WCX
Butterblac's Cruise Control
Breeder: Doug Windsor
Owners:
Dr. & Mrs. F. M. Bourassa
50 Wood Cres.,
Regina, Sask. S4S 6J7

▶Retriever (Labrador)
Can. Am. Ch. Casadelora's
All Spice
Breeders/Owners:
Mr. & Mrs. W. E. Brown
RR 3, Michael Rd.,
Ladysmith, B.C. V0R 2E0
CASADELORA KENNELS REG.

▼Retriever (Labrador)
O.T. Ch. & Ch. Redsky's
Dynamic Duke, Am. C.D.,
C.D.X. (CENTRE), and mother,
grandmother and daughter
Breeder/Owner:
Grace L. McDonald
P.O. Box 15, Dickens P.O.
Winnipeg, Manitoba R3E 1T0
REDSKY KENNELS REG. (PERM.)

▲Retriever (Labrador)
Ch. Springfields Uhuru
Breeder: Mrs. Shirley Costigan
Owner: Miss Joanne Costigan

SPRINGFIELD KENNELS REG.
Mrs. Shirley Costigan
Box 6, Site 12, SS 1,
Calgary, Alta. T2M 4N3

▼Retriever (Labrador)
Ch. Springfields
Fanny Sweet Adams
Breeder/Owner:
Shirley Costigan

▶Retriever (Labrador)
Can. Am. Ch. Sandylands
Royal Envoy
Breeders:
Mrs. Gwen Broadley &
Mr. Garner Anthony
Owners:
Joe & Pierrette Schormann
RR 2, Rang St. Joseph,
Perkins, P.Q.
J0X 2R0
NUTAK KENNELS REG.

**▼Retriever (Nova Scotia
Duck Tolling)**
Ch. Westerlea's White Ensign
Owner/Breeder: Alison Strang
2456-141st St.,
Surrey, B.C. V4A 4K2
WESTERLEA KENNELS REG.

◄Setter (English)
Ch. Ebtide's Lonesome Charlie
Breeder: Robert J. Tait
Owners: Brent & Judith Byers
901 Weldon Ave.,
Saskatoon, Sask.
INGLIS KENNELS REG.

▼Setter (Irish)
Can. Am. Ch. Redpride's
Irish Warlord
Breeder: Mrs. Teryl Ford
Owners:
Frank & Eleonore Rebischke
218 Oakmoor Pl. S.W.,
Calgary, Alta. T2V 4A4
(Photo by Jocelyn)

▶**Setter (Irish)**
Can. Am. Ch.
McCamon Marquis
Breeders/Owners:
Mr. & Mrs. J. S. Korpan
Sub. P.O. 24,
Saskatoon, Sask. S7M 0V0
McCAMON KENNELS REG.

▼**Spaniel (American Cocker)**
Ch. Shadyhill's Frost 'n Fire
Ch. Shadyhill's Basic Black
Ch. Shadyhill's
Painted Trillium
Breeder/Owner:
Jean M. Hallett
RR 1, Ess Rd.,
Elmsdale, N.S. B0N 1M0
SHADYHILL KENNELS (PERM.)

▲**Spaniel (English Cocker)**
Can. Am. Eng. Ch.
Bryansbrook High Society
Breeders:
Mr. & Mrs. B. Fosbrook
Owner: Mr. Eugene Phoa
Box 5, Site 16, RR 2,
South Edmonton, Alta.
T6C 4E6
WITTERSHAM KENNELS REG.

◀**Spaniel (English Cocker)**
Ch. Carnaby Calico
Breeders/Owners:
Mr. & Mrs. E. M. Brangers
Ms. Kerri Brangers
Carnaby Farm,
19th Ave., RR 2,
Markham, Ont. L3P 3J3
CARNABY KENNELS (PERM.)

▲Spaniel (English Cocker)
Can. Am. Ch. Ranzfel
Newsflash
Breeder/Owner:
Virginia L. Lyne
10712 McDonald Park Rd.,
RR 3, Sidney, B.C. V8L 3X9
RANZFEL KENNELS REG.

▼Spaniel (English Cocker)
Can. Am. Ch. Patchwork's
Just In Time
Owners:
Richard & Judy Rochefort
18 Blvd. des Haut-Bois,
Ste. Julie, P.Q. J0L 2S0
ROJU HILLS KENNELS

Spaniel (English Springer)
Linbar's Margaret Rose
Breeder: Mr. J. R. Johnson
Owner: David Withers
971 Wellington St.,
Sarnia, Ont. N7S 1C9

Spaniel (English Springer)
Ch. Linbar's Danny Boy, C.D.
Owner: Miss Dawn Withers
971 Wellington St.,
Sarnia, Ont. N7S 1C9

▲Vizsla (Smooth)
Ch. Janoras Pawlane Suntan
Breeder: John J. Janora
Owner: Dr. P. A. Wright
RR 3, Clair Road E.,
Guelph, Ont.
NAPKELTE KENNELS REG.

▶Weimaraner
Ch. Grayangel Innomine
Tribute
Ch. Beau's Girl Twinkeltoes
Breeder/Owner:
Mary Karen Mayo
3735 E.N. Territorial,
Ann Arbor, Michigan 48105
GRAYANGEL KENNELS REG.

▲Afghan Hound
Ch. Tessa's Chelsea Morning
Breeder: Steve van de Weghe
Owner: Shirley M. Clark
General Delivery,
Stettler, Alta.
SHIR-KAM KENNELS

◄Afghan Hound
Ch. Gold Coast Rasputin
Breeders/Owners:
Jack & Pamela Barnes
RR 1, E. Chezzetcook
Halifax County, N.S. B0J 1N0
WINDWARD KENNELS REG.

▲**Basenji**
Can. Am. Ch. Shantara's
Gentaa Snowdancer, C.D.
Can. Am. Ch. Vikentor's
Tam O'Shandar
Can. Am. Ch. Shantara's
Blactamb Solar Scene

Owner: Marnie Lang
202 Inglewood St.,
Winnipeg, Man. R3J 1W7
SHANTARA KENNELS REG.

▼**Basset Hound**
Can. Am. Ch. Heathrow's
Classic Image
Breeders/Owners:
Richard & Patricia Waterhouse
P.O. Box 35121, Stn. E,
Vancouver, B.C. V6M 4G1
HEATHROW KENNELS REG.

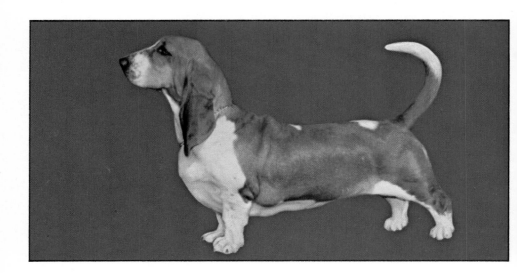

▲**Basenji**
Ch. Kurush Maika Kala
Ben Frederic
Breeders: Mr. & Mrs. R. R. Roy
Owners:
Mr. & Mrs. George Bujea
Box 612
Barrhead, Alta. T0G 0E0

▼**Basset Hound**
Can. Am. Ch. Chantinghall
Airs 'n Graces
Breeder/Owner:
Mrs. Rosemary McKnight
RR 3, Hwy 3,
Wainfleet, Ont. L0S 1V0
CHANTINGHALL KENNELS
(PERM.)

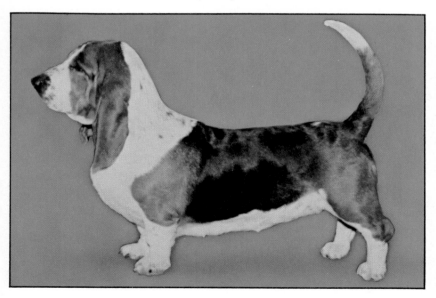

▶Basset Hound
Can. Am. Bda. Ch.
Scotts-Moore's Seymour, C.D.
Breeder: Mrs. Davida Scott
Owners: Davida Scott &
Lorraine Verrault
RR 2, Rigaud, P.Q. J0P 1P0
SCOTTS-MOORE'S KENNELS
REG.

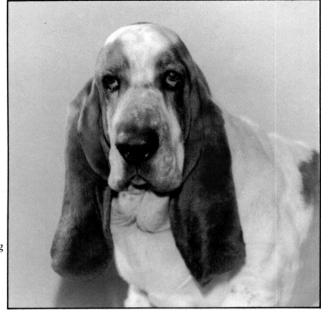

▼Borzoi
Ch. Koroba's Osiris Behzin Lug
Breeders/Owners:
John & Debra Hieter
324 Huron Rd.,
Kitchener, Ont. N2G 3W5
KOROBA KENNELS REG.

Retriever (Chesapeake Bay)

*T*HE HISTORY OF THIS made-in-America breed begins in 1807 when a British brig was shipwrecked off the coast of Maryland. Among the survivors were two puppies, a black male and a drab brown-coloured female. It is thought that these were Newfoundlands, or an early version thereof. The male was already named Sailor and the female was named Canton in honour of the American rescue ship. The puppies are reported to have been good water dogs and were later trained to retrieve goose and duck. But, as one writer observes, these dogs must have been much smaller than the present-day Newfoundlands, if they became efficient retrievers. In time, both dogs were mated to local hunting dogs in variety, it would seem, because suggested crosses include the Coonhound, English water poodle, and Curly and Flat-Coated Retriever.

What emerged from this mixture of sporting dog breeding was a dog that is claimed to have no equal in rough water. One of the breed's most distinctive features is its coat, which is described as being the "colour of dead grass." The outer guard hairs are oily to the touch, enabling the Chesapeake to shed ice particles and water with a few good shakes, while the downy undercoat keeps his skin from getting chilled.

The Chesapeake has always been valued for his utility rather than his looks, and because he is regarded as a rather plain-looking dog, the breed has never become very popular with dog show exhibitors. What is more, the breed is known to be an outdoor dog that does not take well to kennel life. Neither has the Chesapeake won top laurels in field trials, being outclassed by the faster Labrador Retriever. Breed supporters claim this is because the field trial does not present sufficient challenge to the sturdy "Chessy."

The Chesapeake is noted for its fondness of children and in recent years more than one member of the breed has been honoured with life-saving awards for heroism in saving toddlers from drowning. The Chesapeake Bay Retriever was admitted to registration in the United States in 1873 and in Canada in 1892.

Retriever (Chesapeake Bay)

Official Breed Standard for the Retriever (Chesapeake Bay)

General Appearance: The Chesapeake dog should show a bright and happy disposition and an intelligent expression, with general outlines impressive and denoting a good worker. The dog should be well proportioned, a dog with a good coat and well balanced in other points being preferable to the dog excelling in some but weak in others.

The texture of the dog's coat is very important, as the dog is used for hunting under all sorts of adverse weather conditions, often working in ice and snow. The oil in the harsh outer coat and woolly undercoat is of extreme value in preventing the cold water from reaching the dog's skin and aids in quick drying. A Chesapeake's coat should resist the water in the same way that a duck's feathers do. When he leaves the water and shakes himself, his coat should not hold the water at all, being merely moist.

Colour and coat are extremely important, as the dog is used for duck hunting. The colour must be as nearly that of his surroundings as possible and with the fact that dogs are exposed to all kinds of adverse weather conditions, often working in ice and snow, the colour of coat and its texture must be given every consideration when judging on the bench or in the ring.

Temperament: Courage, willingness to work, alertness, nose, intelligence, love of water, general quality, and, most of all, disposition should be given primary consideration in the selection and breeding of the Chesapeake Bay dog.

Size: Weight—males, 65–75 lb. (29–34 kg); females, 55–65 lb. (25–29 kg).
Height—males, 23–26 in. (58–66 cm); females, 21–24 in. (53–61 cm).

Coat and Colour: Coat should be thick and short, nowhere over 1 $\frac{1}{2}$ in. (4 cm) long, with a dense fine woolly undercoat. Hair on face and legs should be very short and straight with tendency to wave on the shoulders, neck, back, and loins only. The curly coat or coat with a tendency to curl not permissible. Any colour varying from a dark brown to a faded tan or deadgrass. Deadgrass takes in any shade of deadgrass, varying from a tan to a dull straw colour. White spot on breast and toes permissible, but the smaller the spot the better, solid colour being preferred.

Head: *Skull* broad and round with medium stop, *nose* medium short, *muzzle* pointed but not sharp. Lips thin, not pendulous. *Eyes* medium large, very clear, of yellowish colour and wide apart. *Ears* small, set well up on head, hanging loosely and of medium leather.

Neck: Of medium length with a strong muscular appearance, tapering to shoulders.

Forequarters: Shoulders sloping and should have full liberty of action with plenty of power without any restrictions of movement. Legs should be medium length and straight, showing good bone and muscle; pasterns slightly bent and of medium length.

Body: Chest strong, deep and wide. Barrel-round and deep. Body of medium length, neither cobby nor roached, but rather approaching hollowness, flanks well tucked up. Back should be short, well coupled and powerful.

Hindquarters: Back quarters should be as high or a trifle higher than the shoulders. They should show fully as much power as the forequarters. There should be no tendency to weakness in either fore or hindquarters. Hindquarters should be especially powerful to supply the driving power for swimming. Good hindquarters are essential. Hocks of medium length, with well-webbed hare feet of good size. The toes well rounded and close. The straighter the legs the better.

Tail: Should be medium length, varying from: males, 12–15 in. (30–38 cm) and females, 11–14 in. (28–36 cm). Medium heavy at base, moderate feathering on stern and tail permissible.

Disqualifications: *Black or liver coloured. White on any part of the body, except breast, belly or spots on feet. Feathering on tail or legs over 1 3/4 in. (4.5 cm) long. Dewclaws on hind legs, undershot, overshot or any deformity. Coat curly or tendency to curl all over body. Specimens unworthy or lacking in breed characteristics.*

Positive Scale of Points:

Head, including lips, ears and eyes   16
Neck   4
Shoulders and body   12
Back quarters and stifles   12
Elbows, legs and feet   12
Colour   4
Stern and tail   10
Coat and texture   18
General conformation   12

TOTAL 100

NOTE: The question of coat and general type of balance takes precedence over any scoring table which could be drawn up.

Approximate Measurements:

	in.	cm
Length head, nose to occiput	$9\frac{1}{2}-10$	$24-25$
Girth at ears	$20-21$	$51-53$
Muzzle below eyes	$10-10\frac{1}{2}$	$25-27$
Length of ears	$4\frac{1}{2}-5$	$11-13$
Width between eyes	$2\frac{1}{2}-2\frac{3}{4}$	$6-7$
Girth neck close to shoulders	$20-22$	$51-56$
Girth of chest to elbows	$35-36$	$89-91$
Girth at flank	$24-25$	$61-64$
Length from occiput to tail base	$34-35$	$86-89$
Girth forearms at shoulders	$10-10\frac{1}{2}$	$25-27$
Girth upper thigh	$19-20$	$48-51$
From root to root of ear, over skull	$5-6$	$13-15$
Occiput to top shoulder blades	$9-9\frac{1}{2}$	$23-24$
From elbow to elbow over the shoulders	$25-26$	$64-66$

Retriever (Curly-Coated)

A BREED OF BRITISH ORIGIN and the first known retriever, the Curly-Coated Retriever is depicted in sporting prints dating back 300 years. He was the first breed to be trained to retrieve game, especially waterfowl, and carry it carefully to the huntsman's hand. From all reports he was so good at his job the curly-coat became the gamekeepers' favourite.

However, because he was a "finished" breed long before stud books and breeding records were maintained, his ancestry must rely on a series of educated guesses. His general conformation and typically curled coat provide the clues. It is assumed that the St. John's Newfoundland (a breed similar to the modern Labrador Retriever), the English Water Spaniel, the poodle, and possibly various types of setters combined to produce the curly-coat. Some claim too that the Irish Water Spaniel was used, submitting that the proof is to be found in coat colour, which in the curly-coat may be either black or liver-coloured, the latter being the only acceptable colour in the Irish Water Spaniel. Those who disagree point to the fact that the curly-coat has not, and never has had, the spaniel's curly topknot.

The curly-coat was first shown in England in 1860 and in 1896 a specialty club was organized to promote the interests of the breed. In this they were successful until about the year 1914, when the popularity of both the Labrador and Golden Retrievers superseded that of the curly-coat. While the breed has never been able to recapture great public interest, it does have a faithful, but limited, following around the world.

It is said that today more curly-coats are registered in New Zealand and Australia than there are in Britain. Large breed entries are usually to be found at their more important championship shows and the breed is widely used for quail hunting. The curly-coat's "down under" supporters claim that the breed works as well on upland game as it does with waterfowl.

The Canadian Kennel Club Stud Book shows that Curly-Coated Retrievers were registered in Canada for the first time in the years 1912—1913.

Retriever (Curly-Coated)

Official Breed Standard for the Retriever (Curly-Coated)

General Appearance: A strong, smart, upstanding dog, showing activity, endurance and intelligence.

Coat and Colour: Coat should be one mass of crisp curls all over—a slightly more open coat not to be severely penalized. A prominent white patch on breast is undesirable, but a few white hairs allowed in an otherwise good dog. Colour: black or liver.

Head: Long and well proportioned, skull not too flat, *jaws* long and strong but not inclined to snipiness, *nose* black, in the black-coated variety, with wide nostrils. *Teeth* strong and level. *Eyes* black or brown, but not yellow, rather large but not too prominent. *Ears* rather small, set on low, lying close to the head, and covered with short curls.

Forequarters: Shoulders should be very deep, muscular, and obliquely placed. Legs should be of moderate length, forelegs straight and set well under the body.

Body: Chest not too wide, but decidedly deep. Body rather short, muscular, and well ribbed up. Loin powerful, deep, and firm to the grasp.

Hindquarters: Quarters strong and muscular, hocks low to the ground with moderate bend to stifle and hock. Feet round and compact with well-arched toes.

Tail: Should be moderately short, carried fairly straight and covered with curls, slightly tapering towards the point.

Faults: A saddle back or patch of uncurled hair behind the shoulder should be penalized.

Retriever (Flat-Coated)

THE FLAT-COAT WAS DEVELOPED from the crossing of continental water dogs (probably of poodle origin), land spaniels, and the Newfoundland dog. The latter was imported into England during the eighteenth and nineteenth centuries. The Newfoundlands undoubtedly reached the island province taken there by British seamen for, we are told, there was much trade between England and Newfoundland. The Newfoundlands were crossed with various sporting dogs and, it is suggested, an infusion of collie blood was used to straighten coat and increase working ability. In addition, a setter cross refined the type and improved scenting power.

Flat-coat type is reported as being stabilized about the year 1880. Credit for this is given to S.E. Shirley, MP, a remarkable man who founded The Kennel Club in 1873 when he was just twenty-nine years old, and who became its first chairman and president. While the term "flat-coat" did exist before Shirley's time, it is thought not to distinguish a specific breed but rather to classify a type of coat as distinct from others prevalent at the time, for example, "curly," "hairy," and "smooth."

Towards the end of the last century flat-coats were among the most popular of show dogs and equally prominent as sporting dogs. The breed standard was intentionally written so that no point of conformation would jeopardize the flat-coat's ability as a gun dog.

Interest in the breed held at a high level until World War I. Then the sportsmen's favour turned to Labrador and Golden Retrievers. Part of the reason for this could be the flat-coat's most notable patron, H.R. Cooke, a follower of Shirley, who lived to the age of 91. His Riverside kennels dominated the breed for sixty years which proved a discouragement to many breeders and they turned their attentions elsewhere.

Early in the 1930s there was a mild upsurge of interest in the breed, but the real impetus came in 1980 when a flat-coat was named Supreme Champion at Crufts'. Fanciers are taking a wary view of this success, fearing there might emerge two types

Retriever (Flat-Coated)

of flat-coat—one for show the other for the field. Many are determined this will not happen. In the world of retrievers these flat-coat breeders are quite satisfied to remain "a distinctive minority."

Official Breed Standard for the Retriever (Flat-Coated)

General Appearance: A bright, active dog of medium size with an intelligent expression, showing power without lumber and raciness without weediness.

Size: Weight—60–70 lb. (27–32 kg).

Coat and Colour: Coat should be dense, of fine quality and texture, flat as possible. Colour: black or liver.

Head: This should be long and nicely moulded, the *skull* flat and moderately broad. There should be a depression or stop between the eyes, slight and in no way accentuated, so as to avoid giving either a down- or a dish-faced appearance. The *nose* of good size with open nostrils. The *jaws* should be long and strong, with a capacity for carrying a hare or pheasant. The *eyes,* of medium size, should be dark brown or hazel, with a very intelligent expression (a round prominent eye is a disfigurement), and they should not be obliquely placed. The *ears* small, and well set on close to the side of the head.

Neck: The head should be well set in the neck which latter should be long and free from throatiness, symmetrically set and obliquely placed in the shoulders.

Forequarters: Shoulders should run well into the back to allow of easily seeking for the trail. The forelegs should be perfectly straight, with bone of good quality carried right down to the feet which should be round and strong.

Body: The back should be short, square, and well ribbed up, with muscular quarters. The chest should be deep and fairly broad, with a well-defined brisket, on which the elbows should work cleanly and evenly. The foreribs should be fairly flat showing a gradual spring and well arched in the centre of the body but rather lighter towards the quarters. Open couplings are to be ruthlessly condemned.

Hindquarters: The stifle should not be too straight or too bent and the dog must neither be cow-hocked nor move too wide behind; in fact, he must stand and move true all round on legs and feet, with toes close and well arched, the soles being thick and strong, and when the dog is in full coat the limbs should be well feathered. The legs and feet are of the greatest importance.

Tail: The stern short, straight and well set on, carried gaily but never above the level of the back.

Retriever (Golden)

UNTIL 1952, the history of the Golden, the most glamorous of the retrievers, read like a fairy-tale. This is how it went: In 1858 Sir Dudley Majoribanks, later Lord Tweedmouth, a Scotsman, was on a visit to the English seaside town of Brighton. While there he attended a circus and was so taken by a troupe of performing Russian sheepdogs he tried to buy a pair. The dogs' trainer would not sell a pair, claiming that this would break up the troupe. Whereupon Majoribanks bought the lot, took them home to his estate, "Guichan," in Scottish Border country, bred them and thus created the Golden Retriever.

The public loved the story but knowledgeable sporting dog people had their doubts. Well founded as it turned out, because in 1952 Majoribanks' breeding records from 1835 to 1890 were made public and they contained no mention of the Russian dogs. They did reveal that the Golden was all sporting blood, having been developed by crossing the wavy-coat Retriever with a yellow-coloured Tweed Water Spaniel, a breed common in the Border country. The first litter of four puppies was whelped in 1868 and named Crocus, Primrose, Cowslip, and Ada. In turn these dogs were crossed with the Red Setter and sandy-coloured Bloodhounds. Eventually line breeding created the Golden.

The breed was first exhibited in Britain in 1908 and was granted separate breed status in 1913. First classified as the Retriever (Golden and Yellow) in 1920, the name was changed to Golden Retriever. Since that year the breed has continued to grow in popularity around the world. Breeders have succeeded in retaining the Golden's sporting instincts as well as promoting it as a beautiful, top winning show dog. Mild mannered and extremely trainable, the Golden has excelled in obedience and has an outstanding record as a guide dog for the blind. It is reported that at the guide dog training schools there are fewer rejects among Golden Retrievers than there are for any other breed.

The Golden Retriever was first registered in Canada in 1927.

Retriever (Golden)

G. STENHOUSE

Official Breed Standard for the Retriever (Golden)

General Appearance: A symmetrical, powerful, active dog, sound and well put together, not clumsy or long in the leg, displaying a kindly expression and possessing a personality that is eager, alert, and self-confident. Primarily a hunting dog, he should be shown in hard working condition. Over-all appearance, balance, gait, and purpose to be given more emphasis than any of his component parts.

Size: Males, 23−24 in. (58−61 cm) in height at withers; females, 21½−22½ in. (55−57 cm). Length from breastbone to buttocks slightly greater than height at withers in ratio of 12:11. Weight for dogs, 65−75 lb. (29−34 kg); bitches, 60−70 lb. (27−32 kg).

Coat and Colour: Dense and water repellent with good undercoat. Texture not as hard as that of a short-haired dog nor silky as that of a setter. Lies flat against body and may be straight or wavy. Moderate feathering on back of forelegs and heavier feathering on front of neck, back of thighs and underside of tail. Feathering may be lighter than rest of coat. Colour lustrous golden of various shades. A few white hairs on chest permissible but not desirable.

Head: Broad in skull, slightly arched laterally and longitudinally without prominence of frontal or occipital bones. Good stop. *Foreface* deep and wide, nearly as long as skull. *Muzzle*, when viewed in profile, slightly deeper at stop than at tip; when viewed from above, slightly wider at stop than at tip. No heaviness in flews. Removal of whiskers for show purposes optional. *Nose* black or dark brown, though lighter shade in cold weather not serious. Scissors bite with lower incisors touching inside of upper incisors. *Eyes* friendly and intelligent, medium large with dark rims, set well apart and reasonably deep in sockets. Colour preferably dark brown, never lighter than colour of coat. No white or haw visible when looking straight ahead. *Ears* rather short, hanging flat against head with rounded tips slightly below jaw. Forward edge attached well behind and just above eye with rear edge slightly below eye.

Neck: Medium long, sloping well back into shoulders, giving sturdy muscular appearance with untrimmed natural ruff. No throatiness.

Forequarters: Forequarters well co-ordinated with hindquarters and capable of free movement. Shoulder blades wide, long, and muscular, showing angulation with upper arm of approximately 90 degrees. Legs straight with good bone. Pastern short and strong, sloping slightly forward with no suggestion of weakness.

Body: Topline level from withers to croup, whether standing or moving. Well balanced, short-coupled, deep through the heart. Chest at least as wide as a man's hand, including thumb. Brisket extends to elbows. Ribs long and well sprung but not barrel shaped, extending well to rear of body. Loin short, muscular, wide and deep, with very little tuck-up. Croup slopes gently.

Hindquarters: Well-bent stifles (angulation between femur and pelvis approximately 90 degrees) with hocks well let down. Legs straight when viewed from rear. Feet medium size, round and compact with thick pads. Excess hair may be trimmed to show natural size and contour.

Tail: Well set on, neither too high nor too low, following natural line of croup. Length extends to hock. Carried with merry action with some upward curve but never curled over back or between legs.

Gait: When trotting, gait is free, smooth, powerful, and well co-ordinated. Viewed from front or rear, legs turn neither in nor out, nor do feet cross or interfere with each other. Increased speed causes tendency of feet to converge toward centreline of gravity.

Faults: White marking beyond a few hairs on chest. Dudley nose (pink without pigmentation). Low, hound-like ear-set. Slab-sidedness, narrow chest, lack of depth in brisket, excessive tuck-up, roach or sway back. Cowhocks and sickle hocks. Open or splayed feet.

Disqualifications:

1. *Deviation in height of more than 1 inch (3 cm) from standard either way.*
2. *Undershot or overshot jaws. This condition not to be confused with misalignment of teeth.*
3. *Trichiasis (abnormal position or direction of the eyelashes).*

Retriever (Labrador)

*T*HE BACKGROUND BREEDING of the Labrador Retriever may never be established, but it is safe to assume that the breed's ancestors were taken to Newfoundland by explorers, fishermen, and settlers from England, Europe, and Norway. Thus the dogs, which subsequently were thought to be native to Labrador and Newfoundland, were in all probability the descendants of dogs left there in early years. They adapted to their environment, and by natural selection had evolved into two distinct types: one was the large heavy-coated dog which became known as the Newfoundland and the other, the smaller shorter-coated, was called the "black Water Dog," the "lesser Newfoundland," and later the "St. John's dog."

Both were excellent water dogs, had strong inherent hunting ability acquired from generations of living off the land and thick double coats which protected them against the elements.

In the early 1800s several keen sportsmen and members of the English nobility acquired a few of the smaller-type dogs that fishermen were bringing back to England. These were found to be excellent retrievers of fish and game. For many years the breed was kept pure, but difficulty arose in obtaining fresh breeding stock, so Labradors were crossed with other sporting breeds, in particular the Flat-Coated Retriever, the Tweed Water Spaniel, and the Curly-Coated Retriever. The Labrador, as we know it today, was thus a British development.

As a sporting dog the Labrador soon took over from the Flat-Coated Retriever as Britain's most popular gun dog, a position the breed has held up to the present time. In addition, the Lab has earned world-wide respect as a war dog, police dog and as a guide dog for the blind.

In 1903 the breed was officially recognized by The Kennel Club (England) and was first registered in Canada in the years 1906–1907.

Retriever (Labrador)

Official Breed Standard for the Retriever (Labrador)

General Appearance: The general appearance of the Labrador should be that of a strongly built, short-coupled, very active dog. He should be fairly wide over the loins, and strong and muscular in the hindquarters. The coat should be close, short, dense and free from feather.

Size: Approximate weights of dogs and bitches in working condition—dogs, 60−75 lb. (27−34 kg); bitches, 55−70 lb. (25−32 kg).
Height at shoulders—dogs, 22½−24½ in. (57−62 cm); bitches, 21½−23½ in. (54−60 cm).

Coat and Colour: The coat is a very distinctive feature; it should be short, very dense and without wave, and should give a fairly hard feeling to the hand. The colours are black, yellow, or chocolate and are evaluated as follows:
a) Blacks: All black, with a small white spot on chest permissible. Eyes to be of medium size, expressing intelligence and good temper, preferably brown or hazel, although black or yellow is permissible.
b) Yellows: Yellows may vary in colour from fox-red to light cream with variations in the shading of the coat on ears, the underparts of the dog, or beneath the tail. A small white spot on chest is permissible. Eye colouring and expression should be the same as that of the blacks, with black or dark brown eye rims. The nose should also be black or dark brown, although "fading" to pink in winter weather is not serious.
c) Chocolates: Shades ranging from light sedge to chocolate. A small white spot on chest is permissible. Eyes to be light brown to clear yellow. Nose and eye rim pigmentation dark brown or liver coloured. "Fading" to pink in winter weather not serious.

Head: The *skull* should be wide, giving brain room; there should be a slight stop, *i.e.*, the brow should be slightly pronounced, so that the skull is not absolutely in a straight line with the nose. The *head* should be clean-cut and free from fleshy cheeks. The *jaws* should be long and powerful and free from snipiness; the *nose* should be wide and the nostrils well developed. *Teeth* should be strong and regular, with a level mouth. The *eyes* should be of a medium size, expressing great intelligence and good temper, and can be brown, yellow or black, but brown or black is preferred. The *ears* should hang moderately close to the head rather far back, should be set somewhat low, and not be large and heavy.

Neck: The neck should be medium length, powerful and not throaty.

Forequarters: The shoulders should be long and sloping. The legs must be straight from the shoulder to ground, and the feet compact with toes well arched, and pads well developed.

Body: The chest must be of good width and depth, the ribs well sprung and the loins wide and strong.

Hindquarters: Stifles well turned, and the hindquarters well developed and of great power. The hocks should be well bent, and the dog must neither be cow-hocked nor be too wide behind; in fact, he must stand and move true all round on legs and feet. Legs should be of medium length, showing good bone and muscle, but not so short as to be out of balance with rest of body. In fact, a dog well balanced in all points is preferable to one with outstanding good qualities and defects.

Tail: The tail is a distinctive feature of the breed; it should be very thick towards the base, gradually tapering towards the tip, of medium length, should be free from any feathering, and should be clothed thickly all round with the Labrador's short, thick, dense coat, thus giving that peculiar "rounded" appearance which has been described as the "otter" tail. The tail may be carried gaily but should not curl over the back.

Gait: Movement should be free and effortless. The forelegs should be strong, straight and true, and correctly placed. Watching a dog move towards one, there should be no signs of elbows being out in front, but neatly held to the body with legs not too close together, but moving straight forward without pacing or weaving. Upon viewing the dog from the rear, one should get the impression that the hind legs, which should be well muscled and not cow-hocked, move as nearly parallel as possible, with hocks doing their full share of work and flexing well, thus giving the appearance of power and strength.

Faults: Dudley nose (pink without pigmentation).

Retriever
(Nova Scotia Duck Tolling)

"TOLLING" MEANS "to entice game to approach by arousing their curiosity." To the huntsman waiting in a duck blind, this means to draw the waterfowl within firing range by using the antics of a made-to-order breed of dog—a trick learned quite by accident from the fox. The story goes that early in the 19th century a huntsman in Maryland, waiting patiently for a flock of ducks to come closer, observed the birds suddenly lift their heads and swim towards shore. What attracted them was a fox dashing back and forth among the rocks flashing his bushy tail while a second waited in ambush. In short order some over-curious ducks became breakfast for two foxes. Putting this curiosity of the waterfowl to practical use, early sportsmen invented a dog closely resembling the fox in appearance, active but silent at work with the ability of a water retriever.

Such dogs have been used in Europe and in the east from Chesapeake Bay to the Maritimes since the mid-19th century. But Yarmouth County, Nova Scotia, is considered the place of origin of the pure-bred officially recognized by The Canadian Kennel Club as the Nova Scotia Duck Tolling Retriever.

Stories that the original tollers resulted from a fox/retriever cross have been discredited. More credible is the story that in 1860 a Mr. Allan mated a liver-coloured Flat-Coated Retriever to a Labrador Retriever-type dog. Females from this breeding then were mated with a brown cocker spaniel. A later cross to the Irish Setter gave the breed its colour and possibly by a cross to the yellow farm collie, its bushy tail. Other bloods may also have been used, including the Brittany Spaniel and the Golden and Chesapeake Bay Retrievers. However it was done, the cross-breedings produced a fox-like dog with the desired working abilities which became known as the Little River Duck Dog after the district of Yarmouth County, the centre of the breed's development.

After generations of pure breeding the toller was granted official breed status by The Canadian Kennel Club in 1945 when

Retriever (Nova Scotia Duck Tolling)

a total of fifteen were registered. For a number of years tollers were seldom seen outside the Maritimes, but today there are breeders across Canada. Fanciers believe their breed finally came of age in 1980 when two Nova Scotia Duck Tolling Retrievers were awarded Best in Show at all-breed championship events.

Official Breed Standard for the Retriever (Nova Scotia Duck Tolling)

Origin and Purpose: The Nova Scotia Duck Tolling Retriever was developed in Nova Scotia in the early 19th century to toll (or lure) and retrieve waterfowl. The tolling dog runs, jumps, and plays along the shoreline in full view of a flock of ducks, occasionally disappearing from sight and then quickly reappearing, aided by the hidden hunter, who throws small sticks or a ball for the dog. The dog's playful actions arouse the curiosity of the ducks swimming offshore and they are lured within gunshot range. The Toller is subsequently sent out to retrieve the dead or wounded birds.

General Appearance: The Toller is a medium-sized, powerful, compact, balanced, well-muscled dog; medium to heavy in bone, with a high degree of agility, alertness, and determination. Many Tollers have a slightly sad expression until they go to work, when their aspect changes to intense concentration and excitement. At work, the dog has a speedy, rushing action, with the head carried out almost level with the back and heavily-feathered tail in constant motion.

Temperament: The Toller is highly intelligent, easy to train, and has great endurance. A strong and able swimmer, he is a natural and tenacious retriever on land and from water, setting himself for springy action the moment the slightest indication is given that retrieving is required. His strong retrieving desire and playfulness are qualities essential to his tolling ability.

Size: Ideal height for males over 18 months is 19—20 in. (48—51 cm); females over 18 months 18—19 in. (45—48 cm). One inch (3 cm) over or under ideal height is allowed. Weight should be in proportion to the height and bone of the dog— guidelines: 45—51 lb. (20—23 kg) for adult males; bitches 37—43 lb. (17—20 kg).

Coat and Colour: The Toller was bred to retrieve from icy waters and must have a water-repellent double coat of medium length and softness with a softer, dense undercoat. The coat may have a slight wave on the back, but is otherwise straight. Some winter coats may form a long, loose curl at the throat. Featherings are soft at the throat, behind the ears and at the back of the thighs, and forelegs are moderately feathered. Colour is various shades of red or orange with lighter featherings and underside of tail, and usually at least one of the following white markings —tip of tail, feet (not extending beyond the pasterns), chest, and blaze. A dog of otherwise high quality is not to be penalized for lack of white. The pigment of the nose, lips, and eye rims to be flesh-coloured, blending with coat, or black.

Head: *Skull:* the head is clean-cut and slightly wedge-shaped. The broad skull is only slightly rounded, the occiput not prominent and the cheeks flat. A good measurement for an average male would be 5½ in. (14 cm) between the ears, tapering to 1½ in. (3.8 cm) at the bridge of the nose. Length of **head** is approximately 9 in. (23 cm) from nose to occiput, but the head must be in proportion to body size. The stop is moderate. *Muzzle* tapers in a clean line from stop to nose, with the lower jaw strong but not prominent. The underline of the muzzle runs almost in a straight line from the corner of the lip to the corner of the jawbone, with depth at the stop being greater than at the nose. Hair on the muzzle is short and fine. *Nose* tapers from bridge to tip, with nostrils well open. Colour should blend with that of the coat or be black. *Mouth:* lips fit fairly tightly, forming a gentle curve in profile, with no heaviness in flews. The correct bite is tight scissors, full dentition is required. Jaws are strong enough to carry a sizeable bird, and softness in mouth is essential. *Eyes* set well apart, almond-shaped, medium-sized. Colour, amber to brown. Expression is friendly, alert, and intelligent. Flesh around the eyes should be the same colour as the lips. *Ears* triangular, of medium size, set high and well back on the skull, with the base held very slightly erect, well feathered at the back of the fold, hair short at the rounded tips.

Neck: Strongly muscled and well set on, of medium length, with no indication of throatiness.

Forequarters: Shoulders should be muscular, with the blade well laid back and well laid on, giving good withers sloping into the short back. The blade and upper arm are roughly equal in length. Elbows should be close to the body, turning neither in nor out, working cleanly and evenly. The forelegs should appear as parallel columns, straight and strong in bone. The pasterns are strong and slightly sloping. The strongly-webbed feet are of medium size, tight and round, with well-arched toes and thick pads. Dewclaws may be removed.

Body: Deep-chested with good spring of rib, brisket reaching to the elbow. The back is short and straight, the topline level, the loins strong and muscular. The ribs are well sprung, neither barrel-shaped nor flat. Tuck-up is moderate.

Hindquarters: Muscular, broad, and square in appearance. Rear and front angulation should be in balance. Thighs are very muscular, upper and lower sections being approximately equal in length. Stifles are well bent and hocks well let down, turning neither in nor out. Dewclaws must not be present.

Tail: Following the natural very slight slope of the croup, broad at the base, luxuriant and heavily feathered, with the last vertebra reaching at least to the hock. The tail may be carried below the level of the back except when the dog is alert when it curves high over, though never touching, the body.

Gait: The Toller combines an impression of power with a springy, jaunty gait, showing good reach in front and a strong driving rear. Feet should turn neither in nor out and the legs travel in a straight line. As speed increases, the dog should single-track, with the topline remaining level.

Faults: (To be penalized according to degree)
Dogs more than 1 inch (3 cm) over or under ideal height.
Overshot bite.
Tail too short, kinked or curled over touching the back.
Lack of substance in adult dog.
Dish- or down-faced.
Abrupt stop.
Large, round eyes.
Nose, eye rims, and eyes not of prescribed colour.
Bright pink nose.
Splayed or paper feet, down in pasterns.

Open coat.
Roached, sway back, slack loins.
Tail carried below level of back when dog gaiting.

Disqualifications:
White on shoulders, around ears, on back of neck, across back or flanks.
Silvery coat, grey in coat, black areas in coat.
Lack of webbing.
Undershot bite, wry mouth.
In adult classes, any shyness.
Butterfly nose.
Overshot by more than $1/8$ inch.
Any colour other than red or orange shades.

Setter (English)

THE ENGLISH SETTER descends from an ancient breed known in Britain since the 14th century and belongs to the family of sporting breeds, the spaniels, said to be of Spanish origin. The early setters were used to "set" game for the sportsman's net, hence the breed name. Later they became known as English Setters to distinguish them from similar breeds that originated in other countries. In early times breeding records were not kept and the sporting dogs were valued for their working ability rather than their appearance. It is safe then to assume that the first English Setters were a far cry from the elegant specimens of the present time.

The first breeder to institute an organized breeding programme and keep accurate records was Edward Laverack who, in 1825, bought a pair of setters from a well-known line. Using them as foundation breeding stock and closely inbreeding, Laverack developed the strain that became known as "Laverack Setters." For almost fifty years, both in the field and on the bench, Laverack's dogs dominated the breed. In 1875 he wrote the first book on the breed and draughted the first breed standard for English Setters which, with minor revisions, is still being used today.

His successor, Purcell Llewellin, purchased his first dogs from Laverack but continued with a breeding programme based more on outcrosses. Llewellin, in turn, became an influential force in the breed and it was a dog of his breeding that in 1869 became the first dual champion of the breed.

The English Setter had become popular on both sides of the Atlantic well before the founding of The Kennel Club (England) in 1873 and was among the first breeds to be admitted to official registration both here and abroad. The breed accounted for the largest entry at this continent's first benched show, the Westminster Kennel Club event, held in New York in May 1877. Many of the entries proudly listed their Laverack or Llewellin lineage in the show catalogue, and several were offered for sale at prices of $1000 and up.

Setter (English)

The Canadian Kennel Club Stud Book lists 157 English Setters registered in the years 1888–1889.

Official Breed Standard for the Setter (English)

Origin and Purpose: Although even our oldest authorities are not entirely in agreement as to the origin of this breed, it is generally agreed that the earliest English Setter had its origins in some of the older of the land spaniels that originated in Spain, or were the product of careful crosses of the Spanish Pointer, the large water spaniel, and the Springer Spaniel. By careful cultivation, the English Setter attained a high degree of proficiency for finding and pointing game in open country. The major credit for the development of the modern English Setter goes to two men of the middle 1800s, Mr. Edward Laverack and Mr. R.L. Purcell Llewellin.

General Appearance: An elegant, stylish and symmetrical gun dog of good substance that projects a heritage of well developed hunting instinct and bird sense. He suggests the ideal blend of strength and stamina combined with grace and style. Flat-coated with feathering of adequate length. Gaiting freely and smoothly with long forward reach and strong rear drive. Males should be decidedly masculine in appearance without coarseness. Females should be decidedly feminine in appearance without over-refinement.

Temperament: A true gentleman by nature, he has a kind and gentle expression and is constantly expressing a willingness to please with an affectionate, happy, and friendly attitude. He has a lovable, mild disposition and is without fear or viciousness.

Size: Dogs about 25 in. (63 cm); bitches about 24 in. (61 cm) in height, when measured at the withers. Symmetry—the balance of all parts to be considered. Symmetrical dogs will have level toplines or will be slightly higher at the shoulders than at the hips. They will have well-angulated fore and rearquarters that work smoothly together. Balance, harmony of proportion, elegance, grace and an appearance of quality, substance, and endurance to be looked for.

Coat: The coat should be flat without curl or woolliness. The dog should be adequately feathered on the ears, the chest, the belly, the underside of the thighs, the back of all legs and on the tail. The feathering, however, should not be so excessive that it hides the true lines and movement of the dog, nor should it affect the dog's appearance or function as a sporting dog.

Colour: Black and white, orange and white, liver and white, lemon and white, white, black-white and tan, orange belton, liver belton, lemon belton, tricolour belton, blue belton. The belton markings may vary in degree from clear, distinctive flecking to roan shading. Dogs without heavy patches of colour on the body, but flecked all over preferred.

Head: The entire head should be in proportion to the body. It should be long and lean with a well-defined stop. The *skull*, when viewed from above, should be oval. The skull should be of medium width, without coarseness, and should be only slightly wider at the base than at the brows. The widest part of the oval should be at the ear set. There should be a moderately defined occipital protuberance. The length of the skull from the occiput to the stop should be equal in length to the muzzle. *Muzzle:* brick-shaped, and the width to be in harmony with the skull. It should be level from the eyes to the tip of the nose. When viewed from the side, the line of the top of the muzzle should be parallel to the line of the top of the skull. A dish face or a Roman nose is objectionable. The flews should be square and pendant. The nose to be black or dark brown in colour except in white, orange and white, lemon and white or liver and white where it may be lighter. The nostrils should be wide apart and large in the openings. *Foreface:* the skeletal structure under the eyes should be well chiseled with no suggestion of fullness. The cheeks, like the sides of the muzzle, should present a smooth and clean-cut appearance. *Jaws:* the lower jaw should extend in length so that the lower teeth form a close scissors bite with the upper teeth, the inner surface of the upper teeth in contact with the outer surface of the lower teeth when the jaws are closed. An even bite is not objectionable. The teeth should be strongly developed with upright incisors. Full dentition is desirable. The *eyes* should be bright, and the expression mild and intelligent. The iris should be brown, the darker the better. The eyelid rims should be fully pigmented. The *ears* should be set low and well back.

Preferably, the set should be even with the eye level. When relaxed the ears should be carried close to the head. They should be of moderate length, slightly rounded at the ends, and covered with long silky hair.

Neck: The neck should be rather long, muscular, and lean. The neck should be slightly arched at the crest, and clean-cut where it joins the head at the base of the skull. The neck should be larger and very muscular toward the shoulders, and the base of the neck should flow smoothly into the shoulders. The neck should not be too throaty or pendulous and should be graceful in appearance.

Shoulder: The shoulder blade (scapula) should be laid back to approach the ideal angle of 45 degrees from the vertical. The upper foreleg (humerus) should be equal in length to the shoulder blade (scapula) and form an angle of 90 degrees with the shoulder blade. This enables the elbow to be placed directly under the back edge of the shoulder blade and brings the heel pad directly under the pivot point of the shoulder thus giving a maximum length of stride. The shoulders should be fairly close together at the tips, but with sufficient width between the blades to allow the dog to easily lower its head to the ground. The shoulder blades should lie flat and meld smoothly with the contours of the body. This structure permits perfect freedom of action for the forelegs.

Forelegs: When seen standing from the front or side, the fore-legs or arms (radius and ulna) should be straight and parallel. The elbows should have no tendency to turn either in or out when standing or gaiting. The upper arm (humerus) should be flat and muscular. The bone should be fully developed and mus-cles hard and devoid of flabbiness. The pastern should be short, strong, and nearly round with the slope from the pastern joint to the foot deviating very slightly forward from the perpendicular.

Feet: The feet should be closely set and strong, pads well developed and tough; toes well arched and protected with short, thick hair.

Forechest: The forechest should be well developed, and the point of the sternum (prosternum) should project about $3/4-1$ in. (2−3 cm) in front of the point of the shoulders.

Rib Cage: The chest should be deep, but not so wide or round as to interfere with the action of the forelegs. The keel should be deep enough to reach the level of the elbow. The ribs should be long, springing gradually to the middle of the body, then tapering as they approach the end of the thoracic cavity.

Topline: The topline of the body of the dog in motion or standing should appear to be level or to slope very slightly from the withers to the tail forming a graceful outline of medium length without sway or drop. The tail should continue as a smooth, level extension of the topline.

Back: The back, the area between the withers and the loin, should be straight and strong at its junction with the loin area. The loins should be strong, moderate in length, slightly arched, but not to the extent of being roached or wheel-backed, and only discernible to the touch.

Hips: The slope and length of the croup determines the tail-set, and the degree of slope should not be more than 15 degrees from the horizontal for an ideal tail-set. The hip bones should be wide apart with the hips nicely rounded and blending smoothly into the hind legs. The pelvis should slope at an angle of 30 degrees from the horizontal. The pelvis governs the forward reach and the backward follow-through of the hind legs, and this angle permits a maximum length of stride. Again for efficiency and balance, the length of the pelvis and the upper thigh (femur) should be equal, and they in turn should be equal in length to the shoulder blade (scapula) and upper arm (humerus).

Hind Legs: The upper thigh (femur) should be well developed and muscular. The well-developed lower thigh (tibia/fibula) in a well-balanced setter should be slightly longer than the upper thigh (femur) and should become wide and flat as it approaches the hock joint. The knee joint (stifle) should be well bent and strong. The pastern from the hock joint to the foot, should be short, strong, and nearly round and perpendicular when viewed from the side. The hind legs, when seen from the rear, should be straight and parallel to each other and the hock joints should have no tendency to turn in or out either at rest or when the dog is in motion.

Tail: The tail should be straight and taper to a fine point with only sufficient length to reach the hock joint or less. The feather must be straight and silky, hanging loosely in a fringe and tapering to a point when the tail is raised. There must be no bushiness. The tail should not curl sideways or curl above the level of the back (sickle tail).

Gait: An effortless graceful movement demonstrating rapidity and endurance while covering the ground efficiently. There must be a long forward reach and strong rear drive with a lively tail and a proud head carriage. Head may be carried slightly lower when moving to allow for greater reach of the forelegs. The back of the dog should remain strong, firm, and level when in motion. When moving at a trot, the properly balanced dog will have a tendency to converge toward a line representing the centre of gravity of the dog.

Faults:
1. Any deviation from the affectionate, happy, friendly attitude which makes the English Setter the true gentleman of the dog world.
2. Undershot or overshot bite.
3. Any dog over 27 in. (69 cm) or under 24 in. (61 cm). Any bitch over 26 in. (66 cm) or under 23 in. (58 cm).
4. Incorrect tail set or tail carriage such as a steep drop from the hips to the tail set or a tail which curls sideways or curls above the level of the back (sickle tails).
5. Incorrect soft and woolly coat texture that will not protect the dog while working in the field.
6. Light eyes. Loose eyes.
7. A lack of long forward reach and strong rear drive.
8. A hackneyed, paddling gait and a rolling, stilted, or lumbering motion.
9. Flat, splayed, or long feet or feet that turn in or out.
10. Too narrow or too wide a front.
11. Barrel-like or slab-sided ribcage.
12. A down-faced or snipey muzzle.
13. Flews in excess of that required to present a square muzzle.
14. A lack of backskull.
15. Cowhocks.
16. Any deviation from a topline that is level or very slightly sloping.

Setter (Gordon)

*T*HE **GORDON SETTER** is the only sporting dog developed in Scotland. It was stabilized by Alexander, the fourth Duke of Gordon, between the years 1770–1820. Originally called the Gordon Castle Setter, the Duke's purpose was to create a larger, heavier type of setter of pleasing conformation, with keen scenting power well adapted to his rugged Scottish environment. It has been strongly suggested that there is some "colley" and possibly some bloodhound breeding in the Gordon's background. This would account for the breed's colour, black with mahogany markings, as well as its habit of hunting with nose to ground. Also the former tendency to circle rather than point the game—a dangerous practice which could put the dog within firing range.

It was a Gordon that was judged best of breed at the world's first dog show—the competition limited to pointers and setters —which was held in Newcastle-on-Tyne, Northumberland, England in 1859. In Britain the breed was among the first forty-six breeds to be officially recognized, and as early as 1840 Gordons were imported to the United States.

Acknowledged to be a strong, dependable bird dog, the Gordon is said to be capable of working for long periods of time without water and in temperatures of extreme heat. But despite his many attributes, the breed's numbers declined drastically in both Britain and on this continent during the first half of this century. Fortunately for the Gordon's survival there has been a steady increase in registrations on both sides of the Atlantic. But it has been dog show fanciers who are chiefly responsible for this, not field trial enthusiasts whose preferences run to the speedier, wider-quartering breeds.

In Canada the breed is usually represented at most championship shows but in limited numbers. The Canadian Kennel Club Stud Book shows thirty-one Gordon Setters were registered in the years 1888–1889, a surprising figure when one considers that in 1962 in Britain Gordon Setter registrations numbered only twenty-eight.

Setter (Gordon)

Official Breed Standard for the Setter (Gordon)

General Appearance: A good-sized, sturdily built dog, well muscled, with plenty of bone and substance, but active, upstanding and stylish, appearing capable of doing a full day's work in the field. Strong, rather short back, well-sprung ribs and short tail, a fairly heavy head, finely chiselled, intelligent, noble and dignified expression, showing no signs of shyness; clear colours and straight or slightly waved coat. A dog that suggests strength and stamina rather than extreme speed.

Symmetry and quality are most essential. A dog well balanced in all points is preferable to one with outstanding good qualities and defects.

Size: Shoulder height for males, 24–27 in. (61–69 cm); for females, 23–26 in. (58–66 cm).
Weight—males, 55–75 lb. (25–34 kg); females, 45–65 lb. (20–29 kg).

As a guide the greater heights and weights are to be preferred provided that character and quality are also combined. Dogs over and under these heights and weights are to be discouraged.

Coat and Colour: Coat should be soft and shining, resembling silk, straight or slightly waved—the latter preferred—but not curly, with long hair on ears, under stomach, on chest, and on back of the fore and hind legs to the feet. Deep, shining coal-black with tan markings, either of rich chestnut or mahogany red colour. The tan should be shining and not dull, yellowish or straw colour and not mixed with black hairs. Black pencilling allowed on toes. The borderlines between black and tan colours should be clearly defined. There should not be any tan hairs mixed in the black.
Tan markings:

a) Two clear spots over the eyes not over ³/₄ inch (2 cm) in diameter.

b) On the sides of the muzzle, the tan should not reach above the base of nose, resembling a stripe around the end of the muzzle from one side to the other.

c) On the throat.

d) Two large, clear spots on the chest.

e) On the inside of the hind legs and inside of thighs showing

down the front of the stifle and broadening out to the outside of the hind legs from the hock to the toes. It must, however, not completely eliminate the black on the back of hind legs.
f)   On the forelegs from the knees or a little above downward to the toes.
g)   Around the vent.
A white spot on the chest is allowed, but the smaller the better.

Head: Deep rather than broad, with plenty of brain room, nicely rounded good-sized skull, broadest between the ears. The head should have a clearly indicated stop. Below and above the eyes should be lean and the cheek as narrow as the leanness of the head allows. The *muzzle* fairly long with almost parallel lines and not pointed either as seen from above or from the side. The flews not pendulous but with clearly indicated lips. The *nose* big, broad with open nostrils and of black colour. *Eyes* of fair size, neither too deep set nor too bulging, dark brown, bright and wise. *Ears* set low on the head, fairly large and thin.

Neck: Long, lean, arched to the head and without throatiness.

Forequarters: Shoulders should be fine at the points, deep and sloping well back, giving a moderately sloping topline. Forelegs big-boned, straight, not bowed either in or out, with elbows free, well let down and not inclined either in or out.

Body: Chest deep and not too broad in front; the ribs well sprung, leaving plenty of lung room.

Hindquarters: The hind legs from hip to hock should be long, flat, and muscular, from hock to heel short and strong. The stifle and hock joints well bent, and not inclined either in or out. Both fore and hind feet should have close knit, well-arched toes with plenty of hair between with full toe pads and deep heel cushions.

Tail: Short and should not reach below the hocks, carried horizontal or nearly so, thick at the root and finishing in a fine point. The feather, which starts near the root of the tail, should be slightly waved or straight and have a three-square appearance growing shorter uniformly toward the end.

Gait: A smooth free movement with high head carriage.

Faults:

1. General Impression—Unintelligent appearance. The Bloodhound type with heavy and big head and ears and clumsy body, as well as the Collie type with its pointed muzzle and curved tail, or showing any signs of shyness.

2. Head—Houndy, pointed, snipey, drooping or upturned muzzle, too small or large mouth.

3. Eyes—Too light in colour, too deep-set, or too prominent.

4. Ears—Set too high or unusually broad or heavy.

5. Neck—Thick and short.

6. Shoulders and Back—Irregularly formed.

7. Chest—Too broad.

8. Legs and Feet—Crooked legs. Out-turned elbows. The toes scattered, flat-footed.

9. Tail—Too long, badly carried or hooked at the end.

10. Coat—Curly like wool, not shining.

11. Colour—Yellow or straw coloured tan or without clearly defined lines between the different colours. White feet. Too much white on the chest. In the black there must be no tan hairs which can appear often around the eyes.

Setter (Irish)

THE RED SETTER that comes from Ireland has often been called the most beautiful of all the show dogs, but it was as a hunting dog that the breed's development began. Bred to set game for the sportsman's net and for the sport of falconry, from all reports the early Irish Setter was a talented field dog. Where the breed acquired these talents is a matter of conjecture. Obviously the setter represents a mixture of many bloods, but their precise nature and the dates when each was introduced is unknown. Suggested breeds include the Irish Water Spaniel, English and Gordon Setters, pointers in variety, and the Bloodhound. Each is thought to have contributed its share to the swift moving, good nosed, boisterous sporting breed.

It is said that by the 18th century a red and white setter was well known in Ireland and that by means of successive outcrosses the white areas disappeared and the all red, mahogany-coloured setter was developed. The dog credited with founding the present-day Irish Setter was whelped in County Tyrone about the year 1862. This was a dog by the name of Ch. Palmerston, a dominant sire, who left his mark on the breed.

Some claim that Palmerston's contribution was a mixed blessing. Because, with the advent of dog shows in 1859, the Irish Setter became more valued for his beauty than for his field ability and his popularity mushroomed among show enthusiasts. The Irish Setter that had scored well at field trials became dangerously close to being lost. It was through the efforts of a few concerned breeders in Britain and on this continent that the Irish Setter was restored to its dual role of efficient field dog and handsome show specimen.

The breed was well represented on this continent before the turn of the century and was among the first breeds to be registered by both The Canadian and American Kennel clubs. It is interesting to note that among the Irish Setter entry at the first benched show held in New York in 1877 the winning female was a red and white, offered for sale with a price-tag of £10,000 sterling.

Setter (Irish)

First registrations for Irish Setters are recorded in The Canadian Kennel Club Stud Book dated 1888–1889.

Official Breed Standard for the Setter (Irish)

General Appearance: The Irish Setter is an active, aristocratic bird-dog, rich red in colour, substantial yet elegant in build. Standing over two feet tall at the shoulder, the dog has a straight, fine, glossy coat, longer on ears, chest, tail and back of legs. Afield he is a swift-moving hunter; at home, a sweet-natured, trainable companion. His is a rollicking personality. At his best the lines of the Irish Setter so satisfy in over-all balance that artists have termed him the most beautiful of all dogs. The correct specimen always exhibits balance whether standing or in motion. Each part of the dog flows and fits smoothly into its neighbouring parts without calling attention to itself.

Size: There is no disqualification as to size. The make and fit of all parts and their over-all balance in the animal are rated more important. A height of 27 in. (69 cm) at the withers with a show weight of about 70 lb. (32 kg) is considered ideal for a dog; the bitch, 25 in. (64 cm), 60 lb. (27 kg). Variance beyond 1 inch (3 cm) up or down to be discouraged.

Coat and Colour: Short and fine on head, forelegs and tips of ears; on all other parts, of moderate length and flat. Feathering long and silky on ears; on back of forelegs and thighs long and fine, with a pleasing fringe of hair on belly and brisket extending onto the chest. Feet well feathered between the toes. Fringe on tail moderately long and tapering. All coat and feathering as straight and free as possible from curl or wave. Colour: mahogany or rich chestnut red, with no trace of black. A small amount of white on chest, throat, or toes, or a narrow centred streak on skull, is not to be penalized.

Head: Long and lean, its length at least double the width between the ears. The brow is raised, showing a distinct stop midway between the tip of the nose and the well-defined occiput (rear point of skull). Thus the nearly level line from occiput to brow is set a little above, and parallel to, the straight and equal line from eye to nose. The *skull* is oval when viewed from above or front; very slightly domed when viewed in profile. Beauty of head is emphasized by delicate chiselling along the muzzle, around and below the eyes, and along the cheeks. *Muzzle* moderately deep, nostrils wide, jaws, of nearly equal length. Upper lips fairly square but not pendulous, the underline of the jaws being almost parallel with the topline of the muzzle. *Nose* black or chocolate. The teeth meet in a scissors bite in which the upper incisors fit closely over the lower, or they may meet evenly. *Eyes* somewhat almond-shaped, of medium size, placed rather well apart; neither deep-set nor bulging. Colour: dark to medium brown. Expression soft yet alert. *Ears* set well back and low, not above level of eye. Leather thin, hanging in a neat fold close to the head, and nearly long enough to reach the nose.

Neck: Moderately long, strong but not thick, and slightly arched; free from throatiness, and fitting smoothly into the shoulders.

Forequarters: Shoulder blades long, wide, sloping well back, fairly close together at the top and joined in front to long upper arms angled to bring the elbows slightly rearward along the brisket. Forelegs straight and sinewy, the elbows moving freely. All legs sturdy, with plenty of bone, and strong, nearly straight pasterns.

Body: Sufficiently long to permit a straight and free stride. Topline of body from withers to tail slopes downward without sharp drop at the croup. Chest deep, reaching approximately to the elbows; rather narrow in front. Ribs well sprung. Loins of moderate length, muscular, and slightly arched.

Hindquarters: Hindquarters should be wide and powerful with broad, well-developed thighs. Hind legs long and muscular from hip to hock, short and nearly perpendicular from hock to ground; well angulated at stifle and hock joints, which, like the elbows, incline neither in nor out. Feet rather small, very firm, toes arched and close.

Tail: Strong at root, tapering to fine point, about long enough to reach the hock. Carriage straight or curving slightly upward, nearly level with the back.

Gait: At the trot the gait is big, very lively, graceful and efficient. The head is held high. The hindquarters drive smoothly and with great power. The forelegs reach well ahead as if to pull in the ground, without giving the appearance of a hackney gait. The dog runs as he stands—straight. Seen from the front or rear, the forelegs, as well as the hind legs below the hock joint, move perpendicularly to the ground, with some tendency towards a single track as speed increases. But a crossing or weaving of the legs, front or back, is objectionable.

Spaniel (American Cocker)

THE ORIGIN AND HISTORY of the American Cocker Spaniel is the same as that of the English Cocker up to the time when a dog called Obo II was exported from Britain to the United States. This dog, whelped in 1880 and known then simply as a Cocker Spaniel, is considered to be the foundation sire of the American Cocker Spaniel. As a show dog, Obo was a great success and attracted many breed fanciers who, in 1883, founded the American Spaniel Club. That year, too, the Cocker Spaniel was granted official breed status in the United States.

But after Obo's reign a gradual change occurred within the breed. Two distinct varieties of Cocker Spaniel began to emerge. One retained the longer bodied, longer muzzled, heavier lines of the original sporting cocker. The other was lighter in weight, higher on leg, shorter backed, had a sloping topline, a short muzzle, domed skull, and heavy coat and leg furnishings. Although the two competed against each other in the show ring and were inter-bred, by the 1930s the differences between them became so obvious that efforts were begun to grant each its own breed classification. When this was finally achieved in 1947 in the United States, the original cocker breed was named the English Cocker while the smaller American version retained the original name of Cocker Spaniel. To the rest of the world this breed is known as the American Cocker Spaniel.

The most illustrious Cocker Spaniel of them all was Ch. My Own Brucie who topped the entry at the Westminster Kennel Club shows in New York in 1940 and 1941. More than any other dog My Own Brucie is responsible for the rise of the cocker to the top of the popularity poll—a position the breed held for some fifteen years.

Spaniel (American Cocker)

G. STENHOUSE

Official Breed Standard for the Spaniel (American Cocker)

Origin and Purpose: The Cocker Spaniel evolved from a very old type of dog classified generally as Spaniels. The name "Spaniel" is mentioned in various literatures and pictured in woodcuts as early as 1328. The English literature and letters of the day always accepted that Spaniels originated in Spain. The partridge and quail hunters of the early 1800s wanted a smaller-sized dog who would simply find the game without disturbing it. Finally in 1892, The Kennel Club (England) recognized the "Cocker" as a classification and being a Spaniel that was less than 25 lb. (11–12 kg) and one that worked. The first Cocker was registered with the American Kennel Club in 1879. The Cockers at this time were long and low-bodied and were generally around 20 lb. (9–10 kg). In the early 1900s, the American Spaniel Club, striving to maintain the Cocker in its sporting dog classification, made the standard call for a dog not less than 28 lb. (13 kg). It was during this time that the American Cocker Spaniel as we know it today really started to evolve into a separate and distinct breed of its own.

General Appearance: The Cocker Spaniel is the smallest member of the Sporting Group. He has a sturdy, compact body and a cleanly chiselled and refined head, with the over-all dog in complete balance and of ideal size. He stands well up at the shoulder on straight forelegs with a topline sloping slightly toward strong, muscular quarters. He is a dog capable of considerable speed, combined with great endurance. Above all he must be free and merry, sound, well balanced throughout, and in action show a keen inclination to work; equable in temperament with no suggestion of timidity.

Size: The ideal height at the withers for an adult dog is 15 in. (38 cm) and for an adult bitch 14 in. (35.5 cm). Height may vary one-half inch (1 cm) above or below this ideal. A dog whose height exceeds 15 $\frac{1}{2}$ in. (39 cm) or a bitch whose height exceeds 14 $\frac{1}{2}$ in. (37 cm) shall be disqualified. An adult dog whose height is less than 14 $\frac{1}{2}$ in. (37 cm) or an adult bitch whose height is less than 14 $\frac{1}{2}$ in. (37 cm) shall be penalized. An adult dog whose height is less than 13 $\frac{1}{2}$ in. (34 cm) shall be penalized.

NOTE: Height is determined by a line perpendicular to the ground from the top of the shoulder blades, the dog standing naturally with its forelegs and the lower hind legs parallel to the line of measurement.

Coat: On the head, short and fine; on the body, medium length, with enough undercoating to give protection. The ears, chest, abdomen, and legs are well feathered, but not so excessively as to hide the American Cocker Spaniel's true lines and movement or affect his appearance and function as a sporting dog. The texture is most important. The coat is silky, flat or slightly wavy, and of a texture which permits easy care. Excessive or curly or cottony textured coat is to be penalized.

Colour: *Black Variety*—Solid colour black, to include black with tan points. The black should be jet; shadings of brown or liver in the sheen of the coat are not desirable. A small amount of white on the chest and/or throat is allowed, white in any other location shall disqualify.

Any Solid Colour Other Than Black and any such colour with tan points. The colour shall be of a uniform shade, but lighter colouring of the feather is permissible. A small amount of white on the chest and/or throat is allowed; white in any other location shall disqualify.

Particolour Variety—Two or more definite, well-broken colours, one of which must be white, including those with tan points; it is preferable that the tan markings be located in the same pattern as for the tan points in the Black and ASCOB varieties. Roans are classified as particolours, and may be of any of the usual roaning patterns. Primary colour which is ninety per cent or more shall disqualify.

Tan Points: The colour of the tan may be from the lightest cream to the darkest red colour and should be restricted to ten per cent or less of the colour of the specimen, tan markings in excess of that amount shall disqualify.

In the case of tan points in the Black or ASCOB variety, the markings shall be located as follows:

a) A clear tan spot over each eye
b) On the sides of the muzzle and on the cheeks
c) On the undersides of the ears
d) On all feet and/or legs
e) Under the tail
f) On the chest, optional—presence or absence not penalized.

Tan markings which are not readily visible or which amount only to traces, shall be penalized. Tan on the muzzle which extends upward, over and joins shall also be penalized. The absence of tan markings in the Black or ASCOB variety in each of the specified locations in an otherwise tan-pointed dog shall disqualify.

Head: To attain a well-proportioned head, which must be in balance with the rest of the dog, it embodies the following: *Skull* rounded but not exaggerated with no tendency toward flatness; the eyebrows are clearly defined with a pronounced stop. The bony structure beneath the eyes is well chiselled with no prominence in the cheeks. *Muzzle* broad and deep, with square, even jaws. The upper lip is full and of sufficient depth to cover the lower jaw. To be in correct balance, the distance from the stop to the tip of the nose is one-half the distance from the stop up over the crown to the base of the skull. *Nose* of sufficient size to balance the muzzle and foreface, with well-developed nostrils typical of a sporting dog. It is black in colour in the blacks and black and tans. In other colours it may be brown, liver or black, the darker the better. The colour of the nose harmonizes with the colour of the eye rim. *Mouth:* the teeth are strong and sound, not too small, and meet in a scissors bite. *Eyes:* eyeballs are round and full and look directly forward. The shape of the eye rims gives a slightly almond-shaped appearance; the eye is not weak or goggled. The colour of the iris is dark brown and in general the darker the better. The expression is intelligent, alert, soft, and appealing. *Ears* lobular, long, of fine leather, well feathered, and placed no higher than a line to the lower part of the eye.

Neck and Shoulders: The neck is sufficiently long to allow the nose to reach the ground easily, muscular and free from pendulous "throatiness." It rises strongly from the shoulders and arches slightly as it tapers to join the head. The shoulders are well laid back forming an angle with the upper arm of approximately 90 degrees which permits the dog to move his forelegs in an easy manner with considerable forward reach. Shoulders are clean-cut and sloping without protrusion and so set that the upper points of the withers are at an angle which permits a wide spring of rib.

Body: The body is short, compact, and firmly knit together, giving an impression of strength. The distance from the highest point of the shoulder blades to the ground is fifteen per cent or approximately two inches (5 cm) more than the length from this point to the set-on of the tail. Back is strong and sloping evenly and slightly downward from the shoulders to the set-on of the docked tail. Hips are wide and quarters well rounded and muscular. The chest is deep, its lowest point no higher than the elbows, its front sufficiently wide for adequate heart and lung space, yet not so wide as to interfere with the straightforward movement of the forelegs. Ribs are deep and well sprung. The American Cocker Spaniel never appears long and low.

Legs and Feet: Forelegs are parallel, straight, strongly boned and muscular and set close to the body well under the scapulae. When viewed from the side with the forelegs vertical, the elbow is directly below the highest point of the shoulder blade. The pasterns are short and strong. The hind legs are strongly boned and muscled with good angulation at the stifle and powerful, clearly defined thighs. The stifle joint is strong and there is no slippage of it in motion or when standing. The hocks are strong, well let down, and when viewed from behind, the hind legs are parallel when in motion and at rest.

Feet: compact, large, round, and firm with horny pads; they turn neither in nor out. Dewclaws on hind legs and forelegs may be removed.

Tail: The docked tail is set on and carried on a line with the topline of the back, or slightly higher; never straight up like a terrier and never so low as to indicate timidity. When the dog is in motion the tail action is merry.

Gait: The American Cocker Spaniel, though the smallest of the sporting dogs, possesses a typical sporting dog gait. Prerequisite to good movement is balance between the front and rear assemblies. He drives with his strong, powerful rear quarters and is properly constructed in the shoulders and forelegs so that he can reach forward without constriction in a full stride to counterbalance the driving force from the rear. Above all, his gait is co-ordinated, smooth, and effortless. The dog must cover ground with his action and excessive animation should never be mistaken for proper gait.

Faults: Dogs under 14½ in. (37 cm), bitches under 13½ in.

(34 cm) penalized. Excessive or curly or cottony textured coat. Tan markings which are not readily visible or which amount only to traces. Tan on muzzle which extends upward, over and joins.

Disqualifications: *Blacks and* ASCOBs–*white markings except on chest and throat.*
Particolour: 90 per cent or more of primary colour.
Tan Points: tan markings in excess of 10 per cent.
Absence of tan markings in the Black or ASCOB *variety in each of the specified locations in an otherwise tan-pointed dog.*
Height: males over 15½ in. (39 cm); females over 14½ in. (37 cm).

Spaniel (American Water)

THE AMERICAN WATER SPANIEL is one of the few breeds entitled to wear the made-in-U.S.A. label. Far from being a glamorous looking sporting dog, the breed is basically a working gun dog seldom seen in the show ring.

There is pictorial evidence which seems to prove that the American Water Spaniel and the Boykin Spaniel, a breed that takes its name from the town of Boykin, South Carolina, are the same dog. The Boykin has been known in the Southern States since before the Civil War (1861—1865) and there are still dogs known as Boykins being bred and used as hunting dogs today.

Except for his feathered tail, the American Water Spaniel looks like a miniature Irish Water Spaniel, so it is reasonable to assume that the Irish dog played a dominant role in its ancestry. It is also assumed that the American Cocker Spaniel was the forbear that brought down size. Other breeds mentioned as possible progenitors are the now extinct English Water Spaniel, the poodle, and the Curly-Coated Retriever. The breed's development took place mainly in the Midwest and the northeastern states. Type was fixed by 1900, but it was not until 1938 that a specialty club was formed in the U.S. and a breed standard written. In 1940, the American Water Spaniel was granted official recognition by the American Kennel Club.

The breed was specifically developed for inland fowling and because of his small size and protective colouring (brown or chocolate) is said to be particularly valuable for hunting duck in country dotted with small lakes and ponds where cover is at a minimum. It is claimed that in addition to waterworking the American Water Spaniel is an efficient retriever of upland game including, despite his small size, the pheasant.

Spaniel (American Water)

Official Breed Standard for the Spaniel (American Water)

General Appearance: Medium in size, of sturdy typical Spaniel character, curly coat; an active muscular dog, with emphasis placed on proper size and conformation, correct head properties, texture of coat and colour.

Temperament: Of amicable disposition; demeanour indicates intelligence, strength, and endurance.

Size: Height—15–18 in. (38–46 cm) at the shoulder. Weight—males, 28–45 lb. (13–20 kg); females, 25–40 lb. (11–18 kg).

Coat and Colour: The coat should be closely curled or have marcel effect and should be of sufficient density to be of protection against weather, water, or punishing cover, yet not coarse. Legs should have medium-short, curly feather. Colour solid liver or dark chocolate, a little white on toes or chest permissible.

Head: Moderate in length, skull rather broad and full, stop moderately defined, but not too pronounced. *Forehead* covered with short smooth hair and without tuft or topknot. *Muzzle* of medium length, square and with no inclination to snipiness, jaws strong and of good length, and neither undershot nor overshot, *teeth* straight and well shaped. *Nose* sufficiently wide and with well-developed nostrils to ensure good scenting power. *Eyes* hazel, brown or of dark tone to harmonize with coat; set well apart. Expression alert, attractive, intelligent. *Ears* lobular, long and wide, not set too high on head, but slightly above the eyeline. Leather extending to end of nose and well covered with close curls.

Neck: Round and of medium length, strong and muscular, free of throatiness, set to carry head with dignity, but arch not accentuated.

Forequarters: Shoulders sloping, clean, and muscular. Legs of medium length and well boned, but not so short as to handicap for field work. Forelegs powerful and reasonably straight.

Body: Well developed, sturdily constructed but not too compactly coupled. General outline is a symmetrical relationship of parts. Well-sprung ribs. Strong loins, lightly arched; and well-furnished deep brisket but not excessively broad.

Hindquarters: Hind legs firm with suitably bent stifles and strong hocks well let down. Feet to harmonize with size of dog. Toes closely grouped and well padded.

Tail: Moderate in length, curved in a slightly rocker shape, carried slightly below level of back; tapered and covered with hair to tip, action lively.

Faults: Coat too straight, soft, fine, or tightly kinked. Very flat skull, narrow across the top, long slender or snipey muzzle. Cowhocks. Rat or shaved tail.

Disqualification: *Yellow eyes.*

Spaniel (Brittany)

THE BRITTANY SPANIEL originated in the French province of Brittany and is thought to be the result of the crossing of English setters with small French land spaniels, an ancestry that many believe is linked to that of the Welsh Springer Spaniel. Such crosses are thought to have taken place about the middle of the 19th century, because over the next fifty years the Breton peasant's hunting dog was a familiar sight throughout the province.

In its compact frame the "Britt" combines the talents of both its progenitors, being able to point game like the setter and retrieve it as does the spaniel. The breed works equally well in open country and thick cover and is especially noted for its ability with woodcock. It is the smallest of the breeds that are known as the versatile gun dogs. The breed can enjoy life as the family companion during the week and double as field or show dog on the weekends.

The Breton spaniel was first exhibited at the Paris dog show in 1900, at which time it was known by a variety of names. Then with the draughting of the first official breed standard, it became known as the Epagneul Breton or Brittany Spaniel and has remained so. Word of the busy pointing spaniel's ability and courage in the field soon spread and caught the interest of sportsmen on this side of the Atlantic. First to bring "Britts" to this continent was Señor Juan Pugibet of Mexico. Then other sportsmen, some in the United States and some in Canada, attracted to the breed for various reasons imported "Britts" during the 1920s, and by 1934 there was sufficient continuing interest in the breed to warrant its official recognition by both The Canadian and American Kennel Clubs.

When the present breed standard was written it was done with the express purpose of describing a dog that would perform as well in the field as it did in the show ring. The committee responsible was determined that the breed should not be split into two types—show and field—as had been the case with other sporting breeds. The Brittany Spaniel's record speaks for itself—it claims more dual champions than any other sporting breed!

Spaniel (Brittany)

Official Breed Standard for the Spaniel (Brittany)

General Appearance: A compact, closely-knit dog of medium size, a leggy spaniel having the appearance as well as the agility of a great ground coverer. Strong, vigorous, energetic, and quick of movement. Not too light in bone, yet never heavy boned and cumbersome. Ruggedness, without clumsiness, is a characteristic of the breed. So leggy is he that his height at the withers is the same as the length of his body. He has no tail, or at most, not more than 4 in. (10 cm).

Size: Weight—should weigh between 30 and 40 lb. (14–18 kg).
Height—17½–20½ in. (44–52 cm) measured from the ground to the highest point of the back, the withers.

Coat and Colour: Hair dense, flat or wavy, never curly. Not as fine as in other Spaniel breeds, and never silky. Furnishings not profuse. The ears should carry little fringe. Neither the front nor hind legs should carry heavy featherings. Skin fine and fairly loose. (A loose skin rolls with briars and sticks, thus diminishing punctures or tearing. But a skin so loose as to form pouches is undesirable.) Colour dark orange and white, or liver and white. Some ticking is desirable, but not so much as to produce belton patterns. Roan patterns or factors of orange or liver shade are permissible. The orange and liver are found in standard particolour, or piebald patterns. Washed out or faded colours are not desirable.

Head: *Skull:* medium length (approximately 4¾ in. (12 cm)). Rounded, very slightly wedge-shaped, but evenly made. Width, not quite as wide as the length (about 4⅜ in. (11 cm)) and never so broad as to appear coarse, or so narrow as to appear racy. Well-defined, but gently sloping stop effect. Median line rather indistinct. The occipital crest only apparent to the touch. Lateral walls well rounded. The Brittany should never be "apple-headed" and he should never have an indented stop. (All measurements of skull are for a 19½ in. (50 cm) dog.) *Muzzle:* medium length, about two-thirds the length of the skull, measuring the muzzle from the tip to the stop, and the skull from the occipital crest to the stop between the eyes. Muzzle should taper gradually in both horizontal and vertical dimensions as it approaches the nostrils. Neither a Roman nose nor a concave curve (dish face) is desirable. Never broad, heavy, or snipey. *Nose:* nostrils well open to permit deep breathing of air and adequate scenting while at top speed. Never shiny. Colour: fawn, tan, light shades of brown or deep pink. *Mouth:* lips tight to the muzzle, with the upper lip overlapping the lower jaw only sufficiently to cover under lip. Lips dry so that feathers do not stick. Well-joined incisors. Posterior edge of upper incisors in contact with anterior edge of lower incisors, thus giving a true scissors bite. *Eyes:* well set in head. Well protected from briars by a heavy, expressive eyebrow. Skull well chiselled under the eyes, so that the lower lid is not pulled back to form a pocket or haw for catching seeds, dirt, and weed dust. Judges should check by forcing head down to see if lid falls away from the eye. Preference should be for darker-coloured eyes, though lighter shades of amber should not be penalized. *Ears:* set high, above the level of the eyes. Short and leafy, rather than pendulous, reaching about half the length of the muzzle. Should lie flat and close to the head, with the tip rounded very slightly. Ears well covered with dense but relatively short hair, and with little fringe.

Neck: Medium length, not quite permitting the dog to place his nose on the ground without bending his legs. Free from throatiness, though not a serious fault unless accompanied by dewlaps. Strong, without giving the impression of being over-muscled. Well set into sloping shoulders. Never concave or ewe-necked.

Forequarters: Shoulder blades should not protrude much. Not too widely set apart with perhaps two thumbs' width or less between the blades. At the withers, the Brittany is slightly higher than at the rump. Shoulders sloping and muscular. Blade and upper arm should form nearly a 90-degree angle when measured from the posterior point of the blade at the withers to the junction of the blade and upper arm, and thence to the point of the elbow nearest the ribs. Straight shoulders do not permit sufficient reach. Viewed from the front, front legs perpendicular, but not set too wide as in the case of a dog loaded in shoulder. Elbows and feet turning neither in nor out. Viewed from the side, practically perpendicular to the pastern. Pastern slightly bent to give cushion to stride. Not so straight as in terriers. Leg bones clean, graceful, but not too fine. One must look for substance and suppleness. Height to the elbows should approximately equal distance from elbows to withers.

Body: Body length approximately the same as the height when measured at the withers. Body length is measured from the point of the forechest to the rear of the haunches. Back short and straight. Slight slope from highest point of withers to the root of the tail. Never hollow, saddle, sway, or roached backed. Chest deep, reaching the level of the elbow. Neither so wide nor so rounded as to disturb the placement of the shoulder bones and elbows, which causes a paddling movement, and often causes soreness from elbow striking ribs. Ribs well sprung, but adequate heart room provided by depth as well as width. Loins short and strong. In motion the loin should not sway sideways, giving a zigzag motion to the back, wasting energy. Distance from last rib to upper thigh short, about three to four finger widths. Slight drop from hips to root of tail. Flanks rounded. Fairly full. Not extremely tucked up, nor yet flabby and falling.

Hindquarters: Broad, strong, and muscular, with powerful thighs and well-bent stifles, giving a hip set well into the loin and the marked angulation necessary for a powerful drive when in motion. Thighs well feathered, but not profusely, halfway to the hock. Stifles well bent. The stifle generally is the term used for knee joint. If the angle made by the upper and lower leg bones is too straight, the dog quite generally lacks drive, since his hind legs cannot drive as far forward at each stride as is desirable. However, the stifle should not be bent so as to throw the hock joint far out behind the dog. Since factors not easily seen by the eye may give the dog his proper drive, a Brittany should not be condemned for straight stifle until the judge has checked the dog in motion from the side. When at a trot, the Brittany's hind foot should step into or beyond the print left by the front foot.

The stifle joint should not turn out making a cowhock. (The cowhock moves the foot out to the side, thus driving out of line, and losing reach at each stride.) Hocks, that is, the back pasterns, should be moderately short, pointing neither in nor out; perpendicular when viewed from the side. They should be firm when shaken by the judge. Feet should be strong, proportionately smaller than other spaniels, with close-fitting, well-arched toes and thick pads. The Brittany is not "up on his toes." Toes not heavily feathered. An ideal foot is halfway between the hare-and cat-foot.

Tail: Naturally tailless, or not over 4 in. (10 cm) long. Natural or docked, set on high, actually an extension of the spine at about the same level.

Faults: Long, curly, or silky hair is a fault. Any tendency towards excessive feathering should be severely penalized as undesirable in a sporting dog which must face burrs and heavy cover. Tight nostrils should be penalized. A two-tone or butter-fly nose should be severely penalized. Drooling to receive a heavy penalty. Flews to be penalized. Overshot or undershot jaw to be penalized heavily. A prominent, full or pop eye should be heavily penalized. It is a serious fault in a hunting dog that must face briars. Light and mean-looking eyes to be heavily penalized. Falling pasterns are a serious fault. An extremely heavy bone is as much a fault as spindly legs. A long body should be heavily penalized. Narrow or slab-sided chests are a fault. Narrow and weak loins are a fault. Fat and falling hindquarters are a fault. Flat feet, splayed feet, paper feet, etc., are to be heavily penalized.

Disqualifications: *Any Brittany Spaniel measuring under 17½ in. (44 cm) or over 20½ in. (52 cm) shall be disqualified from show competition. Any black in the coat or a nose so dark in colour as to appear black shall disqualify. A tail substantially more than 4 in. (10 cm) in length shall disqualify.*

A Guide to the Judge: The points below indicate only relative values. To be also taken into consideration are type, gait, soundness, spirit, optimum height, body length, and gen-eral proportions.

Scale of Points:
Head   25
Body   35
Running gear   40
       TOTAL   100

Spaniel (Clumber)

THE CLUMBER IS THE HEAVIEST and slowest moving of all the spaniel breeds, an ideal shooting companion for the huntsman that travels on foot. Many claim this is also the most aristocratic of the land spaniels. Certainly the breed has had a long association with the aristocracy. It has also been suggested that the breed may have been created by a French nobleman exclusively for his own use and that the most likely ancestors of the Clumber were the basset and a spaniel of continental origin.

The French nobleman was the Duc de Noailles, who transferred his dogs to England at the time of the French Revolution. The Duke returned to France and was killed, but his dogs remained in England.

There they were left in the care of the Duke of Newcastle at his Clumber Park estate, after which the breed was named. A painting dated 1788 entitled "The Return from Shooting" shows the Duke of Newcastle and three of his spaniels believed to be some of the original de Noailles' dogs. The Duke continued to breed the dogs and undoubtedly added a few refinements of his own to complete the creation of a sturdy sporting breed capable of flushing and retrieving game from dense thicket.

The dogs were not sold but given occasionally to shooting companions and it was many years before these spaniels were seen outside the area around Clumber Park. However, after the introduction of dog shows in England (1859), the breed was to be seen entered in the classes for spaniels. The breed became a favourite of the Prince of Wales, later Edward VII, and it is reported that King George V always kept a number of Clumber Spaniels in the Sandringham Kennels.

While the breed performed well in Field Trials and for a time enjoyed a fair bit of popularity, sportsmen began to favour faster moving dogs and the Clumber's numbers declined rather seriously. Today it is making a moderate come-back thanks to the efforts of a few faithful breeders on this continent and overseas.

G.STENHOUSE

Spaniel (Clumber)

The Clumber Spaniel was officially recognized in the United States in 1859 and was among the first of the breeds to be registered in Canada. The Canadian Kennel Club Stud Book for the years 1888–1889 lists twenty-seven registrations.

Official Breed Standard for the Spaniel (Clumber)

General Appearance: A long, low, heavy-looking dog, of a very thoughtful expression, betokening great intelligence. Should have the appearance of great power. Sedate in all movements, but not clumsy.

Size: Weight of dogs averages between 55 and 65 lb. (25–29 kg); bitches from 35–50 lb. (16–23 kg).

Coat and Colour: Coat silky and straight, not too long, extremely dense; feather long and abundant. Colour, lemon and white, and orange and white. Fewer markings on body the better. Perfection of markings, solid lemon or orange ears, evenly marked head and eyes, muzzle and legs ticked.

Head: Head large and massive in all its dimensions; round above eyes, flat on top, with a furrow running from between the eyes upon the centre. A marked stop and large occipital protuberance. *Jaw* long, broad, and deep. Lips of upper jaw overhung. *Muzzle* not square, but at the same time powerful-looking. Nostrils large, open and flesh-coloured, sometimes cherry-coloured. *Eyes* large, soft, deep-set and showing haw. Hazel in colour, not too pale, with dignified and intelligent expression. *Ears* long and broad at the top, turned over on the front edge; vine-shaped; close to the head; set on low and feathered only on the front edge, and there but slightly. Hair short and silky, without the slightest approach to wave or curl.

Neck: Neck long, thick, and powerful; free from dewlap, with a large ruff.

Forequarters: Shoulders immensely strong and muscular, giving a heavy appearance in front. Forelegs short, straight, and very heavy in bone, elbows close.

Body: Long, low, and well ribbed up. The chest is wide and deep, the back long, broad, and level, with very slight arch over the loin.

Hindquarters: Hind legs only slightly less heavily boned than the forelegs. They are moderately angulated, with hocks well let down. Quarters well developed and muscular. No feather above the hocks, but thick hair on the back of the legs just above the feet. Feet large, compact, and well filled with hair between the toes.

Tail: Stern set on a level and carried low.

Scale of Points:

General appearance and size	10
Head	15
Eyes	5
Ears	10
Neck and shoulders	15
Body and quarters	20
Legs and feet	10
Coat and feather	10
Colour and markings	5
TOTAL	100

Spaniel (English Cocker)

THE SUBGROUP OF DOGS known as the spaniels takes its name from *hispania,* the old name for Spain, said to be these dogs' country of origin. Such dogs have been known throughout Europe and in Britain since the 14th century and were used in the sport of falconry. Their job was to flush birds for the hawk. Later they performed the same function flushing birds for the sportsman's net. While their name has been spelled in a variety of ways, among them "spaynel," "spannel," and "spanyett," a description of them written in 1677 has not changed. It was written that the spaniels were dogs "with active feet, wanton tail, and busy nostrils."

By 1800 the spaniels had been divided into those that worked on land—the land spaniels—and those that worked over water—the water spaniels. In 1870 the land spaniels were subdivided into "springing" and "field" spaniels. And it is from the field that the cocker evolved, so named because the small spaniel was an expert at working in thick hedgerows and gorse and flushing the woodcock.

When first exhibited the field spaniels were classified "under and over twenty-five pounds," and it is said that a dog might be exhibited in the morning as an "under" but after a good meal the same dog would compete as an "over." This state of confusion prevailed until after the founding of The Kennel Club (England) in 1873. Varieties were separated and in 1892 the Cocker Spaniel was granted separate breed classification.

Cocker spaniels were first registered in Canada in 1889, but it was not until 1940 that the English Cocker was granted separate breed status. Between these dates two distinct varieties of cocker developed—the American and the English—and although the two differed greatly in appearance they were judged by the same breed standard and frequently inter-bred. After extensive researching of pedigrees the pure English lines were separated from the American and the confusion was resolved with the granting of separate breed classifications.

Spaniel (English Cocker)

Official Breed Standard for the Spaniel (English Cocker)

General Appearance: The English Cocker Spaniel is an attractive, active, merry sporting dog; with short body and strong limbs, standing well up at the withers. His movements are alive with energy; his gait powerful and frictionless. He is alert at all times, and the carriage of head and incessant action of his tail while at work give the impression that here is a dog that is not only bred for hunting but really enjoys it. He is well balanced, strongly built, full of quality and is capable of top speed combined with great stamina. His head imparts an individual stamp peculiar to him alone and has that brainy appearance expressive of the highest intelligence, and is in perfect proportion to his body. His muzzle is a most distinctive feature, being of correct conformation and in proportion to his skull.

Temperament: The character of the English Cocker is of extreme importance. His love and faithfulness to his master and household, his alertness and courage are characteristic. He is noted for his intelligence and merry disposition; not quarrelsome; and is a responsive and willing worker both in the field and as a companion.

Size: Height—ideal heights at withers: males, 16−17 in. (41−43 cm); females, 15−16 in. (38−41 cm).
Weight—the most desirable weights: males, 28−34 lb. (13−15 kg); females, 26−32 lb. (12−15 kg).
  Proper physical conformation and balance should be considered more important than weight alone.

Coat and Colour: Coat on head short and fine; on body flat or slightly wavy and silky in texture. Should be of medium length with enough undercoating to give protection. The English Cocker should be well feathered but not so profusely as to hide the true lines or interfere with his field work. Colour various. In self-colours a white shirt frill is undesirable. In particolours, the colouring must be broken on the body and be evenly distributed. No large portion of any one colour should exist. White should be shown on the saddle. A dog of any solid colour with white feet and chest is not a particolour. In roans it is desirable that the white hair should be distributed over the body, the more evenly the better. Roans come in various colours: blue, liver, red, orange and lemon. In black and tans the coat should be black; tan spots over the eyes, tan on the sides of the muzzle, on the throat and chest, on forelegs from the knees to the toes and on the hind legs on the inside of the legs, also on the stifle and extending from the hock to the toes.

Head: The *skull* and *forehead* should be well developed with no suggestion of coarseness, arched and slightly flattened on top when viewed both from the stop to the end of the skull as well as from ear to ear, and cleanly chiselled under the eyes. The desirable proportion of the head is approximately one-half for the muzzle and one-half for the skull. The *muzzle* should be square with a definite stop where it blends into the skull and in proportion with the width of the skull. As the English Cocker is primarily a sporting dog, the muzzle and jaws must be of sufficient strength and size to carry game; and the length of the muzzle should provide room for the development of the olfactory nerve to ensure good scenting qualities, which require that the nose be wide and well developed. *Nostrils* black in colour except in reds, livers, particolours and roans of the lighter shades where brown is permissible, but black preferred. *Lips* should be square, full and free from flews. *Teeth* should be even and set squarely. The *eyes* should be of medium size, full and slightly oval shaped, set squarely in skull and wide apart. Eyes must be dark brown except in livers and light particolours where hazel is permissible, but the darker the better. The general expression should be intelligent, alert, bright and merry. *Ears* lobular; set low and close to the head; leather fine and extending at least to the nose, well covered with long, silky straight or slightly wavy hair.

Neck: Long, clean and muscular; arched towards the head; set cleanly into sloping shoulders.

Forequarters: Shoulders sloping and fine. Forelegs straight and strong with bone nearly equal in size from elbow to heel; elbows set close to the body with free action from shoulders; pasterns short, straight, and strong.

Body: Back short and strong. Length of back from withers to tail-set should approximate height from ground to withers.

Height of the dog at the withers should be greater than the height at the hip joint, providing a gradual slope between these points. Close coupled, compact and firmly knit, giving the impression of great strength without heaviness. Chest deep and well developed but not too wide and round to interfere with the free action of the forelegs. Depth of brisket should reach to the elbow, sloping gradually upward to the loin. Ribs should spring gradually to middle of body, tapering to back ribs which should be of good depth and extend well back. Loin short and powerful, slightly arched.

Hindquarters: The hips should be rounded; thighs broad, well developed and muscular, giving abundance of propelling power. Stifles strong and well bent. Hock to pad moderately short, strong and well let down. Size of feet in proportion to the legs; firm, round, and cat-like with thick pads and strong toes.

Tail: Set on to conform with the topline of the back. Merry in action.

Faults: Muzzle too short or snipey. Jaw overshot or undershot. Lips snipey or pendulous. Skull too flat or too rounded, cheeky, or coarse. Stop insufficient or exaggerated. Light, round, or protruding eyes. Conspicuous haw. Ears set or carried too high, too wide at the top, insufficient feathering, positive curls or ringlets. Neck short, thick, with dewlap or excessive throatiness. Straight or loaded shoulders. Shoulders loose; elbows turned in or out; legs bowed or set too close or too wide apart; knees knuckled over; light bone. Too long and lacking depth; insufficient spring of rib; barrel rib. Too low at withers; long, sway back, or roach back; flat or narrow loin; exaggerated tuck-up. Excessive angulation; lightness of bone; stifle too short; hocks too long or turned in or out. Feet too large, too small, spreading, or splayed. Tail-set too low, habitually carried too high, too short or too long. White feet are undesirable in any specimen of self-colour. Lack of coat, too soft, curly, or wiry. Excessive trimming to change the natural appearance and coat should be discouraged. Deviations from ideal heights to be severely penalized but not disqualified.

Spaniel (English Springer)

As EARLY AS 1570, dog literature contains references to spaniels, sporting dogs that were brought to Britain from Spain and after which country these breeds take the name of "spaniel." At that time, Dr. Caius, first chronicler of dog breeds, divided the "spanielles" into two groups—those that worked over water and those that were used for hunting on land. It is from the land spaniels that the English Springer descends. Generally regarded as the oldest of the spaniel breeds, it is from the English Springer that all the other land spaniels, except the Clumber, were developed.

By the year 1800 the land spaniel group had been subdivided into two more groups—those weighing up to twenty-five pounds were called "cockers" or "cocking spaniels" because they were used chiefly for hunting woodcock—and the larger dogs, weighing about forty-five pounds, were used for springing game for the net and later for the gun. These became known as "springers," Field Spaniels, or English Spaniels.

Within the next decade a distinct type of robust spaniel had been developed by breeders in the counties of Norfolk and Shropshire. Two strains were predominant and, although these dogs would be considered coarse by today's standards, they are said to have been of true springer type and the forerunners of the present-day breed.

First exhibited in the 1850s as the Norfolk Spaniel, the breed was given its present name after the formation of the Sporting Spaniel Club which was founded in 1885. The first field trial for spaniels, sponsored by this club, was held in 1899, and by 1902 there was sufficient interest in the English Springer to warrant its official recognition as a separate breed by The Kennel Club (England). The following year the breed was shown for the first time at an English championship event.

The breed came to this continent in 1907 and was first registered in Canada in the years 1913–1914. The English Springer has earned a reputation as an outstanding all-purpose sporting dog and has accounted for some spectacular winning in the show ring.

Spaniel (English Springer)

Official Breed Standard for the
Spaniel (English Springer)

General Appearance: The English Springer Spaniel is a medium-sized sporting dog with a most compact body, and a docked tail. His coat is moderately long, glossy, usually liver and white or black and white, with feathering on his legs, ears, chest and brisket. His pendulous ears, soft gentle expression, sturdy build and friendly wagging tail proclaim him unmistakably a member of the ancient family of spaniels. He is above all a well-proportioned dog, free from exaggeration, nicely balanced in every part. His carriage is proud and upstanding, body deep, legs strong and muscular with enough length to carry him with ease. His short level back, well-developed thighs, good shoulders, and excellent feet suggest power, endurance, and agility. Taken as a whole he looks the part of a dog that can go and keep going under difficult hunting conditions, and moreover he enjoys what he is doing. At his best he is endowed with style, symmetry, balance, and enthusiasm and is every inch a sporting dog of distinct spaniel character, combining beauty and utility.

In judging the English Springer Spaniel the over-all picture is a primary consideration. It is urged that the judge look for type which includes general appearance, outline, and temperament and also for soundness, especially as seen when the dog is in motion.

Inasmuch as the dog with a smooth easy gait must be reasonably sound and well balanced, he is to be highly regarded in the show ring; however, not to the extent of forgiving him for not looking like an English Springer Spaniel. A quite untypical dog, leggy, foreign in head and expression, may move well. But he should not be placed over a good all-round specimen that has a minor fault in movement. It should be remembered that the English Springer Spaniel is first and foremost a sporting dog of the spaniel family and he must look and behave and move in character.

Temperament: The typical Springer is friendly, eager to please, quick to learn, willing to obey. In the show ring he should exhibit poise, attentiveness, tractability, and should permit himself to be examined by the judge without resentment or cringing.

Size: The Springer is built to cover rough ground with ability and reasonable speed. He should be kept to medium size—neither too small nor too large and heavy to do the work for which he is intended. The ideal shoulder height for dogs is 20 in. (51 cm); for bitches, 19 in. (48 cm).

Length of topline (the distance from top of the shoulders to the root of the tail) should be approximately equal to the dog's shoulder height—never longer than his height—and not appreciably less. The dog too long in body, especially when long in loin, tires easily and lacks the compact outline characteristic of the breed. Equally undesirable is the dog too short in body for the length of his legs, a condition that destroys his balance and restricts the gait.

Weight is dependent on the dog's other dimensions: a 20 in. (51 cm) dog, well proportioned, in good condition should weigh about 49–55 lb. (22–25 kg). The resulting appearance is a well knit, sturdy dog with good but not too heavy bone, in no way coarse or ponderous.

Coat and Colour: Colour may be liver or black with white markings; liver and white (or black and white) with tan markings; blue or liver roan; or predominantly white with tan, black or liver markings.

On his ears, chest, legs and belly the Springer is nicely furnished with a fringe of feathering (of moderate heaviness). On his head, front of forelegs, and below hocks on front of hind legs the hair is short and fine. The body coat is flat or wavy of medium length, sufficiently dense to be waterproof, weatherproof and thornproof. The texture fine, and the hair should have the clean, glossy, live appearance, indicative of good health. It is legitimate to trim about head, feet, and ears; to remove dead hair; to thin and shorten excess feathering particularly from the hocks to the feet and elsewhere as required to give a smart, clean appearance.

Head: The head is impressive without being heavy. Its beauty lies in a combination of strength and refinement. It is important that the size and proportion be in balance with the rest of the dog. Viewed in profile, the head should appear approximately the same length as the neck and should blend with the body in substance. The *skull* (upper head) to be of medium length, fairly broad, flat on top, slightly rounded at the sides and back.

The occiput bone inconspicuous, rounded rather than peaked or angular.

The *foreface* (head in front of the eyes) approximately the same length as the skull, and in harmony as to width and general character. Looking down on the head the *muzzle* to appear to be about one-half the width of the skull. As the skull rises from the foreface it makes a brow or "stop," divided by a groove or fluting between the eyes. This groove continues upward and gradually disappears as it reaches the middle of the forehead. The amount of "stop" can best be described as moderate. It must not be a pronounced feature as in the Clumber Spaniel. Rather it is a subtle rise where the muzzle blends into the upper head, further emphasized by the groove and by the position and shape of the eyebrows which should be well developed. The stop, eyebrow, and the chiselling of the bony structure around the eye sockets contribute to the Springer's beautiful and characteristic expression.

Viewed in profile, the topline of the skull and the muzzle lie in two approximately parallel planes. The nasal bone should be straight, with no inclination downward towards the tip of the nose which gives a down-faced look so undesirable in this breed. Neither should the nasal bone be concave resulting in a "dish-faced" profile; nor convex giving the dog a "Roman nose."

The *nostrils,* well opened and broad, liver colour or black depending on the colour of the coat. Flesh-coloured ("Dudley noses") or spotted ("butterfly noses") are undesirable. The cheeks to be flat (not rounded, full, or thick) with nice chiselling under the eyes.

The *jaws* to be of sufficient length to allow the dog to carry game easily; fairly square, lean, strong, and even (neither undershot nor overshot). The upper lip to come down full and rather square to cover the line of the lower jaw, but lips not to be pendulous or exaggerated.

The *teeth* should be strong, clean, not too small; and when the mouth is closed the teeth should meet in an even bite or a close scissors bite (the lower incisors touching the inside of the upper incisors).

More than any other feature the eyes contribute to the Springer's appeal. Colour, placement, size influence expression and attractiveness. The *eyes* to be of medium size, neither small, round, full and prominent, nor bold and hard in expression. Set rather well apart and fairly deep in their sockets. The colour of the iris to harmonize with the colour of the coat, preferably a good dark hazel in the liver dogs and black or deep brown in the black and white specimens. The expression to be alert, kindly, trusting. The lids, tight with little or no haw showing.

The correct ear-set is on a level with the line of the eye; on the side of the skull and not too far back. The flaps to be long and fairly wide, hanging close to the cheeks, with no tendency to stand up or out. The leather, thin, approximately long enough to reach the tip of the nose.

Neck: The neck to be moderately long, muscular, slightly arched at the crest, gradually blending into sloping shoulders. Not noticeably upright or coming into the body at an abrupt angle.

Forequarters: Efficient movement in front calls for proper shoulders. The blades sloping back to form an angle with the forearm of approximately 90 degrees which permits the dog to swing his forelegs forward in an easy manner. Shoulders (fairly close together at the tips) to lie flat and mould smoothly into the contour of the body. The forelegs to be straight with the same degree of size to the foot. The bone strong, slightly flattened, not too heavy or round. The knee straight, almost flat; the pasterns short, strong; elbows close to the body with free action from the shoulders.

Body: The topline slopes very gently from withers to tail, the line from withers to back descending without a sharp drop; the back practically level; arch over hips somewhat lower than the withers; croup sloping gently to base of tail; tail carried to follow the natural line of the body. The body to be well coupled, strong, compact; the chest deep but not so wide or round as to interfere with the action of the front legs; the brisket sufficiently developed to reach to the level of the elbows. The ribs fairly long, springing gradually to the middle of the body then tapering as they approach the end of the ribbed section. The back (section between the withers and loin) to be straight and strong, with no tendency to dip or roach. The loins to be strong, short; a slight arch over loins and hip bones. Hips nicely rounded, blending smoothly into hind legs. The bottom line, starting on a level with the elbows, to continue backward with almost no up-curve until reaching the end of the ribbed section, then a more noticeable up-curve to the flank, but not enough to make the dog appear small waisted or tucked up.

Hindquarters: The Springer should be shown in hard muscular condition, well developed in hips and thighs and the whole rear assembly should suggest strength and driving power. The hip joints to be set rather wide apart and the hips nicely rounded. The thighs broad and muscular; the stifle joint strong and moderately bent. The hock joint somewhat rounded, not small and sharp in contour, and moderately angulated. Leg from hock joint to foot pad, short and strong with good bone structure. When viewed from the rear the hocks to be parallel whether the dog is standing or in motion.

The feet to be round, or slightly oval, compact, well arched medium size with thick pads, well feathered between the toes. Excess hair to be removed to show the natural shape and size of the foot.

Tail: The Springer's tail is an index both to his temperament and his conformation. Merry tail action is characteristic. The proper set is somewhat low following the natural line of the croup. The carriage should be nearly horizontal, slightly elevated when dog is excited. Carried straight up is untypical of the breed. The tail should not be docked too short and should be well fringed with wavy feather. It is legitimate to shape and shorten the feathering but enough should be left to blend with the dog's other furnishings.

Gait: In judging the Springer there should be emphasis on proper movement which is the final test of a dog's conformation and soundness. Prerequisite to good movement is balance of the front and rear assemblies. The two must match in angulation and muscular development if the gait is to be smooth and effortless. Good shoulders laid back at an angle that permits a long stride are just as essential as the excellent rear quarters that provide the driving power. When viewed from the front the dog's legs should appear to swing forward in a free and easy manner, with no tendency for the feet to cross over or interfere with each other. Viewed from the rear the hocks should drive well under the body following on a line with the forelegs, the rear legs parallel, neither too widely nor too closely spaced. Seen from the side the Springer should exhibit a good long forward stride, without high-stepping or wasted motion.

Faults: Lack of true English Springer type in conformation, expression, or behaviour.

Excessive timidity, with due allowance for puppies and novice exhibits. But no dog to receive a ribbon if he behaves in a vicious manner towards handler or judge. Aggressiveness towards other dogs in the ring not to be construed as viciousness.

Over-heavy, cloddy build. Legginess, too tall for length and substance. Oversize or undersize (more than 1 inch (3 cm) under or over the breed ideal).

Rough curly coat. Over-trimming especially of the body coat. Any chopped, barbered or artificial effect. Excessive feathering that destroys the clean outline desirable in a sporting dog. Off-colours such as lemon, red or orange not to place.

Oval, pointed, or heavy skull. Cheeks prominently rounded, thick and protruding. Too much or too little stop. Over-heavy muzzle. Muzzle too short, too thin, too narrow. Pendulous slobbery lips. Under or overshot jaws—a very serious fault, to be heavily penalized.

Any deviation from standard for teeth. One or two teeth slightly out of line not to be considered a serious fault, but irregularities due to faulty jaw formation to be severely penalized.

Eyes yellow or brassy in colour or noticeably lighter than the coat. Sharp expression indicating unfriendly or suspicious nature. Loose droopy eyelids. Prominent haw (the third eyelid or membrane in the inside corner of the eye).

Short round ears. Ears set too high or too low or too far back on the head.

Short neck, often the sequence to steep shoulders. Concave neck, sometimes called ewe neck or upside down neck (the opposite of arched). Excessive throatiness.

Shoulders set at a steep angle limiting the stride. Loaded shoulders (the blades standing out from the body by overdevelopment of the muscles). Loose elbows, crooked legs, bone too light or too coarse and heavy. Weak pasterns that let down the feet at a pronounced angle.

Body too shallow, indicating lack of brisket. Ribs too flat sometimes due to immaturity. Ribs too round (barrel-shaped), hampering the gait. Sway back (dip in back), indicating weakness or lack of muscular development, particularly to be seen when dog is in action and viewed from the side. Roach back (too much arch over loin and extending forward into middle section). Croup falling away too sharply, or croup too high—unsightly fault, detrimental to outline and good movement. Topline sloping sharply, indicating steep withers (straight shoulder placement) and a too low tail-set.

Too little or too much angulation. Narrow, underdeveloped thighs. Hocks too short or too long (a proportion of $\frac{1}{3}$ the distance from hip joint to foot is ideal). Flabby muscles. Weakness of joints.

Thin, open or splayed feet (flat with spreading toes). Hare-foot (long, rather narrow foot).

Tail habitually upright. Tail set too high or too low. Clamped down tail (indicating timidity or undependable temperament, even less to be desired than the tail carried too gaily).

Short, choppy stride, mincing steps with up and down movement, hopping. Moving with forefeet wide, giving roll or swing to body. Weaving or crossing of fore or hind feet. Cowhocks—hocks turning in towards each other.

Spaniel (Field)

*U*NTIL 1892 both the English Cocker and the Field Spaniel were classified as "Field Spaniels," the varieties being divided by weight. That is, "Field Spaniels under twenty-five pounds" (Cocker) and "Field Spaniels over twenty-five pounds" (Field). Thus, at one time, both breeds shared a common ancestry. Then in 1892 the two were separated and became two distinct breeds under their present names. The cocker breeders seem to have chosen the right route. Their breed became more elegant, cobbier, and more robust and attracted a large following. Breeders of the Field seem to have gone to the other extreme. They bred for a lower leg and longer back, and succeeded in producing a breed that became the butt of jokes and bad publicity. One specimen, it is said, measured twelve inches at the shoulder and weighed in at forty pounds. They were heavy headed, sluggish, and crooked of leg—not at all the type of sporting breed to give a good account of himself in the field. The breed lost many former supporters and it remained for a group of Field Spaniel devotees to rescue a worthy dog from certain oblivion.

In 1948 the Field Spaniel Society was reformed in Britain, and breeders set about eliminating the exaggerations and recreating an upstanding sporting dog. To accomplish this, crosses to both the springer and cocker were made and eventually the faults were eliminated, and type was fixed. However, such crosses rendered many individuals ineligible for registration with the American Kennel Club.

Even though the Field Spaniel has been restored in both type and working ability, its close relative, the English Cocker, made so many friends during the intervening years, it is doubtful that the Field will ever catch up. Only occasionally is a Field Spaniel exhibited in Canada. The Canadian Kennel Club Stud Book shows that twenty Field Spaniels were registered in the years 1888–1889.

Spaniel (Field)

Official Breed Standard for the Spaniel (Field)

General Appearance: That of a well-balanced, noble, up-standing sporting dog; built for activity and endurance. A grand combination of beauty and utility, and bespeaking of unusual docility and instinct.

Size: Height—about 18 in. (46 cm) to shoulder. Weight—from about 35–50 lb. (16–23 kg).

Coat and Colour: Coat flat or slightly waved, and never curled. Sufficiently dense to resist the weather, and not too short. Silky in texture, glossy, and refined in nature, with neither duffleness on the one hand, nor curl or wiriness on the other. On the chest, under belly and behind the legs, there should be abundant feather, but never too much, especially below the hocks, and that of the right sort, *viz.* setter-like. The hindquarters should be similarly adorned.

Colour black, liver, golden liver, mahogany red, or roan; or any one of these colours with tan over the eyes and on the cheeks, feet, and pasterns. Other colours, such as black and white, liver and white, red or orange and white, while not disqualifying, will be considered less desirable since the Field Spaniel should be clearly distinguished from the Springer Spaniel.

Head: Should be quite characteristic of this grand sporting dog, as that of the Bulldog, or the Bloodhound; its very stamp and countenance should at once convey the conviction of high breeding, character and nobility; **skull** well developed, with a distinctly elevated occipital tuberosity which, above all, gives the character alluded to; not too wide across the **muzzle**, long and lean, never snipey or squarely cut, and in profile curving gradually from nose to throat; lean beneath the eyes—a thickness here gives coarseness to the whole head. The great length of muzzle gives surface for the free development of the olfactory nerve, and thus secures the highest possible scenting powers. **Nose** well developed, with good open nostrils.

Eyes not too full, but not small, receding or overhung, colour dark hazel or brown, or nearly black, according to the colour of the dog. Grave in expression and showing no haw.

Ears moderately long and wide, sufficiently clad with nice Setter-like feather and set low. They should fall in graceful folds, the lower parts curling inwards and backwards.

Neck: Long, strong and muscular, so as to enable the dog to retrieve his game without undue fatigue.

Forequarters: Shoulders long, sloping and well set back, thus giving great activity and speed. Forelegs should be of fairly good length, with straight, clean, flat bone, and nicely feathered. Immense bone is no longer desirable.

Body: Should be of moderate length, well ribbed up to a good strong loin, straight or slightly arched, never slack. Chest deep and well developed, but not too round and wide. Back and loin very strong and muscular.

Hindquarters: Strong and muscular. The stifles should be moderately bent, and not twisted either in or out. Feet not too small; round, with short soft hair between the toes; good, strong pads.

Tail: Well set on and carried low, if possible below the level of the back, in a straight line or with a slight downward inclination, never elevated above the back, and in action always kept low, nicely fringed with wavy feather of silky texture.

Scale of Points:

Head and jaw	15
Eyes	5
Ears	5
Neck	5
Body	10
Forelegs	10
Hind legs	10
Feet	10
Stern	10
Coat and feather	10
General appearance	10
TOTAL	100

Spaniel (Irish Water)

THE IRISH WATER SPANIEL is unique in that he has a naturally short-coated head and tail with a mass of tightly curled ringlets in between. It is as though, over the centuries, Mother Nature had equipped the breed with a natural trim suited to the job of water retrieving.

Most dog historians claim that the Irish Water Spaniel is an ancient breed belonging to the family of water dogs found in many parts of Europe, and that these probably were the progenitors of the poodle. On the other side of the picture there are writers equally convinced that the Irish Water Spaniel is a fairly recent development and derives from a poodle—Curly-Coated Retriever cross. Nevertheless all agree that the Irish Water Spaniel and the poodle share common blood because they have so many traits in common—coat texture, conformation, trainability, and a love of water.

Authoritative information tells us that before 1859 there were two, possibly three, varieties of water spaniel in Ireland—for a certainty in the South Country and the North Country. The variety that may also be included is the Tweed. A Mr. Justin McCarthy is credited with combining the two—or three—and developing the breed we know today as the Irish Water Spaniel. From pictorial evidence it would seem that the South Country variety was dominant. The best known dog of McCarthy's breeding, Boatswain, lived to be eighteen years of age and left a strong impression on the breed.

In 1862 Irish Water Spaniels were first exhibited in Britain where they built up a modest following, and thus it has remained. While the breed works equally well on land and water, has an excellent nose and is keen and intelligent, at one time he was said to be hard-mouthed. Whether this was true or not has been debated, but a dog with such a reputation did not endear himself to the sportsman.

More interest in the breed has been evidenced since the exciting Westminster Kennel Club 1979 Best in Show win of a Canadian-bred Irish Water Spaniel. The Canadian Kennel Club

G. STENHOUSE

Spaniel (Irish Water)

Stud Book lists eight Irish Water Spaniels registered in the years 1888—1889.

Official Breed Standard for the Spaniel (Irish Water)

General Appearance: That of a smart, upstanding, strongly built but not leggy dog, combining great intelligence and rugged endurance with a bold dashing eagerness of temperament.

Size: Height and weight—dogs, 22—24 in. (56—61 cm); bitches, 21—23 in. (53—58 cm). Dogs, 55—65 lb. (25—29 kg); bitches, 45—58 lb. (20—26 kg).

Coat and Colour: Proper coat is of vital importance. The neck, back, and sides should be densely covered with tight crisp ringlets entirely free from woolliness. Underneath the ribs the hair should be longer. The hair on lower throat should be short. The forelegs should be covered all around with abundant hair falling in curls or waves, but shorter in front than behind. The hind legs should also be abundantly covered by hair falling in curls or waves, but the hair should be short on the front of the legs below the hocks. Colour solid liver; white on chest objectionable.

Head: *Skull* rather large and high in dome with prominent occiput; *muzzle* square and rather long with deep mouth opening and lips fine in texture. The head should be cleanly chiselled, not cheeky, and should not present a short wedge-shaped appearance. Hair on face should be short and smooth. *Topknot*, a characteristic of the true breed, should consist of long loose curls growing down into a well-defined peak between the eyes and should not be in the form of a wig; *i.e.*, growing straight across. The *nose* should be large with open nostrils and liver in colour. Teeth strong and level. *Eyes* medium in size and set almost flush, without eyebrows. Colour of eyes hazel, preferably a dark shade. Expression of the eyes should be keenly alert, intelligent, direct, and quizzical. *Ears* long, lobular, set low with leathers reaching to about the end of the nose when extended forward. The ears should be abundantly covered with curls becoming longer towards the tips and extending two or more inches below the ends of the leathers.

Neck: The neck should be long, arching, strong, and muscular, smoothly set into sloping shoulders.

Forequarters: The entire front should give the impression of strength without heaviness. Shoulders should be sloping and clean. Forelegs medium in length, well boned, straight, and muscular with elbows close set. Both fore and hind feet should be large, thick, and somewhat spreading, well-clothed with hair both over and between the toes, but free from superfluous feather.

Body: Body should be of medium length, with ribs well sprung, pear-shaped at the brisket, and rounder towards the hindquarters. Chest deep but not too wide between the legs. Ribs should be carried well back. Loins should be short, wide and muscular. The body should not present a tucked-up appearance.

Hindquarters: The hindquarters should be as high as or a trifle higher than the shoulders and should be very powerful and muscular with well-developed upper and second thighs. Hips should be wide; stifles should not be too straight; and hocks low set and moderately bent. Tail should be set on low enough to give a rather rounded appearance to the hindquarters and should be carried nearly level with the back. Sound hindquarters are of great importance to provide swimming power and drive.

Tail: The so-called "rat tail" is a striking characteristic of the breed. At the root it is thick and covered for 2−3 in. (5−8 cm) with short curls. It tapers to a fine point at the end, and from the root-curls is covered with short, smooth hair so as to look as if the tail had been clipped. The tail should not be long enough to reach the hock joint.

Gait: Should be square, true, precise and not slurring.

Scale of Points:

HEAD

Skull and topknot	6	
Ears	4	
Eyes	4	
Muzzle and nose	6	20

BODY

Neck	5	
Chest, shoulders, back, loin, and ribs	12	17

DRIVING GEAR

Feet, hips, thighs, stifles and continuity of hindquarter muscles	14	
Feet, legs, elbows, and muscles of forequarters	9	23

COAT

Tightness, denseness of curl and general texture	16	
Colour	4	20

TAIL

General appearance and "set on," length, and carriage	5	5

GENERAL CONFORMATION AND ACTION

Symmetry, style, gait, weight, and size	15	15
TOTAL		100

Spaniel (Sussex)

*T*WO FEATURES DISTINGUISH the Sussex. The first is his colour, which is described as "golden liver"—a colour found only in this breed. It is a rich lustrous brown said to be an inheritance from one brood bitch in the breed's founding kennel. His other distinction is the Sussex's unspaniel-like trait of giving tongue when he scents game. It has been claimed that by the tone of the dog's bark the huntsman can tell whether the game is fur or feather and whether the scent is fresh or stale. Because of this vocalizing it is assumed that the Sussex has hound blood in his make-up. The balance of his ancestry comes from various spaniel breeds—the Field, and the now extinct Welsh, and the Springer—found in Britain in 1795, the year when a Mr. Fuller set out to develop the Sussex.

As the name suggests, the breed originated in the county of Sussex, England and was created to be a sturdy, slow moving sporting dog that the hunter could follow comfortably on foot. For fifty years Fuller worked to stabilize his "Rosehill" strain and, on his death in 1847, a breeding pair passed to his head keeper who continued an interest in the Sussex for the next forty years.

The breed was first shown at the Crystal Palace in 1862, and by 1870 the Sussex was in great demand. However, a disease called "dumb madness" had so severely depleted stock, breeders had to resort to intensive in-breeding to keep the Sussex alive. As a consequence the breed suffered from decreased vigour and fertility. Two world wars also took their toll and by the 1940s things were looking pretty bleak. Something had to be done to bring new blood into the breed and because little breeding was taking place outside Britain importing it was out of the question. About the year 1954 a cross to the Clumber Spaniel was successful. Size, temperament, and vigour all improved and the breed continues to enjoy a following in Britain. Few are seen in Canada.

The Canadian Kennel Club Stud Book lists four Sussex Spaniels registered between the years 1888–1889.

Spaniel (Sussex)

Official Breed Standard for the Spaniel (Sussex)

Origin and Purpose: The Sussex Spaniel was developed in Sussex County, England as a working spaniel. His special function was to force his way under low heavy growth and flush birds which were hiding there. He is not designed to cover large areas of ground, nor, contrary to popular opinion, did he have the function of digging. In order that he can be located while hunting, he is gifted with a rich, bell-like voice.

General Appearance: Long, low to the ground, massive, energetic, active and strong, with freedom of movement and nice tail action.

Temperament: Cheerful, tractable, affectionate but somewhat reserved with strangers, having a mind of his own.

Size: Adult males 14–16 in. (35–41 cm) and 45 lb. (20 kg) or more. Adult females 13–15 in. (33–38 cm) and 40 lb. (18 kg) or more.

Coat: Abundant and flat or slightly waved, with no tendency to curl, fine in texture (not woolly) with ample undercoat for weather resistance.

Colour: Rich golden liver, hair shading to a golden tinge towards the tips. A small white spot on the chest, while undesirable, is not grounds for disqualification; no other white is to be tolerated.

Head: The *skull* should be moderately long and also wide, and show a moderate curve from ear to ear, neither flat nor apple-headed, with an indentation in the middle and a pronounced stop. Brows fairly heavy and frowning; occiput full but not pointed, the whole giving an appearance of heaviness without dullness. A well-balanced head is about 8.5 in. (22 cm) from nose to occiput in an adult. *Muzzle:* the adult muzzle should be about 3 in. (8 cm) long and strong, finishing in a deep, square muzzle, and the lips somewhat pendulous, nostrils wide, well developed and liver coloured. Bite scissors or level. *Eyes:* hazel colour, fairly large, not too full but soft in expression, not showing the haw overmuch. *Ears:* thick, fairly large and lobe shaped;

set moderately low, but above eye level; carried close to the head. The entire length being furnished with soft, wavy hair which should not be too profuse.

Neck: Long, strong, and slightly arched, but not carrying the head much above the level of the back. There should not be much throatiness, but a well-marked frill in the coat.

Shoulders and Chest: Shoulders sloping, but not so fine as to bring foreaction in close. The chest is round, especially behind the shoulders, deep and wide, giving a good girth.

Legs: Heavily boned, strong and muscular with large, strong joints; pasterns very short and bony. The forelegs should be very short and strong, with great bone and may show a slight bend in the forearm and be nicely feathered. The hind legs should not appear shorter than the forelegs, nor be too much bent at the hocks. Stifles with sufficient angularity to give power in hind movements. Liberal hair growth above the hocks, but not as profuse below. The hind legs are short from the hock to the ground and wide apart.

Feet: Large, round, well padded, and well feathered between the toes.

Body: The topline should be level. The back and loin is long, well developed and muscular, both in depth and width; for this development the back ribs must be deep and should be carried well back, though not so far as to interfere with movements of stifle joints. There should be no signs of a waist from withers to hips. The whole body is characterized as long, low, and level. Ideally, the body from top of withers to base of tail should be 1½ times the height at the withers. Dogs more than twice as long as tall, or that are not longer than tall, should be heavily penalized; tuck-up should be minimal.

Tail: May be docked or undocked. If docked, should be docked at the halfway point, about 5−7 in. (13−18 cm), set low, and not carried above the level of the back, free actioned and thickly clothed with hair and may have moderate feather.

Gait: The Sussex Spaniel moves slowly with his head at or slightly above the level of the back. Movement is free, sound, and effortless with a decided roll. It is to be kept in mind that the main requirement is brute strength.

Faults: Yellow eyes, overshot or undershot bites, obesity, high head carriage, unfriendly behaviour, movement resembling that of any other spaniel.

Disqualifications: *More than 1 inch (3 cm) over or under recommended height, more than 10 lb. (5 kg) under recommended weight after the age of one (1) year; any colour other than as outlined.*

Spaniel (Welsh Springer)

DOG HISTORIANS BELIEVE that it is quite possible that a white hunting dog with red markings was brought to Wales in pre-Roman times by the Gauls; this dog they assume was the ancestor of both the Brittany Spaniel and the Welsh Springer Spaniel. Wales, being isolated from the rest of England in ancient times, offered ideal conditions for a pure strain to evolve. In its homeland the Welsh Springer first was called the "Starter" and was highly favoured as a sporting dog.

However, until the latter part of the 19th century, outside of his own principality little was known of the Welsh dog. But with the advent of better means of transportation and the introduction of dog shows and field trials, the "Starter's" world grew bigger, thanks to his keenest promoter, Mr. A.T. Williams. In 1899 a dog owned by Williams won the class for working spaniels at the Birmingham show. What is more, for two successive years, a team of Williams' dogs won at trials sponsored by The Sporting Spaniel Society.

Although the breed had its critics, it was hard to ignore success. In 1902 The Kennel Club (England) gave official recognition to the Welsh Springer Spaniel. Up to this time the breed had been listed as "Welsh Cocker." There were those who considered the breed too light and small to be dignified as a springer. An interesting sidelight to this is that in 1901 Williams won with a dog listed as a cocker. The next year he won again with the same dog, now listed as a springer.

For a time after Williams' retirement it seemed that interest in the breed was declining, but not for long. Other breed supporters moved in to take his place and the Welsh Springer continues to have a modest but loyal following. His style, which has never suffered from exploitation, remains as always—smart, active, workmanlike and essentially sporting in character.

G. STENHOUSE

Spaniel (Welsh Springer)

Official Breed Standard for the Spaniel (Welsh Springer)

General Appearance: A symmetrical, compact, strong, merry, very active dog; not stilty, obviously built for endurance and activity.

Size: A dog not to exceed 19 in. (48 cm) in height at the shoulder and a bitch 18 in. (46 cm). Weight should be 35−45 lb. (16−20 kg).

Coat and Colour: Straight or flat and thick, of a silky texture, never wiry or wavy. A curly coat is most objectionable. Rich red and white only.

Head: A short, chubby head is objectionable. *Skull* proportionate, of moderate length, slightly domed, clearly defined stop, well chiselled below the eyes. *Muzzle:* medium length, straight, fairly square; the nostrils well developed, and either flesh coloured, liver, or black acceptable. *Jaw* strong, neither undershot nor overshot. *Eyes* hazel, or dark, medium size, not prominent, nor sunken, nor showing haw. *Ears* set moderately low and hanging close to the cheeks, comparatively small and gradually narrowing towards the tip, covered with nice Setter-like feathering. While the length of feathering on the ears is of little consequence, the leather must be small.

Neck: Long and muscular, clean in throat, neatly set into long and sloping shoulders.

Forelegs: Medium length, straight, well boned, moderately feathered.

Body: Not long; strong and muscular with deep brisket, well-sprung ribs; length of body should be proportionate to length of leg and very well balanced; with muscular loin slightly arched and well coupled up.

Hindquarters: Strong and muscular, wide and fully developed with thick and muscular second thighs.

Hind Legs: Hocks well let down; stifles moderately bent (neither twisted in nor out), moderately feathered.

Feet: Round with thick pads, firm and cat-like, not too large or spreading.

Tail: Well set on and low, never carried above the level of the back, lightly feathered and with lively action.

Faults: Coarse skull, light bone, curly coat, loaded or poorly angulated shoulders, stilted movement.

Disqualifications: *Dogs over 19 in. (48 cm), bitches over 18 in. (46 cm).*

Vizsla (Smooth)

DOG HISTORIANS are of two minds about the development of the Hungarian pointer we know as the Vizsla. Some claim that the breed has a lineage dating back at least to 1000 A.D. because rock carvings of that period show a hunter, his falcon and a dog similar to the present-day Vizsla. Further proof of the breed's antiquity is to be found in a description of falconry in a manuscript dating to the 14th century. Those who believe the Vizsla is of ancient origin claim that such dogs as depicted were crossed with yellow hounds from Turkey during the 18th century and that the eventual standardization of breed type occurred some hundred years later.

The other school of thought holds that the Vizsla is strictly a product of this century, that much as the all-purpose gun dogs of Germany came into being late in the 19th century by the cross breeding of various sporting breeds, so too, in Hungary, the Vizsla was created. The background breeding suggested is the German Weimaraner crossed to different pointing breeds.

In its country of origin the Vizsla became a well-known versatile gun dog and its numbers increased substantially. But two World Wars dealt such destruction to the breed it was feared at one time that the breed might vanish altogether. It was due to the efforts of a few dedicated breeders that the yellow pointer was re-established and is now recognized as Hungary's national dog.

After World War II refugees emigrating to other countries took their gun dogs with them and the Vizsla quickly became known throughout Europe.

Following the success of the Weimaraner on this continent in the 1940s, sportsmen began thinking of importing other breeds of all-purpose gun dogs, among them the Vizsla. First specimens began arriving in the 1950s, and by 1960 there was sufficient interest in the breed to warrant its official recognition by the American Kennel Club followed shortly by its admission to registration with The Canadian Kennel Club.

Vizsla (Smooth)

Official Breed Standard for the Vizsla (Smooth)

Origin and Purpose: The Vizsla (pronounced as if spelled VIZH-LA) is of Hungarian origin, where various records indicate its history as going back many centuries. It was the companion hunting dog of the early warlords and landed aristocracy who used it for general-purpose hunting. It was known in Hungary as the "Yellow" Pointer. In North America it is used primarily as an upland bird dog, where its excellent scenting and retrieving characteristics have been widely acclaimed. It is a strong swimmer and also retrieves well from water.

General Appearance: The Vizsla is a short-haired, medium-sized sporting dog. It conveys the impression of an alert, muscular, well-balanced animal with a distinctive and aristocratic appearance.

Temperament: The Vizsla is intelligent, calm, obedient, and easy to train. It is a sensitive dog which becomes attached to its owner and develops a strong but not overly aggressive protective instinct. In the field, the Vizsla is an eager, happy hunter which is at home on land and in the water.

Size: The standard size, measured at the withers, for the Vizsla is 23 in. (58 cm) for males, and 22 in. (56 cm) for females. A dog of good bone and substance in this size range shall weigh from 50−65 lb. (22−29 kg). A bitch weighs about 10 lb. (5 kg) less. The length to height ratio should be approximately 1:1.

Coat and Colour: The hair of the Vizsla should be short and dense and should lie close to the skin. Each hair should be thick and elastic and the coat should have a glossy sheen.

The correct colour is a golden-rust, sometimes described as the golden colour of a bread crust. In some strains slightly lighter or darker shades may predominate. A white mark on the chest under 2 in. (5 cm) diameter is permissible but not desirable.

Head: *Skull* should convey an impression of being lean and muscular, with a median line down the forehead. The topline of the skull should be straight. The skull tends to be comparatively narrow in relation to its length, with that of the male being slightly wider. The occiput is slightly visible. The stop should be slight and sloping rather than abrupt. *Muzzle:* the muzzle should be approximately the same length as the skull. It should be narrow, end squarely, and have clean straight lines. *Mouth:* the jaws should be strong, and well-developed teeth meeting in a scissors or even bite. The lips should be smooth and well developed and cover the teeth tightly. The lips extend in a level line ¾ of the length of the muzzle. *Eyes:* they should be almond shaped, bright and intelligent in appearance. The colour is in harmony with or darker than the colour of the coat; they should be moderately deep set. The eyelids close neatly and cleanly with no overlap. The nictitating membrane should not be overly exposed. *Ears:* the ears should be thin, silky and moderately tapered with rounded ends. They should just meet under the jaw, or reach to the corner of the mouth, but should not extend as far as the canine teeth. They should be set about ½ inch (1 cm) below the level of the skull and hang close to the cheeks.

Neck: The neck should be of medium length in proportion to the body, it must be well muscled, with a definite arch at the nape and widened to blend smoothly into the forequarters. The skin of the neck should be smooth and tight.

Forequarters: Shoulders: the shoulder blade should be of medium length and must be tightly held in place. The angle formed by the shoulder blade (scapula) and the humerus should be approximately 90 degrees. The musculature should be firm, smooth and clearly defined. Upper-arm (humerus): the bone structure should be heavy, smooth and well covered by strong firm muscles. The skin should be firm, pliable and smooth. The upper-arm should be equal in length to the shoulder blade (scapula). Lower-arm (radius and ulna): strong big bones with good muscles. The legs should be straight whether viewed from the front or side. The angle at the elbow joint should be approximately 135 degrees. Pasterns: the angle that the pastern makes with the lower leg should be nearly straight (about 175 − 180 degrees). Paws: the paws should be cat-like with tightly closed toes and big rough pads. The feet should be webbed. The nails should be short, firm and well curved, and their colour should be similar to that of the eyes, nose and coat. Dewclaws should be removed.

Body: Topline: the topline should be broad and smooth and is slightly arched over the loin and croup to the base of the tail; there is a slight depression at the juncture of the withers and the back. Chest: the chest should be deep, reaching down to the elbows and moderately broad. A cross-section of the chest is oval with well sprung ribs, narrowing between the elbows to permit free and easy leg movement. Width of the chest between the forelegs is at least 6 in. (15 cm) for a male and 5 in. (13 cm) for a bitch. Loin: it should be broad, strong and well muscled. Croup: it should be heavily muscled and smoothly rounded to the base of the tail. Abdomen: the abdomen should be trim and neat with a moderate tuck-up.

Hindquarters: Hip bone (pelvis): this is the framework which forms the basic support for the hind legs. These pelvic bones should be wide and strong. The musculature attaching to these bones should be very well developed and gives strength to the hindquarters. Upper thigh (femur): this bone should be heavy, straight, round, and smooth. Muscle attachments should be very powerful, broad, and evenly distributed. The angle at the hip joint should be 90 degrees. Lower thigh (tibia and fibula) should be well muscled. These bones should be longer than the femur. The angle at the stifle joint should be 110−120 degrees. Hocks: the angle at the hock joint should be from 125−130 degrees. Paws: same as the front.

Tail: The tail-set is lower than on the other continental pointing breeds. In motion it is carried outstretched, at or above the horizontal level. A portion is docked, approximately ⅓ so that the tip of the shortened tail is level with the juncture of the upper and lower thigh. It should be thicker at the base than at the tip.

Gait: Viewed from the front, the dog's legs should appear to swing forward in a free and easy manner, with no tendency for the feet to cross over or swing wide. Viewed from the rear the gait should be true-tracking. The topline is level when dog is in motion, while the head is carried high and the tail "flags" constantly at the proper level.

Faults:
1. Very nervous dogs should be heavily penalized.
2. Very dark or very light colour coat.
3. Hare feet.
4. Light yellow, green, blue or "Pop" eyes.
5. Throatiness.
6. Dogs 10 lb. (5 kg) over or under the standard weight.
7. Dewclaws not removed.
8. Roached, hollow or camel backs.
9. Too steep a croup.
10. Undershot or overshot bites.

Disqualifications:

1. A dog 2 in. (5 cm) or more over or under the standard height.
2. White markings over 2 in. (5 cm) on the chest or white markings anywhere else other than the chest.

Vizsla (Wire-Haired)

*T*HOSE WHO KNOW the Wire-Haired Vizsla describe it as looking like "a Vizsla that needs a shave." Strictly a product of the twentieth century, the wire-haired is said to be a cross between the short coat Vizsla and the German Wire-Haired Pointer. The first litter so produced resulted from an accidental mating of a Vizsla female to a Wire-Haired Pointer. Two of these puppies were on display at a dog show held in Budapest, Hungary, in 1904 and attracted the interest of a Czechoslovakian by the name of Ladislaus Gresnarik who bought the pups and proceeded to use them as the foundation stock of the present-day breed now called the Wire-Haired Vizsla.

Subsequently these dogs were mated back to smooth-coated Vizsla but only the wire-haired puppies were retained for breeding purposes. Within ten years a pure strain had been developed with the yellow-red coloured coat of the Vizsla and the longer, wiry coat of the Wire-Haired Pointer.

In 1950 this newly created breed was accepted for registration by the Hungarian Association of Canine Affairs. At first, breeder interest was rather slow but lately things seem to have improved. Late in the 1970s an American judge was invited to officiate at a dog show while he was on a visit to Hungary. Included in his assignment were both varieties of Vizsla. He reported that both quantity and quality of the Wire-Haireds were extremely high.

In addition to being a well-proportioned, medium-sized gun dog, the Wire-Haired possesses the versatility of his smooth-coated progenitor. Also, it is claimed, that because of his tougher "jacket," this breed is better able to withstand the cold and can work in dense brush with a minimum risk of injury.

Although the breed has been known on this continent for over twenty years, in the United States there has not been sufficient interest in the Wire-Haired to warrant its official recognition by the American Kennel Club. In Canada the Wire-Haired Vizsla has fared much better. In 1978 it was granted full breed status and its name was added to the official roster of The Canadian Kennel Club.

Vizsla (Wire-Haired)

Official Breed Standard for the Vizsla (Wire-Haired)

Origin and Purpose: The Vizsla (Wire-Haired) is of Hungarian origin, formed by the crossing of the Vizsla and the German coarse-haired Setter. In Hungary it was used for general-purpose hunting, but excelled as a pointer. Its keen nose and excellent swimming characteristics have brought it wide acclaim.

General Appearance: The Vizsla (Wire-Haired) is a medium-sized, all-purpose hunting dog bred to work both fur and feather. It is a noble dog, strong in bone and well muscled. Its tough wiry coat is dark yellow in colour. This breed is characterized by a lively and intelligent expression.

Temperament: The Vizsla (Wire-Haired) is a sensible and docile dog, responding well to training, being sensitive to correction. Its keen nose allows it to be an enthusiastic worker in all weather.

Size: The allowable heights for Vizsla (Wire-Haired) when measured at the withers are males, $22^{1}/_{2}-25$ in. (57−64 cm); females, $21-23^{1}/_{2}$ in. (53−60 cm). Dogs and bitches of good bone and substance should weigh between $48^{1}/_{2}$ and 66 lb. (22 and 30 kg). The length of body from withers to tail-set should equal the height from withers to ground.

Coat and Colour: The skin should fit the dog closely, showing no wrinkles or folds. The outer coat should be coarse and hard, about $1^{1}/_{4}-1^{3}/_{4}$ in. (3−4 cm) in length on the neck and body. It is shorter and smoother on the legs forming a slight brush along the back of the forelegs and down to the hock on the hind legs. In winter, the body and neck should have an undercoat. Hair on the muzzle and skull is short and coarse but smooth lying with the exception of the beard which is about $^{3}/_{4}$ inch (2 cm) in length; the eyebrows are prominent and bushy. The tail is densely covered with short, hard hair showing a slight fringe along the bottom. The colour is a dark sandy-yellow and should be even throughout, showing no marks.

Head: The *skull* is of good width and is slightly arched showing a shallow furrow rising from between the eyes toward a moderately prominent occiput. The supra-orbital ridges are of medium development showing a moderate stop. The *muzzle* is strong with a straight nasal bone meeting the skull at a 30–35-degree angle. It is slightly shorter in length than the skull and never snipey but rather blunt in appearance. Lips and flews are dry and not hanging. The *mouth* should close cleanly. The lips are brown in colour. The *nose* is well developed and broad with wide open nostrils and brown in colour. The *teeth* are strong and well developed and meet in a scissors bite. The *ears* are set approximately halfway between the top of the skull and the level of the eye. They should be of good length reaching ³/₄ of the way to the nose, with thin leathers and hanging straight down in a rounded V. The *eyes* are not deep set nor protruding. The eye rim should be close fitting, showing neither white nor haw. The colour should always be a shade darker than the coat colour, but never black or staring. Eye rims are brown in colour.

Neck: The neck is of medium length, muscular and dry, showing a moderate arch.

Forequarters: The shoulders are well muscled, showing good layback and must fit closely to the body. Elbows should be close fitting and straight, neither turning in nor out. The upper arm should equal the shoulder blade in length, the lower arm is strong and of good bone, the pastern is short and strong. Feet are round and tight with a good depth of pad. Nails are short and strong, darker than the coat in colour. Dewclaws are considered to be a fault.

Body: Chest is of medium width, prominent, and well muscled. It should have a good depth and carry well back under the dog with medium spring of rib. The withers are prominent, sloping into a short level muscular back. The loin is strong, of medium length, and showing a slight tuck-up. The croup slopes slightly into the set on of tail.

Hindquarters: The hindquarters do not exhibit extreme angulation, the stifle joint having an angle of approximately 110 degrees. Hocks are well let down. Feet are tight with deep, resilient pads.

Tail: The tail is of moderate thickness and docked to ²/₃ of its original length.

Gait: The gait should be brisk and smooth, indicative of sound conformation. The tail should be carried horizontally when the dog is in action. When coming and going the legs should move neither in nor out.

Faults: A soft, silky or curly coat or hair longer than 1³/₄ in. (4 cm) is considered a fault. Woolly hair on the head is considered a fault. Parting of the coat along the spine is considered a serious fault. Gay tail. Dewclaws.

Disqualifications: *More than ¹/₂ inch (1 cm) over or under the correct size range. Mixed colours, white feet, white mark on chest exceeding 2 in. (5 cm). Cream or brown colour. Spotted or black nose. Drooping eyelids, showing haw. Pendant flews. Long coat. Undershot or overshot more than 2 millimetres.*

Weimaraner

STEEL-GREY HOUNDS similar in colour to the present-day Weimaraner have been known in Germany since the 17th century. And, unlikely as this may seem, it is said that one of the breed's ancestors is the Bloodhound. Others include the German Schweisshund, French hounds, and pointers.

The breed was developed at the court of the Grand Duke Karl August of Weimar, the capital of Thuringen, Germany, as an all-purpose sporting dog for the nobility. That is, a dog that could work equally well with fur and feather. It is said that such a dog was created about 1810 and, once perfected, the breed was carefully guarded. In the hands of a group of sportsmen, the Weimaraner or Weimaraner Vorsthund (Weimar Pointer) as it was known, underwent further development, and in 1896 became an officially recognized breed in Germany. The following year these sportsmen formed the Weimaraner Club of Germany to preserve and protect the breed from exploitation. Only club members were allowed to own the dogs, breeding was strictly controlled, and only infertile dogs were permitted to be exported.

The first Weimaraners were brought to the United States in the late 1930s by an American sportsman who was a member of the German club and had managed to obtain some fertile breeding stock. When it first arrived the breed received tremendous publicity and came to be known as "the dog with the human brain." In the U.S. too, breeding was carefully controlled under regulations set down by the Weimaraner Club of America, which was organized in 1941 and patterned along the lines of the German club. In 1943 the breed was officially recognized by the American Kennel Club and subsequently distinguished itself as a field and obedience dog as well as in the show ring. Since the first Weimaraner was registered in Canada in 1948, breeding kennels have been established coast to coast, founded mainly on stock imported from the United States.

G.Stenhouse

Weimaraner

Official Breed Standard for the Weimaraner

General Appearance: A medium-sized grey dog with light eyes, he should present a picture of great driving power, stamina, alertness and balance. Above all, the dog *should indicate ability to work hard in the field*.

Temperament: The dog should display a temperament that is keen, fearless, friendly, protective, and obedient.

Size: Height at withers—dogs, 25—27 in. (64—69 cm); bitches, 23—25 in. (58—64 cm).

Coat and Colour: Short, smooth and sleek coat in shades of mouse-grey to silver-grey, usually blending to a lighter shade on the head and ears. Small white mark allowable on the chest, but not on any other part of the body. White spots that have resulted from injuries shall not be penalized.

Head: Moderately long and aristocratic, with moderate stop and slight median line extending back over the forehead. Rather prominent occipital bone and trumpets set well back, beginning at the back of the eye sockets. Measurement from tip of nose to stop to equal that from stop to occipital bone. The flews should be moderately deep, enclosing a powerful jaw. *Foreface* perfectly straight, delicate at the nostrils. Skin tightly drawn. Expression kind, keen, intelligent. *Nose* grey. *Teeth* well-set, strong and even; well developed and proportionate to jaw with correct scissors bite, the upper teeth protruding slightly over the lower teeth but not more than $\frac{1}{16}$ inch (.2 cm). Complete dentition is greatly to be desired. *Lips* and *gums* pinkish flesh shades. *Eyes* in shades of light amber, grey or blue-grey, set well enough apart to indicate good disposition and intelligence. When dilated under excitement the eyes may appear almost black. *Ears* long and lobular, slightly folded and set high. The ear when drawn snugly alongside the jaw should end approximately 2 in. (5 cm) from the point of the nose.

Neck: Neck clean-cut and moderately long.

Forequarters: Shoulder well laid on and snug. Forelegs straight and strong, with the measurement from the elbow to the ground approximately equalling the distance from the elbow to the top of the withers. Dewclaws allowable only on forelegs, there optional.

Body: The back should be moderate in length, set in straight line, strong, and should slope slightly from the withers. The chest should be well developed and deep. Ribs well sprung and long. The brisket should drop to the elbow. Abdomen firmly held; moderately tucked-up flank.

Hindquarters: Well-angulated stifles and straight hocks. Musculature well developed. Feet firm and compact, webbed, toes well arched, pads closed and thick, nails short and grey or amber in colour.

Tail: Docked. At maturity it should measure approximately 6 in. (15 cm) with a tendency to be light rather than heavy and should be carried in a manner expressing confidence and sound temperament.

Gait: The walk is rather awkward. The trot should be effort-less, ground-covering, and should indicate smooth co-ordination. When seen from the rear, the hind feet should parallel the front feet. When viewed from the side, the topline should remain strong and level.

Faults: Very serious—Any long-haired coat or coat darker than mouse-grey to silver-grey is considered a most undesirable recessive trait. White, other than a spot on chest. Eyes any other colour than grey, blue-grey or light amber. Black, mottled mouth. Non-docked tail. Cryptorchidism. Dogs exhibiting strong fear. Viciousness.

Serious—Poor gait. Very poor feet. Cowhocks. Faulty back, either roach or sway. Badly overshot or undershot jaw. Monor-chidism. Snipey muzzle. Short ears. Yellow in white marking. Undersize.

Faults—Doggy bitches. Bitchy dogs. Improper muscular con-dition. Badly affected teeth. More than four missing teeth. Back too long or too short. Faulty coat. Neck too short, thick or throaty. Low tail-set. Elbows in or out; feet east and west.

Minor—Tail too short or too long. Pink nose. Oversize should not be considered a serious fault, providing correct structure and working ability are in evidence.

GROUP II: HOUNDS

Afghan Hound

THE HISTORY OF THIS MEMBER of the greyhound family is strongly tied to that of the Persian Greyhound, whose roots trace back several thousands of years. It is written that a pair of these "baboon or monkey-faced hounds" were among the animals in Noah's Ark.

Brought from their homelands of Arabia and Persia to Afghanistan, the breed's long, silky coat is thought to have evolved in response to the harsher environment. Other distinguishing features are the Afghan's naturally short-coated saddle and its prominent hip bones, which are said to give the dog a "free wheeling" action that is thought to have developed from centuries of hunting over rocky terrain. The breed became the hunting dog of the Afghani nobility and was used in the sport of falconry to course the wolf, gazelle, and fox. In later years the breed was also used to herd.

The Afghan was discovered in the latter part of the 19th century by British soldiers stationed on the border between Afghanistan and India. Attracted by these beautiful hounds, an army officer brought the first specimens to England in 1894. There they were first exhibited at the Crystal Palace, London in 1907 in the "Foreign Dog Class" under the breed name "Oriental Greyhound." Model for the original Afghan breed standard was Zardin, the winner at this show and the first champion of record in the breed.

The founding of Afghan breeding kennels in Britain really began in the early 1920s when two English breeders imported a total of seventeen hounds. Each embarked on a separate breeding programme, and in time two strains were developed, markedly different in coat type and colour. Inevitably the two were inter-bred and the modern Afghan is said to embody the best qualities of each.

In 1926 a breed club was formed in England and the Afghan was officially accepted for registration by The Kennel Club. By that year a few English-bred Afghans had arrived in the United States and in 1931 the breed was accepted for registration by the

Afghan Hound

American Kennel Club. Six years later the Afghan was granted breed status in Canada. Since then the growth in popularity of the breed on both sides of the border has been phenomenal.

Official Breed Standard for the Afghan Hound

General Appearance: The Afghan Hound is an aristocrat, his whole appearance one of dignity and aloofness with no trace of plainness or coarseness. He has a straight front, proudly carried head, eyes gazing into the distance as if in memory of ages past. The striking characteristics of the breed—exotic, or "Eastern," expression, long silky topknot, peculiar coat pattern, very prominent hip bones, large feet, and the impression of a somewhat exaggerated bend in the stifle due to profuse trouserings— stand out clearly, giving the Afghan Hound the appearance of what he is, a king of dogs, that has held true to tradition throughout the ages.

Temperament: Aloof and dignified, yet gay.

Size: Height—dogs, 27 in. (69 cm), plus or minus 1 inch (3 cm); bitches, 25 in. (64 cm), plus or minus 1 inch (3 cm). Weight—dogs, about 60 lb. (27 kg); bitches, 50 lb. (23 kg).

Coat and Colour: Hindquarters, flanks, ribs, forequarters, and legs well covered with thick, silky hair, very fine in texture; ears and all four feet well feathered; from in front of the shoulders, and also backwards from the shoulders along the saddle from the flanks and ribs upwards, the hair is short and close forming a smooth back in mature dogs—this is a traditional characteristic of the Afghan Hound.

The Afghan Hound should be shown in its natural state; the coat is not clipped or trimmed; the head is surmounted (in the full sense of the word) with a topknot of long, silky hair—this also an outstanding characteristic of the Afghan Hound. Showing of short hair on cuffs on either front or back legs is permissible.

All colours are permissible, but colour or colour combinations are pleasing; white markings, especially on the head, are undesirable.

Head: The head is of good length, showing much refinement, the *skull* evenly balanced with the foreface. The occipital bone is very prominent. The head is surmounted by a topknot of long silky hair.

There is a slight prominence of the nasal bone structure causing a slightly Roman appearance, the centre line running up over the foreface with little or no stop, falling away in front of the eyes so there is an absolutely clear outlook with no interference; the underjaw showing great strength, the jaws long and punishing. *Nose* is of good size, black in colour. The *mouth* is level, meaning that the teeth from the upper jaw and lower jaw match evenly, neither overshot nor undershot. This is a difficult mouth to breed. A scissors bite is even more punishing and can be more easily bred into a dog than a level mouth, and a dog having a scissors bite, where the lower teeth slip inside and rest against the teeth of the upper jaw, should not be penalized. The *eyes* are almond shaped (almost triangular), never full or bulgy, and are dark in colour. The *ears* are long, set approximately on level with outer corners of the eyes, the leather of the ear reaching nearly to the end of the dog's nose, and covered with long silky hair.

Neck: The neck is of good length, strong and arched, running in a curve to the shoulders.

Forequarters: Shoulders long and sloping and well laid back. Shoulders have plenty of angulation so that the legs are well set underneath the dog. Too much straightness of shoulder causes the dog to break down in the pasterns, and this is a serious fault. Forelegs are straight and strong with great length between elbow and pastern; elbows well held in; pasterns long and straight; forefeet large in both length and width; toes well arched; feet covered with long thick hair, fine in texture; pads of feet unusually large and well down on the ground.

Body: The backline appearing practically level from the shoulders to the loin. The height at the shoulders equals the distance from the chest to the buttocks. The brisket well let down, and of medium width. Strong and powerful loin and slightly arched, falling away towards the stern, with the hip bones very pronounced; well ribbed and tucked up in flanks.

Hindquarters: Hindquarters powerful and well muscled with great length between hip and hock; hocks are well let down; good angulation of both stifle and hock; slightly bowed from hock to crotch. The hind feet are broad and of good length; the toes arched, and covered with long thick hair. All four feet of the Afghan Hound are in line with the body, turning neither in nor out.

Tail: Tail set not too high on the body, having a ring, or a curve on the end; should never be curled over, or rest on the back, or be carried sideways; and should never be bushy.

Gait: When running free, the Afghan Hound moves at a gallop, showing great elasticity and spring in his smooth, powerful stride.

When on a loose lead, the Afghan can trot at a fast pace; stepping along, he has the appearance of placing the hind feet directly in the footprints of the front feet, both thrown straight ahead. Moving with head and tail high, the whole appearance of the Afghan Hound is one of great style and beauty.

Faults: Sharpness or shyness. Lack of short-haired saddle in mature dogs. Coarseness; snipiness; overshot or undershot; eyes round or bulgy or light in colour; exaggerated Roman nose; head not surmounted with topknot. Neck too short or too thick; an ewe neck; a goose neck; a neck lacking in substance. Front or back feet thrown outward or inward; pads of feet not thick enough; or feet too small; or any other evidence of weakness in feet; weak or broken-down pasterns. Roach back, sway back, goose rump, slack loin; lack of prominence of hip bones; too much width of brisket causing interference with elbows. Too straight in stifle; too long in hock.

Basenji

THE BASENJI, commonly known as the "Barkless Dog," is one of the oldest breeds, appearing on ancient Egyptian engravings which date back to 3600 B.C. When the Egyptian civilization declined, the Basenji faded into obscurity. He was, however, preserved in his native land of Central Africa where he was highly prized for his intelligence, courage, speed, keen nose (he can scent at eighty yards), and silence. He was used for driving game into nets and hunting wounded quarry. Due to his silence he wore a bell so the hunter knew where he was. Yet, while the Basenji does not bark, apparently due to a difference from other dogs in the structure of his larynx, he is capable of making all the other usual doggy sounds, plus a variety of unique noises such as his joyous crowing "yodel."

In 1895 the Basenji was rediscovered in Africa by British explorers and a pair was brought back to England and exhibited at Cruft's Show that year as African Bush Dogs. Unfortunately both soon died of distemper. Several more attempts were made to obtain foundation stock, all ending in disaster. Finally in 1936 Mrs. O. Burn successfully imported the famous Bongo of Blean, and Bokoto of Blean. Their puppies made the breed's debut at Cruft's in 1937, causing such a sensation that special police had to be employed to move the crowds past the Basenji benches. The breed had come to Britain to stay.

Four years later the Basenji Club was founded and in 1941 the breed was officially recognized by The Kennel Club (England). It was Mrs. Burn who gave the breed its name. In the language of the tribesmen "Basenji" means Bush Thing.

The Basenji arrived in Canada and the United States early in the 1940s where it subsequently was granted official breed status by both The Canadian and American Kennel Clubs.

Dr. Richmond of Wyndrush Kennels campaigned Ch. Quillo of the Congo in 1940–41 to become the first Basenji champion in the world.

Basenji

G. STENHOUSE

Official Breed Standard for the Basenji

General Appearance: The Basenji is a small, lightly built, short-backed dog, giving the impression of being high on the leg compared to its length. The wrinkled head must be proudly carried, and the whole demeanour should be one of poise and alertness. The Basenji should not bark, but is not mute. The wrinkled forehead and the swift, tireless running gait (resembling a race horse trotting full out) are typical of the breed.

Size: Bitches 16 in. (41 cm) and dogs 17 in. (43 cm) from the ground to the top of the shoulder. Bitches 16 in. (41 cm) and dogs 17 in. (43 cm) from the front of the chest to the farthest point of the hindquarters. Bitches 22 lb. (10 kg) approximately. Dogs 24 lb. (11 kg) approximately.

Coat and Colour: Coat short and silky. Skin very pliant. Colour chestnut red (the deeper the better) or pure black, or black and tan, all with white feet, chest, and tail tip. White legs, white blaze, and white collar optional.

Head: The *skull* is flat, well chiselled and of medium width, tapering towards the eyes. The *foreface* should taper from eye to muzzle and should be shorter than the skull. *Muzzle* neither coarse nor snipey but with rounded cushions. Wrinkles should appear upon the forehead, and be fine and profuse. Side wrinkles are desirable, but should never be exaggerated into dewlap. Black *nose* greatly desired. A pinkish tinge should not penalize an otherwise first-class specimen, but it should be discouraged in breeding. *Teeth* must be level with scissors bite. *Eyes* dark hazel, almond shaped, obliquely set and far seeing. *Ears* small, pointed and erect, of fine texture, set well forward on top of head.

Neck: Of good length, well crested and slightly full at base of throat. It should be well set into shoulders.

Forequarters: Shoulders flat, laid back. The legs straight with clean fine bone, long forearm and well-defined sinews. Pasterns should be of good length, straight and flexible.

Body: The body should be short and the back level. The chest should be deep and of medium width. The ribs well sprung, with plenty of heart room, deep brisket, short-coupled, and ending in a definite waist.

Hindquarters: Should be strong and muscular, with hocks well let down, turned neither in nor out, with long second thighs. Feet small, narrow, and compact, with well-arched toes.

Tail: Should be set on top and curled tightly over to either side.

Faults: Coarse skull or muzzle. Domed or peaked skull. Dewlap. Round eyes. Low set ears. Overshot or undershot mouths. Wide chest. Wide behind. Heavy bone. Creams, shaded or off-colours, other than those defined above, should be heavily penalized.

Basset Hound

*A*LTHOUGH THE BASSET HOUND did not arrive in the English-speaking world until the latter part of the 19th century, low, heavy-set hounds had been known on the continent for at least 300 years. Historians believe that the first of these short-legged dogs appeared in litters of otherwise normal limbed hounds, possibly throw-backs to the now extinct, low-set St. Hubert hound. It is also thought that these "dwarfs" were retained as curiosities and that later, by the process of selective breeding, pure strains of low-set hounds were established.

Named for its appearance by the British (the word "basset" is French for "low set") the breed was first imported into England in 1866 by Lord Galway. The first exhibitor was Sir Everett Millais who showed a dog named Model at Wolverhampton in 1875. Sir Everett wrote a breed text: "Bassets: Their Use and Breeding" and is credited with setting the distinctive long-headed British Basset type by means of a Basset/Bloodhound cross.

After a probationary period The Kennel Club (England) gave official recognition to the breed, and in 1883 the Basset Hound Club was formed. By 1886 the breed's popularity had so increased that a London show drew an entry of 120. Thereafter, for some reason, interest in the low-set hound declined. Happily the same condition does not prevail today.

On this continent too the Basset's popularity has waxed and waned. While the breed had been in the United States since the 18th century, outside of a few sporting hound enthusiasts, the Basset Hound was virtually unknown. Then in the 1920s Basset fanciers in the east imported quality hounds from France and England which were to become the foundation breeding stock of the present-day American Basset Hound. On this continent the breed has been developed into a heavier set hound than the British and European type. As a sporting dog, Bassets were used in Britain and the United States, and to some extent still are, to trail hare, deer, and rabbit. According to his sporting admirers,

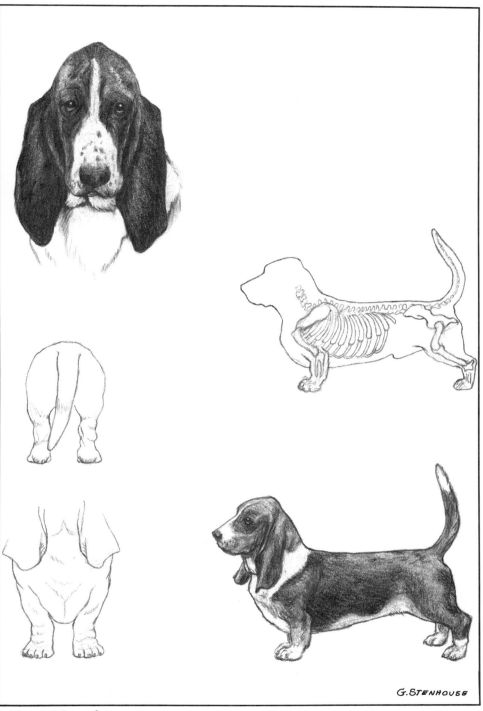

Basset Hound

the breed has a bell-like voice and there is no finer sound than a Basset pack in full cry.

The Basset Hound was officially recognized by The Canadian Kennel Club in 1936. The Stud Book for the years 1936–1937 lists nine individual registrations.

Official Breed Standard for the Basset Hound

Coat and Colour: The coat should be similar to that of the Foxhound, not too fine and not too coarse, but yet of sufficient strength to be of use in bad weather. The skin loose and elastic. No good hound is a bad colour, so that any recognized Foxhound colour should be acceptable to the judge's eye, and only in the very closest competition should the colour of a hound have any weight with a judge's decision.

Head: The head should be large, the *skull* narrow and of good length, the peak being very fully developed, a very characteristic point of the head, which should be free from any appearance of, or inclination to, cheek bumps. It is most perfect when it closest resembles the head of a Bloodhound, with heavy flews and forehead wrinkled to the eyes. The expression when sitting or when still should be very sad, full of reposeful dignity. The whole of the head should be covered with loose skin, so loose in fact, that when the hound brings its nose to the ground the skin over the head and cheeks should fall forward and wrinkle perceptibly. The *nose* itself should be strong and free from snipiness. While the *teeth* of the upper and lower jaws should meet, a pig-jawed hound, or one that is underhung, is distinctly objectionable. The *eyes* should be deeply sunken, showing a prominent haw, and in colour they should be a deep brown. The *ears* are very long, and when drawn forward, folding well over the nose. They are set on the head as low as is possible and hang loose in folds like drapery, the ends curling inward, in texture thin and velvety.

Neck: The neck is powerful, with heavy pendant dewlaps.

Forequarters: The shoulders are muscular, sloping and well laid back. The forelegs should be short, very powerful, very heavy in bone, close fitting to the chest with a crook'd knee and wrinkled ankle, ending in a massive paw. A hound must *not* be "out at *elbows*." He must stand perfectly sound and true on his feet, which should be thick and massive, and the weight of the forepart of the body should be borne equally by each toe of the forefeet so far as it is compatible with the crook of the legs.

Body: The chest should be deep and full. The body should be long and low and well ribbed up.

Hindquarters: The quarters should be full of muscle, which stands out so that when one looks at the dog from behind, it gives him a round, barrel-like effect, with quarters "round as an apple." He should be what is known as "a good dog to follow," and when trotting away from you, his hocks should bend well and he should move true all round. A hound should not be straight on his hocks, nor should he measure more over his quarters than he does at his shoulder.

Tail: The stern is coarse underneath, and carried "gaily" in hound fashion.

Faults: "Out at elbows" is a bad fault. Slackness of loin, flat-sidedness and a roach or razor back are all bad faults. Cowhocks, straight hocks, or weak hocks are all bad faults.

Disqualifications: *Unsoundness in legs or feet should absolutely disqualify a hound from taking a prize.*

Scale of Points:

Head, skull, eyes, muzzle, flews	14
Ears	10
Neck, dewlap, chest, and shoulders	18
Forelegs and feet	18
Back, loins, hocks, and hindquarters	18
Stern	5
Coat and skin	5
Colour and markings	5
Basset Hound character and symmetry	7
TOTAL	100

Beagle

SOME WRITERS CLAIM that the history of the musical-voiced Beagle can be traced back to the year 400 B.C. when similar small hounds were used in packs for hunting in Greece. Whatever its origin, the Beagle is strictly a British development and descends from the Talbot hounds brought to England at the time of the Norman Conquest (1066 A.D.). From these dogs descended the Southern Hound, from which came the present-day Beagle.

First reference to Beagles appears in writings of the 15th century and although there are many explanations as to how the breed name was derived, most acceptable is that it comes from the Celtic word *beag* meaning small. The Beagle is the smallest of the hounds and resembles a Foxhound in miniature. While it was, and still is, used in packs by mounted horsemen to hunt the hare, today it is used more by individuals who hunt on foot. In Canada and the United States the cottontail is the breed's chief quarry and it is claimed that whenever the rabbit population increases, so do Beagle registrations.

Since the 1880s the breed has had a strong following on this continent. In 1888 the National Beagle Club was organized in the United States, and in 1890 a similar club was founded in Britain. In both Canada and the United States Beagle field trials have become a popular sport.

Concurrent with this has been the Beagle's development as a show dog. Show type is somewhat more compact than the sporting hound and although "any true hound colour" is acceptable, those with black "blankets" on the back seem to be preferred. For show purposes the breed is divided into two varieties according to height—13 in. (33 cm) and under, and 15 in. (38 cm) and under. In the United States the winner of each variety competes in the group. In Canada the winner of each variety competes for Best of Breed and only the breed winner competes in the Hound Group. Dogs measuring over 15 in. (38 cm) are disqualified from competition.

13" class

15" class

G. STENHOUSE

Beagle

At one time there was a miniature known as the "Pocket Beagle" which measured 10 in. (25 cm) or less. This variety was a favourite of Queen Victoria and her consort Prince Albert, who are known to have owned packs of "Pocket Beagles." It is written that these were so small a dozen could be carried in a pannier en route to the hunt.

It is the sturdy little Beagle's misfortune that because of his size, temperament, and stamina, he has become the most popular dog for research. In the United States, kennels of genetically pure lines produce Beagles solely for this purpose.

The Beagle was first registered in The Canadian Kennel Club Stud Book of 1888–1889.

Official Breed Standard for the Beagle

General Appearance: A miniature Foxhound, solid and big for his inches, with the wear-and-tear look of the hound that can last in the chase and follow his quarry to the death.

Size: There shall be two varieties: 13 in. (33 cm)—which shall be for hounds not exceeding 13 in. (33 cm) in height; 15 in. (38 cm)—which shall be for hounds over 13 in. (33 cm) but not exceeding 15 in. (38 cm) in height.

Coat and Colour: A close, hard, hound coat of medium length. Any true hound colour.

Head: The *skull* should be fairly long, slightly domed at occiput, with cranium broad and full. *Muzzle* of medium length —straight and square-cut—the stop moderately defined. Nostrils large and open. *Jaws* level. Lips free from flews. *Eyes* large, set well apart—soft and hound-like—expression gentle and pleading; of a brown or hazel colour. *Ears* set on moderately low, long, reaching when drawn out nearly, if not quite, to the end of the nose; fine in texture, fairly broad—with almost entire absence of erectile power—setting close to the head, with the forward edge slightly in-turning to the cheek, rounded at tip.

Neck: Neck rising free and light from the shoulders, strong in substance yet not loaded, of medium length. The throat clean and free from folds of skin; a slight wrinkle below the angle of the jaw, however, may be allowable.

Forequarters: Shoulders sloping—clean, muscular, not heavy or loaded—conveying the idea of freedom of action with activity and strength. Forelegs straight, with plenty of bone in proportion to size of the hound. Pasterns short and straight. Feet close, round, and firm. Pad full and hard.

Body: Back short, muscular, and strong. Chest deep and broad, but not broad enough to interfere with the free play of the shoulders. Loin broad and slightly arched, and the ribs well sprung, giving abundance of lung room.

Hindquarters: Hips and thighs strong and well muscled, giving abundance of propelling power. Stifles strong and well let down. Hocks firm, symmetrical, and moderately bent. Feet close and firm.

Tail: Set moderately high; carried gaily, but not turned forward over the back; with slight curve; short as compared with size of the hound; with brush.

Faults: A short, thin coat, or of a soft quality. A very flat skull, narrow across the top; excess of dome, eyes small, sharp and terrier-like, or prominent and protruding; muzzle long, snipey or cut away decidedly below the eyes, or very short. Roman-nosed, or upturned, giving a dish-faced expression. Ears short, set on high or with a tendency to rise above the point of origin. A thick, short, cloddy neck carried on a line with the top of the shoulders. Throat showing dewlap and folds of skin to a degree termed "throatiness." Straight, upright shoulders. Out at elbows. Knees knuckled over forward, or bent backward. Forelegs crooked or Dachshund-like. Feet long, open or spreading. Very long or swayed or roached back. Chest disproportionately wide or with lack of depth. Flat, narrow loin. Flat ribs. Cowhocks, or straight hocks. Lack of muscle and propelling power. Open feet. A long tail. Teapot curve or inclined forward from the root. Rat tail with absence of brush.

Disqualification: *Any hound measuring more than 15 in. (38 cm) shall be disqualified.*

212 GROUP II: HOUNDS

Scale of Points:

HEAD

Skull	5	
Ears	10	
Eyes	5	
Muzzle	5	25

BODY

Neck	5	
Chest and shoulders	15	
Back, loin and ribs	15	35

RUNNING GEAR

Forelegs	10	
Hips, thighs and hind legs	10	
Feet	10	30
Coat	5	
Stern	5	10
TOTAL		100

Pack of Beagles Score of Points for Judging:

HOUNDS:	General levelness of pack	40	
	Individual merit of hounds	30	70
MANNERS			20
APPOINTMENTS			10
TOTAL			100

Levelness of Pack: The first thing in a pack to be considered is that they present a unified appearance. The hounds must be as near to the same height, weight, conformation, and colour as possible.

Individual Merit of the Hounds: Is the individual bench-show quality of the hounds. A very level and sporty pack can be gotten together and not a single hound be a good Beagle. This is to be avoided.

Manners: The hounds must all work gaily and cheerfully, with flags up—obeying all commands cheerfully. They should be broken to heel up, kennel up, follow promptly and stand. Cringing, sulking, lying down to be avoided. Also, a pack must not work as though in terror of master and whips. In Beagle packs it is recommended that the whip be used as little as possible.

Appointments: Master and whips should be dressed alike, the master or huntsman to carry horn—the whips and master to carry light thong whips. One whip should carry extra couplings on shoulder strap.

Recommendations for Show Livery
Black velvet cap, white stock, green coat, white breeches or knickerbockers, green or black stockings, white spats, black or dark brown shoes. Vest and gloves optional.

Ladies should turn out exactly the same except for a white skirt instead of white breeches.

Bloodhound

THE IMMEDIATE ANCESTOR of the world's most renowned tracking dog was the St. Hubert hound, thought to be descended from the hounds bred by St. Hubert, the patron saint of dogs. As early as the year 1000 A.D. these dogs were being bred in the French monasteries and came to Britain at the time of the Norman invasion (1066). The modern breed is thought to be a blend of three breeds, the black St. Hubert, the white or tricoloured Talbot, and the greyish-red Southern Hound.

There is some disagreement among dog historians as to the origin of the breed's name. Some claim it originated on the continent to distinguish the pure-blooded French strain from the British hounds which, on occasion, were crossed with other breeds to produce a fiercer tracking dog. The true Bloodhound trails, but does not attack, its quarry. The cross-bred British hounds, many of which were used during the continuing English/Scottish border conflicts and did attack their quarry, gave the breed name an entirely different connotation: a bloodthirsty hound. Somewhere along the way the latter type was lost because the modern Bloodhound is an easy going, gentle dog.

At one time the breed was used in packs for stag hunting. Head dog was the "limier" (a word derived from "lyame" meaning leash). The limier, selected because of his superior nose, worked on a long lead, scented out the stag, and then the pack took over the chase.

Because of its long history of pure breeding the Bloodhound was an accepted breed from the earliest days of dog shows. A pair was exhibited at the Birmingham show in 1860 and the breed has been in evidence ever since. On this continent the breed was, and still is, used to some extent in the southern States to track fugitives from justice.

During World War II breeding stock in Britain suffered a serious setback. A Foxhound − Bloodhound cross was used to

Bloodhound

keep the breed alive until imports from Canada and the United States arrived to replenish bloodlines in 1949.

The Canadian Kennel Club Stud Book shows that eight Bloodhounds were registered during the years 1891–1892.

Official Breed Standard for the Bloodhound

General Appearance: The Bloodhound possesses, in a most marked degree, every point and characteristic of those dogs which hunt together by scent (Sagaces). He is very powerful, and stands over more ground than is usual with hounds of other breeds. The skin is thin to the touch and extremely loose, this being more especially noticeable about the head and neck, where it hangs in deep folds. The expression is noble and dignified, and characterized by solemnity, wisdom, and power.

Temperament: In temperament he is extremely affectionate, neither quarrelsome with companions nor with other dogs. His nature is somewhat shy, and equally sensitive to kindness or correction by his master.

Size: Height—the mean average height of adult dogs is 26 in. (66 cm) and of adult bitches 24 in. (61 cm). Dogs usually vary from 25–27 in. (64–69 cm) and bitches from 23–25 in. (58–64 cm); but, in either case, the greater height is to be preferred, provided that character and quality are also combined.

Weight—the mean average weight of adult dogs in fair condition is 90 lb. (41 kg), and of adult bitches 80 lb. (36 kg). Dogs attain the weight of 110 lb. (50 kg), bitches 100 lb. (45 kg). The greater weights are to be preferred, provided (as in the case of height) that quality and proportion are also combined.

Coat and Colour: The colours are black and tan, red and tan, and tawny; the darker colours being sometimes interspersed with lighter or badger-coloured hair, and sometimes flecked with white. A small amount of white is permissible on chest, feet, and tip of stern.

Head: The head is narrow in proportion to its length, and long in proportion to the body, tapering but slightly from the temples to the end of the muzzle, thus (when viewed from above and in front) having the appearance of being flattened at the sides and of being nearly equal in width throughout its entire length. In profile the upper outline of the *skull* is nearly in the same plane as that of the foreface. The length from end of nose to stop (midway between the eyes) should be not less than from stop to back of occipital protuberance (peak). The entire length of head from the posterior part of the occipital protuberance to the end of the muzzle should be 12 in. (30 cm), or more, in dogs, and 11 in. (28 cm), or more, in bitches. The skull is long and narrow, with the occipital peak very pronounced. The brows are not prominent although, owing to the deep-set eyes, they may have that appearance. The *foreface* is long, deep, and of even width throughout, with square outline when seen in profile. The nostrils are large and open. In front the lips fall squarely, making a right angle with the upper line of the foreface; whilst behind they form deep hanging flews and, being continued into the pendant folds of loose skin about the neck, constitute the dewlap, which is very pronounced. These characteristics are found, though in a lesser degree, in the bitch. The *eyes* are deeply sunk in the orbits, the lids assuming a lozenge or diamond shape, in consequence of the lower lids being dragged down and everted by the heavy flews. The eyes correspond with the general tone of colour of the animal, varying from deep hazel to yellow. The hazel colour is, however, to be preferred, although very seldom seen in red and tan hounds. The *ears* are thin and soft to the touch, extremely long, set very low, and fall in graceful folds, the lower parts curling inwards and backwards. The head is furnished with an amount of loose skin, which in nearly every position appears superabundant, but more particularly so when the head is carried low; the skin then falls into loose, pendulous ridges and folds, especially over the forehead and sides of the face.

Neck: The neck is long.

Forequarters: The shoulders are muscular and well sloped backwards. The forelegs are straight and large in bone, with elbows squarely set; the feet strong and well knuckled up.

Body: The ribs are well sprung; and the chest well let down between the forelegs, forming a deep keel. The back and loins are strong, the latter deep and slightly arched.

Hindquarters: The thighs and second thighs (gaskins) are very muscular; the hocks well bent and let down and squarely set.

Tail: The stern is long and tapering, and set on rather high, with a moderate amount of hair underneath.

Gait: The gait is elastic, swinging and free, the stern being carried high, but not too much curled over the back.

Borzoi

THE **BORZOI**, **ONCE KNOWN** as the Russian Wolfhound on this continent, originated in Russia where these coursing hounds have been known since the 13th century. It is thought that the breed is a descendant of the Persian Greyhound and that its luxuriant coat was acquired either in response to the cold Russian climate or as the result of a cross with the boarhound or a collie-type sheepdog.

For practical reasons hunting was the national sport of Russia; the country was overrun with wolves. And, in true Russian style the aristocracy developed the wolf hunt into an elaborate ritual with an entourage numbering in the hundreds. Because of his hunting skills the Borzoi became the favourite dog to course the wolf. Large hunt kennels were established. The Imperial kennels of the Czar dated to 1613.

At first the working ability of the dogs counted for more than their appearance, so if a particular cross to another breed seemed necessary to enhance a characteristic it was made without fear of criticism. However, after the Borzoi was first exhibited at Moscow in 1824, appearance became important and outcrossing was discontinued.

The hounds were not sold but presented as gifts of esteem, and it was as such a gift from Czar Nicholas in 1842 that Queen Victoria received her pair of Borzoi, believed to be the first of the breed in England. Soon other members of Britain's nobility were similarly honoured and by 1917—the time of the Russian revolution—several kennels had become well established in Britain, Canada, and the United States.

In their country of origin the Borzoi suffered at the hands of the Bolsheviks because it was a symbol of the aristocracy. Great numbers of the dogs were slaughtered and it was due to the efforts of a few dedicated breeders and the remoteness of their kennels that the breed managed to survive at all in its homeland.

Prior to this, in 1892, the Borzoi Club of England was organized and in the same year the breed was admitted to registration by

Borzoi

The Canadian Kennel Club. Since its introduction the Borzoi has enjoyed the support of many excellent Canadian breeders who may be justly proud of their contribution to the promotion of the breed.

Official Breed Standard for the Borzoi

General Appearance: Should be that of an elegant, graceful aristocrat among dogs, possessing courage and combining muscular power with extreme speed.

Size: Dogs, average height at shoulder from 28−31 in. (71− 79 cm); average weight from 75−105 lb. (34−48 kg). Larger dogs are often seen, extra size being no disadvantage when it is not acquired at the expense of symmetry, speed, and staying quality. Bitches are invariably smaller than dogs, and 2 in. (5 cm) less in height, and from 15−20 lb. (7−9 kg) less in weight is a fair average.

Coat and Colour: Coat long, silky (not woolly), either flat, wavy or rather curly. On the head, ears and front of legs it should be short and smooth; on the neck the frill should be profuse and rather curly. Feather on hindquarters and tail, long and profuse, less so on the chest and back of forelegs. Any colour, white usually predominating, more or less marked with lemon, tan, brindle, grey or black. Whole-coloured specimens of these tints occasionally appear.

Head: *Skull* slightly domed, long and narrow, with scarcely any perceptible stop, rather inclined to be Roman-nosed. *Nose* large and black. Jaws long, powerful, and deep; teeth strong, clean and even, neither pig-jawed nor undershot. *Eyes* set somewhat obliquely, dark in colour, intelligent, but rather soft in expression, never full nor staring, nor light in colour, eyelids dark. *Ears* small and fine in quality, lying back on the neck when in repose with the tips when thrown back almost touching behind occiput; raised when at attention.

Neck: Clean, free from throatiness, somewhat shorter than in the Greyhound, slightly arched, very powerful and well set on.

Forequarters: Shoulders sloping, should be fine at the withers and free from coarseness or lumber. Forelegs have flat bone, straight, giving free play for the elbows, which should be neither turned in nor out; pasterns strong.

Body: Back rising a little at the loins in a graceful curve. Chest rather narrow, with great depth of brisket. Ribs only slightly sprung, but very deep, giving room for heart and lung play. Loins extremely muscular, but rather tucked up, owing to the great depth of chest and comparative shortness of back and ribs.

Hindquarters: Long, very muscular and powerful, with well bent stifles and strong second thighs, hocks broad, clean and well let down. Feet hare-shaped, with well-arched knuckles, toes close and well padded.

Tail: Long, set on and carried low in a graceful curve.

Scale of Points:

Head	12
Eyes	5
Ears	3
Neck	5
Shoulders and brisket	10
Ribs, back, and loins	15
Hindquarters, stifles, and hocks	12
Legs and feet	10
Coat and feather	10
Tail	3
Conformation and gait	15
TOTAL	**100**

Coonhound
(Black and Tan)

WHEN **WILLIAM THE CONQUEROR** defeated Harold at the Battle of Hastings in 1066, he did more than change the course of English history. He changed the history of English dogs. Along with his invading forces he brought two breeds of French hound, the Talbot and the St. Hubert.

It did not take the Britons long to visualize the variety of possibilities offered by this new canine blood. By cross breeding it with local dogs and selecting for particular traits, before many years had passed they had created a number of specialist hound breeds able to track all manner of four-footed game, as well as the Bloodhound, whose specialty was tracking man.

Why the Bloodhound was selected to be shipped in large numbers to the new English colony of Virginia is not explained. The fact is that they were. There they became best known for tracking runaway slaves. But their secondary service was to help create other sporting hound breeds—the Virginia Foxhound and the coonhounds—whose specialty is nocturnal trailing of the raccoon and opossum.

Altogether six distinct breeds of coonhound were developed: the Plott, English Coonhound, Redbone, Treeing Walker, Bluetick, and the Black and Tan. The last bears the closest resemblance to his forbear, the Bloodhound, and is the only coonhound breed so far accepted for registration with The Canadian and the American Kennel Clubs.

At first the hounds that trailed and treed the nuisance coons offered little more than some after-dark fun for farmers in the southern states. Now night trialing has grown into a popular sport. In the South more than 500 night trials are held annually during the fall and winter months. The championship dog show is a different matter. Black and Tan Coonhound show entries are usually small, but the dogs that are exhibited make their presence felt. One Canadian-bred hound made history by becoming the only member of his breed to be awarded Best in Show in both Canada and the United States.

The breed was first accepted for registration in Canada in 1945.

Coonhound (Black and Tan)

Official Breed Standard for the Coonhound (Black and Tan)

General Appearance: The Black and Tan Coonhound is first and fundamentally a working dog, capable of withstanding the rigours of winter, the heat of summer, and the difficult terrain over which he is called upon to work. Judges are asked by the club sponsoring the breed to place great emphasis upon these facts when evaluating the merits of the dog.

The general impression should be that of power, agility, and alertness. His expression should be alert, friendly, eager, and aggressive. He should immediately impress one with his ability to cover the ground with powerful rhythmic strides.

Size: Measured at the shoulder: males, 25—27 in. (64—69 cm); females, 23—25 in. (58—64 cm). Height should be in proportion to general conformation so the dog appears neither leggy nor close to the ground. Dogs oversized should not be penalized when general soundness and proportion are in favour.

Coat and Colour: The coat should be short but dense to withstand rough going. As the name implies, the colour should be coal black, with rich tan markings above eyes, on sides of muzzle, chest, legs and breeching with black pencil markings on toes.

Head: The head should be cleanly modelled, with medium stop occurring midway between occiput and nose. The head should measure from 9—10 in. (23—25 cm) in males and from 8—9 in. (20—23 cm) in females. Viewed from the profile the line of the *skull* is on a practically parallel plane to the foreface or muzzle. Skull should tend toward oval outline. Nostrils well open and always black. Teeth should fit evenly with slightly scissors bite. *Eyes* should be from hazel to dark brown in colour, almost round and not deeply set. The *ears* should be low set and well back. They should hang in graceful folds giving the dog a majestic appearance. In length they should extend well beyond the tip of the nose. The skin should be devoid of folds or excess dewlap. The flews should be well developed with typical hound appearance.

Neck: The neck should be muscular, sloping, medium length.

Forequarters: Shoulders powerfully constructed. The forelegs should be straight, with elbows well let down, turning neither in nor out; pasterns strong and erect. Feet should be cat-like with compact, well-arched toes and thick strong pads.

Body: The back should be level, powerful and strong, with a visible slope from withers to rump. The chest should be deep. The dog should possess full, round, well-sprung ribs, avoiding flat-sidedness.

Hindquarters: Quarters should be well boned and muscled. From hip to hock long and sinewy, hock to pad short and strong. Stifles and hock well bent and not inclining either in or out. When standing on a level surface the hind feet should set back from under the body, and leg from pad to hock be at right angles to the ground when viewed both from profile and the rear.

Tail: Should be strong, with base slightly below level of backline, carried free, and when in action at approximately right angle to back.

Gait: The stride of the Black and Tan Coonhound should be easy and graceful with plenty of reach in front and drive behind.

Faults: Judges should penalize the following defects: under-size, elbows out at shoulder, lack of angulation in hindquarters, splay feet, sway or roach back, flat-sidedness, lack of depth in chest, yellow or light eyes, shyness and nervousness. Dew-claws are a fault. White on chest or other parts of body is highly undesirable.

Disqualification: *White on chest or other parts of the body if it exceeds 1¹/₂ in. (4 cm) in diameter.*

Dachshund

*I*F EVER A DOG DESERVED to be classified as a terrier, that breed is the dachshund. Its name means "badger-hound" or "badgerdog" in Germany, its country of origin. However, there it is known as the Teckel, a variant of the abbreviated form of dachshund—*dackel*. Dogs of the dachshund type have been used to hunt badger and fox on the continent since the 16th century. The miniature varieties are a later development resulting from selective breeding of small specimens and were used to work on rabbits. Despite the Dachshund's vermin-routing background, when Queen Victoria's consort Prince Albert introduced the breed to Britain, the literal British declared a "hund" was a "hound" and classified the dachshund in the Hound Group where it has stayed ever since.

This may not have been entirely inaccurate because some learned dog historians contend that the original dachshunds were an offshoot of the French Basset, forerunner of that modern hound breed. It is generally assumed that the original dachshunds were smooth coated, the long-haired and the wire-haired varieties resulting from crosses to the field spaniel and various terrier breeds respectively. Thus in both Canada and Britain six separate breeds of dachshund are recognized for show purposes, standards and miniatures (which may not weigh more than ten pounds), each in three coats. The United States recognizes only three breeds. In each coat the standards and the miniatures must compete against each other for show points.

The first dachshund club, for smooths only, was formed in England in 1881, followed in Germany by the formation of the Deutsche Teckelclub in 1888. The breed came to North America during the 1870s, fifteen of the breed being exhibited at the first Westminster Kennel Club show in 1877. Six of these were imports owned by Dr. L.H. Twaddel of Philadelphia. Between 1888–1889 The Canadian Kennel Club registered nine Smooth Dachshunds but the first registrations of the long-haired and wire-haired varieties did not occur until 1933 and 1934 respectively.

Dachshund (Miniature)

Dachshund (Standard)

Official Breed Standard for the Dachshund

Origin and Purpose: Early in the seventeenth century the name Dachshund became the designation of a breed type with smooth and long-haired varieties, and since 1890 wire-hairs have been registered as the third variety. The name Dachshund (*dachs*, badgers; *hund*, dog) at once reveals and conceals the origin of the breed. In medieval European books on hunting, dogs, similar only in possessing the tracking ability of hounds and the proportions and temperament of terriers, because they were used to track badgers were called badger-dogs, or *dachshunds.*

General Appearance: Low to ground, short-legged, long-bodied, but with compact figure and robust muscular development, with bold and confident carriage of head and intelligent facial expression; conformation preeminently fitted for following game into burrows. In spite of his shortness of leg, in comparison with his length of trunk, he should appear neither crippled, awkward, cramped in his capacity for movement, nor slim and weasel-like. Added to this, his hunting spirit, good nose, loud tongue, and small size, render him especially suited for beating the bush. His figure and his fine nose give him an especial advantage over most other breeds of sporting dogs for trailing.

Temperament: He should be clever, lively, and courageous to the point of rashness, persevering in his work both above and below ground; with all the senses being well developed.

Size: Standard Dachshund—over 10 lb. (4.5 kg). Miniature Dachshund—not to exceed 10 lb. (4.5 kg). A Miniature Dachshund over 10 lb. (4.5 kg) is not eligible to compete at shows held under the Dog Show Rules of The Canadian Kennel Club. If, at such a show, a Miniature Dachshund is officially weighed and is found to exceed 10 lb. (4.5 kg) said dog shall be declared absent and not permitted in competition at the show. Within the limits imposed, symmetrical adherence to the general Dachshund conformation, combined with smallness and mental and physical vitality should be the outstanding characteristics of the Miniature Dachshund.

Coat and Colour: Three coat types: Smooth or Short-Haired
—short, dense, shining, glossy. Wire-Haired—like German
Spiky-Haired Pointer, hard with good undercoat. Long-Haired—
like Irish Setter. See later paragraphs in this standard regarding
the Special Characteristics. Colour—Solid red (tan) of various
shades, and black with tan points, should have black noses and
nails, and narrow black line edging lips and eyelids; chocolate
with tan points permits brown nose. Eyes of all, lustrous, the
darker the better.

Special Characteristics of the Three Coat Varieties of Dachshunds
The Dachshund is bred with three varieties of coat: (1) Short-
Haired (or Smooth); (2) Wire-Haired; (3) Long-Haired. All three
varieties should conform to the characteristics already specified.
The long-haired and short-haired are old, well-fixed varieties,
but into the Wire-Haired Dachshund the blood of other breeds
has been purposely introduced; nevertheless, in breeding him,
the greatest stress must be placed upon conformity to the
general Dachshund type.

The following specifications are applicable separately to the
three coat varieties, respectively.

Short-Haired (or Smooth) Dachshund: *Hair:* Short, thick,
smooth and shining; no bald patches. Special faults are: too fine
or thin hair, leathery ears, bald patches, too coarse or too thick
hair in general. *Tail:* Gradually tapered to a point, well but not
too richly haired; long sleek bristles on the underside are
considered a patch of strong-growing hair, not a fault. A brush
tail is a fault, as is also a partly or wholly hairless tail.

Colour of Hair, Nose and Nails:
a)   One-Coloured Dachshund—This group includes red (often
called tan), red-yellow, and yellow, with or without a shading of
interspersed black hairs. Nevertheless a clean colour is preferable, and red is to be considered more desirable than red-yellow
or yellow. Dogs strongly shaded with interspersed black hairs
belong to this class, and not to the other colour groups. No white
is desirable, but a solitary small spot is not exactly disqualifying.
Nose and nails—black; red is admissible, but not desirable.
b)   Two-Coloured Dachshund—These comprise deep black,
chocolate, grey, and white; each with rust-brown or yellow

marks over the eyes, on the sides of the jaw and underlip, on the inner edge of the ear, front, breast, inside and behind the front leg, on the paws and around the anus and from there to about one-third to one-half of the length of the tail on the underside. (The most common Two-Coloured Dachshund is usually called black and tan.) Except on white dogs, no white is desirable, but a solitary small spot is not exactly disqualifying. Absence, or undue prominence of tan markings, is undesirable. Nose and nails—In the case of black dogs, black; for chocolate, brown or black; for grey, grey or even flesh colour, but the last named colour is not desirable; in the case of white dogs, black nose and nails are to be preferred.

c)   Dappled and Striped Dachshund—The colour of the dappled (or tiger) Dachshund is a clear brownish or greyish colour, or even a white ground, with dark irregular patches of dark-grey, brown, red-yellow or black (large areas of one colour not desirable). It is desirable that neither the light nor the dark colour should predominate. The colour of the striped (brindle) Dachshund is red or yellow with a darker streaking. Nose and nails—as for One- and Two-Coloured Dachshunds.

Wire-Haired Dachshund: The general appearance is the same as that of the Short-Haired, but without being long in the legs, it is permissible for the body to be somewhat higher off the ground. *Hair:* With the exception of the jaw, eyebrows, and ears, the whole body is covered with a perfectly uniform tight, short, thick, rough, hard coat, but with finer, shorter hairs (undercoat) everywhere distributed between the coarser hairs, resembling the coat of the German Spiky-Haired Pointer. There should be a beard on the chin. The eyebrows are bushy. On the ears the hair is shorter than on the body; almost smooth, but in any case conforming to the rest of the coat. The general arrangement of the hair should be such that the Wire-Haired Dachshund, when seen from a distance, should resemble a Smooth-Haired. Any sort of soft hair in the coat is faulty, whether short or long, or wherever found on the body; the same is true of long, curly, or wavy hair, or hair that sticks out irregularly in all directions; a flag tail is also objectionable. *Tail:* Robust, as thickly haired as possible, gradually coming to a point and without a tuft. *Colour of Hair, Nose and Nails:* All colours are admissible. White patches on the chest, though allowable, are not desirable.

Long-Haired Dachshund: The distinctive characteristic differentiating this coat from the Short-Haired, or Smooth-Haired, is alone the rather long silky hair. *Hair:* The soft, sleek, glistening, often slightly wavy hair should be longer under the neck, on the underside of the body, and especially on the ears and behind the legs, becoming there a pronounced feather; the hair should attain its greatest length on the underside of the tail. The hair should fall beyond the lower edge of the ear. Short hair on the ear, so-called "leather" ears, is not desirable. Too luxurious a coat causes the Long-Haired Dachshund to seem coarse, and masks the type. The coat should remind one of the Irish Setter, and should give the dog an elegant appearance. Too thick hair on the paws, so-called "mops," is inelegant and renders the animal unfit for use. It is faulty for the dog to have equally long hair over all the body, if the coat is too curly, or too scrubby, or if a flag tail or overhanging hair on the ears are lacking; or if there is a very pronounced parting in the back, or a vigorous growth between the toes. *Tail:* Carried gracefully in prolongation of the spine; the hair attains here its greatest length and forms a veritable flag. *Colour of Hair, Nose and Nails:* Exactly as for the Smooth-Haired Dachshund.

NOTE: Inasmuch as the Dachshund is a hunting dog, scars from honourable wounds shall not be considered a fault.

Head: Viewed from above or from the side, it should taper uniformly to the tip of the nose, and should be clean-cut. The *skull* is only slightly arched, and should slope gradually without stop (the less stop the more typical) into the finely-formed slightly-arched muzzle (ram's nose). The bridge bones over the eyes should be strongly prominent. The nasal cartilage and tip of the nose are long and narrow; lips tightly stretched, well covering the lower jaw, but neither deep nor pointed; corner of the mouth not very marked. Nostrils well open. *Jaws* opening wide and hinged well back of the eyes, with strongly developed bones and teeth. *Teeth:* powerful canine teeth should fit closely together, and the outer side of the lower incisors should tightly touch the inner side of the upper. (Scissors bite.) *Eyes:* medium size, oval, situated at the sides, with a clean, energetic, though pleasant expression; not piercing. Colour: lustrous dark reddish-brown to brownish-black for all coats and colours. Wall (fish or pearl) eyes in the case of grey or dappled-coloured dogs are not a very bad fault, but are also not desirable. *Ears* should be set near the top of the head, and not too far forward, long but not too long, beautifully rounded, not narrow, pointed, or folded. Their carriage should be animated, and the forward edge should just touch the cheek.

Neck: Fairly long, muscular, clean-cut, not showing any dewlap on the throat, slightly arched in the nape, extending in a graceful line into the shoulders, carried proudly but not stiffly.

Forequarters: To endure the arduous exertion underground, the front must be correspondingly muscular, compact, deep, long, and broad. Shoulder Blade long, broad, obliquely and firmly placed upon the fully developed thorax, furnished with hard and plastic muscle. Upper Arm of the same length as the shoulder blade, and at right angles to the latter, strong of bone and hard of muscle, lying close to the ribs, capable of free movement. Lower Arm: this is short in comparison to other breeds, slightly turned inwards; supplied with hard but plastic muscles on the front and outside, with tightly stretched tendons on the inside and at the back. Pasterns: joint between forearm and foot (wrists): these are closer together than the shoulder joints, so that the front leg does not appear absolutely straight. Feet full, broad in front, and a trifle inclined outwards; compact with well-arched toes and tough pads. Toes: there are five of these, though only four are in use. They should be close together, with a pronounced arch; provided on top with strong nails, and underneath with tough toe-pads.

Body: The whole trunk should in general be long and fully-muscled. The back, with sloping shoulders, and short, rigid pelvis, should lie in the straightest possible line between the withers and the very slightly arched loins, these latter being short, rigid, and broad. Topline: the straightest possible line between withers and loin. Chest: the breastbone should be strong, and so prominent in front that on either side a depression (dimple) appears. When viewed from the front, the thorax should appear oval, and should extend downward to the midpoint of the forearm. The enclosing structure of ribs should appear full and oval, and when viewed from above or from the side, full volumed, so as to allow by its ample capacity, complete development of heart and lungs. Well ribbed up, and gradually merging into the line of the abdomen. If the length is correct, and also the anatomy of the shoulder and upper arm, the front leg when viewed in profile should cover the lowest point of the breast line. Loin slightly arched, being short, rigid and broad. Croup long, round, full, robustly muscled, but plastic, only slightly sinking toward the tail. Abdomen slightly drawn up.

Hindquarters: The hindquarters viewed from behind should be of completely equal width. Pelvic Bones not too short, rather strongly developed, and moderately sloping. Thigh robust and of good length, set at right angle to the pelvic bones. Hind Legs robust and well-muscled, with well-rounded buttocks. Knee Joint broad and strong. Calf Bone, in comparison with other breeds, short; it should be perpendicular to the thigh bone, and firmly muscled. The bones at the base of the foot (tarsus) should present a flat appearance, with a strongly prominent hock and a broad tendon of Achilles. The central foot bones (metatarsus) should be long, movable towards the calf bone, slightly bent toward the front, but perpendicular (as viewed from behind). Hind Feet: four compactly-closed and beautifully arched toes, as in the case of the front paws. The whole foot should be posed equally on the ball and not merely on the toes; nails short.

Tail: Set in continuation of the spine, extending without very pronounced curvature, and should not be carried too gaily.

Faults: Serious Faults (which may prevent a dog from receiving any show rating): overshot or undershot jaws, knuckling over, very loose shoulders.

Secondary Faults (which may prevent a dog from receiving a high show rating): a weak, long-legged, or dragging figure; body hanging between the shoulders; sluggish, clumsy, or waddling gait; toes turned inwards or too obliquely outwards; splayed paws; sunken back, roach (or carp) back; croup higher than withers; short-ribbed or too weak chest; excessively drawn up flanks like those of a Greyhound; narrow, poorly muscled hindquarters; weak loins; bad angulation in front or hindquarters; cowhocks; bowed legs; "glass" eyes, except for grey or dappled dogs; a bad coat.

Minor Faults (which may prevent a dog from receiving the highest rating in championship competition): ears wrongly set, sticking out, narrow or folded; too marked a stop, too pointed or weak a jaw; pincer teeth, distemper teeth; too wide or short a head; goggle eyes, "glass" eyes in the case of greys and dappled dogs, insufficiently dark eyes in the case of all other coat-colours; dewlaps; short neck; swan neck; too fine or too thin hair.

A Miniature Dachshund over 10 lb. (4.5 kg) is not eligible to compete at shows held under the Dog Show Rules of The Canadian Kennel Club. If, at such a show, a Miniature Dachshund is officially weighed and is found to exceed 10 lb. (4.5 kg), said dog shall be declared absent and not permitted in competition at the show. Within the limits imposed, symmetrical adherence to the general Dachshund conformation, combined with smallness and mental and physical vitality should be the outstanding characteristics of the Miniature Dachshund.

Deerhound (Scottish)

ONCE KNOWN AS the "Royal Dog of Scotland," there was a time when no person below the rank of earl was permitted by law to own a Scottish Deerhound. Whether this was to preserve the Highland deer exclusively for the sport of "deer driving," a favourite pastime of the nobility, or because the deerhound's character and dignified bearing identified itself with the aristocracy, is not entirely clear. But based on old Scottish tales the breed was highly regarded for its courage and tenacity as a stag hunter and its loyalty to the chieftain and his kin.

Earliest portrayals of the rough-coated hound are found in stone carvings dating from 800 A.D., but how and when the breed came to Scotland is a mystery. Called variously "the Scotch Greyhound," "Highland Greyhound," and "the Highland Deerhound," these names probably provide the best clues to the breed's origin. It is assumed by dog historians that greyhounds were brought to Britain by the Phoenician traders (circa 1000 B.C.) and that these dogs eventually found their way to Scotland where the rough, weather-resistant coat evolved as protection against the harsher environment.

Favoured by Highland chieftains for centuries, the deerhound's usefulness came to an end with the introduction of better firearms. A few hounds were used to find wounded deer, but generally the desire to maintain purity of breeding in the deerhound was lost, especially after the collapse of the clan system in 1745. The numbers of pure-bred deerhounds declined drastically until the early 19th century when Lord Colonsay took up their cause and began a deerstalking revival.

Thereafter the breed increased in numbers and later gained even greater favour through the patronage of Queen Victoria. The renowned animal portraitist Landseer owned a deerhound which appears in many of his paintings. And Sir Walter Scott stated that his pet deerhound was "a most **perfect creature** of heaven."

237

Deerhound (Scottish)

Never numerous, there are still enough dedicated Scottish Deerhound breeders to keep this ancient breed alive, and their dogs are remarkably similar to those being bred more than 100 years ago.

At the first Westminster Kennel Club show held in 1877 the catalogue lists nine deerhounds in competition, two of which had been bred by Her Majesty Queen Victoria and were offered for sale at £10,000 each. The Canadian Kennel Club Stud Book lists seven Scottish Deerhound registrations between the years 1888–1889.

Official Breed Standard for the Deerhound (Scottish)

Size: Height of dogs—from 30–32 in. (76–81 cm), or even more if there be symmetry without coarseness, which is rare.

Height of bitches—from 28 in. (71 cm) upwards. There is no objection to a bitch being large, unless too coarse, as even at her greatest height she does not approach that of the dog, and therefore could not be too big for work as overbig dogs are.

Weight—from 85–110 lb. (39–50 kg) in dogs, and from 75–95 lb. (34–43 kg) in bitches.

Coat and Colour: The hair on the body, neck and quarters should be harsh and wiry, about 3–4 in. (8–10 cm) long; that on the head, breast and belly much softer. There should be a slight fringe on the inside of the forelegs and hind legs but nothing approaching the "feather" of a Collie. A woolly coat is bad. Some good strains have a mixture of silky coat with the hard which is preferable to a woolly coat. The climate of Canada tends to produce the mixed coat. The ideal coat is a thick, close-lying ragged coat, harsh or crisp to the touch.

Colour is a matter of fancy, but the dark blue-grey is most preferred. Next come the darker and lighter greys or brindles, the darkest being generally preferred. Yellow and sandy red or red fawn, especially with black ears and muzzles, are equally high in estimation. This was the colour of the oldest known strains—the McNeil and Chesthill Menzies. White is condemned by all authorities, but a white chest and white toes, occurring as they do in many of the darkest-coloured dogs, are not objected to although the less the better, for the Deerhound is a self-coloured dog. The less white the better but a slight white tip to the stern occurs in some of the best strains.

Head: Should be broadest at the ears, narrowing slightly to the eyes, with the muzzle tapering more decidedly to the nose. The head should be long, the *skull* flat rather than round with a very slight rise over the eyes but nothing approaching a stop. The hair on the skull should be moderately long and softer than the rest of the coat. The *muzzle* should be pointed, but the teeth and lips level. The *nose* should be black (in some blue fawns— blue) and slightly aquiline. In lighter coloured dogs the black muzzle is preferable. There should be a good moustache of rather silky hair and a fair beard. *Eyes* should be dark—generally dark brown, brown, or hazel. A very light eye is not liked. The eye should be moderately full, with a soft look in repose, but a keen, far-away look when the Deerhound is roused. Rims of eyelids should be black. *Ears* should be set on high; in repose, folded back like a Greyhound's, though raised above the head in excitement without losing the fold, and even in some cases semi-erect. A prick ear is bad. The ears should be soft, glossy, like a mouse's coat to the touch and the smaller the better. There should be no long coat or long fringe, but there is sometimes a silky, silvery coat on the body of the ear and the tip. On all Deerhounds, irrespective of the colour of coat, the ears should be black or dark coloured.

Neck: The neck should be long—of a length befitting the Grey-hound character of the dog. Extreme length is neither necessary nor desirable. Deerhounds do not stoop to their work like the Greyhounds. The mane, which every good specimen should have, sometimes detracts from the apparent length of the neck. The neck, however, must be strong as is necessary to hold a stag. The nape of the neck should be very prominent where the head is set on, and the throat clean-cut at the angle and prominent.

Forequarters: Shoulders should be well sloped; blades well back and not too much width between them. Legs should be broad and flat, and good broad forearms and elbows are desirable. Forelegs must, of course, be as straight as possible. Feet close and compact, with well-arranged toes.

Body: General formation is that of a Greyhound of larger size and bone. Chest deep rather than broad but not too narrow or slab-sided. Good girth of chest is indicative of great lung power. The loin well arched and drooping to the tail. A straight back is

▲**Borzoi**
Can. Am. Ch. Kishniga's
Desert Song
Can. Am. Ch. Kishniga's
Dalgarth
Breeders/Owners:
Dr. R. Meen &
Dr. J. Reeve-Newson
P.O. Box 69,
Campbellville, Ont. L0P 1B0
KISHNIGA KENNELS REG.

◄**Borzoi**
Ch. Korolevskii Artico
Zeffiro
Breeder: Penelope Brown
Owner: Christopher Brown
166 Woburn Ave.,
Toronto, Ont. M5M 1K7
KOROLEVSKII KENNELS REG.

► **Dachshund (Standard Long-Haired)**
Ch. Brandachs Beau Diddly, C.D.
Breeder/Owner:
Patricia J. Taylor
146 Madison Cres.,
Brandon, Man. R7A 2H1
BRANDACHS KENNELS REG.

► **Finnish Spitz**
Ch. Jayenn's Jubilant Juniper
Breeder: Joan Grant
Box 1423,
Golden, B.C. V0A 1H0
Owner: Jan Norman
JAYENN KENNELS (PERM.)

◀Finnish Spitz
Ch. Melreva Tagu's Hansom,
C.D.
Breeder:
Mrs. Estelle R. Matthews
75 Mayfair Cres.,
Regina, Sask. S4S 4H6
Owner: Shawn Brooks
MELREVA KENNELS REG. (PERM.)

▼Pharaoh Hound
Ch. Leetbank Amun, C.D.
Breeders:
Dr. & Mrs. B. J. Sproule
Owner: Christine Gillies
385 Amherst St.,
Winnipeg, Man.
AMHERST WOODS KENNELS

▶Rhodesian Ridgeback
Norwesia Fandu
Breeders/Owners:
Dr. C. Elizabeth &
Eleanor C. Mahaffy
RR 3,
High River, Alta. T0L 1B0
NORWESIA KENNELS REG.

▼Rhodesian Ridgeback
Ch. Stalkmoor Falconbridge
Breeder/Owner:
Mrs. M. J. Apostle
579 Valour Rd.,
Winnipeg, Man. R3G 3A7
STALKMOOR KENNELS (PERM.)

Rhodesian Ridgeback
Can. Am. Ch. Wazat Shaka
Breeders/Owners:
John & Pat Wilson
Box 1091, Stn. F,
Thunder Bay, Ont. P7C 4X9
WAZAT KENNELS

▼**Rhodesian Ridgeback**
Can. Am. Ch. Shangani's
Outspanner
Breeders/Owners:
Mr. & Mrs. David Helgesen
26586 98th Ave.,
Whonnock, B.C. V0M 1S0
SHANGANI KENNELS REG.

▲Rhodesian Ridgeback
Chadzombe's Bodie
Ch. Chadzombe's Pearl Oyster
Breeder/Owner:
Alison Fraser
208 Royal Rd.,
Keswick, Ont. L4P 2T7

▶Saluki
Can. Am. Ch. Counterpoint
Hillell Astraea, C.D.
Owners: John & Lynn Ross
11 Selkirk Cres.,
Saskatoon, Sask. S7L 4J4
COUNTERPOINT KENNELS
(PERM.)

▲Saluki
Ch. Iroki Souris, C.D.
Breeder/Owner:
Roberta Pattison
Box 217,
Delisle, Sask. S0L 0P0
IROKI KENNELS REG.

◀Wolfhound (Irish)
Ch. Alberland's Donegal
Toby, C.D.
GrB. Ch. Royden Quire
Breeders: Marni Bersell/
Mr. & Mrs. R. Hollis
Owner: Holly O'Donnell
Site 17, Box 5, RR 2,
Sherwood Park, Alta. T8A 3K2
TYRCONNELL KENNELS REG.

 Akita
Arlberg Kakuteru Sosu
Ch. Shogun Samurai
Shibumi
Owners: Roderick, Terrie,
& Cathy McGlashan
RR 1, Assad Rd.,
Buckingham, P.Q. J8L 2W7
ROTERCATH KENNELS REG.

(Photo by Gleason)

▶**Akita**
Ch. Checan's Subarashii
Checan
Breeders: George & Vera Bohac
Owners: D. Robertson,
D. Van Orsow, & V. Bohac
Rt 1, Box 285A,
Scappoose, OR 97056
CHECAN KENNELS REG.

▲Akita
Ch. Asahi Yama Saisho
No Checan
Breeders:
Werner & Veldta Oetmann
Owner: Mrs. Vera Bohac
Box 640
Lethbridge, Alta. T1J 3Z4
CHECAN KENNELS REG.

▼Australian Cattle Dog
Cattlemaster Sheba, C.D.X.
Breeder:
Cattlemaster Kennels (Aus.)
Owner: K. Scanlon
General Delivery,
Brooks, Alta.
CATTLENIP KENNELS REG.

▲Australian Cattle Dog
Ch. Bluepine Herdsman
Ch. Masked Bandit
Owners:
Carrol Wells & Millicent Pratt
Site 1, Box 17, RR 9,
Calgary, Alta. T2J 5G5
CUBBAROO KENNELS REG.
PITJANTJARA KENNELS REG.

▼Bearded Collie
Ch. Brandylind's Classy
Chassis
Brandylind's Chamois of
Haute Ecole
Brandylind's Dark Rum 'n
Diamonds

Breeder/Owner:
Miss Linda D. Smith
35 George Suttie Bay,
Winnipeg, Man. R2K 3C9
BRANDYLIND KENNELS REG.

Bernese Mountain Dog
Ch. Arno V. Hogerbuur
Ch. Astrid De La Roseliere
Owner: Ernst Brand
Heimberg, Switzerland
SUBMITTED BY THE BERNESE
MOUNTAIN DOG CLUB OF
CANADA

Bearded Collie
Ch. Wishanger Marsh
Pimpernel, C.D.* FRONT
Ch. Raggmopp Gaelin
Image**
Ch. Raggmopp Intrepid
Spirit†
Ch. Bedlam's Go Get 'Em
Garth††
*Owner: Carol Gold
**Breeder/Owner: Carol Gold
†Owner: Jennifer Brewer
††Breeder/Owner:
   Alice Clark
580 Woburn Ave.,
Toronto, Ont. M5M 1L9

▶Boxer
Can. Am. Ch. Haviland's
Count Royal
Breeders/Owners:
Mr. & Mrs. Stanley Whitmore
217 Hwy 7 East,
Thornhill, Ont.
HAVILAND KENNELS REG.

▶Boxer
Tanoak Amber Glory
Breeders/Owners:
Dieter & Helga Liedel
RR 5,
Barrie, Ont. L4M 4S7
TANOAK KENNELS REG.

▲**Boxer**
Tanoak Brutus
Tanoak Amber Glory
Tanoak Dunya

TANOAK KENNELS REG.
Dieter & Helga Liedel
RR 5,
Barrie, Ont. L4M 4S7

◄**Boxer**
Tanoak General
Owner: Alvin Mackey

▲**Boxer**
Ch. Memorylane's
Primavera
Tanoak Holly
Manta's Ambrosius
Memorylane's Kastanie,
C.D.
Owner: Simone Leidel
RR 1,
Queensville, Ont. L0G 1R0
MANTA KENNELS REG.

▶**Bullmastiff**
Can. Am. Ch. Noble Nite
Sir Lancelot, C.D.
Breeders:
John & Deloris Williams
Owner: Kwok Wing Tse
Box 3763 Main Stn.,
Vancouver, B.C.
NITESLATE KENNELS

Canadian Eskimo Dog

Breeder/Owner:
William J. Carpenter
Eskimo Dog Research
Foundation,
Box 1032,
Yellowknife, N.W.T.
QIMMIIT KENNELS REG.

►**Collie (Rough)**
Kirriemuirs Highland Sheba
Breeder: Mrs. E. Pearson
Owner: Layne Tennant
RR 4, Box 242,
Gloucester, Ont. K1G 3N2
TENNS KENNELS

►**Doberman Pinscher**
Can. Am. Ch. Sherluck's
Crimson 'n Clover
Breeders: Faye & Gary Strauss
Owners:
Lana Sniderman and Bob Krol
274 Church St.,
Toronto, Ont. M5B 1Z5
SIMCA KENNELS REG.

not desirable, this formation being unsuited for uphill work, and very unsightly.

Hindquarters: Drooping, and as broad and powerful as possible, the hips being set wide apart. A narrow rear denotes lack of power. The stifles should be well bent, with great length from hip to hock, which should be broad and flat.

Tail: Should be tolerably long, tapering and reaching to within 1½ in. (4 cm) off the ground and about 1½ in. (4 cm) below the hocks. Dropped perfectly down or curved when the Deerhound is still, when in motion or excited, curved, but in no instance lifted out of line of the back. It should be well covered with hair, on the inside, thick and wiry, underside longer and towards the end a slight fringe is not objectionable. A curl or ring tail is undesirable.

Faults: Big thick ears hanging flat to the head or heavily coated with long hair are bad faults. Loaded and straight shoulders are very bad faults. Cowhocks, weak pasterns, straight stifles, and splay feet are very bad faults.

Disqualifications: *A white blaze on the head, or a white collar.*

Points of the Deerhound arranged in order of importance:
1. Typical—a Deerhound should resemble a rough-coated Greyhound of larger size and bone.
2. Movements—easy, active and true.
3. As tall as possible consistent with quality.
4. Head—long, level, well balanced, carried high.
5. Body—long, very deep in brisket, well-sprung ribs and great breadth across hips.
6. Forelegs—strong and quite straight, with elbows neither in nor out.
7. Thighs—long and muscular, second thighs well muscled, stifles well bent.
8. Loins—well arched, and belly well drawn up.
9. Coat—rough and hard, with softer beard and brows.
10. Feet—close, compact, with well-knuckled toes.
11. Ears—small (dark) with Greyhound-like carriage.
12. Eyes—dark, moderately full.
13. Neck—long, well arched, very strong with prominent nape.

14. Shoulders—clean, set sloping.
15. Chest—very deep but not too narrow.
16. Tail—long and curved slightly, carried low.
17. Teeth—strong and level.
18. Nails—strong and curved.

Drever

THE DREVER IS SAID TO BE the most popular of all breeds in Sweden. Some refer to it as the "Swedish Drever," others call it the national dog of Sweden. But strangely enough, the Drever did not originate in Sweden but rather in Germany. Its forbears were the Westfalische Dachsbracken—a short-coated, hound-coloured breed used for hunting hare, fox, wild boar, and occasionally deer.

Early this century some specimens of the Westfalische Dachsbracken were imported into both Sweden and Denmark. In the latter country these dogs were inter-bred with imported Swiss hounds by a breeder by the name of Frandsen. Thus was created a Danish Dachsbracke, a breed Frandsen called the *Strellufstover* after his kennel name. Some of these dogs were then imported into Sweden where they were bred back to the Westfalische Dachsbracken. In 1947 this new breed was given the name Drever, after the Swedish word *drev* which means to hunt. Two years later the breed was officially recognized by the Swedish Kennel Club.

While the Westfalische Dachsbracken is said to be now almost extinct, one descendant, the Drever, is flourishing. It is reported that about 2000 of the breed are registered each year in Sweden but few are ever seen in the show ring. Most, at some time during their lives, are used for hunting.

The Drever is said to have excellent scenting power and a loud, musical voice much larger than his size would seem to warrant. He's been called both "the Swedish beagle" and "the Swedish basset" and looks somewhat like a cross between the two. He is long in body, rather low on leg but lacks the wrinkled brow and the generous basset ear.

The breed is little known outside its homeland. Although officially recognized by The Canadian Kennel Club in 1956, no Drever has been seen in competition in the show ring in Canada for at least the last ten years. The breed is not recognized by the American Kennel Club.

G. STENHOUSE

Drever

Official Breed Standard for the Drever

General Appearance: The Drever should be somewhat less than medium size. Appearance from the side should be rectangular. It must be compact, of good stature, powerful with well-developed musculature, lithe, and agile. It must be alert and self-possessed. External sexual characteristics should be well developed.

Size: The height of the dog at the withers should be 14 in. (36 cm); of the bitch, 13 1/2 in. (34 cm). The dog's height should not exceed 16 in. (40 cm), nor be less than 12 1/2 in. (32 cm). The height of the bitch should not vary from a maximum of 15 in. (38 cm) and minimum of 12 in. (30 cm).

Coat and Colour: The coat should be complete. The hair should be close and straight. On the head, ears, lower legs, upper side of tail it should be relatively short; longer on the neck, back and back part of the thighs. It should be bristly on the underside of the tail, but not feathered. All colours are permitted, but there must be some white visible from front, sides and back. It should preferably appear on the front, including the neck, and at the tip of the tail and on the paws. The colour should be clean.

Head: The head should be relatively large. It should be longish, broadest between the ears, diminishing toward the snout with a slight supraorbital ridge. The snout should be well developed and not snipey either from above or from the side view. The bridge of the *nose* should be straight or slightly convex. The tip of the nose should be well developed with wide nostrils. It is preferably black. The lower edge of the upper lip should overlap the edge of the lower jaw. The lower lip should fit tightly against the lower jaw. The bite should be powerful and upper incisors fit firmly against the lowers. The *eyes* should be clear and expressive. They must not protrude or be stary. They are preferably dark brown. The eyelids should be thin and fit closely over the eyes. The *ears* should be of medium length and wide, bluntly rounded at the tips. They must be set neither especially high nor low. When at attention the forward edge of the ear should be against the head.

Neck: The neck should be long and powerful. It should flow gracefully and smoothly into the trunk. The skin of the neck should be fairly loose though not so loose as to form pouches at the throat or chin.

Forequarters: The shoulders should be muscular with long, sloping shoulder blades, set well into the chest and back. The points of the shoulder blades must not extend up over the apophysis of the spine of the vertebrae of the withers. The front legs should be powerful and in front view, straight and parallel. The upper foreleg should be relatively long and broad and form a good angle with the shoulder blade. The metacarpus should be springy and form only a slight angle with the radius and ulna.

Body: The back should be straight or, from side view, slightly arched at the rear. It should be strong and slope gently from the withers to the sacral region. The hindquarters should flow evenly into the slightly ascending line of the abdomen.

Hindquarters: From rear view the hind legs should be straight and parallel. There should be good bends at knee and back joints. The thighs should be muscular and broad from side view. The metatarsus should be short and almost perpendicular. There should be no dewclaws. Both front and back paws should be firm with toes pointing forward and close together. The pads should be well developed and hard.

Tail: The tail should be long and thick at the root. Preferably, it should be carried hanging, but when the dog is in motion it may be carried higher, though never over the back.

Finnish Spitz

THE FINNISH SPITZ, which is now considered to be the national dog of Finland, has a history stretching to antiquity, although it was not recognized as pure bred in its native land until the first quarter of this century.

The breed is said to descend from a group of wild dogs known as the Pariah dogs, forbears of a number of indigenous breeds throughout the world including the dingo, the wild dog of Australia. It is generally accepted that the Finnish Spitz existed in the northern regions of Lapland and Finland for thousands of years, valued as the fearless hunting dog of the northern tribesmen. Gradually these dogs moved southward to become the most numerous breed in Finland, popular in both town and country. The breed has been used to hunt everything from bear to squirrel and is reported to be particularly good on feathered game. Its habit of giving tongue when it sights wildfowl has earned it the title of "the barking bird dog."

Towards the end of the 19th century nothing had been done in Finland to preserve the purity of the *Suomenpystykorva*, or "Finnish cock-eared dog," the name by which the breed is known in its homeland. Neither had it been granted official recognition by the national kennel club. According to two Finnish sportsmen this was not as it should be, so they travelled north to Lapland in search of good specimens of pure-bred stock. Their fear was that breed type and quality of the dog's working ability would be lost through cross mating with other Scandinavian breeds, a situation that was already occurring in some areas.

They did manage to obtain a number of the brilliantly red-coloured hunting dogs, brought them south and established a breeding colony. By use of this stock and the principles of line breeding, type and working ability were set. In the 1920s the Finnish Spitz became a familiar hunting dog in Finland and was accepted for registration by the Finnish Kennel Club.

In 1927 the first pair was brought to Britain. Interest in the breed took hold and in 1935 the Finnish Spitz was officially

Finnish Spitz

recognized by The Kennel Club (England), where it is now well established. One of the breed pioneers in Britain, the late Lady Kitson, nicknamed the breed the "Finkie," a name by which the Finnish Spitz is now fondly known by its admirers.

In the early 1970s the Finnish Spitz began arriving in Canada in small numbers and by 1974 there was sufficient interest in the breed to warrant its acceptance by The Canadian Kennel Club. Although the breed is well known in the United States it still is not an officially recognized breed in that country.

Official Breed Standard for the Finnish Spitz

General Appearance: Body is almost square. Carriage brisk. The dog's whole being shows liveliness, especially the eyes, ears and tail. The special characteristics of the breed are that it likes hunting, is courageous and faithful. The breed is utilized for bird hunting.

Size: Height at shoulder and length of body are—males $17\frac{1}{2}$–$19\frac{1}{2}$ in. (44–50 cm); bitches $15\frac{1}{2}$–$17\frac{1}{2}$ in. (39–44 cm).

Coat and Colour: The coat on the head and legs is short and close, but longer on the back of the legs. On the body longish, half erect or erect. Stiffer on the neck and back. The stiff hair on the shoulders, especially in males, is noticeably longer and coarser. Hair on the back of the legs is long and thick, also in the tail. Undercoat is short, soft, dense, and lighter coloured. Colour on back is brownish red or yellowish brown, preferably clear. Lighter shade inside of ears, on cheeks, under chin, brisket, stomach, inside of legs, long hair on the back of legs and tail underhair. White is permissible on feet and chest score. Black is permissible a little on lips, and sparse black pointed stiff hairs on the back.

Head: Medium sized and clean. *Skull* a little domed with a good clear stop. Foreface narrow and clean-cut, tapering evenly from above and side. *Nose* coal black. *Lips* tight and thin. *Eyes* medium sized, lively and preferably dark. *Ears* pricked and pointed, with fine hair, very mobile.

Neck: Springy throat. In males it looks rather short, due to the thick coat. Medium length in bitches.

Forequarters: Shoulders fairly straight. Forearms strong and straight.

Body: Back short, straight and strong. Ribs deep. Belly line slightly drawn up.

Hindquarters: Strong, hocks of medium size. Feet preferably round.

Tail: The tail curls from the base in a bow over the back and lies flat against the thigh. The tail must lie tight and finish in the middle of the thigh. When straightened the tail vertebrae usually reach down to the hocks.

Faults: Muscular head. Coarse foreface. Ears carried with a forward, backward, outward or inward inclination; tips drooping and long inner hair. Eyes yellow or watery. Inward turned elbows and too weak pasterns. Tail slackly carried or with too much curl. Coat long, soft, too short, wavy, curly or close coated. Dirty colour. Multicoloured clear borders. Spurs bad looking.

Foxhound (American)

THE FIRST PACK of English Foxhounds, from which the American breed descends, arrived in Maryland in 1650, taken there by an Englishman by the name of Robert Brooke, or Brooks, depending on which dog historian one quotes. This was the beginning of foxhunting in the Southern States; it became a popular sport and has remained so. The quarry was the American grey fox and for the next hundred years descendants of the original pack were quite adequate for the chase. Then, probably about 1730, the red fox was introduced from England: a wilier, faster fox than the grey. For his pursuit a hound more suitable for American hunting conditions was needed and an experimental period of cross breeding began.

Local hounds were crossed with French and Irish hound imports in order to produce a dog that was racier in form and higher on leg. In time the American Foxhound was developed, a dog of great stamina, keen nosed, possessed of good voice, high intelligence and what huntsmen call the "homing instinct," this last characteristic being of great importance to the huntsman whose hounds often wandered far afield during night-time hunts.

In 1889 the first field trials for the American Foxhound were held sponsored by the Brunswick Foxhound Club. And in 1894 this club, in conjunction with the National Foxhunters Association, draughted a breed standard which was later adopted by the American Kennel Club, and remains virtually unchanged to this day.

As a show dog, the American Foxhound has made his mark, accounting for numerous Best in Show awards at championship events. First to be so honoured was Ch. Kentucky Lake Mike, bred and owned by Dr. Braxton B. Sawyer of "The Radio Pulpit" fame. The Kentucky Lake line has been a dominant force in present-day hounds having achieved great success as both bench and field trial champions.

The Canadian Kennel Club Stud Book lists first registrations for the American Foxhound between the years 1891–1892 when nineteen of the breed were recorded.

Foxhound (American)

Official Breed Standard for the Foxhound (American)

Size: Dogs should not be under 22 in. or over 25 in. (56—64 cm). Bitches should not be under 21 in. or over 24 in. (53—61 cm) measured across the back at the point of the withers, the hound standing in a natural position with his feet well under him.

Coat and Colour: A close, hard, hound coat of medium length. Any colour.

Head: *Skull* should be fairly long, slightly domed at occiput, with cranium broad and full. *Muzzle* of fair length, straight and square-cut, the stop moderately defined. *Eyes* large, set well apart, soft and hound-like, expression gentle and pleading; of a brown or hazel colour. *Ears* set on moderately low, long, reaching when drawn out nearly, if not quite, to the tip of the nose; fine in texture, fairly broad, with almost entire absence of erectile power, setting close to the head with the forward edge slightly inturning to the cheek, round at tip.

Neck: Neck rising free and light from the shoulders, strong in substance yet not loaded, of medium length. The throat clean and free from folds of skin, a slight wrinkle below the angle of the jaw, however, is allowable.

Forequarters: Shoulders sloping—clean, muscular, not heavy or loaded—conveying the idea of freedom of action with activity and strength. Forelegs straight, with fair amount of bone. Pasterns short and straight. Feet fox-like. Pad full and hard. Well-arched toes. Strong nails.

Body: Back moderately long, muscular and strong. Chest should be deep for lung space, narrower in proportion to depth than the English hound: 28 in. (71 cm) (*girth*) in a 23 in. (58 cm) hound being good. Well-sprung ribs—back ribs should extend well back—a 3 in. (8 cm) flank allowing springiness. Loins broad and slightly arched.

Hindquarters: Hips and thighs, strong and muscled, giving abundance of propelling power. Stifles strong and well let down. Hocks firm, symmetrical, and moderately bent. Feet close and firm.

Tail: Set moderately high; carried gaily, but not turned forward over the back; with slight curve; with very slight brush.

Faults: A short thin coat, or of a soft quality. A very flat skull, narrow across the top; excess of dome; eyes small, sharp, and terrier-like, or prominent and protruding; muzzle long and snipey, cut away decidedly below the eyes, or very short. Roman-nosed, or upturned, giving a dish-faced expression. Ears short, set on high, or with a tendency to rise above the point of origin. A thick, short, cloddy neck carried on a line with the top of the shoulders. Throat showing dewlap and folds of skin to a degree termed throatiness. Straight, upright shoulders, out at elbow. Knees knuckled over forward, or bent backward. Forelegs crooked. Feet long, open or spreading. Very long or swayed or roached back. Chest disproportionately wide or with lack of depth. Flat ribs. Flat, narrow loins. Cowhocks, or straight hocks. Lack of muscle and propelling power. Open feet. A long tail. Teapot curve or inclined forward from the root. Rat tail, entire absence of brush.

Scale of Points:

HEAD

Skull	5	
Ears	5	
Eyes	5	
Muzzle	5	20

BODY

Neck	5	
Chest and shoulders	15	
Back, loins, and ribs	15	35

RUNNING GEAR

Forelegs	10	
Hips, thighs, and hind legs	10	
Feet	15	35

COAT AND TAIL

Coat	5	
Tail	5	10
TOTAL	100	100

Foxhound (English)

*T*OWARDS THE END of the 17th century, fox hunting came into fashion in Britain as the sport of the landed gentry. Prior to this, stag hunting had been the favourbite chase. However, for a number of reasons the stag became quite scarce, but the fox was everywhere, hunted on foot by farmers who used a hound on a long line to scent the quarry and drive it from its hiding place. The farmers' hounds, descended from the St. Hubert hounds taken to Britain by the Normans, were amiable but slow, not at all suited to setting the pace for huntsmen mounted on horseback. A keener hound was needed.

Early proponents of the foxhunt decided this should be a hound with a keen nose, sound feet, speed, obedience, enthusiasm, a loud voice and enough stamina to run all day. Dogs showing such traits were mated and by the process of selective breeding of their progeny, hounds that were remarkably similar in character and conformation were produced. They were named according to the work for which they were bred—the foxhound.

The first kennel specializing in these hounds dates to 1696. But so popular did the concept of selective breeding become that by 1750 there were fifty foxhound kennels in England owned by large land owners and members of the aristocracy. The most notable breeder was Hugo Meynell, who has been called "the father of foxhunting." Meynell developed the pack of hounds known as "the Quorn," the ultimate in style, workmanship, and uniformity of type. He also established a system of record keeping that others copied. Thus, many of today's hounds have pedigrees that can be traced as far back as 1760.

Times have changed, and the number of packs has dwindled, but enough are still maintained to keep the sport of foxhunting alive. In Canada and in Britain the packs are owned by hunt associations. Having been bred for so many generations as pack dogs, foxhounds are happiest with their own kind. Attempts to turn them into family pets or show dogs have not met with much success. Only the occasional specimen appears in the show ring.

G.Stenhouse

Foxhound (English)

The Canadian Kennel Club Stud Book lists thirty-two Foxhounds registered in 1889. By 1892 these had been separated into two breeds, the English and the American Foxhound. Three registrations were recorded in that year.

Official Breed Standard for the Foxhound (English)

General Appearance: The symmetry of the Foxhound is of the greatest importance, and what is known as "quality" is highly regarded by all good judges.

Coat and Colour: Are not regarded as very important, so long as the latter is a good "hound colour," and the former is short, dense, hard, and glossy. Hound colours are black, tan and white, or any combination of these three, also the various "pies" compounded of white and the colour of the hare and badger, or yellow, or tan.

Head: Should be of full size, but by no means heavy. *Brow* pronounced, but not high or sharp. There should be a good length and breadth, sufficient to give in a dog hound a girth in front of the ears of fully 16 in. (41 cm). The *nose* should be long 4½ in. (11 cm) and wide, with open nostrils. The teeth must meet squarely. *Ears* set on low and lying close to the cheeks. Most English hounds are "rounded" which means that about 1½ in. (4 cm) is taken off the end of the ear.

Neck: Must be long and clean, without the slightest throatiness, not less than 10 in. (25 cm) from cranium to shoulder. It should taper nicely from shoulders to head, and the upper outline should be slightly convex.

Forequarters: Shoulders should be long and well clothed with muscle, without being heavy, especially at the points. They must be well sloped, and the true arm between the front and the elbow must be long and muscular, but free from fat or lumber. Elbows set quite straight, and neither turned in nor out are essentially required. They must be well let down by means of the long true arm above mentioned. Every Master of Foxhounds insists on legs as straight as a post, and as strong; size of bone at the ankle being especially regarded as all important. The desire for straightness had a tendency to produce knuckling-over,

which at one time was countenanced, but in recent years this
defect has been eradicated by careful breeding and intelligent
adjudication, and one sees very little of this trouble in the best
modern Foxhounds. The bone cannot be too large, and the feet
in all cases should be round and cat-like, with well-developed
knuckles and strong horn, which last is of the greatest importance.

Body: The topline of the back should be absolutely level. The
chest should girth over 31 in. (79 cm) in a 24 in. (61 cm) hound,
and the back ribs must be very deep. Back and loin must both be
very muscular, running into each other without any contraction
between them. The couples must be wide, even to raggedness.

Hindquarters: Or propellers are required to be very strong, and
as endurance is of even greater consequence than speed, straight
stifles are preferred to those much bent as in a Greyhound.

Tail: The stern should be well set on and carried gaily but not in
any case curved *over* the back like a squirrel's tail. The end should
taper to a point and there should be a fringe of hair below.

Disqualifications: *Pig-mouth (overshot) or undershot.*

Scale of Points:
Head   5
Neck   10
Shoulders   10
Chest and back ribs   10
Back and loin   15
Hindquarters   10
Elbows   5
Legs and feet   20
Colour and coat   5
Stern   5
Symmetry   5

            TOTAL   100

Greyhound

ORIGINATING IN THE Middle East, the Greyhound is the oldest pure breed in existence. Some claim its history dates back 7000 years, while the more conservative place this at 4000 years. Whichever, there are enough historical references, including the Book of Solomon, and artistic representations of the breed dating from ancient times, to make this a breed of great antiquity yet one whose form and function has altered little through the ages.

Long before the start of the Christian era the breed had journeyed to the Orient, throughout Greece and Europe and into Britain, taken there by traders or visiting noblemen to be presented to their hosts as tokens of esteem.

Everywhere the Greyhound went he became highly regarded as a sporting dog of the gazehound type (those who hunt by sight). His quarry was the stag, fox, gazelle, and hare. Also blessed with a keen nose, the breed has been used to track game including the wild boar. Strong and fleet footed, the Greyhound was an obvious choice for coursing hare when that sport commenced in England during the reign of Elizabeth I (1558–1603). In 1858 the National Coursing Club was formed and drew up a code of coursing rules. A similar organization controls coursing in the U.S.

Still popular, coursing pits the speed and skill of one dog against another in the pursuit of the hare. It is the chase, not the kill that is important. Most hares escape. Even so, there is strong public feeling that the sport should be outlawed.

Possibly more humane and vastly more popular is Greyhound racing which began in England in 1876 and has spread to Australia and the U.S. where it flourishes. An Irish-bred dog, Mick the Miller, who ran in the 1930s, holds the winning record with forty-six wins out of sixty-one starts.

While the breed's strong natural instinct to run and hunt is undeniable, it is said that as a house pet the Greyhound is superb. He also excels as a show dog having for the past several years been among the top contenders in the Hound Group both

Greyhound

in Canada and the U.S. The Canadian Kennel Club Stud Book lists thirty-three Greyhounds registered between the years 1888–1889.

Official Breed Standard for the Greyhound

Size: Dogs, 65–70 lb. (29–32 kg); bitches, 60–65 lb. (27–29 kg).

Coat and Colour: Coat short, smooth, and firm in texture. Colour immaterial.

Head: Long and narrow, fairly wide between the ears, scarcely perceptible stop, little or no development of nasal sinuses, good length of muzzle, which should be powerful without coarseness. *Teeth* very strong and even in front. *Eyes* dark, bright, intelligent, indicating spirit. *Ears* small and fine in texture, thrown back and folded, except when excited, when they are semipricked.

Neck: Long, muscular, without throatiness, slightly arched, and widening gradually into the shoulder.

Forequarters: Shoulders placed as obliquely as possible, muscular without being loaded. Forelegs perfectly straight, set well into the shoulder, neither turned in nor out, pasterns strong.

Body: Back muscular and broad, well arched. Chest deep, and as wide as consistent with speed, fairly well-sprung ribs. Loins have good depth of muscle, well cut up in the flanks.

Hindquarters: Long, very muscular and powerful, wide and well let down, well-bent stifles. Hocks well bent and rather close to ground, wide but straight fore and aft. Feet hard and close, rather more hare than cat-feet, well knuckled up with good strong claws.

Tail: Long, fine, and tapering with a slight upward curve.

Scale of Points:

General symmetry and quality	10
Head and neck	20
Chest and shoulders	20
Back	10
Quarters	20
Legs and feet	20
TOTAL	100

Harrier

*T*HIS BREED WHICH STANDS mid-way between the Beagle and the Foxhound in height is not, as some contend, a small edition of the Foxhound. While the modern Harrier carries the bloods of a variety of hounds it has been known in Britain as a distinct breed since 1130. Hare hunting on foot preceded foxhunting by several hundreds of years, and for this purpose packs of hounds were used. In the year 350 B.C. Xenophon, the Greek historian, wrote of a pack of small hounds he owned whose descriptions are similar to that of today's Harrier.

It is assumed that Greek hounds were brought to Britain at the time of the Roman invasion. There the "harriers," which was the name given to any kind of hunting dog, underwent numerous changes. Crosses to the now extinct St. Hubert and Talbot hounds, the Brachet, and French Basset have been suggested. Later when sportsmen mounted horses to ride to the hunt a faster harrier was needed. This was accomplished by crossing to small Foxhounds. It was in the latter part of the 18th century that the name "Harrier" came to identify the hound with the strong hunting instinct specifically bred to hunt the hare, although in Europe packs of Harriers had been used successfully to hunt the wolf and in Ceylon to hunt the leopard.

Like the Foxhound with its background of centuries of living with his own kind, the Harrier prefers pack life to human companionship. Packs number from forty to fifty dogs and there are still some notable examples being run in Britain. A scheme of placing puppies in private homes where they are tended through their first year of life operates in Britain. While the scheme is said to be successful, it is also reported that those who tend them are not reluctant to give up the hounds when the time comes for them to return to the pack.

Harriers were brought to this continent during colonial times and are still being bred to a limited degree. One Harrier couple competed in the first Westminster Kennel Club show held in New York in 1877. The CKC Stud Book lists one Harrier registered in the years 1891–1892.

G.STENHOUSE

Harrier

Official Breed Standard for the Harrier

General Appearance: The points of the modern Harrier are very similar to those of the English Foxhound. The Harrier, however, is smaller. They should be active, well balanced and full of strength and quality.

Size: The most popular size is 19—21 in. (48—53 cm).

Head: The head should be of a medium size with good bold forehead, and plenty of expression.

Neck: Head must be set well up on a neck of ample length, and not heavy.

Forequarters: Shoulders sloping into the muscles of the back, clean and not loaded on the withers or point. The elbow's point set well away from the ribs, running parallel with the body and not turning outwards. Good straight legs with plenty of bone running well down to the toes, but not overburdened, inclined to knuckle over very slightly but not exaggerated in the slightest degree.

Body: The back level and muscular, and not dipping behind the withers or arching over the loin. Deep, well-sprung ribs, running well back, with plenty of heart room, and a deep chest.

Hindquarters: Hind legs and hocks stand square, with a good sweep and muscular thigh to take the weight off the body. Round cat-like feet, and close toes turning inward.

Tail: Stern should be set well up, long, and well controlled.

Norwegian Elkhound

DOGS BELONGING TO that group known as the Spitz family of dogs, sometimes called Northern Dogs, have existed in the Scandinavian Peninsula since the days of primitive man. Archaeological findings at the Viste Cave at Jaeren, West Norway, include two dog skeletons dating to 4000 to 5000 B.C. which are similar in structure to the Norwegian Elkhound of today. In Viking times (800 to 1000 A.D.) these dogs were used, as they still are, to hunt bear, elk (moose), reindeer, and wolf. They were also known as guardians of the home and tenders of the flock. In time local varieties of these Spitz dogs evolved, among which is the Norwegian Elkhound, now the national dog of Norway.

Although Elkhounds had been breeding pure for centuries, it was not until 1877 that the breed was awarded official status in Norway and made its first appearance at a dog show held in Oslo that same year. According to rules laid down in the breed's country of origin, only those dogs that qualify in Norwegian Hunting Trials may be awarded the title of breed champion.

The Elkhound is a silent worker that hunts by scent to locate and either drive the quarry towards the huntsman or hold it at bay until the arrival of the huntsman who travels on foot. Customarily a pair of Elkhounds works together. Only when the quarry has been located does the Elkhound give voice to signal his position to the huntsman. While not as swift as some hunting breeds the Elkhound is capable of great endurance and able to work over difficult terrain. The breed has also been used to pull sleds and some have been trained for mountain rescue work. The Elkhound is also known as an efficient vermin catcher and has been used successfully for hunting smaller game, both fur and feather.

The Norwegian Elkhound was imported into England before World War I and after the formation of a specialty breed club gained official status in Britain in 1923. In Canada the first registration took place in 1928 with one Norwegian Elkhound being recorded in The Canadian Kennel Club Stud Book.

G.STENHOUSE

Norwegian Elkhound

Official Breed Standard for the Norwegian Elkhound

General Appearance: The Norwegian Elkhound is a typical northern dog, of medium size, with a compact, proportionately short body, with a thick and rich, but not bristling, grey coat, with prick ears, and with a tail that is curled and carried over the back.

Temperament: His temperament is bold and energetic.

Size: Dogs, about 20½ in. (52 cm) at the shoulder; bitches, about 18 in. (46 cm).

Coat and Colour: Coat thick, rich and hard, but rather smooth lying. On head and front of legs, short and even; longest on neck and chest, on buttocks, on hindside of forelegs and on underside of tail. It is made of longer and harder covering hairs, dark at the tips, and of a light, soft, woolly undercoat. Colour grey, with black tips to the long covering hairs; somewhat lighter on chest, stomach, legs, underside of tail, and around anus. The colour may be lighter or darker, with a slight shading towards yellow; but a pronounced variation from the grey colour disqualifies. Too dark or too light individuals should be avoided; also, yellow markings or uneven colouring. There should be no pronounced white markings.

Head: "Dry" (without any loose skin), broad at the ears; the forehead and back of the head only slightly arched; the stop not large, yet clearly defined. The *muzzle* is of medium length, thickest at the base and seen from above or from the side tapers evenly without being pointed. The bridge of the nose is straight; the lips are tightly closed. *Eyes* not protruding, brown in colour, preferably dark, lively, with fearless energetic expression. *Ears* set high, firm and erect, are higher than they are wide at the base, pointed (not rounded) and very mobile. When the dog is listening, the orifices are turned forward.

Neck: Of medium length, "dry" (without any loose skin), strong, and well set up.

Forequarters: Legs firm, straight, and strong; elbows closely set on.

Body: Powerful, *compact*, and short, with broad deep chest, well-sprung ribs, straight back, well-developed loins, and stomach very little drawn up.

Hindquarters: Hind legs with little angulation at knees and hocks. Seen from behind, they are straight. Feet comparatively small, somewhat oblong, with tightly closed toes, not turned out. There should be no dewclaws on hind legs.

Tail: Set high, short, thickly and closely haired, but without brush; tightly curled, not carried too much to one side.

Disqualification: *Pronounced variation from grey colour.*

Otterhound

THE OTTERHOUND IS A WATER DOG with strongly webbed feet and, it is claimed, the ability to swim for hours without tiring. The breed has been known in Britain since before the time of King John (1212), where it was used in packs to hunt out and kill the otter that robbed the streams and rivers of their fish.

While the breed's ancestry is uncertain it is generally believed that the Bloodhound, the Southern Harrier and various griffon breeds of continental origin played important roles. Over the centuries outcrosses have been used, always with discretion, so as not to lose the breed's scenting power and love of the water.

Prior to World War I, otter hunting in Britain was at its peak of popularity and still persisted, to some extent, between World Wars. But as pollution took over the otter's water habitat the fish grew scarce, and the otter even scarcer. In 1978 the die was cast. By law in England the otter became a protected species, thus otter hunting had to be abandoned. Many Otterhounds were destroyed but the two remaining pure-bred packs, numbering about 100 hounds, the Kendal and the Dumfriesshire, determined to keep the breed alive. The Otterhound Club of Great Britain was formed and the first official breed standard for the Otterhound in Britain was draughted. To the displeasure of those British diehards who insisted that the Otterhound was a pack and kennel dog and should remain so, the breed has joined the ranks of the show dog. When the Otterhound made its championship show debut at Crufts', in London in 1979, Kendal Nimrod was named Reserve Winner of the Hound Group.

The breed's history is quite different on this continent. While the Otterhound has never been used for pack hunting of the otter it has been used to hunt mink, raccoon, mountain lion, and bear. Brought over in 1900 and officially recognized by the American Kennel Club shortly afterwards, the breed was first exhibited in 1907. While it has never achieved great popularity and is only seen in small numbers at even the largest championship events, the Otterhound has accounted for a number of Best in Show wins in both Canada and the United States.

Otterhound

Among its other accomplishments, the Otterhound is generally considered to be one of the progenitors of the Airedale Terrier.

Official Breed Standard for the Otterhound

General Appearance: In general appearance—always excepting the coat—the Otterhound much resembles the Bloodhound; he should be perfect in symmetry, strongly built, hard and enduring, with unfailing powers of scent, and a natural antipathy to the game he is bred to pursue.

Coat and Colour: The colours are generally grizzle or sandy, with black and tan more or less clearly defined.

Head: The head should be large, broader in proportion than the Bloodhound's, the forehead high, the *muzzle* a fair length and the nostrils wide. The *ears* are long, thin and pendulous, fringed with hair.

Neck: The neck is not naturally long, and looks shorter than it really is from the abundance of hair on it.

Forequarters: The shoulders should slope well, the legs be straight and the feet a good size, but compact.

Body: The back is strong and wide, the ribs, and particularly the back ribs, well let down.

Hindquarters: The thighs should be big and firm, and the hocks well let down.

Tail: The stern is well and thickly covered with hair and carried well up but not curled.

Scale of Points:

Skull	10
Jaws	10
Eyes	5
Ears	10
Chest and shoulders	15
Body and loin	15
Legs and feet	10
Coat	10
Stern	5
Symmetry and strength	10
TOTAL	100

Pharaoh Hound

*T*HE EARLIEST DOG RELIC in existence dating from the Stone Age (prior to 3000 B.C.) is a disc discovered on the banks of the Nile which depicts two hounds at chase. The dogs are similar to the breed we now call the Pharaoh Hound, a member of the oldest known group of dogs, the greyhounds.

Originating in Egypt, the breed's likeness appears on tomb carvings and it is easy to imagine that a Pharaoh Hound served as the model for the sculpture of the dog-god Anubis of Egyptian mythology whose duty was to accompany the souls of the departed into the afterworld. The Phoenicians, who were maritime traders, brought these hounds to the Mediterranean Islands of Malta and Gozo, where they were known as the *Kelb-tal Fewek*, or rabbit dogs. Isolated from the mainland the dogs bred true for almost 2000 years before being introduced to other parts of the world.

The breed has a strong hunting instinct and has been used successfully to hunt hare and rabbit as well as feathered game. The Pharaoh Hound is almost unique among the breeds classified as "gazehounds" (those that hunt by sight) in that it hunts by scent as well as sight.

Although first imported into Britain in the 1920s, it was not until the breed was reintroduced in the early 1960s that it received any recognition. It was because of its resemblance to the hounds of antiquity that the breed was given its present name. In 1968 a specialty club was organized to promote the Pharaoh's interests and thereafter official breed status was granted by The Kennel Club (England).

On this continent the Pharaoh Hound is still comparatively new. In 1979 because there was sufficient interest in the breed The Canadian Kennel Club added the Pharaoh Hound to its roster of recognized breeds. So far, in the United States it has not achieved similar status but has been admitted into the Miscellaneous Class and is exhibited occasionally in this class, in obedience classes, and at unofficial "rare breed" dog events.

Pharaoh Hound

Official Breed Standard for the Pharaoh Hound

Origin and Purpose: The Pharaoh Hound is of great antiquity, bearing a striking resemblance to the hounds with large, erect ears depicted in the sculptured delineations in the Egyptian temples from before 4000 B.C. A keen hunter, the Pharaoh Hound hunts by scent and sight, as well as using its large ears to a marked degree when working close.

General Appearance: The Pharaoh Hound is medium sized, of noble bearing, with clean-cut lines. Graceful yet powerful. Very fast with free easy movement.

Temperament: An intelligent, friendly, affectionate, and playful breed.

Size: Males 22−25 in. (55−63 cm). Females 21−24 in. (53−61 cm). Over-all balance must be maintained.

Coat and Colour: Short and glossy, ranging from fine and close to slightly harsh, with no feathering. Tan, rich tan with white markings permitted as follows:
a) White tip on tail strongly desired.
b) White on chest (called the "star").
c) White on toes.
d) Slim white blaze on centre line of face.
Flecking, or white other than above undesirable.

Head: *Skull:* long, lean, and well chiselled. *Foreface:* slightly longer than skull. Only slight stop. Top of skull parallel with foreface, the whole head representing a blunt wedge when viewed in profile and from above. *Nose:* flesh-coloured only, blending with the coat. *Mouth:* powerful jaws with strong teeth. Scissors bite. *Eyes:* amber colour, blending with the coat; oval, moderately deep set, with keen intelligent expression. *Ears:* medium high set; carried erect when alert, but very mobile; broad at base, fine and large.

Neck: Long, lean muscular and slightly arched. Clean throat line.

Forequarters: Shoulders: strong, long, and well laid back. Forelegs: straight and parallel. Elbows well tucked in. Pasterns strong. Feet: strong, well knuckled and firm, turning neither in nor out. Paws well padded. Dewclaws may be removed.

Body: Length of body from breast to haunch bone slightly longer than height at withers. Topline: lithe and almost straight. Slight slope down from croup to root of tail. Chest: deep brisket extending down to point of elbow. Ribs well sprung. Abdomen: moderate tuck-up.

Hindquarters: Strong and muscular. Limbs parallel when viewed from behind. Thigh: well developed second thigh. Stifle: moderate bend. Hocks: well let down.

Tail: Medium set, fairly thick at the base and tapering (whiplike), reaching just below the point of hock in repose. Carried high and curved when the dog is in action. The tail should not be tucked between the legs. A screw tail is a fault.

Gait: Free and flowing with the head held fairly high, the dog should cover the ground well without any apparent effort. The legs and feet should move in line with the body. Any tendency to throw the feet sideways, or a high stepping "hackney" action is a fault.

Faults: The foregoing description is that of the ideal Pharaoh Hound. Accident blemishes should not be considered faults. Any deviation from the above described dog must be penalized to the extent of the deviation. Male animals should have two apparently normal testicles fully descended into the scrotum.

Rhodesian Ridgeback

THIS IS THE ONLY breed of dog originating in South Africa to have gained official status. Unique to the Rhodesian Ridgeback is the ridge of hair growing forward on its spine and its natural antagonism for and courage to face the "king of beasts," the African lion.

It is thought that the first ridged dogs were probably related to the Saluki and Pharaoh Hound and were taken by the Hottentot tribe, or "Khoikoi" (the tribal name preferred by anthropologists), on their thousand-year-long migration to Southern Africa. First description of the ridged dogs appears in writings which describe conditions in Southern Africa prior to 1505. It was noted that these dogs were fiercely loyal to their masters, brave and hardy.

Undoubtedly some interbreeding with dogs imported from the continent occurred, but it was not until the late 1870s that the ridged dogs assumed any prominence. At that time, near Bulawayo (now Zimbabwe), a few of the dogs were obtained by Cornelius van Rooyen, a South African who hunted big game for a living. For thirty-five years he refined his pack of "lion dogs" or "van Rooyen" dogs as they were first known. To the speed of the basic greyhound blood in his first dogs he added the Pointer for scenting ability, collie, terrier and Great Dane to give his dogs endurance, agility, biting power and a short, wheaten-coloured coat. His dogs retained the ridge. They also retained the ability to protect wagon teams of oxen from lions at night and to track and bay lions and other big game by day, either to be shot or captured alive for zoos.

After van Rooyen's death a group of fanciers in the Bulawayo area met together in 1922 to standardize the breed. A few days after this meeting a breed standard was draughted, a specialty club formed and official breed recognition sought for the Rhodesian Lion Dog from the South African Kennel Club. Because of the rather fierce connotation the name was later changed to Rhodesian Ridgeback.

G.STENHOUSE

Rhodesian Ridgeback

During the 1950s the breed achieved official status in Britain and the United States. First Canadian registrations were recorded in 1949.

Official Breed Standard for the Rhodesian Ridgeback

General Appearance: The Ridgeback should represent a strong muscular and active dog, symmetrical in outline, and capable of great endurance with a fair amount of speed.

The peculiarity of this breed is the ridge on the back, which is formed by the hair growing in the opposite direction to the rest of the coat. The ridge must be regarded as the escutcheon of the breed. The ridge should be clearly defined, tapering and symmetrical. It should start immediately behind the shoulders and continue up to a point between the prominence of the hips (haunch bones), and should contain two identical crowns opposite each other. The lower edges of the crown should not extend further down the ridge than one-third of the ridge.

Size: A mature Ridgeback should be a handsome, upstanding dog; dogs should be of a height of 25−27 in. (63−69 cm), and bitches 24−26 in. (61−66 cm). Minimum bench standard: dogs 25 in. (63 cm), bitches 24 in. (61 cm).
Weight (desirable): dogs, 75 lb. (34 kg); bitches, 65 lb. (29 kg).

Coat and Colour: The coat should be short and dense, sleek and glossy in appearance, but neither woolly nor silky. Colour light wheaten to red wheaten. A little white on the chest and toes permissible but excessive white here and on the belly and above paws is undesirable.

Head: The head should be of a fair length, and *skull* flat and rather broad between the ears and should be free from wrinkles when in repose. The stop should be reasonably well defined, and not in one straight line from the nose to the occiput bone, as required in a Bull Terrier. The *muzzle* should be long, deep, and powerful; *jaws* level and strong with well-developed teeth, especially the canines or holders. The lips clean, closely fitting the jaws. The *nose* should be black, or brown, in keeping with the colour of the eyes. No other coloured nose is permissible. A black nose should be accompanied by dark eyes, a brown nose by amber eyes. The *eyes* should be moderately well apart, and should be round, bright, and sparkling, with intelligent expression, their colour harmonizing with the colour of the nose. The *ears* should be set rather high, of medium size, rather wide at the base, and tapering to a rounded point. They should be carried close to the head.

Neck: The neck should be fairly strong and free from throatiness.

Forequarters: The shoulder should be sloping, clean, and muscular, denoting speed. The forelegs should be perfectly straight, strong and heavy in bone; elbows close to the body. The feet should be compact, with well-arched toes, round, tough, elastic pads, protected by hair between the toes and pads.

Body: The chest should not be too wide, but very deep and capacious; ribs moderately well sprung, never rounded like barrel hoops (which would indicate want of speed), the back powerful, and loins strong, muscular and slightly arched.

Hindquarters: In the hind legs the muscles should be clean, well defined, and hocks well down.

Tail: The tail should be strong at the insertion, and generally tapering towards the end, free from coarseness. It should not be inserted too high or too low, and should be carried with a slight curve upwards, never curled.

Scale of Points:

Ridge   20
Head   15
Neck and shoulders   10
Body, back, chest, loins   10
Legs and feet   15
Coat   5
Tail   5
Size, symmetry, general appearance   20

       TOTAL   100

Saluki

ANCIENT REPRESENTATIONS in art confirm that the Saluki is the oldest of breeds with a heritage dating back 9000 years. The breed is thought to have originated in Syria, from which it spread to Egypt, Persia, India, and Afghanistan and is undoubtedly a close relative of another coursing hound, the Afghan.

The Saluki was, and still is, held in high esteem by the sheikhs who used the swift desert hound in the sport of falconry, to course the fox, the hare and the fleet-footed gazelle. Over the years it has been called many names including "Eastern Greyhound," "Persian Greyhound," "Arabian Gazelle Hound," and "Slughi." The present name is a general mideast word meaning "running hound," and is thought to have been taken either from the name of an Arabian town "Saluk" which was noted for its dogs, or from the Syrian town Seleukia.

The Saluki was never sold but given as a tribute gift to those the sheikhs considered worthy recipients. And it was probably in exchange for favours that the dogs were presented to the Crusaders (1095–1271) who introduced the breed to Europe. There the breed became a symbol of royalty and as such has been depicted in several works of art. One, a Tintoretto painting, circa 1550, "Washing of Feet," now in the Art Gallery of Ontario, shows a Saluki in the foreground. Catherine the Great, the Russian empress, had a favourite hound of definite Saluki-type that has been immortalized in several works of art and there is evidence that the breed was known in China in the mid-15th century.

With all this globe-trotting the desert hound did not arrive in Britain until 1895 when two puppies that had been presented to a British army officer were given to the Hon. Florence Amherst. Although the dogs created great interest when they were first shown, the Saluki did not become popular until after the first World War. In 1920 foundation breeding stock came from Egypt and Mesopotamia and in 1923 the Saluki was granted official breed status by The Kennel Club (England). At about the same time breeding stock came to the United States from England,

smooth-coated

G.STENHOUSE

Saluki

Egypt, Arabia, and Persia. In 1927 the breed was officially recognized by the American Kennel Club and by The Canadian Kennel Club in 1938.

Official Breed Standard for the Saluki

Origin and Purpose: The Saluki is one of the oldest known breeds of dogs. It has existed, virtually unchanged, for many thousands of years. It was originally bred by the Arab tribesmen for bringing down game, and was considered a sacred gift of God by the tribesmen. In Arabic, an ordinary dog is called *kelb* while the Saluki is *El Hor,* The Noble One.

General Appearance: The whole appearance of this breed should give an impression of grace and symmetry and of great speed and endurance coupled with strength and activity to enable it to kill gazelle or other quarry over deep sand or rocky mountains. The expression should be dignified and gentle with deep, faithful, far-seeing eyes.

Size: Dogs should average in height from 23–28 in. (58–71 cm), and bitches may be considerably smaller, this being very typical of the breed.

Coat: Smooth and of a soft silky texture, slight feather on the legs, feather at the back of the thighs and sometimes with slight woolly feather on the thigh and shoulder.

Colour: White, cream, fawn, golden, red, grizzle, and tan tricolour (white, black and tan), black and tan, or any of the aforementioned colours and white.

Head: Long and narrow, *skull* moderately wide between the ears, not domed, stop not pronounced, the whole showing great quality. *Nose* black or liver; *teeth* strong and level; *eyes* dark to hazel and bright; large and oval, but not prominent; *ears* long and covered with long silky hair hanging close to the skull and mobile.

Neck: Long, supple, and well muscled.

Forequarters: Shoulders sloping and set well back, well mus-cled without being coarse. Forelegs straight and long from the elbow to the knee.

Loin and Back: Back fairly broad, muscles slightly arched over loin. Chest deep and moderately narrow.

Hindquarters: Strong, hip bones set well apart and stifle moderately bent, hocks low to the ground, showing galloping and jumping power.

Feet: Of moderate length, toes long and well arched, not splayed out, but at the same time not cat-footed; the whole being strong and supple and well feathered between the toes.

Tail: Long, set on low and carried naturally in a curve, well feathered on the underside with long silky hair, not bushy.

The Smooth Variety: In this variety the points should be the same with the exception of the coat, which has no feathering.

Whippet

*T*HERE SEEMS TO BE NO DOUBT that the Whippet and the Greyhound derive from the same ancient stock.

The breed chiefly responsible is thought to have been the Pharaoh Hound which was brought to Britain at the time of the Roman Invasion in 55 B.C. The smaller breed was developed to course rabbit while hare was the quarry of the Greyhound.

For a certainty the Whippet was bred to its present form in Britain, but exactly how this was accomplished remains a matter of conjecture. Some authorities claim the breed represents a cross between the Italian Greyhound and the terrier, while others maintain that small greyhounds were crossed with various terrier breeds. Thus the Whippet inherited his gameness from the terriers, and his conformation and speed from the Greyhound. There seems to be no firm evidence to prove either theory, but, Todd, in his text *The Popular Whippet*, claims that if terrier blood had been introduced there must inevitably be some throwbacks exhibiting long, coarse-textured terrier coats. To his knowledge this has not occurred. He concludes simply: "the Whippet is a small dog of great antiquity of the Greyhound type" and leaves it at that. And there is ample evidence to support this. Works of art, sculptures, and paintings of the fourteenth century depict small dogs of the make and shape of the Whippet as we know the breed today.

His speed is legendary (200 yards in twelve seconds is not uncommon) and Whippet racing became a popular sport in the north of England particularly among the working class. This earned for him the name "the poor man's racehorse." In the early days of Whippet racing the dogs were slipped to chase live rabbits. However, when this practice was outlawed as cruel, lure or "rag racing" became the substitute. Whippet racing was introduced to America by the Lancashire textile workers who came to work in the New England mills early this century. Since then it has grown in popularity both on this continent and abroad.

The Whippet's greatest charm is the pleasure he gives as family pet and companion. Elegant, neat and an "easy keeper,"

Whippet

English breeders find it difficult to keep up with the demand for puppies. Happily the same situation seems to be developing on this continent. Our version is slightly taller than the British counterpart because of differences in height specified in the breed standards. In Canada and the U.S. heights range from nineteen to twenty-two inches for males, eighteen to twenty-one inches for females, with disqualifications above or below these limits in the U.S. In Britain the ideal height for dogs is eighteen and one-half inches, and one inch less for females.

Official Breed Standard for the Whippet

General Appearance: The Whippet should be a dog of moderate size, very alert, that can cover a maximum of distance with a minimum of lost motion, a true sporting hound. Should be put down in hard condition but with no suggestion of being muscle-bound.

Size: Ideal height for dogs 19−22 in. (48−56 cm); for bitches, 18−21 in. (46−53 cm). These are not intended to be definite limits, only approximate.

Coat and Colour: Coat close, smooth, and firm in texture. Colour immaterial.

Head: Long and lean, fairly wide between the ears, scarcely perceptible stop, good length of *muzzle* which should be powerful without being coarse. Nose entirely black. Teeth white, strong and even. Teeth of upper jaw should fit closely over the lower. *Eyes* large, intelligent, round in shape and dark hazel in colour, must be at least as dark as the coat colour. Expression should be keen and alert. A sulky expression and lack of alertness to be considered most undesirable. *Ears* small, fine in texture, thrown back and folded. Semipricked when at attention.

Neck: Long and muscular, well arched and with no suggestion of throatiness, widening gradually into the shoulders. Must not have any tendency to an "ewe" neck.

Forequarters: Shoulders long, well laid back with long, flat muscles. Forelegs straight and rather long, held in line with the shoulders and *not* set under the body so as to make a forechest.

Elbows should turn neither in nor out and move freely with the point of the shoulder. Fair amount of bone, which should carry right down to the feet. Pasterns strong.

Body: Back strong and powerful, rather long with a good, natural arch over the loin creating a definite tuck-up of the underline but covering a lot of ground. Brisket very deep and strong, reaching as nearly as possible to the point of the elbow. Ribs well sprung but with no suggestion of barrel shape. Should fill in the space between the forelegs so that there is no appearance of a hollow between them.

Hindquarters: Long and powerful, stifles well bent, hocks well let down and close to the ground. Thighs broad and muscular, the muscles should be long and flat. A steep croup is most undesirable. Feet must be well formed with strong, thick pads and well-knuckled-up paws.

Tail: Long and tapering, should reach to a hip bone when drawn through between the hind legs. Must not be carried higher than the top of the back when moving.

Gait: Low, free moving and smooth, as long as is commensurate with the size of the dog.

Faults: Light yellow or oblique eyes should be strictly penalized. Gay ears are incorrect and should be severely penalized. Loaded shoulders are a *very* serious fault. A thin, flat, open foot is a serious fault. A short, mincing gait with high knee action should be severely penalized.

Disqualification: *An undershot mouth shall disqualify.*

Wolfhound (Irish)

*F*ROM PRE-CHRISTIAN TIMES a large, rough-coated dog of greyhound form called the *cu* has been known in Ireland. The word *cu* denotes outstanding qualities and it is certain this canine giant was held in high esteem. Irish legends abound with stories of the great dog's prowess as a hunter of Irish elk, wild boar, and the wolf. He was a ferocious dog in battle but gentle and trustworthy as guardian of hearth and home.

By law, ownership of the *cu* was restricted to kings, nobles, and poets. The dog's collar was often fashioned in precious metals. And as a gesture of esteem a *cu* would be presented as a gift to visiting noblemen.

In writings from earliest times descriptions of the *cu* are identical to the Irish Wolfhound of today. And although the point at one time was the subject of heated debate, all authorities now agree that the *cu* is the present-day Irish Wolfhound.

It was said that when the last wolf left Ireland the Irish Wolfdog vanished with it; but early in the 19th century Captain G.A. Graham, a Scottish officer in the British army, disputed this. He contended that although the breed had deteriorated in bone and substance, it was still in existence. He made it his life's avocation to locate whatever strains were still being bred and restore the national dog of Ireland to its former magnificence. Captain Graham obtained stock which he felt to be directly descended from the ancient hounds, although diminished in stature. Other individuals attempting restoration experimented with crosses to the Great Dane and the Scottish Deerhound.

While early efforts were not entirely successful, by the end of the 19th century both size and type had been restored. The world's largest breed of dog, the Irish Wolfhound, had been returned to the dog scene and has been a fixture ever since. The Canadian Kennel Club Stud Book lists one Irish Wolfhound registered in the years 1888–1889 with the next registration not occurring until 1909.

G.STENHOUSE

Wolfhound (Irish)

Official Breed Standard for the Wolfhound (Irish)

General Appearance: Of great size and commanding appearance, the Irish Wolfhound is remarkable in combining power and swiftness with keen sight.

The largest and tallest of the galloping hounds, in general he is a rough coated, Greyhound-like breed; very muscular, strong though gracefully built; movements easy and active; head and neck carried high, the tail carried with an upward sweep with a slight curve towards the extremity.

Size: The minimum height and weight of dogs should be 32 in. (81 cm) and 120 lb. (54 kg); of bitches 30 in. (76 cm) and 105 lb. (48 kg), these to apply only to hounds over 18 months of age. Anything below this should be debarred from competition. Great size, including height at shoulder and proportionate length of body, is the desideratum to be aimed at, and it is desired to firmly establish a race that shall average from 32–34 in. (81–86 cm) in dogs, showing the requisite power, activity, courage, and symmetry.

Coat and Colour: Hair rough and hard on body, legs and head; especially wiry and long over eyes and underjaw. The recognized colours are grey, brindle, red, black, pure white, fawn, or any other colour that appears in the Deerhound.

Head: Long, the frontal bones of the forehead very slightly raised and very little indentation between the eyes. *Skull* not too broad. *Muzzle* long and moderately pointed. *Ears* small and Greyhound-like in carriage.

Neck: Rather long, very strong and muscular, well arched, without dewlap or goose skin about the throat.

Forequarters: Shoulders muscular, giving breadth of chest, set sloping. Elbows well under, neither turned inwards nor outwards. Forearm muscular, and the whole leg strong and quite straight.

Body: Back rather long than short. Chest very deep. Breast wide. Loins arched. Belly well drawn up.

Hindquarters: Muscular thighs and second thigh long and strong as in the Greyhound, and hocks well let down and turning neither in nor out. Feet moderately large and round, neither turned inwards nor outwards. Toes well arched and closed. Nails very strong and curved.

Tail: Long and slightly curved, of moderate thickness, and well covered with hair.

Faults: Too light or heavy a head, too highly arched frontal bone; large ears and hanging flat to the face; short neck; full dewlap; too narrow or too broad a chest; sunken or hollow or quite straight back; bent forelegs; overbent fetlocks; twisted feet; spreading toes, too curly a tail; weak hindquarters and a general want of muscle; too short in body. Lips or nose liver-coloured or lacking pigmentation.

List of Points in Order of Merit:
1. Typical—The Irish Wolfhound is a rough-coated Greyhound-like breed, the tallest of the coursing hounds and remarkable in combining power and swiftness.
2. Great size and commanding appearance.
3. Movements—easy and active.
4. Head—long and level, carried high.
5. Forelegs—heavily boned, quite straight; elbows well set under.
6. Thighs—long and muscular; second thighs, well muscled, stifles nicely bent.
7. Coat—rough and hard, specially wiry and long over eyes and under jaw.
8. Body—long, well ribbed up, with ribs well sprung, and great breadth across hips.
9. Loins—arched, belly well drawn up.
10. Ears—small, with Greyhound-like carriage.
11. Feet—moderately large and round; toes, close, well arched.
12. Neck—long, well arched and very strong.
13. Chest—very deep, moderately broad.
14. Shoulders—muscular, set sloping.
15. Tail—long and slightly curved.
16. Eyes—dark.

NOTE: The above in no way alters the "Standard of Excellence" which must in all cases be rigidly adhered to; they simply give the various points in order of merit. If in any case they appear at variance with Standard of Excellence, it is the latter which is correct.

GROUP III: WORKING DOGS

Akita

THREE BREEDS BELONGING TO the Spitz or Northern family of dogs are native to the Japanese Islands. In outline they resemble the Chow Chow of China except for their coats, which are short to medium-long haired. In order of size the Shiba is the smallest; the Sanshu is the medium sized, and the largest is the Shishu Inu or Akita Inu, the latter being the best known of the Japanese dogs and the only one of the three recognized as a distinct breed in Canada.

The Akita is said to have originated in the polar regions, and that it has a history dating back 300 years. It is named for the Akita Prefecture, the northernmost province of Honshu Island, and was used originally for hunting large game such as the Japanese black bear, wild boar, and deer. The Akita has a dense weather-resistant coat and strong, webbed feet enabling it to be a powerful swimmer.

At one time ownership of the strong hunting dog was restricted to royalty and the nobility. But in later years the Akita has become best known as a police and guard dog as well as trusted family pet. In Japan it is now classified along with the guard and police dog breeds, not as a hunting breed. Highly esteemed in its country of origin, the Akita is now regarded as one of Japan's natural treasures and has been named that country's national dog.

It is thought that the first Akita came to this continent in 1937 imported by Helen Keller, renowned American author and lecturer. But it was not until after the close of World War II that the breed began arriving in numbers, brought home by members of the American occupation troops who served in Japan.

In time, sufficient continuing interest in the Akita resulted in its acceptance by the American Kennel Club in the Miscellaneous Class, and in 1973 it was elevated to official breed status. Interest spread to Canada, and in 1975 the Akita was added to the list of breeds officially recognized by The Canadian Kennel Club.

G.STENHOUSE

Akita

Official Breed Standard for the Akita

Origin and Purpose: The Akita, whose history dates back some 300 years, derives its name from the Prefecture of Akita, in northern Japan. At one time, in the early days of the breed, Akitas were considered a national treasure and only nobles could own one. In 1931, this beautiful dog was proclaimed a natural monument by the Japanese Ministry of Education, and the government took all necessary steps to preserve the breed. The Akita is primarily a working dog and has been used for guard work, a guide for the blind, a protector of children and home, a hunting companion and sled work.

General Appearance: Large, powerful, alert, with much substance and heavy bone, the broad head, forming a blunt triangle, with deep muzzle, small eyes and erect ears carried forward in line with back of neck, is characteristic of the breed. The large, curled tail, balancing the broad head, is also a characteristic of the breed.

Temperament: Alert and responsive, dignified and reserved but courageous, friendly towards people and often aggressive towards other dogs. The Akita barks infrequently and then only as a warning signal. The demeanour suggests activity and agility.

Size: Height—dogs 26 in. (66 cm) or more at the shoulder, bitches 24 in. (61 cm) or more at the shoulder. The male's body length to height ratio is approximately 10:9 and the female's slightly greater. The dog is powerfully built, with bone and substance proportionate to height.

Coat and Colour: Double-coated. Undercoat soft and very dense and shorter than outer coat. Outer coat straight, harsh and standing somewhat off body. Hair on head, legs and ears short. Length of hair at withers and rump approximately two inches, which is slightly longer than the rest of body except tail, where coat is longest and most profuse. Any colour, brindle, white (no mask) or pinto. Colours are brilliant and clear and markings are well balanced, with or without mask or blaze. Pinto has a white background with large, evenly-placed patches covering head and more than one-third of body. Undercoat may be a different colour from outer coat. The white Akita should have pigmented eyes, dark nose and lips.

Head: *Skull* massive but in balance with the body, tending to be flat on top with the rest of the head forming a blunt triangle when viewed from top, free from excessive wrinkle when at ease, median fissure clearly visible, and stop well defined. *Muzzle* broad and full, distance from nose to stop is the distance from stop to occiput as two is to three. *Nose* broad and black, liver nose permitted on light Akitas but black always preferred. *Mouth* clean, powerful jaws, lips black and heavy but not pendulous, tongue pink, teeth strong with scissors bite preferred but level bite acceptable. *Eyes* dark brown, small, deep set and triangular in shape, eye rims black and tight. *Ears:* the ears of the Akita are characteristic of the breed. They are strongly erect and small in relation to rest of head. If ear is folded forward for measuring length, tip will touch upper eye rim. Ears are triangular, slightly rounded at tip, wide at base, set wide on head but not too low, and carried slightly forward over eyes in line with back of neck.

Neck: The neck is thick and muscular; comparatively short, widening gradually towards shoulders. A pronounced crest blends in with base of skull.

Forequarters: Shoulders strong and powerful with moderate layback. Upper arm heavy boned and straight as viewed from front. Elbows neither turning in nor out. Lower arm heavy boned and straight as viewed from front. Dewclaws generally not removed. Pasterns: angle of pastern 15 degrees from vertical. Feet: cat feet, well knuckled up with thick pads. Feet straight ahead.

Body: Topline: level back. Chest is wide and deep; depth of chest is one-half height of dog at shoulder. Ribs well sprung, brisket well developed. Loin firmly muscled and moderate tuck-up. Croup slightly rounded. Abdomen is drawn up and tucked up.

Hindquarters: Hipbone: width, muscular development and bone comparable to forequarters. Upper thigh well developed and powerful. Lower thigh should be comparable to forequarters. Dewclaws permissible. Hocks less angular than many breeds 145 to 160 degrees, turning neither in nor out. Stifle Bend: stifle is moderately bent. Feet same as front.

Tail: Large and full, set high and carried over back or against flank in a three-quarter, full or double curl, always dipping to or below level of back. On a three-quarter curl, tip drops well down flank. Root large and strong. Tail reaches hock when let down. Hair coarse, straight and full, with no appearance of a plume.

Gait: Brisk and powerful with strides of moderate length. Back remains strong, firm and level. Rear legs move in line with front legs.

Faults:
1. Narrow or snipey head.
2. Round or light eyes.
3. Excessive dewlap.
4. Light bone, rangy body.
5. Elbows in or out, loose shoulders.
6. Indication of ruff or feathering of coat.
7. Coarseness in bitches.
8. Over-refinement in males.

Disqualifications:
1. *Monorchids or Cryptorchids.*
2. *Viciousness, instability.*
3. *Excessively overshot or undershot.*
4. *Albinos.*
5. *Pink noses, eyelids, or rims, butterfly nose.*
6. *Uncurled tail.*
7. *Drop or broken ears.*
8. *Deafness.*
9. *Excessive entropion or ectropion.*
10. *Altering of coat or general appearance by scissoring or clipping.*

Scale of Points:

General appearance	20
Characteristic	10
Head	20
Back, fore and hindquarters	10
Chest and abdomen	10
Members, feet and soles	10
Coat	10
Gait, pace	10
TOTAL	100

Alaskan Malamute

CONSIDERED TO BE one of the five breeds of dog native to the Western Hemisphere, the Alaskan Malamute was first discovered by Russian explorers in an area around the mouth of the Yukon River. There it was being bred as a dog-of-all-work by an Inuit tribe called Mahlemut or Malemuit, skilled hunters and fishermen who are reported to have taken great care of their dogs, as well they might. These powerful members of the Spitz family of dogs were used to guard herds of caribou, track quarry such as the polar bear, moose, and wolf, and help in the attack. Then they hauled the meat, by sled during the winter and as pack dogs in the summer months. Malamutes have been known to transport packs weighing fifty pounds a distance of twenty miles per day. In addition they have an incredible sense of direction, being able to follow a track during a blinding snowstorm and withstand the hard Arctic winter with little food. In camp the Malamutes served as beloved family pets and guard dogs who helped keep the Eskimo children warm through long nights of bitter cold.

The breed will forever be linked with the history and development of Canada. Early English and French explorers used sleds drawn by teams of Malamutes in their search for a Northwest passage to the Orient. They accompanied explorers on polar expeditions and during both World Wars were used to transport munitions and supplies and evacuate the wounded.

During the 1920s, when sled dog racing came into prominence as a winter sport, Malamutes were crossed with lighter-boned "huskies," a general term given to sled dogs. The cross was made to give more stamina to the racing dogs and, had it not been for the efforts of a few breeders who were determined to preserve the Alaskan Malamute as a distinct breed, the purebred "Mal" could have become extinct.

Despite rumours to the contrary, the Alaskan Malamute adapted well to more temperate climates than those found in the Yukon and Alaska and today ranks high in popularity as a show dog in both Canada and the United States.

Alaskan Malamute

Official Breed Standard for the Alaskan Malamute

General Appearance: The Alaskan Malamute is a powerful and substantially built dog with deep chest and strong, compact body, not too short coupled, with a thick, coarse guard coat of sufficient length to protect a dense, woolly undercoat, from 1–2 in. (3–5 cm) in depth when dog is in full coat. Stands well over pads, and this stance gives the appearance of much activity, showing interest and curiosity. The head is broad, ears wedge-shaped and erect when alerted. The muzzle is bulky with only slight diminishing in width and depth from root to nose, not pointed or long, but not stubby. The Malamute moves with a proud carriage, head erect and eyes alert. Face markings are a distinguishing feature. These consist of either cap over head and rest of face solid colour, usually greyish white, or face marked with the appearance of a mask. Combination of cap and mask are not unusual. The tail is plumed and carried over the back, not like a fox brush, or tightly curled, more like a plume waving.

Malamutes are of various colours, but are usually wolfish grey or black and white. Their feet are of the ''snowshoe'' type, tight and deep, with well-cushioned pads, giving a firm and compact appearance. Front legs are straight with big bone. Hind legs are broad and powerful, moderately bent at stifles, and without cowhocks. The back is straight, gently sloping from shoulders to hips. The loin should not be so short or tight as to interfere with easy tireless movement. Endurance and intelligence are shown in body and expression. The eyes have a ''wolf-like'' appearance by their position, but the expression is soft and indicates an affectionate disposition.

In judging Alaskan Malamutes their function as a sledge dog for heavy freighting must be given consideration above all else. The judge must bear in mind that this breed is designed primarily as the working sledge dog of the North for hauling heavy freight and therefore he should be a heavy-boned, powerfully built, compact dog with sound legs, good feet, deep chest, powerful shoulders, steady, balanced tireless gait, and the other physical equipment necessary for the efficient performance of his job. He isn't intended as a racing sled dog designed to compete in speed trials with the smaller Northern breeds. The Malamute as a sledge dog for heavy freighting is designed for strength and endurance and any characteristics of the individual specimen, including temperament, which interfere with the accomplishment of this purpose are to be considered the most serious of faults.

Temperament: The Alaskan Malamute is an affectionate, friendly dog, not a "one-man" dog. He is a loyal, devoted companion, playful on invitation, but generally impressive by his dignity after maturity.

Size: There is a natural range in size in the breed. The desirable freighting sizes are: Males, 25 in. (63 cm) at the shoulders—85 lb. (39 kg). Females, 23 in. (58 cm) at the shoulders—weighing 75 lb. (34 kg). However, size consideration should not outweigh that of type, proportion, and functional attributes, such as shoulders, chest, legs, feet, and movement. When dogs are judged equal in type, proportion, and functional attributes, the dog nearest the desirable freighting size is to be preferred.

Coat and Colour: The Malamute should have a thick, coarse, guard coat, not long and soft. The undercoat is dense, from 1 in. (3 cm) to 2 in. (5 cm) in depth, oily and woolly. The coarse guard coat stands out, and there is a thick fur around the neck. The guard coat varies in length as does the undercoat, however, in general, the coat is moderately short to medium along the sides of the body with the length of the coat increasing somewhat around the shoulders and neck, down the back and over the rump, as well as in the breeching and plume. Malamutes usually have shorter and less dense coats when shed out during the summer months.

The usual colours range from light grey through the intermediate shadings to black, always with white on underbodies, parts of legs, feet and part of mask markings. Markings should be either caplike and/or masklike on face. A white blaze on forehead and/or collar or spot on nape is attractive and acceptable, but broken colour extending over the body in spots or uneven splashings is undesirable. One should distinguish between mantled dogs and splash-coated dogs. The only solid colour allowable is the all-white.

Head: The head should indicate a high degree of intelligence, and is broad and powerful as compared with other "natural" breeds, but should be in proportion to the size of the dog so as not to make the dog appear clumsy or coarse.

The *skull* should be broad between the ears, gradually narrowing to eyes, moderately rounded between ears, flattening on top as it approaches the eyes, rounding off to cheeks, which should be moderately flat. There should be a slight furrow between the eyes; the topline of skull and topline of the muzzle showing but little break downward from a straight line as they join. The *muzzle* should be large and bulky in proportion to size of skull, diminishing but little in width and depth from junction with skull to nose; lips close fitting.

Nose: black. *Mouth:* upper and lower jaws broad with large teeth, front teeth meeting with a scissors grip but never overshot or undershot. *Eyes:* brown, almond shaped, moderately large for this shape of eye, set obliquely in skull. Dark eyes preferred. The *ears* should be of medium size, but small in proportion to head. The upper halves of the ears are triangular in shape, slightly rounded at tips, set wide apart on outside back edges of the skull with the lower part of the ear joining the skull on a line with the upper corner of the eye, giving the tips of the ears the appearance, when erect, of standing off from the skull. When erect, the ears point slightly forward, but when the dog is at work the ears are sometimes folded against the skull.

Neck: The neck should be strong and moderately arched.

Forequarters: Shoulders should be moderately sloping; forelegs heavily boned and muscled, straight to pasterns, which should be short and strong and almost vertical as viewed from the side. The feet should be large and compact, toes tight-fitting and well arched, pads thick and tough, toenails short and strong. There should be a protective growth of hair between toes.

Body: The back should be straight and gently sloping to the hips. The chest should be strong and deep; body should be strong and compactly built but not short coupled. The loins should be well muscled and not so short as to interfere with easy, rhythmic movement with powerful drive from the hindquarters. No excess weight.

Hindquarters: Hind legs must be broad and powerfully muscled through thighs; stifles moderately bent, hock joints broad and strong, moderately bent and well let down. As viewed from behind, the hind legs should not appear bowed in bone, but stand and move true, in line with movement of the front legs, and not too close or too wide. The legs of the Malamute must indicate unusual strength and tremendous propelling power. Dewclaws on the hind legs are undesirable and should be removed shortly after pups are whelped.

Tail: Moderately set and following the line of the spine at the start, well furred and carried over the back when not working, not tightly curled to rest on back, or short-furred and carried like a fox brush, a waving plume appearance, instead.

Faults: High set ears are a fault. A long loin which weakens the back is also a fault. Any indication of unsoundness in legs or feet, standing or moving, is to be considered a serious fault. Faults under the provision for worthiness for heavy freighting would be splayfootedness, any indication of unsoundness or weakness in legs, cowhocks, bad pasterns, straight shoulders, lack of angulation, stilted gaits or any gait which is not balanced, strong and steady; ranginess, shallowness, ponderousness, light-ness of bone, poor over-all proportion and similar characteristics.

Scale of Points:
General appearance 20
Head 15
Body 20
Legs and movement 20
Feet 10
Coat and colour 10
Tail 5

        TOTAL 100

Australian Cattle Dog

THE **AUSTRALIAN CATTLE DOG** was made-to-order for the job of controlling sheep and cattle in a country of wide open spaces where fences were few, and ranch hands even fewer. The breed's creation began in the 1830s with a breed called the "Smithfield." While this dog seems to have been an efficient worker, he barked so much he stampeded the livestock. A stockman by the name of Timmins crossed the Smithfield with Australia's wild dog, the Dingo, which was renowned as a silent worker. The result was a quiet working dog but rather uncontrollable. He earned the name of Timmins Biter.

To bring things under better control, the Biter was crossed with smooth-coated blue merle collies that had been imported from Scotland. These dogs, known as Hall's Heelers, did improve control but again there was a barking problem. So there was another cross to the Dingo, and more temperament problems, especially when the dogs worked in the vicinity of horses.

To correct this, the logical move was to cross Hall's Heelers with the Dalmatian, a breed well known for its steadiness when in the company of horses. The result was a dog with the typical red or blue speckled coat, reliable temperament but a bit lacking in working ability. A final cross to the Kelpie, an Australian herding dog used mainly with sheep, did the trick. The breed, originally called the Queensland Heeler, was not only a superb worker of controllable temperament but, somewhere along the line, he had picked up a remarkable power of reasoning.

In 1893 Robert Kaleski began breeding these working dogs and in 1897 draughted a breed standard for them complete with interpretations of why each point of conformation was considered desirable. With minor revisions the standard was adopted in 1903 by the New South Wales Kennel Club. Later the name was changed to the Australian Heeler and finally to the Australian Cattle Dog, by which name it is known today.

The breed is an outstanding example of genetic engineering and a tribute to the ability of the many Australian stockmen

Australian Cattle Dog

who knew what they wanted in a cattle dog and, with limited breeding stock at their disposal, produced it. From his protective colouration which helps to camouflage him as he works close in to livestock to his sturdy, agile frame, the Australian Cattle Dog combines form with function. He is alert, quiet, strong and tireless, able to work equally well over rough terrain and dry grassland or in the confines of a stockyard.

Official Breed Standard for the Australian Cattle Dog

Origin and Purpose: The Australian Cattle Dog was developed to assist with the development of the cattle industry in early Australian conditions. The principal requirement was a strong biting dog capable of mustering and moving wild cattle. The long distances to be travelled made it essential that such a dog possess great stamina. Although there is still some disagreement as to the actual breeds used, it is generally thought that the Cattle Dog developed chiefly from cross breeding a Dingo and the Blue Merle Collie.

General Appearance: The general appearance is that of a sturdy, compact, symmetrically-built working dog. With the ability and willingness to carry out any task, however strenuous, its combination of substance, power, balance, and hard muscular condition to be such that it must convey the impression of great agility, strength, and endurance.

Temperament: The utility purpose is assistance in the control of cattle, in both wide open and confined areas. Ever alert, extremely intelligent, watchful, courageous, and trustworthy. With an implicit devotion to duty, making it an ideal dog, its loyalty and protective instincts make self-appointed guardians to the stockman, his herd, his property, whilst suspicious of strangers, must be amenable to handling in the show ring.

Size: The desirable height at the withers to be within the following:
Dogs,   18−20 in. (45−51 cm).
Bitches, 17−19 in. (43−48 cm).

Dogs or bitches over or under these specified sizes are undesirable. Dogs over 20$\frac{1}{2}$ in. (52 cm) or under 17$\frac{1}{2}$ in. (44 cm) and bitches over 19$\frac{1}{2}$ in. (50 cm) or under 16$\frac{1}{2}$ in. (42 cm) are disqualified. Desirable weight: 33−50 lb. (15−23 kg).

Coat and Colour: The weather-resisting outer coat is moderately short, straight, and of medium texture, with short dense undercoat. Behind the quarter, the coat is longer, forming a mild feathering. The tail is furnished sufficiently to form a good brush. The head, forelegs, and hind legs from hock to ground are coated with short hair. The Australian Cattle Dog should be shown in natural state. The coat is not clipped or trimmed.

There are two recognized colours in the breed:

Blue: The colour should be blue or blue mottled with or without other markings. The permissible markings are black, blue, or tan markings on the head, evenly distributed for preference, the forelegs tan midway up the legs, the hindquarters tan on the inside of the hind legs and inside of the thighs, showing down the front of the stifles and broadening out to the outside of the hind legs from hock to toes. Tan undercoat is permissible on the body, providing it does not show through the blue outer coat.

Red: The colour should be of good even red speckle all over, including the undercoat (not white or cream), with or without darker red markings on the head. Even head markings are desirable. Solid red or solid black markings on the body are not desirable.

Head: A blunt wedge-shaped head, in balance with other proportions of the dog, and in keeping with its general conformation, is broad of *skull*, and only slightly curved between the ears, flattening to a slight but definite stop. The cheeks are muscular, but not coarse or prominent. The underjaw is strong, deep and well developed. The *foreface* is broad and well filled in under the eye, tapering gradually to a medium length; a deep powerful *muzzle*. The *nose* is black irrespective of the colour of the dog. The lips are tight and clean. The teeth should be sound, strong and regularly spaced, gripping with a scissorlike action, the lower incisors close behind and just touching the upper. Undershot or overshot jaw should be disqualified. The *eyes* to be oval shaped and of medium size, neither prominent nor sunken, and must express alertness and intelligence. A warning or suspicious glint characteristic. Eye colour is brown with a very dark pupil. Yellow eye is disqualified. The *ears* should be of moderate size, preferably small rather than large, broad at the base, muscular, pricked, and moderately pointed (not spoon or bat ears). Ears are set wide apart on the skull, inclined outwards, sensitive in their use and firmly erect. The inside of the ear should be fairly well furnished with hair.

Neck: The neck is of exceptional strength, muscular and of medium length, about ⅓ the length of the body, broadening to blend into the body and free from throatiness.

Forequarters: The shoulders are broad of blade, sloping, muscular and at the point of the withers should be well laid back. The upper arm is well angulated to the shoulders. The lower arm should have strong round bone, extending to the feet. They should be perfectly straight viewed from the front. The pasterns should have no weakness between the feet and lower arm and should show a slight angle with the lower arm when regarded from the side. The feet should be round, toes short, strong, well arched and held close together. The pads are hard and deep and the nails must be short and strong, (cat paws). Dewclaws are found on the front feet only and may be removed.

Body: The length of the body from point of the breastbone in a straight line to the buttocks is greater than the height of the withers as 10 is to 9. The topline is level, back strong, with ribs well sprung and ribbed back, (not barrel chested). The chest is deep and muscular and moderately broad. The loins are broad, deep and muscular with deep flanks and showing strength joining the fore and hindquarters. The croup is slightly sloping, broad, strong and muscular. The abdomen does not cut up into the flank.

Hindquarters: The line from the point of the hip to the point of buttock is rather long and sloping. The upper thigh is long, broad and well developed. The lower thigh is long and well muscled. The hocks are strong and well let down and when viewed from behind the hind legs from hocks to the feet are straight and placed neither close nor too wide apart. They should have a moderate bend of stifle.

Tail: The set of the tail is low. Following the slope of the croup, and at rest, the tail should hang in a slight curve of a length to reach approximately to the hock. During normal movement it may be raised, but a gay tail should be severely penalized. The tail is never docked.

Gait: Soundness is of paramount importance. The action is true, free, supple and tireless. The movement of the shoulders and forelegs, with the powerful thrust of the hindquarters, should be in unison. Capability of quick, sudden movement is essential.

Faults: Any tendency to grossness or weediness is a serious fault. Ears: ears other than pricked. Colour: solid red or black markings on the body. Tail: gay tail is a fault. Other: stiltiness, loaded or slack shoulders, straight shoulders, weakness of elbows, pasterns or feet, straight stifles, cow or bowhocks must be regarded as serious faults.

Disqualifications: *Mouth: overshot or undershot jaw. Eye: yellow eye. Size: bitches over 19½ in. (50 cm) or under 16½ in. (42 cm) and dogs over 20½ in. (52 cm) or under 17½ in. (44 cm).*

Bearded Collie

*T*HERE IS SOME EVIDENCE to suggest that the forbears of the Bearded Collie existed in Britain at the time
of the Roman invasion. There are even those who
claim the breed's ancestry can be traced as far back as 2000 B.C.,
citing dog skeletons dating back to that time as proof. Be that as
it may, because one dog skeleton looks much like any other of
comparable size such antiquity for a specific breed is somewhat
difficult to verify.

The most reliable information brings us into the 16th century
when a Polish vessel landed in Scotland to pick up a shipment of
sheep. The ship's owner had brought some Polish Lowland
Shepherd dogs with him which he used to separate the sheep he
wished to buy from the rest of the flock. The shepherd was so
impressed by the work these efficient herders did he offered to
exchange "a good horned ram" for a pair of dogs. The deal was
made. One ram and one ewe were traded for one herding dog
and two females. These, inter-bred with local Highland Collies,
became the foundation stock of today's Beardies.

At one time there were two distinct strains of Bearded
Collie—the Border, which was grey and white, and the Highland
strain which was brown and white. Now the two have been
inter-bred to develop a single strain and black as well as the
fawns and greys are recognized colours.

Headed by Dr. Russell Greig, a specialty club was formed in
Edinburgh in 1912. The purpose was to promote the breed but
public interest was slow in coming. It was not until 1944 that the
breed was officially recognized by The Kennel Club in Britain.
Reason for this seems to be that the Beardie was a working
breed of the stockman who had little interest in promoting it as
a show specimen or maintaining accurate breeding records.

The breed gained official recognition in Canada in August
1970 when seven imported Beardies were registered with The
Canadian Kennel Club. A few years later the breed was accepted
in the United States.

Bearded Collie

Official Breed Standard for the Bearded Collie

Origin and Purpose: One of the oldest of the British herding breeds, the Bearded Collie has for centuries been the Scottish hill shepherd's dog, used to hunt and gather free-ranging sheep on the Highlands. The breed was also popular as a cattle drover. Both jobs required a hardy constitution and intelligence, initiative, strength, stamina, and speed.

General Appearance: This is a lean active dog, longer than it is high in an approximate proportion of 5:4, measured from point of chest to point of buttock. Bitches may be slightly longer. The dog, though strongly made, should show plenty of daylight under the body and should not look too heavy. A bright, enquiring expression is a distinctive feature of the breed.

Characteristics and Temperament: The Bearded Collie must be alert and self-confident, and should be lively and active. The temperament should be that of a steady, intelligent working dog and must show no signs of nervousness or aggression.

Size: Ideal height at the shoulder: dogs, 21–22 in. (53–56 cm); bitches, 20–21 in. (51–53 cm). Over-all quality and proportions should be considered before size but excessive variation from the ideal height should be discouraged.

Coat: The coat must be double with the undercoat soft, furry and close. The outer coat should be flat, harsh and strong, shaggy, free from woolliness and curl, though a slight wave is permissible. The length and density of the hair should be sufficient to provide a protective coat and to enhance the shape of the dog, but not enough to obscure the natural lines of the body. The adult coat may break along the spine, but must not be artificially parted. The coat must not be trimmed in any way. On the head, the bridge of the nose should be sparsely covered with hair which should be slightly longer on the sides just to cover the lips. From the cheeks, the lower lips and under the chin, the coat increases in length towards the chest, forming the typical beard.

Colour: Bearded Collies are born dark, pure black, brown, blue or fawn, with or without white markings. The base colours mature to any shade of black, grey, blue, brown, or fawn, with the coat usually having a mixture of many shades at once and individual hairs showing bands of light and dark. Grey hairs may be lightly interspersed with all colours. Where white occurs, it should only appear on the foreface, as a blaze on the skull, on the tip of the tail, on the chest, legs and feet and, if round the collar, the roots of the white hair should not extend behind the shoulder. White should not appear above the hocks on the outside of the hind legs. Slight tan markings are acceptable on the eyebrows, inside the ears, on the cheeks, under the root of the tail, and on the legs where white joins the main colour.

Head: The head should be in proportion to the size of the dog. The *skull* is broad and flat, the distance between stop and occiput being equal to the width between the orifices of the ears. The *muzzle* is strong and equal in length to the distance between the stop and the occiput, the whole effect being that of a dog with strength of muzzle and plenty of brain room. The stop should be moderate. The *nose* is large and square. Pigmentation of nose leather, lips, and eye rims follows coat colour at birth and should be of a solid colour without spots or patches. The *eyes* should be set widely apart and are large, soft and affectionate, but not protruding. The eyebrows are arched up and forward but are not so long as to obscure the eyes. Eyes should tone with coat in colour. Born blues and fawns will have lighter eyes with all shades of coat than born blacks or browns. The *ears* are of medium size and drooping. When the dog is alert, the ears lift at the base, level with, but not above, the top of the skull, increasing the apparent breadth of the skull. The *teeth* are large and white, the incisors of the lower jaw fitting tightly behind those of the upper jaw. However, a level bite is acceptable. A full set of forty-two teeth is desirable.

Neck: The neck must be of a fair length, muscular, and slightly arched.

Forequarters: The shoulders should slope well back, a line drawn through the centre of the shoulder blade should form a right angle (90 degrees) with the humerus. The shoulder blades at the withers should only be separated by the vertebrae but must slope outwards from there sufficiently to accommodate the desired spring of rib. The legs are straight and vertical, with good bone, and covered with shaggy hair all-round. The pasterns should be flexible without weakness.

Body: The length of the back should come from the length of the rib cage and not that of the loin. The ribs are well sprung but angled back, making the rib cage appear flat, and the chest is deep, giving plenty of heart and lung room. The back must be level and the loins should be strong. The level back blends smoothly into the curve of the rump and must not fall away in croup.

Hindquarters: The hindquarters are well muscled with good second thighs, well-bent stifles and low hocks. Below the hock, the leg falls at a right angle to the ground and, in normal stance, will be just behind a line vertically below the point of the buttock. The distance between the hocks should approximate the distance from hock to ground.

Feet: The feet are oval in shape with the soles well padded. The toes are arched and close together, well covered with hair including between the pads.

Tail: The tail is set low, without kink or twist, and is long enough for the end of the bone to reach at least the point of the hock. It is carried low with an upward swirl at the tip while standing. When the dog is excited or in motion the tail may be extended or raised, but must not be carried forward over the back.

Gait: Seen from the side, a correctly moving dog appears to flow across the ground with the minimum of effort. Movement should be supple, smooth, and long-reaching, with good driving power in the hindquarters and feet lifted just enough to clear the ground. The forelegs should track smoothly and straight. Each hind leg should move in line with the foreleg on the same side. The back should remain level and firm.

Belgian Sheepdog

Up to the end of the 19th century there was a vast number of sheepherding breeds on the continent, quite similar in type, that were bred for their working abilities rather than their appearance. With the advent of the Machine Age, however, the dog's usefulness seemed to come to an end. Fanciers feared that in time these clever dogs might disappear from the scene altogether. So it was that in the late 19th century shepherd dog fanciers met together to agree on the ideal type and character of the breed that was to be given the official name of Belgian Sheepdog.

While they did agree on the matter of structure and character, they could not agree on coat type or colour. Thus today the breed continues to be found with differing coats which form the basis of the four varieties within the single breed. Each is named after the Belgian town or area where that particular variety was favoured.

In almost all countries of the world, including Canada (not, however, in the U.S.A.), these varieties are recognized as being one breed: the Belgian Sheepdog. In the United States in 1959, it was decided to recognize the Belgian Sheepdog (Groenendael), the Belgian Tervuren, and the Belgian Malinois as three separate breeds. The Laeken is denied registration in the U.S.A.

The earliest recorded arrival of a Belgian Sheepdog in North America was in 1907. However, it was not until after World War I that the breed attracted much attention on this side of the Atlantic due, no doubt, to tales told by returning servicemen who praised the distinguished record of this breed as messenger and Red Cross dogs.

Although some of these early imports came to Canada, it was not until the late 1950s and early 1960s that the Belgian Sheepdog gained any degree of popularity in this country. Today the Belgian Sheepdog enjoys good support across Canada and excels in obedience work. Most championship events, especially the larger shows, draw entries of the three better known varieties. The rarest, the Rough-Haired Laeken, is seldom exhibited.

Groenendael

Laeken

Tervuren

Malinois

G.STENHOUSE

Belgian Sheepdog

Official Breed Standard for the Belgian Sheepdog

Origin and Purpose: The Belgian Sheepdog has an ancestry which is common to many of the herding dogs used throughout the modern world. His type is a result of the rugged Belgian climate and the requirements of the Belgian shepherd for a bright, strong, and agile dog. In addition to sheepherding, the Belgian Sheepdog has been widely used for police and war work and is noted for his intelligence and alertness in obedience work.

General Appearance: The first impression of the Belgian Sheepdog should be that of a well-balanced square dog, elegant in appearance, with an exceedingly proud carriage of head and neck. He should be a strong, agile, well-muscled animal who is alert and full of life. His whole conformation should give the impression of depth and solidity without bulkiness. The dog should be somewhat more impressive and grand than the bitch. The bitch should have a distinctively feminine look.

Like many European breeds, different coat colours, textures, and lengths were preferred by the original fanciers. Today, however, only four distinct coat types are recognized and have become the distinguishing characteristics of the four varieties of Belgian Sheepdog. The long-haired Groenendael and Tervuren, the short-haired Malinois, and the rough-haired variety differ in coat colour, length and texture but are unmistakably the same breed.

Temperament: The Belgian Sheepdog should reflect the qualities of intelligence, courage, alertness, and devotion to his master. To his inherent aptitude as guardian of flocks should be added protectiveness of the person and property of his master. He should be watchful, attentive, and always in motion when not under command. In his relationship with humans, he should be observant and vigilant with strangers but not apprehensive. He should not show fear or shyness. He should not show viciousness by unwarranted or unprovoked attack. With those he knows well, he is most affectionate, friendly, zealous of their attention, and very possessive.

Size: Males should be 24–26 in. (61–66 cm) in height and females 22–24 in. (56–61 cm), measured at the withers. The length, measured from the front of the forechest to the rear projection of the pelvis, should equal the height. Bitches may be slightly longer. Bone structure should be moderately heavy in proportion to height so that he is well balanced throughout and neither spindly and leggy nor cumbersome and bulky.

Coat and Colour: Coat length, colour, and texture is the one distinguishing feature between the different varieties of the Belgian Sheepdog.

a) Longhaired: The guard hairs of the coat must be long, well fitting, straight, and abundant. The texture should be a medium harshness. The undercoat should be extremely dense, commensurate, however, with climatic conditions. The hair is shorter on the head, outside of the ears, and lower part of the legs. The opening of the ear is protected by tufts of hair. There should be long and abundant hair forming a collarette around the neck; forming a fringe along the back of the forearm; forming the breeches in the hindquarters and forming a nicely plumed tail. Two colour types are found in the long-haired variety:

   i. The dog should be completely black or be black with white limited as follows: small to moderate patch on forechest, between the pads of the feet, on tips of hind toes, and frost on the chin and muzzle. White on the tips of the front toes is allowable but is a fault. The black, longhaired variety is known as the GROENENDAEL.

   ii. The dog should be either rich fawn to russet mahogany or distinctly grey, each with a black overlay. The coat is characteristically double pigmented, wherein the tip of each hair is blackened. On mature males, this blackening is especially pronounced on the shoulders, back, and rib section. The chest colour is a mixture of black and grey. The face has a black mask and the ears are mostly black. The underparts of the dog, tail, and breeches are light beige or grey. A small white patch is permitted on the chest but should not extend into the neck or breast. Frost on the chin or muzzle is normal. Too light a colour or too black a colour is a serious fault. This variety is known as the TERVUREN.

b) Short-haired: The coat should be comparatively short and straight with a dense undercoat. It is very short on the head, the ears and lower legs. The hair is somewhat longer around the neck where it forms a collarette and on the tail and back of the thighs. The colour should be from a rich fawn to mahogany with a black overlay. There should be a black mask and black ears.

The underparts of the body, tail, and breeches are lighter fawn. A small white patch on the chest is permissible as is white on the tips of the toes. A washed-out fawn colour is undesirable. This variety is known as the MALINOIS.

c) Rough-haired: The coat should have a rough or dry texture and appear unkempt. The undercoat is thick and woolly. The coat is of medium length on all parts of the body except the head where the hair on the skull is short while the hair on the muzzle is slightly longer forming a beard or whiskers. The coat should be light fawn to red brown in colour. Grey is acceptable as well. Blackening may appear on the muzzle, ears, and tail. The underparts of the dog, tail, and breeches are light beige or grey. The tail should not form a plume. A small amount of white is permitted on the chest and the tips of the toes. This variety is known as the LAEKEN.

Head: Should be clean-cut and strong with size in proportion to the body. *Skull* should be flattened on top rather than rounded. The width should be approximately the same as, but not wider than the length. The stop should be moderate. *Muzzle* should be moderately pointed, avoiding any tendency to snipiness, and approximately equal in length to that of the top skull. *Nose* should be black without spots or discoloured areas. *Mouth:* the jaw should be strong and powerful. The lips should be tight and black with no pink showing on the outside. There should be a full complement of strong, white, evenly-set teeth. There should be either an even or a scissors bite. An overshot or undershot bite is a serious fault. *Eyes* should be dark brown, medium sized, slightly almond shaped and should not protrude. *Ears* should be triangular in shape, stiff, erect, and in proportion in size to the head. The base of the ear should not come below the centre of the eye.

Neck: Should be round and rather outstretched, tapered from head to body and well muscled with tight skin.

Body: Forequarters—Chest should be deep but not broad. The lowest point should reach the elbow of the front leg and should form a smooth ascending curve to the abdomen. Shoulder should be long and oblique, laid flat against the body and should form a sharp angle (approximately 90 degrees) with the upper arm. Legs should be straight, strong and parallel to each other. The bone should be oval rather than round. The length should be in proportion to the size of the dog. Pasterns should be of medium length and should be strong and very slightly sloped.

Back—Should be level, straight and firm from withers to hip. The withers should be slightly higher than and slope into the back.

Loin—The loin section viewed from above should be relatively short, broad, and strong, and should blend smoothly into the back. The abdomen should be moderately developed and should be neither tucked up nor paunchy.

Hindquarters—Croup should be medium long with a gradual slope. Thighs should be broad and heavily muscled. The upper and lower thigh bones form a relatively sharp angle at the stifle joint. Hocks: the angle at the hock is relatively sharp although the angulation is not extreme. Metatarsus should be of medium length, strong, and slightly sloped. Dewclaws, if any, should be removed.

Tail—Should be strong at the base and the bone should reach the hock. At rest, it should be held low and in action it should be raised with a slight curl which is strongest toward the tip. It should not curl over the dog's back or form a hook.

Feet—The front feet should be round (cat-footed). The rear feet should be slightly elongated. Toes on both front and back feet should be curved and close together. They should be well padded. Nails should be strong and black except that they may be white to match white toe tips.

Gait: Should be smooth, free and easy, seemingly never tiring and exhibiting facility of movement rather than a hard driving action. He should single track on a fast gait—*i.e.*, the legs, both front and rear, converge toward the centre line of the body. The backline should remain firm and level, parallel to the line of motion, with no crabbing. He should show a marked tendency to move in a circle rather than a straight line.

Faults: Any deviation from these specifications is a fault. In determining whether a fault is minor, serious, or major, these two factors should be used as a guide:
1. The extent to which it deviates from the standard.
2. The extent to which such deviation would actually affect the working ability of the dog.

Disqualifications:

1. *Viciousness.*
2. *Excessive shyness.*
3. *Any colour or colour combination not allowed in the standard.*
4. *Ears hanging (as on a hound).*
5. *Tail cropped or stump.*
6. *Males under 23 in. (58 cm) or over 27 in. (69 cm) in height. Females under 21 in. (53 cm) or over 25 in. (64 cm) in height.*

Bernese Mountain Dog

ONLY RECENTLY ADDED to The Canadian Kennel Club's roster of officially recognized breeds, the Bernese Mountain Dog has a history dating back to Roman times, when large mastiff-type dogs accompanied the legions in their marches across the Alps. Some of these huge dogs were left behind to guard the Alpine outposts which the Romans established along the route.

From these guard dogs have descended four distinct breeds of Swiss mountain dog—the Appenzell, the Entlebuch, the Greater Swiss Mountain Dog, and the Bernese. The latter was named for the Swiss Canton of Berne where it was most numerous prior to the turn of the century.

While the mountain dogs are said to have lost some of their stature because of cross matings with local herding dogs, their loyalty in the service of man has remained unchanged. Over the centuries they developed a remarkable facility to negotiate steep Alpine paths. Because of this, the breeds were used primarily as cart dogs to transport dairy products and weavers' baskets to market. They also served as cattle dogs.

With his long, distinctively marked, silky coat, the Bernese is said to be the most beautiful of the four breeds of mountain dog and unrivalled as a family pet. Nevertheless, with the coming of the Machine Age the breed's usefulness seemed to be at an end. Had it not been for the efforts of two Swiss dog enthusiasts the Bernese might have vanished.

To prevent this from happening, in 1892 these dog fanciers searched the country for good specimens and succeeded in establishing a breeding colony. In 1907 a specialty club for the Bernese Mountain Dog was formed in Burgdorf, Switzerland and the breed began appearing at dog shows. Today it is extremely popular in its country of origin accounting for large exhibits at most championship events.

During the 1930s the breed was introduced to the United States and some forty years later there was sufficient interest in the Bernese Mountain Dog in Canada to warrant its inclusion on the official list of recognized breeds.

Bernese Mountain Dog

Official Breed Standard for the Bernese Mountain Dog (Bouvier Bernois)

Origin and Purpose: The Bernese is a descendant of the ancient Molossian dog. He is one of four breeds generally referred to as Swiss Mountain Dogs and is the only one to wear a long coat. He takes his name from the Canton of Berne in Switzerland where he traditionally was used to haul the wares of the basket weavers to market. The Bernese, as well as a cart dog and an excellent companion dog, is used as a herder or drover.

General Appearance: An above middle size, well-balanced working dog. Square in appearance from withers to ground and withers to tail-set. The Bernese is active and alert, a combination of sagacity, fidelity, and utility.

Temperament: The Bernese temperament is one of his strongest assets. He is consistent and dependable and always appears to be in command of the situation. He usually directs his affection towards one master while remaining an excellent family companion and protector. He possesses a very strong desire to please. He is suspicious of strangers but not aggressive towards them unless threatened.

Size: Dogs, 23−27½ in. (58−70 cm); bitches, 22−26 in. (56−66 cm). Weights may range from 71−110 pounds (32−50 kg). The stocky well-balanced appearance must be maintained.

Coat and Colour: The coat is soft and silky, with a short soft undercoat. The guard coat has a bright natural sheen; it is long and somewhat wavy, but should never curl. Compulsory Markings: Jet-black with russet or deep tan markings on all four legs, a spot above the forelegs on each side of the white chest markings, on the cheeks, and a spot over each eye. Brown on the legs must come between the black on the leg and the white of the feet. There shall be a white blaze (slight to middle sized) and a white cross shaped marking on the chest. Preferable Markings: White feet with white reaching at the highest the pastern and a white tip of tail. The markings should be symmetrical.

Head: The *skull* is flat, with a defined but not too pronounced stop. The *muzzle* is strong, square and reasonably short. The distance from nose to eyes and eyes to occiput is a ratio of 1 to 1.8. Dewlaps are very slightly developed, flews not too pendulous. The jaw is strong with good teeth meeting in a scissor or level bite. The *eyes* are dark red brown, full of fire, almond shaped and well set apart. The *ears* are V-shaped, set high, short and not too pointed at the tips. They hang close to the head in repose and are brought slightly forward and raised at the base when at the alert. *Nostrils* well open and black in colour.

Neck: The neck is strong, muscular and well set on the shoulders.

Forequarters: The shoulders are well muscled and slope back at an angle of 45 degrees. The forelegs are straight, well boned, and muscular. Pasterns are slightly sloping but not weak. Feet are proportionate in size, round and compact.

Body: The body is square when measured from ground to withers and withers to tail-set. The topline is firm and level between the withers and croup. The chest is broad with good depth of brisket reaching at least the elbows. The loins are strong and muscular. The croup is fairly broad and well muscled.

Hindquarters: The hindquarters are very important in a working dog. As such, the whole hindquarter should be powerful, with broad, well-muscled thighs and strong well-developed bones. Stifles should be well bent and hocks should be wide and straight. The hock to equal approximately ⅓ the length of the leg. The feet are proportionate in size, round and compact. Rear dewclaws should be removed.

Tail: The tail should reach the hock, be fairly thick, and covered with long hair. When in repose, it should be carried low; an upper swirl is permissible. When alert, it may be carried gaily but not curl over the back.

Gait: The general movement should give an impression of effortless power. He is well reaching in front and possesses plenty of drive in the rear. In travelling, the legs should be carried straight forward while maintaining the topline in all gaits.

Faults: All deviations from the standard, deficiency of type, and insufficient expression of sex. Unbalanced build. Too massive or too light head. Light or staring eyes. Ectropis or entropia (out- or in-rolled eyelids). Too heavy or long ears. Too narrow or snipey muzzle. Undershot or overshot mouth. Too flat or too pronounced stop. Pendulous dewlaps. Overly long or thin body. Splayed feet. Unsymmetrical markings, especially facial. Too light brown or impure colour.

Disqualifications: *Cryptorchid or monorchid males. Split nose. White neck ring. Absent markings as described as Compulsory Markings in* Coat and Colour.

Bouvier des Flandres

ORIGINATING IN THE AGRICULTURAL PLAIN of Flanders, Belgium, this breed has been known by various names—Vuilbaard (Dirty Beard), Koe Hund (Cow Dog), Toucheur de Boeuf (Cattle Drover), and Bouvier (Cowherder). Used mainly for herding and driving cattle, the background breeding of the Bouvier remains in question. Some claim the breed is a product of the 20th century and that the bloods of several continental herding breeds are in his makeup. Others contend that the breed descends from the Schnauzer which would make his lineage old indeed.

It is enough to know that when the Machine Age arrived and cattle were transported to market by truck the work of these droving dogs seemed to be at an end. Fortunately for the Bouvier, there were enough concerned breed fanciers who wished to preserve this handsome working dog. But it took some time before all could agree on type.

In 1910 the Bouvier was first exhibited in Belgium in four varieties—a situation that displeased the purists who, in 1912, formed a group whose aim it was to standardize a single Bouvier variety. Of necessity work was suspended during World War I, but recommenced after the close of hostilities. The war dealt harshly with the Bouvier. Many became war casualties. Good breeding stock was at a premium. It is said that the breed today owes its existence to a Belgian army veterinarian, Captain Darby, who saved some stock and whose dog Ch. Nic de Sottegem became the foundation sire of the breed.

By 1922 the Club National Belge du Bouvier des Flandres had agreed on a single type and had draughted a breed standard for the guidance of Bouvier breeders.

The breed excels as a police and army dog as well as personal guard dog. In Belgium a Bouvier may not hold the title of breed champion unless it has also won a prize as a working dog.

The Bouvier des Flandres was introduced to this continent in the 1930s where it is slowly but surely gaining in popularity as show dog and family pet.

Bouvier des Flandres

Official Breed Standard for the Bouvier des Flandres

Origin and Purpose: The Bouvier des Flandres is a dog of notably rugged appearance as befitting an erstwhile cattle driver and farmer's helper of Flandres, and later, an ambulance dog and messenger in World War I.

General Appearance: He is a compact bodied, powerfully built dog of upstanding carriage and alert, intelligent expression.

Size: Dogs from 23 $^{1}/_{2}$–27 $^{1}/_{2}$ in. (59–70 cm); bitches a minimum of 22 $^{5}/_{8}$ in. (58 cm).

Coat and Colour: Rough, tousled, and unkempt in appearance, the coat is capable of withstanding the hardest work in the most inclement weather. Topcoat harsh, rough, and wiry, and so thick that when separated by the hand the skin is hardly visible. Undercoat fine and soft in texture, and thicker in winter. On the skull the hair is shorter and almost smooth. On the brows it is longer, thus forming eyebrows. Longer growth on muzzle and underjaw form moustache and beard. On the legs it is thick and rough, on the feet rather short. Colour from fawn to black; pepper and salt, grey and brindle. A white star on the chest is allowed.

Head: The head is medium long, with the skull slightly longer than the muzzle. *Skull* almost flat on top, moderately wide between the ears, and sloping slightly toward the muzzle. The brow is noticeably arched over the eyes. The stop is shallow, and the under-eye fill-in good. *Muzzle* wide, deep and well filled out, the width narrowing gradually towards the tip of the nose. Cheeks are clean or flat-sided. *Nose* black and well developed, the nostrils wide open. Across the top the contour is a trifle rounded as opposed to flat. Jaws powerful, and the lips dry and tight-fitting. *Teeth* strong and white, with the canines set well apart; the teeth meet in a scissors bite. Neither protruding nor sunken, the *eyes* are set a trifle obliquely in the skull and not too far apart. They are of medium size and very nearly oval. Preferred colour, a dark nut-brown. Black eyes, although not considered faulty, are less desirable as contributing to a sombre expression. *Ears* rough coated, set high on the head and cropped to a triangular contour. They stand erect and are carried straight up.

Neck: The neck is well rounded, slightly arched, and carried almost upright, its thickness gradually increasing as it fits gracefully into the shoulders. Clean and dry at the throat.

Forequarters: The shoulders are long and sloping. The leg bones, although only moderate in girth, are made to appear heavy because of their covering with thick, rough hair. Forelegs straight as viewed from the front or side, with elbows turned neither in nor out.

Body: Back short, strong, and straight. The brisket is deep, extending down at least to the point of the elbows, and of moderate width. Ribs are deep and well sprung. Loins short, taut and slightly arched in topline, while the rump is broad and square rather than sloping. As advantageous for breeding purposes, slightly greater length of loin is permissible in bitches.

Hindquarters: Hindquarters are firm and well muscled, with large, powerful hams. Legs are strong and sturdy, with hocks well let down and wide apart. They are slightly angulated at stifle and hock joints. Viewed from the back they are absolutely parallel. Feet round, compact, with toes arched and close. The nails are black, the pads thick and tough.

Tail: Set high, carried up, and docked to about 4 in. (10 cm).

Faults: Soft, silky, or woolly topcoats. Chocolate brown with white spots. A narrow muzzle, suggestive of weakness. Brown, pink and spotted noses. Light-coloured eyes, and staring or wild expression.

Scale of Points:

Coat   20
Head (eyes, ears, skull, foreface)   20
Shoulders and style   10
Hindquarters (hams and legs)   10
Back, loin, brisket, belly   15
Feet and legs   10
Symmetry, size, and character   15

       TOTAL   100

Boxer

*T*HE **BOXER WAS DEVELOPED** in Munich, Germany, towards the end of the 19th century and represents a cross between a mastiff-type breed, the Brabanter Bullenbeisser (smaller bull-baiter), and the British Bulldog. It is said that because one of the breed's progenitors was a white Bulldog, the occasional all-white puppy appears in a litter of otherwise correctly coloured puppies. Because the Boxer was developed to work as a security dog, the white-coloured dogs were considered completely unacceptable. For a time in Germany there was some effort made to develop an all-black Boxer but results were indifferent. Today the only allowable colours, for show purposes, are fawn and brindle.

The origin of the breed name is uncertain. One writer states that it was derived from a south German dialect, but the most frequently stated explanation is that it comes from the English word "to box" because of the dog's habit of playfully using its forepaws like the hands of a pugilist.

The breed was first registered in its homeland in 1904 and a few Boxers were brought to Britain about this time. They did not attract much notice there or on this continent until after the end of World War I when interest was sparked by returning servicemen who brought many of the attractive dogs home with them. Breeding kennels became established in the United States and Canada and by the time of the outbreak of the Second World War there was a good reservoir of excellent breeding stock available. The most influential stud dog of all time is said to be Ch. Sigurd von Dom, imported from Germany by Barmere Kennels.

On this continent Boxers are shown with cropped ears as a rule, a practice that was introduced during the time when the dog was used for security work and the larger, hanging ear could easily get torn during a fight. In Britain ear cropping is prohibited by law, thus the Boxer must be shown with natural ears which give a different, but nevertheless attractive, appearance to head and expression.

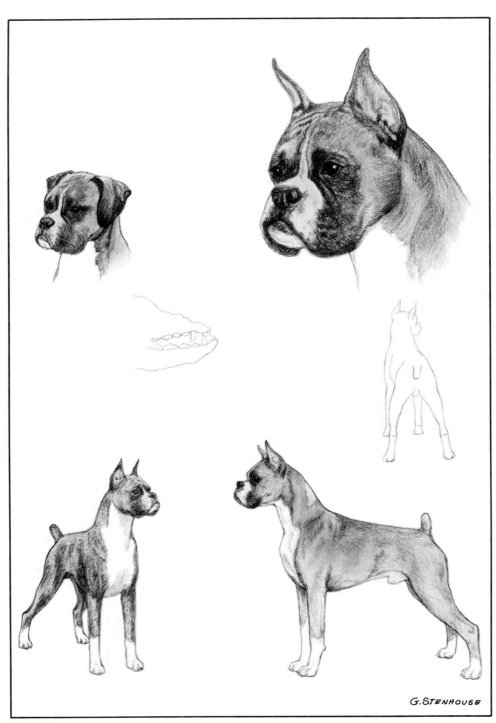

G.Stenhouse

Boxer

The first Boxer was registered in Canada in The Canadian Kennel Club Stud Book for the years 1934–1935 under the breed name Boxer Spaniel.

Official Breed Standard for the Boxer

General Appearance: The Boxer is a medium-sized sturdy dog, of square build, with short back, strong limbs and short tight-fitting coat. His musculation, well developed, should be clean, hard, and appear smooth (not bulgy) under taut skin. Developed to serve the multiple purposes of guard, working, and escort-dog, he must combine elegance with substance and ample power, not alone for beauty but to ensure the speed, dexterity, and jumping ability essential to an arduous hike, riding expedition, police or military duty. Only a body whose individual parts are built to withstand the most strenuous efforts, assembled as a complete and harmonious whole, can respond to these combined demands. Therefore, to be at his highest efficiency he must never be plump or heavy, and while equipped for great speed, he must never be racy.

The head imparts to the Boxer a unique individual stamp peculiar to him alone. It must be in perfect proportion to his body, never small in comparison to the over-all picture. His muzzle is his most distinctive feature and the greatest value to be placed on its being of correct form and in absolute proper proportion to the skull.

In judging the Boxer, the first thing to be considered is general appearance, then balance; the relation of substance to elegance and the desired proportion of the individual parts of the body to each other.

Consideration is to be given to an attractive colour, after which the individual parts are to be examined for their correct constructions and their functions. Special attention is to be devoted to the head.

Temperament: The character of the Boxer is of the greatest importance and demands the most solicitous attention. He should be alert and fearless; willing to make friends, but not necessarily effusive.

Size: Height—males, 22 in. (56 cm) to 24 in. (61 cm) at the withers; females, 21 in. (53 cm) to 23 in. (59 cm) at the withers.

Males should not go under 22 in. (56 cm), and females should not go over 23 in. (59 cm).

Coat and Colour: Coat short, shiny, lying smooth and tight to the body. The colours are fawn and brindle. Fawn in various shades from light yellow to dark deer red. The brindle variety should have clearly defined black stripes on fawn background. White markings in fawn and brindle dogs are not to be rejected; in fact, they are often very attractive in appearance. The black mask is absolutely required. When white occurs on the muzzle it should be edged by remnants of the black mask. Black toenails are preferred but not essential. Even distribution of head markings is desirable.

Head: The top of the *skull* is slightly arched, not rotund, or flat or noticeably broad, and the occiput must not be too pronounced. The forehead forms a distinct stop with the topline of the muzzle, which must not be forced back into the forehead like that of a Bulldog. It should not slant up or down (down-faced), or be dished. The forehead shows a suggestion of furrow which, however, must never be too deep, especially between the eyes. Corresponding with the powerful set of teeth, the cheeks are accordingly well developed, without protruding from the head with too bulgy an appearance; preferably they should taper into the muzzle in a slight, graceful curve.

The beauty of the head depends upon the harmonious proportion between the muzzle and the skull. The *muzzle* should always appear powerful, never small in its relationship to the skull. The head should be clean, not showing deep wrinkles. Folds will normally appear upon the forehead when the ears are erect, and they are always indicated from the lower edge of the stop running downward on both sides of the muzzle. The dark mask is confined to the muzzle and is in distinct contrast to the colour of the head. Any extension of the mask to the skull, other than dark shading around the eyes, creates a sombre, undesirable expression. The muzzle is powerfully developed in length, width, and depth. It is not pointed, narrow, short or shallow. Its shape is influenced first through the formation of both jaw-bones, second through the placement of teeth, and third through the texture of the lips.

The two *jawbones* do not terminate in the usual scissors bite; instead the lower jaw protrudes moderately beyond the upper and bends slightly upward. The Boxer is normally undershot. The upper jaw is broad where attached to the skull and maintains this breadth except for a very slight tapering to the front. The lower jaw incisor teeth are in a straight line. In the upper jaw they are slightly rounded. The middle incisors should not project. This formation creates frontal width in both jaws and results in the canine teeth being widely separated from each other. The upper corner incisors should fit snugly back of the lower canine teeth, the premolars, anterior palative foramen (a technical term pertaining to the placing of teeth), and molars fitting in the most normal possible manner, creating a sound, powerful bite.

The *lips* complete the formation of the muzzle. The upper lip is thick and padded, filling out the frontal space formed by the projection of the lower jaw and it is supported by the jaw's fangs. Therefore, these fangs must stand far apart and be of good length so that the front surface of the muzzle shall become broad and squarish and, when viewed from the side, form a rounded angle with the topline of the muzzle. The lower edge of the upper lip rests on the edge of the lower lip. The repandous (bent upward) part of the underjaw with the lower lip (sometimes called the chin) must not rise above the front of the upper lip, but much less may it disappear under it. It must be perceptible when viewed from the front as well as the side, without protruding and bending upward in the manner of the English Bulldog. The Boxer must not show his teeth or his tongue when his mouth is closed. Excessive flews are not desirable.

The tip of the *nose* lies somewhat higher than the root of the muzzle. The nose is broad and black, very slightly turned up; the nostrils are broad with the naso-labial line running between them. The dark brown *eyes*, not too small, not protruding or deep set, disclose an alert and intelligent expression, and must never appear gloomy, threatening or piercing; they should be encircled by dark hair. The *ears* are cut rather long, well trimmed and carried erect.

Neck: Round, of ample length, not too short; strong and muscular and clean throughout, without dewlap, with a distinctly marked nape and an elegant arch running down to the back.

Forequarters: The shoulders are long and sloping, close lying and not excessively covered with muscle. The upper arm is long, closely approaching a right angle to the shoulder blade. The fore-legs, when seen from the front, must be straight, stand parallel to each other, and have strong firmly joined bones. The elbows must not press too closely to the chest wall nor stand off visibly from it. The forearm is straight, long and firmly muscled. The pastern (knee) joint of the foreleg is clearly defined but not distended. The pastern is short, slightly slanting, but standing almost perpendicular to the ground. Feet compact, turning neither in nor out, with tightly arched toes and hard soles (cat's paws).

Body: The withers should be clearly defined, the whole back short, straight and very muscular. Body is square. Measured in profile, a horizontal line from the front of the forechest to the rear projection of the upper thigh should equal a vertical line dropped from the top of the withers to the ground. The brisket is deep, reaching down to the elbows; the depth of the body at the lowest point of the brisket amounts to half the height of the dog at the withers. Chest of fair width, and forechest well defined. The ribs, extending far to the rear, are well arched but not barrel-shaped. The loins are short and muscular; the lower stomach line, lightly tucked up, blending into a graceful curve to the rear. The croup is very slightly sloped, broad.

Hindquarters: In balance with forequarters; strongly muscled. The pelvis should be long and especially broad in females. The thighs broad and curved, the breech musculation strongly developed. Upper and lower thigh long, leg well angulated. In standing position, the leg below the hock joint should be practically perpendicular to the ground (a slight slope is permissible). Viewed from behind the hind legs are straight. The hocks (metatarsus) clean, strong, and short, supported by powerful rear pads with hock joint clean-cut and clearly defined. The rear toes just a little longer than the front toes, but similar in all other respects.

Tail: Tail attachment high, rather than low. Tail clipped, carried upward.

Faults: Head not typical, plump bull-doggy appearance, light bone, lack of balance, bad condition, deficiency in nobility.
   Shyness—A dog should be considered shy if he shrinks away from a friendly approach or displays timidity when approached

from the rear, or displays cowardice over sudden and unusual noises.

Viciousness—A dog should be considered vicious that attempts to attack either his handler or the judge. Belligerency towards other dogs should not be considered viciousness.

Lack of nobility and expression, sombre face, unserviceable bite. Pinscher or Bulldog head, badly trimmed ears, visible conjunctiva (haw), drivelling, showing teeth or tongue, light so-called "Bird-of-Prey" eyes. Sloping topline of muzzle, too pointed or too light a bite (snipey). Dewlap.

Loose shoulders, tied-in elbows, hare's feet, turned feet.

Too broad and low in front, chest hanging between the shoulders, hollow flanks, hanging stomach. Roach back, sway back, thin lean back, long narrow loins, weak union with croup, falling off or too rounded or narrow croup, higher in back than in front.

Steep, stiff or too slightly angulated hindquarters, light thighs, cowhocks, bowlegs and crooked legs, rear dewclaws, soft hocks, narrow heel, tottering, waddling gait, hare feet, hindquarters too far under or too far behind. Low-set tail.

Disqualifications: *Boxers with white or black ground colour, or entirely white or black or any colour other than fawn or brindle. (White markings are allowed but must not exceed one-third ($1/3$) of the ground colour.)*

Briard

THE BRIARD OR "CHIEN BERGER DE BRIE" as the breed is known in its homeland, France, belongs to an ancient family of continental herding dogs and is related to such breeds as the Komondor, the Puli, Bearded Collie, and the Old English Sheepdog. Of these it is claimed that the Briard is the most ancient. Charlemagne (742–814) is said to have owned one of these sheepdogs, and there are records which trace the breed's history back to the 12th century.

Other notable Briard owners have been the Marquis de Lafayette, who brought the first specimens to the New World to work with sheep. Napoleon is reported to have used Briards to drive livestock during his Egyptian campaign.

Probably the best known and most numerous of the French sheepdogs, the Briard is named after the French province of Brie. During the Middle Ages it was used as a guard and watchdog, somewhat later as herder and drover. At the first dog show held in Paris, in 1863, a Briard placed first in the class for sheepdogs, but it was not until 1897 that the Club Français du Chien Berger was founded on behalf of the French sheepdogs and, three years later, Les Amis du Briard, whose specific interest was the promotion of the Briard. It was the latter society which draughted the first breed standard and instituted breeding regulations which did much to improve breed type and quality.

During the first World War Briards were used to carry ammunition and small equipment to the front lines and for sentry duty. As Red Cross dogs they were used to carry first aid supplies and to locate the wounded. Many were killed on the battlefield. Because of their valour the Briards earned the respect of servicemen, and soon after the Armistice was signed in 1918, the first members of the breed began arriving on this continent. The breed remains the most numerous sheepdog in France where it is now also being used in police work.

A unique feature of the breed is the double dewclaws on the hind legs, lack of which constitutes a disqualification under both the Canadian and American breed standards.

The Briard was first registered on this continent in 1922.

double dewclaws

G. STENHOUSE

Briard

Official Breed Standard for the Briard

General Appearance: A strong and substantially built dog, fitted for field work, lithe, muscular, and well proportioned, alert and active.

Size: Height at shoulders—dogs, 23–27 in. (58–69 cm); bitches, 22–25½ in. (55–65 cm). Young dogs may be below the minimum.

Coat and Colour: Coat long, slightly wavy, stiff and strong. All solid colours are allowed except white. Dark colours are preferable. Usual colours: black, and black with some white hairs, dark and light grey, tawny, and combinations of two of these colours, provided there are no marked spots and the transition from one to the other takes place gradually and symmetrically.

Head: Large and rather long. Stop well marked and placed at equal distance from top of head and tip of nose. Forehead very slightly rounded. Line from stop to tip of nose straight. *Muzzle* neither narrow nor pointed. Hair heavy and long on top of head, the ears, and around the muzzle, forming eyebrows standing out and not veiling the eyes too much. *Nose* rather square than rounded, always black. Teeth strong, white, and meet exactly evenly. *Eyes* horizontal, well opened, dark in colour and rather large, intelligent and gentle in expression. *Ears* placed high, not too large and not carried too flat. In France the tips of the ears are generally cropped, causing the ear to be semi-erect.

Neck: Muscular and distinct from the shoulders.

Forequarters: Legs muscular with heavy bones. Feet strong, round, with toes close together and hard pads, nails black.

Body: Back straight. Rump slightly sloped. Chest broad and deep.

Hindquarters: Hock not too near the ground, making a well-marked angle, the leg below the hock being not quite vertical. Two dewclaws on each hind leg are required. A dog with only one cannot be given a prize.

Tail: Well feathered, carried low and twisted neither to the right nor to the left, curled at the end, tip when straightened reaching to point of hock.

Faults: Muzzle pointed. Eyes small, almond shaped, or light in colour. Rump straight or too sloped. White spot on the breast (a large white spot is very bad). Tail too short or carried over the back. White nails.

Disqualifications: *Size below the limit. Absence of dewclaws. Short hair on the head, face, or feet. Tail lacking or cut. Nose light in colour or spotted. Eyes spotted. Hair curled. White hair on feet. Spotted colours of the coat.*

Bullmastiff

THE **B**ULLMASTIFF **IS A PRODUCT** of this century but combines, in predetermined proportions, the bloods of two ancient British breeds: the Bulldog and the Mastiff. The breed was developed to fill a specific need and was generally known as "the gamekeeper's nightdog," a name descriptive of the Bullmastiff's job.

Poaching game on large estates in Britain was an age-old trick, but at the end of the 19th century to be caught poaching carried the death penalty. Such lawbreakers went well-armed to their job and would rather risk killing the gamekeeper than be caught. The keeper's job became a dangerous one indeed, especially at night. What was needed was a dog to warn him of poachers and, if need be, help him in a fight. A dog, in fact, combining the best qualities of both the Bulldog and the Mastiff.

The specifications were laid down. The ideal nightdog should be more agile and faster than the Mastiff; and like the Bulldog a silent worker aggressive enough to attack on command, able to throw and hold a man without mauling or biting him. By melding these two breeds in the proportion of sixty per cent Mastiff, forty per cent Bulldog, the "gamekeeper's nightdog" was created; christened appropriately the Bullmastiff.

Such a cross was not a new idea. It had been used to produce guard dogs on the continent which bear a strong resemblance to the British creation, especially the Dogue de Bordeaux. Similar dogs may have existed in Britain, but this was the first time breeders worked to stabilize the cross and seek official recognition of the new breed. Prime mover in this effort was Mr. S.F. Mosley. A breed club was formed and in 1924 The Kennel Club (England) gave official recognition to the Bullmastiff on condition that only dogs with three generations of pure breeding behind them could be registered. There was to be no more crossing to the parent breeds.

In addition to fighting off armed poachers, the Bullmastiff has been used successfully as a police and army dog and as a guard dog by diamond companies in South Africa.

344

Bullmastiff

The breed made its debut on this continent in 1931 where it is now a frequent, although not large, entry at most dog shows.

Official Breed Standard for the Bullmastiff

NOTE: Faults are classified as Serious or Minor, indicated as (S) and (M) respectively. Note the *minor* faults are either points which would not of themselves contribute to unsoundness in the dog, or are the result of poor conditioning, which might be controlled, and are not likely to be hereditary.

Origin and Purpose: The Bullmastiff was developed in England by gamekeepers for protection against poachers. The foundation breeding of the modern pure-bred was 60 per cent Mastiff and 40 per cent Bulldog. It is a guard and companion dog, and should be loyal, obedient, and thus suitable for training.

General Appearance: The Bullmastiff is a powerfully built, symmetrical dog, showing great strength and activity, but not cumbersome; upstanding and compact in appearance, with breadth and depth of skull and body, the latter set on strong, sturdy, well-boned legs. The height measured vertically from the ground to the highest point of the withers, should nearly equal the length measured horizontally from the forechest to the rear part of the upper thigh, and should slightly exceed the height at the hips. Bitches are feminine in appearance, of somewhat lighter bone structure than the male, but should still convey strength. Faults: (S) Lack of balance. Poor or light bone structure. (M) Lack of muscular development. Ranginess.

Temperament: The Bullmastiff should be bold, fearless and courageous, a dependable guard dog; alert and intelligent. Faults: (S) Viciousness. Shyness. (Such dogs should not be used for breeding.) (M) Apathy and sluggishness.

Size: Height at the highest point of the withers—dogs, 25–27 in. (63–69 cm); bitches, 24–26 in. (61–66 cm).
Weight—dogs, 110–130 lb. (50–59 kg); bitches, 100–120 lb. (45–55 kg). It is important that weight be in proportion to height and bone structure, to ensure balance. Faults: (S) Over maximum height. Under minimum height. (M) Over maximum weight. Under minimum weight.

Coat and Colour: Coat short and dense, giving good weather protection. Faults: (s) Long, soft coat. (M) "Staring" coat, which means poor condition. Colour: any shade of red, fawn or brindle, but the colour to be pure and clear. A small white marking on chest permissible but not desirable. Faults: (s) White markings other than on chest. (M) Black shading on body, legs or tail (of reds or fawns).

Head: The *skull* should be large, equal in breadth, length and depth, with a fair amount of wrinkle when the dog is interested; well-developed cheeks. The skull in circumference may measure the height of the dog. Forehead flat, with furrow between the eyes. Stop definite. Faults: (s) Narrow skull. Shallow skull. (M) Domed forehead. Insufficient stop.

The *muzzle* should be short, broad and deep, in the same proportion as the skull. The distance from the tip of the nose to the stop should not exceed one-third of the length from the tip of the nose to the centre of the occiput. Broad under the eyes and nearly parallel in width to the end of the nose; blunt and cut off square, appearing in profile in a plane parallel to the line of the skull. A black mask is *essential*. The *nose* should be black, flat, and broad with widely spreading nostrils when viewed from the front. Flews not too pendulous. The lower jaw broad. Faults: (s) Muzzle too long, too narrow, pointed or lacking in depth. Muzzle too short; nostrils set on top; nose pointed, upturned or laid back; lower jaw narrow. (M) Lack of wrinkle; flews too pendulous.

Teeth preferably level bite or slightly undershot. Canine teeth large and set wide apart; other teeth strong, even and well placed. Faults: (s) Teeth overshot. Teeth more than ¼ inch (.6 cm) undershot. Wry mouth. (M) Irregular or poorly placed teeth. Small teeth.

Eyes dark or hazel, and of medium size; set apart the width of the muzzle. Faults: (M) Light eyes. Eyes too close together, too large, too small.

Ears V-shaped and carried close to the cheeks; set on wide and high, level with the occiput, giving a square appearance to the skull which is most important. They should be darker in colour than the body, and the point of the ear, when alert, should be level with the eye. Faults: (s) Rose ears. (M) Ears too long or too short. Lack of darker colour.

Neck: Well arched of moderate length, very muscular, and almost equal in circumference to the skull. Faults: (s) Neck too short; too long. Neck weak and scrawny.

Forequarters: Proper angulation and proportionate bone lengths of the forequarters are very important. The shoulder bone should slope forward and downward from the withers at an angle of 45 degrees from the vertical. The humerus (upper arm) should form a right angle with the shoulder bone, 45 degrees from the vertical. The shoulder bone and humerus should be approximately equal in length. The length of the foreleg from the ground to the elbow should be a little more than half the distance from the ground to the withers, approximately 52 per cent. The shoulders and upper arms should be muscular and powerful, but not overloaded. Forelegs powerful, with round heavy bone, vertical and parallel to each other, set well apart; elbows set close to the body. Pasterns straight and strong. Feet of medium size, not turning in or out, with round toes, well arched. Pads thick and tough. Nails black. Faults: (s) Lack of proportion in bone. Shoulder too steep. Shoulders overloaded. Elbows turned in or out. Lack of bone in forelegs. Forelegs bowed. Weak pasterns. Splay feet. (m) Feet turned in or out. White nails.

Body and Tail: Body compact. Chest wide and deep, with ribs well sprung and well set down between the forelegs. Back short and level. Loins wide, muscular; croup slightly arched, with fair depth of flank. Faults: (s) Body too long. Shallow chest. Narrow chest. Lack of ribspring. Sway back. Roach back. Tip of hip bone higher than withers. (m) Too much tuck-up.

Tail set on high, strong at the root and tapering to the hocks. It may be carried straight or curved. Faults: (s) Screw tail. Crank tail. Tail set too low. (m) Tail carried hound fashion. Too long. Too short. Too heavily coated.

Hindquarters: It is important that structure, angulation, and proportionate bone lengths of the hindquarters be in balance with the forequarters. The pelvis (hip bone) should slope backward and downward from the spine at an angle of 30 degrees. The femur (upper thigh bone) should form a right angle with the pelvis. The lower thigh bone (stifle) should set at an angle of 45 degrees to the vertical. The pelvis and femur should be approximately equal in length. The ratio of the lengths of the femur, to the tibia/fibula, to the hock should be approximately as 4:5:3. The length of the lower leg, from the ground to the hock joint, should be a little less than 30 per cent of the distance from the ground to the top of the hip bones. The lower leg should be vertical to the ground. The hips should be broad, in balance with shoulders and rib cage. Hind legs strong and muscular, with well-developed second thighs, denoting power and activity, but not cumbersome, set parallel to each other and well apart, in balance with forelegs and body. Feet as in forequarters. Faults: (S) Lack of proportion in bone. Poor angulation at hip bone. Narrow hip structure. Stifle too straight or over-angulated. Cowhocks. Bowed hind legs. Splay feet. (M) Feet turned in or out. White nails.

Gait: The gait should be free, balanced and vigorous. When viewed from the side the dog should have good reach in the forequarters and good driving power in the hindquarters. The back should be level and firm, indicating good transmission from rear to front. When viewed from the front (coming toward) or from the rear (going away), at a moderate pace, the dog shall track in two parallel lines, neither too close together nor too far apart, so placed as to give a strong well-balanced movement. The toes (fore and hind) should point straight ahead.

Direction to exhibitors and judges: The dog should be moved in the ring at a sufficient speed to show fluidity of movement, and not at a slow walk. Faults: (S) Rolling, paddling, or weaving when gaited. Any crossing movement, either front or rear. Stilted and restricted movement. (Dogs with structural weakness as evidenced by poor movement should not be used for breeding.)

Disqualifications: *Liver mask. No mask. Yellow eyes.*

Canadian Eskimo Dog

THE ESKIMO DOG, which is the only breed of dog associated with the aboriginal people of the Arctic, has a history dating back between 1100 and 2000 years. Authorities suggest that the breed was probably taken to the North American arctic by the Thule Eskimos and that the dogs gradually spread from Alaska to Greenland. The Eskimo people call this dog the "Kingmik" and for centuries have used him to pull their sleds in winter, a job the dogs do joyfully despite low or non-existent rations. In summer the Kingmik is a pack dog, and in all seasons he is a companion on the hunt being keen enough of nose to locate seal breathing holes in the ice, and brave enough to hold large game at bay for the hunter to come in for the kill.

The Eskimo Dog figured prominently in polar expeditions and was highly regarded by the explorer Robert Peary who said this was the only dog in the world that could work "so long in the lowest temperatures with practically nothing to eat." In addition, contrary to much that has been written about the Eskimo Dog, the breed has a loving, happy nature.

Why then has the breed not been taken up by sled dog fanciers farther south? Possibly because the breed is said not to fare well in temperate climates. What is more probable is that the Eskimo is an in-between breed—not so swift as the Siberian Husky nor so strong as the Alaskan Malamute.

Because the breed has been left to the fortunes of the Northland his future seems uncertain. In the 1920s it is reported there were 20,000 Eskimo Dogs in the north. Fifty years later there were less than 200 pure-breds left. While the breed is still being used extensively for sled work in northern Greenland, this job has been taken over by the snowmobile in other regions. Struck with the seriousness of these declining figures, early in the 1970s William Carpenter, with the help of The Canadian Kennel Club, began a project to re-establish the Eskimo Dog and save it from extinction. Funding came from private citizens and a grant from The Canada Council. Carpenter's goal was to bring breed registrations to a total of 300 over a three-year period.

G.STENHOUSE

Canadian Eskimo Dog

Official Breed Standard for the Canadian Eskimo Dog

Origin and Purpose: The Canadian Eskimo Dog is an aboriginal breed of dog that has gone through many name changes. As a breed, The Canadian Kennel Club has, in the past, referred to the dog as the "Eskimo," "Exquimaux Husky," "Esquimaux Dog," and "Husky." The Inuit of Arctic Canada called this dog "Qimmiq." The breed has an 1100- to 2000-year history of being interdependent with the Thule culture of Inuit (Eskimo people) who, following the Dorset culture, occupied the coastal and archipelago area of what is now Arctic Canada. Although within the spitz family of dogs, the Canadian Eskimo Dog's origin prior to this is lost in the Inuit prehistory which includes the migration of the Mongolian race from the Asian continent to North America. The existing strain of Canadian Eskimo Dog originated from stock primarily bred by the Eskimo Dog Research Foundation in the Northwest Territories. The foundation's work over a six-year period was primarily funded by the Governments of Canada and the Northwest Territories and involved the purchase of specimens from the remnant population of dogs kept by the Inuit of the Boothia Peninsula, Melville Peninsula and parts of Baffin Island. The Canadian Eskimo Dog, as a primitive dog, is primarily a carnivorous breed, whose natural diet consisted of seal, walrus, fish, or caribou. For centuries this breed was used as a draught animal and was capable of pulling between 45 and 80 kg per dog, covering distances from 15 to 70 miles per day. He was also used as a hunting dog, to locate seal breathing holes for the Inuit hunters. As a hunting dog he would also attack and hold at bay musk ox and polar bear for the Inuit hunters. In the summer the dog was used as a pack dog carrying up to 15 kg.

General Appearance: The Canadian Eskimo Dog is a powerfully built, moderately sized dog with a thick neck and chest and medium length legs. Typical of the spitz family of dogs he has a wedge-shaped head held high with thick erect ears. The eyes are obliquely set giving a serious appearance. The dog has a bushy tail carried up or curled over the back. Of almost equal height at the hips as at the withers, medium to large boned and well muscled the dog displays a majestic and powerful physique giving the impression that he is not built for speed but rather for hard work. During the winter the body is thickly clothed with an outer coat of straight or erect hair; below is dense underfur which enables the animal to easily withstand the rigours of high latitudes. A mane-like growth of longer hair over the neck and shoulder will appear on male specimens. The whole conformation of the Canadian Eskimo Dog should be one of strength, power and endurance balanced with agility, alertness and boldness. The female of the breed will usually have a shorter coat than the male and will always be significantly smaller than the male. As young bitches, they will be finer boned giving among other things a narrower head which tends to produce a friendlier looking face than with males. Both males and females of the breed are known to have a rapid growth rate reaching working size around seven months. However, the maturing process extends to at least three years of age giving them a very majestic appearance. Puppies have often been described as miniature adults, with erect ears and a curly tail at the young ages between three to five weeks. There may be occasional periods during adolescent growth stages when the ears may not be fully erect but it is important to note that the ears of the Canadian Eskimo Dog do not have the same gradual growth of becoming erect around four months of age as is seen in some other breeds.

Temperament: The temperament of the Canadian Eskimo Dog should reflect the tough, hard-working breed that he is. He is not to be viewed as a domestic pet but rather as a primitive dog originally domesticated by Inuit for specific tasks in a harsh arctic environment. In general disposition, the mature Canadian Eskimo Dog is gentle and affectionate with the average individual, enjoying attention. Even with total strangers the dogs are rarely standoffish. Usually they will exhibit a rather quiet friendliness and harmless curiosity or become completely distant. The dog is very pack oriented and if raised as a group, dominant and subordinate roles will be acted out under the leadership of a totally dominant or boss dog. Behaviour within a group or pack is usually well structured and controlled but it is not uncommon to see battle scars or torn ears on dogs originating from kennel areas where the dogs are raised in groups or packs. Compared to modern domestic breeds, the Canadian Eskimo Dog has an almost over response to any stimulus whether it be food, work, fighting or play. For this reason, the dog should be a companion for adults and is not to be considered a child's pet.

Size: Height of males should range from 23–27½ in. (58–70 cm) at the withers and approximately the same height at the hip. Weight of males in working condition will generally range from 66–88 lb. (30–40 kg) in relation to the height. Height of females should be 19½–23½ in. (50–60 cm) at the withers and approximately the same height at the hip. Weight of females in working condition should range from 40–66 lb. (18–30 kg).

Coat and Colour: Subject to an annual moult usually in August or September, the coat is thick and dense with guard hairs being hard and stiff. This outer coat will vary from 3–6 in. (7–15 cm) in length. In males it will occur in a mane-like growth over the shoulder and neck making the male appear much larger in size and taller at the withers than he actually is. The undercoat is very dense to give excellent protection during the most extreme winter conditions. During the moult this underfur will come loose in clumps over a period of a few days. Females will usually have a shorter coat over-all partially because of the additional moult that will occur following the birth of pups. No one colour or colour pattern should dominate the breed with the colour and colour patterns of the Canadian Eskimo Dog ranging from:

a) An all white body with pigmentation around the eyes, nose and lips (*e.g.* not albino).
b) White body with only the smallest amount of red, buff (including cinnamon shades), grey or black around the ears or eyes.
c) White bodies with either red, buff, cinnamon, grey, or black head marks around ears and eyes or the entire head and the occasional small patch of the same colour on the body usually around the hip or flank.
d) Red and white, or buff and white, or cinnamon and white or black and white with about 50/50 distribution of the two colours, on various parts of the body.
e) Red body or buff body or cinnamon body with white on chest and/or legs and underside of body.
f) Sable or black body or dark grey body with white on chest and/or legs and underside of body occasionally extending around part of the neck in a collar-like fashion.
g) Silver grey or greyish white body.
h) Buff to brown undercoat with black guard hairs.

Very common to dogs with solid colour to most of the head is a mask-like shading of white around the eyes and/or muzzle with or without white spots over the eyes. On very rare occasions the spots over the eyes as well as cheek-marks will be buff coloured thus adding a third colour to a normally two-coloured animal. Pigmentation of the nose will vary from black to light brown (especially on lighter coloured dogs with red, buff, or cinnamon on the body). Butterfly noses have, on occasion, appeared with the light brown nose.

Head: Over-all the *skull* would be described as massive but well proportioned being broad and wedge-shaped. Although often described as wolf-like in appearance the head of the Canadian Eskimo Dog has a more elevated forehead. Immature females will have a much narrower skull than the male. The *muzzle* is tapered and of medium length. *Mouth:* the jaws are heavy and powerful possessing large teeth with well-developed canine teeth. The incisors meet in a scissor bite. The teeth are perfectly adapted for the dog's instinctive approach to ripping and tearing his meat or fish. Lips are black or brown with pink. The *eyes* are generally dark-coloured but hazel or yellow-coloured eyes will appear in the breed. They are small, wide spaced and placed obliquely in the head which tends to impart much more of a wild and deceitful appearance than the dog deserves. The *ears* are short, thick and have slightly rounded ends. They are carried erect, turned forward and are covered with dense short hair. Width of the forehead between the ears on the males will be from 5—6 in. (13—15 cm). On the females the distance will be from 4 1/2—5 1/2 in. (11—14 cm).

The natural voice is a howl, not a bark. When in a group the dogs often give voice in a chorus of strangely woven tones and this is one of the thrilling sounds of the Arctic. A number of dogs will produce a mass crescendo persisting for varying periods until as if cued by a special note all will abruptly stop.

Neck: The neck is short, straight, thick, and very muscular.

Forequarters: The dog has broad shoulders obliquely set with moderate muscling. The forelegs are straight but may give the appearance of being bowed because of the well developed triceps muscle above and behind the elbow and the pronounced muscle on the forearm itself. Feet are large, nearly round, well arched with thick pads being well furred between; however, under extremely cold winter conditions, this fur will grow to be very long so as to cover the bottom of the pads.

Body: The body should further accentuate the over-all power and endurance of the dog through a deep, wide and well muscled chest to a well-developed loin. There is very little curve to the flank. Interestingly, the spinal column when felt through the furred body is well pronounced. Above all the body should be muscled and not fat. The skin of the dog should feel thick and tough. Females will have a smaller and less muscled body than the males.

Hindquarters: The hips may appear as pronounced and bony as the spine, and are about the same height as the withers. The legs will be very muscular with the width of the thigh being carried well down towards the hock. The stifles are well bent. The hind feet are similar in design to the front but slightly longer. From the rear the legs will appear straight with the hocks turning neither in nor out.

Tail: The tail is large and bushy and generally carried up or curled over the back. Mature bitches may on occasion carry their tails down.

Gait: The working gait of this dog is a powerful and brisk trot with the rear legs moving in line with the front legs on the force motion but showing some abduction during the forward movement of the stride. This may be especially pronounced in mature male dogs with many miles in harness. This gait may appear awkward to the untrained eye but is a result of a wide stance caused by well-developed thighs. This particular gait is a well-balanced efficient stride for heavy pulling day after day. The movement of the dog should in no way appear as a choppy or paddling motion. The females are much faster and freer in movement than the heavier males and are capable of break-ing stride from the natural trot and running or galloping for much longer distances than the males.

Faults: Head: square muzzle or loose lips, round or bulging eyes. Legs: thin, fine boned or cow hocked. Neck: long and thin. Coat: short, off prime. Body: narrow chest, over-all lack of muscle, excess fat, sloping back, coarseness or lack of finer bones in bitches. Feet: flat or open.

Disqualifications: *Blue eyes, dewclaws on rear legs; floppy ears, the exception being battle torn ears; clipping or altering the coat by scissoring; no evidence at all of a curled or upright tail in male dogs (recognizing that a tail may occasionally be kept down as a sign of subordination or stress); excessive undershot or overshot jaw.*

Scale of Points:
General appearance and gait 25
Head 5
Teeth 5
Body 15
Coat condition and texture 20
Coat colour 0
Legs 10
Feet 20
                          TOTAL 100

Collie (Rough)
Collie (Smooth)

DOG HISTORIANS AGREE that the Collie descends from herding dogs brought to Britain at the time of the Roman Conquest. Later, when England was invaded by the Picts and Scots, it is surmised that some of these dogs were taken north to Scotland, where a breed of intelligent sheepherders slowly emerged. Scotland is regarded as the homeland of the Collie and the breed is often erroneously referred to as the "Scotch Collie."

Earliest reference to the "colley" appears in *The Canterbury Tales* written in the 14th century. A later work, dated 1570, describes the way these herders worked in response to the shepherd's whistled commands. The dogs were used to tend the flocks, gather in the strays and, at sale time, drive the sheep to market.

So familiar were the dogs that they received little attention until after the introduction of the dog show in Britain in 1859. The following year some of the breed were exhibited at the Birmingham show where they were classified as "sheep dogs." They failed to excite much interest until later in that same year when Queen Victoria saw some Collies while on a visit to Balmoral Castle in Scotland. She was so taken with the cleverness of the working dogs that she brought some Collies back with her to the Royal Kennels at Windsor. From that date onward the Collie "had it made."

It is suggested that some Borzoi blood may have been introduced to give a touch of elegance to the breed's appearance. Whatever magic was worked, the Collie leapt from the obscurity of being the lowly shepherd's helper to one of the world's most fashionable and beloved breeds. Much of the breed's fame and popularity was generated by the stories of Albert Payson Trehune and later by the "Lassie" films.

The origin of the breed name is a continuing subject of speculation. Most generally accepted is that the name derives from the Anglo-Saxon word for black, "col," and that the

Collie (Rough)

Collie (Smooth)

black-faced sheep of Scotland were called "colleys." Thus the dog that drove them was the "colley dog."

While there are two breeds of Collie, the Rough and the Smooth, identical in all respects except for length of coat and judged by the same breed standard, the Smooth has never achieved the popularity of his longer coated brother.

The breed standard in Canada and the United States calls for a somewhat taller dog than does the British. Also, in Britain white is not considered an acceptable Collie colour.

In the first Stud Book issued by The Canadian Kennel Club (1888–1889) there were 123 Rough Collies registered.

Official Breed Standard for the Collie (Rough)

Origin and Purpose: Both breeds of Collie originated in the British Isles. The Rough Collie was originally used as a herding dog, while the Smooth Collie was the drover's dog.

General Appearance: The Collie is a lithe, strong, responsive, active dog, carrying no useless timber, standing naturally straight and firm. The deep moderately wide chest shows strength, the sloping shoulders and well-bent hocks indicate speed and grace and the face shows high intelligence. The Collie presents an impressive, proud picture of true balance, each part being in harmonious proportion to every other part and to the whole. Except for the technical description that is essential to this Standard and without which no Standard for the guidance of breeders and judges is adequate, it could be stated simply that no part of the Collie ever seems to be out of proportion to any other part. Timidity, frailness, sullenness, viciousness, lack of animation, cumbersome appearance, and lack of over-all balance impair the general character.

Size: Dogs are from 24–26 in. (60–67 cm) at the shoulder and weigh from 60–75 lb. (27–34 kg). Bitches are from 22–24 in. (55–61 cm) at the shoulder, weighing from 50–65 lb. (22–30 kg). An undersized or an oversized Collie is penalized according to the extent to which the dog appears to be undersized or oversized.

Coat and Colour: The well-fitting, proper-textured coat is the crowning glory of the Rough variety of Collie. It is abundant except on the head and legs. The outer coat is straight and harsh to the touch. A soft, open outer coat or a curly outer coat, regardless of quantity, is penalized. The undercoat, however, is soft, furry and so close together that it is difficult to see the skin when the hair is parted. The coat is very abundant on the mane and frill. The face or mask is smooth. The forelegs are smooth and well feathered to the back of the pasterns. The hind legs are smooth below the hock joints. Any feathering below the hocks is removed for the show rings. The hair on the tail is very profuse and on the hips it is long and bushy. The texture, quantity, and the extent to which the coat "fits the dog" are important points.

The five recognized colours are "Sable and White," "Tricolour," "Blue Merle," "Sable Merle," and "White." There is no preference among them. The "Sable and White" is predominantly sable (a sable colour of varying shades from light gold to dark mahogany) with white markings usually on the chest, neck, legs, feet and the tip of the tail. A blaze may appear on the foreface or backskull or both. The "Tricolour" is predominantly black, carrying white marking as in a sable and white and has tan shadings on and about the head and legs. The "Blue Merle" is a mottled or "marbled" colour, predominantly blue-grey and black with white markings as in the "Sable and White" and usually has tan shadings as in the "Tricolour." The "Sable Merle" is predominantly a light sable with darker sable mottling or marbling as in the "Blue Merle" and with white markings as in the "Sable and White." The "White" is predominantly white, with sable, tricolour, blue merle, or sable merle markings on the head and elsewhere.

Head: The head properties are of great importance. When considered in proportion to the size of the dog the head is inclined to lightness and never appears massive. A heavy-headed dog lacks the necessary bright, alert, full-of-sense look that contributes so greatly to expression.

Both in front and profile view the head bears a general resemblance to a well-blunted wedge, being smooth and clean in outline and nicely balanced in proportion. On the sides it tapers gradually and smoothly from the ears to the end of the black nose, without being flared out in backskull (cheeky) or pinched-in muzzle (snipey). In profile view the top of the backskull and the top of the muzzle lie in two approximately parallel, straight planes of equal length, divided by a very slight but perceptible stop or break.

There is a very slight prominence of the eyebrows. The backskull is flat, without receding either laterally or backward and the occipital bone is not highly peaked. The proper width of backskull necessarily depends upon the combined length of skull and muzzle and the width of the backskull is less than its length. Thus the correct width varies with the individual and is dependent upon the extent to which it is supported by length of muzzle.

A midpoint between the inside corners of the eyes (which is the centre of the correctly placed stop) is the centre of balance in length of head.

The end of the smooth, well-rounded *muzzle* is blunt but not square. The underjaw is strong, clean-cut and the depth of skull from the brow to the under part of the jaw is not excessive.

The *teeth* are of good size, meeting in a scissors bite.

Because of the combination of the flat skull, the arched eyebrows, the slight stop and the rounded muzzle, the foreface must be chiselled to form a receptacle for the eyes and they are necessarily placed obliquely to give them the required forward outlook. Except for the blue merles, they are required to be matched in colour. They are almond shaped, of medium size and never properly appear to be large or prominent. The colour is dark and the eye does not show a yellow ring or a sufficiently prominent haw to affect the dog's expression.

The *eyes* have a clear, bright appearance, expressing intelligent inquisitiveness, particularly when the ears are drawn up and the dog is on the alert.

In blue merles, dark brown eyes are preferable, but either or both eyes may be merle or china in colour without specific penalty.

A large, round, full eye seriously detracts from the desired "sweet" expression.

The *ears* are in proportion to the size of the head and, if they are carried properly and unquestionably "break" naturally, are seldom too small. Large ears usually cannot be lifted correctly off the head and even if lifted they will be out of proportion to the size of the head. When in repose the ears are folded lengthwise and thrown back into the frill. On the alert they are drawn well up on the backskull and are carried about three-quarters erect, with about one-fourth of the ear tipping or "breaking" forward.

Expression is one of the most important points in considering the relative value of Collies. "Expression," like the term "Character," is difficult to define in words. It is not a fixed point as in colour, weight, or height and it is something the uninitiated can properly understand only by optical illustration. In general, however, it may be said to be the combined product of the shape and balance of the skull and muzzle, the placement, size, shape, and colour of the eyes, and the position, size and carriage of the ears. An expression that shows sullenness or which is suggestive of any other breed is entirely foreign. The Collie cannot be judged properly until its expression has been carefully evaluated.

Neck: The neck is firm, clean, muscular, sinewy, and heavily frilled. It is fairly long, is carried upright with a slight arch at the nape and imparts a proud, upstanding appearance showing off the frill.

Forequarters: The forelegs are straight and muscular, with a fair amount of bone considering the size of the dog. A cumbersome appearance is undesirable. The forearm is moderately fleshy and the pasterns are flexible, but without weakness.

Body: The back is strong and level, supported by powerful hips and thighs and the croup is sloped to give a well-rounded finish. The body is firm, hard and muscular, a trifle long in proportion to the height. The ribs are well rounded behind the well-sloped shoulders and the chest is deep, extending to the elbows. The loin is powerful and slightly arched.

Hindquarters: The hind legs are less fleshy than the forelegs, are muscular at the thighs, very sinewy and the hocks and stifles are well bent. The comparatively small feet are approximately oval in shape. The soles are well padded and tough and the toes are well arched and close together. When the Collie is not in motion, the legs and feet are judged by allowing the dog to come to a natural stop in a standing position so that both the forelegs and the hind legs are placed well apart, with the feet extending straight forward. Excessive "posing" is undesirable.

Tail: The tail is moderately long, the bone reaching to the hock joint or below. It is carried low when the dog is quiet, the end having an upward twist or "swirl." When gaited or when the dog is excited it is carried gaily, but not over the back.

Gait: Gait is sound. When the dog is moved at a slow trot towards an observer, its straight front legs track comparatively close together at the ground. The front legs are not out at the elbows, do not "cross over," neither does the dog move with a choppy, pacing, or rolling gait. When viewed from the rear the hind legs are straight, tracking comparatively close together at the ground. At a moderate trot the hind legs are powerful and propelling. Viewed from the side the reasonably long, "reaching" stride is smooth and even, keeping the back line firm and level.

As the speed of the gait is increased, the Collie single tracks, bringing the front legs inward in a straight line from the shoulder toward the centre line of the body and the hind legs inward in a straight line from the hip toward the centre line of the body. The gait suggests effortless speed combined with the dog's herding heritage, requiring it to be capable of changing its direction of travel almost instantaneously.

Faults: A soft, open outer coat or a curly outer coat, regardless of quantity, is penalized. Because of the importance of the head characteristics, prominent head faults are severely penalized. Overshot or undershot jaws are undesirable, the latter being more severely penalized. Eye faults are heavily penalized. A dog with prick ears or low ears cannot show true expression and is penalized accordingly. Both narrow and wide placement of the forelegs are penalized. Noticeably fat dogs or dogs in poor flesh or with skin diseases or with no undercoat are out of condition and are moderately penalized accordingly. A dog which moves cow-hocked, or a dog with straight stifles, should be penalized.

Disqualifications: *Monorchid or cryptorchid in grown males. In sables and sable merles, blue eyes is a disqualification.*

Official Breed Standard for the Collie (Smooth)

The Smooth variety of Collie is judged by the same standard as the Rough variety, except that the references to the quantity and distribution of the coat are not applicable to the Smooth variety, which has a short, hard, dense, flat coat of good texture, with an abundance of undercoat.

Doberman Pinscher

THE DOBERMAN PINSCHER, known in Britain and on the continent simply as the Dobermann, is named after the breed's creator, Louis Dobermann, a tax collector in Apolda, a town in Thuringia, Germany. Dobermann was a dog lover and, as it has transpired, a skilled breeder. What he wanted was an alert, aggressive companion dog to protect him while making his rounds. Because Dobermann was also the keeper of the local animal shelter he had a continuing supply of breeding stock to use in his creation. He began his project in the 1880s and although he kept no breeding records, educated guesses have it that the Dobe was built around the German Pinscher, the Rottweiler, the Manchester Terrier, and the Greyhound.

By 1899 Dobermann's creation was complete. A specialty club was organized for the breed's promotion and improvement and the Dobe was introduced to the public at a dog show. The reception was less than enthusiastic. Early specimens were considered coarse, rough, and ill-tempered. Nevertheless, the breed did attract those interested in an alert, medium-sized security dog. Dobermann was joined in his efforts by a fellow breeder, Herr Goeller, who worked towards improving elegance and refinement. It was Goeller who draughted the first breed standard and obtained official recognition of the Dobermann from the German Kennel Club in 1900.

First specimens came to the United States in 1908 and it is American breeders who are credited with developing the handsome, elegant, tractable present-day Dobe.

Two world wars dealt harshly with the breed. Many of the dogs were conscripted for war service. Many were put to sleep or starved to death. But after 1945 there was sufficient breeding stock still available on the continent to give new impetus to the breed. More imports came to America, and in 1947 the first Dobes were brought to Britain. There the breed has overcome much prejudice to become one of the country's most popular working breeds. On this side of the Atlantic the Dobe has gone from strength to strength. Renowned as an intelligent security

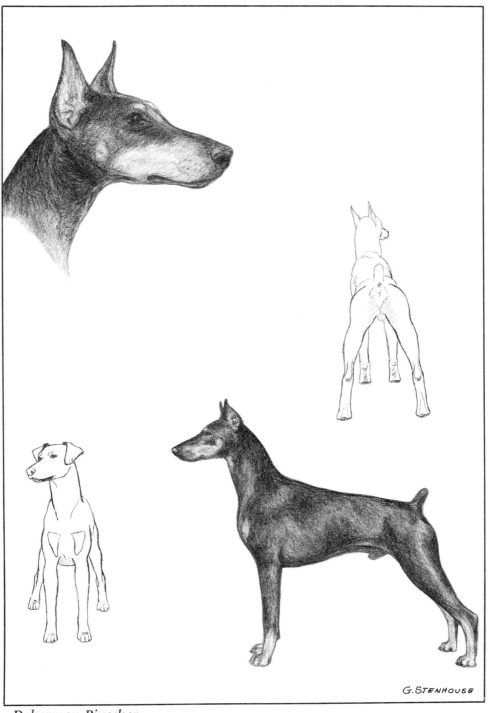

Doberman Pinscher

dog, the breed has also earned the reputation as a reliable, affectionate family pet.

The breed's most influential stud is said to have been Ch. Dictator of Glenhugel who passed on his outstanding temperament and, as far down as the tenth generation, a cowlick on the nape of the neck that has come to be known as the "mark of Dictator."

The Doberman Pinscher was first registered in Canada in 1912.

Official Breed Standard for the Doberman Pinscher

Origin and Purpose: The Doberman Pinscher originated in Germany around 1890, and takes its name from Louis Dobermann. Originally it was used almost exclusively as a guard dog. In today's society, the properly bred and trained specimen makes a loving and obedient family companion.

General Appearance: The appearance is that of a dog of good middle size, with a body that is square: the height measured vertically from the ground to the highest point of the withers equalling the length, measured horizontally from the forechest to the rear projection of the upper thigh. The Doberman should be elegant in appearance, with proud carriage, reflecting great nobility, and should be compactly built, muscular and powerful for great endurance and speed.

Temperament: Energetic, watchful, determined, alert, fearless, loyal, and obedient.

Size: Height at withers—males, ideal 27$\frac{1}{2}$ in. (70 cm); females, ideal 25$\frac{1}{2}$ in. (65 cm). Males, decidedly masculine, without coarseness. Females, decidedly feminine, without over-refinement. Deviation from ideal height to be penalized in proportion to the amount of deviation.

Coat and Colour: Smooth haired, short, hard, thick and close lying. Invisible grey undercoat on neck permissible. Allowed colours: black, red, blue, and fawn. In each colour the more strongly pigmented coat is the more desirable.

Markings: rust red, sharply defined, and appearing above each eye, and on muzzle, throat, and forechest, and on all legs and feet, and below tail. White on chest not exceeding one-half square inch permissible.

Head: Long and dry, resembling a blunt wedge, both frontal and profile views. When seen from the front, the head widens gradually towards the base of the ears in a practically unbroken line. Top of *skull* flat, turning with slight stop to bridge of muzzle, with muzzle line extending parallel to the topline of the skull. Length of *muzzle* equal to length of skull. Cheeks flat and muscular. Lips lying close to the jaws, and not drooping. Jaws full and powerful, well filled under the eyes. *Nose* solid black in black dogs, dark brown in reds, dark grey in blues, and dark tan in fawns. Teeth strongly developed. Lower incisors upright and touching inside of upper incisors—a true scissors bite. Forty-two teeth (22 in lower jaw and 20 in upper jaw) correctly placed. Distemper teeth not to be penalized. *Eyes* almond shaped, not round, moderately deep set, not prominent, with vigorous, energetic expression. Iris of uniform colour, ranging from medium to darkest brown in black dogs, the darker shade being the more desirable. In reds, blues and fawns, the colour of the iris should blend with that of the markings, but not be of a lighter hue than that of the markings. *Ears* either cropped or uncropped. The upper attachment of the ear, when alert, should be on a level with the top of the skull. If cropped, the ears should be well trimmed and carried erect. If uncropped, they should be small and neat, and set high on the head.

Neck: Carried proudly, well muscled and dry. Well arched, and with nape of neck widening gradually toward body. Length of neck proportioned to body and head. Head may be carried slightly lower when moving, for greater reach of the forequarters.

Forequarters: Shoulder blade sloping forward and downward at a 45-degree angle to the ground, and meeting the upper arm at an angle of 90 degrees. Shoulder to be as close to 45 degrees as possible and set well back. Relative length of shoulder and upper arm should be as one to one, excess length of shoulder blade is more a fault than excess length of upper arm. Height from elbow to withers approximately equals height from ground to elbow. Legs seen from the front and side perfectly straight and parallel to each other from elbow to pastern; muscled and sinewy, with round, heavy bone. In a normal position, and when gaiting, the elbow should lie close to the brisket. Pasterns firm, with an almost perpendicular position to the ground. Feet well arched, compact and cat-like, turning neither in nor out. Slight toeing out much less undesirable than toeing in. Dewclaws may be removed.

Body: Back short, firm, of sufficient width, and muscular at the loin extending in a straight line from withers to the slightly rounded croup. Withers pronounced and forming the highest point of the body. Brisket full and broad, reaching deep to the elbow. Chest broad, and forechest well defined. Ribs well sprung from the spine, but flattened at lower end to provide elbow clearance. Belly well tucked up, extending in a curved line from chest. Loins well muscled. Hips broad in proportion to body, breadth of hips being approximately equal to breadth of body at rib spring.

Hindquarters: In balance with forequarters. Upper shanks long, wide, and well muscled on both sides of thigh, with clearly defined stifles. Hocks while the dog is at rest: hock to heel should be perpendicular to the ground. Upper shanks, lower shanks and hocks parallel to each other, and wide enough apart to fit in with a properly built body. The hip bone should fall away from the spinal column at an angle of about 30 degrees. Upper shank and lower shank are equal in length. The upper shank should be at right angles to the hip bone. Croup well filled out. Cat feet, as on front legs, turning neither in nor out. Dewclaws, if any, may be removed.

Tail: Tail docked at approximately the second joint, should appear to be the continuation of the spine, without material drop.

Gait: The gait should be free, balanced, and effortless with good reach in the forequarters and good driving power in the hindquarters. When trotting there should be a strong rear action drive. Hocks should fully extend. Each rear leg should move in line with the foreleg on the same side. Rear and front legs should be thrown neither in nor out. Back should remain strong, firm and level. When moving at a fast trot the properly built dog will single track.

Faults: Feminine dogs, masculine. Light tan or muddied markings. Overly large markings. Head out of balance in proportion to both Ram's, dish-faced, cheeky or snipey head. Any deviation from the correct number or placement of teeth to be penalized in direct proportion to the amount of deviation. Slit eyes, glassy eyes, round eyes. Weak or knuckled-over pasterns. Hare feet, splay feet. Overly rounded or flat croup.

Major Faults: Coarseness, fine Greyhound build. Loose shoulder, straight shoulder. Sway or roach back. Straight stifles, cowhocks, spread hocks, sickle hocks.

Scale of Points:

GENERAL CONFORMATION AND APPEARANCE

Proportions	8	
Bone and substance	8	
Temperament and expression	8	
Nobility and condition	5	29

HEAD

Shape	6	
Teeth	5	
Eyes	3	
Ears	1	15

NECK	3	3

BODY

Backline, withers, loins	8	
Tail placement, chest, brisket, rib spring	8	
Tuck-up, shape, and proportions	4	20

FOREQUARTERS

Shoulders, upper arms, legs	5	
Pasterns, angulation	4	
Paws	2	11

HINDQUARTERS

Upper thigh, stifle	5	
Hocks, angulation	4	
Paws	2	11

GAIT	6	6

COAT, COLOUR, AND MARKINGS	5	5

TOTAL		100

Disqualifications: *Shyness, viciousness. Overshot more than* $^3/_{16}$ *inch (.5 cm), undershot more than* $^1/_8$ *inch (.3 cm). Four or more missing teeth.*

Shyness—A dog shall be judged fundamentally shy if, refusing to stand for examination, it shrinks away from the judge; if it fears an approach from the rear; if it shies at sudden and unusual noises to a marked degree.

Viciousness—A dog that attacks, or attempts to attack either the judge or its handler, is definitely vicious. An aggressive or belligerent attitude towards other dogs shall not be deemed vicious.

German Shepherd Dog

THE MOST VERSATILE working dog of them all, the German Shepherd Dog, owes its existence to the efforts of a German cavalry officer, Captain Max von Stephanitz who, in the 1890s, envisioned a super-herding dog that would be intelligent, sound in mind and body, and noble and elegant in appearance. At that time Germany's farm dogs were a mixed lot, valued more for their working ability than their good looks. The best of them, although they varied greatly in appearance, shared two things in common: their body structure was compatible with long hours of hard outdoor work and they had an instinct to guard and herd.

Selecting quality specimens, Stephanitz commenced breeding towards his ideal. His work attracted others and in 1899 a group of eleven men founded the Verein für Deutsche Schaferhund (Society for German Shepherd Dogs) commonly referred to as SV. This society has grown to be the largest and most influential breed club in the world. The society draughted a breed standard for the Shepherd, set up a system of registration and established strict breeding regulations. In that same year it sponsored the first Sieger Show, an event which is held annually at which the best male and female German Shepherd Dog are named the *sieger* and *siegerin* for the year, titles which compare to the North American "victor" and "victrix." This prestigious show draws a huge entry and is attended by Shepherd fanciers from all parts of the world who pay enormous prices for top German breeding stock.

The German Shepherd was first imported to this continent early in the 1900s but did not achieve much popularity until after the First World War. Returning servicemen were high in their praise of the intelligent German breed that had served so valiantly as army dogs. Imports increased, and between the years 1918–1926 the breed's popularity peaked. Dog actors such as Rin Tin Tin and Strongheart brought fame to the breed.

The Shepherd has become renowned around the world for its loyalty and intelligence. As sentry, police dog, tracker, drug dog,

German Shepherd Dog

search and rescue and avalanche dog the breed has no equal. It excels as a guide dog for the blind, has been used successfully to search out gasline leaks, minerals, bodies of dead servicemen buried under desert sand as well as nests of the elusive gypsy moth for the U.S. Department of Agriculture.

Despite his outstanding contribution to man, because of anti-German sentiment in Britain the breed was called the "Alsatian" until the late 1970s at which time the name was revised to German Shepherd Dog (Alsatian).

The breed was first registered in Canada in 1919.

Official Breed Standard for the German Shepherd Dog

General Appearance: The first impression of a good German Shepherd Dog is that of a strong, agile, well-muscled animal, alert and full of life. It should both be and appear to be well balanced, with harmonious development of the forequarter and hindquarter. The dog should appear to the eye, and actually be, longer than tall; deep-bodied, and present an outline of smooth curves rather than corners. It should look substantial and not spindly, giving the impression both at rest and in motion of muscular fitness and nimbleness without any look of clumsiness or soft living.

The Shepherd should be stamped with a look of quality and nobility, difficult to define but unmistakable when present. The good Shepherd Dog never looks common.

Secondary sex characteristics should be strongly marked, and every animal should give a definite impression of masculinity or femininity, according to its sex. Dogs should be definitely masculine in appearance and deportment; bitches, unmistakably feminine, without weakness of structure or apparent softness of temperament.

The condition of the dog should be that of an athlete in good condition, the muscles and flesh firm and the coat lustrous.

Temperament: The breed has a distinct personality marked by a direct and fearless, but not hostile, expression, and self-confidence and a certain aloofness which does not lend itself to immediate and indiscriminate friendships. The Shepherd Dog is not one that fawns upon every new acquaintance. At the same time, it should be approachable, quietly standing its ground and showing confidence and a willingness to meet overtures without itself making them. It should be poised, but when the occasion demands, eager and alert, both fit and willing to serve in any capacity as companion, watch dog, blind leader, herding dog or guardian, whichever the circumstances may demand.

The Shepherd Dog must not be timid, shrinking behind its master or handler; nervous, looking about or upward with anxious expression or showing nervous reactions to strange sounds or sights, or lackadaisical, sluggish, or manifestly disinterested in what goes on about him. Lack of confidence under any surroundings is not typical of good character; cases of extreme timidity and nervous unbalance sometimes give the dog an apparent, but totally unreal, courage and it becomes a "fear biter," snapping not for any justifiable reason but because it is apprehensive of the approach of a stranger. This is a serious fault subject to heavy penalty.

Size: The ideal height for dogs is 25 in. (64 cm), and for bitches, 23 in. (58 cm) at the shoulder. This height is established by taking a perpendicular line from the top of the shoulder blade to the ground with the coat parted or so pushed down that this measurement will show only the actual height of the frame or structure of the dog. The working value of dogs above or below the indicated heights is proportionately lessened, although variations of an inch (3 cm) above or below the ideal height are acceptable, while greater variations must be considered as faults. Weights of dogs of desirable size in proper flesh and condition average between 75 and 85 lb. (34 and 39 kg); and of bitches, between 60 and 70 lb. (27 and 32 kg).

Coat: The Shepherd is normally a dog with a double coat, the amount of undercoat varying with the season of the year and the proportion of the time the dog spends out of doors. It should, however, always be present to a sufficient degree to keep out water, to insulate against temperature extremes, and as a protection against insects. The outer coat should be as dense as possible, hair straight, harsh and lying close to the body. A slightly wavy outer coat, often of wiry texture, is equally permissible. The head, including the inner ear, foreface, and legs and paws are covered with short hair, and the neck with longer and thicker hair. The rear of forelegs and hind legs has somewhat longer hair extending to the pastern and hock respectively. Faults in coat include complete lack of any undercoat, soft, silky or too long outer coat and curly or open coat.

Colour: The German Shepherd Dog differs widely in colour and all colours are permissible. Generally speaking, strong, rich colours are to be preferred, with definite pigmentation and without the appearance of a washed-out colour. White dogs are not desirable and are to be disqualified if showing albino characteristics.

Head: Clean-cut and strong, the head of the Shepherd is characterized by nobility. It should seem in proportion to the body and should not be clumsy, although a degree of coarseness of head, especially in dogs, is less of a fault than over-refinement. A round or domey *skull* is a fault. The *muzzle* is long and strong with the lips firmly fitted, and its topline is usually parallel with an imaginary elongation of the line of the forehead. Seen from the front, the forehead is only moderately arched and the skull slopes into the long wedge-shaped muzzle without abrupt stop. Jaws are strongly developed. Weak and too narrow underjaws, snipey muzzles, and no stop are faults.

Teeth: the strong teeth—42 in number, 20 upper and 22 lower—are strongly developed and meet in a scissors grip in which part of the inner surface of the upper teeth meets and engages part of the outer surface of the lower teeth. This type of bite gives a more powerful grip than one in which the edges of the teeth meet directly, and is subject to less wear. The dog is overshot when the lower teeth fail to engage the inner surfaces of the upper teeth. This is a serious fault. The reverse condition —an undershot jaw—is a very serious fault. While missing premolars are frequently observed, complete dentition is decidedly to be preferred. So-called distemper teeth and discoloured teeth are faults whose seriousness varies with the degree of departure from the desired white, sound colouring. Teeth broken by accident should not be severely penalized but worn teeth, especially the incisors, are often indicative of the lack of a proper scissors bite, although some allowance should be made for age.

Eyes of medium size, almond shaped, set a little obliquely and not protruding. The colour as dark as possible. Eyes of lighter colour are sometimes found and are not a serious fault if they harmonize with the general colouration, but a dark brown eye is always to be preferred. The expression should be keen, intelligent, and composed.

The *ears* should be moderately pointed, open towards the front, and are carried erect when at attention, the ideal carriage being one in which the centre lines of the ears, viewed from the front, are parallel to each other and perpendicular to the ground. Puppies usually do not permanently raise their ears until the fourth or sixth month, and sometimes not until later. Cropped and hanging ears are to be discarded. The well-placed and well-carried ear of a size in proportion to the skull materially adds to the general appearance of the Shepherd. Neither too large nor too small ears are desirable. Too much stress, however, should not be laid on perfection of carriage if the ears are fully erect.

Neck: The neck is strong and muscular, clean-cut and relatively long, proportionate in size to the head and without loose folds of skin. When the dog is at attention or excited, the head is raised and the neck carried high, otherwise typical carriage of the head is forward rather than up and but little higher than the top of the shoulder, particularly in motion.

Body: The whole structure of the body gives an impression of depth and solidity without bulkiness. Forechest, commencing at the prosternum, should be well filled and carried well down between the legs with no sense of hollowness. Chest: deep and capacious with ample room for lungs and heart. Well carried forward, with the prosternum, or process of the breastbone, showing ahead of the shoulder when the dog is viewed from the side. Ribs should be well sprung and long, neither barrel shaped nor too flat, and carried down to a breastbone which reaches to the elbow. Correct ribbing allows the elbow to move back freely when the dog is at a trot, while too round a rib causes interference and throws the elbow out. Ribbing should be carried well back so that loin and flank are relatively short. Abdomen firmly held and not paunchy. The bottom line of the Shepherd is only moderately tucked up in flank, never like that of a Greyhound.

Legs: The bone of the legs should be straight, oval rather than round or flat, and free from sponginess. Its development should be in proportion to the size of the dog and contribute to the over-all impression of substance without grossness. Crooked leg bones and any malformation such as, for example, that caused by rickets, should be penalized. Pastern should be of medium length, strong and springy. Much more spring of pastern is desirable in the Shepherd Dog than in many other breeds, as it contributes to the ease and elasticity of the trotting gait. The upright terrier pastern is definitely undesirable.

Metatarsus (the so-called "hock"): short, clean, sharply defined, and of great strength. This is the fulcrum upon which much of the forward movement of the dog depends. Cowhocks are a decided fault, but before penalizing for cowhocks, it should be definitely determined, with the animal in motion, that the dog has this fault, since many dogs with exceptionally good hindquarter angulation occasionally stand so as to give the appearance of cowhockedness which is not actually present.

Feet: rather short, compact, with toes well arched, pads thick and hard, nails short and strong. The feet are important to the working qualities of the dog. The ideal foot is extremely strong with good gripping power and plenty of depth of pad. The so-called cat-foot, or terrier foot, is not desirable. The thin, spread or hare-foot is, however, still more undesirable.

Topline: The withers should be higher than, and sloping into, the level back to enable a proper attachment of the shoulder blades. The back should be straight and very strongly developed without sag or roach, the section from the wither to the croup being relatively short. (The desirable long proportion of the Shepherd Dog is not derived from a long back but from over-all length with relation to height, which is achieved by breadth of forequarter and hindquarter viewed from the side.) Loin: viewed from the top, broad and strong, blending smoothly into the back without undue length between the last rib and the thigh, when viewed from the side. Croup should be long and gradually sloping. Too level or flat a croup prevents proper functioning of the hindquarter, which must be able to reach well under the body. A steep croup also limits the action of the hindquarter.

Structure: A German Shepherd is a trotting dog and his structure has been developed to best meet the requirements of his work in herding. That is to say, a long, effortless trot which shall cover the maximum amount of ground with the minimum number of steps, consistent with the size of the animal. The proper body proportion, firmness of back and muscles and the proper angulation of the forequarters and hindquarters serve this end. They enable the dog to propel itself forward by a long step of the hindquarter and to compensate for this stride by a long step of the forequarter. The high withers, the firm back, the strong loin, the properly formed croup, even the tail as balance and rudder, all contribute to this same end.

Proportion: The German Shepherd Dog is properly longer than tall with the most desirable proportion as 10 is to 8½. We have seen how the height is ascertained; the length is established by a dog standing naturally and four-square, measured on a horizontal line from the point of the prosternum, or breastbone, to the rear edge of the pelvis, the ischium tuberosity, commonly called the sitting bone.

Angulation: Forequarter: the shoulder blade should be long, laid on flat against the body with its rounded upper end in a vertical line above the elbow, and sloping well forward to the point where it joins the upper arm. The withers should be high, with shoulder blades meeting closely at the top, and the upper arm set on at an angle approaching as nearly as possible a right angle. Such an angulation permits the maximum forward extension of the foreleg without binding or effort. Shoulder faults include too steep or straight a position of either blade or upper arm, too short a blade or upper arm, lack of sufficient angle between these two members, looseness through lack of firm ligamentation, and loaded shoulder with prominent pads of flesh or muscles on the outer side. Construction in which the whole shoulder assembly is pushed too far forward also restricts the stride and is faulty.

Hindquarters: The angulation of the hindquarter also consists ideally of a series of sharp angles as far as the relation of the bones to each other is concerned, and the thigh bone should parallel the shoulder blade while the stifle bone parallels the upper arm. The whole assembly of the thigh, viewed from the side, should be broad, with both thigh and stifle well muscled and of proportionate length, forming as nearly as possible a right angle. The metatarsus (the unit between the hock joint and the foot commonly and erroneously called the hock) is strong, clean and short, the hock joint clean-cut and sharply defined.

Tail: Bushy, with the last vertebra extended at least to the hock joint, and usually below. Set smoothly into the croup and low rather than high, at rest the tail hangs in a slight curve like a sabre. A slight hook—sometimes carried to one side—is faulty only to the extent that it mars general appearance. When the dog is excited or in motion, the curve is accentuated and the tail raised, but it should never be lifted beyond a line at right angles with the line of the back. Docked tails, or those which have been operated upon to prevent curling, disqualify. Tails too short, or with clumpy ends due to the ankylosis or the growing together of the vertebrae, are serious faults.

Gait: General Impression: the gait of the German Shepherd Dog is outreaching, elastic, seemingly without effort, smooth and rhythmic. At a walk it covers a great deal of ground, with long step of both hind leg and foreleg. At a trot, the dog covers still more ground and moves powerfully but easily with a beautiful co-ordination of back and limbs so that, in the best examples, the gait appears to be the steady motion of a well-lubricated machine. The feet travel close to the ground, and neither fore nor hind feet should lift high on either forward reach or backward push.

The hindquarter delivers, through the back, a powerful forward thrust which slightly lifts the whole animal and drives the body forward. Reaching far under, and passing the imprint left by the front foot, the strong arched hind foot takes hold of the ground; then hock, stifle, and upper thigh come into play and sweep back, the stroke of the hind leg finishing with the foot still close to the ground in a smooth follow-through. The overreach of the hindquarter usually necessitates one hind foot passing outside and the other hind foot passing inside the track of the forefeet and such action is not faulty unless the locomotion is crabwise with the dog's body sideways out of the normal straight line. In order to achieve ideal movement of this kind, there must be full muscular co-ordination throughout the structure with the action of muscles and ligaments positive, regular and accurate.

Back Transmission: the typical smooth, flowing gait of the Shepherd Dog cannot be maintained without great strength and firmness (which does not mean stiffness) of back. The whole effort of the hindquarter is transmitted to the forequarter through the muscular and bony structure of the loin, back, and withers. At full trot, the back must remain firm and level without sway, roll, whip or roach. To compensate for the forward motion imparted by the hindquarter, the shoulder should open to its full extent—the desirability of good shoulder angulation now becomes apparent—and the forelegs should reach out in a stride balancing that of the hindquarter. A steep shoulder will cause the dog either to stumble or to raise the forelegs very high in an effort to co-ordinate with the hindquarter, which is impossible when shoulder structure is faulty. A serious gait fault results when a dog moves too low in front, presenting an unlevel topline with the wither lower than the hips. The Shepherd Dog does not track on widely separated parallel lines as does the terrier, but brings the feet inward toward the middle line of the body when at trot in order to maintain balance. For this reason a dog viewed from the front or rear when in motion will often seem to travel close. This is not a fault if the feet do not strike or cross, or if the knees or shoulders are not thrown out, but the feet and hocks should be parallel even if close together. The excellence of gait must also be evaluated by viewing from the side the effortless, properly co-ordinated covering of ground.

Summary: It should never be forgotten that the ideal Shepherd is a working animal which must have an incorruptible character combined with body and gait suitable for the arduous work which constitutes its primary purpose. All its qualities should be weighed in respect to their contribution to such work, and while no compromise should be permitted with regard to its working potentiality, the dog must nevertheless possess a high degree of beauty and nobility.

Evaluation of Faults: NOTE: Faults are important in the order of their group, as per group headings, irrespective of their position in each group.
Very Serious Faults: Major faults of temperament; undershot lower jaw.
Serious Faults: Faults of balance and proportion; poor gait, viewed either from front, rear or side; marked deficiency of substance (bone or body); bitchy male dogs; faulty backs; too level or too short croup; long and weak loin; very bad feet; ring tails; tails much too short; rickety condition; more than four missing premolars or any other missing teeth, unless due to accident; lack of nobility; badly washed-out colour; badly overshot bite.
Faults: Doggy bitches; poorly carried ears; too-fine in head; weak muzzles; improper muscular condition; faulty coat, other

than temporary condition; badly affected teeth.

Minor Faults: Too coarse head; hooked tails; too light, round or protruding eyes; discoloured teeth; condition of coat, due to season or keeping.

Disqualifications: *Albino characteristics; cropped ears; hanging ears (as in a hound); docked tails; male dogs having one or both testicles undescended (monorchids or cryptorchids).*

Great Dane

LARGE DOGS RESEMBLING the Great Dane have been known since the start of recorded history. Carvings on Egyptian tombs dating to 3000 B.C. depict such dogs, and there is a Grecian coin dated 500 B.C. showing a dog's head much like that of the Dane.

Strong and swift, the large dogs were used by Celtic and Germanic tribes as war dogs and to hunt big game. It is claimed that the breed was already established in Britain before the time of the Roman Conquest and that the Romans took these dogs home with them to Rome where they were used as fighting dogs.

While both Linnaeus and Buffon, 18th century naturalists who made detailed chronicles of species, give a Danish origin for the breed, it is Germany that claims to be the breed's country of origin. Certainly this was the country of the Dane's development. There it is called the Deutsche Dogge (German Mastiff) and was proclaimed the national dog of Germany in 1876. Since the Middle Ages the German nobility have used the "Dogge" to hunt wild boar and protect their country estates. It is recorded that in 1592 the Duke of Braunschweig arrived at a boar hunt with a pack of 600 male Great Danes!

The breed was first exhibited at a dog show held in Hamburg in 1863, but it was not until 1888 that the first specialty club was founded in Germany. It is a source of pride among British Great Dane fanciers that the founding of a similar club in Britain pre-dates this by six years.

The Great Dane began arriving in the United States in the mid-19th century. One of the earliest owners of a Dane was the venturesome scout, William "Buffalo Bill" Cody. The breed was first exhibited in 1877 under the breed name "Siberian or Ulm Dog." It is reported that the first dogs to be shown were ferocious, having been imported directly from German estates where they had been used as attack dogs. To the credit of American breeders, within a twenty-year period the breed had been transformed into an even-tempered dog still possessed of its protective instinct. Dog writers agree that today the best Great Danes in the world are being bred on this continent.

Great Dane

There were eleven Great Danes registered in the first Stud Book published by The Canadian Kennel Club for the years 1888-1889.

Official Breed Standard for the Great Dane

General Appearance: The Great Dane combines in its distinguished appearance dignity, strength and elegance with great size and a powerful, well-formed, smoothly muscled body. He is one of the giant breeds, but is unique in that his general conformation must be so well balanced that he never appears clumsy and is always a unit—the Apollo of dogs. He must be spirited and courageous—never timid. He is friendly and dependable. This physical and mental combination is the characteristic which gives the Great Dane the majesty possessed by no other breed. It is particularly true of this breed that there is an impression of great masculinity in dogs as compared to an impression of femininity in bitches. The male should appear more massive throughout than the bitch, with larger frame and heavier bone. In the ratio between length and height, the Great Dane should appear as square as possible. In bitches, a somewhat longer body is permissible.

Faults: Lack of unity; timidity; bitchy dogs; poor musculature; poor bone development; out of condition; rickets; doggy bitches.

Size: The male should not be less than 30 in. (76 cm) at the shoulders, but it is preferable that he be 32 in. (81 cm) or more, providing he is well proportioned to his height. The female should not be less than 28 in. (71 cm) at the shoulders, but it is preferable that she be 30 in. (76 cm) or more, providing she is well proportioned to her height. Substance is that sufficiency of bone and muscle which rounds out a balance with the frame.

Faults: Lightweight whippety Danes; coarse, ungainly proportioned Danes; there should be balance always.

Coat and Colour: The coat should be very short and thick, smooth and glossy.

Faults: Excessively long hair (stand-off coat); dull hair (indicating malnutrition, worms, and negligent care).

Colour:

a) Brindle Danes. Base colour ranging from light golden yellow to golden yellow always brindled with strong black cross stripes.

The more intensive the base colour and the more intensive the brindling, the more attractive will be the colour. Small white marks at the chest and toes are not desirable.

Faults: Brindle with too dark a base colour; silver-blue and greyish-blue base colour; dull (faded) brindling; white tail tip.

b) Fawn Danes. Golden yellow up to deep golden yellow colour with a deep black mask. The golden deep-yellow colour must always be given the preference. Small white spots at the chest and toes are not desirable.

Faults: Yellowish-grey, bluish-yellow, greyish-blue, dirty-yellow colour (drab colour), lack of black mask.

c) Blue Danes. The colour must be pure steel blue as far as possible without any tinge of yellow, black, or mouse grey.

Faults: Any deviation from a pure steel-blue colouration.

d) Black Danes. Glossy black.

Faults: Yellow black, brown black or blue-black. White markings, such as stripes on the chest, speckled chest and markings on the paws are permitted but not desirable.

e) Harlequin Danes. Base colour: pure white with black torn patches irregularly and well distributed over the entire body; pure white neck preferred. The black patches should never be large enough to give the appearance of a blanket or so small as to give a stippled or dappled effect. (Eligible but less desirable are a few small grey spots, also pointings where instead of a pure white base with black spots there is a white base with single black hairs showing through which tend to give a salt and pepper or dirty effect.)

Faults: White base colour with a few large spots; bluish-grey pointed background.

Head: Long, narrow, distinguished, expressive, finely chiselled, especially the part below the eyes (which means that the *skull* plane under and to the inner point of the eye must slope without any bony protruberance in a pleasing line to the full square jaw), with strongly pronounced stop. The masculinity of the male is very pronounced in the expression and structure of head (this subtle difference should be evident in the dog's head through massive skull and depth of muzzle); the bitch's head may be more delicately formed. Seen from the side, the forehead must be sharply set off from the bridge of the nose. The forehead and the bridge of the nose must be straight and parallel to one another. Seen from the front, the head should appear narrow, the bridge of the nose should be as broad as possible. The cheek muscles must show slightly but under no circumstances should they be too pronounced (cheeky). The *muzzle* part must have full flews and must be as blunt vertically as possible in front; the angles of the lip must be quite pronounced. The front part of the head, from the tip of the nose up to the centre of the stop should be as long as the rear part of the head from the centre of the stop to the only slightly developed occiput. The head should be angular from all sides and should have definite flat planes and its dimensions should be absolutely in proportion to the general appearance of the Dane.

Faults: Any deviation from the parallel planes of skull and foreface; too small a stop; a poorly defined stop or none at all; too narrow a nose bridge; the rear of the head spreading laterally in a wedgelike manner (wedge head); an excessively round upper head (apple head); excessively pronounced cheek musculature; pointed muzzle; loose lips hanging over the lower jaw (fluttering lips) which create an illusion of a full deep muzzle. The head should be rather shorter and distinguished than long and expressionless.

The *nose* must be large and in the case of brindled and "single-coloured" Danes, it must always be black. In harlequins, the nose should be black; a black spotted nose is permitted; a pink-coloured nose is not desirable.

Teeth strong, well developed and clean. The incisors of the lower jaw must touch very lightly the bottoms of the inner surface of the upper incisors (scissors bite). If the front teeth of both jaws bite on top of each other, they wear down too rapidly.

Faults: Even bite; undershot and overshot; incisors out of line; black or brown teeth; missing teeth.

Eyes of a medium size, as dark as possible, with lively intelligent expression; almond-shaped eyelids, well-developed eyebrows.

Faults: Light-coloured, piercing, amber-coloured, light blue to a watery blue, red or bleary eyes; eyes of different colours; eyes too far apart; Mongolian eyes; eyes with pronounced haws; eyes with excessively drooping lower eyelids. In blue and black Danes, lighter eyes are permitted but are not desirable. In harlequins, the eyes should be dark. Light-coloured eyes, two eyes of different colour and walleyes are permitted but not desirable.

Ears should be high, set not too far apart, medium in size, of moderate thickness, drooping forward close to the cheek. Top line of folded ear should be about level with the skull. Cropped ears; high set; not set too far apart, well pointed but always in proportion to the shape of the head and carried uniformly erect.

Faults: Hanging on the side, as on a Foxhound.

Neck: The neck should be firm and clean, high set, well arched, long, muscular and sinewy. From the chest to the head, it should be slightly tapering, beautifully formed, with well-developed nape.

Faults: Short, heavy neck, pendulous throat folds (dewlaps).

Forequarters: The shoulder blade must be strong and sloping and seen from the side, must form as nearly as possible a right angle in its articulation with the humerus (upper arm) to give a long stride. A line from the upper tip of the shoulder to the back of the elbow joint should be as nearly perpendicular as possible. Since all dogs lack a clavicle (collar bone) the ligaments and muscles holding the shoulder blades to the rib cage must be well developed, firm and secure to prevent loose shoulders. The upper arm should be strong and muscular. Seen from the side or front the strong lower arms run absolutely straight to the pastern joints. Seen from the front, the forelegs and the pastern roots should form perpendicular lines to the ground. Seen from the side, the pastern root should slope only very slightly forward. Paws round and turned neither toward the inside nor toward the outside. Toes short, highly arched and well closed. Nails short, strong and as dark as possible.

Faults: Steep shoulders, which occur if the shoulder blade does not slope sufficiently; overangulation; loose shoulders which occur if the Dane is flabbily muscled, or if the elbow is turned towards the outside; loaded shoulders. Elbows turned towards the inside or towards the outside, the former position caused mostly by too narrow or too shallow a chest, bringing the front legs too closely together and at the same time turning the entire lower part of the leg outward; the latter position causes the front legs to spread too far apart, with the pastern roots and paws usually turned inward. Seen from the side, a considerable bend in the pastern toward the front indicates weakness and is in most cases connected with stretched and spread toes (splay foot); seen from the side a forward bow in the forearm (chair leg); an excessively knotty bulge in the front of the pastern joint. Spreading toes (splay foot), bent, long toes (rabbit paws);

toes turned toward the outside or towards the inside; light-coloured nails.

Body: The withers form the highest part of the back which slopes downward slightly toward the loins, which are imperceptibly arched and strong. The back should be short and tensely set. Chest deals with that part of the thorax (rib cage) in front of the shoulders and front legs. The chest should be quite broad, deep and well muscled. Ribs and brisket deals with that part of the thorax back of the shoulders and front legs. Should be broad, with the ribs sprung well out from the spine and flattened at the side to allow proper movement of the shoulders extending down to the elbow joint. The belly should be well shaped and tightly muscled, and with the rear part of the thorax, should swing in a pleasing curve (tuck-up).

Faults: Receding back; sway back; camel or roach back; a back line which is too high at the rear; an excessively long back. A narrow and poorly muscled chest; strong protruding sternum (pigeon breast). Narrow (slab-sided) rib cage; round (barrel) rib cage; shallow rib cage not reaching the elbow joint. Poor tuck-up.

Hindquarters: The croup must be full, slightly drooping and must continue imperceptibly to the tail root. Hind legs, the first thighs (from hip joint to knee) are broad and muscular. The second thighs (from knee to hock joint) are strong and long. Seen from the side, the angulation of the first thigh with the body, of the second thigh with the first thigh, and the pastern root with the second thigh should be very moderate, neither too straight nor too exaggerated. Seen from the rear, the hock joints appear to be perfectly straight, turned neither towards the inside nor towards the outside. Paws, round and turned neither towards the inside nor towards the outside. Toes short, highly arched and well closed. Nails short, strong and as dark as possible.

Faults: A croup which is too straight; a croup which slopes downward too steeply; and too narrow a croup. Hind legs: soft, flabby, poorly muscled thighs; cowhocks which are the result of the hock joint turning inward and the hock and rear paws turning outward; barrel legs, the result of the hock joints being too far apart; steep rear. As seen from the side, a steep rear is the result of the angles of the rear legs forming almost a straight line; overangulation is the result of exaggerated angles between the first and second thighs and the hocks and is very conducive to weakness. The rear legs should never be too long in proportion to the front legs. Spreading toes (splay foot); bent, long toes (rabbit paws); toes turned towards the outside or towards the inside. Furthermore, the fifth toe on the hind legs appearing at a higher position and with wolf's claw or spur; excessively long nails; light-coloured nails.

Tail: Should start high and fairly broad, terminating slender and thin at the hock joint. At rest, the tail should fall straight. When excited or running, slightly curved (sabre-like).

Faults: A too high, or too low-set tail (the tail-set is governed by the slope of the croup); too long or too short a tail; tail bent too far over the back (ring tail); a tail which is curled; a twisted tail (sideways); a tail carried too high over the back (gay tail); a brush tail (hair too long on lower side). Cropping tail to desired length is forbidden.

Gait: Long, easy, springy stride with no tossing or rolling of body. The back line should move smoothly, parallel to the ground. The gait of the Great Dane should denote strength and power. The rear legs should have drive. The forelegs should track smoothly and straight. The Dane should track in two parallel straight lines.

Faults: Short steps. The rear quarters should not pitch. The forelegs should not have a hackney gait (forced or choppy stride). When moving rapidly the Great Dane should not pace for the reason that it causes excessive side-to-side rolling of the body and thus reduces endurance.

Faults: The faults below are important according to their grouping (very serious, serious, minor) and not according to their sequence as placed in each grouping:

Very Serious: Lack of unity. Poor bone development. Poor musculature. Lightweight whippety Danes. Rickets. Timidity. Bitchy dog. Sway back. Roach back. Cowhocks. Pitching gait. Short steps. Undershot teeth.

Serious: Out of condition. Coarseness. Any deviation from the standard on all colouration. Deviation from parallel planes of skull and foreface. Wedge head. Poorly defined stop. Narrow nose bridge. Snipey muzzle. Any colour but dark eyes in fawns and brindles. Mongolian eyes. Missing teeth. Overshot teeth. Heavy neck. Short neck. Dewlaps. Narrow chest. Narrow rib cage; round rib cage; shallow rib cage. Loose shoulders; steep shoulders. Elbows turned inward. Chair legs (front). Knotty bulge in pastern joint (adult dog). Weak pastern roots. Receding back. Too long a back. Back high in rear. In harlequins, a pink nose. Poor tuck-up (except in bitches that have been bred). Too straight croup; too sloping croup; too narrow croup. Over-angulation. Steep rear. Too long rear legs. Poorly muscled thighs. Barrel legs. Paws turned outward; rabbit paws. Wolf's claw. Hackney gait.

Minor: Doggy bitches. Small white marks on chest and toes—blues, blacks, brindles, and fawns. Few grey spots and pointings on harlequins. Excessively long hair. Excessively dull hair. Apple head. Small stop. Fluttering lips. Eyes too far apart. Drooping lower eyelids. Haws. Any colour but dark eyes in blacks, blues and harlequins. Discoloured teeth. Even bite. Pigeon breast. Loaded shoulders. Elbows turned outward. Paws turned inward. Splay foot. Excessively long toenails. Light nails (except in harlequins). Low set tail. Too long a tail. Too short a tail. Gay tail. Curled tail. Twisted tail. Brush tail.

Disqualifications: *Danes under minimum height. White Danes without any black marks (albinos). Merles, a solid mouse-grey colour or a mouse-grey base with black or white or both colour spots or white base with mouse-grey spots. Harlequins and solid-coloured Danes in which a large spot extends coatlike over the entire body so that only the legs, neck and the point of the tail are white. Brindle, fawn, blue and black: Danes with white forehead line, white collars, high white stockings and white bellies. Danes with predominantly blue, grey, yellow or also brindled spots. Docked tails. Split noses.*

Scale of Points:

GENERAL CONFORMATION

General appearance	10	
Colour and markings	8	
Size	5	
Condition of coat	4	
Substance	3	30

MOVEMENT

Gait	10	
Rear end (croup, legs, paws)	10	
Front end (shoulders, legs, paws)	8	28

HEAD

Head conformation	12	
Teeth	4	
Eyes (nose and ears)	4	20

TORSO

Neck	6	
Loin and back	6	
Chest	4	
Ribs and brisket	4	20

TAIL	2	2
TOTAL		100

Great Pyrenees

THE GREAT PYRENEES, or Pyrenean Mountain Dog as the breed is known in Britain, descends from the Tibetan Mastiff, a Chinese guard dog of ancient origin. His immediate forbears were the Molossian Hounds which were brought to Spain by the Romans. There the dogs became established in the Pyrenees Mountains on the border between Spain and France where they apparently remained isolated for a period of some 1000 years. The big white dogs were used to guard sheep against both human and animal predators. Often left alone with the flocks for days at a time, the dogs wore spiked iron collars to protect their throats from injury.

During the Middle Ages the dogs were used to guard French fortresses and to prevent the escape of prisoners. In the 18th century, while on a visit to Bareges, a watering place in the Pyrenees, the Dauphin of France was so taken with the magnificent breed he was allowed to take some puppies home with him, where the breed soon became the official dog of the court of Louis XIV.

The dog writer "Idstone" reports that at one time the Pyr was used to restore the vigour and numbers of the dogs at the Hospice of St. Bernard in the Swiss Alps. It is also written that early French settlers brought some of the breed with them when they emigrated to Newfoundland in 1662 where the breed became a progenitor of the giant breed now known as the Newfoundland.

Queen Victoria is said to have imported the first Pyr to Britain, but not until the early 1930s did the breed make much of an impression there or on this continent. In 1931 Mrs. Frances Crane founded her Basquaerie Kennels based on breeding stock of excellent type imported from France. Shortly afterwards breeding kennels were established in Britain and the translation of the original French breed standard, which had been draughted after the close of World War I, was adopted as the criterion in both countries. One writer suggests that some of the standard's accuracy may have been lost in the translation.

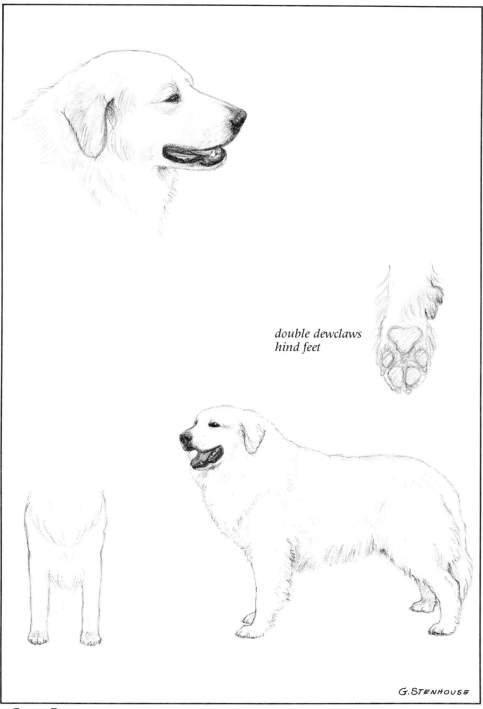

*double dewclaws
hind feet*

G. STENHOUSE

Great Pyrenees

Double dewclaws on the hind legs are a distinguishing feature of the Great Pyrenees, but lack of them does not constitute a disqualification.

The breed was granted official recognition by both The Canadian and American Kennel Clubs in 1935.

Official Breed Standard for the Great Pyrenees

General Appearance: A dog of immense size, great majesty, keen intelligence, and kindly expression; of unsurpassed beauty and a certain elegance, all white or principally white with markings of badger, grey, or varying shades of tan. In the rolling, ambling gait it shows unmistakably the purpose for which it has been bred—the strenuous work of guarding the flocks in all kinds of weather on the steep mountain slopes of the Pyrenees. Hence soundness is of the greatest importance and absolutely necessary for the proper fulfilment of his centuries' old task.

Temperament: In addition to his original age-old position in the scheme of pastoral life as protector of the shepherd and his flock, the Great Pyrenees has been used for centuries as a guard and watchdog on the large estates of his native France, and for this he has proven ideal. He is as serious in play as he is in work, adapting and moulding himself to the moods, desires and even the very life of his human companions, through fair weather and foul, through leisure hours and hours fraught with danger, responsibility and extreme exertion; he is the exemplification of gentleness and docility with those he knows, of faithfulness and devotion for his master even to the point of self-sacrifice; and of courage in the protection of the flock placed in his care and of the ones he loves.

Size: The average height at the shoulder is 27–32 in. (68–81 cm) for dogs, and 25–29 in. (63–74 cm) for bitches.

The average length from shoulder blades to root of tail should be the same as the height in any given specimen.

The average girth is 36–42 in. (91–107 cm) for dogs and 32–36 in. (81–91 cm) for bitches.

The weight for dogs runs 100–125 lb. (45–57 kg) and 90–115 lb. (40–52 kg) for bitches.

A heavily boned dog.

Coat and Colour: Coat created to withstand severe weather, with heavy fine white undercoat and long flat thick outer coat of coarser hair, straight or slightly undulating. All white or principally white with markings of badger, grey, or varying shades of tan.

Head: The head is in brief that of a brown bear, but with the ears falling down. It is large and wedge-shaped, measuring 10–11 in. (25–28 cm) from dome to point of nose, with rounding crown; furrow only slightly developed and with no apparent stop. Cheeks flat. Lips close-fitting, edged with black. *Eyes* of medium size set slightly obliquely, dark rich brown in colour with close eyelids, well pigmented. *Ears* V-shaped, but rounded at the tips, of medium size, set parallel with the eyes, carried low and close to the head except when raised at attention.

Neck: Short, stout and strongly muscular. Dewlaps developed but little.

Forequarters: Well-placed shoulders set obliquely, close to the body. Single dewclaws in front.

Body: Back and loin well coupled, straight and broad. Chest deep. Ribs flat-sided. Rump sloping slightly.

Hindquarters: Haunches fairly prominent. Double dewclaws behind. Close cupped feet.

Tail: Of sufficient length to hang below the hocks, well plumed, carried low in repose, and curled high over the back, ''making the wheel'' when alert.

(Breed Standard continued)

Scale of Points:

HEAD

Shape of skull	5	
Ears	5	
Eyes	5	
Muzzle	5	
Teeth	5	25

GENERAL CONFORMATION

Neck	5	
Chest	5	
Back	5	
Loins	5	
Feet	5	25

COAT	10	10
SIZE AND SOUNDNESS	25	25
EXPRESSION AND GENERAL APPEARANCE	15	15
TOTAL		100

Karelian Bear Dog

THIS MEDIUM-SIZED MEMBER of the spitz family of dogs is considered to be a close relative of the Russian Laiki but more domesticated. Authorities believe both breeds descend from the Russian Spitz, the Karelian Bear Dog originating in an area of Northern Europe, Karelia, which was once a part of Finland but now is called the Karelo-Finnish Soviet Socialist Republic.

The breed has been pure bred in Finland since 1930 where it is highly regarded by huntsmen who use the dog to hunt bear, elk, moose, deer, hare, and wolf. The breed is renowned for its scenting ability and can, it is reported, locate the bear's winter sleeping quarters. All authorities agree that the Karelian Bear Dog's single drawback is his personality which has been variously described as "sullen," "stubborn," and aggressive towards other dogs. For this reason the Karelian Bear Dog works alone, not with other dogs. To its credit the breed is said to be devoted to its master.

The Karelian Bear Dog was recognized as a pure-bred by the Finnish Kennel Club in 1935 and in 1946 by the Federation Cynologique Internationale (FCI).

Principal breeders today are the Russians who are said to have crossed the *Karjalankarhukoira*—the breed's original Finnish name—with the Utchak Sheepdog to produce a Russian version of the Karelian Bear Dog. The intention was to produce a dog of greater courage and stamina and, from all reports, the cross has been successful. It is said that this super bear dog will, if necessary, attack its quarry or put it to flight.

The Karelian Bear Dog was added to The Canadian Kennel Club's list of officially recognized breeds in 1980, but is still a rarity in this country. The breed is not, as yet, recognized in the United States.

Karelian Bear Dog

Official Breed Standard for the Karelian Bear Dog

Origin and Purpose: The Karelian Bear Dog is a native of the area once known as Karelia in Northern Europe but which, since 1946, has been known as the Karelo-Finnish Soviet Socialist Republic, where for centuries he hunted moose, roebuck, and hare, and fought the wolf. Over the last decades, the principal breeders of Karelians, the Russians, have tried to strengthen the breed to give it the power and aggressiveness needed to fight bears. Thus the *Karjalankarhukoira* (this being its original Finnish name) has become a Russian bear dog through crossing with the Utchak Sheepdog, an intrepid animal who has no fear of fighting wild beasts. The Karelian Bear Dog not only warns the hunter of the presence of bear, but does not hesitate to attack him and put him to flight.

General Appearance: The Karelian Bear Dog is medium sized, of robust build, strong, slightly longer than high, has a thick coat, cocked ears, is of an inbound character, brave and persevering; its senses, particularly scent, are sharp, wherefore it is suitable for big-game hunting.

Size: Height at withers—dogs, $21^{1}/_{4}$–$23^{1}/_{2}$ in. (54–60 cm); bitches, $19^{1}/_{4}$–$21^{1}/_{4}$ in. (49–54 cm).

Coat and Colour: Outer coat straight and stiff, undercoat soft and dense. Outer coat on the neck, back and rear parts of the thighs longer than elsewhere. Colour black, preferably slightly brownish or dull, mostly with distinct white markings or spots on the head, neck, chest, abdomen, and legs. So far allowed but not desirable are: dewclaws, white colour with black markings, wolf-grey colour or spots.

Head: Shaped as a blunt wedge, fairly broad at the forehead and cheeks. *Forehead* slightly arched, stop gently sloping, protuberances above the eyes only slightly developed. The *muzzle* is high and its bridge preferably straight only slightly tapering towards the nose. *Nose* black and well developed. Lips thin and tight fitting. *Eyes* rather small, brown. Look alert, often fiery. *Ears* cocked, pointing slightly outward, medium sized and fairly blunt at the points.

Neck: Muscular, medium sized, curving, covered with thick coat.

Forequarters: Sturdy, shoulders relatively sloping and muscular. Elbows pointing straight backward. Forearm straight, pastern only slightly bent. Paws thick, high and roundish.

Body: Sturdy; back with well-developed muscles nicely sloping without bulges or hollows. Chest spacious, extending approximately to the level of the elbow. Abdomen slightly drawn up.

Hindquarters: The knee pointing straight forward, hock straight backward. Thighs look very broad due to the profuse coat, particularly in their upper parts. Front line of leg curving without sudden bends. Hock comparatively straight. Hind paws slightly longer and lower than forepaws.

Tail: Of medium length, usually arched, a full arch is most desirable.

Faults: Weak bones, snipey muzzle, curly or wavy coat, bat-like ears, domed forehead, light or walleyes, loose skin under the neck, too deep chest, barrel-like chest, straight shoulders and straight hocks, flat paws, straight or whiplike tail, unusual colours and savage disposition towards humans.

Komondor

*T*HE BIG WHITE DOG with the coat that hangs to the ground in ribbonlike cords is a native of Hungary where his reputation as trustworthy guardian of the flock has earned him the title "King of the Working Dogs." The Komondor is the largest of the Hungarian herding breeds and is thought to be of Asian origin descending from the dogs brought to Hungary by the Magyars in the 10th century. The breed is a close kin of the Russian herding dog, the Afscharka, and possibly the Puli.

Out in the pastures the Komondor keeps vigil over the sheep which, at the first sign of danger, are said to converge behind their protector. The Komondor will fight any predator to the death and for this reason one European authority suggests that early nomadic tribes who bred these sheepdogs may have used a cross to the wolf to give the breed its fiercely protective nature. The Komondor's corded coat which is the hallmark of the breed is functional as well as unusual. It provides him with insulation against inclement weather and protects him from serious injury in fights. Traditionally the breed's chief work has been to guard sheep but it has been used successfully to herd cattle and in police work.

The Komondor was introduced to this continent in the early 1930s, where it is officially recognized by both The Canadian and the American Kennel Clubs, but it is not recognized in Britain.

In recent years sheep ranchers across the United States have been experimenting with using the Komondor to protect their flocks from coyotes, which are blamed for killing more than a million sheep per year. Results so far are excellent—losses have been sharply cut.

Komondor

Official Breed Standard for the Komondor

General Appearance: The Komondor is characterized by imposing strength, courageous demeanour and pleasing conformation. In general he is a big muscular dog with plenty of bone and substance.

Temperament: As a houseguard as well as a guardian of herds he is, when grown up, an earnest, courageous, and very faithful dog. The young dog, however, is just as playful as any other puppy. He is much devoted to his master and will defend him against attack by any stranger. On account of this trait he is not used for driving the herds, but only for guarding them. His special task is to protect the animals, and he lives during the greater part of the year in the open air without protection against strange dogs and all kinds of beasts of prey.

Size: The height at the top of shoulders is $23\frac{1}{2}-31\frac{1}{2}$ in. (59–80 cm). The bigger the Komondor, the better. A minimum height of 25 in. (63 cm) at top of shoulders for males and $23\frac{1}{2}$ in. (59 cm) for females is required. The body and the legs should form a rectangle.

Coat and Colour: The entire body of the Komondor is covered with a long, soft, woolly, dense hair of different length on the different parts of the body, with inclination to entanglement and shagginess. If the dog is not taken care of, the hair becomes shaggy on the forelegs, chest, belly, rump and on the sides of the thigh and the tail. The longer and the more ragged, the better, though as above stated, the length of the hair varies on the different parts of the body. The longer hair begins on the head and ears and lengthens gradually on the body, being longest on the thighs and the tail. A somewhat shorter, but still long hair is found on the legs, the muzzle and the cheeks. Too curly hair is undesirable. The colour of the hair is white. Any other colour is disqualifying.

Head: The head of the Komondor is covered all over with long hair, and thus the head looks somewhat short, in comparison to the seemingly wide forehead. When the hair is smoothed, it will be seen that the *skull* is somewhat arched if viewed from the side; the forehead is not wide, but appears, however, wider through the rich growth of hair. The stop is moderate, it is the starting point of the muzzle which is somewhat shorter than the length of the skull. The topline of the *muzzle* is straight and about parallel with the line of the top of the skull. The muzzle should be fairly square. In comparison to the length given in the head description, the muzzle is wide, coarse and not pointed. The lips cover the teeth closely and are black. The muzzle is mostly covered by long hair. The edges of the muzzle are black or steel blue-grey. The nostrils are wide. The colour of the *nose* is black. Komondors with flesh-coloured noses must absolutely be excluded from breeding. A slate-coloured or dark brown nose is undesirable but may, however, be accepted for breeding purposes. The jaws are powerful, and the teeth are level and close together evenly. The *eyes* express fidelity. They are medium sized and almond shaped, not too deeply set and surrounded by rough, unkempt hair. The iris of the eyes is of a coffee or darker brown colour; a light colour is not desirable. Blue-white eyes are disqualifying. The edges of the eyelids are slate-grey. The *ears* are rather low-set and hang along the side of the head. They are medium sized, and their surface is covered with long hair.

Neck: The neck is covered with long hair, is muscular, of medium length, moderately arched. The head erect. No dewlap is allowed.

Forequarters: The shoulders slope into the neck without apparent protrusion. The forelegs should be straight, well boned and muscular. Viewed from any side, the legs are like vertical columns. The upper arm joins the body closely, without loose elbows. The legs are covered all around by long, evenly hanging hair.

Body: The body is moderately long and level. It is characterized chiefly by the powerful, deep chest which is muscular and proportionately wide. Back and loins are wide. The rump is wide, muscular, moderately sloping towards the root of the tail. The body should be somewhat drawn up at the rear, but not Greyhound-like.

Hindquarters: The steely, strong bone structure is covered with highly developed muscles, and the legs are evenly covered with long hair, hanging down in matted clods. The legs should be straight as viewed from the rear. Stifles well bent. Dewclaws must be removed. The feet should be strong, rather large and with close, well-arched toes. The hind feet are stronger, and all are covered with long hair. The nails are black or slate-grey. The pads are hard, elastic, and black.

Tail: The tail is as a straight continuation of the rump-line, and reaches down to the hocks slightly curved upwards at its end. It is covered in its full length with long hair, which when the dog is at ease almost touches the ground. When the dog is excited the tail is raised up to the level of the back. The tail should not be docked. Komondors born with short tails must be excluded even for breeding purposes.

Faults: Light or flesh-coloured nose, albino or blue eyes, highly set and small ears. Short, smooth hair on the head and legs, strongly curled tail, colour other than white.

Disqualifications: *Blue-white eyes; colour other than white.*

Kuvasz

*I*T IS SAID that the history of the Kuvasz can be traced back almost 7000 years to its country of origin, Sumeria, where herdsmen used the large white dog to watch over their sheep and protect them from predators, and is thought to be descended from the Tibetan Mastiff. The Kuvasz is closely related to the Maremma Sheepdog which it strongly resembles and is possibly an ancestor of the Great Pyrenees. The breed was brought to Hungary, its country of development, by the Kurds in 1100 A.D. where it became the favourite guard dog of the nobility. The name Kuvasz (plural Kuvaszok) is thought to come from the Turkish *Kawasz* which means "guard of the noblemen." History tells us that King Mathias I (1458—1490) thought more highly of his Kuvasz than he did of his courtiers, and is reported to have used his dogs for hunting wild boar as well as using them as his personal guardians.

The Kuvasz is a strong dog with a thick, weather resistant coat. He is very suspicious of strangers, devoted to his master and gentle with children. While his age-old job has been that of guardian of the flock, the Kuvasz hâs also been used to herd cattle.

Today the breed's chief function is as guard dog on farms and estates. At present his services are being used with great success in the United States. The Kuvasz and his cousin the Maremma Sheepdog are among the breeds being used by American sheep ranchers to protect their flocks from the ravages of the coyote.

The Kuvasz has been an officially recognized breed on this continent since the 1930s. So far the breed is not recognized in Britain.

In Canada in 1978 a Hungarian import made breed history by becoming the first Kuvasz to be awarded Best in Show at an all-breed championship event.

G.STENHOUSE

Kuvasz

Official Breed Standard for the Kuvasz

Origin and Purpose: A Hungarian breed whose forbears can almost certainly be traced back to the Tibetan Mastiff, the present-type Kuvasz was first recorded in Hungary in the ninth century. Since that time, they have been widely used in their native land, primarily as guardians but also for tracking, hunting, herding, and as companions.

General Appearance: The Kuvasz is a large working dog with a pure white, medium length wavy coat. Although strongly built, he possesses grace and lightness of foot, with no hint of bulkiness or lethargy, and is exaggerated in no aspect.

Temperament: Temperamentally, the Kuvasz is an intelligent dog with a great deal of independence of spirit. He has been used for centuries as a guardian and has very strongly developed protective instincts.

Size: The recommended sizes are: males, 28–29½ in. (71–75 cm) high at the withers with a corresponding weight of approximately 88–115 lb. (40–52 kg); females, 26–27½ in. (66–70 cm) high at the withers with a corresponding weight of approximately 66–93 lb. (30–42 kg).

Coat and Colour: The double coat is formed by a coarse outer guard coat and a thick, woolly undercoat. The texture of the guard coat is rough so that the coat readily sheds dirt and shows no tendency to mat. The length of the hair follows a definite pattern: head, ears, front of forelegs, and feet are covered with short, straight, dense hair ³/₈– ³/₄ in. (1–2 cm) in length. The guard coat on the body and thighs is medium length 1½–4³/₄ in. (4–12 cm). Some coats have long, loose waves, some have smaller, tighter waves. Both are correct, as is anything in between. On the adult dog, the coat must not be tightly curled nor should it lie completely flat, but the degree of waviness will vary considerably from one specimen to another. There is a ruff and mane of longer hair about the neck and chest, more prominent on the males, and feathering of 2–3¼ in. (5–8 cm) on the back of the legs. The tail is thickly covered in long wavy hair 4–6 in. (10–15 cm) in length. Puppies may have either straight or curly coats but should lose these characteristics with their first adult coat. The coat is a lustrous, pure white, although ivory is permissible, but not preferred. A yellow saddle is to be severely penalized. The skin is well pigmented, preferably grey in colour. The nose, eyerims, lips, and flews are black. The roof of the mouth should be dark. Pads of the feet are black or slate grey and slate-coloured nails are preferred.

Head: From the tip of the nose to the top of the occiput should measure slightly less than half the dog's height at the withers. Viewed from above, the head should narrow, gradually and smoothly, from the ears to the nose. The *skull* and muzzle are of equal length and the width of the skull should be slightly less than its length. While there is a gentle and graceful arch of the forehead above the eyes, the stop should be only slightly marked. A distinct furrow runs from between the eyes to the top of the occiput. The *muzzle*, which tapers gently from root to nose, is strongly built with a punishing bite. It is never snipey but neither should it be coarse or clumsy. Skin on the skull and muzzle should be clean, dry and close-fitting. The *lips* should be tight and show no flews. The *eyes* should be as dark as possible, ideally a coffee-black. They are almond shaped with close-fitting rims, set well apart and a trifle obliquely. The *nose* is of good size with well-developed nostrils. The *teeth* are large and very strong. Dentition should be complete, and the teeth meet in a scissors bite. The Kuvasz has drop-ears of a triangular shape with a gently rounded tip. Set well to the side and nearly at a level with the top of the head, the upper portion stands slightly away from the head while the lower third falls close to the cheek. When the dog is alert he brings the whole ear slightly toward the front giving him a keen and alert appearance. The *ear* should be small and neat and when pulled over the face should just cover the eye.

Neck: The neck should be powerful, slightly arched, and of medium length. There should be no dewlap.

Forequarters: The shoulders are well covered with good, hard muscle. The shoulder blade and upper arm should be at right angles to each other and of good length, allowing the dog ample reach and follow-through of stride. Elbows are close without being constricted and the whole foreleg should describe a straight line from shoulder to forepaw when viewed from the front. The leg should be of good, strong bone, without being coarse or clumsy. The pasterns should have ample spring and the feet should be of the type known as "cat feet," tight and well arched with deep, resilient pads. There should not be much hair between the toes.

Body: The withers are prominent and slope gently into a strong, level back of medium length. The chest reaches to the elbow, with a well-developed forechest and medium spring of rib. The ribs behind the forelegs must taper inward to allow complete freedom for long, easy stride. The loin is strong and gently arched. There is a distinct but moderate tuck-up. There should be a well-formed, slightly sloping croup which is broad and well muscled.

Hindquarters: The hindquarters are well angulated. The angle between pelvis and upper thigh should be 90 degrees to correspond with the proper angle in the forequarters. The upper thigh itself should be of good length, creating the correct bend of stifle (110−120 degrees). The bend of the hock joint should be about 130−140 degrees with the metatarsus being short, strong, and perpendicular to the ground. Rear paws are somewhat longer than forepaws but should nevertheless be tight and well arched with deep, resilient pads. Dewclaws are undesirable and should be removed.

Tail: The tail is set on low, a smooth continuation of the slope of croup. The tip, when straightened, should reach the hock. The tail hangs straight down and may be slightly turned up at the tip but should not curl when the dog is relaxed. When the dog is excited the tail will curl up to the level of the loin, but should not be carried over the back.

Gait: The trot is smooth, elastic and far-reaching, often showing a tendency for the hind foot to overreach the front. As the dog's speed increases, he will tend to single-track. When he is moving fast, he will carry his head low, at a level with his shoulders. The Kuvasz should move effortlessly, enabling him to travel great distances without fatigue.

Faults: Since the Kuvasz is a working breed any faults of soundness should be considered serious. Faults in type which should be guarded against are: too short a muzzle, apple head or bulging skull, no visible supraorbital ridge, too much stop; giving an uncharacteristic setter-like appearance, drooping haws or pendulous flews, hound ears, lying back in the ruff. Too long a neck, barrel chest, loose or sloppy shoulder assembly, yellow eyes or yellow markings, sullen appearance or distrustful expression (not to be confused with reserve), extreme nervousness, overshot or undershot mouth, gay tail.

Disqualifications: *Over or undersize as follows—males, over 32 in. (81 cm) or under 25½ in. (65 cm); females, over 30 in. (76 cm) or under 23½ in. (60 cm). So pronounced a lack of pigmentation as to have flesh-coloured eye rims. Colour other than white.*

Mastiff

*I*T IS THOUGHT that both the Mastiff, sometimes referred to as the Old English Mastiff, and the Bulldog descend from *Canis Pugnaces*, large, mastiff-type dogs brought to Britain by the Phoenician traders in the 6th century B.C. The dogs were bartered in exchange for metals and were welcomed by the Britons who cross bred them with local fighting dogs to increase size and aggressiveness. The resultant dogs were used to hunt and kill the wolf, and later as combatants in bear, lion, and bull-baiting competitions.

Over the years the breed has been known by a variety of names, including Molossus, Alan, Alaunt, Tie-dog, and Bandog. Writings dating to the 16th century refer to the breed as the Mastiff, by which name it has since been known. The large dog became well known as a companion and protection dog and when dog fighting came into vogue the Mastiff was the first breed to be so employed.

Two of the oldest strains were owned by Mr. Leigh of Lyme Hall in Cheshire and the Duke of Devonshire. It is said that most Mastiffs of today trace back to these early lines. These were longer-headed dogs than the present square-muzzled Mastiff. A change that was brought about by a committee of breeders who laid down a breed standard calling for a short-headed dog led to the indiscriminate use of an ideal-headed but otherwise faulty stud and almost spelled doom for the breed. From an entry of sixty-three Mastiffs at the Crystal Palace show in 1871, they dropped to zero a few years later indicating a total lack of interest in the breed. Added to this came the devastating effects of two world wars. A breed census taken after the close of World War II showed that there were only eight Mastiffs of breeding age still in Britain, the former stronghold of the breed. Two puppies donated by H.W. and Mrs. Mellish from their Heatherbelle Kennels in Canada are credited with restoring the Mastiff in Britain to its present high level of popularity.

Among the first breeds to be recognized in Canada, The Canadian Kennel Club Stud Book lists forty-nine Mastiffs registered in the years 1888–1889.

Mastiff

Official Breed Standard for the Mastiff

General Appearance: Large, massive, symmetrical, and well-knit frame. A combination of grandeur and good nature, courage and docility.

Size: Dogs, minimum 30 in. (76 cm) at the shoulder; bitches, minimum 27½ in. (70 cm) at the shoulder.

Coat and Colour: Outer coat moderately coarse. Undercoat dense, short, and close lying. Colour apricot, silver fawn or dark fawn-brindle. Fawn-brindle should have fawn as a background colour which should be completely covered with very dark stripes. In any case muzzle, ears, and nose must be dark in colour, the blacker the better, with similar colour tone around the orbits, extending upwards between them.

Head: In general outline giving a massive appearance when viewed from any angle. Breadth greatly to be desired.
   Skull: broad and somewhat rounded between the ears, forehead slightly curved, showing marked wrinkles which are particularly distinctive when at attention. Brows (superciliary ridges) moderately raised. Muscles of the temples well developed, those of the cheeks extremely powerful. Arch across the skull a flattened curve with a furrow up the centre of the forehead. This extends from between the eyes to halfway up the skull.
   Muzzle: short, broad under the eyes and running nearly equal in width to the end of the nose. Truncated, *i.e.*, blunt and cut off square, thus forming a right angle with the upper line of the face. Of great depth from the point of the nose to underjaw. Underjaw broad to the end and slightly rounded. Lips diverging at obtuse angles with the septum and sufficiently pendulous so as to show a modified square profile. Muzzle dark in colour, the blacker the better. Muzzle should be half the length of the skull, thus dividing the head into three parts—one for the foreface and two for the skull. In other words, the distance from tip of nose to stop is equal to one-half the distance between the stop and the occiput. Circumference of muzzle (measured midway between the eyes and nose) to that of the head (measured before the ears) as 3 is to 5.

Nose: broad and always dark in colour, the blacker the better, with spread flat nostrils (not pointed or turned up) in profile.

Mouth: canine teeth healthy, powerful and wide apart. Scissors bite preferred but a moderately undershot jaw permissible providing the teeth are not visible when the mouth is closed.

Eyes: set wide apart, medium in size, never too prominent. Expression alert but kindly. The stop between the eyes well marked but not too abrupt. Colour of eyes brown, the darker the better and showing no haw.

Ears: small, V-shaped, rounded at the tips. Leather moderately thin, set widely apart at the highest points on the sides of the skull continuing the outline across the summit. They should lie close to the cheeks when in repose. Ears dark in colour, the blacker the better, conforming to the colour of the muzzle.

Neck: Powerful and very muscular, slightly arched, and of medium length. The neck gradually increases in circumference as it approaches the shoulder. Neck moderately "dry" (not showing an excess of loose skin).

Forequarters: Shoulder slightly sloping, heavy and muscular. No tendency to looseness of shoulders. Legs straight, strong and set wide apart, heavy bones. Elbows parallel to body. Pasterns strong and bent only slightly. Feet heavy, round and compact with well-arched toes. Black nails preferred.

Body: Back muscular, powerful, and straight. Chest wide, deep, rounded, and well let down between the forelegs, extending at least to the elbow. Forechest should be deep and well defined. Ribs extremely well rounded. False ribs deep and well set back. Loins wide and muscular, slightly rounded over the rump. There should be a reasonable, but not exaggerated, cut-up.

Hindquarters: Hindquarters broad, wide and muscular. Second thighs well developed, hocks set back, wide apart and parallel when viewed from the rear.

Tail: Set on moderately high and reaching to the hocks or a little below. Wide at the root, tapering to the end, hanging straight in repose, forming a slight curve but never over the back when dog is in action.

Scale of Points:

General character and symmetry   10
Height and substance   10
Skull   10
Face and muzzle   12
Ears   5
Eyes   5
Chest and ribs   10
Forelegs and feet   10
Back, loins, and flanks   10
Hind legs and feet   10
Tail   3
Coat and colour   5

TOTAL   100

Newfoundland

THERE IS SOME DISAGREEMENT among dog historians as to when and how the Newfoundland dog arrived on the island after which it is named. Newfoundland folklore, which is unconfirmed by present-day writings, claims that the breed's progenitor was the Tibetan Mastiff which had migrated in two directions, the one line winding across the Canadian North to Newfoundland, and the other finding its place amongst the Vikings. In 1001 A.D., when Leif Ericsson brought the Viking "bear dog" strain with him to the island of Newfoundland, they joined their "long-lost cousins" who for the previous 4000 years had lived with the Maritime Indians on the island.

For 500 years they bred and developed in geographical isolation until the summer visits of European fishing fleets brought dogs of other varieties. The original breed characteristics were secured, however, since the "resident" breed mated with only their own kind during the winter season when no foreign human habitation was allowed, and the Newfoundlands living in the interior remained isolated.

During the 19th century, the big, family-oriented dog became a popular status symbol in England, and to a lesser extent on the European continent, especially after Sir Edwin Landseer featured a white and black Newfoundland in his famous painting "A Distinguished Member of the Humane Society." This two-coloured variety (developed in England) has since been called the "Landseer."

The Newfoundland is an excellent swimmer and has a strong life-saving instinct. There are many tales, authenticated in the rich, oral history used by Newfoundlanders, citing heroic rescues of drowning victims. One modern kennel alone has had five instances of its progeny saving lives. In the service of man the Newfoundland has been used as a draught and sled dog, fisherman's helper, children's protector and playmate. In the service of his own kind, in 1856 a careful selection of the best of the breed from Newfoundland was used to help re-establish the St. Bernard when the kennels of the Hospice du Grand Saint

G. STENHOUSE

Newfoundland

Bernard were almost wiped out of breeding stock because of a distemper epidemic.

In 1886 a specialty club for the Newfoundland was organized and a breed standard drawn up. With minor revisions this is still in use today. At the Westminster Kennel Club show, 1877, there were twelve Newfoundlands in competition and the breed was among the first to be registered in Canada. The Canadian Kennel Club Stud Book lists seven Newfoundlands registered between 1888–1889.

Official Breed Standard for the Newfoundland

Origin and Purpose: The breed originated in Newfoundland from dogs indigenous to the island, and the big black bear dogs introduced by the Vikings in 1001 A.D. With the advent of European fishermen, a variety of new breeds helped to shape and re-invigorate the breed, but the essential characteristics of the Newfoundland dog remained. By the time colonization was permitted in 1610, the distinct physical characteristics and mental attributes had been established in the breed for all time.

The large size, heavy coat and webbed feet permit him to withstand the rigours of the extreme climate and sea while serving both as lifeguard and draught animal.

General Appearance: The Newfoundland is massive, deep bodied, well muscled and co-ordinated, projecting dignity in stance and head carriage. The appearance is square in that the length of the dog, from the top of the withers to the base of the tail, is equal to the distance from the top of the withers to the ground. The distance from the top of the withers to the underside of the chest is greater than the distance from the underside of the chest to the ground. The body of the bitch may be slightly longer, and is less massive than that of the dog. A mature dog should never appear leggy or lacking substance. The Newfoundland is free moving with a slight roll perceptible. Substantial webbing of the toes is always present. Large size is desirable but never at the expense of gait symmetry and balance. Fine bone is to be faulted.

Temperament: The Newfoundland's expression is soft and reflects the character of the breed—benevolent, intelligent, dignified but capable of fun. He is known for his sterling gentleness and serenity. Any show of ill temper or timidity is to be severely faulted. Bad temperament is a disqualification.

Size: The average height for adult dogs is 28 in. (71 cm), for adult bitches, 26 in. (66 cm). The average weight for adult dogs is 150 lb. (68 kg), for adult bitches, 120 lb. (54 kg). Large size is desirable but it is not to be favoured over correct gait, symmetry, soundness and structure.

Coat and Colour: The Newfoundland has a water resistant double coat. The outer coat is moderately long and straight with no curl. A slight wave is permissible. When rubbed the wrong way, the coat tends to fall back into place. The undercoat is soft and dense, but less dense during summer months, but always found to some extent on the rump and chest. A completely open coat is to be faulted. The hair on the head, muzzle, and ears is short and fine. The front and rear legs are feathered. The tail is completely covered with long dense hair, but does not form a flag. A short, flat, smooth coat (Labrador Retriever type) is a disqualification. The traditional colour is black. A sunburned black is permissible. White markings on chest, toes and/or tip of tail are permissible. Markings of any colour other than white are most objectionable and the dog is to be disqualified. The Landseer Newfoundland is white with black markings, and is of historical significance to the breed. The preferred pattern of markings for the Landseer is black head with white blaze extending onto the muzzle, black saddle and black rump and upper tail. All remaining parts are to be white with a minimum of ticking. The symmetry of markings and beauty of pattern characterize the best marked Landseers. Landseers are to be shown in the same classes as blacks unless special classes are provided for them.

Head: The head is massive with a broad *skull,* slightly arched crown and strongly developed occipital bone. The forehead and face are smooth and free from wrinkles. The stop is not abrupt. The *muzzle* is clean-cut and covered with short fine hair. It is rather square, deep and moderately short. The nostrils are well developed. The bitch's head follows the same general conformation, but is feminine and less massive. A narrow head, snipey or long muzzle is to be faulted. Pronounced flews are not desirable. The *eyes* are dark brown, relatively small and deep set. They are spaced wide apart and show no haw. Round. Protruding or yellow eyes are objectionable. The *ears* are relatively small and triangular with rounded tips. They are set well back on the side of the head and lie close. When the ear of the adult dog is brought forward, it reaches to the inner corner of the eye on the same side. The teeth meet in a scissors or level bite.

Neck: The neck is strong, muscular, and well set on the shoulders. It is long enough to permit dignified head carriage, and should not show surplus dewlap.

Forequarters: When the dog is not in motion, the forelegs are straight and parallel, with the elbows close to the chest. The shoulders are well muscled and well laid back at an angle approaching 45 degrees. The pasterns are slightly sloping. Down in the pasterns is to be faulted. The feet are proportionate to the body in size, well rounded and tight, with firm compact toes (cat-foot type). Splayed toes are a fault. Toeing in or out is undesirable.

Body: The Newfoundland's chest is broad, full and deep, with the brisket reaching to the elbows. The back is broad, with good spread of rib, and the topline is level from the withers to croup, never roached, slack, or swayed. The loins are strong and well muscled, and the croup is broad. The pelvis slopes at an angle of about 30 degrees. Viewed from the side, the body is deep, showing no discernible tuck-up. Bone structure is massive throughout but does not give sluggish appearance.

Hindquarters: Because driving power for swimming, pulling loads or covering ground efficiently is largely dependent upon the hindquarters, the rear structure of the Newfoundland is of prime importance. The hip assembly is broad, strong and well developed. The upper thighs are wide and muscular. The lower thighs are strong and fairly long. The stifles are well bent, but not so as to give a crouching appearance. The hocks are well let down, well apart and parallel to each other. They turn neither in nor out. The feet are firm and tight. Dewclaws, if present, should have been removed. Straight stifles, cowhocks, barrel legs, and pigeon toes are to be faulted.

Tail: The tail acts as a rudder when the Newfoundland is swimming; therefore it is strong and broad at the base. When the dog is standing the tail hangs straight down, possibly a little curved at the tip, reaching to or slightly below the hocks; when the dog is in motion or excited, the tail is carried straight out or with slight upward curve but never curled over the back nor curved inward between the legs. A tail with a kink or curled at the end is very objectionable.

Gait: The Newfoundland has good reach and strong drive, giving the impression of effortless power. In motion, the legs move straight forward, parallel to the line of travel. A slight roll is present. As the speed increases, the dog tends to single track, with the topline remaining level. Mincing, shuffling, crabbing, too close moving, weaving, crossing over in front, toeing out or distinctly toeing-in in front, hackney action and pacing are all faults.

Faults: Legginess, narrow head, snipey or long muzzle, pronounced flews, short tail, long tail, tail with a kink, tail with curled end, fine bone, any show of ill temper or timidity, open coat, eyes showing pronounced haw, round, protruding or yellow eyes, splayed feet, down pasterns, mincing, shuffling, crabbing, weaving, crossing over in front, toeing out or distinctly toeing-in in front, hackney action or pacing, straight stifles, cowhocks, barrel legs, roached, slack or sway back, lack of webbing between toes, overshot or undershot or wry mouth.

Disqualifications: *Bad temperament, short flat-coat (Labrador Retriever type), markings of any other colour than white on a black dog, any colours other than the traditional black, or Landseer (white and black).*

Old English Sheepdog

THE NAME "OLD ENGLISH" SHEEPDOG is something of a misnomer, because this bobtailed breed has only been known in Britain for about 200 years. How or exactly when the breed arrived there has not been recorded. But the Old English, who is now prized more for his gentle manners and appearance than for his working ability, is thought to be related to several European herding breeds that once were noted for their bad temper and ferocity.

Undoubtedly such temperament was useful during the time when the wolf still flourished in Britain. Then, as conditions changed, the sheepdog's working role became that of drover—an agile, intelligent, hardy dog that drove the livestock to market. At that time dogs who worked for a living were exempt from tax. So, to distinguish the droving dogs, owners began the practice of removing tails. Thus the Old English Sheepdog came to be called "the bobtail."

By the mid-nineteenth century the bobtail was to be found in rural areas throughout England where his natural herding instincts are still being used. On seeing an Old English Sheepdog for the first time many have asked: "How could he possibly see to work with all that hair hanging over his eyes?" First, it should be noted that working farm dogs do not carry the abundant coat of the show specimens, and also that these dogs are sheared at the same time as the sheep. During World War I these shearings were put to good use. They were spun into yarn from which warm garments were fashioned. One sheepdog was said to yield from three to five pounds of wool per year. In addition to his herding talents it is said that the trainable bobtail makes a good, light-mouthed retriever.

The breed was first exhibited in Britain in 1873 when three rather mediocre specimens were shown. Notwithstanding an inauspicious start, fanciers organized a specialty club and drew up a breed standard and established ideal type which remains virtually unchanged today. The Canadian Kennel Club Stud Book lists first registrations in the years 1902–1903 when two Old English Sheepdogs are recorded.

Old English Sheepdog

Official Breed Standard for the Old English Sheepdog

General Appearance: A strong, compact-looking dog of great symmetry, practically the same in measurement from shoulder to stern as in height, absolutely free from legginess or weaselness, very elastic in his gallop, but in walking or trotting he has a characteristic ambling or pacing movement, and his bark should be loud, with a peculiar "pot-casse" ring in it. Taking him all round, he is a profusely, but not *excessively* coated, thick-set, muscular, able-bodied dog with a most intelligent expression, free from all Poodle or Deerhound character. *Soundness should be considered of greatest importance.*

Size: Twenty-two in. (56 cm) and upwards for dogs and slightly less for bitches. Type, character, and symmetry are of the greatest importance and are on no account to be sacrificed to size alone.

Coat and Colour: Coat profuse, but not so excessive as to give the impression of the dog being overfat, and of a good hard texture; not straight, but shaggy and free from curl. *Quality and texture of coat to be considered above mere profuseness.* Softness or flatness of coat to be considered a fault. The undercoat should be a waterproof pile, when not removed by grooming or season. Colour any shade of grey, grizzle, blue or blue-merled with or without white markings or in reverse. *Any shade of brown or fawn to be considered distinctly objectionable and not to be encouraged.*

Head: *Skull:* capacious and rather squarely formed, giving plenty of room for brain power. The parts over the eyes should be well arched and the whole well covered with hair. *Muzzle:* fairly long, strong, square, and truncated. The top should be well defined to avoid a Deerhound face. *(The attention of judges is particularly called to the above properties, as a long, narrow head is a deformity.) Nose:* always black, large and capacious. *Mouth:* teeth strong and large, evenly placed and level in opposition. *Eyes* vary according to the colour of the dog. Very dark preferred, but in the glaucous or blue dogs a pearl, walleye, or china eye is considered typical. *(A light eye is most objectionable.) Ears:* medium sized, and carried flat to side of head, coated moderately.

Neck: The neck should be fairly long, arched gracefully and well coated with hair.

Forequarters: The shoulders sloping and narrow at the points. The forelegs should be dead straight, with plenty of bone, removing the body a medium height from the ground, without approaching legginess, and well coated all around.

Body: The dog stands lower at the shoulder than at the loin. Rather short and very compact, ribs well sprung and brisket deep and capacious. *Slab-sidedness highly undesirable.* The loin should be very stout and gently arched.

Hindquarters: Should be round and muscular and with well-let-down hocks, and the hams densely coated with a thick, long jacket in excess of any other part. Feet small, round; toes well arched, and pads thick and hard.

Tail: It is preferable that there should be none. Should never, however, exceed 1 $\frac{1}{2}$–2 in. (4–5 cm) in grown dogs. When not natural-born bobtails, puppies should be docked at the first joint from the body and the operation performed when they are from three to four days old.

Faults: Softness or flatness of coat to be considered a fault. Any shade of brown or fawn to be considered distinctly objectionable and not to be encouraged. A long, narrow head is a deformity. A light eye is most objectionable. Slab-sidedness highly undesirable.

Scale of Points:

Skull 5
Eyes 5
Ears 5
Teeth 5
Nose 5
Jaw 5
Foreface 5
Neck and shoulders 5
Body and loins 10
Hindquarters 10
Legs 10
Coat (texture, quality and condition) 15
General appearance and movement 15

               TOTAL 100

Puli

RESEARCHERS BELIEVE THAT because the Puli (plural Pulik) and the Tibetan Terrier share so many physical characteristics, the breeds must also share a common ancestry. This would seem highly probable. Both breeds originated in Asia and both found their way into new territories in the company of nomadic tribes.

From ancient times, it is reported, dogs known as the Puli drove the sheep that accompanied the Magyars, a tribe that came originally from the central steppes of Asia and settled in Hungary in the 9th century A.D. This tribe was related to the legendary Huns who once were known as Puli Hou or "destroyer Huns." Thus, the breed name Puli is of ancient origin. Now part of the Hungarian language, the word may mean either "drover" or "destroyer."

For centuries the Puli was noted for its herding instinct and was to be found in great numbers in the rural areas of Hungary. Not until the end of the 19th century, with the advent of dog shows, was any attempt made to classify it as a pure Hungarian breed or maintain accurate breeding records. Both biologists and veterinarians researched the breed's history and, despite the interruption of World War I, by 1918 ideal type had been established and the first breed standard for the Puli had been draughted.

A few years later, the U.S. Department of Agriculture became interested in the Puli's inherent ability to herd and protect livestock. Four specimens were imported for experimental breeding crosses to larger herding breeds. The purpose was to create a super herd-dog that would protect pasturing livestock from the ravages of predators.

With the outbreak of World War II this experiment was terminated. But the breed did have a foothold on this continent. More imports followed and in time there was sufficient interest in the breed to warrant the Puli's recognition as an official breed by the American Kennel Club. The first Puli to enter Canada was the German bred Ch. Adolar von der Herlingsburg, CDX, brought

Puli

in by Mrs. R.D. McLellan of Montreal in January 1948. Official breed recognition was granted by The Canadian Kennel Club later that same year.

One of the breed's distinguishing features is its corded coat. While the Puli may be shown with brushed out coat in the United States, this is considered unacceptable in Canada.

Official Breed Standard for the Puli

Origin and Purpose: The Puli is a medium-sized Hungarian sheepdog of Asiatic origin, and has been prized for centuries for his ability to do the strenuous work of herding the flocks of sheep, and sometimes cattle, swine, and horses, on the great plains, or Puszta, of Hungary. It follows that he must be sturdy, richly muscled, and alert, and exhibit great courage and stamina to perform his tasks. The correct mental image of the Puli should be that of a true working dog, and it is appropriate to think of him as one of the basic sheepdogs of the world.

General Appearance: The most striking breed characteristic is the unusual but typical corded coat, the result of many years of natural development, adapted to outdoor living and extreme climates. There is nothing artificial in this coat; it is a unique and ancient style fitting the dog for his work. It is difficult to make an assessment of the body purely on a visual examination, for the whole dog should be covered with the profuse coat. The Puli does not impress by a beautiful clean-cut shape, but by his distinctive shaggy appearance. The head appears to be round because of the long hair overshadowing the eyes, and the rump may appear to be higher due to the fullness of the tail coat. The body should be square, measured from the top of the withers to the ground, and from the foremost point of the forechest to the rear point of the pelvis, but the heavy coat may create a rectangular appearance. Beneath the coat, the Puli is wiry, muscular, and fine-boned, but never light or shelly.

Temperament: Lively, nimble, and intelligent, the Puli is by nature affectionate, and a devoted and home-loving companion, sensibly suspicious of strangers and therefore an excellent guard. He has a certain aloofness which does not lend itself to immediate and indiscriminate friendship, but extreme timidity and shyness are serious faults.

◀**German Shepherd Dog**
Odessa Dawn, C.D.
Breeder: Mr. Seigmund
Owner: Miss Linda D. Smith
35 George Suttie Bay,
Winnipeg, Man. R2K 3C9
BRANDYLIND KENNELS REG.

▼**German Shepherd Dog**
Ch. Kolbrook's Piper Cub
Breeder: Kolbrook Kennels
Owner: Dr. R. A. Alexander
Box 37,
Midnapore, Alta. T0L 1J0
FELSENHOLZ KENNELS REG.

► **Great Dane**
Heldre Reagan Lovett
V. Reaper*
Ch. Reaper Madness**
Breeders:
*Andre Schoen
**Peter & Dorothy Rozins
Owners:
Peter & Dorothy Rozins
RR 2,
Alliston, Ont. L0M 1A0
REAPER KENNELS REG.

▼ **Komondor**
Can. Am. Ch. Bundas
Myosho Gaspar
Breeder: Grace Lush
Owners:
Barbara & Bill Mooney
RR 5,
Rockwood, Ont. N0B 2K0
MYOSHO KENNELS (PERM.)

Kuvasz
Ch. Whitewoods Wrayle
Lofranco
Budavari Deven of Lofranco
Owners:
Mr. & Mrs. F. Lofranco
RR 2,
Acton, Ont. L7J 2L8
LOFRANCO KENNELS REG.
(Photo by Lofranco)

▼**Kuvasz**
Ch. Alcsi Rattenfanger
Von Laxenburg (Aus)
Godollokerti Potyi (Hgy)
Ch. Thunderbell Centaurus
The Riff, C.D.
Owners:
Mr. & Mrs. Guy Beesley
RR 1, Murillo, Ont. P0T 2G0
THUNDERBELL KENNELS REG.

▲ **Newfoundland**
Ch. Demon V. St. Silvester
Breeder: Felix Buntschu
Owner: Andrew C. Crosbie
P.O. Box 398,
St. John's, Nfld. A1C 5K3
KAEGUDECK KENNELS REG.
(Photo by Rostotsky)

▶ **Old English Sheepdog**
Ch. Tegglewend Caesar
Breeders:
Clifton & Barbara Davis
Owners:
Kenneth & Louise Graham
167 Manitou Cres. W.,
Amherstview, Ont.

Puli
Can. Am. Ch. Immerzu
Moorva, C.D., Am. C.D.
Breeders/Owners:
Terry & Stephanie Horan
Box 1403,
Cochrane, Alta. T0L 0W0
IMMERZU KENNELS (PERM.)

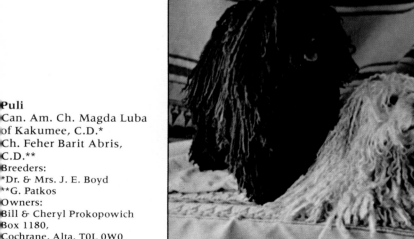

Puli
Can. Am. Ch. Magda Luba
of Kakumee, C.D.*
Ch. Feher Barit Abris,
C.D.**
Breeders:
*Dr. & Mrs. J. E. Boyd
**G. Patkos
Owners:
Bill & Cheryl Prokopowich
Box 1180,
Cochrane, Alta. T0L 0W0
KAKUMEE KENNELS REG.

▲**Rottweiler**
▼Ch. Rintelna The Dragoon
  Breeder: Jim Miller
  Owners:
  Pat Johnson & Jim Miller
  Box 10, GR 355, RR 3,
  Winnipeg, Man.
  RINTELNA KENNELS REG.

Samoyed
Can. Am. Ch. Jasam's
Viktor
Breeders:
Mr. & Mrs. John A. Post
Owners:
John B. & Barbara A. Meyer
P.O. Box 626,
Coeur d'Alene, Idaho 83814
SNOWBLAZE KENNELS REG.

▼**Shetland Sheepdog**
Ch. Sheldon Korshelt
Classic Look
Breeders/Owners:
Bill & Doreen Randall
RR 1,
Mount Brydges, Ont. N0L 1W0
SHELDON KENNELS REG. (PERM.)

▲**Shetland Sheepdog**
Ch. Sovereign Ring's Legacy
Breeder/Owner:
Mrs. Ariel J. Sleeth
RR 1,
Seeley's Bay, Ont. K0H 2N0
SOVEREIGN KENNELS REG.

▶**Siberian Husky**
Ch. Loboden's Tuavi
Kiggiak
Breeder: Judith Meakin
Owner: Glenys I. Morgan
3-414 Carpathia Rd.,
Winnipeg, Man. R3N 1Y4
SNOWALKER KENNELS REG.

◀**Siberian Husky**
Breeders/Owners:
Ken & Jan Weagle
Box 4688,
Whitehorse, Yukon Y1A 3V7
TAKKALIK KENNELS REG.

◀**Siberian Husky**
Ch. Jophil's Sweet
Valentine
Breeder/Owner:
Jo-Ann Moffatt
Box 12,
Ste. Agathe, Man. R0G 1Y0
JOPHIL KENNELS REG.

▶Siberian Husky
Ch. Coppermine's Silver
Spring
Breeders/Owners:
Randy & Cathryn Kyle
8720 Harvie Rd., RR 10,
Surrey, B.C. V3S 5X7
COPPERMINE KENNELS REG.

▼St. Bernard
Can. Am. Ch. Arlberg's
Kondor
Breeders/Owners:
John & Ann Gauthier
RR 1, Donaldson Rd.,
Buckingham W., P.Q. J8L 2W7
ARLBERG KENNELS REG.

Australian Terrier
Can. Am. Ch. Yaralla's
The Fonz
Breeder/Owner:
Rose Parker
Box 519,
Yarrow, B.C. V0X 2A0
YARALLA KENNELS REG.

▼**Bull Terrier**
Proycon & Casey
Owners:
Renée & Mel Trottier
22 Bertmount Ave.,
Toronto, Ont.
MINOTAURUS KENNELS REG.

▲**Kerry Blue Terrier**
Can. Ire. Bda. Am. Ch.
Arigna Lucky Strike
Owner: E. C. "Gene" Banks
18 Manners Sutton Rd.,
Saint John, N.B. E2K 1K6
BALLACHULISH KENNELS REG.

▼**Norwich Terrier**
Norwesia Lady Gwendolyn
Breeders/Owners:
Dr. C. Elizabeth &
Eleanor C. Mahaffy
RR 3,
High River, Alta. T0L 1B0
NORWESIA KENNELS REG.
(Photo by Gray)

▲**Schnauzer (Miniature)**
Can. Am. Ch. Dow's
Twenty One Gunn Salute
Breeder: David O. Williams
Owner: Dr. Dorothy Griggs
285 Downey Rd.,
Guelph, Ont.
SYLVA SPRITE KENNELS REG.

◄**Schnauzer (Miniature)**
Ch. Frontenac Don't Step
On My Foot
Breeders/Owners:
Jacline & Armand Gratton
450 Ch. St. Antoine,
Les Cedres, P.Q. J0P 1L0
FRONTENAC KENNELS REG.

▲Scottish Terrier
Brunnoch Bee & Puppies
Breeder: Dr. E. M. King
Owner: Mrs. Joyce Holdham
Whites Rd., RR 2,
Trenton, Ont. K8V 5P5
ARDYCE KENNELS REG. (PERM.)

▼Scottish Terrier
Can. Am. Ch. Anstamm
Daring Venture
Breeder: Mrs. Miriam Stamm
Owner: Joyce Alleyne Wyler
Box 101,
Millarville, Alta. T0L 1K0
GREATBEAR KENNELS REG.

◀Skye Terrier
Ch. Ceilidh's Adam
MacTavish
Breeder: Mr. Donald Drury
Owner: Mrs. Joyce Thornhill
299 Portland St.,
Dartmouth, N.S. B2Y 1K3
(Photo by Keseluk)

▼Staffordshire Bull Terrier
Can. Am. Ch. Pride of
Black King, C.D.
Breeder:
Miss R. J. A. Swindells
Owners: Joan & Ian Trott
36-3175 Kirwin Ave.,
Mississauga, Ont. L5A 3M4
JUBILEE KENNELS REG.

▲Staffordshire Terrier
Revol-te Sibelle de Froja
Breeder/Owner:
Gaétan Couturier
5526 8ᵉ Ave.
Montreal, P.Q.
CHENIL REVOL-TE ENRG.

**▶West Highland
White Terrier**
Ch. Thornemore Hello Dolly
Breeder: Mrs. M. E. Brady
Owners: Dr. J.E.H. Wait &
Mrs. Marian Wait
Box 18, Morna Heights,
Saint John W., N.B. E2L 3W7
ISLAND VIEW KENNELS REG.

Size: Height at the top of the withers—males, ideal 16–18 in. (40–46 cm); females, ideal 14–16 in. (35–41 cm). Weight—males, 28–33 lb. (13–15 kg); females, 22–28 lb. (10–13 kg).

Coat and Colour: Characteristic of the breed is its dense weather-resisting double coat. The undercoat is soft, dense, and fine, and it interweaves with the topcoat, which is long, and wavy or curly, and is of a fairly coarse texture. The ideal proportions of topcoat and undercoat create the desired cords, which consist of uniform, tightly interwoven hair. These cords are less inclined to mat together. The cords may vary from wide flat strands, to narrow flat strands, to small round cords, and these variations are all correct, provided that the coat shows the tendency to form cords. This tendency should be noticeable even in the puppy coat, the hair forming into bunches. Both puppies and young dogs will have coats of a softer texture than mature dogs, but in Pulik of all ages the tendency to cord must always be present in the coat. Cording is generally complete all over the body by the age of two years, although variations will occur. The coat should be long all over the body, the length depending on the age of the dog, and is generally longest on the hindquarters and shortest on the head and paws. With age the coat can become quite long, even reaching to the ground; however, only enough length to properly evaluate quality and texture is considered necessary so as not to penalize the working specimen or younger dog.

An excess of topcoat and a sparse undercoat result in an open coat which will not cord, while too much undercoat and a sparse topcoat result in excessive matting and felting. Such coats are objectionable. A brushed-out coat is highly objectionable, as is a neglected coat. Accepted colours are: black, reddish-black, grey-reddish-black, all shades of grey, and white. The colour should always appear solid, although the greys are mostly a mixture of black and white hair, but should always look either all light, or all dark grey. A white spot on the chest of not more than 2 in. (5 cm) in diameter is permissible, and a few scattered white hairs in between the pads may be tolerated. The skin should be blue, blue-grey, or slate-grey.

Head: From the front, the head should appear round, from the side almost elliptical. Disregarding the hair, the head should be rather small and fine. The *skull* should be smooth, moderately wide, and slightly domed, with the stop clearly defined but not abrupt. The *muzzle* should be straight and rather short, about one-third of the total length of the head, and should never be snipey, but bluntly rounded, ending in a relatively large nose. The upper and lower jaws should be well developed to accommodate a full set of teeth. The *teeth* should be large, regular, and strong, with a scissors bite, the lower incisors touching the inside of the upper incisors. A level bite, the upper and lower incisors meeting edge to edge, is acceptable. The flews should fit tightly to the set of teeth, and the roof of the mouth should be uniformly dark, or variegated with deeply pigmented spots on a dark base. The arches of the eye sockets should be well defined. The *eyes* should be medium sized, slightly slanted with eyelids tight, and should be dark brown in colour. Their expression should be lively and intelligent. The *ears* should be set medium-high, pendant, and V-shaped, measuring about half the length of the head, reaching to the inner corner of the eye when pulled forward. Movement of the ears is practically imperceptible. *Nose*, flews, and eyelids should always be black. Head, neck, and ears should be covered with long hair which blends in with the body, not showing noticeably separate features.

Neck: Should be set at an angle of 45 degrees to the horizontal, of medium length, tight and muscular, and slightly arched. It should seem to merge with the body because of the long hair.

Forequarters: The shoulder blade and the upper arm should be about the same length, forming an angle of 90 degrees at the shoulder joint. The shoulder blade should be well laid back. Elbows set close to the chest. The forelegs should be muscular, and viewed from any angle they should be vertical. Fore pasterns should be slightly sloping. Feet should be round and tight, with a full and springy pad, dark grey in colour. Nails should be strong, and black or slate-grey. Dewclaws, if they occur, should be removed from both fore and hind legs.

Body: The withers should be slightly higher than the level of the back, which should be of medium length, tight and straight. The loin should be short, broad, and tucked up. Rump slightly sloping towards the root of the tail, but this is not obvious because of the tail curling over the back. Chest should be medium-broad and deep, with well-sprung ribs reaching well back. The depth of the chest from the top of the withers to the brisket should be about 45 per cent of the dog's height.

Hindquarters: The pelvis should form an angle of 90 degrees to the femur, approximately the angle at the shoulder joint and resulting in structural balance. The stifle should be well bent, but not excessively, with hocks well developed and short.

Tail: Should be of medium length, and should curl quickly well up over the back and touch the body, falling to one side or the other or curling on the midline of the back. The tail should not be noticeable because of the long hair on it mixing indistinguishably with the hair on the rump.

Gait: The gait of the Puli is short-striding, very quick and typical, in harmony with its lively disposition. It should never be heavy, lethargic, or lumbering. The legs should swing straight forward with no twisting in or out of the elbows, pasterns or hocks, and the feet should not interfere or cross. When at a full trot, the Puli covers ground smoothly and efficiently with good reach and drive, the feet naturally tending to converge towards a median line of travel beneath the body in order to keep the body in balance and offset pitching from side to side. The tendency to converge should never be confused with moving close, where the lower part of the legs moves parallel. The Puli should be capable of great speed and agility, and shows the unique quality of being a bundle of springs, able to leap straight up from a standstill, or to change direction suddenly in mid-air.

Faults: Any departure from the foregoing should be considered a fault, the seriousness of the fault depending upon its degree.

Disqualifications: *Particolours. Large markings of any colour other than a white spot on the chest of not more than 2 in. (5 cm) in diameter.*
   Males under 13 in. or over 20 in. (33 and 51 cm). Females under 12 in. or over 19 in. (30 and 48 cm) respectively. Colours other than those mentioned as acceptable. Coats showing no tendency to form cords.

Rottweiler

When the Roman legions crossed the Alps, the beef that was to feed the soldiers accompanied them "on the hoof," driven during the day and watched over at night by strong, mastiff-type cattle dogs. Not all the dogs completed the march into newly conquered lands. Many were left behind to guard the outposts that the Romans established along the route. There they remained, adapted to their new environments and eventually became the progenitors of several European working breeds.

One such outpost was in the small community of Rottweil, Germany, which was to become the centre of an important cattle-producing area. There the large working dogs seem to have flourished and, continuing in their service to man, came to be known as "the butcher's dog of Rottweil." The dog's work consisted of accompanying the butcher on his cattle buying trips. When the pair set out, the dog carried his master's money in a leather purse fastened to his collar. Then, the purchase completed, on the return trip the dog drove the cattle back to his master's place of business.

It was a unique working arrangement that protected the butcher from thieves on the outward trip and kept his livestock under control when he was homeward bound. But, as happened with many of the cattle driving breeds, the Rottweiler's usefulness came to an end when the transport of livestock became mechanized. Although cattle dealers still used the dogs for draught work, the "butcher's dog" was almost forgotten until late in Victorian times, when there was an upsurge of interest in locating and re-establishing the rare and unusual breeds. Thus the Rottweiler was rediscovered and the breed was to prove its usefulness in other ways, first as a police dog, and later with the outbreak of World War I as a war dog.

In Germany, which is considered the Rottweiler's country of origin, breeding is strictly controlled by the breed society. Only the best specimens may be bred from and litters are culled to permit the raising of no more than six puppies per litter.

G.STENHOUSE

Rottweiler

First specimens came to this continent in the early 1930s. In 1935 the Rottweiler was accepted for registration by the American Kennel Club, and in 1938 the first two Rottweilers were recorded in The Canadian Kennel Club Stud Book.

Official Breed Standard for the Rottweiler

Origin and Purpose: The Rottweiler was developed from the dogs used by the Roman legions to herd and guard the cattle brought by them to feed their legions. The butchers of Rottweil, Germany, developed the dogs to drive cattle to market and to protect their money bags which were tied around the dogs' necks. It was an arduous task to drive the cattle and a strong dog with staying power, full of self will and physical strength was needed. In the beginning of the 20th century these dogs were found particularly well suited as a police dog, a function they still fulfil especially in Europe.

General Appearance: The ideal Rottweiler is an above medium-sized, robust, and powerful dog, black with clearly defined rich tan markings. His compact build denotes great strength, agility, and endurance. Males are characteristically larger, heavier boned and more masculine in appearance.

Temperament: The Rottweiler should possess a fearless expression with a self-assured aloofness that does not lend itself to immediate and indiscriminate friendships. He has a strong willingness to work. In examining a Rottweiler, one should bear in mind that this dog reacts with alertness to his master and his surroundings, and in performing his function in life, the Rottweiler is not expected to submit to excessive handling by strangers. However, the judge shall dismiss from the ring any shy or vicious Rottweiler. A dog shall be judged fundamentally shy if, refusing to stand for examination it shrinks away from the judge; if it fears an unexpected approach from the rear; if it shies at sudden or unusual noises to a marked degree. A dog that attacks or attempts to attack, without provocation, either the judge, or its handler is definitely vicious. An aggressive or belligerent attitude towards other dogs shall not be deemed viciousness.

Size: Dogs 24–27 in. (60–68 cm). Bitches 22–25 in. (55–63 cm).

Proportion should always be considered rather than height alone. The length of the body, from the breastbone (sternum) to the rear edge of the pelvis (ischium) is slightly longer than the height of the dog at the withers, the most desirable proportion being as 10 to 9. Depth of chest should be fifty per cent of the height.

Coat and Colour: Outer coat is straight, coarse, dense, medium length, lying flat. Undercoat must be present on neck and thighs. The Rottweiler should be exhibited in a natural condition without trimming, except to remove whiskers, if desired. The colour is always black with rich tan to mahogany markings. The borderline between the black and the colour should be clearly defined. The markings should be located as follows: a spot over each eye; on cheeks; as a strip around each side of the muzzle, but not on the bridge of the nose; on throat; a proportionate triangular mark on either side of the breastbone not to exceed 25 per cent of the forechest; on forelegs from carpus downward to toes; on inside of rear legs showing down the front of the stifle and broadening out to front of rear legs from hock to toes but not eliminating the black from the back of the legs; under tail. Black pencilling markings on the toes. The undercoat is grey or black. Quantity and location of markings are important. Insufficient or excessive markings should be penalized.

Head: Of medium length, broad between the ears; forehead line seen in profile is moderately arched. The cheekbones and stop are well developed. The length of the *muzzle* should not exceed the distance between the stop and the occiput. The *skull* is preferred dry; however, some wrinkling may occur when the dog is alert. The bridge of the muzzle is straight. The muzzle is broad at the base with slight tapering towards the tip but not snipey. The *nose* is broad rather than round, with black nostrils. The lips are always black with the corners tightly closed. The flews should not be too pronounced. The inner mouth pigment is dark. A pink mouth is to be penalized. The teeth are 42 in number (20 upper and 22 lower). They are strong and should be correctly placed meeting in a scissors bite—lower incisors touching the inside of the upper incisors. *Eyes* should be of medium size, moderately deep set, almond shaped with well-fitting lids.

The iris should be of uniform colour, from medium to dark brown, the darker shade always preferred. **Ears** should be pendant, proportionately small, triangular in shape, set well apart and placed on skull so as to make it appear broader when the dog is alert. The ear should terminate at approximately mid-cheek level. When correctly held, the inner edge will lie tightly against the cheek.

Neck: Powerful, well muscled, moderately long with slight arch and without loose skin.

Forequarters: The shoulder blade should be long and well laid back at a 45-degree angle. The elbows are tight and under the body. The distance from the withers to the elbow and the elbow to the ground is equal. The legs are strongly developed with straight, heavy bone. They are not set close together. The pasterns are strong, springy and almost perpendicular to the ground. Feet are round, compact with well arched toes, turning neither in nor out. Pads are thick and hard. Nails are short, strong and black. Dewclaws may be removed.

Body: The topline is firm and level, extending in a straight line from the withers to the croup. The brisket should be deep, reaching to the elbow. The chest is roomy and broad with a well-developed forechest. The ribs are well sprung. The loins short, deep, and well muscled. The flank should not be tucked up. The croup is broad, of medium length and slightly sloping.

Hindquarters: The angulation of the hindquarters balances that of the forequarters. The slope of the pelvis from the horizontal is between 20–30 degrees. The bone of the upper thigh is fairly long and the thigh is broad and well muscled. The stifle joint is moderately angulated. The lower thigh is long, powerfully muscled leading to a strong hock joint. The metatarsus is perpendicular to the ground. Viewed from the rear, the hind legs are straight and perpendicular to the ground. The feet are somewhat longer than the front feet, with well arched toes turning neither in nor out. Dewclaws must be removed.

Tail: The tail is normally carried in an horizontal position giving the appearance of an elongated topline. It is carried above the horizontal when the dog is excited. The tail is normally docked short close to the body. The set of the tail is more important than length.

Gait: The Rottweiler is a trotter; the motion is harmonious, sure, powerful and unhindered, with a strong fore-reach and a powerful rear drive. Front and rear legs are not thrown either in or out, as the imprint of the hind feet should touch that of the forefeet. In a trot, the forequarters and hindquarters are mutually co-ordinated while the back remains firm. As speed increases the legs will converge under the body towards the centre line.

Faults: The foregoing is a description of the ideal Rottweiler. Any structural fault that detracts from the ideal must be penalized to the extent of the deviation. Included as faults are: pink mouth, wavy coat, insufficient markings, undercoat showing through outercoat. Faults considered serious are: lack of proportion, undersize, oversize, level bite, yellow eyes, eyes not of same colour, eyes unequal in size or shape, hairless eyelids, excessively short coat, curly or open coat, lack of undercoat, white markings any place on dog (a few white hairs do not constitute a marking), excessive markings, light-coloured markings, up to four missing pre-molars.

Disqualifications: *Undershot, overshot, more than four missing pre-molars and/or any other missing tooth, long coat, any base colour other than black, total absence of markings.*

Samoyed

*T*HIS MEMBER OF THE spitz family of dogs has been described as "the dog with Christmas in its face," while those who know the Sammy best claim the breed may be too pretty for its own good. Centuries of working on his own initiative have given the breed an independence of spirit that makes him more than a cuddly bundle of fur.

The breed is native to the northeast area of Siberia, which lies north of the Arctic Circle. The Samoyed was first discovered by fur traders who had gone to this frozen wilderness to buy sables. Named after the Samoyedes, a nomadic people, the dogs were used to guard and drive herds of reindeer from one feeding ground to another. They were also used as sled and draught animals. So important were the dogs to the Samoyedes' livelihood that they were regarded as members of the family and it was not unusual for them to share sleeping quarters with their masters.

Unknown outside of its country of origin until the latter part of the 19th century, the Samoyed was brought to Britain in 1889. Early specimens came from Siberia, Finland, and, oddly enough, from the zoo in Sydney, Australia where a survivor of Sir Robert Scott's second expedition to the South Pole was kept.

The original dogs brought to Britain are reported to have been a variety of colours, black showing occasionally. They were of smaller build and not so heavily coated as the modern Samoyed. The profuse, glistening white or biscuit-coloured coat so admired in today's show specimens is a comparatively recent development.

From a small number of imports British fanciers, one of whom was Queen Alexandra, developed the first breeding lines. Notable among the early breeders were Mr. and Mrs. Kilburn-Scott, whose Farninghan Kennels became known world-wide and to whose dogs many of today's Samoyeds can be traced. It was the Kilburn-Scotts who were largely responsible for drawing up the breed standard which, with slight modifications, remains the accepted blueprint for the breed.

Samoyed

While it is reported that an entry of Samoyeds was shown at a dog show held on the west coast in 1913, first official Canadian registrations did not take place until 1925.

Official Breed Standard for the Samoyed

General Appearance: The Samoyed, being essentially a working dog, should present a picture of beauty, alertness and strength, with agility, dignity, and grace. As his work lies in the cold climate, his coat should be heavy and weather resistant, and of good quality rather than quantity. The male carries more of a "ruff" than the female. He should not be long in the back as a weak back would make him practically useless for his legitimate work, but at the same time a close-coupled body would also place him at a great disadvantage as a draught dog. Breeders should aim for the happy medium, a body not long but muscular, allowing liberty, with a deep chest and well-sprung ribs, strong arched neck, straight front and especially strong loins. Males should be masculine in appearance and deportment without unwarranted aggressiveness; bitches feminine without weakness of structure or apparent softness of temperament. Bitches may be slightly longer in back than males. They should both give the appearance of being capable of great endurance but be free from coarseness. Because of the depth of chest required, the legs should be moderately long. A very short-legged dog is to be depreciated. Hindquarters should be particularly well developed, stifles well bent and any suggestion of unsound stifles or cowhocks severely penalized. General appearance should include movement and general conformation indicating balance and good substance.

Temperament: Alert and intelligent and should show animation. Friendly, but conservative.

Size: Dogs, 20—22 in. (51—56 cm) at the shoulder; bitches, 18—20 in. (45—51 cm); weight in proportion to size.

Coat and Colour: The body should be well covered with a thick, close, soft and short undercoat, with harsh hair growing through it, forming the outer coat, which should stand straight away from the body and be quite free from curl. The legs should have good feathering. Colour pure white, cream, biscuit, or white and biscuit.

Head: Powerful and wedge-shaped with a broad, flat *skull*, *muzzle* of medium length, a tapering foreface, not too sharply defined. The stop should not be too abrupt—nevertheless well defined. *Nose* and eye rims black for preference, but may be brown. Lips black, flews should not drop predominantly at corners of the mouth. Strong jaws with level teeth. *Eyes* dark, set well apart and deep with alert intelligent expression. *Ears* should not be too long but rounded at the tips, set well apart and well covered inside with hair. Hair short and smooth before the ears.

Forequarters: Forelegs straight and muscular. Good bone.

Body: Back medium in length, broad and very muscular. Bitches may be slightly longer in back than males. Chest broad and deep. Ribs well sprung, giving plenty of heart and lung room.

Hindquarters: Very muscular, stifles well let down. Feet long, flattish and slightly spread out. Soles well padded with hair.

Tail: Long and profuse, carried over the back when alert, sometimes dropped when at rest. A judge should see the tail over the back once when judging.

Gait: A Samoyed should gait with a good, well-balanced movement. He should move with an easy, agile stride that is well timed. The gait should be free with a good reach in the fore-quarters and a sound, driving power in the hindquarters.

Faults: Unprovoked aggressiveness. Over and under allowed height. In or out at the elbow. Cowhocks or straight stifles. Double hook in the tail. Choppy or stilted gait.

Disqualifications: *Blue eyes. Dewclaws on the hind legs. Any colour other than pure white, cream, biscuit, or white and biscuit.*

Scale of Points:

Gait	15
General appearance	10
Coat	10
Head	10
Back	10
Chest and ribs	10
Hindquarters	10
Forelegs	10
Feet	10
Tail	5
TOTAL	100

Schnauzer (Giant)

THE LARGEST OF THE three breeds of schnauzer, the giant is said to have originated in southern Bavaria in the area around Munich. Over the years it has been known by a variety of names among which are the Russian Bear Schnauzer, Münchener Dog, and the Riesenschnauzer.

From the 15th century until the time when livestock was transported by rail, these big dogs were used to drive the cattle. But, as happened with many of the droving dogs, once the need for their services had passed, so did the interest in breeding them. Many such breeds disappeared from the scene. Fortunately for the Giant Schnauzer, his efficiency as a guard dog was well known and there were enough interested fanciers to keep the strain alive.

While his ancestry is obscure, it is theorized that the present-day Giant Schnauzer was developed from crosses with smooth-coated drovers, rough-coated shepherd dogs, black Great Danes, and Bouviers des Flandres. Also, it is further suggested that because the resultant dog resembled a larger edition of the already well-known Standard Schnauzer, breeders decided to create a third size of schnauzer. To reinforce type, the Münchener Dog was therefore given a small infusion of Standard Schnauzer blood.

The product of this cross was first called the Münich Schnauzer; then, as type came closer to that of its smaller cousin, the name Giant Schnauzer was adopted. This breed was introduced to dog shows at Munich in 1909 and attracted so much attention that within a month a specialty club was formed to promote its interests.

During two world wars the Giant Schnauzer gave valiant service as a police and war dog and suffered so many casualties it was once thought the breed might be in danger of dying out. Thanks to the dedication of German breeders, it is again well established in Europe where it is one of the principal breeds used for security work.

Schnauzer (Giant)

G.STENHOUSE

Introduced to Canada early in the 1930s, the breed has excelled in obedience work and as a handsome show exhibit. The Canadian Kennel Club Stud Book records the first Giant Schnauzer registrations in the years 1932–1933.

Official Breed Standard for the Schnauzer (Giant)

Origin and Purpose: The Giant Schnauzer is generally considered to have originated in the mountains of Bavaria in the 1810s. Rather than being bred for a specific purpose he was bred, and is noted for, his versatility. He has been used over the years as a drover's dog, a brewery guard, a cart dog, a herding dog, and a superlative police dog.

General Appearance: The Giant Schnauzer is robust, more heavy-set than slender dog, square in build. He should resemble a larger and more powerful version of the Standard Schnauzer. The sound, reliable temperament, rugged build, and dense, weather-resistant wiry coat make for one of the most useful, powerful, and enduring working breeds.

Temperament: Combines spirit and alertness with intelligence and extreme reliability; amiable in repose and a commanding figure when aroused. Shy or vicious dogs shall be dismissed from the ring.

Size: Height at the withers for males is $25\,^1/_2$–$27\,^1/_2$ in. (65–70 cm); for females $23\,^1/_2$–$25\,^1/_2$ in. (60–65 cm), mediums preferred. Size alone should never take precedence over type, balance, soundness, and proper temperament. It should be noted that too small dogs generally lack the power and too large dogs the agility and manoeuvrability desired in a working dog.

Coat and Colour: Coat close, strong, hard and wiry, shorter on ears, skull, throat, and under tail. Slightly longer on legs and under chest, with beard and eyebrows adding to the rectangular appearance of the head. The eyes are not obscured by too-long eyebrows. The undercoat is soft and dense. Colour may be black, or salt and pepper. Black: deep, solid black. A small white patch on the chest is allowed. Salt and pepper: outer coat to a combination of banded hairs (white and black) and some solid black and solid white hairs, appearing as a medium to dark grey, peppering evenly distributed with no trace of patterning, and a grey undercoat. Dark facial mask to emphasize the expression. Eyebrows, inside ears, whiskers, cheeks, throat, chest, legs, and under tail are lighter in colour but include peppering.

Head: Strong and elongated, gradually narrowing from the ears to the tip of the powerful, ferretting snout, rectangular in appearance and in proportion to the sex and substance of the dog. The length of the head is one-half the length of the back from withers to the base of the tail. The masseters (cheek muscles) are strongly developed, though no strongly-marked cheek form is to disturb the rectangular appearance of the head and beard. The *skull* is flat and unwrinkled, in width not more than two-thirds the length. Occiput not prominent. *Muzzle* is well filled under the eyes, both parallel and equal in length to the skull, ending in a moderately blunt wedge. The *lips* are tight, not overlapping, black, and the *nose* is large, black and full. The tongue may be either pink, or pink with black or grey spots. Bite: a full complement of sound, white teeth (6/6 incisors, 2/2 canines, 8/8 premolars, 4/6 molars) with scissors bite. The upper and lower jaws are powerful and well formed. *Eyes:* medium sized, dark, oval, turned forward with tight lids. *Ears:* small and V-shaped button ears, of moderate thickness set high on the head, and dropping forward closely to the cheek, or cropped, evenly cut, not overly long, with as little bell as possible, placed high and carried erect in excitement with the inner edges parallel.

Neck: Strong and well arched, of moderate length, blending cleanly into the shoulders, with skin close-fitting at the throat, in harmony with the dog.

Forequarters: Shoulders slanting, well angled, and flat, but strongly muscled, well set on, giving no appearance of a terrier front. The upper end of the scapulae (shoulder blades) are, from the side, in a vertical line above the elbows. The angle between the scapula and humerus (upper arm) is 90 degrees. Elbows are set close to the body. Forelegs from the elbow down, seen from all sides, are vertical without any curve, with strong pasterns and good bone. Feet are short, round, extremely compact, with close, arched toes (cat's paws), dark nails, and thick, tough pads.

Body: Compact, substantial, short-coupled, and strong, with great power and agility. Topline is short, strong and straight, sloping moderately to the rear, extending into a slightly rounded croup. Chest is moderately broad with visible, strong sternum (breastbone), reaching at least down to the elbow, and slowly tapering up and back to a moderate tuck-up. The loin (distance from the last rib to the pelvis) is short, giving the impression of a compact body. The length of the dog from sternum to point of rump is equal to the height at the withers.

Hindquarters: Strongly muscled, in balance with the fore-quarters; femurs (upper thighs) are strong and slanting, the stifles well bent, with tibiae (second thighs) approximately parallel to the extension of the upper neckline. The hocks are short, perpendicular to the ground while the dog is standing, and, from the rear, parallel to each other. The hind feet are slightly smaller than the forefeet. The hindquarters do not appear over-built or higher than the withers.

Tail: Set moderately high, carried high in excitement, from 2−4 in. long (5−10 cm), docked to the second or third joint.

Gait: The trot is free, balanced, and vigorous, with good reach in the forequarters and good driving power in the hindquarters. When moving at a fast trot a properly built dog will single track. Back remains strong, firm, and flat. Movement from the front and rear should be clean and true, the legs being thrown neither in nor out.

Faults: Soundness (both temperament and conformation) and type are of prime importance. The foregoing description is that of the ideal Giant Schnauzer. Any deviation from the standard must be penalized to the extent of the deviation. The Giant Schnauzer should always be considered and judged as a working dog.

Disqualifications: *Overshot, undershot. The judge shall dismiss from the ring any shy or vicious Giant Schnauzer.*

Shyness: A dog shall be judged fundamentally shy if, refusing to stand for examination, it repeatedly shrinks away from the judge; if it fears unduly any approach from the rear; if it shies to a marked degree at sudden and unusual noises.

Viciousness: A dog that attacks or attempts to attack either the judge or its handler is definitely vicious. An aggressive or belligerent attitude toward other dogs, while not desirable, shall not be deemed viciousness.

Schnauzer (Standard)

OLDEST MEMBER OF THE schnauzer family, the Standard Schnauzer is the medium-sized member from which the other two breeds, the giant and the miniature, were developed. Originating in Germany, there are several theories as to which breeds form the schnauzer's ancestry. Some dog historians claim that the breed represents a cross between a rough-coated ratting dog and the now-extinct Middle Ages Beaver Dog, others that it descends from shepherd dogs only. Still others claim its ancestors were the German Black Poodle and the Gray Wolf Spitz, or crosses of the extinct Schafer Pudel and the Wirehaired German Pinscher.

Whichever, there is no doubt that the breed has been known for several centuries and was renowned as a herder and outstanding ratter. It was also a favourite of the German artists, the best known being Albrecht Dürer who owned a schnauzer and included his dog in several of his paintings dated circa 1492.

The breed was first exhibited in 1879 in Hanover at the third German International Show under the breed name "Wire-Haired Pinscher." The winning dog was named "Schnauzer" and it is a moot point whether the breed was renamed in honour of the winning dog or whether it relates to the whiskered snout for which the German word is "schnauzer." The following year German breeders draughted a breed standard and in 1895 the first specialty club was organized.

Known as "the dog with the human brain," the schnauzer excels in obedience and police work. He has proved himself as both herder and guard dog and was used extensively during wartime as a dispatch carrier and Red Cross dog.

After the close of World War I the breed was introduced to the United States where it was first classified in the Terrier Group. In 1925, The Schnauzer Club of America was formed, a name that was changed to The Standard Schnauzer Club of America in 1933 at the time when The American Miniature Schnauzer Club was formed. In 1945 the breed was transferred to the Working Group where it has remained.

Schnauzer (Standard)

First registrations of the Standard Schnauzer in Canada were recorded in The Canadian Kennel Club Stud Book in the years 1926–1927.

Official Breed Standard for the Schnauzer (Standard)

General Appearance: The Standard Schnauzer is a robust, sinewy, heavy-set dog of the terrier type, sturdily built, square in the proportion of body length to height, with good muscle and plenty of bone. His nature combines high-spirited temperament with extreme reliability. His rugged build and dense, harsh coat are accentuated by arched eyebrows, bristly moustache and luxurious whiskers.

Size: At withers, from 18–20 in. (45–51 cm) for males, and from 17–19 in. (43–48 cm) for females.

Coat and Colour: Coat hard and wiry, standing up on the back and, when seen against the course of the hair, neither short nor lying flat. The outer coat should be harsh, the undercoat soft. It should be trimmed only to accent the body outline and should not be more than an inch long except on the ears and skull. Colour pepper and salt or similar equal mixtures, light or dark including pure black.
    Faults: Soft, smooth, curly; too long or short; too closely trimmed, dyed or excessively powdered. Solid colours other than black, also very light or whitish, spotted or tiger colours. A small white spot on the breast is not a fault.

Head: Strong and rectangular, diminishing slightly from the ear to the eyes, and again to the tip of the nose. Total length about one-third the length of the back, measuring from the withers to the beginning of the tail. *Skull:* moderately broad between the ears, width not exceeding two-thirds of the length. Forehead flat and unwrinkled. Cheeks well muscled, but not too strongly developed. *Muzzle:* strong and in proportion to the skull, ending in moderately blunt manner, with wiry whiskers accenting the rectangular shape of the head. *Nose:* powerful, black and full, with ridge running almost parallel to the extension of the forehead. *Mouth:* lips tight and not overlapping. Jaw level, powerful and square. Teeth sound, strong, and white, with canines meeting in scissors bite. *Eyes:* medium size, dark brown, oval and turned forward. Vision should not be obstructed from the front or profile by too long an eyebrow. The brow should be arched and wiry. *Ears* evenly shaped, set high and carried erect when cropped. If uncropped, they should be small and V-shaped, of moderate thickness and carried rather high and close to the head.

Faults: Skull too narrow or pronounced. Protruding cheekbones. Muzzle too long or too short, pointed or lacking whiskers; dish-faced or down-faced. Overshot or undershot. Teeth pointed or irregular. Eyes too large, round or protruding; light or yellow-ringed eyes. Low set, houndy ears and badly cut ears.

Neck: Nape should be strong, slightly arched and set cleanly on the shoulders. Skin should be tight, fitting closely to the throat.

Faults: Too short, thick, long and throaty.

Forequarters: Shoulders somewhat sloping, strongly muscled. Forelegs straight and vertical when seen from all sides, with bone carried well down to the feet; elbows set close to body and pointing directly backward.

Faults: Loose, straight or low shoulders, or steep-set front. Legs too high, low, thin, or weak; elbows turned out or in. Pasterns sunken or any weakness of joint, bone, or muscular development.

Body: Compact, strong, short-coupled and substantial so as to permit great flexibility. Back strong, stiff, straight, and short, with a well-developed short loin section, the ribs well sprung. Length of the back from the withers to the set-on of tail should approximate the height at withers. Chest moderately broad, with the breastbone plainly discernible and reaching at least to the height of the elbows, extending slowly backwards. Belly well drawn up towards the back, but no tuck-up.

Faults: Back too long, sunken, or roached. Too broad or too narrow, shallow or false chest.

Hindquarters: Strongly muscled, with thighs slanting and flat, never appearing over-built or higher than the shoulders. Feet small and compact; round with thick pads, strong nails. Toes well arched and pointing straight ahead.

Faults: Hocks let down, cowhocks, or any weakness of joint. Toed-in or toed-out and long or spreading feet.

Tail: Set moderately high and carried erect. Cut down to two joints and should not be longer than 2 in. (5 cm).

Faults: Too steep, level, or too long a croup.

Gait: Should be sound, strong, quick, free, true and level.

Faults: Soft, smooth, curly coat; too long or short coat; too closely trimmed, dyed or excessively powdered. Solid colours other than black, also very light or whitish, spotted or tiger colours. Skull too narrow or pronounced. Protruding cheekbones. Muzzle too long or too short, pointed or lacking whiskers; dish-faced or down-faced. Overshot or undershot. Teeth pointed or irregular. Eyes too large, round or protruding; light or yellow-ringed eyes. Low set, houndy ears and badly cut ears. Neck too short, thick, long and throaty. Loose, straight or low shoulders, or steep-set front, legs too high, low, thin, or weak; elbows turned out or in. Pasterns sunken or any weakness of joint, bone or muscular development. Back too long, sunken, or roached. Too broad or too narrow, shallow or false chest. Hocks let down, cow-hocks, or any weakness of joint. Toed-in or toed-out and long or spreading feet. Too steep, level, or too long a croup.

Disqualifications: *Shy, savage, or highly nervous dogs and dogs which are in excess of or less than the standard in height.*

Shetland Sheepdog

THE SHETLAND SHEEPDOG originated in the Shetland Islands, a group of rugged, sparsely vegetated islands which lie off the northeast coast of Scotland, noted for miniature livestock—sheep, cattle, ponies, and sheepdogs.

The islands were once occupied by Norwegians and it is thought that the Shelty descends from dogs of the Spitz family similar to the Norwegian Buhund, or possibly from the "Yakki," a breed of dog brought to the islands by whaling fleets from Iceland. The Shelty was once known as the "toonie," a name derived from the Norwegian word *tun* which means farm. Thus the farm dog was the "toonie." The farm dog's job was to tend small flocks of sheep and to keep them from wandering into the home garden. It was beloved as a family pet and is said often to have filled the role of babysitter.

Before the turn of this century it is said that the dogs were a nondescript lot. Some were taken to the mainland by fishermen, where they attracted the interest of dog enthusiasts who crossbred them to various toy breeds and later to small collies. The blue merle colour of the Shelty is said to be a direct result of the collie cross.

This cross is said to have done much to smarten up the breed's appearance, and in 1906 Shelties were exhibited at Crufts' dog show in London under the name Shetland Collies. Some time later a specialty club was founded under the same name but there was so much objection to it from the Collie breeders it was revised to Shetland Sheepdog.

Members of the Royal Navy who visited the Shetlands during World War I did much to popularize the breed in Britain. The sailors were attracted by the fluffy little Shelty and breeders are said to have done a brisk business selling puppies to the crew men who took them home to England as pets.

The breed was granted official recognition by The Kennel Club (England) in 1909 but was not registered in Canada until 1930. The British breed standard calls for a considerably smaller Shelty than do the Canadian or American breed standards.

Shetland Sheepdog

Official Breed Standard for the Shetland Sheepdog

Origin and Purpose: The Shetland Sheepdog, like the Collie, traces to the Border Collie of Scotland which, transported to the Shetland Islands and crossed with small, intelligent, longhaired breeds, was reduced to miniature proportions. Subsequently crosses were made from time to time with Collies. This breed now bears the same relationship in size and general appearance to the Rough Collie as the Shetland Pony does to some of the larger breeds of horses. Although the resemblance between the Shetland Sheepdog and the Rough Collie is marked, there are differences which may be noted.

General Appearance: The Shetland Sheepdog is a small, alert, rough-coated, long-haired working dog. He must be sound, agile and sturdy. The outline should be so symmetrical that no part appears out of proportion to the whole. Dogs should appear masculine, bitches feminine.

Temperament: The Shetland Sheepdog is intensely loyal, affectionate, and responsive to his owner. However, he may be reserved towards strangers but not to the point of showing fear or cringing in the ring.
   Faults: Shyness, timidity, or nervousness. Stubbornness, snappiness, or ill temper.

Size: The Shetland Sheepdog should stand between 13 and 16 in. (33−41 cm) at the shoulder. NOTE: Height is determined by a line perpendicular to the ground from the top of the shoulder blades, the dog standing naturally, with forelegs parallel to line of measurement.

Coat and Colour: The coat should be double, the outer coat consisting of long, straight, harsh hair; the undercoat short, furry, and so dense as to give the entire coat its "stand-off" quality. The hair on face, tips of ears and feet should be smooth. Mane and frill should be abundant, and particularly impressive in males. The forelegs well feathered, the hind legs heavily so, but smooth below the hock joint. Hair on tail profuse. NOTE: Excess hair on ears, feet, and on hocks may be trimmed for the show ring. Colour black, blue merle, and sable (ranging from golden through mahogany); marked with varying amounts of white and/or tan.

Faults: Coat short or flat, in whole or in part; wavy, curly, soft or silky. Lack of undercoat. Smooth-coated specimens. Rustiness in a black or a blue coat. Washed out or degenerate colours, such as pale sable and faded blue. Self-colour in the case of blue merle, that is, without any merling or mottling and generally appearing as a faded or dilute tricolour. Conspicuous white body spots. Specimens with more than 50 per cent white shall be so severely penalized as to effectively eliminate them from competition.

Head: The head should be refined and its shape, when viewed from top or side, be a long, blunt wedge tapering slightly from ears to nose, which must be black. Top of *skull* should be flat, showing no prominence at nuchal crest (the top of the occiput). Cheeks should be flat and should merge smoothly into a well-rounded muzzle. Skull and *muzzle* should be of equal length, balance point being the inner corner of eye. In profile, the topline of skull should parallel the topline of muzzle, but on a higher plane due to the presence of a slight but definite stop. *Jaws* clean and powerful. The deep, well-developed underjaw, rounded at chin, should extend to base of nostril. Lips tight. Upper and lower lips must meet and fit smoothly together all the way around. Teeth level and evenly spaced. Scissors bite. *Eyes* medium size with dark, almond-shaped rims, set somewhat obliquely in skull. Colour must be dark, with blue or merle eyes permissible in blue merles only. *Ears* small and flexible, placed high, carried three-fourths erect, with tips breaking forward. When in repose the ears fold lengthwise and are thrown back into the frill. Contours and chiselling of the head, the shape, set and use of ears, the placement, shape and colour of the eyes, combine to produce expression. Normally the expression should be alert, gentle, intelligent and questioning. Towards strangers the eyes should show watchfulness and reserve, but no fear.

Faults: Two-angled head. Too prominent stop, or no stop. Over-fill below, between or above eyes. Prominent nuchal crest. Domed skull. Prominent cheekbones. Snipey muzzle. Short, receding, or shallow underjaw, lacking breadth and depth. Overshot or under-shot, missing or crooked teeth. Teeth visible when mouth is closed. Light, round, large or too small eyes. Prominent haws.

Ears set too low. Hound, prick, bat, twisted ears. Leather too thick or too thin.

Neck: Neck should be muscular, arched, and of sufficient length to carry the head proudly.
Faults: Too short and thick.

Forequarters: From the withers the shoulder blades should slope at a 45-degree angle forward and downward to the shoulder joint. At the withers they are separated only by the vertebra, but they must slope outward sufficiently to accommodate the desired spring of rib. The upper arm should join the shoulder blade as nearly as possible at a right angle. Elbow joint should be equidistant from the ground or from the withers. Forelegs straight viewed from all angles, muscular and clean, and of strong bone. Pasterns very strong, sinewy and flexible. Dewclaws may be removed.
Faults: Insufficient angulation between shoulder and upper arm. Upper arm too short. Lack of outward slope of shoulders. Loose shoulders. Turning in or out of elbows. Crooked legs. Light bone.

Body: In over-all appearance the body should appear moderately long as measured from shoulder joint to ischium (rearmost extremity of the pelvic bone), but much of this length is actually due to the proper angulation and breadth of the shoulder and hindquarter, as the back itself should be comparatively short. Back should be level and strongly muscled. Chest should be deep, the brisket reaching to point of elbow. The ribs should be well sprung, but flattened at their lower half to allow free play of the foreleg and shoulder. There should be a slight arch at the loins, and the croup should slope gradually to the rear. The hip bone (pelvis) should be set at a 30-degree angle to the spine. Abdomen moderately tucked up.
Faults: Back too long, too short, swayed or roached. Barrel ribs. Slab-sides. Chest narrow and/or too shallow. Croup higher than withers. Croup too straight or too steep.

Hindquarters: The thigh should be broad and muscular. The thighbone should be set into the pelvis at a right angle corresponding to the angle of the shoulder blade and upper arm. Stifle bones join the thighbone and should be distinctly angled at the stifle joint. The over-all length of the stifle should at least equal the length of the thighbone, and preferably should slightly exceed it. Hock joint should be clean-cut, angular, sinewy, with good bone and strong ligamentation. The hock (metatarsus) should be short and straight viewed from all angles. Dewclaws should be removed. Feet should be oval and compact with the toes well arched and fitting tightly together. Pads deep and tough, nails hard and strong.

Faults: Narrow thighs. Cowhocks. Hocks turning out. Poorly defined hock joint. Feet turning in or out. Splay feet. Hare feet. Cat feet.

Tail: The tail should be sufficiently long so that when it is laid along the back edge of the hind legs the last vertebra will reach the hock joint. Carriage of tail at rest is straight down or in a slight upward curve. When the dog is alert the tail is normally lifted, but it should not be curved forward over the back.

Faults: Too short, twisted at end.

Gait: The trotting gait of the Shetland Sheepdog should denote effortless speed and smoothness. There should be no jerkiness, nor stiff, stilted, up-and-down movement. The drive should be from the rear, true and straight, dependent upon correct angulation, musculation, and ligamentation of the entire hindquarter, thus allowing the dog to reach well under his body with his hind foot and propel himself forward. Reach of stride of the foreleg is dependent upon correct angulation, musculation and ligamentation of the forequarters, together with correct width of chest and construction of rib cage. The foot should be lifted only enough to clear the ground as the leg swings forward. Viewed from the front, both forelegs and hind legs should move forward almost perpendicular to ground at the walk, slanting a little inward at a slow trot, until at a swift trot the feet are brought so far inward towards centre line of body that the tracks left show two parallel lines of footprints actually touching a centre line at their inner edges. *There should be no crossing of the feet or throwing of the weight from side to side.*

Faults: Stiff, short steps, with a choppy, jerky movement. Mincing steps, with a hopping up and down, or a balancing of weight from side to side (often erroneously admired as a "dancing gait" but permissible in young puppies). Lifting of front feet in hackneylike action, resulting in loss of speed and energy. Pacing gait.

Faults: Shyness, timidity, or nervousness. Stubbornness, snappiness, or ill temper. Coat short or flat, in whole or in part; wavy, curly, soft or silky. Lack of undercoat. Smooth-coated specimens. Rustiness in a black or a blue coat. Washed out or degenerate colours, such as pale sable and faded blue. Self-colour in the case of blue merle, that is, without any merling or mottling and generally appearing as a faded or dilute tricolour. Conspicuous white body spots. Specimens with more than 50 per cent white shall be so severely penalized as to effectively eliminate them from competition. Two-angled head. Too prominent stop, or no stop. Overfill below, between or above eyes. Prominent nuchal crest. Domed skull. Prominent cheekbones. Snipey muzzle. Short, receding, or shallow underjaw, lacking breadth and depth. Overshot or undershot, missing or crooked teeth. Teeth visible when mouth is closed. Light, round, large or too small eyes. Prominent haws. Ears set too low. Hound, prick, bat, twisted ears. Leather too thick or too thin. Too short and thick a neck. Insufficient angulation between shoulder and upper arm. Upper arm too short. Lack of outward slope of shoulders. Loose shoulders. Turning in or out of elbows. Crooked legs. Light bone. Back too long, too short, swayed or roached. Barrel ribs. Slab-sides. Chest narrow and/or too shallow. Croup higher than withers. Croup too straight or too steep. Narrow thighs. Cowhocks. Hocks turning out. Poorly defined hock joint. Feet turning in or out. Splay feet. Hare feet. Cat feet. Tail too short, twisted at end. Stiff, short steps, with a choppy, jerky movement. Mincing steps, with a hopping up and down, or a balancing of weight from side to side (often erroneously admired as a "dancing gait" but permissible in young puppies). Lifting of front feet in hackneylike action, resulting in loss of speed and energy. Pacing gait.

Disqualifications: *Cryptorchidism in adults over 12 months of age. Heights below or above the desired range, i.e., 13—16 in. (33—41 cm). Brindle colour.*

Scale of Points:

GENERAL APPEARANCE

Symmetry	10	
Temperament	10	
Coat	5	25

HEAD

Skull and stop	5	
Muzzle	5	
Eyes, ears, and expression	10	20

BODY

Neck and back	5	
Chest, ribs and brisket	10	
Loin, croup, and tail	5	20

FOREQUARTERS

Shoulder	10	
Forelegs and feet	5	15

HINDQUARTERS

Hip, thigh, and stifle	10	
Hocks and feet	5	15

GAIT

Smoothness and lack of waste motion when trotting	5	5
TOTAL		100

Siberian Husky

*A*LTHOUGH THE SOVIETS DISPUTE the claim, there is evidence to show that the Siberian Husky descends from the Chukchi Sled Dog which had been breeding true in the Soviet Arctic for 3000 years prior to its introduction to this continent. These were the dogs of a nomadic Siberian tribe used to pull sleds and herd reindeer. Not highly regarded in their native country because of their small size, it was nevertheless conceded that the Chukchi was the breed that could travel the greatest distance. Like all sled dog breeds, they were able to work hard for long periods on little food.

In a primitive way the women of the tribe practised a form of selective breeding—the "best bred to the best"—and being isolated from crossbreeding by nature of the environment, in time a strain of intelligent, fast, sled dogs evolved.

A fur trader and explorer, Olaf Swenson, is credited with bringing the breed to the continental United States. Over a twenty-five-year period, Swenson had dealt with the Chukchi buying or trading for good dogs when he could. His eye for quality was infallible, and several of the dogs he managed to obtain were subsequently sent to the eastern United States to become the foundation stock of some of the first Siberian Husky kennels.

While Swenson's prime interest in the sled dog was its value as a reliable means of transportation, there were others who valued the Chukchi for its speed. At the turn of the century sled dog racing was becoming a popular sport and in 1909 the first team of Siberian Huskies was entered in the All-Alaska Sweepstake by William Goosak, but it was a Norwegian, Leonhard Seppala, who has been called the "World's greatest dog driver," who brought the Chukchi into public prominence. Seppala and his team won the All-Alaska Sweeps three years running and he was the hero of the historic "serum drive" that averted a diphtheria epidemic in Nome in the winter of 1925. A statue in memory of one of Seppala's dogs now stands in Central Park, New York, commemorating this historic run.

Siberian Husky

Seppala's dogs came with him when he later moved to the United States where they contributed much to the breeding programmes of early Siberian Husky kennels, and also the foundation stock of the first breeding kennel in Canada, which was located at St. Jovite, Quebec.

Since becoming an officially recognized breed in 1939, the Siberian Husky's popularity has grown enormously. As well as being the favourite of sled dog racing enthusiasts, the breed accounts for large entries at most championship dog shows.

Official Breed Standard for the Siberian Husky

General Appearance: The Siberian Husky is an alert, gracefully built, medium-sized dog, quick and light on his feet, and free and graceful in action. He has a strong, moderately compact body; a deep, strong chest; well-muscled shoulders and hindquarters; and straight, strong legs with medium bone. His coat is dense and very soft, and his brush tail is carried curved over his back when at attention, and trailing when in repose. His head presents a finely chiselled and often fox-like appearance, and his eyes have a keen and friendly expression. Bitches are smaller than dogs, averaging up to 2 in. (5 cm) shorter and 10 lb. (5 kg) less in weight. Siberians range in build from moderately compact (but never cobby) to moderately rangy; in all builds the bone must be medium, the back powerful (never slack, from excessive length), and the shoulder height never exceeding 23 1/2 in. (60 cm). (Any ranginess is merely a matter of proportion, not of actual height.) The most important and characteristic points in a Siberian Husky are *medium* size and bone, *soft* coat, *high-set* ears, freedom and ease of action, and good disposition.

Size: Dogs from 21—23 1/2 in. (53—60 cm) at the shoulder; bitches, from 20—22 in. (51—56 cm). Dogs, from 45—60 lb. (20—27 kg); bitches, from 34—50 lb. (15—23 kg).

Coat and Colour: The Siberian Husky has a thick, soft, double coat consisting of a soft, dense, downy undercoat of fur next to the skin; and an outer coat of soft, smooth texture, giving a smooth, full-furred appearance and a clean-cut outline (in contrast to the harsh, coarse coat of the Alaskan Malamute or the bear-like Eskimo coat). The coat is usually medium in length; a longer coat is allowed, but the texture must remain the same in any length. All colours and white are allowed, and all markings. The commonest colours are various shades of wolf and silver greys, tan (a light sable), and black with white points. A large variety of markings, especially head markings, is found in the Siberian, including many striking and unusual ones not found in any other breed. Frequently found are the caplike mask and spectacle markings.

Head: *Skull* of medium size in proportion to the body; width between ears medium to narrow, gradually tapering to eyes, and moderately rounded. *Muzzle* of medium length. Both skull and muzzle are finely chiselled. *Nose* black for preference, brown allowed in occasional specimens of reddish colouring; flesh-coloured nose and eye rims allowed in white dogs. Some dogs, especially black-and-white ones, have what is often termed a "snow nose," or "smudge nose," *i.e.*, a nose normally solid black, but acquiring a pink streak in winter. This is permissible, but not preferable. Lips dark and close-fitting; jaws and teeth strong, meeting with a scissors bite. *Eyes* either brown or blue ("watch" or "China") in colour, one blue and one brown eye permissible but not preferable; set only very slightly obliquely in skull. *Eyes* have a keen, friendly and fox-like expression; this expression is distinctly "interested," sometimes even mischievous. *Ears* of medium size, erect, close-fitting, set high on head, and well covered with hair on the inside. There is an arch at the back of the ears. Ears are slightly taller than width at base, and moderately rounded at tips. When dog is at attention, ears are usually carried practically parallel on top of head, with inner edges quite close together at base.

Forequarters: Shoulder well developed and powerful. Legs straight and well muscled, with good bone (but *never* heavy boned like the Eskimo or Alaskan Malamute).

Body: Back of medium length, not too long, nor cobby like the Elkhound's, and strongly developed. Chest should be deep and strong, but not too broad. Ribs should be well arched and deep. Loins well muscled and slightly arched, and should carry no excess weight of fat.

Hindquarters: Powerful, and showing good angulation. Stifles well bent. Dewclaws occasionally appear on the hind legs: they are not a sign of impure breeding, but as they interfere with the dog's work, they should be removed, preferably at birth. Feet oblong in shape, and not so broad as the Eskimo's or Malamute's; well furred between pads which are tough and thickly cushioned; compact; neither too large (like the Malamute's) nor too small (like many Samoyeds'). The Siberian's foot, like that of other true Arctic dogs, is a "snowshoe foot," *i.e.*, it is somewhat webbed between the toes, like a retriever's foot. Good feet are very important, and therefore feet should always be examined in the ring.

Tail: A well-furred brush carried over back in a sickle curve when running or at attention, and trailing out behind when working or in repose. Tail should not "snap" flat to back. Hair on tail is usually of medium length, varying somewhat with the length of the dog's coat.

Gait: His characteristic gait is free, tireless, and almost effortless when free or on loose leash; but showing great strength when pulling; the trot is brisk and smooth, and quite fast.

Faults: Any clumsy, heavy, or unwieldy appearance or gait should be penalized. Any harshness of coat (except while actually shedding); rough or shaggy appearance (like Samoyed, Malamute, or Eskimo); absence of undercoat (except when shedding). Head clumsy or heavy; muzzle bulky (like the Malamute's); skull too wide between ears; snipiness, coarseness. Eyes set too obliquely (like a Malamute's). Low set ears; ears too large; "flat" ears; lop ears. Weak shoulders; heavy bone; too light bone. Weak or slack back; chest too broad, like Malamute's; weak or flat chest. Any weakness of hindquarters; lack of proper angulation in hind legs. Soft or splayed feet; feet too large or clumsy; feet too small or delicate. In addition to the faults stated herein, obvious structural faults common to all breeds (such as cowhocks) are just as undesirable in a Siberian Husky as in any other breed, although not specifically mentioned in this standard.

Disqualifications: *Weight over 60 lb. (27 kg) in a male or over 50 lb. (23 kg) in a female. (Anything over these weights indicates cross* *breeding.) Height and weight are **very** important, and the upper limit in each must be rigidly maintained.*

Scale of Points:

General appearance and conduct   20
Head and ears   20
Body and shoulders   20
Legs and feet   15
Coat   15
Tail   10

        TOTAL   100

St. Bernard

*T*HE BREED WHICH BECAME renowned for saving the lives of travellers lost in the snow, the St. Bernard, takes its name from the Hospice du Grand St. Bernard where the monks bred the dogs as guards and to guide them along treacherous Alpine paths. Established in the 10th century high in the Jural Mountains, the Hospice became a refuge for travellers. Records show that dogs were first bred at the Hospice in the 17th century and it is thought that the "Alpine" or "Hospice" dogs, as they were first known, combined the bloods of the Great Dane, the local Senna hounds, the Bloodhound and the Mastiff, the latter being descended from the ancient Roman Molossian dogs. The result was a strong, short-coated breed with an uncanny sense of direction and the ability to locate avalanche victims buried many feet under the snow. The Hospice dogs are credited with saving over 2500 lives.

Dog historians write that occasionally an oversize, long-coated pup would occur in a litter and, because the monks did not consider either great size or overcoating suited to Alpine rescue work, these pups were given away. It is these dogs which founded the giant breed we know today as the St. Bernard.

The breed was introduced to Britain in 1810 and first exhibited at a dog show in 1863. In 1865 it was officially named the St. Bernard and in 1887 at a congress held in Zurich, Switzerland, a breed standard was laid down which was accepted internationally the following year.

In 1856, the Hospice kennels suffered the dual calamity of an avalanche and a distemper epidemic which almost wiped out the breeding stock. Remaining stock was crossed to various breeds and the line was saved from extinction. Dogs are still being bred at the Hospice kennels, mainly as a tourist attraction because their Alpine rescue work has now been taken over by the German Shepherd.

The "Saints" achieved early and continuing popularity because of their romantic history. There were seventeen benched at the first Westminster Kennel Club show, held in 1877, several being

G. STENHOUSE

St. Bernard

offered for sale at prices of $1000 and up. The Canadian Kennel Club Stud Book records 249 registrations for St. Bernards in the years 1888–1889.

Official Breed Standard for the St. Bernard

SHORT-HAIRED

Origin and Purpose: The St. Bernard likely originated in Switzerland from dogs brought back from Asia by conquering Roman armies. They have been connected with rescue work in the Great St. Bernard Pass in the Swiss Alps for several centuries. They are still bred in the famous Hospice founded by St. Bernard de Menthon, and many people have been saved from death in the snow by representatives of the breed.

General Appearance: Powerful, proportionately tall figure, strong and muscular in every part, with powerful head and most intelligent expression. In dogs with a dark mask the expression appears more stern, but never ill-natured.

Size: Height at shoulder of the dog ought to be 27½ in. (70 cm) minimum, of the bitch 25½ in. (65 cm). Female animals throughout are of a more delicate and finer build.

Coat and Colour: Coat very dense, short-haired (*stockhaarig*), lying smooth, tough, without however feeling rough to the touch. The thighs are slightly bushy. The tail at the root has longer and denser hair which gradually becomes shorter towards the tip. The tail appears bushy, not forming a flag. Colour white with red or red with white, the red in its various shades; brindle patches with white markings. The colours red and brown-yellow are of entirely equal value. Necessary markings are: white chest, feet and tip of tail, nose band, collar or spot on the nape; the latter blaze are very desirable. Never of one colour or without white. Faulty are all other colours, except the favourite dark shadings on the head (mask) and ears. One distinguishes between mantle dogs and splash-coated dogs.

Head: Like the whole body, very powerful and imposing.
   Skull: the massive skull is wide, slightly arched and the sides slope in a gentle curve into the very strongly developed, high

cheek bones. Occiput only moderately developed. The supra-orbital ridge is very strongly developed and forms nearly a right angle with the horizontal axis of the head. Deeply imbedded between the eyes and starting at the root of the muzzle, a furrow runs over the whole skull. It is strongly marked in the first half, gradually disappearing towards the base of the occiput. The lines at the sides of the head diverge considerably from the outer corner of the eyes towards the back of the head. The skin of the forehead, above the eyes, forms rather noticeable wrinkles, more or less pronounced, which converge toward the furrow. Especially when the dog is in action, the wrinkles are more visible without in the least giving the impression of morosity. Too strongly developed wrinkles are not desired. The slope from the skull to the muzzle is sudden and rather steep.

Muzzle: the muzzle is short, does not taper, and the vertical depth at the root of the muzzle must be greater than the length of the muzzle. The bridge of the muzzle must be greater than the length of the muzzle. The bridge of the muzzle is not arched, but straight; in some dogs, occasionally, slightly broken. A rather wide, well marked, shallow furrow runs from the root of the muzzle over the entire bridge of the muzzle to the nose. *Nose* (Schwamm) very substantial, broad, with wide open nostrils and, like the lips, always black. *Mouth:* the flews of the upper jaw are strongly developed, not sharply cut, but turning in a beautiful curve into the lower edge, and slightly overhanging. The flews of the lower jaw must not be deeply pendant. The teeth should be sound and strong and should meet in either a scissors or an even bite, the scissors bite being preferable. The undershot bite although sometimes found with good specimens is not desirable. The overshot bite is a fault. A black roof to the mouth is desirable.

Eyes set more to the front than the sides, are of medium size, dark brown, with intelligent, friendly expression, set moderately deep. The lower eyelids, as a rule, do not close completely and, if that is the case, form an angular wrinkle towards the inner corner of the eye. Eyelids which are too deeply pendant and show conspicuously the lachrymal glands, or a very red, thick haw, and eyes that are too light, are objectionable.

Ears of medium size, rather high set, with very strongly developed burr (Muschel) at the base. They stand slightly away from the head at the base, then drop with a sharp bend to the side and cling to the head without a turn. The flap is tender and forms a rounded triangle, slightly elongated towards the point, the front edge lying firmly to the head, whereas the back edge may stand somewhat away from the head, especially when the dog is at attention. Lightly set ears, which at the base immediately cling to the head, give it an oval and too little marked exterior, whereas a strongly developed base gives the skull a squarer, broader and much more expressive appearance.

Neck: Set high, very strong and in action is carried erect. Otherwise horizontally or slightly downward. The junction of head and neck is distinctly marked by an indentation. The nape of the neck is very muscular and rounded at the sides which makes the neck appear rather short. The dewlap of throat and neck is well pronounced; too strong development, however, is not desirable.

Forequarters: Shoulders sloping and broad, very muscular and powerful. Forearms very powerful and extraordinarily muscular. Forelegs straight, strong.

Body: The withers are strongly pronounced. The back very broad, perfectly straight as far as the haunches, from there gently sloping to the rump, and merging imperceptibly into the root of the tail. Chest very well arched, moderately deep, not reaching below the elbows. Belly distinctly set off from the very powerful loin section, only a little drawn up.

Hindquarters: Well developed. Legs very muscular. Hocks of moderate angulation. Dewclaws are not desired; if present, they must not obstruct gait. Feet broad, with strong toes, moderately closed, and with rather high knuckles. The so-called dewclaws which sometimes occur on the inside of the hind legs are imperfectly developed toes. They are of no use to the dog and are not taken into consideration in judging. They may be removed by surgery.

Tail: Starting broad and powerful directly from the rump is long, very heavy, ending in a powerful tip. In repose it hangs straight down, turning gently upwards in the lower third only, which is not considered a fault. In a great many specimens the tail is carried with the end slightly bent and therefore hangs down in the shape of an "f". In action all dogs carry the tail more or less turned upwards. However, it may not be carried too erect or by any means rolled over the back. A slight curling of the tip is sooner admissible.

Faults: Considered as faults are all deviations from the standards, as for instance a sway back, and a disproportionately long back, hocks too much bent, straight hindquarters, upward growing hair in spaces between the toes, out at elbows, cowhocks, and weak pasterns.

LONG-HAIRED

The Long-Haired variety completely resembles the Short-Haired variety except for the coat which is not short-haired (*stockhaarig*) but of medium length, plain to slightly wavy, never rolled or curly and not shaggy either. Usually, on the back, especially from the region of the haunches to the rump, the hair is more wavy, a condition, by the way, that is slightly indicated in the short-haired dogs.

The tail is bushy dense with hair of moderate length. Rolled or curly hair on the tail is not desirable. A tail with parted hair, or a flag tail, is faulty. Face and ears are covered with short and soft hair; longer hair at the base of the ear is permissible. Forelegs only slightly feathered; thighs very bushy.

Welsh Corgi (Cardigan)

*F*OLKLORE HAS IT that the two breeds of Welsh cattle dogs, the Cardigan and the Pembroke Welsh Corgis, were "a gift from the fairies." Imaginative as that may seem, it is only slightly more fanciful than some of the theories that have been advanced as to these breeds' origins.

Some dog historians claim separate origins for the two. But the most plausible would seem to be that both breeds had a common ancestor in the Vallhund, a Swedish herding dog, short-legged like the Corgis. It is reported that the Vallhund arrived in Wales when the Vikings invaded that country in the 9th century A.D. There this dog bred with local farm dogs. The result—a low, long-bodied herding breed that controlled the cattle by nipping at their heels.

In the case of the Cardigan Welsh Corgi, that was the extent of his backgroud breeding. He developed to become a dog-of-all-trades—drover, guard, companion, even a sporting dog. Isolated in his native land, little was known of the breed until the 1920s, when Corgis were introduced to the world of dog shows.

If his background remains a moot point, so does the origin of the breed name "Corgi." Etymologists claim the word derives from two Welsh words, *cor* which means dwarf, and *gi* which means dog. While this is not the only opinion, it seems the most logical. Certainly, despite crosses to other, probably longer-legged breeds, the dwarf characteristic has remained dominant throughout the centuries.

The Cardigan differs from his cousin the Pembroke Corgi in several respects. He is somewhat larger, longer-bodied, has rounded ears, the tail is left undocked, and he comes in a greater variety of colours.

Corgis were first shown in Britain in 1925 with both types classified as a single breed and, to the dismay of each type's supporters, under a single breed standard. This situation prevailed until 1934 when The Kennel Club (England) gave them separate breed status. For reasons which are rather difficult to understand, the Cardigan has failed to achieve the popularity of the Pembroke.

G.Stenhouse

Welsh Corgi (Cardigan)

Official Breed Standard for the
Welsh Corgi (Cardigan)

Origin and Purpose: The Cardigan Welsh Corgi originated in the hill country of Cardiganshire in western Wales. The time of origin is uncertain, but perhaps a thousand years ago. The breed was originally a general-purpose farm dog, frequently used for driving cattle.

General Appearance: Sturdy, mobile, and capable of endurance. Over-all silhouette long in proportion to height, terminating in a fox-like brush, set in line with the body. Alert expression.

Temperament: Alert, active, and intelligent, with steady temperament.

Size: Height as near as possible to 12 in. (30 cm) at the shoulder. Weight in proportion to size, with over-all balance as prime consideration.

Coat: Short or medium of hard texture. Weatherproof with good undercoat. Preferably straight.

Colour: Any colour, with or without white markings, but white should not predominate.

Head: *Skull:* head foxy in shape and appearance, skull wide and flat between the ears tapering towards the eyes above which it should be slightly domed. Moderate amount of stop. Length of foreface in proportion to skull as 3 is to 5, tapering moderately towards the nose, which should be black, slightly projecting and in no sense blunt. Underjaw clean-cut, strong but without prominence. *Eyes:* medium size, clear, giving a kindly, alert but watchful expression. Rather widely set with corners clearly defined. Eyes preferably dark, or to blend with the coat, rims dark. One or both eyes pale blue, blue or blue flecked, permissible only in blue merles. *Ears:* erect, proportionately rather large to the size of the dog. Tips slightly rounded, moderately wide at the base and set about 3 ½ in. (9 cm) apart. Carried so that the tips are slightly wide of a straight line drawn from the tip of the nose through the centre of the eyes, and set well back so that they can be laid flat along the neck. *Mouth:* teeth strong, with a perfect regular and complete scissors bite, *i.e.*, the upper teeth closely overlapping the lower teeth and set square to the jaw. Pincer bite permissible. The teeth should be evenly arranged and not crowded in relation to one another.

Neck: Muscular, well developed and in proportion to the dog's build, fitting into well-sloped shoulders.

Forequarters: Shoulders well laid and angulated at approximately 90 degrees to the upper arm; muscular, elbows close to sides. Strong bone carried down to feet. Legs short but body well clear of the ground, forearms slightly bowed to mould round the chest. Feet turned only slightly outwards.

Body: Chest moderately broad with prominent breast bone. Body fairly long and strong with deep brisket, well sprung ribs and clearly defined waist. Topline level.

Hindquarters: Strong, well angulated and aligned with muscular thighs and second thighs, strong bone carried down to feet, legs short; when standing, hocks should be vertical viewed from the side and rear.

Feet: Round, tight, rather large and well padded. All dewclaws should be removed.

Tail: Like a fox's brush set in line with the body and moderately long (to touch or nearly touch the ground). Carried low when standing but may be lifted a little above the body when moving, but not curled over the back.

Gait: The gait should be free, smooth, and appear effortless. In forequarters there should be good forward reach, without exaggerated lift, and with good follow-through. The elbows should work close to the body, neither loose nor tight. Viewed from in front, the forefeet should approach a single track at a brisk trot. In hindquarters there should be good forward reach and moderate rear extension, giving the appearance of a powerful driving action. The stifles must bend, giving appearance that the hocks are lifted, not swung from the hip. From the rear, tendency towards single tracking is preferred. At a trot, the top-line should remain relatively level, without pronounced bobbing in front or rear.

Faults: Any departure from the foregoing points should be considered a fault and the seriousness with which the fault is regarded should be in exact proportion to its degree.

NOTE: Male animals should have two apparently normal testicles fully descended into the scrotum.

Welsh Corgi (Pembroke)

DOG HISTORIANS WHO THEORIZE that the Cardigan and Pembroke Corgis originated from a Swedish Vallhund/Welsh herd dog cross claim that further crosses account for the obvious physical differences between the two breeds. The fox-like head of the Pembroke Corgi, they claim, was accentuated by cross breeding to members of the Spitz family of dogs. Both the Schipperke and the Pomeranian are suggested because these breeds were brought to Wales early in the 12th century by Flemish weavers who settled in Pembrokeshire, Wales. It is also thought that the Lancashire Heeler, a small black and tan cattle dog similar in type to the Pembroke Corgi, could share in the breed's ancestry.

Whatever his background, the final product exerted enormous appeal. It is reported that every farm in the county had at least two Pembroke Corgis. And with the Corgi's introduction to dog shows it was the Pembroke that dominated the breed. While both the Cardigan and Pembroke varieties were still being shown as a single breed, the first Corgi to become a champion was a red Pembroke female. The first male Corgi champion was also a Pembroke.

While this was enough to assure a following for the engaging little Pembroke, it was royal patronage that brought the breed international fame. In 1933 King George VI, then the Duke of York, purchased a Pembroke Corgi puppy for his daughters, Elizabeth and Margaret Rose. Later a mate was added to the family and descendants of these Pembroke Corgis are pets of the Royal Family today.

In 1975 The Kennel Club (England) commissioned a portrait of its patron, Queen Elizabeth II. This work shows Her Majesty surrounded by some of her dogs. The little fellow with its forefeet on her lap that Queen Elizabeth II is patting, is one of her favourites, the Pembroke Corgi "Windsor Brush." Centred in the portrait is the cross-bred "Tinker" whose dam was a Pembroke Corgi, his sire a Dachshund—a breed the Royal Family calls the "Windsor Dorgi."

Welsh Corgi (Pembroke)

In 1934, the year the Cardigan and Pembroke Corgis were accorded separate breed status in Britain, The Canadian Kennel Club Stud Book lists nine Pembroke Corgis were registered in Canada.

Official Breed Standard for the Welsh Corgi (Pembroke)

General Appearance: Low-set, strong, sturdily built, alert and active, giving an impression of substance and stamina in a small space; outlook bold, expression intelligent and workman-like.

Size: Dogs, 20–24 lb. (9–11 kg); bitches, 18–22 lb. (8–10 kg). Height—from 10–12 in. (25–30 cm) at shoulder.

Coat and Colour: Coat of medium length and dense; not wiry. Self-colours in red, sable, fawn, black and tan, or with white markings on legs, chest and neck. Some white on head and foreface is permissible.

Head: Head to be foxy in shape and appearance, with alert and intelligent expression, *skull* to be fairly wide and flat between the ears; moderate amount of stop. Length of foreface to be in proportion to the skull as three is to five. *Muzzle* slightly tapering. *Nose* black. Teeth level, or with the inner side of the upper front teeth resting closely on the front of the under ones. *Eyes* well set, medium size, hazel in colour and blending with colour of coat. *Ears* pricked, medium sized, slightly pointed. A line drawn from the tip of the nose through the eye should, if extended, pass through, or close to, the tip of the ear.

Neck: Fairly long.

Forequarters: Legs short and as straight as possible. "Straight as possible" means straight as soundness and deep broad chest will permit. It does not mean terrier-straight. Ample bone carried right down to the feet. Elbows should fit closely to the sides, neither loose nor tied. Forearm should curve slightly round the chest.

Body: Of medium length, with well-sprung ribs. Not short-coupled or terrier-like. Level topline. Chest broad and deep, well let down between the forelegs.

Hindquarters: Strong and flexible, slightly tapering. Legs short. Ample bone carried right down to the feet. Hocks straight when viewed from behind. Feet oval, the two centre toes slightly in advance of two outer toes, pads strong and well arched. Nails short.

Tail: Short, preferably natural.

Gait: The movement should be free and active, elbows fitting closely to the sides, neither loose nor tied. Forelegs should move well forward, without too much lift, in unison with thrusting action of hind legs.

GROUP IV: TERRIERS

Airedale Terrier

THE AIREDALE CAN HARDLY QUALIFY as a dog that goes to ground for its quarry; it is just too big. However, it is probably the most versatile of terriers, having been bred to hunt fur and feather, retrieve over land and water, and used as a pit fighter, ratter, herder, guard and police dog, and as a guide dog for the blind. Needless to say that dogs of such a multitalented heritage have also excelled in obedience.

The Airedale originated in an area of Yorkshire, England, between the Aire and the Wharfe Rivers as the working man's sporting dog. Otters fished the rivers and rats were an ever-present problem. Under such circumstances the ideal sporting dog combination would be a few water dogs to hunt the otter, and a couple of terriers to take care of the rats—a combination beyond the means of the average working man.

The next best thing was to combine the bloods of both types of dog in the hope that the progeny would inherit all the desired working abilities. Such a cross was made in 1853. A Rough-Coated Black and Tan Terrier was mated to an Otterhound and the result was a dog that could swim and scent game, and was possessed of the keenness of the terrier. More such crosses followed, and within twelve years the Waterside Terrier, as these cross-breds were known, became a popular local sporting terrier. Working ability counted for more than appearance and it is said that these early dogs were a mixed lot.

In 1864 these terriers were exhibited for the first time at a championship dog show sponsored by the Airedale Agricultural Society classified under various names including Rough-Coated, Bingley, and Waterside Terrier. This situation prevailed for the next few years. Then in 1879 fanciers decided to call their breed the Airedale Terrier, a name that was accepted by The Kennel Club (England) in 1886.

Subsequent crosses to other terrier breeds have been suggested in order to improve outline and standardize breed type. Thus the present-day Airedale has come a long way from its rough-looking progenitor. By selectively mating the "best to the best," breeders have created a dog rightly known as "the king of terriers."

Airedale Terrier

The 1880s saw the first imports of Airedales to this continent. First Canadian registrations are recorded in the Stud Book of 1888–1889.

Official Breed Standard for the Airedale Terrier

Size: Dogs should measure approximately 23 in. (58 cm) in height at the shoulder; bitches, slightly less. Both sexes should be sturdy, well-muscled and well-boned.

Coat and Colour: Coat should be hard, dense and wiry, lying straight and close, covering the dog well over the body and legs. Some of the hardest are crinkling or just slightly waved. At the base of the hard very stiff hair should be a shorter growth of softer hair termed the undercoat. The head and ears should be tan, the ears being of a darker shade than the rest. Dark markings on either side of the skull are permissible. The legs up to the thighs and elbows and the underpart of the body and chest are also tan and the tan frequently runs into the shoulder. The sides and upper parts of the body should be black or dark grizzle. A red mixture is often found in the black and is not to be considered objectionable. A small white blaze on the chest is a characteristic of certain strains of the breed.

Head: Should be well balanced with little apparent difference between the length of skull and foreface. *Skull* should be long and flat, not too broad between the ears and narrowing very slightly to the eyes. Scalp should be free from wrinkles, stop hardly visible, and cheeks level and free from fullness. *Muzzle* should be deep, powerful, strong, and muscular. Should be well filled up before the eyes. *Nose* should be black and not too small. *Mouth:* lips should be tight. Teeth should be strong and white, free from discolouration or defect. Bite either level or vise-like. A slightly overlapping or scissors bite is permissible without preference. *Eyes* should be dark, small, not prominent, full of terrier expression, keenness and intelligence. *Ears* should be V-shaped with carriage rather to the side of the head, not pointing to the eyes, small but not out of proportion to the size of the dog. The topline of the folded ear should be above the level of the skull.

Neck: Should be of moderate length and thickness gradually widening towards the shoulder. Skin tight, not loose.

Forequarters: Shoulders long and sloping well into the back. Shoulder blades flat. Forelegs should be perfectly straight, with plenty of muscle and bone. Elbows should be perpendicular to the body, working free of sides.

Body: Back should be short, strong and level. From the front, chest deep but not broad. The depth of the chest should be approximately on a level with the elbows. Ribs well sprung. Loins muscular and of good width. There should be but little space between the last rib and the hip joint.

Hindquarters: Should be strong and muscular with no droop. Thighs should be long and powerful with muscular second thigh, stifles well bent, not turned either in or out, hocks well let down, parallel with each other when viewed from behind. Feet should be small, round, and compact with a good depth of pad, well cushioned; the toes moderately arched, not turned either in or out.

Tail: The root of the tail should be set well up on the back. It should be carried gaily but not curled over the back. It should be of good strength and substance and of fair length.

Gait: Movement or action is the crucial test of conformation. Movement should be free. As seen from the front the forelegs should swing perpendicular from the body free from the sides, the feet the same distance apart as the elbows. As seen from the rear the hind legs should be parallel with each other, neither too close nor too far apart, but so placed as to give a strong, well-balanced stance and movement. The toes should not be turned either in or out.

Faults: Yellow eyes, hound ears, white feet, soft coat, being much over or under the size limit, being undershot or overshot, having poor movement, are faults which should be severely penalized.

   The use of any and all foreign agents for the improvement of dogs in the show ring, such as colouring, dilating the pupil, and stiffening the coat, is forbidden. Such acts are unsportsmanlike and unfair to those exhibitors who live up to the rules.

Scale of Points:

Head 10
Neck, shoulders and chest 10
Body 10
Hindquarters and tail 10
Legs and feet 10
Coat 10
Colour 5
Size 10
Movement 10
General characteristics and expression .... <u>15</u>

       TOTAL 100

Australian Terrier

THE AUSTRALIAN TERRIER and the Australian Silky Terrier, a toy breed, share the same ancestry. Both breeds were developed in Australia, a process that began in the early 1800s when a puppy from the mating of a pair of broken-coated dogs, blue with tan markings, was taken to England, when her owner emigrated from Tasmania. There this female was mated to a Dandie Dinmont Terrier and some of her offspring eventually came to Australia, taken there by a settler.

Then the experimenting began. It must be remembered that in the mid-19th century Australia was much more isolated from the rest of the world than it is today. And if the Australians wanted a dog of a particular type, they created it out of the materials at hand. Such was the history of the Australian Terrier. From the Dandie Dinmont it was given its topknot; from the Skye Terrier its short legs, long coat, and length of body; from the Irish Terrier the colour of the reds and sandies; and from the Manchester Terrier the rich tan markings of the blue and tans. It has also been said that there were several crosses to the Yorkshire Terrier, presumably to control size.

The end product of all these crosses was a lively little dog of typical terrier character and temperament, an efficient rodent killer and watchdog. In short, just what the breeders wanted.

Within a few years these terriers were breeding true to type and made their debut in 1872 at a dog show held in Melbourne. In 1896 the first Australian Terrier Club was founded in that city and a breed standard draughted. Originally both the erect and drop ear was correct, and a slightly smaller dog was called for. The present standard was approved by the Australian National Kennel Council in 1961 and has remained the blueprint for the breed throughout the world.

First specimens were introduced to Britain in 1906, but it was to be another thirty years before the Australian Terrier was granted official recognition by The Kennel Club (England). First Canadian registrations were recorded in The Canadian Kennel Club Stud Book for the years 1936-1937. The breed's most illustrious member was Australian-bred Ch. Tinee Town Talcbac who

Australian Terrier

won a total of eleven Best in Show awards in his homeland and three all-breed Best in Show awards in the United States.

Official Breed Standard for the Australian Terrier

General Appearance: A sturdy, low-set dog rather long in proportion to height with strong terrier character, alertness, activity, and soundness. Its untrimmed harsh coat, with a definite ruff around the neck, extending to the breastbone, assists its hard-bitten and rugged appearance. Essentially a working terrier, it is equally suited as a companion dog owing to its loyalty and even disposition.

Size: Weight—the desirable weight is approximately 14 lb. (6 kg). Height—the desirable height is approximately 10 in. (25 cm).

Coat and Colour: The body coat consists of a harsh, straight dense topcoat approximately 2½ in. (6 cm) long, with short soft textured undercoat. The muzzle, lower legs and feet to be free from long hair. Colour: *a)* Blue, steel-blue or dark grey-blue, with rich tan (not sandy) on face, ears, under body, lower legs and feet and around the vent (puppies excepted). The richer the colour and more clearly defined the better. Topknot blue, silver or a lighter shade than head colour. *b)* Clear sandy or red, smuttiness, or dark shadings undesirable. Topknot a lighter shade.

Head: Long with flat *skull* of moderate width, full between the eyes, with slight but definite stop. The *muzzle*, strong and powerful, of equal length to that of the skull, which is covered with a soft, silky topknot. *Nose* black, of moderate size; the leather extending to bridge of muzzle. Jaw strong and punishing, teeth large and evenly spaced, the upper incisors fitting closely over the lower; lips black, tight and clean. The *eyes* are small, with keen expression, and of dark brown colour, set well apart and not prominent. The *ears* are small, erect, pointed, well carried, set on moderately wide, free from long hair and sensitive in their use (puppies under six months excepted).

Neck: Long, slightly arched, shapely and strong.

Forequarters: Shoulders long and well laid. Forelegs well boned and perfectly straight, parallel when viewed from the front.

Pasterns strong, without slope (slightly feathered to the knee).

Body: Topline level. Long in proportion to height, strongly constructed, with well-sprung ribs and chest of moderate depth and width. Loins strong, flanks deep.

Hindquarters: Moderate length of quarters, broad with strong muscular thighs. Stifles well turned and hocks well bent and let down. Viewed from behind they should be parallel, neither too wide nor too close. Feet small, well padded, toes closely knit and moderately arched, turned neither in nor out, with strong black or dark toenails.

Tail: Docked $^2/_3$, set on high, and well carried, but not over the back.

Gait: The action to be free, springy and forceful. When viewed from the front, the forelegs should move truly without looseness of shoulder, elbows, or pasterns. The hindquarters to have drive and power, with free movement of stifles and hocks. Seen from the rear, the legs from the hocks to the ground to be parallel, neither too close nor too wide.

Faults: Flesh-coloured or butterfly nose. White or light-coloured toenails. Soft, woolly, or wavy coat. Black and tan (puppies excepted). Sandy marking in place of tan. Tan smut in blue coat. Shading or smut in sandy or red. Crooked forelegs. Unsoundness. Light eyes. Under or oversize. Under or overshot mouth. Over gay tail. White markings on chest or feet.

Scale of Points:

Skull	5
Muzzle	5
Eyes	5
Ears	5
Neck	5
Body	15
Feet and legs	15
Coat	10
Colour	10
Tail	5
General appearance	20
TOTAL	100

Bedlington Terrier

BOTH THE DANDIE DINMONT and the Bedlington Terrier are thought to share the same ancestry, and both are equally obscure. Although today their appearance is quite different, early specimens of both breeds bore a close resemblance to each other. Both were valued as vermin killers and both originated in the north of England.

It is thought that the Bedlington was first known in Cumberland County towards the end of the 18th century, and that some specimens found their way into the adjoining county of Northumberland, where they were bred with local terriers. The resultant cross became known by the regional name of Rothbury Terrier.

The breed became popular with coal miners who cross bred the Rothbury to create a terrier-of-all-work, that is, a dog that could work equally well on land and in water, and fleet enough to catch a rabbit. Thus the Rothbury was crossed with the Whippet, and it was at this point that the present-day conformation of the Bedlington was set. While there seems to be some difference of opinion among dog historians as to when the present name, Bedlington, was adopted, all agree on the Rothbury/ Whippet cross. Whether the breed had been renamed before or after the cross, which is said to have occurred in the 1870s, is not significant; what does matter is that the miners had created one of the gamest of terriers, able to swim down an otter, course a rabbit and give a good account of himself in the fighting pit. The Bedlington is said to have become the poacher's greatest ally and in some parts of England is still known as the "Gypsy Dog."

It is known too that in the 1870s the Bedlington made its debut in the show ring and soon attracted public attention. In 1875 the National Bedlington Terrier Club was formed, and in 1895 the first breed standard was draughted. Slowly but surely ever since, the breed has been transformed from a rough-looking creature valued more for his working ability than his appearance to a gentle-mannered, elegant show dog and companion.

Bedlington Terrier

Towards the end of the 19th century, the Bedlington was introduced to this continent where it was boosted to immediate acclaim when a member of the breed was awarded Best in Show at the prestigious Morris and Essex Kennel Club event in 1947 followed by a similar win at the Westminster Kennel Club show in New York in 1948.

The Bedlington Terrier was first registered in Canada in the years 1888–1889.

Official Breed Standard for the Bedlington Terrier

Origin and Purpose: The Bedlington Terrier originated in the mining country of Northumberland early in the nineteenth century. The breed was known for drawing badgers and vermin. Shown in 1877, he later became much of a housepet, but never lost his working proclivity.

General Appearance: A graceful, lithe, well-balanced dog with no sign of coarseness, weakness, or shelliness. Noteworthy for endurance, Bedlingtons also gallop at great speed, as their body outline clearly shows.

Temperament: In repose, the expression is mild and gentle, not shy or nervous. Aroused, the dog is particularly alert and full of immense energy and courage.

Size: Height—the preferred Bedlington Terrier dog measures 16½ in. (42 cm) at the withers, the bitch 15½ in. (39 cm). Under 16 in. or over 17½ in. for dogs (40 cm and 45 cm), and under 15 in. or over 16½ in. for bitches (38 cm and 42 cm) are serious faults. Only where comparative superiority of a specimen outside these ranges clearly justifies it, should greater latitude be taken.

Weight—to be proportionate to height, within the range of 17–23 lb. (7–10 kg).

Coat and Colour: Coat—a very distinctive mixture of hard and soft hair standing well out from the skin. Thick and linty, crisp to the touch but not wiry, having a tendency to curl, especially on the head and face. When in show trim must not exceed 1 inch (3 cm) on body; hair on legs is slightly longer.

Colour—blue, sandy, liver, blue and tan, sandy and tan, liver and tan. In bicolours the tan markings are found on the legs, chest, under the tail, inside the hindquarters and over each eye. The topknots of all adults should be lighter than the body colour. Patches of darker hair from an injury are not objectionable, as these are only temporary. Darker body pigmentation of all colours is to be encouraged.

Head: Narrow, but deep and rounded. Shorter in *skull* and longer in jaw. Covered with a profuse topknot which is lighter than the colour of the body, highest at the crown, and tapering gradually to just back of the nose. *Muzzle:* there must be no stop and the unbroken line from crown to nose end reveals a slender head without cheekiness or snipiness. Strong muzzle well filled up with bone beneath the eye. *Nose:* nostrils large and well defined. Blues and blue and tans have black noses. Livers, liver and tans, sandies, sandy and tans have brown noses. *Mouth:* jaws long and tapering. Close-fitting lips, no flews. Teeth—large, strong and white. Level or scissors bite. Lower canines clasp the outer surface of the upper gum just in front of the upper canines. Upper premolars and molars lie outside those of the lower jaws. *Eyes:* almond shaped, small, bright and well sunk with no tendency to tear or water. Set is oblique and fairly high on the head. Blues have dark eyes; blue and tans, less dark with amber lights; sandies, sandy and tans, light hazel; liver, liver and tans, slightly darker. Eye rims are black in the blue and blue and tans, brown in all other solid and bicolours. *Ears:* filbert shaped, triangular with rounded tips. Set on low and hanging flat to the cheek in front with a slight projection at the base. Point of greatest width approximately 3 in. (8 cm). Ear tips reach the corners of the mouth. Thin and velvety in texture, covered with fine hair forming a small silky tassel at the tip.

Neck: Long, tapering neck with no throatiness, deep at the base and rising well up from the shoulders. The head is carried high.

Forequarters: Shoulders flat and sloping with no excessive musculature. Upper and lower arm lithe and muscular. Forelegs are straight and wider apart at the chest than at the feet. Pasterns: slight bend to pasterns which are long and sloping without weakness. Feet: long hare feet with thick, well-closed-up, smooth pads. Dewclaws should be removed.

Body: Muscular and markedly flexible. Topline: the back should be roached and the loin markedly arched. Body slightly greater in length than height. Chest deep, flat-ribbed and deep through the brisket, which reaches to the elbows. Loin, croup, abdomen: the arch over the loin creates a definite tuck-up of the underline.

Hindquarters: Hip bone and upper thigh, lower thigh: well-muscled quarters are also fine and graceful. Hocks strong and well let down, turning neither in nor out. Stifles well angulated. Feet: as in forefeet.

Tail: Set low, scimitar-shaped, thick at the root and tapering to a point which reaches the hock. Not carried over the back or tight to the underbody.

Gait: Unique lightness of movement, springy in the slower paces, not stilted or hackneyed, must not cross, weave or paddle.

Faults: Shyness, nervousness. Dogs over 17½ in. (45 cm) or under 16 in. (40 cm), bitches over 16½ in. (42 cm) or under 15 in. (38 cm); wiry coat; head too wide or lacking correct proportions; cheekiness, snipiness; overshot or undershot; large eyes, too light eyes in blues; ears set high; too short neck, throatiness; steep shoulders, too narrow chest, shallow chest, splayed feet, lack of arch over loin, hocks turning in or out, lack of rear angulation; tail carried over back or tight to the underbody; stilted or hackneyed gait, crossing, weaving or paddling.

Border Terrier

PRIOR TO THE MID-19TH CENTURY, the background breeding of the working terriers native to the country bordering the Cheviot Hills in the north of England was so intermingled it is impossible to trace the history of a particular breed farther back than this. And while they now bear little resemblance to one another, it is thought that the Dandie Dinmont, Bedlington, Lakeland, and Border Terriers share the same ancestry. Each has been developed along different lines but all were essentially hard-working terriers used to control the fox population that preyed on livestock.

The birthplace of the Border is considered to be the Northumberland valley of Coquetdale, an area renowned for its terriers. At one time the breed was known as the Coquetdale Terrier. Another local terrier, the now extinct white Redesdale, is thought to be a common ancestor of the Dandie, Bedlington, and Border. As evidence, terrier authorities cite the occasional Border puppy that carries the distinctive topknot and the occurrence of puppies born with white feet and white chest markings.

In 1880 the name Border Terrier took preference over all the local names by which the breed had been known probably because the breed was a favourite hunt terrier and worked with packs of Border Foxhounds. Credit for standardizing type, draughting the first breed standard, and helping to obtain official recognition for the breed belongs to three hunt masters whose families had been associated with working terriers for generations. In 1920 the Border Terrier Club was formed, and shortly thereafter The Kennel Club (England) added this breed to its official list.

For a time a group of breed fanciers were angered that the Border had been elevated to the ranks of the show dog, fearing that such prettifying would be the ruination of the working terrier. However, the Border has remained sturdy and natural, able if need be to run with the hounds all day. The breed's most distinctive feature is its head which resembles that of an otter.

The Border Terrier was first registered in Canada in the years 1929–1930.

G. STENHOUSE

Border Terrier

Official Breed Standard for the Border Terrier

General Appearance: Since the Border Terrier is a working terrier of a size to go to ground and able, within reason, to follow a horse, his conformation should be such that he be ideally built to do his job. No deviations from this ideal conformation should be permitted, which would impair his usefulness in running his quarry to earth and in bolting it therefrom. For this work he must be alert, active and agile, and capable of squeezing through narrow apertures and rapidly traversing any kind of terrain. His head, "like that of an otter," is distinctive.

It should be the aim of Border Terrier breeders to avoid such over-emphasis of any point in the standard as might lead to unbalanced exaggeration.

The Border Terrier is an active terrier of medium bone, strongly put together, suggesting endurance and agility, but rather narrow in shoulder, body, and quarter. The body is covered with a somewhat broken though close-fitting and intensely wiry jacket. The characteristic "otter" head with its keen eye, combined with a body poise which is "at the alert," gives a look of fearless and implacable determination characteristic of the breed. The proportions should be that the height at the withers is slightly greater than the distance from the withers to the tail, *i.e.*, by possibly 1–1½ in. (3–4 cm) in a 14 lb. (6.4 kg) dog.

Temperament: His temperament ideally exemplifies that of a Terrier. By nature he is good-tempered, affectionate, obedient, and easily trained. In the field he is hard as nails, "game as they come," and driving in attack.

Size: Weight—dogs, 13–15½ lb. (5.9–7 kg); bitches, 11½–14 lb. (5–6.4 kg), are appropriate weights for Border Terriers in hard-working condition.

Coat and Colour: A short and dense undercoat covered with a very wiry and somewhat broken topcoat which should lie closely, but it must not show any tendency to curl or wave. With such a coat a Border should be able to be exhibited almost in his natural state, nothing more in the way of trimming being needed than a tidying-up of the head, neck, and feet. The hide is very thick and loose fitting. Colour red, grizzle and tan, blue and tan, or wheaten. A small amount of white may be allowed on the chest but white on the feet should be penalized.

Head: Similar to that of an otter. Moderately broad and flat in *skull* with plenty of width between the eyes and between the ears. A slight, moderately broad curve at the stop rather than a pronounced indentation. Cheeks slightly full. *Muzzle* short and "well filled." A dark muzzle is characteristic and desirable. A few short whiskers are natural to the breed. *Nose* black, and of a good size. Teeth strong, with a scissors bite, large in proportion to size of dog. *Eyes* dark hazel and full of fire and intelligence. Moderate in size, neither prominent nor small and beady. *Ears* small, V-shaped and of moderate thickness, dark preferred. Not set high on the head but somewhat on the side, and dropping forward close to the cheeks. They should not break above the level of the skull.

Neck: Clean, muscular, and only long enough to give a well-balanced appearance. It should gradually widen into the shoulder.

Forequarters: Shoulders well laid back and of good length, the blades converging to the withers gradually from a brisket not excessively deep or narrow. Forelegs straight and not too heavy in bone and placed slightly wider than in a Fox Terrier.

Body: Deep, fairly narrow and of sufficient length to avoid any suggestion of lack of range and agility. Deep ribs carried well back and not oversprung in view of the desired depth and narrowness of the body. The body should be capable of being spanned by a man's hands behind the shoulders. Back strong but laterally supple, with no suspicion of a dip behind the shoulder. Loin strong and the underline fairly straight.

Hindquarters: Muscular and racy, with thighs long and nicely moulded. Stifles well bent and hocks well let down. Feet small and compact. Toes should point forward and be moderately arched with thick pads.

Tail: Moderately short, thick at the base, then tapering. Not set on too high. Carried gaily when at the alert, but not over the back. When at ease, a Border may drop his stern.

Gait: Straight and rhythmical before and behind, with good length of stride and flexing of stifle and hock. The dog should respond to his handler with a gait which is free, agile and quick.

Scale of Points:

Head, ears, neck and teeth	20
Legs and feet	15
Coat and skin	10
Shoulders and chest	10
Eyes and expression	10
Back and loin	10
Hindquarters	10
Tail	5
General appearance	10
TOTAL	100

Bull Terrier

THE BULL TERRIER is the gladiator of the canine race, who has earned the title "the white cavalier."

The Bull Terrier was developed in England early in the 19th century primarily for bull baiting, but was also used extensively in the pits against dogs, badgers, and vermin. In keeping with these pursuits, the breed is noted for its courage, resistance to pain, and quick thinking—qualities that were inherited from the breed's immediate forbears, the Bulldog and the Terrier. The original name for these feisty cross-breds was, quite logically, the Bull and Terrier.

It is reported that the early dogs were an inconsistent lot, blocky headed and variously coloured. But, as breeding progressed, the terrier characteristics predominated. More all-white dogs were being bred, heads became smoother and legs longer. Then, after the abolishment of the bull baiting and dog fighting in Britain in 1835, breeders turned their attentions to the gentler art of breeding dogs for show.

The developer of the present-day Bull Terrier is acknowledged to be James Hinks, who had been experimentally crossing the gamest of his Bull and Terriers with the white English Terrier and the Dalmatian to produce a strain of all-white dogs he called Bull Terriers. A female of Hinks' breeding, Puss, first of this new breed to be shown, made her debut in 1862. Hard-line Bull and Terrier enthusiasts scoffed at Hinks' refinement, claiming he had destroyed the breed's pugnacity. Despite the fact that it was against the law, Hinks took up the challenge. That evening, Puss was matched against a tough Bull and Terrier; she quickly took care of him and not being the worse for wear and tear was returned to the dog show the next morning. Other crosses are assumed to have brought further refinement to the breed. Among the breeds suggested are the Greyhound, Spanish Pointer, and Dalmatian.

In 1888, the Bull Terrier Club of England was formed and official status granted to the breed. At first the only recognized Bull Terrier was white, coloureds not being accepted until 1919.

Bull Terrier

Canada first registered the Bull Terrier in the years 1888–1889 and has the honour of being the birthplace of the first Bull Terrier to win an all-breed Best in Show, Ch. Haymarket Faultless, who defeated all comers at the prestigious Westminster Kennel Club event held in New York City in 1918.

Official Breed Standard for the Bull Terrier

Origin and Purpose: The Bull Terrier originated in England and is the Gladiator of the canine race.

General Appearance: Must be strongly built, muscular, symmetrical and active, with a keen, determined, and intelligent expression, full of fire and courage but of even temperament and amenable to discipline. Irrespective of size, dogs should look masculine and bitches feminine.

Size: There are neither weight nor height limits but there should be the impression of maximum substance to the size of the dog.

Coat and Colour: The coat should be short, flat, even and harsh to the touch, with a fine gloss. The skin should fit the dog tightly. For white, pure white coat. Skin pigmentation and markings on the head should not be penalized. For coloured, the colour should predominate, all other things being equal, brindle to be preferred.

Head: The head should be long, strong and deep, right to the end of the muzzle, but not coarse. Viewed from the front it should be egg shaped and completely filled, its surface being free from hollows or indentations. The top of the *skull* should be almost flat from ear to ear. The profile should curve gently downwards from the top of the skull to the tip of the *nose*, which should be black and bent downwards at the top. The nostrils should be well developed. The distance from the tip of the nose to the eyes should be perceptibly greater than that from the eyes to the top of the skull. The underjaw should be strong.
The *teeth* should be sound, clean, strong, of good size, and perfectly regular with full dentition. Either a level bite or scissors bite is acceptable. If a scissors bite, the upper front teeth should

fit in front of and closely against the lower front teeth. The lips should be clean and tight.

The *eyes* should appear narrow, obliquely placed and triangular, well sunken, as dark as possible and with a piercing glint. The *ears* should be small, thin, and placed closely together. The dog should be able to hold them stiffly erect, when they should point straight upwards.

Neck: The neck should be very muscular, long, arched, tapering from the shoulders to the head, and free from loose skin.

Forequarters: The shoulders should be strong and muscular but without loading. The shoulder blades should be wide, flat, and attached closely to the chest wall, and should have a very pronounced backward slope of the front edge from bottom to top. The forelegs should have the strongest type of round quality bone and the dog should stand solidly upon them; they should be moderately long and perfectly parallel. The elbows should be held straight and the strong pasterns upright. The feet should be round and compact with well-arched toes.

Body: The body should be well rounded with marked spring of rib, and a great depth from withers to brisket, so that the latter is nearer the ground than the belly. The back should be short and strong with the topline level behind the withers and arching or reaching slightly over the loin. The underline from the brisket to belly should form a graceful upward curve. The chest should be broad viewed from the front.

Hindquarters: The hind legs should be parallel viewed from behind. The thighs must be muscular and the second thigh well developed. The stifle joint should be well bent and the hock well angulated, with the bone to the foot short and strong.

Tail: The tail should be short, set on low. It should be carried horizontally. Thick at the root, it should taper to a fine point.

Gait: The moving dog shall appear well knit, smoothly covering the ground with free, easy strides and with a typical jaunty air. Fore and hind legs moving smoothly at the hip and flexing well at the stifle and hock with great thrust.

Faults: Any departure from the foregoing points should be considered a fault and the seriousness of the fault should be in exact proportion to its degree.

Disqualifications: *Deafness, blue eyes.*

Cairn Terrier

SMALL "EARTH DOGS," or terriers, as we now know them, have existed in the Western Highlands and Islands of Scotland for close to 500 years. It is recorded that every Scottish chieftain had his pack of hounds and his pack of terriers which were used to control small fur-bearing vermin such as fox, otter, weasels, and rodents. And while these "earth dogs" may have differed in appearance from the modern Cairn, it is assumed that it was from these short-legged, game, and tenacious little dogs that the breed was developed. Fanciers claim that the Cairn is one of the oldest, if not the oldest, breed of pure British terrier.

Stronghold of the breed was the Isle of Skye, where it is reported that the purest strains were developed and had been known as working terriers since 1810. Thus it seemed appropriate that when the breed made its show debut at Inverness in 1909, the dogs should be classified as "Shorthaired Skyes." This name did not sit well with Skye Terrier adherents, who had laid claim to the "Skye" appellation many years before. A lengthy dispute followed, the issue finally being resolved when one of the breed's strongest supporters suggested that to persist in using "Skye" could lead to confusion. Or, even worse, it might give the impression this should be a long-bodied dog.

In 1910 the committee charged with defining breed characteristics was persuaded to rename the breed the Cairn Terrier. Two years later the Cairn was granted official breed status by The Kennel Club (England). Since that time the breed has grown in popularity not only in Great Britain but throughout the world. Fanciers fondly call the Cairn "the best little pal in the world."

The first Cairn Terrier was imported into the United States by a Mrs. Price in 1913, and was registered with the American Kennel Club. First Canadian registrations were recorded in The Canadian Kennel Club Stud Book of 1920.

Cairn Terrier

Official Breed Standard for the Cairn Terrier

General Appearance: That of an active, game, hardy, small, working Terrier of the short-legged class; very free in its movements, strongly but not heavily built, standing well forward on its forelegs, deep in the ribs, well coupled with strong hindquarters and presenting a well-proportioned build with a medium length of back, having a hard, weather-resisting coat; head shorter and wider than any other terrier and well furnished with hair giving a general foxy expression.

Dogs should be shown in good hard flesh, well muscled and neither too fat nor thin. Should be in full good coat with plenty of head furnishings, be clean, combed, brushed and tidied up on ears, tail, feet, and general outline. Should move freely and easily on a loose lead, should not cringe on being handled, should stand up on their toes and show with marked terrier characteristics.

Size: Ideal size involves the weight, the height at the withers and the length of body. Weight for bitches, 13 lb. (5.9 kg); for dogs, 14 lb. (6.4 kg). Height at the withers—bitches, 9½ in. (24 cm); dogs, 10 in. (25 cm). Length of body from 14½–15 in. (37–38 cm) from the front of the chest to back of hindquarters. The dog must be of balanced proportions and appear neither leggy nor too low to ground; and neither too short nor too long in body. Weight and measurements are for matured dogs at two years of age. Older dogs may weigh slightly in excess and growing dogs may be under these weights and measurements.

Coat and Colour: Coat hard and weather resistant. Must be double-coated with profuse harsh outer coat and short, soft, close furry undercoat. May be of any colour except white. Dark ears, muzzle, and tail tip are desirable.

Head: *Skull* broad in proportion to length with a decided stop and well furnished with hair on the top of the head, which may be somewhat softer than the body coat. *Muzzle* strong but not too long or heavy. *Nose* black. Teeth large—mouth neither overshot nor undershot. *Eyes* set wide apart, rather sunken, with shaggy eyebrows, medium in size, hazel or dark hazel in colour, depending on body colour, with a keen terrier expression. *Ears* small, pointed, well carried erectly, set wide apart on the side of the head. Free from long hairs.

Forequarters: A sloping shoulder, medium length of leg, good but not too heavy bone; forelegs should not be out at elbows, and be perfectly straight, but forefeet may be slightly turned out. Forefeet larger than hind feet. Legs must be covered with hard hair. Pads should be thick and strong and dog should stand well up on its feet.

Body: Well muscled, strong, active body with well-sprung, deep ribs, with a level back of medium length, giving an impression of strength and activity without heaviness.

Hindquarters: Strong.

Tail: In proportion to head, well furnished with hair but not feathery. Carried gaily but must not curl over back. Set on at back level.

Faults:
1. Skull—too narrow in skull.
2. Muzzle—too long and heavy a foreface; mouth overshot or undershot.
3. Eyes—too large, prominent, yellow, and ringed are all objectionable.
4. Ears—too large, round at points, set too close together, set too high on the head; heavily covered with hair.
5. Legs and feet—too light or too heavy bone. Crooked forelegs or out at elbow. Thin, ferrety feet; feet let down on the heel or too open and spread. Too high or too low on the leg.
6. Body—too short back and compact a body, hampering quickness of movement and turning ability. Too long, weedy and snaky a body, giving an impression of weakness. Tail set on too low. Back not level.
7. Coat—open coats, blousy coats, too short or dead coats, lack of sufficient undercoat, lack of head furnishings, lack of hard hair on the legs. Silkiness or curliness. A slight wave permissible.
8. Nose—flesh- or light-coloured nose.
9. Colour—white on chest, feet or other parts of body.

Dandie Dinmont Terrier

*I*T IS GENERALLY CONCEDED that the origin of the Dandie Dinmont is unknown. But this has not stopped the theorists who, over the years, have proposed some rather bizarre combinations as the breed's ancestors. The most plausible explanation of the Dandie's origin is that it was developed from the numerous native terrier breeds that abounded in the hill country along the border between Scotland and England, particularly in Coquetdale, an area of Northumberland famous for its terriers.

What is known is that as far back as the 17th century these dogs were owned by several families who lived near Coquetdale and were used to kill badger, fox, and otter. One family in particular, the Allans, is closely associated with the breed. Willy "Piper" Allan, the family head who died in 1704, kept a pack of terriers which, despite handsome offers to buy, he refused to sell. After Piper's death, two generations of Allans kept the strain alive, parting with the occasional dog in exchange for favours received. Presumably a tenant farmer by the name of James Davidson obtained a pair of the Allan dogs, bred them and named each according to its colour: "Mustard" or "Pepper," varying these names with such adjectives as old, young, big, little and so on.

Outside of their local area the terriers were unknown until 1814, when Sir Walter Scott published his novel *Guy Mannering*. In it, one of the characters was patterned after Davidson. Scott called him "Dandie Dinmont" and, like Davidson, he kept a pack of pepper and mustard terriers. Soon the breed, then called the "Pepper and Mustard," was very much in demand. By the time of Davidson's death in 1820 the breed had been renamed the Dandie Dinmont and they were being extensively bred in farms along the border as well as in other parts of England.

So much confusion prevailed as to correct breed points that in 1876 the Dandie Dinmont Terrier Club was formed and a breed standard draughted that, with minor weight changes, remains the same today.

The Dandie Dinmont Terrier was first registered in Canada in the years 1888–1889.

Dandie Dinmont Terrier

Official Breed Standard for the Dandie Dinmont Terrier

Size: The height should be from 8–11 in. (20–28 cm) at the top of the shoulder. Length from top of shoulder to root of tail should not be more than twice the dog's height, but preferably 1–2 in. (3–5 cm) less.

Weight—the preferred weight from 18–24 lb. (8–11 kg). These weights are for dogs in good working condition.

Coat and Colour: The coat is a very important point; the hair should be about 2 in. (5 cm) long; that from skull to root of tail, a mixture of hardish and soft hair, which gives a sort of crisp feel to the hand. The hair should not be wiry; the coat is what is termed piley or pencilled. The hair on the underpart of the body is lighter in colour and softer than on the top. The skin on the belly accords with the colour of dog. The colour is pepper or mustard. The pepper ranges from a dark bluish black to a light silvery grey, the intermediate shades being preferred, the body colour coming well down the shoulder and hips, gradually merging into the leg colour. The mustards vary from a reddish brown to a pale fawn, the head being a creamy white, the legs and feet of a shade darker than the head. The claws are dark as in other colours. (Nearly all Dandie Dinmont Terriers have some white on the chest, and some have also white claws.)

Head: Strongly made and large, not out of proportion to the dog's size, the muscles showing extraordinary development, more especially the maxillary. *Skull* broad between the ears, getting gradually less towards the eyes, and measuring about the same from the inner corner of the eye to back of skull as it does from ear to ear. The forehead well domed. The head is *covered* with very soft silky hair, which should not be confined to a mere topknot, and the lighter in colour and silkier it is the better. Cheeks starting from the ears proportionately with the skull have a gradual taper towards the muzzle. *Muzzle* deep and strongly made, and measures about 3 in. (8 cm) in length, or in proportion to skull as 3 is to 5. It is covered with hair of a little darker shade than the topknot, and of the same texture as the feather of the forelegs. The top of the muzzle is generally bare for about 1 inch (3 cm) from the back part of the nose, the bareness coming to a point towards the eye, and being about 1 inch (3 cm) broad at the nose.

Nose black or dark-coloured. **Mouth** black or dark-coloured inside. Teeth very strong, especially the canines, which are of extraordinary size for such a small dog. The canines fit well into each other, so as to give the greatest available holding and punishing power, and the teeth are level in front, the upper ones very slightly overlapping the under ones. (Many of the finest specimens have a "swine mouth," which is very objectionable, but is not so great an objection as the protrusion of the underjaw.)

Eyes set wide apart, large, full, round, bright, expressive of great determination, intelligence and dignity; set low and prominent in front of the head; colour a rich dark hazel. *Ears* pendulous, set well back, wide apart, and low on the skull, hanging close to the cheek, with a very slight projection at the base, broad at the junction of the head and tapering almost to a point, the forepart of the ear tapering very little—the tapering being mostly on the back part, the forepart of the ear coming almost straight down from its junction with the head to the tip. They should harmonize in colour with the body colour. In the case of a Pepper dog they are covered with a soft straight brownish hair (in some cases almost black). In the case of a Mustard dog the hair should be mustard in colour, a shade darker than the body, but not black. All should have a thin feather of light hair starting about 2 in. (5 cm) from the tip, and of nearly the same colour and texture as the topknot, which gives the ear the appearance of a *distinct point*. The animal is often one or two years old before the feather is shown. The cartilage and skin of the ear should not be thick, but rather thin. Length of ear from 3–4 in. (8–10 cm).

Neck: Very muscular, well developed and strong, showing great power of resistance, being well set into the shoulders.

Forequarters: The forelegs short, with immense muscular development and bone, set wide apart, the chest coming well down between them. The feet well formed *and not flat,* with very strong brown or dark-coloured claws. Bandy legs and flat feet are objectionable. The hair on the forelegs and feet of a Pepper dog should be tan, varying according to the body colour from a rich tan to a pale fawn; of a Mustard dog they are of a darker shade than its head, which is a creamy white. In both colours there is a nice feather, about 2 in. (5 cm) long, rather lighter in colour than the hair on the forepart of the leg.

Body: Long, strong, and flexible; the back rather low at the shoulder, having a slight downward curve and a corresponding arch over the loins, with a very slight gradual drop from top of loins to root of tail; both sides of backbone well supplied with muscle; ribs well sprung and round, chest well developed and let well down between the forelegs.

Hindquarters: The hind legs are a little longer than the forelegs, and are set rather wide apart but not spread out in an unnatural manner, while the feet are much smaller; the thighs are well developed, and the hair of the same colour and texture as the forelegs, but having no feather or dewclaws; the whole claws should be dark; but the claws of all vary in shade according to the colour of the dog's body.

Tail: Rather short, say from 8–10 in. (20–25 cm), and covered on the upper side with wiry hair of darker colour than that of the body, the hair on the underside being lighter in colour and not so wiry, with nice feather about 2 in. (5 cm) long, getting shorter as it nears the tip; rather thick at the root, getting thicker for about 4 in. (10 cm), then tapering off to a point. It should not be twisted or curled in any way, but should come up with a curve like a scimitar, the tip, when excited, being in a perpendicular line with the root of the tail. It should neither be set on too high nor too low. When not excited it is carried gaily, and a little above the level of the body.

Scale of Points:
The relative value of the several points in the standard are apportioned as follows:

Head	10
Eyes	10
Ears	10
Neck	5
Body	20
Tail	5
Legs and feet	10
Coat	15
Colour	5
Size and weight	5
General appearance	5
TOTAL	100

Fox Terrier
(Smooth and Wire)

SINCE THE 15TH CENTURY terriers have been known in Britain, homeland of the Fox Terriers. These have been described as small, sturdy, and game, noted for going to earth for their quarry. With the introduction of fox-hunting in the 18th century, these terriers found their place as useful members of the hunt whose job it was to kill the fox. Thus it was that most of the terriers were bred in hunt kennels and were developed according to the hunt master's preference. A dash of this and a bit of that blood would be added to basic terrier stock. Breeding records were not kept until after the introduction of the championship dog show in the 1860s, so it is impossible to sort out the various breeds that form the ancestry of the Fox Terriers. Educated guesses have it that the white English Terrier, Bulldog, smooth-coated Black and Tan, Greyhound, and Beagle were used to develop the smooth variety, the first fox terrier. This breed was then crossed with the rough-coated Black and Tan Terrier to create the wire-haired variety.

Paintings dating from the mid-18th century depict dogs resembling the fox terrier in both coat types, but it was not until 1860 that any attempt was made to standardize the breed. Smooth fox terriers were introduced to the public at the Birmingham show in 1862 and they quickly won popularity as the working man's favourite. Later the wire-haired made its debut, but until 1878 the two were classified as separate breeds. The smooth was known simply as the Fox Terrier, a sporting breed. The wirehaired was called the Wire-Haired Terrier and classified as a Non-Sporting breed. After the first breed standard was written, both were granted separate terrier classification.

Shortly after its recognition the fox terrier came to America. Most notable import was Ch. Nornay Saddler, a smooth, brought over by James Austin. Saddler was a dominant force in the breed who produced at least one champion in every litter he sired.

Among the first breeds to be recognized by The Canadian Kennel Club, the comparative popularity of the two varieties is

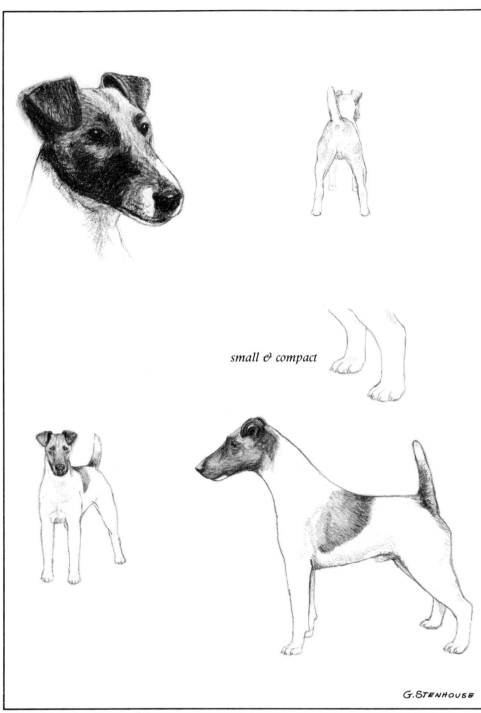

small & compact

G.Stenhouse

Fox Terrier (Smooth)

Fox Terrier (Wire)

evident in registration figures. In the years 1888–1889 there were 180 smooths registered in contrast to fourteen wires. Today those positions are reversed.

Official Breed Standard for the Fox Terrier

SMOOTH

The following shall be the standard of the Fox Terrier amplified in part in order that a more complete description of the Fox Terrier may be presented. The standard itself is set forth in ordinary type, the amplification in italics.

General Appearance: The dog must present a generally gay, lively, and active appearance; bone and strength in a small compass are essentials, but this must not be taken to mean that a Fox Terrier should be cloddy, or in any way coarse—speed and endurance must be looked to as well as power, and the symmetry of the Foxhound taken as a model. The terrier, like the hound, must on no account be leggy, nor must he be too short in the leg. He should stand like a cleverly made hunter, covering a lot of ground, yet with a short back, as before stated. He will then attain the highest degree of propelling power, together with the greatest length of stride that is compatible with the length of his body.

Balance may be defined as the correct proportions of a certain point, or points, when considered in relation to a certain other point or points. It is the keystone of the terrier's anatomy. The chief points for consideration are the relative proportions of skull and foreface; head and back; height at withers and length of body from shoulder-point to buttock—the ideal of proportion being reached when the last two measurements are the same. It should be added that, although the head measurements can be taken with absolute accuracy, the height at withers and length of back and coat are approximate, and are inserted for information of breeders and exhibitors rather than as a hard and fast rule.

Size: Weight is not a certain criterion of a terrier's fitness for his work—general shape, size, and contour are the main points; and if a dog can gallop and stay, and follow his fox up a drain, it matters little what his weight is to 1 lb. (.5 kg) or so. *According to present-day requirements, a full-sized, well-balanced dog should not exceed 15½ in. (39 cm) at the withers, the bitch being proportionately lower—neither should the length of back from withers to root of tail* *exceed 12 in. (30 cm), while, to maintain the relative proportions, the head should not exceed 7¹/₄ in. (18.4 cm) or be less than 7 in. (17.8 cm). A dog with these measurements should scale 18 lb. (8 kg) in show condition—a bitch weighing some 2 lb. (1 kg) less—with a margin of 1 lb. (¹/₂ kg) either way.*

Coat and Colour: The coat should be smooth, flat, but hard, dense and abundant. The belly and underside of the thighs should not be bare. White should predominate; brindle, red, or liver markings are objectionable. Otherwise colour is of little or no importance.

Head: The *skull* should be flat and moderately narrow, gradually decreasing in width to the eyes. Not much stop should be apparent, but there should be more dip in the profile between the forehead and the top jaw than is seen in the case of a Greyhound. The cheeks must not be full. The *jaws*, upper and lower, should be strong and muscular and of fair punishing strength, but not so as in any way to resemble the Greyhound or modern English Terrier. There should not be much falling away below the eyes. This part of the head should, however, be moderately chiselled out, so as not to go down in a straight slope like a wedge. The *nose*, toward which the muzzle must gradually taper, should be black. *It should be noticed that although the foreface should gradually taper from eye to muzzle and should tip slightly at its juncture with the forehead, it should not "dish" or fall away quickly below the eyes, where it should be full and well made up, but relieved from "wedginess" by a little delicate chiselling.* The teeth should be as nearly as possible together, *i.e., the points* of the upper (*incisors*) teeth on the ouside of *or slightly overlapping* the lower teeth. *There should be apparent little difference in length between the skull and foreface of a well-balanced head.* The *eyes* and the rims should be dark in colour, *moderately* small and rather deep-set, full of fire, life and intelligence and as nearly as possible circular in shape. *Anything approaching a yellow eye is most objectionable.* The *ears* should be V-shaped and small; of moderate thickness, and dropping forward close to the cheek, not hanging by the side of the head like a Foxhound. *The topline of the folded ear should be well above the level of the skull.*

Neck: Should be clean and muscular, without throatiness, of fair length, and gradually widening to the shoulders.

Forequarters: Shoulders should be long and sloping, well laid back, fine at the points, and clearly cut at the withers. The forelegs viewed from any direction must be straight with bone strong right down to the feet, showing little or no appearance of ankle in front, and being short and straight in pasterns. Both forelegs and hind legs should be carried straight forward in travelling, the stifles not turning outward. The elbows should hang perpendicularly to the body, working free of the sides.

Body: Back should be short, straight (*i.e.*, level), and strong, with no appearance of slackness. Chest deep and not broad. *Brisket should be deep, yet not exaggerated.* Loin should be very powerful, *muscular* and very slightly arched. The foreribs should be moderately arched, the back ribs deep *and well sprung*, and the dog should be well ribbed up.

Hindquarters: Should be strong and muscular, quite free from droop or crouch; the thighs long and powerful; *stifles well curved and turned neither in nor out;* hocks *well bent* and near the ground *should be perfectly upright and parallel each with the other when viewed from behind,* the dog standing well up on them like a Foxhound, and not straight in the stifle. *The worst possible form of hindquarters consists of a short second thigh and a straight stifle.* Feet should be round, compact, and not large; the soles hard and tough; the toes moderately arched and turned neither in nor out.

Tail: Stern should be set on rather high and carried gaily, but not over the back or curled. It should be of good strength, anything approaching a "pipe-stopper" tail being especially objectionable.

Gait: *Movement, or action, is the crucial test of conformation. The terrier's legs should be carried straight forward while travelling, the forelegs hanging perpendicular and swinging parallel with the sides, like the pendulum of a clock. The principal propulsive power is furnished by the hind legs, perfection of action being found in the terrier possessing long thighs and muscular second thighs well bent at the stifles, which admit of a strong forward thrust or "snatch" of the hocks. When approaching, the forelegs should form a continuation of the straight line of the front, the feet being the same distance apart as the elbows. When stationary, it is often difficult to determine whether a dog is slightly out at shoulder, but, directly he moves, the defect—if it* *exists—becomes more apparent, the forefeet having a tendency to cross, "weave," or "dish." When, on the contrary, the dog is tied at the shoulder, the tendency of the feet is to move wider apart, with a sort of paddling action. When the hocks are turned in—cowhock—the stifles and feet are turned outwards, resulting in a serious loss of propulsive power. When the hocks are turned outwards the tendency of the hind feet is to cross, resulting in an ungainly waddle.*

N.B.—Old scars or injuries, the result of work or accident, should not be allowed to prejudice a terrier's chance in the show ring, unless they interfere with its movement or with its utility for work or stud.

Disqualifications: *Nose white, cherry, or spotted to a considerable extent with either of these colours. Ears prick, tulip, or rose. Mouth much undershot, or much overshot.*

Scale of Points:

Head and ears   15
Neck   5
Shoulders and chest   10
Back and loin   10
Hindquarters   15
Stern   5
Legs and feet   15
Coat   15
Symmetry, size and character   10

> TOTAL   100

WIRE

This variety of the breed should resemble the smooth sort in every respect except the coat, which should be broken. The harder and more wiry the texture of the coat is, the better. On no account should the dog look or feel woolly; and there should be no silky hair about the poll or elsewhere. The coat should not be too long, so as to give the dog a shaggy appearance, but, at the same time, it should show a marked and distinct difference all over from the smooth species.

Irish Terrier

*T*HE IRISH HAS THE DISTINCTION of being the only all-red terrier, and originated, as the name suggests, in Ireland. But how the breed was created is another matter. Dog historians are very unsure in this regard. Its ancestry seems to be linked to that of the Welsh Terrier for it is suggested that both descend from a type of wire-haired black and tan terrier which had been known in Britain since the 17th century. To confirm this is the fact that some black and tan puppies frequently occurred in early litters of Irish Terriers.

When the breed was first introduced fanciers claimed all manner of virtues for the Irishman. And while some exaggeration may have existed in these claims, it is true that the breed is a superb ratter and guard dog which, despite its vermin killing instinct, is also a soft-mouthed retriever of game. In truth it is a breed deserving of its earlier name, the "Irish Sporting Terrier."

Most dog historians begin their accounts of the breed with its introduction to the public at a dog show held in Dublin in 1875. Classes were offered for dogs over and under nine pounds and it is written that the event drew an entry of fifty terriers of all colours and sizes, with and without cropped ears. This heterogeneous gathering caused such a stir among breed fanciers they formed a specialty club and draughted the first breed standard, which remains virtually unchanged today.

The public was quick to take a liking to the Irish Terrier, and within a very few years the breed ranked among the three most popular terrier breeds in Britain. But this was not to last. Commencing in the 1920s, the demand for Irish Terriers moved steadily downward. One breed enthusiast, Gordon Selfridge, owner of one of London's largest department stores, tried to revive interest in the breed by staging an Irish Terrier exhibition in one of his store's departments. Another Irish Terrier supporter, the Duke of Atholl, opened the exhibition; attendants were dressed in Irish national costume and souvenir programmes were given to all visitors. While this gesture did little to restore the Irish Terrier's popularity, it remains a colourful part of the breed's history.

Irish Terrier

The Irish Terrier was first registered in Canada in the years 1888–1889.

Official Breed Standard for the Irish Terrier

General Appearance: This terrier must be active, lithe, and wiry in movement, with great animation; sturdy and strong in substance and bone structure, but at the same time free from clumsiness, for speed, power, and endurance are most essential. The Irish Terrier must be neither cobby nor cloddy, but should be built on lines of speed, with a graceful, racing outline.

Temperament: The Irish Terrier is game and asks no quarter. He is of good temper, most affectionate, and absolutely loyal to mankind. Tender and forebearing with those he loves, this rugged, stout-hearted terrier will guard his master, his mistress, children in his charge, or their possessions, with unflinching courage and with utter contempt of danger or hurt. His life is one continuous and eager offering of loyal and faithful companionship, and devoted, loving service. He is ever on guard, and stands between his house and all that threatens.

Size: The most desirable weight in show condition is 27 lb. (12 kg) for the dog and 25 lb. (11 kg) for the bitch. The height at the shoulder should be approximately 18 in. (46 cm).

The weights herein mentioned are ideal and serve as a guide to both breeder and judge. In the show ring, however, the informed judge readily identifies the oversized or undersized Irish Terrier by its conformation and general appearance. The weights named should be regarded as limit weights, as a rule, but it must be considered that a comparatively small, heavily-built and cloddy dog—which is most undesirable, and not at all typical—may easily be of standard weight, or over it; whereas another Terrier which is long in leg, lacking in substance and built somewhat upon the lines of a Whippet—also undesirable and not at all typical—may be of the exact weight, or under it; therefore, although the standard weights must be borne well in mind, weight is not the last word in judgement. It is of the greatest importance to select, in so far as possible, terriers of moderate and generally accepted size, possessing the other various necessary characteristics.

Coat and Colour: Coat should be dense and wiry in texture, rich in quality, having a broken appearance, but still lying fairly close to the body, the hairs growing so closely and strongly together that when parted with the fingers the skin is hardly visible; free of softness or silkiness, and not so long as to alter the outline of the body, particularly in the hindquarters. At the base of the stiff outer coat there should be a growth of finer and softer hair, differing in colour, termed the undercoat. Single coats, which are without any undercoat, and wavy coats, are undesirable; the curly coat is most objectionable. On the sides of the body the coat is never as harsh as on the back and the quarters, but it should be plentiful and of good texture. Should be whole-coloured; the bright red, red wheaten, or golden red colours are preferable. A small patch of white on the chest, frequently encountered in all whole-coloured breeds, is permissible but not desirable. White on any other part of the body is most objectionable.

Head: Long, but in nice proportion to the rest of the body; the *skull* flat, rather narrow between the ears, and narrowing slightly towards the eyes; free from wrinkle, with the stop hardly noticeable except in profile. The *jaws* must be strong and muscular, but not too full in the cheek, and of good punishing length. The *foreface* must not fall away appreciably between or below the eyes; instead, the modelling should be delicate and in contradistinction, for example, to the fullness of foreface of the Greyhound. An exaggerated foreface, which is out of proportion to the length of the skull from the occiput to the stop, disturbs the proper balance of the head, and is not desirable. Also, the head of exaggerated length usually accompanies oversize or disproportionate length of body, or both, and such conformation is not typical. On the other hand, the foreface should not be noticeably shorter than is the skull from occiput to stop. Excessive muscular development of the cheeks, or bone development of the temples, conditions which are described by the fancier as "cheeky," or "strong in head," or "thick in skull," are objectionable. The "bumpy" or "alligator" head, sometimes described as the "taneous" head, in which the skull presents two lumps of bony structure with or without indentations above the eyes, is unsightly and to be faulted. The hair on the upper and lower jaws should be similar in quality and texture to that on the body, and only of sufficient length to present an appearance of additional strength and finish to the foreface. The profuse, goat-like beard is unsightly and undesirable, and almost invariably it betokens the objectionable linty and silken hair in the coat. *Nose* must be black. Lips should be close and well fitting, almost black in colour. Teeth should be strong and even, white and sound; and neither overshot nor undershot. *Eyes* dark hazel in colour; small, not prominent; full of life, fire and intelligence. The light or yellow eye is most objectionable. *Ears* small and V-shaped; of moderate thickness; set well on the head, and dropping forward closely to the cheek. The ear must be free of fringe, and the hair much shorter and somewhat darker in colour than on the body. A "dead" ear, hound-like in appearance, must be severely penalized. It is not characteristic of the Irish Terrier. An ear which is too slightly erect is undesirable.

Neck: Should be of fair length and gradually widening towards the shoulders; well and proudly carried, and free from throatiness. Generally there is a slight frill in the hair at each side of the neck, extending almost to the corner of the ear.

Forequarters: Shoulders must be fine, long, and sloping well into the back. Legs moderately long, well set from the shoulders, perfectly straight, with plenty of bone and muscle; the elbows working clear of the sides; pasterns short, straight, and hardly noticeable. The feet should be strong, tolerably round, and moderately small; toes arched and turned neither out nor in, with black toenails. The pads should be deep, not hard, but with a pleasing velvety quality and perfectly sound; they must be entirely free from cracks or horny excrescenses. Corny feet, so-called, are to be regarded as an abominable blemish, as a taint which must be shunned. Cracked pads frequently accompany corny growths, and these conditions are more pronounced in hot and dry weather. In damp weather and in winter such pads may improve temporarily, but these imperfections inevitably reappear and the result is unsound feet, a deplorable fault which must be heavily penalized. There seems to be no permanent cure for this condition, and even if a temporary cure were possible, the disease is seldom, if ever, eradicated, and undoubtedly it is transmitted in breeding. The one sure way to avoid corny and otherwise unsound feet is to avoid breeding from dogs or bitches which are not entirely free from this taint.

Body: The body should be moderately long—neither too long nor too short. The short back, so coveted and so appealing in the Fox Terrier, is *not* characteristic of the Irish Terrier. It is objectionable. The back must be symmetrical, strong and straight, and free from an appearance of slackness or "dip" behind the shoulders. The chest should be deep and muscular, but neither full nor wide. The ribs fairly sprung, deep rather than round, with a well-ribbed back. The loin strong and muscular, and slightly arched. The bitch may be slightly longer in appearance than the dog.

Hindquarters: Should be strong and muscular; powerful thighs; hocks near the ground; stifles moderately bent. Cowhocks—that is, where the hocks are turned in, and the stifles and feet turned out, are intolerable. The legs should be free from feather, and covered, like the head, with hair of similar texture to that on the body, but not so long.

Tail: Should be docked, and set on rather high, but not curled. It should be of good strength and substance; of fair length and well covered with harsh, rough hair, and free from fringe or feather. The three-quarters dock is about right.

Gait: Both forelegs and hind legs should move straight forward when travelling; the stifles should not turn outwards.

Disqualifications: *Nose any other colour than black. Mouth much undershot or overshot. Ears cropped. Any other colour than red, golden red, or red wheaten. A small patch of white on the chest is permissible; otherwise particoloured coats disqualify.*

(Breed Standard continued)

Scale of Points:

Head, ears and expression	20
Legs and feet	15
Neck	5
Shoulders and chest	10
Back and loin	5
Hindquarters and stern	10
Coat	15
Colour	10
Size and symmetry	10
TOTAL	100

Negative Points: MINUS

White nails, toes and feet	10
Much white on chest	10
Dark shadings on face	5
Mouth undershot or cankered	10
Coat shaggy, curly, or soft	10
Uneven in colour	5
TOTAL	50

Kerry Blue Terrier

To EXPECT THE HISTORY of this Irish breed to be well documented is to expect the impossible. There is a long period of uncertainty between the year 1588, when ships of the Spanish Armada were wrecked off the coast of Ireland and some elegant Spanish "puddle dogs" swam ashore, and the year 1808 when the first Irish Blue Terrier is mentioned in writings. Nevertheless, it is believed that the shipwrecked dogs interbred with local terriers to found the breed we now call the Kerry Blue. In 1808, it is said that a race of silver blue dogs had been breeding true in County Kerry for 150 years, where they were used for fighting, ratting, controlling such farm pests as badger and rabbit, herding, hunting, guarding the flock and the homestead, even operating the butter churn when there was nothing else to do. Because these were dogs of the humble crofter who was forbidden by law to own sporting hounds, it is suggested that some of the blue dogs' versatility came from Irish Wolfhound and Otterhound blood that had been introduced on the sly.

However the breed was created, after the introduction of dog shows, classes were offered for the dogs in Ireland commencing in 1887. Over the years they were variously classified as "silver-haired Irish Terrier," Irish Terrier (blue) and Blue Terrier (working). This muddled state of affairs continued until 1922 when Mrs. Casey Hewitt of Tralee, one of the breed pioneers who had helped standardize type, introduced the blue terrier to Britain. In that year, ten of the breed were exhibited at Crufts' show in London, the Kerry Blue Terrier Club of England was formed and a breed standard written. At first the Kerry's unkempt appearance was held against him, but once the British had persuaded exhibitors to trim their dogs so they could compete on equal terms with other terrier breeds, the Kerry made a fine account of himself in the show ring. In Ireland the Kerry must still be shown in its natural state, and since 1926 before a dog may be confirmed as a breed champion it must qualify in two working tests. In one it must tackle a badger and

Kerry Blue Terrier

draw it to ground; in the other it must demonstrate its natural hunting ability with rabbit and rat.

The first Kerry Blues came to this continent in 1918. Canadian registrations were first recorded in 1924—1925.

Official Breed Standard for the Kerry Blue Terrier

General Appearance: The typical Kerry Blue Terrier should be upstanding, well knit and in good balance, showing a well-developed and muscular body with definite terrier style and character throughout. A low-slung Kerry is not typical.

Size: The ideal Kerry should be 18½ in. (47 cm) at the withers for a dog, slightly less for a bitch.

In judging Kerries, a height of 18—19½ in. (46—50 cm) for a dog, and 17½—19 in. (44—48 cm) for a bitch should be given primary preference. Only where the comparative superiority of a specimen outside of the ranges noted clearly justifies it, should greater latitude be taken. In no case should it extend to a dog over 20 in. (51 cm) or under 17½ in. (44 cm), or to a bitch over 19½ in. (50 cm) or under 17 in. (43 cm). The minimum limits do not apply to puppies.

Weight—the most desirable weight for a fully developed dog is from 33—40 lb. (15—18 kg), bitches weighing proportionately less.

Coat and Colour: Coat soft, dense, and wavy. A harsh wire or bristle coat should be severely penalized. In show trim, the body should be well covered but tidy, with the head (except for the whiskers) and the ears and cheeks clear.

The correct mature colour is any shade of blue grey or grey blue from deep slate to light blue grey, of a fairly uniform colour throughout except that distinctly darker to black parts may appear on the muzzle, head, ears, tail, and feet.

Kerry colour, in its process of "clearing" from an apparent black at birth to the mature grey blue or blue grey, passes through one or more transitions—involving a very dark blue (darker than deep slate), shades or tinges of brown, and mixtures of these, together with a progressive infiltration of the correct mature colour.

Up to 18 months such deviations from the correct mature colour are permissible without preference and without regard for uniformity. Thereafter, deviation from it to any significant extent must be severely penalized.

Solid black is never permissible in the show ring. Up to 18 months any doubt as to whether a dog is black or a very dark blue should be resolved in favour of the dog, particularly in the case of a puppy. Black on the muzzle, head, ears, tail, and feet is permissible at any age.

Head: Long, but not exaggerated and in good proportion to the rest of the body. Well balanced, with little apparent difference between the length of the skull and foreface. *Skull* flat, with very slight stop, of but moderate breadth between the ears, and narrowing very slightly to the eyes. Cheeks clean and level, free from bumpiness. *Muzzle:* jaws deep, strong and muscular. *Foreface* full and well made up, not falling away appreciably below the eyes but moderately chiselled out to relieve the foreface from wedginess. *Nose* black, nostrils large and wide.

Mouth: teeth strong, white and either level or with the upper (incisors) teeth slightly overlapping the lower teeth. *Eyes* dark, small, not prominent, well placed and with a keen terrier expression. Anything approaching a yellow eye is very undesirable. *Ears* V-shaped, small but not out of proportion to the size of the dog, of moderate thickness, carried forward close to the cheeks with the top of the folded ear slightly above the level of the skull. A "dead" ear, hound-like in appearance, is very undesirable.

Neck: Clean and moderately long, gradually widening to the shoulders upon which it should be well set and carried proudly.

Forequarters: Shoulders fine, long and sloping, well laid back and well knit. Legs moderately long with plenty of bone and muscle. The forelegs should be straight from both front and side view, with the elbows hanging perpendicularly to the body and working clear of the sides in movement, the pasterns short, straight, and hardly noticeable.

Body: Back short, strong, and straight (*i.e.,* level), with no appearance of slackness. Chest deep and of but moderate breadth. Loin short and powerful with a slight tuck-up, the ribs fairly well sprung, deep rather than round.

Hindquarters: Strong and muscular with full freedom of action, free from droop or crouch, the thighs long and powerful, stifles well bent and turned neither in nor out, hocks near the ground and when viewed from behind, upright and parallel with each other, the dog standing well up on them. Feet should be strong, compact, fairly round and moderately small, with good depth of pad free from cracks, the toes arched, turned neither in nor out, with black toenails.

Tail: Should be set on high, of moderate length and carried gaily erect; the straighter the tail the better.

Gait: Both forelegs and hind legs should move straight forward when travelling, the stifles turning neither in nor out.

Faults: An undershot mouth should be strictly penalized.

Disqualifications:
1. *Solid black.*
2. *Faking or dyeing.*
3. *Dewclaws on hind legs.*

Scale of Points:

Head	20
Neck	5
Shoulders and chest	10
Legs and feet	10
Body	10
Hindquarters and stern	10
Colour	10
Coat	15
General conformation and character	10
TOTAL	100

Lakeland Terrier

THE LAKELAND IS A SMALL, working terrier developed in the border county of Cumberland in the north of England. The Lakeland's job was to hunt fox and other vermin that preyed on the farmers' lambs and poultry. Unlike the terriers in the south of England who were used to bolt the fox from its hiding place, the Lakeland was bred to go in for the kill. For this job, strong, punishing jaws were essential. Also, because the little dog accompanied the hunt which usually travelled on foot, the Lakeland needed great stamina and endurance. The dog also needed a slender, agile body to aid him in following the wily fox over rocky ledges and through narrow crevices. It is said that "the body of a Lakeland should be able to follow into any rocky crevice that his head and shoulders can enter."

The background breeding used to create the tough little Lakeland varies with the authority quoted. Breeds suggested include the Border, Bedlington, Fox, Dandie Dinmont, and Old English Black and Tan Terriers. One writer includes the Otterhound.

The breed was also known by a variety of names, these in accordance with the district where the Lakeland was bred. They include Patterdale, Fell, Cumberland and Westmoreland. Small wonder that when the Lakeland was exhibited, it was first classified under the all-embracing title "coloured working terrier." It is said that first specimens were much rougher looking and higher on leg than today's smartly groomed Lakelands.

Prior to World War I some effort was made to organize a breed association but it was not until 1921 that this became a reality. The association's first president was Lord Lonsdale, whose family had been breeding Lakelands for some fifty years.

By 1928 a breed standard had been adopted and in that same year The Kennel Club (England) renamed "the coloured working terrier" the Lakeland Terrier, and granted it official recognition. Three specimens competed at their first championship show at the Crystal Palace, London, in 1928. Succeeding years have seen ever increasing numbers of Lakelands in competition and the breed has accounted for some outstanding show wins both in Britain and on this continent. First Canadian registrations were recorded in 1931.

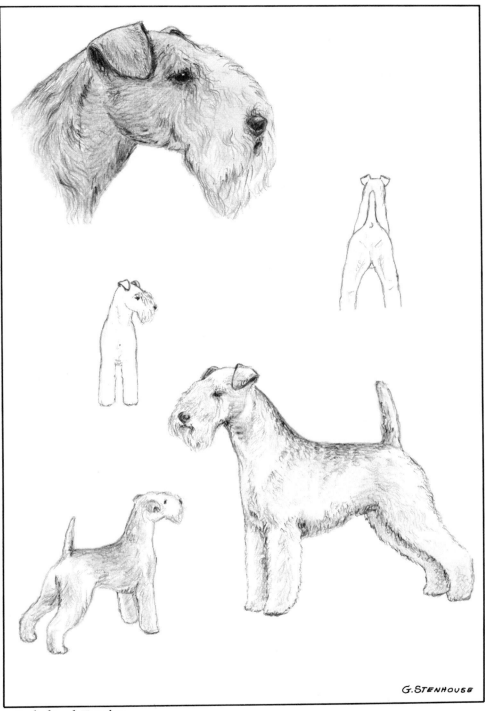

Lakeland Terrier

Official Breed Standard for the Lakeland Terrier

Origin and Purpose: The Lakeland Terrier originated in the early nineteenth century in Cumberland, and was developed by the farmers, using a couple of hounds, as a working terrier to destroy the foxes found raiding the sheepfolds and was known and bred for the qualities of gameness, courage and endurance.

General Appearance: The Lakeland Terrier is a small, workmanlike dog of square, sturdy build and gay, friendly, self-confident demeanour. He stands on his toes as if ready to go, and he moves, lithe and graceful, with a straight-ahead, free stride of good length. His head is rectangular in contour, ears V-shaped, and wiry coat finished off with fairly long furnishings on muzzle and legs.

Temperament: The typical Lakeland Terrier is bold, gay and friendly, with a self-confident cock-of-the-walk attitude. Shyness, especially shy-sharpness in the mature specimen, is to be heavily penalized.

Size: The ideal height of the mature dog is 14½ in. (37 cm) from the withers to the ground, with up to a ½-inch deviation either way permissible. Bitches may measure as much as 1 inch (3 cm) less than dogs. The weight of the well-balanced, mature specimen in hard, show condition, averages approximately 17 lb. (8 kg), those of other heights proportionately more or less.

Size is to be considered of lesser importance than other qualities; that is, when judging dogs of equal merit, the one nearest the ideal size is to be preferred. Symmetry and proportion, however, are paramount in the appraisal, since all qualities together must be considered in visualizing the ideal.

Coat and Colour: Two-ply or double, the outer coat is hard and wiry in texture, the undercoat soft. Furnishings on muzzle and legs are plentiful as opposed to profuse.

The colour may be blue, black, liver, black and tan, blue and tan, red, red grizzle, grizzle and tan, or wheaten. Tan, as desirable in the Lakeland Terrier, is a light wheaten or straw colour, with rich red or mahogany tan to be penalized. Otherwise, colours as specified are equally acceptable. Dark-saddled specimens (whether black grizzle or blue) are nearly solid black at birth, with tan points on muzzle and feet. The black recedes and usually turns greyish or grizzle at maturity, while the tan also lightens.

Head: Well balanced, rectangular, the length of skull equalling the length of the muzzle when measured from occiput to stop and from stop to nosetip. The *skull* is flat on top and moderately broad, the cheeks almost straight-sided, and the stop barely perceptible. *Muzzle* is broad with straight nose bridge and good fill-in beneath the eyes. *Nose* is black, except that liver-coloured noses shall be permissible on liver-coated dogs. *Mouth:* jaws are powerful. The teeth, which are comparatively large, may meet in either a level, edge-to-edge bite, or a slightly overlapping scissors bite. Specimens with teeth overshot or undershot are to be disqualified.

Eyes moderately small and somewhat oval in outline, are set squarely in the skull, fairly wide apart, their normally dark colour may be a warm brown or black. The expression depends upon the dog's mood of the moment. Although typically alert, it may be intense and determined, or gay and even impish. *Ears* are small, V-shaped, their fold just above the top of the skull, the inner edge close to the cheeks, and the flap pointed down.

Neck: Reachy and of good length; refined but strong; clean at the throat, slightly arched and widening gradually into the shoulders. The withers, that point at the back of the neck where neck and body meet, are noticeably higher than the level of the back.

Forequarters: Shoulder blades are sloping, that is, well laid back, their musculature lean and almost flat in outline. Upper and Lower Arm: forelegs are strongly boned, clean and absolutely straight as viewed from the front or side, devoid of appreciable bend at the pasterns. Feet are small, round, the toes compact and well padded, the nails strong. Dewclaws, if any, are to be removed.

Body: In over-all length-to-height proportion, the dog is approximately square. Topline: the back is short and level in topline. Chest moderately narrow, deep; it extends to elbows which are held close to the body. The ribs are well sprung and moderately round. Loins taut and short, although they may be a trifle longer in bitches than in dogs. Croup and Abdomen: quarters are strong, broad and muscular.

Hindquarters: Hip Bone and Upper Thigh: hind legs are strong and sturdy. Lower Thigh long and nicely angulated at the stifles and the hocks. Hocks are well let down, with the bone from hock to toes straight and parallel to each other. Feet small, round (as in forefeet), toes compact and well padded.

Tail: Set high on the body, the tail is customarily docked so that when the dog is set up in show position, the tip of the docked tail is on an approximate level with the skull. In carriage it is gay or upright, although a slight curve in the direction of the head is considered desirable. The tail curled over the back is faulty.

Gait: Movement straight and free, with good length of stride. Paddling, moving close and toeing-in are faulty.

Faults: Shyness, shy-sharpness; soft outer coat, no undercoat; rich red or mahogany tan; lack of balance between skull and muzzle; nose other than black (except in liver-coated dogs); weak jaws; very large or light eyes; poorly placed ears, too short neck, throatiness; steep shoulders, over muscled; weak bone in forelegs, down at pasterns, splay feet; roached or soft back, out at elbows, too wide in front; lack of angulation in hindquarters, cowhocks, feet turning in; low tail-set, tail curled over back; paddling, moving close, toeing-in.

Disqualifications: *The front teeth overshot or undershot.*

Scale of Points:

Head	15
Eyes, ears, expression	15
Neck	5
Body	10
Coat	15
Legs and feet	10
Size and symmetry	10
Movement	10
Temperament	10
TOTAL	100

Manchester Terrier

W‌RITINGS DATING BACK ALMOST 400 years are thought to refer to a breed of English terrier similar to the modern Manchester. Originally called "the black and tan terrier," the Manchester was bred as a "ratting machine," not a show dog. Early specimens were valued more for their working ability than their good looks, and it is reported that the black and tans were rough coated, quick, strong-jawed and generally more rugged in type than the Manchester as it is known today. On farms these terriers were used as barnyard ratters and to control the rabbit population. Apparently this was the extent of their gameness, the breed being unequal to the task of routing the fox or larger predators.

In the days when blood sports flourished the black and tan was highly favoured in the rat pit. Most famous was a dog called Billy, who is on record as having killed 100 large rats in six minutes and thirteen seconds. The dogs' ears were cropped to protect them from painful rat bites.

Two events were to influence the change in breed type and the eventual drop in the black and tan's popularity. The first was the abolition of blood sports in England. The second was the banning of ear cropping in 1895. The ear that took well to cropping gave an ungainly appearance when left natural. To further complicate matters a breed standard was adopted which spelled out precise, compulsory tan markings on an otherwise solid black dog. This made ideal specimens extremely difficult to breed and public favour switched to other terriers. Presumably about this time a whippet cross was introduced to give the black and tan its sleek coat, more refined outline, whip tail and finer head. One of the foremost breeders was Samuel Handley of Manchester, Lancashire. Because of his efforts in stabilizing breed type the name was changed to Manchester, although until his death in 1878 Handley protested that black and tan was a sufficiently honourable name for the breed and that good specimens were being bred in many parts of England.

Manchester Terrier

While the Manchester has never regained its former popularity, it does continue to have a small but loyal following around the world.

The Canadian Kennel Club Stud Book first recorded the Manchester Terrier in 1889 when twenty were registered.

Official Breed Standard for the Manchester Terrier

General Appearance: A terrier calculated to take his own part in the rat pit and not of the Whippet type.

Size: Weight—12–22 lb. (5–10 kg).

Coat and Colour: Coat close, short, and glossy; not soft. Colour black and tan, as distinct as possible; the tan should be a rich mahogany colour. A tan spot over each eye, and another on each cheek, the latter as small as possible; the lips of the upper and lower jaws should be tanned, the tan extending under the jaw to the throat, ending in the shape of the letter V; the inside of the ear is partly tanned; the forelegs tanned to the knee, with a black patch "thumb mark" between the pastern and the knee; the toes have a distinct black mark running up each, called the "pencil mark"; the tan on the hind legs should continue from the pencilling on the feet up the inside of the legs to a little below the stifle joint, and the outside of the legs should be *perfectly black*. There should be tan under tail, and on the vent, but only of such size as to be covered by the tail. In every case the tan should meet the black abruptly.

Head: Narrow, almost flat, with a slight indentation up the forehead, long and tight-skinned. Slightly wedge-shaped, tapering to the nose, and well filled up under the eyes, with tight-lipped jaws. *Nose* should be perfectly black. Level in *mouth*, with no visible cheek muscles. *Eyes* small, bright, and sparkling, set moderately close together, as near black as possible; oblong in shape, slanting upwards on the outside; they should neither protrude nor sink in the skull. *Ears* erect, or button, small and thin; smaller at the root and set as close together as possible at the top of the head. If cropped, to a point, long and carried erect.

Neck: The neck should be slim and graceful, gradually becoming larger as it approaches the shoulders, and perfectly free from throatiness; slightly arched from the occiput.

Forequarters: The shoulders slope off elegantly. Legs perfectly straight, and well under the body; strong, and of proportionate length. Feet compact, split up between the toes, and well arched, with jet-black nails; the two middle toes in the front feet rather longer than the others.

Body: Short, with powerful loins; the back being slightly arched at the loin, and falling again to the joining of the tail to the same height as the shoulder. Chest narrow between the legs, deep in the brisket; ribs well sprung out behind the shoulders.

Hindquarters: The hind feet shaped like those of a cat.

Tail: Should be moderately short, and set on where the arch of the back ends; thick where it joins the body, and gracefully tapering to a point; not carried higher than the back.

Norfolk Terrier

WHATEVER BACKGROUND BREEDING was used to create the Norwich Terrier also applies to the Norfolk. It is assumed that small Irish Terriers were used initially. Later these were crossed with other terrier breeds. Two that are suggested are the Border and the Cairn.

For thirty years two ear types persisted in the Norwich Terrier—the drop and the prick. Both varieties were shown together under the same breed classification and the two varieties were inter-bred. However, it seems that such inter-breeding created problems with ear carriage, and breeders discontinued the practice. Thus only prick-eareds were mated to like, and drop-eareds to drop-eareds. After a few generations of this it became evident that two quite different types of terrier were evolving, and what seemed grossly unfair was that in the show ring the prick-eareds were consistent winners over the "drops." Because of this, supporters of the drop-eareds sought to have this variety recognized as a distinct breed.

In 1963 separate breed standards for the two varieties were submitted to The Kennel Club (England), and two years later separate breed status was granted. The newly recognized breed became known as the Norfolk Terrier.

Like his very close relative, the Norfolk is a game, working terrier that loves horses and the stableyard. These are the smallest of the terriers weighing about eleven pounds (5 kg) and standing about ten inches (25 cm) at the shoulder. It is said that their harsh, wiry, close lying coats make them the ideal companion for those wanting a terrier that stays neat with a minimum amount of grooming attention.

Following Britain's example The Canadian Kennel Club recognized the Norfolk Terrier as a separate breed in 1978.

Norfolk Terrier

Official Breed Standard for the Norfolk Terrier

General Appearance: The Norfolk Terrier is one of the smallest of the Terriers, but a "demon" for its size. Of a lovable disposition, not quarrelsome, with a hardy constitution. A small, low, keen dog, compact and strong with short back, good substance and bone. Honourable scars from fair wear and tear should not be penalized unduly.

Temperament: Alert and fearless.

Size: Ideal height 10 in. (25 cm) at withers.

Coat and Colour: Coat hard, wiry and straight, lying close to the body. It is longer and rougher on the neck and shoulders. Hair on head and ears short and smooth, except for slight whiskers and eyebrows. Colour all shades of red, red wheaten, black and tan, or grizzle. White marks or patches are undesirable but shall not disqualify.

Head: *Skull* wide and slightly rounded with good width between the ears. Stop should be well defined. *Muzzle* wedge-shaped and strong; length of muzzle slightly less than half the length of skull. *Mouth* tight lipped, jaw strong; teeth strong and rather large; scissors bite. *Eyes* oval shaped and deep set, in colour dark brown or black. Expression alert, keen and intelligent. *Ears* medium sized, V-shaped but slightly rounded at tip, dropping forward close to the cheek.

Neck: Medium length and strong.

Forequarters: Clean and powerful shoulders with short, powerful and straight legs.

Body: Compact with short back, level topline, well-sprung ribs.

Hindquarters: Well muscled, good turn of stifle, hocks well let down and straight when viewed from rear; with great powers of propulsion. Feet round with thick pads.

Tail: Medium docked, not excessively gay.

Faults: Any departure from the foregoing points should be considered a fault and the seriousness of the fault should be in exact proportion to its degree.

NOTE: Male animals should have two apparently normal testicles fully descended into the scrotum.

Norwich Terrier

DURING THE MID-19TH CENTURY it became the vogue to create local strains of terriers particularly suited to various districts in England. Each would be of a size, structure, and working ability compatible with local conditions. In this way, it is assumed, the Norwich Terrier—the working terrier of East Anglia—came into being. The interesting point is that while many breeds so created failed to stand the test of time, the Norwich not only survived but from the original breed a second breed now called the Norfolk was derived. It is not known for certain which breeds were used to create the little red terrier but most authorities assume that small specimens of the Irish Terrier played a major role.

What has been recorded is that in the 1870s a breeder by the name of Lawrence did a brisk business in small red terriers, many of which were sold to students of Cambridge University—so many, in fact, that at one time the little dogs were known as Cantab Terriers. Over the years other names have been given them, including Trumpington and Jones Terriers.

As working terriers the little dogs proved their gameness and many were adopted as hunt club favourites. They became dual-purpose dogs that could go to ground for the fox when necessary and act as stableyard and house pet at other times.

The record states that early specimens were of mixed type until about 1914 when a Mr. Fagan became interested in stabilizing breed type. This was achieved by 1923 when the breed became known as the Norwich Terrier and in 1932 it was granted separate breed status by The Kennel Club (England).

At this time both the prick- and drop-eared varieties were classified under the single breed name of Norwich Terrier. In 1936 the breed was recognized in the United States, where both varieties are still known under the single Norwich classification. In Canada, as in Britain, the drop-eared variety now has separate breed status under the name of Norfolk Terrier.

Norwich Terrier

Official Breed Standard for the Norwich Terrier

General Appearance: The Norwich Terrier is one of the smallest of the terriers. Of a lovable disposition, not quarrelsome, tremendously active and with a hardy constitution. A small, low, keen dog, compact and strong with good substance and bone. Honourable scars from fair wear-and-tear should not be penalized unduly.

Temperament: Gay and fearless.

Size: Ideal height 10 in. (25 cm) at withers. This ideal height should not be attained by excessive length of leg.

Coat and Colour: Coat hard, wiry, and straight, lying close to the body with a thick undercoat. Longer and rougher on the neck forming a ruff to frame the face. Hair on head and ears short and smooth, except for slight whiskers and eyebrows. Colour all shades of red, wheaten, black and tan, or grizzle. White marks or patches are undesirable.

Head: *Skull* wide, good width between the ears, and slightly rounded. *Muzzle* wedge-shaped and strong; length about one-third less than a measurement from the occiput to the bottom of the stop, which should be well defined. *Mouth* tight-lipped, jaws clean and strong. Teeth strong, rather large. Scissors bite. *Eyes* small and oval shaped, dark, full of expression, bright and keen. *Ears* erect, set well apart on top of skull. Of medium size with pointed tips. Held perfectly erect when aroused. Can be laid back when not at attention.

Neck: Strong, of good length, commensurate with correct over-all balance, flowing into shoulders.

Forequarters: Shoulders well laid back. Legs short, powerful and straight; elbows close to body. Pasterns firm and upright.

Body: Level topline. Short back, compact body with good depth. Rib cage should be long and well sprung with short loin.

Hindquarters: Broad, strong and muscular, with well-turned stifle. Low-set hock with great powers of propulsion. Feet round, well padded and cat-like. To point straight forward, standing and moving.

Tail: Medium docked. Set on high to complete a perfectly level topline. Carried erect.

Gait: Forelegs should be moving straight forward when travelling. Hind legs should follow in the track of the forelegs when moving, showing the pads and with hocks parallel.

Faults: Any departure from the foregoing points should be considered a fault and the seriousness of the fault should be in exact proportion to its degree.

NOTE: Male animals should have two apparently normal testicles fully descended into the scrotum.

Schnauzer (Miniature)

THERE ARE THREE SIZES of schnauzer, of which the miniature is the smallest and the only one of the three breeds to be classified as a terrier, the other two being classified as working breeds. The miniature was developed in Germany towards the end of the 19th century and is thought to represent a cross between small specimens of the Standard Schnauzer and a toy breed, either the Affenpinscher or the Miniature Pinscher or possibly a bit of both. The oldest known specimen to be registered in Germany was a black female according to the stud book of 1888. Some authorities also claim that the Pomeranian, the Fox Terrier and the Scottish Terrier may have played a part in the breed's ancestry. If so, this would account for the appearance of the occasional "mismark" still said to occur in present-day litters.

The breed name derives from the German word *schnauze* meaning snout or muzzle, or perhaps, more specifically, *schnauzbart* meaning conspicuous moustache, a characteristic with which the schnauzers are all well endowed. Intended to resemble its larger cousins in all respects, the Miniature Schnauzer was first used as a barnyard ratter, an instinct many of the breed still carry although the schnauzer's role today is chiefly that of family pet and watchdog.

The breed was first exhibited as a distinct breed in its country of origin in 1899 but did not make its debut on this continent until 1925. It is from a very small number of dogs imported into the United States between the years 1925–1935 from the continent, mostly from Germany, that the majority of present-day Miniature Schnauzers in Canada and the United States descend. In America the breed was not an overnight success. But in 1946, after a Miniature Schnauzer won Best in Show at a prestigious event, its popularity was assured.

In 1933 a national specialty club was founded in the United States, and in 1951 a similar organization came into being in Canada. First called The Miniature Schnauzer Club of Ontario,

Schnauzer (Miniature)

since 1955 this group has been known as The Miniature Schnauzer Club of Canada.

First official registration took place in Canada under the breed name "Schnauzer-Pinscher" in 1933.

Official Breed Standard for the Schnauzer (Miniature)

General Appearance: The Miniature Schnauzer is a robust, active dog of terrier type, resembling his larger cousin, the Standard Schnauzer, in general appearance, and of an alert, active disposition. He is sturdily built, nearly square in proportion of body length of height, with plenty of bone, and without any suggestion of toyishness. Faults: Type-Toyishness, raciness, or coarseness.

Temperament: The typical Miniature Schnauzer is alert and spirited, yet obedient to command. He is friendly, intelligent and willing to please. He should never be over-aggressive or timid. Faults: Temperament—shyness or viciousness.

Size: From 12–14 in. (30–36 cm).

Coat: Double, with hard, wiry, outer coat and close under-coat. Head, neck, and body coat must be plucked. When in show condition the body coat should be of sufficient length to determine texture. Close covering on neck, ears, and skull. Faults: Coat too soft or too smooth and slick in appearance.

Colour: The recognized colours are salt and pepper, black and silver, and solid black. The typical colour is salt and pepper in shades of grey; tan shading is permissible. The salt and pepper mixture fades out to light grey or silver white in the eyebrows, whiskers, cheeks, under throat, across chest, under tail, leg furnishings, under body, and inside legs. The light underbody hair is not to rise higher on the sides of the body than the front elbows.

The black and silvers follow the same pattern as the salt and peppers. The entire salt and pepper section must be black.

Black is the only solid colour allowed. It must be a true black with no grey hairs and no brown tinge except where the whiskers may have become discoloured. A small white spot on the chest is permitted, not to exceed one inch in diameter.

Head: Strong and rectangular, its width diminishing slightly from ears to eyes, and again to the tip of the nose. The forehead is unwrinkled. The top *skull* is flat and fairly long. The foreface is parallel to the top skull, with a slight stop; and it is at least as long as the top skull. The *muzzle* is strong in proportion to the skull; it ends in a moderately blunt manner, with thick whiskers which accentuate the rectangular shape of the head. Faults: Head coarse and cheeky.

The teeth meet in a scissors bite. That is, the upper front teeth overlap the lower front teeth in such a manner that the inner surface of the upper incisors barely touches the outer surface of the lower incisors when the mouth is closed. Faults: Bite— undershot or overshot jaw. Level bite.

Eyes: small, dark brown and deep-set. They are oval in appearance and keen in expression. Faults: Eyes—light and/or large and prominent in appearance or excessively small.

Ears: when cropped, the ears are identical in shape and length, with pointed tips. They are in balance with the head and not exaggerated in length. They are set high on the skull and carried perpendicularly at the inner edges, with as little bell as possible along the outer edges. When uncropped, the ears are small and V-shaped, folding close to the skull.

Neck: Strong and well arched, blending into the shoulders, and with the skin fitting tightly at the throat.

Forequarters: The forequarters have flat, somewhat sloping shoulders and high withers. Forelegs are straight and parallel when viewed from all sides. They have strong pasterns and good bone. They are separated by a fairly deep brisket which precludes a pinched front. The elbows are close, and the ribs spread gradually from the first rib so as to allow space for the elbows to move close to the body. Faults: Loose elbows.

Body: Short and deep, with the brisket extending at least to the elbows; ribs are well sprung and deep, extending well back to a short loin. The underbody does not present a tucked up appearance at the flank. The topline is straight; it declines slightly from the withers to the base of the tail. The over-all length from chest to stern bone appears to equal the height at the withers. Faults: Chest too broad or shallow in brisket. Sway or roach back.

Hindquarters: The hindquarters have strong-muscled, slanting thighs; they are well bent at the stifles and straight from hock to so-called heel. There is sufficient angulation so that, in stance, the hocks extend beyond the tail. The hindquarters never appear overbuilt or higher than the shoulders. Feet short and round (cat feet) with thick, black pads. The toes are arched and compact. Faults: Bowed or cowhocked hindquarters.

Tail: Set high and carried erect. It is docked only long enough to be clearly visible over the topline of the body when the dog is in proper length of coat. Faults: Tail-set low.

Gait: The trot is the gait at which movement is judged. When approaching, the forelegs, with elbows close to the body, move straight forward, neither too close nor too far apart. Going away, the hind legs are straight and travel in the same planes as the forelegs.

NOTE: It is generally accepted that when a full trot is achieved, the rear legs continue to move in the same planes as the forelegs, but a very slight inward inclination will occur. It begins at the point of the shoulder in front and at the hip joint in the rear. Viewed from the front or rear, the legs are straight from these points to the pads. The degree of inward inclination is almost imperceptible in a Miniature Schnauzer that has correct movement. It does not justify moving close, toeing-in, crossing, or moving out at the elbows.

Viewed from the side, the forelegs have good reach, while the hind legs have strong drive, with good pickup of hocks. The feet turn neither inward nor outward. Faults: Sidegaiting. Paddling in front, or high hackney knee action. Weak rear action.

Faults: Toyishness, raciness, or coarseness. Shyness or viciousness. Coat too soft or too smooth and slick in appearance. Head coarse and cheeky. Undershot or overshot jaw. Level bite. Eyes light and/or large and prominent in appearance or excessively small. Loose elbows. Chest too broad or shallow in brisket. Sway or roach back. Bowed or cowhocked hindquarters. Tail-set low.

Sidegaiting. Paddling in front, or high hackney knee action. Weak rear action.

Disqualifications: *Dogs or bitches under 12 in. (30 cm) or over 14 in. (36 cm). Colour solid white or white patches on the body.*

Scottish Terrier

*I*F EVER THERE WAS A TIME when small terriers did not abound in Scotland, it has not been recorded.

They were true working dogs, whose job it was to rout such vermin as the fox, otter, and wild cat, and because of their efficiency and gameness the terriers were highly regarded as gamekeepers' helpers.

The first writers to describe these dogs under the broad name "Scotch Terriers" wrote that they were of two distinct types: one being rather high on leg with a short, smooth coat; the other short-legged with a rough coat. Colours ranged from white through wheaten to black. It is from the latter type that particular strains and later distinct breeds of terriers were developed. Each was bred for a specific purpose and thus acquired unique characteristics and conformation. Today we know them as the Cairn, the West Highland White and Scottish Terriers. But it took several years before the three were sorted out, agreement on breed names achieved, and uniformity of type established.

The sorting out process began with the advent of the dog show in 1859. The following year at the Birmingham event in the north of England the Scotch terriers were first exhibited under a variety of names. These included the Roughhaired, Paisley, Highland, Aberdeen, and to add to the confusion, the Skye. The most persistent of these was Aberdeen because many of the early winners were exhibited by a breeder from Aberdeen.

Eventually some order was brought to bear and in 1881 the name "Hard-Haired Scotch Terrier" was agreed to by breed supporters. The following year a specialty club was formed in Scotland and in 1883 the first breed standard was adopted. Later the breed name was revised to the present one.

Evidently Canada was the first country on this side of the Atlantic to import the Scottish Terrier. The first Scotty to be registered in America was a Canadian-bred whelped in April 1881. The dog's name was Prince Charlie and he was bred by D. O'Shea of London, Ontario.

The first Canadian Kennel Club Stud Book (1888–1889) records that five Scottish Terriers were registered.

*planes should
be parallel*

G.STENHOUSE

Scottish Terrier

Official Breed Standard for the Scottish Terrier

General Appearance: The face should wear a keen, sharp, and active expression. Both head and tail should be carried well up. The dog should look very compact, well muscled and powerful, giving the impression of immense power in a small size.

Size: Equal consideration must be given to height, length of back and weight. Height at shoulder for either sex should be about 10 in. (25 cm). Generally, a well-balanced Scottish Terrier dog of correct size should weigh from 19—22 lb. (9—10 kg), and a bitch, from 18—21 lb. (8—9.5 kg). The principal objective must be symmetry and balance.

Coat and Colour: Coat rather short, about 2 in. (5 cm), dense undercoat with outer coat intensely hard and wiry. Colour steel or iron grey, brindled or grizzled, black, sandy or wheaten. White markings are objectionable and can be allowed only on the chest and that to a slight extent only.

Head: *Skull* long, of medium width, slightly domed and covered with short, hard hair. It should not be quite flat, as there should be a slight stop or drop between the eyes. *Muzzle* in proportion to the length of skull, with not too much taper towards the nose. *Nose* should be black and of good size. The jaws should be level and square. The nose projects somewhat over the mouth, giving the impression that the upper jaw is longer than the lower. The teeth should be evenly placed, having a scissors or level bite, with the former being preferable. *Eyes* set wide apart, small and of almond shape, not round. Colour to be dark brown or nearly black. To be bright, piercing, and set well under the brow. *Ears* small, prick, set well up on the skull, rather pointed but not cut. The hair on them should be short and velvety.

Neck: Moderately short, thick and muscular, strongly set on sloping shoulders, but not so short as to appear clumsy.

Forequarters: Shoulders sloping. Both forelegs and hind legs should be short and very heavy in bone in proportion to the size of the dog. Forelegs straight or slightly bent with elbows close to the body. Scottish Terriers should not be out at the elbows.

Body: Moderately short and well ribbed up, chest broad and very deep, well let down between the forelegs. Loin strong, flanks deep.

Hindquarters: Very muscular. Stifles should be well bent and legs straight from hock to heel. Thighs very muscular. Feet round and thick with strong nails, forefeet larger than the hind feet.

Tail: Never cut and about 7 in. (18 cm) long, carried with a slight curve but not over the back.

Gait: The gait of the Scottish Terrier is peculiarly its own and is very characteristic of the breed. It is not the square trot or walk that is desirable in the long-legged breeds. The forelegs do not move in exact parallel planes—rather in reaching out incline slightly inward. This is due to the shortness of leg and width of chest. The action of the rear legs should be square and true and at the trot both the hocks and stifles should be flexed with a vigorous motion.

Faults: Soft coat, round or very light eye, overshot or under-shot jaw, obviously oversize or undersize, shyness, timidity, or failure to show with head and tail up are faults to be penalized. No judge should put to Winners or Best of Breed any Scottish Terrier not showing real terrier character in the ring.

Scale of Points:

Skull	5
Muzzle	5
Eyes	5
Ears	10
Neck	5
Chest	5
Body	15
Legs and feet	10
Tail	2 1/2
Coat	15
Size	10
Colour	2 1/2
General appearance	10
TOTAL	100

Sealyham Terrier

IN THE MID-19TH CENTURY in Pembrokeshire, Wales, a sportsman by the name of Captain John Edwardes set out to develop his ideal of the perfect working terrier, one that performed equally well as a hunt terrier in company with Edwardes' pack of Otterhounds and as a vermin router that was small enough to slip down a badger hole.

Edwardes kept no records of the breeds he used to create the Sealyham—so named after his family's Wales estate. Nor did he imagine that his terrier would become a recognized breed destined to achieve great honour in the show ring. His only concern was to develop an uncommonly game terrier and, to this end, young dogs had to survive harsh testing before Edwardes considered them acceptable.

Thus the breeds used to develop the courageous Sealyham remain a matter of guesswork. Those assumed to be included in the breed's ancestry are the Welsh Corgi, Flanders Basset, Dandie Dinmont, Bull, West Highland White, Wire Fox, and Old English White Terriers.

After Edwardes' death in 1891 others took up the cause of the Sealyham. Most significant was the work done by Fred Lewis, who is regarded as the father of the breed. It was Lewis who founded the Sealyham Club in Britain in 1908, an organization which was successful in gaining official breed recognition from The Kennel Club (England) in 1911. In that same year the Sealyham was also accorded breed status by the American Kennel Club. The first registration of a Sealyham Terrier in Canada is recorded in The Canadian Kennel Club Stud Book for the years 1916–1917 when one individual was registered.

Although still not seen in great numbers at championship shows on this continent, the quality of the entry remains high.

Sealyham Terrier

G.STENHOUSE

Official Breed Standard for the Sealyham Terrier

Origin and Purpose: The Sealyham Terrier was originally developed in the region of Haverfordwest in South Wales for the purpose of digging out badger and fox and later was used in otter-hunting also. His short legs were ideal for "going to earth" and his rough coat protected him against attack by his prey.

General Appearance: The Sealyham should be the embodiment of power and determination, ever keen and alert, of extraordinary substance, yet free from clumsiness.

Temperament: As well as a keen, reliable, hunting terrier, the Sealyham makes an ideal companion and pet.

Size: Height at withers about $10\frac{1}{2}$ in. (26 cm).
Weight—23−24 lb. (10−11 kg) for dogs, bitches slightly less. It should be borne in mind that size is more important than weight.

Coat and Colour: Coat weather-resisting, comprised of soft, dense undercoat and hard, wiry topcoat. Silky or curly coat a bad fault. Colour: all white, or with lemon, tan or badger markings on head and ears. Heavy body markings and excessive ticking should be discouraged.

Head: Long, broad and powerful, without coarseness. It should, however, be in perfect balance with the body, joining neck smoothly. Length of head roughly three-quarters height at withers, or about an inch longer than neck. Breadth between ears a little less than one-half length of head. *Skull* very slightly domed, with a shallow indentation running down between the brows, and joining the muzzle with a moderate stop. *Muzzle:* cheeks smoothly formed and flat, without heavy jowls. Jaws powerful, square. *Nose* black, with large nostrils. White, cherry, or butterfly bad faults. *Mouth:* bite level or scissors. Overshot or undershot bad faults. Teeth sound, strong and white, with canines fitting closely together. *Eyes* very dark, deeply set and fairly wide apart, of medium size, oval in shape with keen terrier expression. Light, large, or protruding eye bad faults. *Ears* folded level with top of head, with forward edge close to cheek. Well rounded at tip, of length to reach outer corner of eye. Thin, not leathery, and of sufficient thickness to avoid creases. Prick, tulip, rose, or hound ears bad faults.

Neck: Length slightly less than two-thirds of height of dog at withers. Muscular without coarseness, with good reach, refinement at throat, set firmly on shoulders.

Forequarters: Shoulders well laid back and powerful, but not over-muscled. Sufficiently wide to permit freedom of action. Upright or straight shoulder placement highly undesirable. Upper and Lower Arm: forelegs strong, with good bone, and as straight as is consistent with chest being well let down between them.

Pasterns: down on pasterns, knuckled over, bowed and out at elbow bad faults. Feet large but compact, round with thick pads, strong nails. Toes well arched and pointing straight ahead. Forefeet larger, though not quite so long as hind feet. Thin, spread or flat feet bad faults.

Body: Topline level, neither roached nor swayed. Length from withers to set-on of tail should approximate height at withers, or 10½ in. (26 cm). Any deviations from these measurements undesirable. Chest: brisket deep and well let down between forelegs. Ribs well sprung. Loin, croup, abdomen strong, short-coupled and substantial, so as to permit great flexibility.

Hindquarters: Hind legs longer than forelegs and not so heavily boned. Hip Bone protruding well behind the set-on of tail. Upper Thigh—very powerful. Lower Thigh—strong second thighs. Hocks well let down. Cowhocks bad fault. Stifles well bent. Feet compact, longer than forefeet, thick pads, strong nails. Thin, spread, or flat feet bad faults.

Tail: Docked and carried upright. Set on far enough forward so that spine does not slope down to it.

Gait: Action sound, strong, quick, free, true, and level.

Faults: Silky or curly coat; heavy body markings and excessive ticking; lack of balance and proportion in head; cheekiness, heavy jowls; white, cherry, or butterfly nose; overshot or undershot; light, large or protruding eyes; prick, tulip, rose, or hound ears; coarseness at neck; upright or straight shoulders; poor bone in forelegs; down on pasterns, knuckled over, bowed out at elbow; small, thin, spread or flat feet; roached or sway back; too short or too long back; shallow chest; weak hindquarters, cowhocks, straightness in stifle; low tail-set; lack of drive in gait.

Scale of Points:

General character, balance and size	15	15
Head	5	
Eyes	5	
Mouth	5	
Ears	5	
Neck	5	25
Shoulders and brisket	10	
Body, ribs and loin	10	
Hindquarters	10	
Legs and feet	10	
Coat	10	50
Tail	5	
Colour (body marking and ticking)	5	10
TOTAL		100

Skye Terrier

*A*S EARLY AS THE sixteenth century a dog fitting the Skye Terrier's description was written of by Dr. Caius, master of Gonville and Caius College, Cambridge University. But, despite the fact that the Skye is one of the oldest breeds in existence, little factual information as to its origin is available. Suffice it to say that for several hundreds of years the sturdy, short-legged dog with the long, lank hair has been known in the Western Islands of Scotland as an efficient, fearless vermin catcher. How the breed got to these islands in the first place remains in doubt.

Most writers agree that the Skye is a member of that family of dogs once known as the "Terriers of Scotland." Being protected from crossbreeding because of its remote island habitat, this member of the family evolved into a distinct breed ideally suited to its environment. Known originally as the Terrier of the Western Islands, its name was later changed to the Skye Terrier.

In addition to being a true working terrier, the Skye was much favoured as a house pet by the Scottish lairds. It has been called "the Heavenly breed" and appears in numerous paintings of Landseer, the renowned animal artist.

From 1842 onwards the breed became a favourite of Queen Victoria and greater public acceptance followed. By 1877 the breed had arrived on this continent, but the first registration, of a dog named Romach, was not until 1887. There were seven Skyes registered in Canada in 1889 and most notable among the earliest exhibitors was a Mr. Caverhill of Montreal. Up until 1890 the majority of Skyes were of the drop-eared type, but after this time, the erect ear came into vogue. Although both types of ear are correct according to the breed standard preference for the erect ear has continued.

The most notable Canadian breeder of Skyes was the late Mrs. Percy Adams who owned her first Skye, Oban Jock, in 1904. Five years later she imported a breeding pair from Scotland who were to found the famous "Talisker" line which remained dominant in the breed in Canada and the U.S. for over fifty years.

Skye Terrier

Official Breed Standard for the Skye Terrier

General Appearance: An alert terrier with great style, elegance and dignity, gay with friends and reserved with strangers. A working terrier, capable of overtaking its game and going to ground, displaying stamina, courage, strength and agility. Must be of a size suitable for its work. Strong in body, quarters, and jaws. Of good bone and hard muscle. Neither slight, heavy, lethargic, or nervous. Hair on head and body should be of such length and texture to protect it in the brush and in a serious argument. Long, low and lank. Level back. Flattish appearance to sides. Strong head. Dark eyes, full of life and intelligence. Ears prick or drop. Graceful neck. Straight front and rear, with hindquarters moderately angulated. Feathered tail. Hard, straight, 5½ in. (14 cm) outercoat, well furnished on ears, face and tail; any colour so long as muzzle is dark. A good mover. Ideal height for male 10 in. (25 cm), for female 9½ in. (24 cm) and length measured chest over tail at rump, twice the height.

Temperament: Fearless, good-tempered, loyal and canny; never shy or ill-tempered.

Size: Ideal measurements—dogs, height at shoulder 10 in. (25 cm); length, chest bone over tail at rump 20 in. (51 cm); head, 8½ in. (22 cm); tail 9 in. (23 cm). Bitch, height at shoulder 9½ in. (24 cm); length, chest bone over tail at rump 19 in. (48 cm); head, 8 in. (20 cm); tail 8½ in. (22 cm).

A slightly higher or lower dog of either sex is acceptable, providing body, head, and tail dimensions are proportionately longer or shorter. It should be noted that the ideal ratio of body length to shoulder height is 2 to 1.

The height and length measurements should be taken with the Skye standing in a natural position with the feet well under it. A box caliper is used, vertically and horizontally. For the height, the top bar should be across the back at the highest point of the withers. The head is measured from the tip of the nose to the back of the occipital bone, and the tail from its root to tip.

Coat and Colour: Coat double. Undercoat short, close, soft and woolly. Outercoat 5½ in. (14 cm) with no extra credit for any greater length. Hard, straight and flat. Body coat hanging straight down each side, parting from head to tail. Hair on head shorter, softer and veiling forehead and eyes, with moderate beard and apron. On ears, overhanging inside, falling down and mingling with side locks, surrounding the ears like a fringe and allowing their shape to appear.

Any colour, including but not limited to black, dark or light blue, grey, fawn, or cream. Shade of head and legs should approximate that of body. In dogs of all colours, muzzle, ears, and tip of tail are preferably dark.

Head: Should be long and powerful, with slight stop, but never coarse. Strength should not be sacrificed for extreme length. Moderate width at back of skull tapering gradually to a strong muzzle. *Muzzle* dark and nose always black. Powerful jaws and mouth, incisor teeth closing level or upper teeth just fitting over lower. *Eyes* brown, preferably dark brown. Medium size, close set, full of life and intelligence. *Ears* (prick or drop) gracefully feathered and symmetrical. When prick, not large, erect at outer edges and slightly wider apart at peak than at skull; should be placed high on skull. When drop, placed lower on head; larger ears are permitted and they should hang flat against the skull.

Neck: Long and gracefully arched.

Forequarters: Straight front. Good layback of shoulders with tight placement of shoulder blades at withers. Elbows close to body. Legs short, muscular and straight.

Body: Pre-eminently long and low. Back level. Chest deep. Ribs a deep oval giving a flattish appearance to sides.

Hindquarters: Full, well developed and moderately angulated. Legs short, muscular and straight when viewed from behind. No dewclaws. Large hare feet, pointing forward. Pads thick. Nails strong and preferably black.

Tail: When hanging, upper section pendulous, and following line of rump; lower section thrown back in a gentle arc. When raised, a prolongation of the line of the back. Though not preferred, sometimes carried high when happy, excited, or angry. When this is a matter of spirit, not conformation, no penalty should follow. Well feathered.

Gait: The legs should be carried straight forward when travelling. When approaching, the forelegs should form a continuation of the straight line of the front, without paddling or weaving, the feet being the same distance apart as the elbows. The principal propelling power is furnished by the hind legs and should be straight forward without weaving. The whole movement should be fluid without waddle or bounce. Movement is important in a Skye Terrier since conformation may be concealed by a profuse coat. Therefore, the dog must be in motion to reveal its true conformation.

Faults: Dogs at shoulder over 12 in. (30 cm) and bitches over 11$\frac{1}{2}$ in. (29 cm). Dogs under 8 in. (20 cm) and bitches under 7$\frac{1}{2}$ in. (19 cm). These measurements are definite limits and any height over or under is to be considered a very serious fault.

Any softness or curl of outercoat. A single or sparse coat. Lack of ear or face curtains.

Short, weak or coarse head. Snipey muzzle. Nose any colour other than black. Wry mouth. Undershot or overshot jaw. Light- or yellow-coloured eyes. Ears that are not symmetrical. Prick ears that are low set. Semi-prick ears. Drop-ears with a lift. Lazy carriage of prick ears. Short neck.

Fiddle front or out at elbows. Straight shoulders. Shoulder blades wide apart at withers. Weak or crooked front legs. High on leg or cobbiness. Sway back or roach back. Shallow or barrel chest.

Weak hindquarters. Straight stifles. Weak or crooked hind legs as viewed from behind. Cowhocks. Dewclaws on hind legs. Splay, paper, or cat-foot.

Tail with twist or curl or continuously carried above the line of the back. Tail poorly feathered.

Scale of Points:

BODY
Back and neck. Chest and ribs.
Forequarters and hindquarters. Feet. Movement 40

HEAD
Skull. Jaws and teeth. Eyes and ears 20

SIZE
Dog: height at shoulder 10 in. (25 cm).
Length, chest bone over tail at rump 20 in. (51 cm).
Head 8½ in. (22 cm) and tail 9 in. (23 cm).
Bitch: height at shoulder 9½ in. (24 cm).
Length, chest bone over tail at rump 19 in. (48 cm).
Head 8 in. (20 cm). Tail 8½ in. (22 cm).
A slightly higher or lower dog of either sex, providing body,
head and tail are proportionately longer or shorter 15

COAT
Outercoat hard and straight with a length of 5½ in. (14 cm),
with no extra credit for any greater length.
Undercoat short, close, soft and woolly 15

TAIL
Carriage and feather 10

                          TOTAL 100

Soft-Coated Wheaten Terrier

YOU COULD CALL THE Soft-Coated Wheaten Terrier the breed that was almost forgotten—not that it wasn't well known, and had been for more than 200 years. Wheatens abounded on farms throughout Ireland because at one time only the aristocracy was permitted by law to own hunting dogs. So the cotters had to settle for native terriers who earned their keep as the poor man's hunting dog, vermin killer, herder, watchdog, and family pet. But the farmers had no interest in such things as seeking official breed status or competing with their shaggy, wheaten-coloured terriers at dog shows.

Puppies were whelped and reared on the "survival of the fit" principle which meant little human care. And thus a robust, healthy breed evolved. There was certainly no shortage of willing wheaten mates for the sole survivor of a shipwreck, a large blue dog who found a home in County Kerry. This cross was the start of the Irish terrier breed called the Kerry Blue which gained fame and popularity long before anyone noticed one of its progenitors—the wheaten. It is claimed that occasionally a light-coloured puppy would appear in a litter of dark-coated Kerries, attesting to its wheaten ancestry. The last such incident was reported in 1945.

The wheaten was not to remain unnoticed forever. In 1932 at a terrier match the breed attracted a group of fanciers who decided to do something for the shaggy dogs. A club was formed and the dog given the name of the Irish Wheaten Terrier. This was too similar to Irish Terrier, a breed already recognized, so it was changed to the present name. In 1937 the breed first appeared on exhibition in Ireland at a championship show and later that year the Soft-Coated Wheaten was placed on the list of native Irish breeds. In 1938 wheatens were permitted to compete at championship events as a distinct breed. At first the breed was shown in a completely natural state. Then, after several years of arguing the point, fanciers agreed to show wheatens in the now familiar scissored trim.

pups may have black tipping

G. STENHOUSE

Soft-Coated Wheaten Terrier

The breed was rather slow in gaining recognition outside its country of origin. In 1973 the American Kennel Club accepted the Soft-Coated Wheaten and added its name to the official roster followed in 1975 by The Kennel Club in England and in 1978 by The Canadian Kennel Club.

Official Breed Standard for the Soft-Coated Wheaten Terrier

Origin and Purpose: The Soft-Coated Wheaten Terrier originated in Ireland. It was an all-purpose working farm dog used for destroying vermin, hunting small animals and guarding against intruders.

General Appearance: The Soft-Coated Wheaten Terrier is a medium-sized, hardy, well-balanced sporting terrier, covered abundantly with a soft, wavy coat of clear wheaten colour. The breed requires moderation in all points and any exaggerated features are to be shunned. The Soft-Coated Wheaten Terrier should present a square outline with an over-all appearance of a strong, well co-ordinated, happy animal.

Temperament: Good tempered, spirited and game. Affectionate and loyal. Alert and intelligent. Defensive without aggression. He does not start a fight, but should always stand his ground; exhibits less aggressiveness than is sometimes encouraged in other terriers.

Size: Ideal height for males is 18½ in. (47 cm); for bitches 17½ in. (44 cm). Ideal weight for males is 35–40 lb. (16–18 kg), for bitches 30–35 lb. (14–16 kg).

Coat and Colour: Abundant, single coated, soft textured and wavy, showing no trace of woolliness or harshness at maturity. The hair does not shed. Colour is pale gold to warm honey. Some dark shading may be found on the ears and muzzle, but should not be present in the body coat. Latitude in coat colour must be given to dogs less than twenty-four months of age. For show purposes the coat should be trimmed to present a neat outline.

The head, with the exception of the fall and beard, should be trimmed to present a rectangular outline and should be in balance with the rest of the body. The ears should be relieved of fringe, but not taken down to the leather. The tail should be trimmed enough to be tidy. Overstylizing is to be penalized.

Head: Well balanced and moderately long with *skull* and foreface of equal length and in good proportion to the body. The skull is flat and not too wide. Cheeks are clean; moderate stop. The *muzzle* is square, powerful and strong, with no suggestion of snipiness. The *nose* is black and large for the size of the dog. Lips are tight and black. Teeth are strong and white, meeting in a scissors or level bite with scissors preferred. The *eyes* are dark hazel or brown, medium sized and well protected under a strong brow. Eye rims are black. Coat should fall forward over the eyes. The *ears* are small to medium in size, breaking level with the skull, and dropping slightly forward, close to the cheeks, pointing to the ground rather than the eye. "Rose" or "flying" ears are objectionable.

Neck: Medium in length and set well upon the shoulders, sloping into the back.

Forequarters: The Soft-Coated Wheaten Terrier should have good reach in front. The shoulders should be well laid back at a 45-degree angle with a clean smooth appearance. The forelegs are straight when viewed from all angles and are well boned and muscled. Dewclaws should be removed. Feet are round and compact with good depth of pad. Nails are dark, pads black.

Body: The body is compact. The chest is deep but not round. The ribs are well sprung. The back is strong with relatively short coupling. The anatomical slope of the croup is 10 degrees, but with muscle fill-in must appear level.

Hindquarters: The Soft-Coated Wheaten Terrier requires good drive from behind, so requires a strong, well-muscled rear assembly. The legs should be well developed with powerful muscles, well-bent stifles, turning neither in nor out. The hocks are well let down and parallel when viewed from behind. Dewclaws on rear legs must be removed. The nails are dark.

Tail: The tail is docked so that half to two-thirds of its original length remains. It is high set, carried gaily but never over the back.

Gait: The gait is free, graceful and lively, having good reach in front and strong drive from behind, straight action fore and aft.

Faults: Coat texture deviations, any colour other than wheaten (with latitude given to young dogs), black hairs throughout the body coat, cowhocks, shuffling, crabbing, roach or slack back, poor pigment, snipey muzzle, rose or flying ears, overstylizing of the coat.

Disqualifications: *Over or undershot mouth, over aggression, nose not solid black, yellow, or light eyes.*

Staffordshire Bull Terrier

*T*HE STAFFORDSHIRE BULL TERRIER is acknowledged to be a British breed dating back at least 175 years. However, because breeding records of that time were virtually non-existent, the exact breeds that were combined to create the Staff are unknown. Courage, not show points or pedigrees, was all that mattered to the dogs' breeders, for the Staff was bred to be a fighter even as late as 1930, well after the time when dog fighting had been outlawed in Britain. Fortunately, times have changed. Although the Staff will rise to the occasion if provoked no breed is more tractable or more trustworthy with children.

While facts as to his heritage are few, dog historians believe that the breed descends from the mastiff of ancient times, of which there were two types—a large and a small. From the latter, it is thought, came the Old English Bulldog which when crossed with one or more terrier breeds, produced the Bull and Terrier, the dog which is today called the Staffordshire Bull Terrier. This is not entirely conjecture on the part of the historians. If old-time breeders were careless record keepers they left behind them enough portraits and drawings of their more noteworthy dogs to give credence to this reasoning.

Early in the 1930s and perhaps, as one writer suggests, because the law was making things difficult for the dog fighting fraternity, a group of fanciers led by Joseph Dunn determined to raise the status of the Bull and Terrier and have it officially recognized by The Kennel Club. In 1935 they succeeded. All that remained to be done was to select a suitable name. That of Bull Terrier had already been given to a closely related breed, so it was decided to name the breed for the English county where it was most popular (as well as being the home area of its patrons). The breed has become very popular in Britain and frequently accounts for the largest terrier entry at prestigious championship dog shows.

The Staffordshire Bull Terrier was officially recognized by The Canadian Kennel Club in 1952, followed some years later by the United States.

Staffordshire Bull Terrier

Official Breed Standard for the Staffordshire Bull Terrier

General Appearance: The Staffordshire Bull Terrier is a smooth-coated dog. He should be of great strength for his size, and although muscular, should be active and agile.

Temperament: From the past history of the Staffordshire Bull Terrier, the modern dog draws his character of indomitable courage, high intelligence, and tenacity. This, coupled with his affection for his friends, and children in particular; his off-duty quietness and trustworthy stability, makes him the foremost all-purpose dog.

Size: Weight—dogs, 28–38 lb. (13–17 kg); bitches, 24–33½ lb. (11–15 kg). Height—(at shoulder), 14–16 in. (36–41 cm), these heights being related to the weights.

Coat and Colour: Coat smooth, short and close to the skin. Colour red, fawn, white, black or blue, or any of these colours with white. Any shade of brindle, or any shade of brindle with white. Black and tan or liver colour not to be encouraged.

Head: Short, deep through, broad *skull,* very pronounced cheek muscles, distinct stop, short foreface, black *nose.* The *mouth* should be level, *i.e.,* the incisors of the bottom jaw should fit closely inside the incisors of the top jaw, and the lips should be tight and clean. *Eyes:* dark preferable but may bear some relation to coat colour. Round, of medium size, and set to look straight ahead. *Ears* rose or half-pricked and not large.

Neck: Muscular, rather short, clean in outline and gradually widening towards the shoulders.

Forequarters: Legs straight and well boned, set rather wide apart, without looseness at the shoulders, and showing no weakness at the pasterns, from which point the feet turn out a little.

Body: The body should be close-coupled, with a level topline, wide front, deep brisket, well-sprung ribs and rather light in the loins.

Hindquarters: Should be well muscled, hocks let down with stifles well bent. Legs should be parallel when viewed from behind. The feet should be well padded, strong and of medium size.

Tail: Should be of medium length, low set, tapering to a point and carried rather low. It should not curl much and may be likened to an old-fashioned pump handle.

Faults: To be penalized in accordance with the severity of the fault: Light eyes or pink eye rims. Tail too long or badly curled. Non-conformation to the limits of weight or height. Full drop and prick ears. Undershot or overshot mouths. The following faults should debar a dog from winning any prize: Pink (Dudley) nose. Badly undershot or overshot mouth. Badly undershot— where the lower jaw protrudes to such an extent that the incisors of the lower jaw do not touch those of the upper jaw. Badly overshot—where the upper jaw protrudes to such an extent that the incisors of the upper jaw do not touch those of the lower jaw.

Staffordshire Terrier

A BREED DEVELOPED IN America, the Staffordshire Terrier is closely related to the Staffordshire Bull Terrier.

Both breeds were derived from crossing the Bulldog with various terrier breeds. But, unlike the Staffordshire Bull, this breed is taller, heavier, straighter in forelimb and somewhat smoother in over-all outline, His ears may be either cropped or uncropped.

The breed was first known early in the 19th century when dog fighting was a popular spectator sport in parts of the United States. The Staffordshire was intentionally designed as a fighting dog combining the tenacity and courage of the Bulldog with the agility and spirit of the terrier. And he was good at his job, so good, in fact, that at first the American Kennel Club refused to acknowledge the Staffordshire Terrier as a pure breed. But he was admitted to registration by another American-based organization, the United Kennel Club.

Then the breed's fortunes took a turn for the better. Dog fighting was outlawed in most States in 1900, and breeders of the Staffordshire turned their attentions to producing a more docile animal that would function well as family pet and guardian. Their efforts were successful and the Staffordshire Terrier was admitted to the American Kennel Club's official roster of pure-breds in 1935.

Later, in January 1972, in order to avoid confusion with the Staffordshire Bull Terrier, which was then in process of gaining official acceptance, the American Kennel Club changed the breed name to the American Staffordshire Terrier.

This was to be the last of a series of names for the breed that over the years had included the Yankee Terrier, Pit Bull Terrier, Half and Half, and the American Bull Terrier. In Canada it is still known as the Staffordshire Terrier.

The breed has a loyal following in the United States with good entries at most of the larger championship shows. For some reason it has failed to achieve the same acceptance in Canada. Only rarely is a Staffordshire Terrier seen at a dog show in Canada.

Staffordshire Terrier

G. Stenhouse

Official Breed Standard for the Staffordshire Terrier

General Appearance: The Staffordshire Terrier should give the impression of great strength for his size, a well put-together dog, muscular, but agile and graceful, keenly alive to his surroundings. He should be stocky, not long-legged or racy in outline. His courage is proverbial.

Size: Height and weight should be in proportion. A height of about 18–19 in. (46–48 cm) at shoulders for the male and 17–18 in. (43–46 cm) for the female is to be considered preferable.

Coat and Colour: Coat short, close, stiff to the touch, and glossy. Any colour, solid, parti, or patched is permissible, but all white, more than 80 per cent white, black and tan, and liver not to be encouraged.

Head: Medium length, deep through, broad *skull*, very pronounced cheek muscles, distinct stop; *muzzle* medium length, rounded on upper side to fall away abruptly below eyes. Jaws well defined. Underjaw to be strong and have biting power. Lips close and even, no looseness. *Nose* definitely black. Upper teeth to meet tightly outside lower teeth in front. *Eyes* dark and round, low down in skull and set far apart. No pink eyelids. *Ears* set high; cropped or uncropped, the latter preferred. Uncropped ears should be short and held half rose or prick.

Neck: Heavy, slightly arched, tapering from shoulders to back of skull. No looseness of skin. Medium length.

Forequarters: Shoulders strong and muscular with blades wide and sloping. Forelegs set rather wide apart to permit chest development. The front legs should be straight, large or round bones, pastern upright. No resemblance of bend in front.

Body: Back fairly short. Slight sloping from withers to rump with gentle short slope at rump to base of tail. Well-sprung ribs, deep in rear. All ribs close together. Chest deep and broad. Loins slightly tucked.

Hindquarters: Well muscled, let down at hocks, turning neither in nor out. Feet of moderate size, well arched and compact.

Tail: Short in comparison to size, low set, tapering to a fine point; not curled or held over back. Not docked.

Gait: Must be springy but without roll or pace.

Faults: Faults to be penalized are Dudley nose, light or pink eyes, undershot or overshot mouth, full drop ears, tail too long or badly carried.

Welsh Terrier

ORIGINATING IN WALES, this sturdy member of the Terrier Group was bred to hunt badger, fox, and otter. Historians generally agree that the Welsh Terrier is descended from the Old English Black and Tan Terrier. Some of England's earliest sporting prints portray couples of rough-coated black and tan terriers, similar to the modern Welsh Terrier. It is reported that as far back as 1737 considerable in-breeding took place in order to preserve the purity of the breed—a practice which, no doubt, established the strong Welsh character of today.

The first show at which separate classes were held for Welsh Terriers was held at Caernarfon, Wales in 1885. Then, as the popularity of the breed grew, classes were put on throughout the British Isles. In 1886 The Kennel Club (England) sanctioned the Welsh Terrier breed standard and, basically, this same standard is in use today. In Britain a slightly larger dog is preferred. This is one of the characteristics that distinguishes this breed from the Lakeland Terrier, whom the Welsh Terrier closely resembles. Another is his coat which is always black (or black grizzle) and tan. Because of this colouration the Welsh Terrier is popularly compared to a "miniature Airedale." But the Welshman is very much his own breed. Spunky, loyal, and an excellent watchdog, the breed still retains much of its hunting instinct. It is said that with very little training he could be used as a gun dog.

The first two specimens of the breed came to America in 1885. Both were imported and shown by Mr. Prescott Lawrence. The Welsh were first shown in separate classes in 1888 and in 1903 the first Welsh Terrier champion was recorded in the American Kennel Club Stud Book.

In Canada the breed was first shown at a Toronto dog show held in conjunction with Canada's Industrial Exhibition. These were British-bred Welsh Terriers imported from Glansevin Kennels by Miss Beardmore of Torrington Farm, Toronto.

G.STENHOUSE

Welsh Terrier

Official Breed Standard for the Welsh Terrier

Size: The height at shoulder should be 15 in. (38 cm) for dogs, bitches proportionately less. Twenty lb. (9 kg) shall be considered a fair average weight in working condition, but this may vary 1 lb. (.5 kg) or so either way.

Coat and Colour: The coat should be wiry, hard, very close and abundant. The colour should be black and tan, or black grizzle and tan, free from black pencilling on toes.

Head: The *skull* should be flat, and rather wider between the ears than the Wire-Haired Fox Terrier. Stop not too defined, fair length from stop to end of nose, the latter being of a black colour. The jaw should be powerful, clean-cut, rather deep, and more punishing—giving the head a more masculine appearance than that usually seen on a Fox Terrier. The *eyes* should be small, not being too deeply set in or protruding out of skull, of a dark hazel colour, expressive and indicating abundant pluck. The *ears* should be V-shaped, small, not too thin, set on fairly high, carried forward and close to the cheek.

Neck: The neck should be of moderate length and thickness, slightly arched and sloping gracefully into the shoulders.

Forequarters: The shoulders should be long, sloping, and well set back. The legs should be straight and muscular, possessing fair amount of bone, with upright and powerful pasterns. The feet should be small, round, and cat-like.

Body: The back should be short, and well ribbed up, good depth, moderate width of chest, and the loin strong.

Hindquarters: The hindquarters should be strong, thighs muscular and of good length, with the hocks moderately straight, well let down, and fair amount of bone.

Tail: The stern should be set on moderately high, but not too gaily carried.

Disqualifications:

1. *Nose white, cherry, or spotted to a considerable extent with either of these colours.*
2. *Ears prick, tulip, or rose.*
3. *Undershot jaw or pig-jawed mouth.*
4. *Black below hocks or white to a considerable extent.*

Scale of Points:

Head and jaws	10
Ears	5
Eyes	5
Neck and shoulders	10
Body	10
Loins and hindquarters	10
Legs and feet	10
Coat	15
Colour	5
Stern	5
General appearance	15
TOTAL	100

West Highland White Terrier

ALL THE LITTLE VERMIN CATCHERS that were once collectively known as the "Terriers of Scotland" are related to one another. But the closest kin to the West Highland White Terrier is said to be the Cairn. In fact it is reported that frequently white puppies appeared in litters of Cairns, and when they did they were promptly put to sleep because the white puppies were not considered fit to survive. But, in various regions of Scotland, some breeders thought differently. They considered that white terriers had an advantage because when on the hunt for vermin they were easily distinguishable from the foxes and badgers. Not being earth-coloured, they were readily visible as they worked among the rocks.

Thus the little white dogs came to be known by various regional names such as the Poltalloch and the Roseneath Terrier. Then around the turn of the century, after the commencement of dog shows at the time when the "Terriers of Scotland" were being classified separately prior to gaining official breed recognition, all the regional names of the white terriers were merged to become the West Highland White Terrier.

Colonel E.D. Malcolm of Poltalloch, whose family had been breeding the white terriers for two generations before him, is credited with developing the modern Westie. In 1900 Malcolm introduced the breed to dog shows under the name Poltalloch Terrier. In 1905 the first specialty club was organized, a breed standard was adopted and in 1907 the West Highland White Terrier was granted official breed status by The Kennel Club (England).

It did not take long for the Westie to find supporters on this side of the Atlantic and in 1909 a national breed club was organized in the United States, followed by a similar organization in Canada in 1911. While the Westie retains the instincts of the working terrier and is still being used to keep down the vermin population on farms, the breed is best known today because of its outstanding record as a show dog, having captured top wins at the world's major dog events.

G.STENHOUSE

West Highland White Terrier

First registrations of the West Highland White Terrier in Canada are recorded in The Canadian Kennel Club Stud Book for the years 1908–1909.

Official Breed Standard for the West Highland White Terrier

Origin and Purpose: The "Westie" or "Highlander," as he is sometimes called, is a smallish dog stemming from the basic branch of the Terrier family. He has great agility and is quick in movement with tremendous stamina and courage, attributes which he needed as a hunter of fox and otter in his native Scotland, where rocks and crags and generally rough terrain made ease and quickness of movement vital. By selection and inter-breeding, the white colour was purposely bred so that the dog could be easily distinguished from his foe during the hunt, while his double coat gave necessary protection against the teeth of his foe and the climate. The West Highlander is not an argumentative terrier but is a plucky individual who will not back down and who will stand against a larger animal in matters of moral rights; yet he is fun-loving and a devoted companion.

General Appearance: The West Highland White Terrier is that of a small, game, well-balanced, hardy-looking Terrier exhibiting good showmanship, possessed of no small amount of self-esteem, strongly built, deep in chest and back ribs, straight back and powerful hindquarters on muscular legs, and exhibiting in marked degree a great combination of strength and activity. The coat should be about 2 in. (5 cm) long, white in colour, hard, with plenty of soft undercoat. The dog should be neatly presented. The ruff of hair around the head should act as a frame for the face to yield a typical Westie expression.

Temperament: Must be alert, gay, courageous, and self-reliant, and friendly. Faults: Excess timidity or excess pugnacity.

Size: Dogs should measure 11 in. (28 cm) at the withers, bitches 1 in. (3 cm) less. Faults: any specimens as much as 1 in. (3 cm) over or under the height standard are very objectionable.

Coat and Colour: Coat, very important, and seldom seen to perfection, must be double-coated. The outer coat consists of straight, hard hair, at least 2 in. (5 cm) long on the body of mature dogs, with proper blending of the shorter coat on neck and shoulders. Faults: Any silkiness or tendency to curl is a serious fault, as is an open or single coat. Colour and Pigmentation: coat must be white, as defined by the breed's name. Nose must be black. Black pigmentation is most desirable on lips, eye rims, pads of feet, nails and skin. Faults: Any coat colour other than white, and nose colour other than black are serious faults.

Head: *Skull* should be fairly broad, being in proportion to the powerful jaw, not too long, slightly domed, and gradually tapering to the eyes. There should be a defined stop, eyebrows heavy. Faults: A too long or too narrow skull.

Muzzle should be slightly shorter than the skull, powerful, and gradually tapering to the nose, which should be large. The *jaws* should be level and powerful, the *teeth* well set and large for the size of the dog. There shall be six incisor teeth between the canines of both lower and upper jaws. A tight scissors bite with upper incisors slightly overlapping the lower incisors or level mouth are equally acceptable. Faults: Muzzle longer than skull. Teeth much undershot are a serious fault as are teeth defective or missing.

Eyes widely set apart, medium in size, dark in colour, slightly sunk in the head, sharp and intelligent. Looking from under heavy eyebrows, they give a piercing look. Faults: Too small, too full or light-coloured eyes are very objectionable.

Ears small, carried tightly erect, set wide apart and terminating in a sharp point. They must never be cropped. The hair on the ears should be short, smooth and velvety. Ears should be free of fringe at the tips. Faults: Round-pointed, drop, broad and large ears are very objectionable, as are mule-ears, ears set too closely together or not held tightly erect.

Neck: Should be sufficiently long to allow the proper set-on of head required, muscular and gradually thickening towards the base, allowing the neck to merge into nicely sloping shoulders. Faults: Short neck or too long neck, thus upsetting the over-all balance.

Forequarters: Forelegs should be muscular and relatively short, but with sufficient length to set the dog up so as not to be too close to the ground. Height from the highest point of the withers to the ground should be approximately equal to the length from withers to set-on of tail; height from elbow to withers and elbow to the ground should be approximately equal. The shoulder blades should be well laid back and well knit at the backbone. The chest should be relatively broad and the front legs spaced apart accordingly. The front legs should be set in under the shoulder blades with definite body overhang before them, and should be reasonably straight and covered with short, hard hair. The forefeet are larger than the hind ones, are round, proportionate in size, and strong; thickly padded, and covered with short, hard hair; they may properly be turned out a slight amount. Faults: Steep shoulders, loaded shoulders, or out at the elbows. Too light bone. A "fiddlefront" is a serious fault.

Chest and Body: Chest very deep and extending at least to the elbows with breadth in proportion to the size of the dog. Body compact and of good substance, level back, ribs deep, and well arched in the upper half of rib, presenting a flattish side appearance; loins broad and strong, hindquarters strong, muscular, and wide across the top. Faults: Shallow chest, long or weak back, barrel ribs, high rump.

Hindquarters: Should be muscular, the hind legs relatively short and sinewy, the thighs very muscular, well angulated, and not set wide apart. The hocks well bent and parallel viewed from the rear. The hind feet are smaller than the forefeet, and thickly padded. Faults: Too light in bone, cowhocks, weak hocks, lack of angulation.

Tail: Relatively short, when standing erect it should be approximately level with the top of the skull, thus maintaining a balanced appearance. It should be covered with hard hairs, no feather, as straight as possible, carried gaily but not curled over the back. The tail should be set on high enough so that the spine does not slope down to it. The tail must never be docked. Faults: Tail-set too low; tail too long or carried at half mast or over back.

Gait: Should be free, straight and easy all around. In front, the leg should be freely extended forward by the shoulder. The hind movement should be free, strong and fairly close. The hocks should be freely flexed and drawn close under the body, so that when moving off the foot the body is thrown or pushed forward with some force. Faults: Stiff, stilted or too wide movement behind. Lack of reach in front, and/or drive behind.

Summary of Faults: Excess timidity or excess pugnacity; any specimens as much as 1 inch (3 cm) over or under height standard; silky or curling coat, open or single coat; any coat colour other than white, or nose colour other than black; skull too long or too narrow; muzzle longer than skull; undershot or overshot bite, missing or defective teeth; eyes too small, too full or light-coloured; ears round-pointed, drop, broad and large, mule-ears, ears set too close, or not held tightly erect; neck too short or too long; steep shoulders, loaded shoulders, out at elbows, too light bone in forelegs, fiddle-front; shallow chest; long or weak back, barrel ribs, high rump; cowhocks, weak hocks, too light bone in hind legs, lack of angulation; tail set too low, tail too long, carried at half-mast or over back; stiff stilted movement, too wide movement behind, lack of reach in front and/or drive behind.

GROUP V: TOYS

Affenpinscher

THE COMICAL LITTLE Affenpinscher is a toy breed of German origin whose ancestry is unknown. Nevertheless, the breed's fanciers claim this is a very old breed, as proven by paintings by Jan van Eyck and Albrecht Dürer dating from the 15th century, which depict small dogs similar to the modern Affenpinscher. Literally translated the breed name means "monkey terrier," a name derived more from the little dog's fun-loving behaviour than its appearance. In France the breed is sometimes called the *Diablotin Moustachée*, or "Moustached Little Devil." For it is a fact that both the Affenpinscher's moustache and chin whiskers contribute to his mischievous expression.

It is reported that in Germany, at one time, both the Affenpinscher and the Miniature Pinscher were regarded as two varieties of the same breed with different types of coat. Both were known under the name of Affenpinscher until 1896 when it was decided to grant them separate breed status, the rough-coated variety retaining the Affenpinscher name.

The breed is claimed to be a progenitor of both the Miniature Schnauzer and the Brussels Griffon. While the relationship to the modern Schnauzer seems remote, the skull shape, jaw formation, and general demeanour make the Affenpinscher's kinship to the Belgian breed highly probable. In addition, both were known to be useful barnyard ratters whose endearing personalities elevated them to the role of household pet. The breed is reported to make an excellent watchdog as well as an engaging, affectionate companion.

The Affenpinscher was admitted to registration on this continent in 1936 but it is still comparatively rare here as it is in its country of origin. The breed is practically unknown in Britain according to dog authorities.

G.STENHOUSE

Affenpinscher

Official Breed Standard for the Affenpinscher

General Appearance: As in most toys, general appearance is one of, if not the most, important single points in the Affenpinscher. Details are of secondary importance and anatomical variations are of small concern.

The Affenpinscher is small, but rather sturdy in build and not delicate in any way. He carries himself with comical seriousness and he is generally quiet and a very devoted pal. He can get vehemently excited, however, when attacked and is fearless towards any aggressor.

Size: The smaller dog, if of characteristic type, is more valuable, and the shoulder height should not exceed 10¼ in. (26 cm) in any case.

Coat and Colour: Coat is a very important factor. It is short and dense in certain parts and shaggy and longer in others, but should be hard and wiry. It is longer and more loose and shaggy on the legs and around the eyes, nose and chin, giving the typical monkey-like appearance from whence comes his name. The best colour is black, matching his eyes and fiery temperament. However, black with tan markings, red, grey and other mixtures are permissible. Very light colours and white markings are a fault.

Head: Should be round and not too heavy, with well-domed forehead. *Muzzle* must be short and rather pointed with a black nose. The upper jaw is a trifle shorter than the lower jaw, while the teeth should close together; a slight undershot condition is not material. The teeth, however, should not show. *Eyes* should be round, of good size, black and very brilliant. *Ears* rather small, set high, pointed and erect, usually clipped to a point.

Neck: Short and straight.

Forequarters: Front legs should be straight as possible.

Body: The back should be straight with its length about equal to the height at the shoulder. Chest should be reasonably deep and the body should show only a slight tuck-up at the loin.

Hindquarters: Hind legs without much bend at the hocks and set well under the body. Feet should be round, small, and compact. Turned neither in nor out, with preferably black pads and nails.

Tail: Cut short, set and carried high.

Cavalier King Charles Spaniel

SMALL TOY SPANIELS have been known in Europe and Great Britain since the 16th century. Several appear in paintings of old masters, and they were great favourites at the court of Charles II (1660–1685). Packs of the little dogs are said to have been kept by members of the nobility as sporting dogs. As lap dogs they were popular with the ladies, and it is also claimed that they were of great comfort to those afflicted with febrile diseases.

After William of Orange ascended the throne, the Pug took over as court pet and it is assumed, but not recorded, that this breed was crossed with the toy spaniels. Breed type was thereby changed to the snub-nosed, domed breed known today as the King Charles Spaniel.

Thus in 1926, when an American by the name of Roswell Eldridge visited Britain in search of dogs resembling the original toy spaniels, he was dismayed to find that the breed carrying the monarch's name bore little resemblance to the dogs in the early portraits. To rectify this Eldridge offered money prizes to be awarded at Crufts' Dog Show (London) for the dog and the bitch that came closest to "the dogs as shown in the pictures of King Charles II's time."

Breeders accepted the challenge. In 1928 a club was organized in England and the name for the recreated breed, Cavalier King Charles Spaniel, chosen. A breed standard was drawn up which remains basically unchanged. The breeders' objective was to develop a completely natural dog which needed no trimming. Within a few years they had such a spaniel and by 1945 the Cavalier was standardized and breeding true to type. In that year it was granted separate breed status by The Kennel Club (England) and subsequently added to The Canadian Kennel Club's roster of recognized breeds.

Although not officially recognized in the United States, the Cavalier does have a strong following in that country, and American-bred Cavaliers are eligible for registration in Canada and may compete in Canadian championship events.

Cavalier King Charles Spaniel

Official Breed Standard for the Cavalier King Charles Spaniel

Origin and Purpose: The Cavalier King Charles Spaniel is a much admired Royal Spaniel. Descended from the Toy Spaniels of Europe, the breed was variously known as the "Comforter" or "Spaniel Gentle" and first appeared in the courts of England with the reign of Queen Mary I. The breed, which appears in many of the great paintings by the Masters, received its name from King Charles II. It became virtually extinct in the Victorian and Edwardian eras as short-nosed breeds took the fore. By 1923 the King Charles Spaniel (today's English Toy), with its flat nose, had replaced the old-type Toy Spaniel. In 1926 the incentive for revitalization of the old-type Toy Spaniel was provided by Mr. Roswell Eldridge, an American, who offered prizes of £25 for the Best Dog and Best Bitch of this type at Crufts'. The name Cavalier was added when the Cavalier King Charles Spaniel Club was founded in 1928 to further develop the breed. It was not until 1945 that The Kennel Club (England) granted separate registration from the King Charles. The popularity of these companion dogs has spread around the world and in 1957 the breed gained Canadian Kennel Club recognition.

General Appearance: An active, graceful, well-balanced dog, very gay and free in action.

Temperament: Fearless and sporting in character, yet at the same time gentle and affectionate.

Size: Height 12–13 in. (30–33 cm). Weight proportionate to height between 12 and 18 lb. (5–8 kg). Slight variations permissible. Penalize only in comparison with equal quality, appearance and type. A small well-balanced dog well between these measurements is desirable.

Coat: Long, silky, and free from curl, though a slight wave is permissible. Feathering on ears, legs, and tail should be long, and the feathering on the feet is a feature of the breed. No trimming or artificial colouring of the dog is permitted. However, it is permissible, and often desirable, to remove the hair growing between the pads on the underside of the foot.

Colour: Blenheim: bright chestnut red markings well broken up on a pearly white ground. The red on the head must extend around the eyes as well as down over the ears. There should be a white blaze between the eyes and ears in the centre of which is the lozenge or "Blenheim Spot" unique within the Blenheim Cavalier King Charles Spaniel, a highly desirable, but not essential, characteristic of the Blenheiml.

Tricolour: jet black markings well broken up on a pearly white ground. The black on the head must extend around the eyes as well as down over the ears. There should be a white blaze between the eyes. Rich tan markings appear over the eyes, on cheeks, inside ears, inside legs, under the tail and around the vent.

Ruby: whole-coloured rich red.

Black and Tan: jet black with rich tan markings over the eyes, on the sides of the muzzle, inside the ears, on the throat and chest, on the forelegs from the knees to the toes and on the hind legs on the inside of the legs, also extending from the hock to the toes, and on the underside of the tail and surrounding the vent.

Head: Head almost flat between the ears, without dome. Stop shallow; length from base of stop to tip of nose about $1\frac{1}{2}$ in. (4 cm). Nostrils should be well developed and the pigment black. *Muzzle* tapered. Lips well covering but not hound-like. There should be cushioning beneath the eyes, which contributes much to the sweet, gentle expression characteristic of the breed.

Mouth: teeth strong and even, preferably meeting in a scissors bite, although a level bite is permitted. Undershot mouths are greatly to be discouraged. It should be emphasized, however, that a slightly undershot bite in an otherwise well-balanced head with the correct sweet expression should not be penalized in favour of a level mouth with a plain or hard expression.

Eyes should be large, round and set well apart; colour a warm, dark brown, giving a lustrous limpid look. Faults: White ring surrounding the iris. Bulging eyes.

Ears set high, but not close to the top of the head. Leather long with plenty of silky feathering, and wide enough so that when the dog is alert, the ears fan slightly forward to frame the face.

Neck: Moderate length, without throatiness. Well enough muscled to form a slight arch at the crest. Set smoothly into nicely sloping shoulders.

Forequarters: Forelegs straight and well under the dog. Bone moderate. Elbows close to the sides. Shoulders should slope back with moderate angulation to give the characteristic look of top class and presence. Pasterns strong and feet compact, well feathered, and with well-cushioned pads.

Body: Short-coupled with ribs well sprung but not barrelled. Chest moderately deep leaving ample heart room. Back level. Slightly less body at the flank than at the last rib, but with no tucked up appearance.

Hindquarters: Hind legs moderately muscled, well angulated at the stifles. Hocks relatively short and at right angles to the ground when standing. Hind legs should parallel each other from hock to heel. The dog should stand level on all four feet.

Tail: Set so as to be carried level with the back. Tail should be in constant characteristic motion when the dog is in action. Docking is optional, but whether or not it is docked, the tail must balance the body. If docked, two-thirds is the absolute minimum to be left on the body, and the tails of broken-coloured dogs should always be docked to leave a white tip.

Disqualifications: *Colours other than the four above. Clown faces (white around one or both eyes or white ears). Undue aggressiveness, bad temper, snapping at judge.*

Chihuahua

THE WORLD'S SMALLEST DOG, the Chihuahua, seems to be the subject of the biggest disagreement among dog historians as to this breed's country of origin. Some authorities write that the tiny dog evolved in Egypt and that the mummified remains of a small dog with the unique "molera," or fontanelle, was unearthed in a tomb dating back 3000 years. From here it is assumed the little breed was taken to Mediterranean countries and eventually to Mexico at the time of the Spanish Conquest (1519).

Those who hold a contrary view state that four breeds of dog were domesticated in Mexico long before the Spanish Conquest. One was a dog resembling the Chihuahua which played an important role in religious ceremonies. To support this claim there are artifacts dating to ancient Mexican culture. It is further claimed that the Spanish took some of these small dogs with them when they returned to Spain. Thus they became established throughout Europe and the islands of the Mediterranean. Yet another theory has been put forth that claims the dogs were brought to Mexico by Chinese traders just over 100 years ago.

Wherever the Chihuahua originated, it is known that the little dogs were discovered late in the 19th century by American tourists who were visiting Mexico. On their return to the United States they brought some of the dogs with them. It is from these first specimens, probably crossed with English black and tan toy terriers, that the present-day Smooth-Coat was developed and named for Chihuahua, the Mexican state where the breed was discovered.

It is said that the Long-Coat variety was developed entirely in the United States by crossing the smooth variety with other toy breeds which are thought to have been the Papillon and Pomeranian. The Pekingese, Yorkshire Terrier, and Toy Poodle are also mentioned as other possibilities.

The Chihuahua was first registered in Canada in 1928.

Chihuahua (Short Coat)

G.STENHOUSE

Chihuahua (Long Coat)

Official Breed Standard for the Chihuahua

SHORT COAT

General Appearance: A graceful, alert, swift-moving little dog with saucy expression. Compact, and with terrier-like qualities.

Size: One—6 lb. (.5—3 kg), with 2—4 lb. (1—2 kg) preferable. If two dogs are equally good in type, the more diminutive is preferred.

Coat and Colour: In the smooth, the coat should be soft texture, close and glossy. (Heavier coats with undercoats permissible.) Coat placed well over body with ruff on neck, and more scanty on head and ears. Any colour—solid, marked, or splashed.

Head: A well-rounded apple dome *skull*, with or without molera. Cheeks and jaws lean. *Nose* moderately short, slightly pointed, self-coloured, in blond types, or black. In moles, blues, and chocolate, they are self-coloured. In blond types, pink nose permissible. Teeth level. *Eyes* full, but not protruding, balanced, set well apart—dark, ruby, or luminous. (Light eyes in blond type, permissible.) *Ears* large, held erect when alert, but flaring at the sides at about an angle of 45 degrees when in repose. This gives breadth between the ears.

Neck: Slightly arched, gracefully sloping into lean shoulders, may be smooth in the very short types, or with ruff about neck preferred.

Forequarters: Shoulders lean, sloping into a slightly broadening support above straight forelegs that are set well under, giving a free play at the elbows. Shoulders should be well up, giving balance and soundness, sloping into a level back. This gives a chestiness, and strength of forequarters, yet not of the ''Bulldog'' chest.

Body: Level back (never down or low), slightly longer than height. Shorter backs desired in males. Plenty of brisket. Ribs rounded (but not too ''barrel-shaped'').

Hindquarters: Muscular, with hocks well apart, neither out nor in, well let down, with firm sturdy action. Feet small, with toes well split up, but not spread, pads cushioned, with fine pasterns. (Neither the hare- nor the cat-foot.) A dainty, small foot with nails moderately long.

Tail: Moderately long, carried sickle either up or out, or in a loop over the back, with tip just touching the back. (Never tucked under.) Hair on tail in harmony with the coat of the body, preferred furry. A natural bobtail or tailless permissible, if so born, and not against a good dog.

Disqualifications: *Cropped tail, broken down or cropped ears.*

Scale of Points:

Head, including ears	20
Body	20
Coat	10
Tail	5
Colour	5
Legs	15
Weight	10
General appearance and action	15
TOTAL	100

LONG COAT

The long-coated variety of the Chihuahua is judged by the same standard as the smooth-coated variety, except for the following:

Coat: In the Long Coats, the coat should be of a soft texture, either flat or slightly curly, with undercoat preferred. Ears fringed (heavily fringed ears may be tipped slightly, never down), feathering on feet and legs, and pants on hind legs. Large ruff on neck desired and preferred. Tail full and long (as a plume).

Disqualifications: *Cropped tail, broken down or cropped ears, too thin a coat that resembles bareness.*

Scale of Points:

Head, including ears	20
Body	20
Coat	20
Tail	5
Colour	5
Legs	10
Weight	5
General appearance and action	15
TOTAL	100

English Toy Spaniel

THE TOY SPANIEL is presumed to have originated in Japan, and to have been brought to Britain via Spain prior to the 16th century. These dogs were favourites of the nobility; Mary, Queen of Scots, is known to have kept a pack of toy spaniels as sporting dogs. History records that one of these little dogs crept beneath her skirts at the time of her execution and could not be removed "except by force." Perhaps for this reason the little breed came to be known as "the comforter."

Most renowned patron of the breed was King Charles II and it was during his reign (1660—1685) that the breed reached the peak of its popularity. After Charles' death the Pug took over as the favourite pet of royalty and little was heard of the toy spaniel until the mid-19th century.

When it did emerge, again as a parlour pet, its appearance was greatly changed. Bowing to the public preference for oriental-type breeds it is assumed that the toy spaniels had been inter-bred with dogs of Asiatic origin, probably the Pug, Pekingese, and the Japanese Spaniel. The result was a smaller dog, round headed and short in foreface which looked more like a Pekingese than a spaniel.

In 1860 a Toy Spaniel club was formed in England and from the first days of dog shows in Britain the breed was shown under two different headings. There was the King Charles Spaniel named for its royal patron. This was a black dog with tan markings. The other variety was the Blenheim, a white dog with chestnut markings named for Blenheim Palace, the home of the Duke of Marlborough, who bred spaniels of this colour. By 1902 two more colours had been added, the Ruby (solid red) and the Prince Charles (tricolour). But when The Kennel Club (England) suggested these four colours be classified under the single heading "Toy Spaniel," Edward VII, also a breed fancier, let it be known that he did not approve. Thus in Britain the breed remains the King Charles Spaniel. In Canada and the United States "King Charles" denotes one of four colours of the breed known as the English Toy Spaniel.

The Canadian Kennel Club Stud Book lists seven English Toy Spaniels registered in the years 1888—1889.

English Toy Spaniel

Official Breed Standard for the English Toy Spaniel (King Charles, Prince Charles, Ruby, and Blenheim)

General Appearance: In compactness of shape these spaniels almost rival the Pug, but the length of coat adds greatly to the apparent bulk, as the body, when the coat is wetted, looks small in comparison with that dog. Still, it ought to be decidedly cobby, with strong, stout legs, short broad back, and wide chest.

Size: The most desirable size is from 9–12 lb. (4–5.5 kg).

Coat and Colour: The coat should be long, silky, soft and wavy, but not curly. There should be a profuse mane, extending well down in the front of the chest. The feather should be well displayed on the ears and feet, and in the latter case so thickly as to give the appearance of being webbed. It is also carried well up the backs of the legs. In the Black and Tan, the feather on the ears is very long and profuse, exceeding that of the Blenheim by 1 inch (3 cm) or more. The feather on the tail (which is cut to the length of about 1½ in. (4 cm)) should be silky, and from 3–4 in. (8–10 cm) in length, constituting a marked "flag" of a square shape, and not carried above the level of the back.

Colours of the two varieties:

King Charles and Ruby—The King Charles and Ruby types which comprise one show variety are solid-coloured dogs. The King Charles are black and tan (considered a solid colour), the black rich and glossy with deep mahogany tan marks over the eyes and on the muzzle, chest and legs. The presence of a few white hairs intermixed with the black on the chest is to be faulted, but a white patch on the chest or white appearing elsewhere disqualifies. The Ruby is a rich chestnut red and is whole-coloured. The presence of a few white hairs intermixed with the red on the chest is to be faulted, but a white patch on the chest or white appearing elsewhere disqualifies.

Blenheim and Prince Charles—The Blenheim and Prince Charles types which comprise the other show variety are broken-coloured dogs. The Blenheim is red and white. The ground colour is a pearly white which has bright red chestnut or ruby red markings evenly distributed in large patches. The ears and cheeks should be red, with a blaze of white extending from the nose up the forehead and ending between the ears in a crescentic curve. In the centre of the blaze at the top of the forehead, there should be a clear "spot" of red, the size of a dime. The Prince Charles, a tricoloured dog, is white, black and tan. The ground colour is a pearly white. The black consists of markings which should be evenly distributed in large patches. The tan appears as spots over the eyes, on the muzzle, chest, and legs; the ears and vent should also be lined with tan. The Prince Charles has no "spot," that being a particular feature of the Blenheim.

Head: *Skull* should be well domed, and in good specimens is absolutely semiglobular, sometimes even extending beyond the half-circle, and absolutely projecting over the eyes, so as nearly to meet the upturned nose. The stop, or hollow between the eyes, is well marked, as in the Bulldog, or even more so; some good specimens exhibit a hollow deep enough to bury a small marble in it. The *nose* must be short and well turned up between the eyes, and without any indication of artificial displacement afforded by a deviation to either side. The colour of the end should be black, and it should be both deep and wide with open nostrils. A light-coloured nose is objectionable, but shall not disqualify. The *muzzle* must be square and deep, and the lower jaw wide between the branches, leaving plenty of space for the tongue, and for the attachment of the lower lips, which should completely conceal the teeth. It should also be turned up or "finished," so as to allow of its meeting the end of the upper jaw, turned up in a similar way as above described. A protruding tongue is objectionable, but does not disqualify. The *eyes* are set wide apart, with the eyelids square to the line of the face—not oblique or fox-like. The eyes themselves are large and dark as possible, so as to be generally considered black, their enormous pupils, which are absolutely of that colour, increasing the description. The *ears* must be long, so as to approach the ground. In an average-sized dog they measure 20 in. (51 cm) from tip to tip, and some reach 22 in. (56 cm) or even a trifle more. They should be set low down on the head and hang flat to the sides of the cheeks, and be heavy feathered.

Disqualifications: *King Charles and Ruby—a white patch on the chest, or white on any other part.*

(Breed Standard continued)

Scales of Points:
KING CHARLES, OR BLACK AND TAN. PRINCE CHARLES, WHITE, WITH BLACK AND TAN MARKINGS. RUBY, OR RED.

Symmetry, condition, size, and soundness of limb	20
Head	15
Stop	5
Muzzle	10
Eyes	10
Ears	15
Coat and feathering	15
Colour	10
TOTAL	100

BLENHEIM OR WHITE WITH RED MARKINGS.

Symmetry, condition, size, and soundness of limb	15
Head	15
Stop	5
Muzzle	10
Eyes	10
Ears	10
Coat and feathering	15
Colour and markings	15
Spot	5
TOTAL	100

Griffon (Brussels)

A PAINTING BY JAN VAN EYCK, "The Marriage of Giovanni Arnolfini," dated 1434, shows a small dog in the foreground of the picture that fanciers declare to be a Brussels Griffon. This seems to prove the claim that this is a very old breed. Of Belgian origin, the little dog is thought to descend from the German rat dog, and was first used as a stable ratter where hansom cabs were housed. The little dogs were so engaging that it became the custom for the cabbies to drive with a Griffon seated on a box beside them. With this improvement in lifestyle the dogs are said to have assumed the duties of guardians and attracted much notice as they rode through the streets barking at passers-by.

Early in the 19th century it is thought that the Griffon was crossed with the Pug, the Affenpinscher, and the English Miniature Spaniel. From the Pug the breed got its shorter muzzle and this cross produced the short-haired variety which is called the Petit Brabançon. The Affenpinscher is credited with reducing size and the spaniel contributed the round head. Other crosses suggested are the Miniature Black and Tan Terrier, the Yorkshire and the Irish Terriers.

After 1870 the Brussels Griffon became a fashionable pet in Belgium because of royal patronage. In 1886 separate classes for the breed were offered at dog shows on the continent. Thereafter it attracted British interest, and the first specimens arrived in England about 1890. There, in 1898, a specialty club was formed to promote the Belgian toy breed.

Fanciers claim that both coat varieties may occur in the same litter and that the personalities of each, as well as their outward appearance, are markedly different. The colours of both varieties are similar but in the United States and Canada the all black, smooth coat is not an allowable colour, although it is quite acceptable in Britain and on the continent.

The first Brussels Griffon was registered in Canada in the years 1911–1912.

G.STENHOUSE

Griffon (Brussels)

Official Breed Standard for the Griffon (Brussels)

General Appearance: A toy dog, intelligent, alert, sturdy, with a thick-set short body, a smart carriage and set-up, attracting attention by its almost human expression.

Size: For the class of dogs and bitches of a small size, the weight should not exceed 7 lb. (3 kg). For the class of dogs and bitches of a large size, that is weighing more than 7 lb. (3 kg), the weight should not exceed 11 lb. (5 kg) for dogs and 12 lb. (5.5 kg) for bitches. **NOTE:** Type and quality are of greater importance than weight, and a smaller dog that is sturdy and well proportioned should not be penalized.

Coat and Colour: There are two distinct types of coat—rough and smooth. The rough coat should be wiry and dense, the harder and more wiry the better. On no account should the dog look or feel woolly, and there should be no silky hair anywhere. The coat should not be so long as to give a shaggy appearance, but should still be distinctly different all over from the smooth coat. The head should be covered with wiry hair, slightly longer around the eyes, nose, cheeks, and chin, thus forming a fringe. The smooth coat is similar to that of the Boston Terrier or English Bulldog, with no trace of wire hair.
In the rough-coated type, coat is either: *a)* reddish brown, with a little black at the whiskers and chin allowable, or *b)* black and reddish brown mixed, usually with black mask and whiskers, or *c)* black with uniform reddish brown markings, usually appearing under the chin, on the legs, over the eyebrows, around the edges of the ears and around the vent, or *d)* solid black. The colours of the smooth-coated type are the same as those of the rough-coated type. Any white hairs in either the rough or smooth coat are a serious fault, except for "frost" on the black muzzle of a mature dog, which is natural.

Head: *Skull* large and round, with a domed forehead. *Nose* very black, extremely short, its tip being set back deeply between eyes so as to form a lay-back. The nostrils large, the stop deep. *Lips* edged with black, not pendulous but well brought together, giving a clean finish to the mouth. Chin must be undershot, prominent, and large with an upwards sweep. The incisors of the lower jaw should protrude over the upper incisors and the lower jaw should be rather broad. Neither teeth nor tongue should show when the mouth is closed. *Eyes* should be set well apart, very large, black, prominent, and well open. The eyelashes long and black. Eyelids edged with black. *Ears* small and set rather high on the head. May be shown cropped or natural. If natural they are carried semi-erect.

Neck: Medium length, gracefully arched.

Forequarters: Forelegs of medium length, straight in bone, well muscled, set moderately wide apart and straight from the point of the shoulders as viewed from the front. Pasterns short and strong.

Body: Back level and short, brisket should be broad and deep, ribs well sprung.

Hindquarters: Hind legs set true, thighs strong and well muscled, stifles bent, hocks well let down, turning neither in nor out. Feet round, small and compact, turned neither in nor out. Toes well arched. Black pads and toenails preferred.

Tail: Set and held high, docked to about one-third.

Faults: Any white hairs in either the rough or smooth coat are a serious fault. A wry mouth is a serious fault.

Disqualifications: *Dudley or butterfly nose, white spot or blaze anywhere on coat, hanging tongue, jaw overshot.*

Scale of Points:

HEAD

Skull	5	
Nose and stop	10	
Eyes	5	
Chin and jaws	10	
Ears	5	35

COAT

Colour	12	
Texture	13	25

BODY AND GENERAL CONFORMATION

Body (brisket and rib)	15	
Legs	10	
Feet	5	
General appearance (neck, topline, and tail carriage)	10	40
TOTAL		100

Italian Greyhound

*T*HROUGHOUT ITS HISTORY, which dates back at least 2000 years, this smallest member of the greyhound family has been favoured by royalty. Mummified remains of a dog resembling the present-day Italian Greyhound were discovered in a tomb of a pharaoh. And, while the breed name would suggest its origin was Italy, dog historians believe that the little greyhound originated in Egypt, and was the result of matings between small-sized greyhounds. Subsequently the breed was brought to Italy by Roman soldiers and soon became popular throughout Europe as a pet of the nobility.

Cleopatra was among the more illustrious owners of the I.G., as it has been nicknamed. Others include Catherine the Great, Charles I of England, and Frederick the Great of Prussia. The little dog's likeness has been painted many times by old masters and there are two statues in the Vatican honouring the breed. It is thought that the plaques uncovered in the ruins of Pompeii inscribed *Cave Canem* (Beware of the Dog) do not mean "Watch out for the Mastiff lest you get bitten," but rather "Watch where you place your feet, don't step on the I.G."

In the mid-19th century in Europe, the fad for miniaturization almost spelled the ruin of the breed. Irresponsible inbreeding and, in Britain, crosses to the toy terrier, resulted in dogs of low fertility and grotesque appearance. Through the efforts of a group of dedicated breeders the Italian Greyhound's former elegance was restored. In 1900 in England a specialty club was organized, and the breed standard draughted following the lines of the one that had been in use since 1860.

Two world wars dealt harshly with the breed in Europe. Fortunately the Italian Greyhound had become well established in North America and imports from both the U.S. and Canada helped to re-establish the breed in Britain and on the continent. It is now quite usual to see good entries of the small greyhound with its characteristic high-stepping prance at most British championship shows. For some reason the breed has remained

G.STENHOUSE

Italian Greyhound

comparatively rare both in Canada and the United States. Among the first breeds to be registered in Canada, The Canadian Kennel Club Stud Book records that three Italian Greyhounds were registered in the years 1888–1889.

Official Breed Standard for the Italian Greyhound

General Appearance: A miniature English Greyhound, more slender in all proportions, and of ideal elegance and grace in shape, symmetry, and action.

Size: Two classes, one of 8 lb. (4 kg) and under, and one over 8 lb. (4 kg). A good small dog is preferable to an equally good large one but a good larger dog is preferable to a poor smaller one.

Coat and Colour: Skin fine and supple, hair thin and glossy, like satin. Colour all shades of fawn, red, mouse, blue, cream, and white are recognized. Black and Tan Terrier markings not allowed.

Head: *Skull* long, flat, and narrow. *Muzzle* very fine, *nose* dark, teeth level. *Eyes* rather large, bright, and full of expression. *Ears* rose shaped, placed well back, soft, and delicate.

Neck: Long and gracefully arched.

Forequarters: Shoulders long and sloping. Forelegs straight, set well under the shoulders, fine pasterns, small delicate bones.

Body: Back curved and drooping at the hindquarters. Chest, deep and narrow.

Hindquarters: Thighs muscular, hocks well let down, long hare-foot.

Tail: Rather long, fine, and with low carriage.

Gait: High stepping and free.

Scale of Points:

Skull	6
Muzzle	8
Ears	8
Eyes	5
Neck	8
Shoulders	5
Chest	5
Back	8
Forelegs	8
Hind legs	8
Feet	8
Tail	8
Coat	4
Colour	3
Action	8
TOTAL	100

Japanese Spaniel

*T*HERE SEEMS TO BE general agreement among dog historians that the Japanese Spaniel, or "Chin," as it is known in Japan, shares ancestry with the Pug and the Pekingese. It is thought that small dogs were brought to Japan as tribute gifts to the Mikado about 500 B.C. There the forerunners of the present-day Chin underwent further development as well as becoming the favourite pets of Japan's Imperial family. It is said that the Chin were carefully fed, mostly on rice, and that they were given sake, a Japanese liquor made from fermented rice, in order to stunt their growth. Some of the dogs were so small, it is reported, they were kept in hanging cages much as cage birds are.

The Japanese Spaniel was brought to the Western world about 1860, and some were exhibited at a British dog show in 1862. Then, in 1879, further show entries were reported. This time the breed was entered under the name "Japanese Pug." The following year royal patronage set the breed on the road to popularity both in Britain and on the continent. Queen Alexandra acquired several Japanese Spaniels and the Mikado presented a pair to the Empress of Germany. Two years later the breed was introduced to America when the first Japanese Spaniels appeared in competition at a dog show held in New York City. Subsequently, breed clubs were organized on both sides of the Atlantic, and the respective breed standards adopted. Some authorities believe that the Canadian and American breed standards err in that they do not define correct expression. The English standard requires that some white be shown at the inner corners of the eyes thus imparting the characteristic look of astonishment.

In its native land the Chin's ownership is no longer restricted to the royal family. It has become enormously popular with the Japanese people with about 8000 registrations being recorded annually.

The Japanese Spaniel was first registered in Canada in the years 1909–1910.

G. Stenhouse

Japanese Spaniel

Official Breed Standard for the Japanese Spaniel

General Appearance: That of a lively, high-bred little dog with smart, dainty appearance, compact carriage and profuse coat.

Size: In size they vary considerably, but the smaller they are the better, provided type and quality are not sacrificed. When divided by weight, classes should be under and over 7 lb. (3 kg).

Coat and Colour: Coat profuse, long, straight, rather silky. It should be absolutely free from wave or curl, and not lie too flat, but have a tendency to stand out, especially at the neck, so as to give a thick mane or ruff, which with profuse feathering on thighs and tail gives a very showy appearance. The dogs should be either black and white or red and white, *i.e.*, particoloured. The term red includes all shades of sable, brindle, lemon and orange, but the brighter and clearer the red the better. The white should be clear white, and the colour, whether black or red, should be evenly distributed, patches over the body, cheek, and ears.

Head: Should be large for the size of the dog, with broad *skull*, rounded in front. *Nose* very short in the muzzle part. The end or nose proper should be wide, with open nostrils, and must be the colour of the dog's markings, *i.e.*, black in black-marked dogs, and red or deep flesh colour in red or lemon-marked dogs. It shall be a disqualification for a black and white Japanese Spaniel to have a nose any other colour than black. *Eyes* large, dark, lustrous, rather prominent and set wide apart. *Ears* small and V-shaped, nicely feathered, set wide apart and high on the head and carried slightly forward.

Neck: Should be short and moderately thick.

Forequarters: The bones of the legs should be small, giving them a slender appearance, and they should be well feathered.

Body: Should be squarely and compactly built, wide in chest, cobby in shape. The length of the dog's body should be about its height.

Hindquarters: Feet small and shaped somewhat long; the dog stands up on its toes somewhat. If feathered, the tufts should never increase in width of the foot, but only its length a trifle.

Tail: Must be well twisted to either right or left from root and carried up over back and flow on opposite side; it should be profusely covered with long hair (ring tails not desirable).

Gait: These dogs should be essentially stylish in movement, lifting the feet high when in action, carrying the tail (which is heavily feathered, proudly curved or plumed) over the back.

Disqualifications: *In black and whites, a nose any other colour than black.*

Scale of Points:

Head and neck	10
Eyes	10
Ears	5
Muzzle	10
Nose	5
Body	15
Tail	10
Feet and legs	5
Coat and markings	15
Action	5
Size	10
TOTAL	100

Maltese

THE MALTESE IS THE OLDEST European toy breed; his likeness has been depicted on art objects dating back 3000 years. In 200 B.C. the breed was described in writings under the Latin name *Canis Melitaeus* from which, obviously, the breed name was derived. Whether *Melitaeus* referred to the Island of Malta (which was once called Melita), or to the town of Melita in Sicily, continues to be in question.

From earliest times the breed appears to have been well known throughout Europe, where it was enjoyed for its beauty and companionship, especially by the ladies. It is assumed that the reason the little breed became so widespread was that it was used as an object of barter in exchange for goods. Thus it was left behind at many points along the trade routes. Wherever it travelled, the Maltese seems to have attracted the interest of artists because down through the ages the little breed has had its portrait painted sitting on the laps of gentle ladies.

The breed was already well known in Britain at the time of Elizabeth I (1558–1603). There are two theories as to how the Maltese came to be there. One is that returning Crusaders brought the little dogs home with them as gifts for their ladies. The other places the breed's arrival in Britain much earlier than this, claiming that the Maltese was brought in at the time of the Roman invasion.

It is reported that during the 17th and 18th centuries the breed faced near disaster when attempts were made to miniaturize it even more. Crosses to other toy breeds were used to restore vigour.

The breed was first shown in Britain in 1862 and made its first appearance at an American show at the Westminster Kennel Club event held in 1877, when one imported dog by the name of Leo was shown under the breed name of the Maltese Lion Dog. It was in strange company. One of the entries in the Miscellaneous Group in which the Maltese was included was a dog, aged two years, of uncertain breed that had been born with only two legs.

G. STENHOUSE

Maltese

Happily the Maltese has come up in the world since that time and accounts for a beautiful entry in the Toy Group wherever dog shows are held.

The first Maltese registration in Canada was recorded in The Canadian Kennel Club Stud Book for the years 1901–1902.

Official Breed Standard for the Maltese

Origin and Purpose: The Maltese is of spaniel origin, and has been a household pet for many centuries.

General Appearance: Should suggest a vigorous, well-balanced dog with a mantle of long white straight coat hanging evenly down each side.

Temperament: The Maltese is among the gentlest mannered of all little dogs. They are intelligent, vigorous, very affectionate and seemingly fearless. Over-aggressive or too timid behaviour is to be severely penalized.

Size: Weight under 7 lb. (3 kg) with from 4–6 lb. (2–2.7 kg) preferred. Over-all quality is to be favoured over size.

Coat and Colour: Should be of good length, but not so as to impede action. The coat is single, that is, with no undercoat. It hangs flat, straight and silky on either side of the centre part, which should run from tip of nose to tip of tail. The texture should be even throughout with no suggestion of woolliness, curliness, or cosmetic alteration. The long head hair may be tied up in a single topknot or divided into two. White colour is preferred, but light beige or lemon markings are permissible.

Head and Skull: Head in proportion to the size of the dog. From stop to centre of the skull (centre being between forepart of the ears) and stop to tip of the nose should be equally balanced. The *skull* is slightly rounded, rather broad between the ears and moderately well defined at the temples. The stop is moderate. The *muzzle* is fine and slightly tapered, but not snipey, with a good firm underjaw. The *nose* is small, black, and in balance with the size of the eyes. Teeth may meet in an even edge to edge bite or in a scissors bite. The lips should be black.

Eyes should be dark brown with black eye rims. Halos of pigmentation around the eyes give a more beautiful expression. The shape is not quite round but not almond shaped, and their size should be in proportion to the size of the face, there should be no suggestion of bulging or prominence and the expression should be gentle but very alert. *Ears* should be low set, the hair long and well feathered and hanging close to the side of the head, the hair to be mingled with the coat at the neck and shoulders.

Neck: Of sufficient length and proportion to the body to give a high carriage of head.

Forequarters: The shoulder blades are sloping at an approximate 45-degree angle, elbows are well knit and held close to the body. Forelegs are straight, their pastern joints well knit and devoid of appreciable bend. The feet should be round and small. Pads of the feet are black. The hair around the feet may be trimmed to give a neater appearance.

Body: Should be in every way well balanced. The dog should be compact, with the height from the withers to the ground to equal the length from the withers to the root of the tail. The topline should be straight and level from the tip of the shoulders to the root of the tail. Ribs should be well sprung, chest fairly deep, at least to the elbows, the loins taut, strong and well tucked up underneath.

Hindquarters: Legs are fine boned and nicely feathered. Hind legs are strong and moderately angulated at the stifles and hock. The hock is straight, turning neither in nor out.

Tail: Is set high and should be long haired and carried well arched over the back with the tip resting on the hindquarter on either side.

Gait: The gait should be smooth and flowing without weaving. In stride the forelegs reach forward, straight and free from the shoulders, elbows close. The hind legs move in a straight line with good driving action. The topline is level, head held high and tail carried gracefully over the back resting on the hindquarters.

Scale of Points:

SCALE OF POSITIVE POINTS

Balance and size	20
Movement and carriage	20
Head, eyes, nose, pigmentation	15
Legs, feet, action	10
Tail and tail carriage	10
Coat, colour and texture	15
Condition, presentation, body substance	10
TOTAL	100

SCALE OF NEGATIVE POINTS

Lack of pigmentation	10
Cowhocks, or hind legs toeing-in or out	10
Weaving in front, toeing in or out	10
Gay tail, or low-set tail	5
Roach back, topline not level	10
Undershot or overshot jaws	10
Prominent, bulging eyes, or too wide set	5
Lacking in body substance, poor condition	10
Kinky coat, curly coat, or undercoat	10
Timid or snapping	10
Poorly balanced	10
TOTAL	100

Mexican Hairless

THE MEXICAN HAIRLESS is one of several hairless breeds found throughout the world and is named for the country where it was discovered. Some authorities believe that the Mexican dog may be of Turkish origin but fail to explain when or how it reached Mexico.

At any rate, in 1840 it is said that the breed was fairly common along the border between the United States and Mexico, where it was a popular house pet. Many folk tales surround the Mexican Hairless. One is that the breed has great curative powers. If held close to the body it can cure a patient of arthritis by drawing the "poison" into its own body. This stems, no doubt, from the belief that the Mexican Hairless has a body temperature normally above that of other breeds of dog. While the skin does feel warm to the touch because it is not insulated by a covering of hair, those familiar with the Mexican Hairless state that its temperature is no higher than that of any other dog.

An oddity of the breed is that in most litters one puppy will be born with hair and, so it has been reported, a full set of teeth! The haired puppy is called a "Powder Puff" because its coat is downy soft. It is claimed this puppy is born to keep its littermates warm until they have enough vitality to move about and keep themselves warm.

The Mexican Hairless was first shown in the United States in 1883 and remained an officially recognized breed until 1959. Then, because of apparent lack of interest in the breed, the American Kennel Club withdrew the Mexican Hairless from its official roster. There is, however, a group of enthusiasts who continue to breed the Hairless in the hope that one day the breed may be restored to its former status.

No such organization exists in Canada but The Canadian Kennel Club does still recognize the Mexican Hairless. In 1980, for the first time in many years, the breed was exhibited at a few championship shows in southwestern Ontario.

Mexican Hairless

Official Breed Standard for the Mexican Hairless

General Appearance: The Mexican Hairless is a small, active dog, about the size of a small Fox Terrier, symmetrical and well proportioned, with rather broad chest and ribs, and slender legs.

Skin: Smooth and soft, not wrinkled, any colour, hot to touch, no hair whatever. There should be a tuft of coarse hair on top of the skull, in the centre but a bit forward, in some cases shadowing the brow. A little fuzz or hair on lower half of tail permitted. Absence of tuft on top of the head is undesirable but not a disqualification.

Head: Should be slender and skull narrow, cheeks lean, *muzzle* long and pointed. *Eyes* should not be too deep-set but balanced and not bulging. Eye rims pink or dark and the eyes themselves hazel, yellow, or dark.

Neck: Should be of good length, slender, and well arched into shoulders.

Forequarters: Shoulders flat. Muscles and sinews well developed. A nervous tremor of muscles and sinews is characteristic, like that of a nervous race horse.

Body: Back should be level, rump slightly rounded. The chest rather broad, ribs well rounded and chest rather deep.

Hindquarters: Legs fairly long and slender. Feet should be hare feet; nails black in dark skin or pale in pale-skinned dogs.

Tail: Long, smooth tail, carried out similar to that of Manchester Terrier.

Disqualifications: *Cut or broken ears or tail are disqualifications, likewise a fuzz or any hair, except as described above.*

Papillon

*T*HIS IS A SMALL ELEGANT BREED of European origin which, as evidenced by paintings of the Old Masters, has been breeding true to type for over 700 years. The breed is thought to have originated in Italy, a descendant of the dwarf spaniel. But today it is generally thought of as a Franco-Belgian breed.

The Papillon's most distinguishing feature is its erect, fringed ears which resemble the wings of a butterfly. The French word *papillon* means butterfly. Enhancing this appearance is a narrow blaze of white running up the forehead. While the erect ear is the most frequently seen variety today, this is a comparatively recent development which was standardized in the breed early this century by Belgian breeders. The older and original variety of the breed is the drop ear which is known as the Phalene, taken from the French word for "moth," because it is said that these ears are carried much like the folded wings of the moth. Another characteristic is the Papillon's plumed tail which is carried in a graceful arc over the back and falls to one side or the other. For this reason the little dog is sometimes called *chien écureuil* or squirrel dog.

Throughout Europe the Papillon was a favourite pet of ladies of the court, especially in France. It is written that Marie Antoinette carried her pet Papillon with her to the guillotine.

Nevertheless, despite royal patronage on the continent, it was some time before the Papillon made much of an impression elsewhere. The breed was brought to South America by the Spaniards in 1915 and to Britain and the United States a few years later. When the breed was exhibited in England for the first time in 1923 under the classification "Foreign Dogs" it immediately attracted attention. One year later it was elevated to full breed status. On this continent the Papillon has been officially recognized in the United States and Canada since 1935.

phalene

G. STENHOUSE

Papillon

Official Breed Standard for the Papillon

Pronunciation: Papillon—"Pappy-yon."

Origin and Purpose: The first Papillons may have been Spanish (Spaniel) or Italian. Today, both the French and the Belgians claim the breed. Since the Renaissance, no known cross has been used in its development although two or three other breeds probably trace their ancestry in part to the Papillon. It is one of the oldest pure-bred Toys, seen in the company of 17th and 18th century Royal children and ladies at Court in paintings of the Old Masters.

General Appearance: The Papillon is a small, friendly, elegant toy dog of fine-boned structure; light, dainty and of lively action; distinguished from other breeds by its beautiful butterfly-like ears.

Size: Ideal height at highest point of shoulder blades, 8–11 in. (20–28 cm). Weight is in proportion to height. Fault: Over 11 in. (28 cm). Disqualification: under 8 in. (20 cm) and over 12 in. (30 cm).

Coat: Abundant, long, fine, silky, flowing, straight with resilient quality, flat on back and sides of body. A profuse frill on chest. There is no undercoat. Hair short and close on skull, muzzle, front of forelegs and from hind feet to hocks. Ears well fringed with the inside covered with silken hair of medium length. Backs of the forelegs are covered with feathers diminishing to the pasterns. Hind legs are covered to the hocks with abundant breeches (culottes). Tail is covered with a long flowing plume. Hair on feet is short but fine, tufts may appear over toes and grow beyond them forming a point.

Colour: Particolour—white with patches of any colour. Tricolour—black and white with tan spots over the eyes, inside the ears, on cheeks, and may have tan under root of tail. On the head, colour other than white must cover both ears, back and front, and extend without interruption from the ears over both eyes. A clearly defined white blaze and noseband are preferred to a solidly marked head. Symmetry of facial markings is desirable. The size, shape, placement, or absence of patches on the body are without importance. Papillons may be any particolour, provided nose, eye rims and lips are well-pigmented black. Among the colours there is no preference. The following faults shall be severely penalized:

1. Nose not black.
2. Colour other than white not covering both ears, back and front, or not extending from the ears over both eyes. A slight extension of the white collar onto the base of the ears or a few white hairs interspersed among the colour shall not be penalized provided the butterfly appearance is not sacrificed. Disqualification: an all-white dog or a dog with no white.

Head: Small. The *skull* of medium width, and slightly rounded between the ears. A well-defined stop is formed where the muzzle joins the skull. The *muzzle* is fine, abruptly thinner than the head, tapering to the nose. The length of the muzzle from the tip of nose to stop is approximately one-third the length of the head from tip of nose to occiput. *Nose:* black, small, rounded and slightly flat on top. *Mouth:* lips are tight, thin, and black. Teeth meet in a scissors bite. Tongue must not be visible when jaws are closed. Fault: Overshot or undershot.

Eyes: dark, round, not bulging, of medium size and alert in expression. The inner corner of the eyes is on a line with the stop. Eye rims black. *Ears:* the ears of either the erect or drop type should be large with rounded tips and set on the sides and toward the back of head. Ears of the erect type are carried obliquely and move like the spread wings of a butterfly. When alert, each ear forms an angle of approximately 45 degrees to the head. The leather should be of sufficient strength to maintain the erect position. Ears of the drop type, known as Phalene, are similar to the erect type, but are carried drooping and must be completely down. Faults: Ears small, pointed, set too high, one ear up or ears partly down, set too low.

Neck: Of medium length.

Forequarters: Shoulders well developed and laid back to allow freedom of movement. Forelegs slender, fine-boned and must be straight. Removal of dewclaws on forelegs optional.

Body: Must be slightly longer than the height at withers. It is not a cobby dog. Topline straight and level. The chest is of medium depth with well-sprung ribs. The belly is tucked up.

Hindquarters: Well developed and well angulated. Hocks inclined neither in nor out. The hind legs are slender, fine-boned, and parallel when viewed from behind. Dewclaws, if any, must be removed from hind legs.

Feet: Thin and elongated (hare-like), pointing neither in nor out.

Tail: Long, set high and carried well arched over the body. The plume may hang to either side of the body. Fault: Low-set tail, one not arched over back or too short.

Gait: Free, quick, easy, graceful, not paddle-footed, or stiff in hip movements.

Disqualifications: *Height under 8 in. (20 cm) or over 12 in. (30 cm). An all-white dog or a dog with no white.*

Pekingese

THE ORIGIN OF THE PEKINGESE is veiled in Oriental mystery and romance. It is believed that the breed is a miniature version of the ancient "Fo Dogs" of China which, because of their terrifying lion-like appearance, were thought to ward off evil spirits. Such dogs appear in Chinese works of art dating to 900 A.D. and bear a striking resemblance to the present-day Pekingese. The small dogs became favourites of the Chinese Imperial court where they were bred in great numbers but only those within the royal circle were permitted to own one. The dogs were lavishly tended, considered to be bringers of good fortune and possessed of the courage of the lion.

Closely watched over within the palace precincts, the breed did not reach the Western world until after British troops stormed the Summer Palace in Peking in 1860. There they found five small dogs protecting the body of the Imperial Princess who had taken her own life. These dogs were of the "sleeve" type—that is, all weighed about five pounds. The five were looted and taken back to England. A pair was presented to the Duchess of Wellington and to the Duchess of Richmond, and one female was given to Queen Victoria, who promptly named her Looty. In the years that followed, by various means, more Pekingese were smuggled out of China, brought to England, and became the foundation stock of what was soon to become the most popular toy breed in Britain.

The Pekingese was first exhibited in the show ring in 1894 and in 1898 was accepted for registration by The Kennel Club (England). In that same year the first standard for the breed was draughted.

News of the breed's romantic background quickly travelled, and created great interest in the Pekingese. First imports began arriving in the United States early in the 1900s, and in 1909 the Pekingese Club of America was founded. The following year the first of the breed were registered in Canada.

The most illustrious Pekingese of them all was International Champion Chik T'Sun of Caversham, bred in England, who was to become the world's top winner of Best in Show awards. His record of 125 top awards still stands.

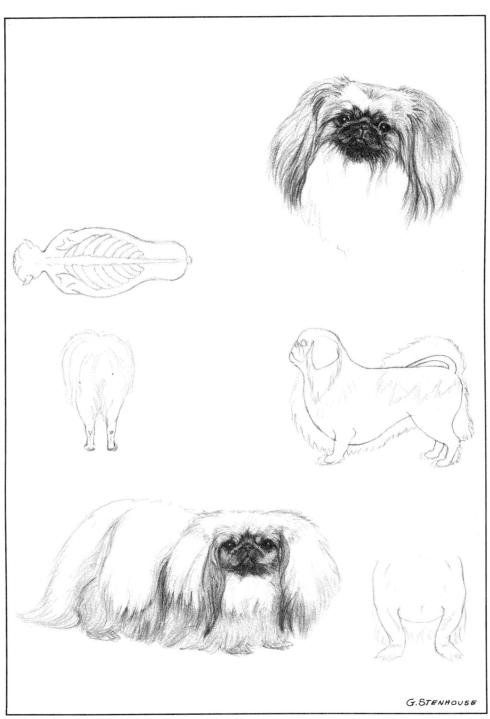

G. STENHOUSE

Pekingese

Official Breed Standard for the Pekingese

General Appearance: Expression must suggest the Chinese origin of the Pekingese in its quaintness and individuality, resemblance to the lion in directness and independence and should imply courage, boldness, self-esteem and combativeness rather than prettiness, daintiness, or delicacy.

Size: Being a toy dog, medium size preferred, providing type and points are not sacrificed; extreme limit 14 lb. (6 kg).

Coat and Colour: Coat long, with thick undercoat, straight and flat, not curly nor wavy, rather coarse, but soft; feather on thighs, legs, tail, and toes long and profuse. Mane profuse, extending beyond the shoulder blades, forming ruff or frill round the neck. All colours are allowable. Red, fawn, black, black and tan, sable, brindle, white and particolour well defined: black masks and spectacles around the eyes, with lines to ears are desirable. The colouring of a particoloured dog must be broken on the body. No large portion of any one colour should exist. White should be shown on the saddle. A dog of any solid colour with white feet and chest is *not* a particolour.

Head: Skull massive, broad, wide and flat between the ears (not dome shaped), wide between the eyes. Stop deep. Muzzle wrinkled, very short and broad, not overshot nor pointed. Strong, broad underjaw, teeth not to show. Nose black, broad, very short and flat. Eyes large, dark, prominent, round, lustrous. Ears heart shaped, not set too high, leather never long enough to come below the muzzle, nor carried erect, but rather drooping, long feather.

Forequarters: Firm at shoulder, bones of forearm bowed, short forelegs.

Body: Back level. Not too long in body; allowance made for longer body in bitch. Heavy in front, well-sprung ribs, broad chest, falling away lighter behind, lion-like.

Hindquarters: Hind legs lighter than forelegs but firm and well shaped. Feet flat, toes turned out, not round, should stand well up on feet, not on ankles.

Tail: Set high; lying well over back to either side; long, profuse, straight feather.

Gait: Fearless, free and strong, with slight roll.

Faults: Protruding tongue, badly blemished eye, overshot, wry mouth.

Disqualifications: *Weight over 14 lb. (6 kg); Dudley nose.*

Scale of Points:

Expression	5
Skull	10
Nose	5
Eyes	5
Stop	5
Ears	5
Muzzle	5
Shape of body	15
Legs and feet	15
Coat, feather, and condition	15
Tail	5
Action	10
TOTAL	100

Pinscher (Miniature)

THE MINIATURE PINSCHER originated in Germany where terrier-like breeds known as "pinschers" have been used as ratters for at least 300 years. It is thought that the Miniature Pinscher evolved from breeding small specimens of the German smooth-haired pinscher possibly crossed to the Italian Greyhound and the Smooth Dachshund. It is not, as some believe, the miniature version of the Doberman Pinscher although its clean lines, colouring, and general activity are remarkably similar. The Miniature Pinscher was a recognized breed in Germany many years before the Doberman was developed. In Germany the breed is often called the *Reh Pinscher* because of its resemblance to the Roe deer, a small deer that is said to abound in the forests of the Rhineland.

The breed standard was first recorded in the German Stud Book in 1880 and was officially recognized by the Pinscher-Schnauzer Klub in Germany in 1895. Undoubtedly the little dog was very popular in its country of origin; when it was first shown at the Stuttgart show in 1900, there were ninety-three Miniature Pinschers in competition.

The Miniature Pinscher was first brought to the United States in 1920, and that country is credited with much of the breed's development. Since the organization of the Miniature Pinscher Club of America in 1929, the breed has become extremely popular on this continent both in the United States and Canada.

Its progress has been somewhat slower in the United Kingdom, probably due to the ban on ear cropping. It has taken breeders some years to breed dogs whose ear size and placement were in pleasing balance with the rest of the head. One of the Miniature Pinscher's most attractive characteristics is its high-stepping "hackney" gait, which would seem to verify the fact that somewhere in its ancestry the Italian Greyhound can be found.

In Canada the first Miniature Pinschers were registered in The Canadian Kennel Club Stud Book for the years 1937—1938.

G. STENHOUSE

Pinscher (Miniature)

Official Breed Standard for the Pinscher (Miniature)

General Appearance: The Miniature Pinscher originated in Germany and named the *Reh Pinscher* due to his resemblance in structure and animation to a very small species of deer found in the forests. This breed is structurally a well-balanced, sturdy, compact, short-coupled, smooth-coated toy dog. He is naturally well groomed, proud, vigorous, and alert. The natural characteristic traits which identify him from other toy dogs are his precise Hackney gait, his fearless animation, complete self-possession, and his spirited presence. Faults: Structurally lacking in balance, too long or short-coupled, too coarse or too refined (lacking in bone development causing poor feet and legs), too large or too small, lethargic, timid or dull, shy or vicious, low in tail placement and poor in action (action not typical of the breed requirements). Knotty overdeveloped muscles.

Size: Desired height 11−11½ in. (28−29 cm) at the withers. A dog of either sex measuring under 10 in. (25 cm) or over 12½ in. (32 cm) shall be disqualified.

Coat and Colour: Coat smooth, hard and short, straight, and lustrous, closely adhering to and uniformly covering the body. Colour: *a)* Solid red or stag red. *b)* Lustrous black with sharply defined tan, rust-red markings on cheeks, lips, lower jaw, throat, twin spots above eyes, and chest, lower half of forelegs, inside of hind legs and vent region, lower portion of hocks and feet. Black pencil stripes on toes. *c)* Solid brown or chocolate with rust or yellow markings. Faults: Thin, too long, dull coat; upstanding coat; curly coat; dry coat; area of various thickness or bald spots. Any colour other than listed; very dark or sooty spots.

Head: In correct proportion with the body. From top: Tapering, narrow with well-fitted but not too prominent foreface which should balance with the skull. No indication of coarseness.

From front: *Skull* appears flat, tapering forward towards the muzzle. *Muzzle* itself strong rather than fine and delicate, and in proportion to the head as a whole; cheeks and lips small, taut and closely adherent to each other. Teeth in perfect alignment and apposition.

From side: Well balanced with only a slight drop to the muzzle, which should be parallel to the top of the skull.

Nose black only (with the exception of chocolates, which may have a self-coloured nose). *Eyes* full, slightly oval, almost round, clear, bright and dark, even to a true black; set wide apart and fitted well into the sockets. *Ears* well set and firmly placed, upstanding (when cropped, pointed, and carried erect in balance with the head).

Faults: Too large or too small for the body, too coarse or too refined, pinched and weak in foreface, domed in skull, too flat and lacking in chiselling, giving a vapid expression. Nose any colour other than black (with the exception of chocolates which may have a self-coloured nose). Jaws and teeth overshot or undershot. Eyes too round and full, too large, bulging, too deep-set or set too far apart; or too small, set too close (pig eyes). Light-coloured eyes not desirable. Ears poorly placed, low-set hanging ears (lacking in cartilage) which detract from head conformation. (Poorly cropped ears if set on the head properly and having sufficient cartilage should not detract from head points, as this would be a man-made fault and automatically would detract from general appearance.)

Neck: Proportioned to head and body. Slightly arched, gracefully curved, clean and firm, blending into shoulders, length well balanced, muscular and free from a suggestion of dewlap or throatiness. Faults: Too straight or too curved; too thick or too thin; too long or short; knotty muscles; loose, flabby or wrinkled skin.

Forequarters: Shoulders clean, sloping with moderate angulation, co-ordinated to permit the true action of the Hackney pony. Strong bone development and small clean joints. As viewed from the front, straight and upstanding; elbows close to body, well knit, flexible yet strong with perpendicular pasterns.

Faults: Shoulders too straight, too loose, or too short and overloaded with muscles. Forelegs bowed or crooked, weak pasterns, feet turning in or out, loose elbows.

Body: From top: Compact, slightly wedge-shaped, muscular with well-sprung ribs.

From side: Back level or slightly sloping towards the rear. Length of males equal height at withers. Females may be slightly longer. Forechest well developed and full, moderately broad. Depth of brisket, the base line of which is level with the points of the elbows; short and strong in loin with belly moderately tucked up to denote grace in structural form.

From rear: High tail-set; strong, sturdy upper shanks, with croup slope at about 30 degrees; vent opening not barrelled.

Faults: From top—too long, too short, too barrelled, lacking in body development. From side—too long, too short, too thin, or too fat, hips higher or considerably lower than the withers, lacking depth of chest, too full in loin, sway back, roach back or wry back. Forechest and spring of rib too narrow (or too shallow and underdeveloped). From rear—quarters too wide or too close to each other, overdeveloped, barrelled vent, underdeveloped vent, too sloping croup, tail-set low.

Hindquarters: Well-knit muscular quarters set wide enough apart to fit into a properly balanced body. All adjacent bones should appear well angulated with well-muscled thighs or upper shanks, with clearly well-defined stifles, hocks short, set well apart turning neither in nor out, while at rest should stand perpendicular to the ground and upper shanks, lower shanks and hocks parallel to each other. Feet cat-like, toes strong, well arched and closely knit with deep pads and thick, blunt nails.

Faults: Too narrow, undermuscled or overmuscled, too steep in croup. Too thick or thin bone development, large joints, spreading flat feet. Thin underdeveloped stifles, large or crooked hocks, loose stifle joints.

Tail: Set high, held erect, docked to $\frac{1}{2}$–1 inch (1–3 cm). Faults: Set too low, too thin, drooping, hanging or poorly docked.

Faults: Structurally lacking in balance, too long or short-coupled, too coarse or too refined (lacking in bone development causing poor feet and legs), too large or too small, lethargic, timid or dull, shy or vicious, low in tail placement and poor in action (action not typical of the breed requirements). Knotty overdeveloped muscles. Thin, too long, dull coat; upstanding coat; curly coat; dry coat; area of various thickness or bald spots. Any colour other than listed; very dark or sooty spots. Head too large or too small for the body, too coarse or too refined, pinched and weak in foreface, domed in skull, too flat and lacking in chiselling, giving a vapid expression. Nose any colour other than black (with the exception of chocolates which may have a self-coloured nose). Jaws and teeth overshot or undershot. Eyes too round and full, too large, bulging, too deep-set or set too far apart; or too small, set too close (pig eyes). Light-coloured eyes are not desirable. Ears poorly placed, low-set hanging ears (lacking in cartilage) which detract from head conformation. (Poorly cropped ears if set on the head properly and having sufficient cartilage should not detract from head points, as this would be a man-made fault and automatically would detract from general appearance.) Neck too straight or too curved; too thick or too thin; too long or short; knotty muscles; loose, flabby or wrinkled skin on neck. Shoulders too straight, too loose, or too short and overloaded with muscles. Forelegs bowed or crooked, weak pasterns, feet turning in or out, loose elbows. Body from top—too long, too short, too barrelled, lacking in body development. Body from side—too long, too short, too thin or lacking depth of chest, too full in loin, sway back, roach back or wry back. Forechest and spring of rib too narrow (or too shallow and underdeveloped). Body from rear—quarters too wide or too close to each other, overdeveloped, barrelled vent, underdeveloped vent, too sloping croup, tail-set low. Hindquarters too narrow, undermuscled or overmuscled, too steep in croup, too thick or thin bone development, large joints, spreading flat feet. Thin underdeveloped stifles, large or crooked hocks, loose stifle joints. Tail-set too low, too thin, drooping, hanging, or poorly docked.

Disqualifications: *Thumb marks or any area of white on feet or forechest exceeding ½ inch (1 cm) in its longest dimension. A dog of either sex measuring under 10 in. (25 cm) or over 12½ in. (32 cm) shall be disqualified.*

Scale of Points:

General appearance and movement (very important)	30
Skull	5
Muzzle	5
Mouth	5
Eyes	5
Ears	5
Neck	5
Body	15
Feet	5
Legs	5
Colour	5
Coat	5
Tail	5
TOTAL	100

◄**Cavalier King Charles Spaniel**
Ch. Lady Lou
Owner: Mrs. Bette Harris
RR 1, Site 123 C10,
Qualicum Beach, B.C. V0R 2T0
BEAUCHAMPS KENNELS REG.

▼**Cavalier King Charles Spaniel**
Ch. Pharos of Chandlers and
Italia at Charlescote
Breeder: Mrs. Viktor Strelcs
Owner: Janice M. Koehler
1719 Osgood St.,
N. Andover, MA. 01845
CHARLESCOTE KENNELS REG.
(Photo by Barry Kaplan)

▶**Cavalier King Charles Spaniel**
Ch. Beaverdam's Edward
Breeders: Chuck & Carol Purser
Owners: J. P. Bracey, Chuck,
Carol & Robert Purser
(Photo by Alex Smith)

BEAVERDAMS KENNELS (PERM.)
Chuck & Carol Purser
52 Alexander St., Box 416,
Burford, Ont. N0E 1A0

▼**Cavalier King Charles Spaniel**
Ch. Beaverdam's Briar Rose
Owners: Chuck & Carol Purser
(Photo by Stonham)

▲Chihuahua
Can. Am. Wisherwood's
Tamara
Breeder/Owner:
Jean Westwood
795 Meaford Ave.,
Victoria, B.C.
WISHERWOOD KENNELS (PERM.)

▼Chihuahua
Can. Am. Ch. Chanté,
Céline, Soleil, Pata,
Chozette, Quita, Minuit,
Scellé, Pistache, Chayon
Breeder/Owner:
Edna St. Hilaire
2114 Dublin St.,
New Westminster, B.C.
V3M 3A9
HILAIRE'S KENNELS REG.

▶Griffon (Brussels)
Ch. Wild Rock's
Van Counterpoint
Breeders: Flora & Susan Hewitt
Owners: Lynn Ross, Flora &
Susan Hewitt
11 Selkirk Cres.,
Saskatoon, Sask. S7L 4J4
WILD ROCK & COUNTERPOINT
KENNELS REG. (PERM.)

▼Japanese Spaniel
Can. Am. Ch. Valleja's
Una-Theodore
Breeder/Owner:
Jean S. Whitford
25 Mountain St.,
Sutton, P.Q. J0E 2K0
VALLEJA KENNELS (PERM.)

Italian Greyhound
Can. Am. Ch. Bugatti
Scarlet Speedster*
Can. Am. Ch. Arabesque
Anticipation**

Owners:
*A. Arthur & C. Haslam
**D. & Anne-Marie Arthur
4350 Arbutus St.,
Vancouver, B.C. V6J 4A2
SCARRA KENNELS REG.
(Photo by Arthur)

▼**Maltese**
Ch. Kuri Nino Tesoro
Owner: Margaret J. Garland
151 Waterford Bridge Rd.,
St. John's, Nfld. A1E 1C7
KURI KENNELS (PERM.)

▶Maltese
Can. Am. Ch. Four Halls
Conversation Piece
Breeder/Owner:
Mrs. Glenna Fierheller
4184 Musqueam Dr.,
Vancouver, B.C. V6N 3R7
FOUR HALLS KENNELS REG.

▼Papillon
Ch. Glenmargo's The Red
Nugget & Candyman
Breeder/Owner:
Mrs. Vincent T. Scott
539 Carlisle Rd. E., RR 3,
Campbellville, Ont. L0P 1B0
GLENMARGO KENNELS (PERM.)

▲Pug
Can. Am. Ch. Shiralee's
Free 'n Easy
Breeders/Owners:
Mr. & Mrs. C. &
Karen Zimmerman
6415-133 Ave.,
Edmonton, Alta. T5A 0K6
SHIRALEE KENNELS (PERM.)

▶Yorkshire Terrier
Can. Am. Ch. Checkmates
Man of The Year
Breeders:
Ernie & Nancy Chrustawka
Owners:
Ernie & Nancy Chrustawka,
Gordon & Gillian Salls
RMD 133, RR 8,
Edmonton, Alta. T5L 4H8
CHECKMATE KENNELS REG.

▲**Yorkshire Terrier**
Can. Am. Ch. Farrkee's
Diamond Jim
Breeders/Owners:
Shirley & Cliff Farrier
16 Alice Cres.,
Petersburg, Ont. N0B 2H0
FARRKEE KENNELS REG.

◄**Bulldog**
Ch. Joymuir Smirnoff Salty
Breeder: Mr. M. C. Dennett
Owner: Joan M. Railton
RR 1, Lake Charlotte,
Halifax County, N.S. B0J 1Y0
TAUNTON KENNELS (PERM.)

▶Chow Chow
Can. Am. Ch. Mi-Pao's
Timang
Breeder/Owner:
F. P. A. Odenkirchen
P.O. Box 863,
Waterdown, Ont. L0R 2H0
MI-PAO KENNELS REG. (PERM.)

▶Chow Chow
Can. Am. Ch. Mi-Tu's Han
Su Shang
Owners:
John C. Frederick Peddie
Herbert E. & Joan I. Williams
21 Lorraine Gardens,
Toronto, Ont. M9B 4Z5
BU DYNASTY KENNELS REG.

▲Dalmatian
Can. Am. Ch. Camosun's Bryony
Breeder: Mrs. C.D. Blinko
Owners:
Mrs. Blinko & Mrs. N. Dorini
4865 Cherry Tree Bend,
Victoria, B.C. V8Y 1S1
CAMOSUN KENNELS (PERM.)
(Photo by Carl Lindemaier)

◀Dalmatian
Ch. Camosun's Arabella
Breeder: Mrs. C. D. Blinko
Owners:
Dr. & Mrs. J. Hamilton Brooks
Site 444, Box 5, RR 4,
Sherwood Park, Alta. T8A 3K4
HIGHWAY KENNELS REG.

▶French Bulldog

Mister LEFT
Ch. Balihai's Contessa RIGHT
Prince, Angel, Tuffy LOWER

Owners: LEFT
Mel & Renée Trottier
22 Bertmount Dr.,
Toronto, Ont. M4M 2X9
MINOTAURUS KENNELS REG.

Owner: RIGHT Mr. James Groulx
3818 Lawrence Ave. E.,
Scarborough, Ont. M1G 1R6
IRLEES KENNELS (PERM.)

Breeder/Owner: LOWER
Linda Marshall
185 Elizabeth St. S.,
Brampton, Ont. L6Y 1R9
EL TORRO KENNELS REG.

▶Keeshond

Ch. Keesbrook's Billigo
Bingo
Ch. Star-Kees' Hobbit of
Keesbrook*
Ch. Keesbrook's Elf
Princess**
*Breeder: Robin Stark
**Owner: Robert Kane
KEESBROOK KENNELS REG.
Brenda Brookes
Steeple Hill Cres., RR 2,
Richmond, Ont. K0A 2Z0

▲Keeshond
Ch. Kendol's Chinook of
Gates, C.D.
Owner: Gladys H. Gates
Box 17, Site 21, RR 1,
Tantallon, N.S. B0J 3J0
SEAWIND KENNELS REG.

◄Keeshond
Ch. Baronwood Sassy Cassy
Ch. Keewinds Southern
Vixen
Ch. Keewinds Kountry
Studd
Owners:
Ross & Shirley Henderson
Box 214,
Aberdeen, Sask. S0K 0A0
KEEWINDS KENNELS REG. (PERM.)
(Photo by Gibson)

▶**Lhasa Apso**
Can. Am. Bda. Ch.
Shangrelu Rainy Days
O'Irlees
Breeder: Wendy F. Penn
Owner: Catherine L. Freedman
3818 Lawrence Ave. E.,
Scarborough, Ont. M1G 1R6
IRLEES KENNELS (PERM.)

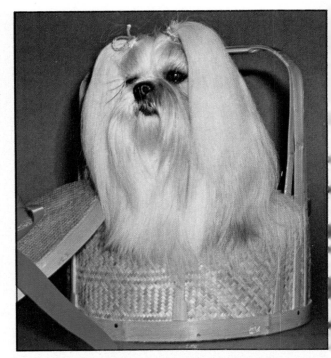

▼**Lhasa Apso**
Totem's Chief Golden
Sunset
Ch. Potala's Keke's
Daybreak
Breeder/Owner:
Mrs. H. D. "Peggy" Bishop
RR 3, Lakeshore Rd.,
Port Alberni, B.C. V9Y 7L7
TOTEM KENNELS (PERM.)

◄Poodle (Standard)
Ch. Wentworth Hapi
Breeder: G. Ellwood Smith
Owner: Mrs. Dorothy Hansen
P.O. Box 624,
Keewatin, Ont. P0X 1C0
(Photo by Coultman)

◄Poodle (Standard)
Ch. Griggswood Barrister,
C.D.
Breeder: Mrs. D. E. Griggs
Owner: Mrs. J. Harbour
1154 Hwy. 2 W.,
Ancaster, Ont. L9G 3K9
TUDOROSE KENNELS REG.

▲Schipperke
Ch. Skipakey's Burglar Bob
Breeder/Owner: Tom Burke
P.O. Box 61,
Charlottetown, P.E.I. C1A 7K2
SKIPAKEY KENNELS (PERM.)

▼Shih Tzu
Ch. Arvind vom
Tschomo-Lungma
Breeder:
Frau Erika Geusendam

Owner: Trudy V. Kerr
3615 Elbow Dr., S.W.,
Calgary, Alta. T2S 2J6
TA YA CHAI KENNELS REG.
(Photo by Gold)

Pomeranian

THE POMERANIAN IS THE SMALLEST member of the family of spitz, or northern breeds, which all originated in the Arctic Circle and gradually made their way southward. With its prick ears, pointed muzzle, mane of hair around the neck, and plumed tail carried over the back, the diminutive Pom is a true spitz breed in miniature. The breed name is taken from Pomerania, a country on the Baltic Sea and once a part of Germany, from which the first of the breed were imported into England. The original dog was much larger than the present-day Pom, weighing up to thirty pounds and was used in its homeland as a herding dog and beast of burden.

First imports came to Britain early in the 19th century but failed to make much impression. Then breeders discovered that often in a litter of otherwise normal puppies, an undersized pup would appear. Most breeders considered them runts and had them put to sleep, but those who kept the tinies were surprised to find out that they did not mature into misshapen adults. Instead they were tiny replicas of their littermates. These became known as Toy Pomeranians and were in great demand.

In 1870 the "Spitz Dog" was officially recognized by The Kennel Club (England), and classes were offered for the breed at dog shows. Early specimens were usually white in colour, but in time blacks appeared, even later a wide range of colours.

The real boost to the breed came in 1888 when Queen Victoria took an interest in the Pom and exhibited extensively at dog shows. She favoured dogs in the twelve to eighteen-pound range. But even this smaller size was to become large as breeders managed to reduce size even further. Today the preferred weight for the Pom both here and abroad is from four to five pounds.

It was not long before the Pomeranian was brought to this continent, and in 1900 the breed was granted official recognition by the American Kennel Club. The first Canadian registrations of the breed are recorded in the Stud Book for the years 1903–1904.

G.STENHOUSE

Pomeranian

Official Breed Standard for the Pomeranian

General Appearance: The Pomeranian in build and appearance should be a compact, short-coupled dog, well knit in frame. He should exhibit great intelligence in his expression, docility in his disposition, and activity and buoyancy in his deportment, and be sound in action.

Size: The weight of a Pomeranian for exhibition is 3–7 lb. (1–3 kg). The ideal size for show specimens is from 4–6 lb. (1.8–2.7 kg).

Coat and Colour: There should be two coats, an under and an outer coat; the first a soft, fluffy undercoat, and the other a long, perfectly straight and glistening coat covering the whole body, being very abundant around the neck and forepart of the shoulders and chest where it should form a frill of profuse, standing-off, straight hair extending over the shoulders. The hindquarters should be clad with long hair or feathering from top of rump to the hocks. The texture of the guard hairs must be harsh to the touch.

Twelve colours, or colour combinations, are permissible and recognized, namely: black, brown, chocolate, beaver, red, orange, cream, orange-sable, wolf-sable, blue, white, and particolour. The beaver colour is a dark beige. A particolour dog is white with orange or black, colour distributed in even patches on the body, with white blaze on head desirable. Where whole-coloured and particoloured Pomeranians compete together, the preference should, other points being equal, be given to the whole-coloured specimen. Sable-coloured dogs must be shaded throughout as uniformly as possible, with no self-coloured patches. In orange-sable, the undercoat must be a light tan colour with deeper orange guard hairs ending in black tippings. In wolf-sable the undercoat is light grey with a deeper shade of steel grey guard hairs ending in black tippings. A shaded muzzle on the sables is permissible, but a black mask on sables is a minor fault. Orange Pomeranians must be self-coloured throughout with light shadings of the same tone (not white) on breechings permitted. A black mask on an orange Pomeranian is a major fault. White chest, white foot, or white leg on whole-coloured dogs are major faults. White hairs on black, brown, blue, or sable Pomeranians are objectionable.

Tinges of lemon, or any other colour, on white dogs are objectionable. The above colours, as described, are the only allowable colours or combination of colours for Pomeranians.

The classes for Pomeranians may be divided by colour in Open Classes as follows: black and brown; red, orange, or cream; sables; any other allowable colour.

Head: The head should be wedge-shaped, somewhat foxy in outline, the *skull* being slightly flat, large in proportion to the muzzle. In its profile it has a little stop which must not be too pronounced, and the hair on the head and face must be smooth or short-coated. The *muzzle* should finish rather fine. The *nose* should be self-coloured in blues and browns. In all other colours should be black. The teeth should meet in a scissors grip, in which part of the inner surface of the upper teeth meets and engages part of the outer surface of the lower teeth. This type of bite gives a firmer grip than one in which the edges of the teeth meet directly, and is subject to less wear. The *mouth* is considered overshot when the lower teeth fail to engage the inner surfaces of the upper teeth. The mouth is undershot when the lower teeth protrude beyond the upper teeth. One tooth out of line does not mean an undershot or overshot mouth. The *eyes* should be medium in size, rather oblique in shape, not set too wide apart, or too close together, bright and dark in colour. The eye rims of the blues and browns are self-coloured. In all other colours the eye rims must be black. The *ears* should be small, not set too far apart or too low down, and carried perfectly erect, and should be covered with soft, short hair. Trimming unruly hairs on edges of ears permissible.

Neck: The neck rather short, well set in, and lion-like, covered with a profuse mane and frill of long, straight hair sweeping from the underjaw and covering the whole of the front part of the shoulders and chest as well as the top part of the shoulders.

Forequarters: The shoulders must be clean and laid well back. The forelegs must be well feathered and perfectly straight, of medium length and strength in due proportion to a well-balanced frame. The feet small, compact in shape, standing well up on toes.

Body: The back must be short and level, and the body compact, being well ribbed up and rounded. The chest must be fairly deep.

Hindquarters: The hind legs and thighs must be well feathered down to the hocks, and must be fine in bone and free in action. Trimming around the edges of the toes and up the back of the legs to the first joint is permissible.

Tail: The tail is characteristic of the breed, and should be turned over the back and carried flat, set high. It is profusely covered with long, spreading hair.

Faults:
Major—Round, domey skull. Too large ears. Undershot. Pink eye rims. Light or Dudley nose. Out at elbows or shoulders. Flat-sided dogs. Down in pasterns. Cowhocks. Soft, flat, open coat. Whole-coloured dogs with white chest, or white foot or leg. Black mask on an orange.
Objectionable—Overshot. Large, round or light eyes. High or low on legs. Long toes. Too wide in hind legs. Trimming too close to show-date. Tail-set too low on rump. Black, brown, blue and sable should be free from white hairs. Whites should be free from lemon or any other colour. Black and tan. Underweight or overweight.
Minor—Must be free from lippiness, wide chest. Tail should not curl back. Black mask on sable. White shadings on orange.

Poodle (Toy)

*T*HE HISTORY OF THE Toy Poodle is identical to that of both the Standard and the Miniature Poodles. This breed is the tiniest descendant of the continental water dogs known in Europe, especially in Germany and Russia, at least since the 16th century. In every respect, except height, the Toy Poodle is identical to his larger relatives, and is judged in the show ring by the same breed standard.

While there are a number of references to tiny poodles throughout the breed literature, it would seem that no attempt was made to develop a true, toy-sized Poodle until after the Miniature had been granted separate breed classification by The Kennel Club (England) in 1910. Dog writers do state that there are artistic representations of "little" Poodles dating to pre-Christian times. How "little" they do not state. Also it is reported that the early Russian Poodles varied in size from eighty-pound hunting dogs down to tinies weighing as little as the present-day Toy. It is also a matter of record that the Germans were the first to grade their *Pudel* into *grosse, mittlere,* and *kleine Pudel,* meaning large, medium, and small. But it was because of the work done by 20th-century breeders in both Britain and on this continent that the modern Toy Poodle came into being.

With the success of the Miniature, the challenge to reduce size even further was just too much for breeders to resist. Besides, the tremendous world-wide popularity that the Miniature was achieving promised an equal, if not greater, success for the more diminutive size. Spurred on by the challenge of creating a new breed and, in some cases unfortunately, the prospect of a lucrative market, the process of miniaturization began.

Undoubtedly the Toy was developed by mating small-sized Miniatures. It has been suggested that on this continent smaller breeds such as the Maltese and Bichon Frise may have been used to reduce size. Progress was slow, but by the late '40s and early '50s the Toy was so well established on both Continents that it was granted a separate registry for show purposes in Canada, and

G. STENHOUSE

Poodle (Toy)

in 1957 was granted official breed recognition in Britain. The English breed standard calls for a dog measuring under eleven inches at the shoulder. The Canadian and American standards state this measurement must be ten inches or less.

Like the Standard and the Miniature, the Toy Poodle comes in a wide range of solid colours. Particolours are not acceptable in the show ring.

Official Breed Standard for the Poodle (Toy)

FOR SHOW PURPOSES, THERE ARE THREE VARIETIES OF THE POODLE BREED—STANDARD, MINIATURE, AND TOY.

Origin and Purpose: The breed probably dates back to the late Roman period but certainly the variety we know as the Standard Poodle was well established across the whole of Europe by the 16th century. The Miniature and Toy varieties developed in the next two hundred or so years. The Poodle is the world's oldest water retriever, circus performer, and truffle hunter. The ubiquitous Poodle is such a versatile dog he can be all things to all people.

General Appearance, Carriage and Condition: That of a very active, gay, intelligent, smart, and elegant-looking dog, squarely built, well proportioned and carrying himself proudly. Properly clipped in the traditional fashion and carefully groomed, the Poodle has about him an air of distinction and dignity peculiar to himself.

Size: The Standard Poodle is over 15 in. (38.1 cm) at the highest point at the shoulder. Any Poodle 15 in. or less in height shall be disqualified from competition as a Standard Poodle. The Miniature Poodle is 15 in. (38.1 cm) or under at the highest point at the shoulder, with a minimum height in excess of 10 in. (25.4 cm). Any Poodle which is over 15 in., or 10 in. or under at the highest point at the shoulder, shall be disqualified from competition as a Miniature Poodle. The Toy Poodle is 10 in. (25.4 cm) or under at the shoulder. Any Poodle which is more than 10 in. at the highest point at the shoulder shall be disqualified from competition as a Toy Poodle.

Coat: Quality—Curly Poodles—dense, naturally harsh texture, even length, frizzy or curly. Corded Poodles—all hair hanging in tight even cords of varying lengths.

Clip—A Poodle under 12 months may be shown in the "Puppy Clip." In all regular classes, Poodles 12 months or over must be shown in the "English Saddle" or "Continental" Clip. A Poodle shown in competitive classes in any other clip shall be disqualified. However, the Brood Bitch and Stud Dog may be shown in any clip.

a) Puppy Clip: A Poodle under a year old may be shown in the Puppy Clip with the coat long. The face, throat, feet, and base of the tail are shaved. The entire shaven foot is visible. There is a pompon on the end of the tail. In order to give a neat appearance and a smooth unbroken line, shaping of the coat is permissible.

b) English Saddle Clip: In the English Saddle Clip, the face, throat, feet, forelegs and base of tail are shaved, leaving bracelets on the forelegs and a pompon on the end of the tail. The hindquarters are covered with a short blanket of hair except for a curved shaved area on each flank and two shaved bands on each hind leg at the stifle and hock joints. The entire shaven foot and a portion of the shaven foreleg above the bracelets are visible. The rest of the body is left in full coat but may be shaped in order to ensure over-all balance.

c) Continental Clip: In the Continental Clip, the face, throat, feet and base of the tail are shaved. The hindquarters are shaved with pompons (optional) on the hips. The legs are shaved leaving bracelets on the forelegs and rear legs. There is a pompon on the end of the tail. The entire shaven foot and a portion of the shaven foreleg above the bracelets are visible. The rest of the body is left in full coat but may be shaped to ensure over-all balance.

In all three clips the hair of the topknot may be left free, or shaped, or held in place by not more than three elastic bands.

Colour: Any solid colour. The coat is an even solid colour at the skin. In the blues, greys, silvers, browns, café-au-laits, apricots and creams, the coat may show varying shades of the same colour. This is frequently present in the somewhat darker feathering of the ears and in the tipping of the ruff. While clear colours are definitely preferred, such natural variations in the shading of the coat are not to be considered faults. Brown and café-au-lait Poodles may have brown-coloured noses, eye rims and lips, dark toenails and dark amber eyes. Black, blue, grey, silver, cream, and white Poodles have black noses, eye rims and lips, and black or self-coloured toenails, and very dark eyes. In the apricots, while the foregoing colour is preferred, brown noses, eye rims and lips and dark amber eyes are permitted but not desirable. Particoloured Poodles shall be disqualified. Particolour is at least two definite colours appearing in clearly defined markings at the skin.

Head and Expression: *Skull* should be slightly full and moderately peaked with a slight but definite stop. Cheekbones and muscles flat. Length from occiput to stop about the same as the length of muzzle. Viewed from the side, the plane of the top of the skull should extend parallel to the plane of the top of the muzzle. *Muzzle* long, straight and fine, but strong without lippiness. Moderate chiselling under the eyes. The chin definite enough to preclude snipiness. Teeth (42) white and strong. Tight scissors or level bite. Nose sharp with well-defined nostrils. *Eyes* oval shaped, very dark. Happy, alert and full of fire and intelligence. *Ears* hanging close to the head, set at or slightly below eye level. The ear leather is long, wide and thickly feathered, and when drawn forward almost reaches the nose.

Neck: Well proportioned, strong and long enough to admit of the head being carried high and with dignity. Skin snug at the throat.

Shoulders: Strong and smoothly muscled. The shoulder blade (scapula) is well laid back and is about the same length as the forearm (humerus).

Body: The chest deep and moderately wide. The ribs well sprung and braced up. To ensure the desirable squarely built appearance, the length of the body measured from the breastbone (sternum) to the pinbone (ischiatic tuberosity) approximates the height from the highest point at the shoulders to the ground. The back short and strong and very slightly hollowed immediately behind the withers. The loins short, broad, and muscular. Bone in proportion to the size of the dog.

Legs: Forelegs—straight, parallel when viewed from the front. When viewed from the side, the perpendicular line falls through the fourth thoracic vertebra, the rear point of the scapula, the elbow at the deepest point of the brisket, and the back of the pastern. The pasterns are strong.

Hind legs—straight and parallel when viewed from the rear. When viewed from the side, muscular with width in the region of the stifles, which are well bent. Pelvis and femur are about equal in length; pad to heel short and perpendicular to the ground. When standing, the rear toes are only slightly behind the point of the rump. The angulation of the hindquarters balances that of the forequarters.

Feet: Rather small and oval in shape. Toes well arched and close with webbing. Pads thick and firm. Nails short. The feet turn neither in nor out. Dewclaws may be removed.

Tail: Set on high, docked and carried up. Never curled nor carried over the back.

Gait: A straight, smooth, forward trot, verging on the single track, showing balanced reach and drive; pasterns, hocks and feet showing light springing action. Head and tail carried high. It is imperative that all three varieties be moved in the ring fully and decidedly to show correct gait.

Major Faults: Any distinct deviation from the desired characteristics described in the breed standard with particular attention to the following:

Temperament:	Shyness or viciousness
Bad mouth:	Undershot, overshot, wry mouth, missing teeth
Eyes:	Round protruding, large or very light
Muzzle:	Down faced, dish-faced, Roman nose, snipiness
Tail:	Set low, curled or carried over the back
Hindquarters:	Cowhocks or sicklehocks
Feet:	Flat or spread, thin pads, no webbing

Disqualifications: *Particolours, unorthodox clip, size—a Poodle over or under the height limits specified.*

Scale of Points:

General appearance, temperament, carriage, and condition	25
Head and expression	15
Neck and shoulders	10
Body, tail, and hindquarters	10
Legs and feet	10
Coat, colour, and texture	10
Gait	20
TOTAL	100

Pug

So MANY POTTERY REPLICAS of the Pug have come down to us from Victorian times that the breed seems almost synonymous with Victoriana. But these colourful, often comical likenesses merely bespeak the breed's popularity, especially with the ladies. The Pug had been known in Britain since the time of William of Orange (1689–1704) whose entourage included some pet Pugs. From that date onward the breed enjoyed royal favour, the most recent royal personages to be devoted to their Pugs being the Duke and Duchess of Windsor.

How the breed originated is another story. Some claim its ancestry dates to the time of the pharaohs; others that this was the result of cross breeding small Bulldogs, as evidenced by the pushed-in face. The much more likely, and more accepted, theory is that the breed originated in the Orient and was the smooth-coated, long-legged variety of the Pekingese.

Paintings from the period show that the Pug was well known on the continent in the sixteenth century and after William III's accession to the throne this became the fashionable pet in Britain.

Almost as much controversy surrounds the origin of the breed's name. There are those who claim it derives from the Latin and means "closed fist." Breed devotees prefer to think the name comes from the old English word *pugg* which meant "someone tenderly loved." To substantiate the latter claim fanciers state that the word *pugg* was in common use in Britain long before the dog arrived.

The breed was first shown in Britain in 1861, all the specimens being fawn in colour. Then in 1877 Lady Brassey returned from the Orient with two black Pugs purchased in China. These she bred to the darkest fawns, and by inter-breeding their progeny established a line of blacks, forerunners of the modern blacks.

The Pug Dog Club was formed in 1883, and soon after a breed standard was drawn up which remains essentially the same today. There was an entry of twenty-seven Pugs at the Westminster Kennel Club show in 1877. A total of forty-five were registered in Canada in the years 1888–1889.

G.STENHOUSE

Pug

Official Breed Standard for the Pug

General Appearance: Symmetry and general appearance, decidedly square and cobby. A lean, leggy Pug and a dog with short legs and a long body are equally objectionable.

Size: The Pug should be *multum in parvo*, but this condensation (if the word may be used) should be shown by compactness of form, well-knit proportions, and hardness of developed muscle. Weight from 14−18 lb. (6−8 kg) (dog or bitch) desirable.

Coat and Colour: Coat fine, smooth, soft, short and glossy, neither hard nor woolly. Colour silver or apricot-fawn. Each should be decided, to make the contrast complete between the colour and the trace and the mask. Black. Markings clearly defined. The muzzle or mask, ears, moles on cheeks, thumb mark or diamond on forehead, back-trace should be as black as possible. The mask should be black. The more intense and well defined it is the better. The trace is a black line extending from the occiput to the tail.

Head: Large, massive, round—not apple-headed, with no indentation of the skull. *Muzzle* short, blunt, square, but not up-faced. *Eyes* dark in colour, very large, bold and prominent, globular in shape, soft and solicitous in expression, very lustrous, and when excited, full of fire. *Ears* thin, small, soft, like black velvet. There are two kinds—the "rose" and "button." Preference is given to the latter.

Forequarters: Legs very strong, straight, of moderate length and well under.

Body: Short and cobby, wide in chest and well ribbed up. Wrinkles large and deep.

Hindquarters: Feet neither so long as the foot of the hare, nor so round as that of the cat; well-split-up toes, and the nails black.

Tail: Curled as tightly as possible over the hip. The double curl is perfection.

Scale of Points:

	Fawn	Black
Symmetry	10	10
Size	5	10
Condition	5	5
Body	10	10
Legs and feet	5	5
Head	5	5
Muzzle	10	10
Ears	5	5
Eyes	10	10
Mask	5	—
Wrinkles	5	5
Tail	10	10
Trace	5	—
Coat	5	5
Colour	5	10
TOTALS	100	100

Silky Toy Terrier

MOST DOG WRITERS state that the Silky Toy Terrier is a cross between the Yorkshire Terrier and the Australian Terrier. But there is more to the breed's history than that. While both of these breeds did contribute their share to the final product, the breed's beginnings date back to some time between 1820–30, when the daughter of the commandant of the penal settlement in Tasmania travelled to England, taking a blue-coloured, Broken-Coated Terrier with her. While in England, this dog was crossed with a Dandie Dinmont Terrier. The result was a litter of soft-coated blue puppies with the distinctive Dandie topknot which the Silky carries today.

Some of the puppies from this litter were bought by a Mr. Macarthur Little who did further experimental breeding, and when he emigrated to Australia he took some of this stock with him. By further selective breeding, both type and colour were well established, and this made-in-Australia breed attracted followings in both Victoria and New South Wales. In the early 1900s specialty clubs were formed in both areas and each drew up a separate breed standard, one for the Victorian Silky, the other for the Sydney Silky Terrier. It was by the latter name that the breed became known world wide until 1959, when the Australian National Kennel Council adopted a single standard for the breed and renamed it the Australian Silky Terrier. In the United States the breed is called the Silky Terrier; in Canada it is the Silky Toy Terrier.

Probably no other breed has been known by so many different names. No matter, for the Silky was designed with a single purpose in mind. He was bred to be a toy dog that would fill the role of family pet and companion while possessing the courage and keenness of a terrier. In this his creators succeeded. During World War II the breed made many friends among the American servicemen who were stationed in Australia, and it was through them that the Silky was introduced to the U.S. By 1959 there was sufficient interest in the breed to warrant its

Silky Toy Terrier

official recognition by the American Kennel Club. In the mid-sixties The Canadian Kennel Club added the Silky to its roster of recognized breeds.

Official Breed Standard for the Silky Toy Terrier

General Appearance: The Silky Toy Terrier is a lightly built, moderately low set, toy dog of pronounced terrier character and spirited action.

Temperament: The keen, alert air of the terrier is characteristic, with shyness or excessive nervousness to be faulted. The manner is quick, friendly, responsive.

Size: Weight ranges from 8–10 lb. (4–5 kg). Shoulder height from 9–10 in. (23–25 cm). Pronounced diminutiveness (such as a height of less than 8 in. (20 cm)) is not desired; it accentuates the quality of toyishness as opposed to the breed's definite terrier character.

Coat and Colour: Coat flat, in texture fine, glossy, silky; on matured specimens the desired length of coat from behind the ears to the set on of the tail is from 5–6 in. (13–15 cm). On the top of the head the hair is so profuse as to form a topknot, but long hair on face and ears is objectionable. Legs from knee and hock joints to feet should be free from long hair. The hair is parted on the head and down over the back to the root of the tail. Colour blue and tan. The blue may be silver blue, pigeon blue or slate blue, the tan deep and rich. The blue extends from the base of the skull to the tip of the tail, down the forelegs to the pasterns, and down the thighs to the hocks. On the tail the blue should be very dark. Tan appears on muzzle and cheeks, around the base of the ears, below the pasterns and hocks, and around the vent. There is a tan spot over each eye. The topknot should be silver or fawn.

Head: The head is strong, wedge-shaped, and moderately long. The *skull* is a trifle longer than the muzzle, in proportion about three-fifths for the skull, two-fifths for the muzzle. Skull flat, and not too wide between the ears. Stop shallow. The *nose* is black. Teeth strong and well aligned. Scissors bite. *Eyes* dark in colour, and piercingly keen in expression. *Ears* small, V-shaped and pricked. They are set high and carried erect without any tendency to flare obliquely off the skull.

Neck: The neck fits gracefully into sloping shoulders. It is medium long, fine and to some degree crested along its topline.

Forequarters: Well-laid-back shoulders, together with good angulation at the upper arm, set the forelegs nicely under the body. Forelegs are strong, straight, and rather fine boned.

Body: Low-set, about one fifth longer than the dog's height at the withers. The backline is straight, with a just perceptible rounding over the loins. Brisket medium wide, and deep enough to extend down to the elbows.

Hindquarters: Thighs well muscled and strong, but not so developed as to appear heavy. Legs moderately angulated at stifles and hocks, with the hocks low and equidistant from the hock joints to the ground. Feet small, cat-like, round, compact. Pads are thick and springy while the nails are strong and dark coloured. The feet point straight ahead, with no turning in or out. Dewclaws, if any, are removed.

Tail: The tail is set high and carried erect or semi-erect but not over gay. It is docked and well coated but devoid of plume.

Gait: Should be free, light footed, lively, and straight forward. Hindquarters should have strong propelling power.

Faults: Shyness or excessive nervousness. A bite markedly undershot or overshot is a serious fault. Light eyes are a fault. A too-short body is a fault. White or flesh-coloured nails are a fault. Toeing in or out on the move is to be faulted.

Toy Manchester Terrier

FOR A SMALL DOG, the Toy Manchester Terrier has had more than its share of names. Over the years it has been known as the Black and Tan Terrier (miniature), the Toy Black and Tan, and the name by which it has been known in Britain since 1960, the English Toy Terrier (black and tan). In Canada and the United States the original name, Toy Manchester, is still used.

This seems most appropriate because the little dog was developed from small specimens of the old English Black and Tan Terrier, which has a history dating back 400 years and from which the modern Manchester Terrier was developed. Like the Manchester, the smaller version was bred as a ratter and was able to give a good account of itself in the rat pit. One contest is on record in which the owner of a Toy Manchester called "Tiny, the Wonder," a five-and-a-half pounder, wagered that his dog could kill 300 rats in three hours. The match was held at the Queen's Hotel Tavern in London in 1848. Tiny killed the lot in the record time of fifty-four minutes, fifty seconds.

It is reported that towards the mid-19th century the toy black and tan almost became extinct because of the fad towards miniaturization. Ill-informed breeders bred from stock on the basis of small size only, without regard to the health or soundness of the dogs used. The result was dogs of decreased size but very faulty and lacking resistance to disease.

Fortunately for the Toy Manchester, more knowledgeable breeders took over and the breed has shown steady improvement since 1950. Crosses to the Italian Greyhound are said to have been used, giving the breed more elegance and lighter bone.

The temporary set-back, plus the very precise markings called for in the standard have kept the Toy Manchester from its deserved popularity. It was, and is, a game little terrier in miniature with all the attributes of an effective watch dog. Its fortunes may be on the upswing. Judged by the Toy Manchester Terriers seen in the show ring today, quality has reached a new high.

The Canadian Kennel Club Stud Book lists six Toy Manchester Terriers registered in the years 1888–1889.

Toy Manchester Terrier

Official Breed Standard for the Toy Manchester Terrier

Size: Weight not exceeding 12 lb. (5.5 kg). All dogs weighing more than 12 lb. (5.5 kg) shall be disqualified. It is recommended that at all dog shows the open class shall be (and any or all other classes, except puppy class, may be) divided as: *a)* under 7 lb. (3 kg); *b)* 7−12 lb. (3−5.5 kg).

Coat and Colour: Coat smooth, short, thick, dense, close, and glossy; not soft. Jet black and rich mahogany tan, which should not run or blend into each other but meet abruptly forming clear, well-defined lines of colour division. A small tan spot over each eye; a very small tan spot on each cheek; the lips of the upper and lower jaws should be tanned, extending under the throat, ending in the shape of the letter V; the inside of the ears partly tanned. Tan spots, called rosettes, on each side of the chest above the front legs, more pronounced in puppies than in adults. There should be a black "thumb mark" patch on the front of each foreleg between the pastern and the knee. There should be a distinct black "pencil mark" line running lengthwise on the top of each toe on all four feet. The remainder of the forelegs to be tan to the knee. Tan on the hind legs should continue from the pencilling on the feet up the inside of the legs to a little below the stifle joint; the outside of the hind legs to be black. There should be tan under tail, and on the vent, but only of such size as to be covered by the tail. (White in any part of the coat is a serious fault and shall disqualify whenever the white shall form a patch or stripe measuring as much as ½ inch (1 cm) in its longest dimension.)

Head: Long, narrow, tight skinned, almost flat, with a slight indentation up the forehead; slightly wedge-shaped, tapering to the nose, with no visible cheek muscles, and well filled up under the eyes; level in *mouth*, with tight-lipped jaws. *Nose* black. *Eyes* small, bright, sparkling and as near black as possible; set moderately close together; oblong in shape, slanting upwards on the outside; they should neither protrude nor sink in the skull. *Ears* of moderate size; set well up on skull and rather close together; thin, moderately narrow at base; with pointed tips; naturally erect carriage. Wide, flaring, blunt tipped or "bell" ears are a serious fault; cropped or cut ears shall disqualify.

Neck: The neck should be of moderate length, slim and graceful; gradually becoming large as it approaches, and blend smoothly with the sloping shoulders; free from throatiness; slightly arched from the occiput.

Forequarters: Shoulders sloping. Forelegs straight, and well under body. Feet compact, well arched, with jet-black nails; the two middle toes in the front feet rather longer than the others.

Body: Back slightly arched at the loin, and falling again to the joining of the tail to the same height as the shoulder; body moderately short, with robust loins; chest narrow between the legs; deep in the brisket; ribs well sprung out behind the shoulders.

Hindquarters: Hind legs should not turn in or out as viewed from the rear, carried back; hocks well let down. The hind feet shaped like those of a cat.

Tail: Moderately short, and set on where the arch of the back ends; thick where it joins the body, tapering to a point; not carried higher than the back.

Faults: White in any part of the coat is a serious fault. Wide, flaring, blunt tipped or "bell" ears are a serious fault.

Disqualifications: *Cropped or cut ears. White whenever it shall form a patch or stripe measuring as much as ¹/₂ inch (1 cm) in its longest dimension. Weight, more than 12 lb. (5.5 kg).*

Scale of Points:
Head (including eyes, nose, and ears)   30
Neck and shoulders   10
Body (including chest, and tail)   15
Legs and feet   15
Coat   10
Colour   20

        TOTAL   100

Yorkshire Terrier

ONE OF THE MOST GLAMOROUS and popular of the toy breeds, the Yorkshire Terrier was originally bred for the unglamorous job of keeping down the rats in the Yorkshire coal pits and cotton mills. It was also used by the miners as a sporting terrier in rat-killing contests.

If this seems a far cry from the dainty, profusely coated darling of today's show ring it should be remembered that this all took place in the mid-19th century, when the Yorky was bred to do the work of a terrier and when it weighed in the area of fifteen pounds.

How the breed was created remains a secret. It is assumed that the black and tan terrier, the Dandie Dinmont, and the Skye Terrier were crossed to produce the original ratter. What is known is that the Yorky was developed in the west riding of Yorkshire, and was first shown at a dog show held in Leeds in 1861 under the broad classification "Scotch Terriers."

Further "behind closed doors" breeding (this time a cross to the Maltese is assumed), resulted in a smaller dog with a very long coat that by 1880 was classified as a "Broken-Haired or Yorkshire Terrier." Somewhere about this time it was being regarded as a toy breed, not a terrier, and by 1886 it was officially given the breed name of Yorkshire Terrier.

When the Yorky first appeared as a distinct breed there were many critics who prophesied that the breed had no future and referred to it scathingly as "the Dresser Drawer Dog," this because in Yorkshire a cottage industry in breeding the little dogs flourished and they could be housed in very small quarters. While the men were not enthused about the Yorkshire Terrier, the breed made a big hit with the ladies and was soon in great demand especially among the wealthy.

Because of its unique coat and diminutive size, the Yorkshire Terrier is one of the most difficult dogs to breed. Nevertheless it ranks as the most popular toy breed in Britain today, and is high in the listings in both Canada and the United States.

The breed was first registered in Canada in the years 1888–1889.

Yorkshire Terrier

G. STENHOUSE

Official Breed Standard for the Yorkshire Terrier

General Appearance: Should be that of a long-coated toy terrier, the coat hanging quite straight and evenly down each side, a parting extending from the nose to the end of the tail.

The animal should be very compact and neat, the carriage being very upright, and having an important air. The general outline should convey the existence of a vigorous and well-proportioned body.

Coat and Colour: The hair on body moderately long and perfectly straight (not wavy), glossy like silk, and of a fine silky texture. Colour, a dark steel blue (not silver blue) extending from the occiput (or back of skull) to the root of the tail, and on no account mingled with fawn, bronze or dark hairs. All tan hair (on the head and legs) should be darker at the roots than in the middle, shading to a still lighter tan at the tips.

Head: Should be rather small and flat, not too prominent or round in the *skull*, nor too long in the *muzzle*, with a perfect black nose. The fall on the head to be long, of a rich golden tan, deeper in colour at the sides of the head about the ear roots, and on the muzzle where it should be very long. On no account must the tan on the head extend on to the neck, nor must there be any sooty or dark hair intermingled with any of the tan. *Mouth* perfectly even, with teeth as sound as possible. An animal having lost any teeth through accident not a fault, providing the jaws are even. *Eyes* medium, dark and sparkling, having a sharp, intelligent expression, and placed so as to look directly forward. They should not be prominent, and the edge of the eyelids should be of a dark colour. *Ears* small, V-shaped, and carried semi-erect, or erect, and not far apart, covered with short hair, colour to be of a very deep rich tan.

Forequarters: Legs quite straight, well covered with hair of a rich golden tan a few shades lighter at the ends than at the roots, not extending higher on the forelegs than the elbow.

Body: Level on the top of the back. Very compact, and a good loin. The hair on the chest a rich bright tan.

Hindquarters: Tan on the hind legs not extending higher on the hind legs than the stifle. Feet as round as possible, and the toenails black.

Tail: Cut to medium length; with plenty of hair, darker blue in colour than the rest of the body, especially at the end of the tail, and carried a little higher than the level of the back.

Scale of Points:

Formation and terrier appearance   15
Colour of hair on body   15
Richness of tan on head and legs   15
Quality and texture of coat   10
Quantity and length of coat   10
Head   10
Mouth   5
Legs and feet   5
Ears   5
Eyes   5
Tail (carriage of) . . . .   <u>5</u>

TOTAL   100

GROUP VI:
NON-SPORTING DOGS

Bichon Frise

ONE OF **CANADA'S** **MOST** recently recognized breeds, the Bichon Frise originated on the Spanish mainland, and has been known throughout Europe for many centuries. This is one of four varieties of Bichon: the Bichon Maltaise, Bichon Bolognese, Bichon Havanese, and the little dog now called the Bichon Frise, the Bichon Teneriffe. All are descended from the Barbet or Water Spaniel and named for the areas where they were most abundant. It is believed that some of these little dogs were taken to the Canary Islands (where they became well established on the island of Teneriffe), and were rediscovered in the 14th century by visiting sailors who returned with some of them to the mainland.

Back again on the continent the little Bichon's happy ways soon won him friends in high places. He became the favourite pet of the aristocracy, pampered by kings and ladies of the court, and was painted many times by masters of the French and Spanish schools. Then fashions in royal pets changed, and after four centuries of high living, the Bichon Teneriffe became the little street dog. But he was not without friends. He became the pet of the common people and because the Bichon was a master at performing tricks many earned their keep travelling with the circus and as the organ grinder's dog.

After World War I many Bichons were brought home as pets by returning soldiers, but nothing was done to establish the little dog as a pure breed until the 1930s when four French breeders began to take the Bichon seriously. They established bloodlines through controlled breeding programmes, and in 1933 a breed standard was draughted. The more suitable name *Bichon à poil frisé* or "Bichon of the curly coat" was selected, and in October 1934 the breed was admitted to the Stud Book of the French Kennel Club.

By 1971 there was sufficient interest in the Bichon Frise to warrant its admission into the Miscellaneous Class of the American Kennel Club, and subsequently the Bichon Frise was granted official breed status. Similar recognition followed in Canada in 1975.

Bichon Frise

Official Breed Standard for the Bichon Frise

Origin and Purpose: The Bichon Frise originated in the Canary Islands, and was formerly called the Teneriffe after the largest of this group of Islands. It has been bred as a companion dog because of its friendly and affectionate nature.

General Appearance: A small, sturdy, lively dog projecting an air of dignity and intelligence. Having a powder-puff appearance with the tail carried gaily over the back.

Temperament: Stable, outgoing and alert.

Size: Not under 9 in. (23 cm) and not over 12 in. (31 cm) at the withers with preference given to dogs 10–11 in. (25–28 cm), and bitches 9½–10½ in. (24–27 cm).

Coat and Colour: The coat should be white, with shadings of cream or apricot permissible in the ears and/or body. The coat is double with the outer hair profuse, soft, silky and loosely curled. Two in. (5 cm) or longer on adults. The skin pigmentation is preferably dark. Nose, lips and eye rims must be black.

Head: The circumference of the skull equals the height at the withers which should be approximately 10½ in. (27 cm). *Skull* broad and rather flat, not coarse, covered with a topknot of hair giving it a rounded appearance. *Muzzle:* the skull is longer than the muzzle in the ratio of 8:5. Not heavy or snipey, with a slightly accentuated stop. *Nose* black, round, and pronounced. *Mouth:* lips black, fine, and never drooping. Scissors bite. *Eyes* black or dark brown, large, round, expressive and alert, surrounded by halos which are dark grey to black pigmentations extending ¼ in. (.6 cm) or more around the eye. The *ear* is dropped, set level with the eyes and, when alerted, brought slightly forward but placed in such a way that the front edge touches the skull and does not angle away from the skull. Well covered with long, finely curled hair with the ear leather reaching the mid-point of the muzzle.

Neck: Fairly long, carried high and proudly. Round and slender near the skull, broadening gradually and fitting smoothly into the shoulders. Length of neck measures one-third that of body.

Forequarters: The shoulders are well laid back with upper and lower arms of equal length. The forelegs are perfectly straight, close to the body, with pasterns slightly bent.

Body: Length of body measured from sternum to pinbones longer than the height at the withers, the ideal ratio being 10:13. There is a gradual slant upwards from the withers to the rump. The sternum well pronounced with a good spring of ribs rather round and blending smoothly into the loin. The chest is deep, extending to the elbows. The loin is large and muscular. The tail is set on level with the back.

Hindquarters: The upper thigh is well muscled with stifle well bent.

Feet: Round and tight (cat's paw); pads thick.

Tail: The tail is carried upwards, elegantly curled, in line with the spine without being rolled up; the tail is not docked. The tailbone should not touch the back, however the feathering may.

Gait: Balanced and vigorous, with good reach in the forequarters and good drive in the hindquarters. The legs must move straight fore and back along the line of travel.

Faults: Cowhocks, snipey muzzle, poor pigmentation, protruding eyes, yellow eyes, undershot or overshot bite in excess of 1.6 mm. Corkscrew tail, too short a coat in adult dogs.

Disqualifications: *Over 12 in. (30 cm) or under 9 in. (23 cm). Black hair in the coat, pink eye rims.*

Boston Terrier

THE BOSTON TERRIER, sometimes erroneously called the Boston Bull or Toy Bulldog, is unique in that it originated and was developed to its present standard of excellence in the United States. Originally bred as a pit fighter, (the sport flourishing in and around the Boston area in the mid-19th century), the Boston Terrier represents a cross between the Bulldog and the Bull Terrier. First specimens are said to have been much heavier than the modern Boston, more similar in type to the Staffordshire Bull Terrier, and were popularly known as "round heads." For this reason, since the Boston's debut in the show ring, some authorities suggest that a further cross to the French Bulldog was used to give the breed its needed touch of elegance.

The breed might have passed into limbo when dog fighting was outlawed in the United States had it not been for a group of breeders who worked to promote official recognition of the Boston (at that time as yet unnamed). First of the breed to be exhibited was at the Massachusetts Kennel Club show held in 1878, when a ten-month-old puppy competed as a Bull Terrier. Obviously this classification was incorrect, so four years later classes were provided for "Round Heads and Bull Terriers, any colour."

In 1891 Boston area breeders organized a specialty club under the name of "The American Bull Terrier Club"—a title that was not acceptable to the prevailing kennel authority, so the group was renamed the Boston Terrier Club, and in 1893 the breed was granted official status by the American Kennel Club.

The Boston Terrier became the most popular breed in the States between the years 1929–1935 and is well represented in most countries around the world. It is said that because of its conformation (large head, narrow pelvis) the Boston is a difficult and often expensive breed to produce. Therefore only the best breed representatives are used for breeding purposes. Thus, despite a period of immense popularity, over-all quality within the breed has been maintained.

The Boston Terrier was first registered in Canada in the years 1888–1889.

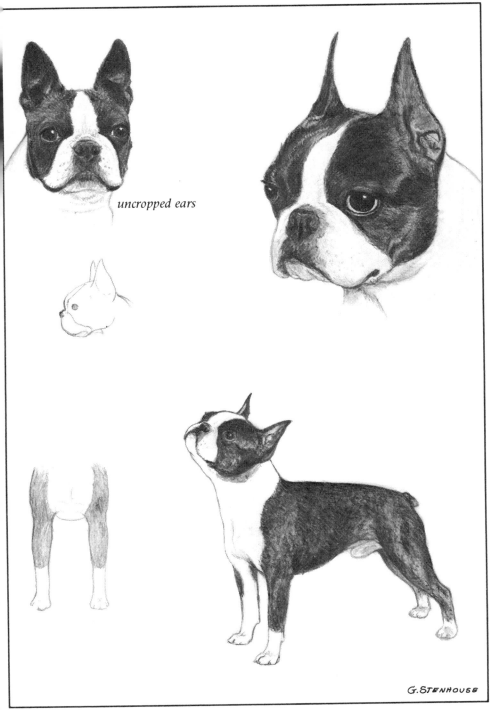

uncropped ears

G. STENHOUSE

Boston Terrier

Official Breed Standard for the Boston Terrier

General Appearance: The general appearance of the Boston Terrier should be that of a lively, highly intelligent, smooth-coated, short-headed, compactly built, short-tailed, well-balanced dog of medium station, of brindle colour and evenly marked with white. The head should indicate a high degree of intelligence, and should be in proportion to the size of the dog; the body rather short and well knit, the limbs strong and neatly turned; tail short; and no feature be so prominent that the dog appears badly proportioned.

The dog should convey an impression of determination, strength and activity, with a style of a high order; carriage easy and graceful.

A proportionate combination of "colour" and "ideal markings" is a particularly distinctive feature of a representative specimen, and a dog with a preponderance of white on body, or without the proper proportion of brindle and white on head, should possess sufficient merit otherwise to counteract its deficiencies in these respects.

The ideal "Boston Terrier expression" displays "a high degree of intelligence," and is an important characteristic of the breed.

"Colour and markings" and "expression" should be given particular consideration in determining the relative value of "general appearance" to other points.

Size: Not exceeding 25 lb. (11 kg), divided by classes as follows: lightweight, under 15 lb. (7 kg); middleweight, 15 lb. and under 20 lb. (7−9 kg); heavyweight, 20 lb. and not exceeding 25 lb. (9−11 kg).

Coat and Colour: Coat short, smooth, bright and fine in texture. Colour brindle with white markings. The brindle to be evenly distributed and distinct. Black with white markings permissible but brindle with white markings preferred. Ideal markings: white muzzle, even white blaze over head, collar, breast, part or whole of forelegs, and hind legs below hocks. Faults: Long or coarse coat; coat lacking lustre. All white; absence of white marking; preponderance of white on body; without the proper proportion of brindle and white on head; or any variation detracting from the general appearance.

Head: *Skull* square, flat on top, free from wrinkles; cheeks flat; brow abrupt, stop well defined. *Muzzle* short, square, wide and deep, and in proportion to skull; free from wrinkles; shorter in length than in width and depth, not exceeding in length approximately one-third of length of skull; width and depth carried out well to end; the muzzle from stop to end of nose on a line parallel to the top of the skull.

Nose black and wide, with well-defined line between nostrils. *Mouth:* the jaws broad and square, with short regular teeth. Bite even or sufficiently undershot to square muzzle. The chops of good depth but not pendulous, completely covering the teeth when mouth is closed. *Eyes* wide apart, large and round, dark in colour, expression alert, but kind and intelligent. The eyes should be set square in the skull, and the outside corners should be on a line with the cheeks as viewed from the front. *Ears* carried erect, either cropped to conform to the shape of the head, or natural bat, situated as near the corners of skull as possible.

Faults: Skull "domed" or inclined; furrowed by a medial line; skull too long for breadth, or vice versa; stop too shallow; brow and skull too slanting. Muzzle wedge-shaped or lacking depth; down-faced; too much cut out below the eyes; pinched or wide nostrils; butterfly nose; protruding teeth; weak lower jaw; showing turn-up, lay back; wrinkled. Eyes small or sunken; too prominent; light colour or walleye; showing too much white or haw. Ears poorly carried or in size out of proportion to head.

Neck: Of fair length, slightly arched and carrying the head gracefully; setting neatly into shoulders. Faults: Ewe-necked; throatiness; short and thick.

Forequarters: Shoulders sloping. Elbows standing neither in nor out. Forelegs set moderately wide apart and on a line with the point of the shoulders; straight in bone and well muscled; pasterns short and strong. Faults: Loose shoulders or elbows; long or weak pasterns.

Body: Deep with good width of chest; back short; ribs deep and well sprung, carried well back to loins; loins short and muscular; rump curving slightly to set-on of tail; flank very slightly cut up. The body should appear short but not chunky. Faults: Flat sides; narrow chest; long or slack loins; roach back; sway back; too much cut-up in flank.

Hindquarters: Hind legs set true; bent at stifles; short from hocks to feet; hocks turning neither in nor out; thighs strong and well muscled. Feet round, small, and compact and turned neither in nor out; toes well arched. Faults: Hind legs too straight at stifles; hocks too prominent; splay feet.

Tail: Set-on low; short, fine and tapering; straight or screw; devoid of fringe or coarse hair, and not carried above horizontal.
   Faults: A long or gaily carried tail; extremely gnarled or curled against body. (**NOTE:** The preferred tail should not exceed in length approximately half the distance from set-on to hock.)

Gait: The gait of the Boston Terrier is that of a sure-footed straight-gaited dog, forelegs and hind legs moving straight ahead in line with perfect rhythm, each step indicating grace with power. Faults: There shall be no rolling, paddling, or weaving when gaited, and any crossing movement, either front or rear, is a serious fault.

Faults: Long or coarse coat; coat lacking lustre. All white; absence of white marking; preponderance of white on body; without the proper proportion of brindle and white on head; or any variations detracting from the general appearance. Skull "domed" or inclined; furrowed by a medial line; skull too long for breadth, or vice versa; stop too shallow; brow and skull too slanting. Muzzle wedge-shaped or lacking depth; down-faced; too much cut out below the eyes; pinched or wide nostrils; butterfly nose; protruding teeth; weak lower jaw; showing turn-up, layback, or wrinkled. Eyes small or sunken; too prominent; light colour or walleye; showing too much white or haw. Ears poorly carried or in size out of proportion to head. Ewe-necked; throatiness; neck short and thick. Loose shoulders or elbows; long or weak pasterns. Flat sides; narrow chest; long or slack loins; roach back; sway back; too much cut-up in flank. Hind legs too straight at stifles; hocks too prominent; splay feet. A long or gaily carried tail; extremely gnarled or curled against body. Rolling, paddling or weaving when gaited; any crossing movement, either front or rear.

Disqualifications: *Solid black; black and tan; liver or mouse colours. Dudley nose.*

Scale of Points:

General appearance	10
Skull	10
Eyes	5
Muzzle	10
Ears	2
Neck	3
Body	15
Elbows	4
Forelegs	5
Hind legs	5
Gait	10
Feet	5
Tail	5
Colour	4
Ideal markings	5
Coat	2
TOTAL	100

Bulldog

*I*T IS BELIEVED that the ancester of both the Bulldog and the Mastiff, the Molossian dog, was brought to Britain by Phoenician traders in the 6th century B.C. From this dog evolved the Alaunt, a powerful breed that was used to hunt wild boar and to drive beef cattle. Thus it became known as "the butcher's dog" and, sometime later, the Bulldog.

It is reported that in the 13th century a member of the aristocracy was so amused by two Bulldogs that were chasing an enraged bull that he donated land for the purpose of "bull running," a diversion which became an annual event in three districts in England until it was outlawed in 1778.

Another pastime popular in all parts of England was bull baiting, which had survived since Roman times. In this competition the dog attempted to bring the bull down by fastening onto its lip, tongue, or eye. A dog that attacked the bull in any other area, for example the leg or throat, was not considered to be pure-bred. To be the winner in such a contest the dog needed his unique head and body characteristics for power and to protect him from serious injury.

In the latter part of the 18th century, dog fighting took over as the popular sport, an activity for which the Bulldog was ill-suited. To please the public fancy a longer-jawed, more aggressive dog was needed for the fighting pit, so the Bulldog was crossed with the terrier. Thus fewer pure-blooded Bulldogs were being produced. Then in the first quarter of the 19th century bull baiting was outlawed, and the breed's usefulness seemed to be at an end. Had it not been for a handful of bulldoggers who appreciated the breed for its character and as a symbol of British tenacity, the pure-bred Bulldog would have become extinct.

Because of these breeders' efforts a Bulldog Club was formed whose motto was "Hold Fast." A breed standard was draughted, and the Bulldog was among the first breeds to be recognized when The Kennel Club (England) was organized in 1873. The breed was first shown on this continent at the New York show in 1880. The Canadian Kennel Club Stud Book lists four English Bulldogs registered in the years 1888–1889.

rose ear

G. STENHOUSE

Bulldog

Official Breed Standard for the Bulldog

General Appearance: The perfect Bulldog must be of medium size and smooth coat; with heavy, thick-set, low-swung body, massive short-faced head, wide shoulders and sturdy limbs. The general appearance and attitude should suggest great stability, vigour, and strength. The demeanour should be pacific and dignified. These attributes should be countenanced by the expression and behaviour.

The "points" should be well distributed and bear good relation one to the other, no feature being in such prominence from either excess or lack of quality that the animal appears deformed or ill-proportioned.

In comparison with specimens of different sex, due allowance should be made in favour of the bitches which do not bear the characteristics of the breed to the same degree of perfection and grandeur as do the dogs.

Temperament: The disposition should be equable and kind, resolute and courageous (not vicious or aggressive).

Size: The size for mature dogs is about 50 lb. (23 kg); for mature bitches about 40 lb. (18 kg).

Coat and Colour: The coat should be straight, short, flat, close, of fine texture, smooth and glossy. (No fringe, feather, or curl.) The colour of coat should be uniform, pure of its kind and brilliant. The various colours found in the breed are to be preferred in the following order: *a)* red brindle; *b)* all other brindles; *c)* solid white; *d)* solid red, fawn, or fallow; *e)* piebald; *f)* inferior qualities of all the foregoing.

NOTE: A perfect piebald is preferable to a muddy brindle or defective solid colour.

Solid black is very undesirable, but not so objectionable if occurring to a moderate degree in piebald patches. The brindles, to be perfect, should have a fine, even and equal distribution of the composite colours.

In brindles and solid colours a small white patch on the chest is not considered detrimental. In piebalds the colour patches should be well defined, of pure colour and symmetrically distributed.

The skin should be soft and loose, especially at the head, neck and shoulders.

Head: The head and face should be covered with heavy wrinkles. The *skull* should be very large, and in circumference, in front of the ears, should measure at least the height of the dog at the shoulders. Viewed from the front, it should appear very high from the corner of the lower jaw to the apex of the skull, and also very broad and square. Viewed at the side, the head should appear very high, and very short from the point of the nose to occiput. The forehead should be flat (not rounded or domed), neither too prominent nor overhanging the face. The cheeks should be well rounded, protruding sideways and outward beyond the eyes.

The temples or frontal bones should be very well defined, broad, square and high, causing a hollow or groove between the eyes. This indentation, or stop, should be both broad and deep and extend up the middle of the forehead, dividing the head vertically, being traceable to the top of the skull.

Muzzle: the face, measured from the front of the cheekbone to the tip of the nose, should be extremely short, the muzzle being very short, broad, turned upwards and very deep from the corner of the eye to the corner of the mouth. The chops or flews should be thick, broad, pendant, and very deep, completely overhanging the lower jaw at each side. They join the underlip in front and almost or quite cover the teeth, which should be scarcely noticeable when the mouth is closed.

The *nose* should be large, broad and black, its tip being set back deeply between the eyes. The distance from bottom of stop, between the eyes, to the tip of nose should be as short as possible and not exceed the length from the tip of nose to the edge of underlip. The nostrils should be wide, large and black, with a well-defined line between them. Any nose other than black is objectionable and Dudley or flesh-coloured nose absolutely disqualifies from competition.

Mouth: the jaws should be massive, very broad, square and undershot, the lower jaw projecting considerably in front of the upper jaw and turning up. The teeth should be large and strong, with the canine teeth or tusks wide apart; the six small teeth in front, between the canines, in an even, level row.

The *eyes*, seen from the front, should be situated low down in the skull, as far from the ears as possible, and their corners should be in a straight line at right angles with the stop. They should be quite in front of the head, as wide apart as possible, provided their outer corners are within the outline of the cheeks when viewed from the front. They should be quite round in form, of moderate size neither sunken nor bulging, and in colour should be very dark. The lids should cover the white of the eyeball, when the dog is looking directly forward, and the lid should show no haw.

The *ears* should be set high in the head, the front inner edge of each ear joining the outline of the skull at the top back corner of skull, so as to place them as wide apart, and as high, and as far from the eyes as possible. In size they should be small and thin. The shape termed "rose ear" is the most desirable. The rose ear folds inward at its back lower edge, the upper front edge curving over, outwards and backwards, showing part of the inside of the burr. (The ears should not be carried erect or prick-eared or buttoned and should never be cropped.)

Neck: The neck should be short, very thick, deep and strong and well arched at the back. At the throat, from jaw to chest, there should be two loose pendulous folds, forming the dewlap.

Forequarters: The shoulders should be muscular, very heavy, widespread and slant outward, giving stability and great power. The elbows should be low and stand well out and loose from the body. The forelegs should be short, very stout, straight and muscular, set wide apart, with well-developed calves, presenting a bowed outline, but the bones of the legs should not be curved or bandy, nor the feet brought too close together. The feet should be moderate in size, compact and firmly set. Toes compact, well split up, with high knuckles and with short stubby nails. The front feet may be straight or slightly out-turned.

Body: The back should be short and strong, very broad at the shoulders and comparatively narrow at the loins. There should be a slight fall in the back, close behind the shoulders (its lowest part), whence the spine should rise to the loins (the top of which should be higher than the top of the shoulders), thence curving again more suddenly to the tail forming an arch (a very distinctive feature of the breed) termed roach back or, more correctly "wheel-back."

The brisket and body should be very capacious, with full sides, well-rounded ribs and very deep from the shoulders down to its lowest part, where it joins the chest. The chest should be very broad, deep, and full. It should be well let down between the shoulders and forelegs, giving the dog a broad, low, short-legged appearance.

The body should be well ribbed up behind with the belly tucked up and not rotund.

Hindquarters: The hind legs should be strong and muscular and longer than the forelegs, so as to elevate the loins above the shoulders.

Hocks should be slightly bent and well let down, so as to give length and strength from loins to hock.

The lower leg should be short, straight and strong, with the stifles turned slightly outward and away from the body. The hocks are thereby made to approach each other, and the hind feet to turn outward.

The hind feet should be pointed well outward.

Tail: The tail may be either straight or screwed (but never curved or curly), and in any case must be short, hung low, with decided downward carriage, thick root and fine tip. If straight, the tail should be cylindrical and of uniform taper. If screwed, the bends or kinks should be well defined, and they may be abrupt and even knotty, but no portion of the member should be elevated above the base or root.

Gait: The style and carriage are peculiar, his gait being a loose-jointed, shuffling, sidewise motion, giving the characteristic "roll." The action must, however be unrestrained, free and vigorous.

Disqualification: *Dudley or flesh-coloured nose.*

(Breed Standard continued)

Scale of Points:

GENERAL PROPERTIES

Proportion and symmetry	5	
Attitude	3	
Expression	2	
Gait	3	
Size	3	
Coat	2	
Colour of coat	4	22

HEAD

Skull	5	
Cheeks	2	
Stop	4	
Eyes and eyelids	3	
Ears	5	
Wrinkle	5	
Nose	6	
Chops	2	
Jaws	5	
Teeth	2	39

BODY, LEGS, ETC.

Neck	3	
Dewlap	2	
Shoulders	5	
Chest	3	
Ribs	3	
Brisket	2	
Belly	2	
Back	5	
Forelegs and elbows	4	
Hind legs	3	
Feet	3	
Tail	4	39
TOTAL		100

Chow Chow

THE CHOW CHOW has been known in China (Mongolia) since 150 B.C. A member of the Spitz family of dogs, some authorities claim that the breed descends from the Tibetan Mastiff, while others hold that the Chow Chow is an original breed. Some experts believe the first specimens were black but when smoky blues appeared in a litter, dogs of this colour were elevated to the role of temple dogs which guarded the Buddhist monasteries.

The Chow's guarding ability is legendary in China where the breed has been known variously as "the black-tongued," "wolf," and "bear dog." This is the only breed of dog possessing a blue-black tongue, and authorities claim this gives credence to the "original" theory.

The breed was brought to England during the latter part of the 18th century, but it was not until Queen Victoria took an interest in Chow Chows that they began to become popular. A breed club was formed in England in 1895, and since becoming a recognized breed in the United States in 1901, the Chow has made steady progress on this continent.

Different styles of Chow Chow seem to prevail in different parts of the world. However, international authorities state that the breed style is becoming more uniform around the world.

The Chow Chow is valued most today as a pet and guardian of the home and is classified among the breeds in the Non-Sporting Group. First registrations for the breed in Canada are recorded in The Canadian Kennel Club Stud Book for the years 1911–1912.

G.STENHOUSE

Chow Chow

Official Breed Standard for the Chow Chow

General Appearance: A massive, cobby, powerful dog, active and alert, with strong, muscular development, and perfect balance. Body squares with height of leg at shoulder; head, broad and flat, with short, broad, and deep muzzle, accentuated by a ruff; the whole supported by straight, strong legs. Clothed in a shining, offstanding coat, the Chow is a masterpiece of beauty, dignity, and untouched naturalness.

Coat and Colour: Coat abundant, dense, straight, and offstanding; rather coarse in texture with a soft, woolly undercoat. It may be any clear colour, solid throughout, with lighter shadings on ruff, tail, and breechings.

Head: Large and massive in proportion to size of dog, with broad, flat *skull*; well filled under the eyes; moderate stop; and proudly carried. *Muzzle* short in comparison to length of skull; broad from eyes to end of nose, and of equal depth. *Nose* large, broad, and black in colour. The *lips* somewhat full and overhanging. *Teeth* strong and level, with a scissors bite; should neither be overshot, nor undershot. Tongue a blue-black. The tissues of the *mouth* should approximate black. *Eyes* dark, deep set, of moderate size, and almond shaped. *Ears* small, slightly rounded at tip, stiffly carried. They should be placed wide apart, on top of the skull, and set with a slight, forward tilt. Expression essentially dignified, lordly, scowling, discerning, sober, and snobbish—one of independence.

Neck: Strong, full, set well on the shoulders.

Forequarters: Shoulders muscular, slightly sloping. Forelegs perfectly straight, with heavy bone and upright pasterns.

Body: Short, compact. Back short, straight, and strong. Chest broad, deep, and muscular, with well-sprung ribs. A narrow chest is a serious fault. Loins broad, deep, and powerful, and let down in the flank.

Hindquarters: Hind legs straight-hocked, muscular, and heavy boned. Feet compact, round, cat-like, with thick pads.

Tail: Set well up and carried closely to the back, following line of spine at start.

Gait: Completely individual. Short and stilted because of straight hocks.

Disqualifications: *Nose spotted or distinctly any other colour than black, except in blue Chows, which may have solid blue or slate noses. Tongue red, pink, or obviously spotted with red or pink. Drop ear or ears. A drop ear is one which is stiffly carried or stiffly erect, but which breaks over at any point from its base to its tip.*

Dalmatian

THERE ARE SEVERAL THEORIES concerning the origin of the Dalmatian, none proven. One is that the breed originated in northern India and was brought to Dalmatia, now a part of Yugoslavia, by bands of travelling gypsies. Certainly the breed has been known throughout Europe since the Middle Ages as a sporting dog, as evidenced by paintings dating from the 16th century which depict dogs of the Dalmatian type in hunting scenes.

This is the only breed of dog with spots, and this is the reason for many of the Dalmatian's nicknames: among them "the Plum Pudding Dog," "Spotted Dick," and "the Bengal Harrier." Other nicknames relate to the breed's affinity for horses. These include "Coach Dog," "Carriage Dog," and "Fire House Dog." It is in these roles that the Dalmatian is most familiar.

A dog of extreme stamina capable of travelling great distances, the Dalmatian trotted with the carriages, at first to protect the travellers from highwaymen. Later their function was strictly ornamental. The Dalmatian also enjoyed life as a fire house mascot, particularly in the United States. At the first alarm the dog would race onto his perch on the horse-drawn fire wagon and often did his bit by locating fire victims and helping in their rescue.

These are but two of the useful careers the Dalmatian has followed over the years. He's been used as a cattle drover, as draught dog, and ratter. In wartime he's served as tracker and sentinel. In Australia he's been used to hunt wild pig, and because the breed is so adaptable and easily trained he has often been seen as a circus performer.

In 1890 in Britain, a group of fanciers organized a club for the breed and in the same year the Dalmatian breed standard was draughted. But, despite all his talents, when the automobile replaced the horse-drawn carriage, the Dalmatian's popularity dwindled. Then, in the mid-1950s, the breed was swept into prominence with the publication of Dodie Smith's book *101 Dalmatians*, later made into a Disney motion picture. Since then the breed's popularity has been assured.

The Dalmatian was first registered in Canada in 1902.

G.STENHOUSE

Dalmatian

Official Breed Standard for the Dalmatian

Origin and Purpose: The Dalmatian is thought to be of Central European or Mediterranean origin and is known at least from the Middle Ages. Because of its affinity for horses, and capacity to travel great distances at a steady pace, it came to be used as a dog to run with and guard coaches and was known as a stable dog. Even later, the Dalmatian became popular as a dog to travel with and guard horse-drawn fire-fighting equipment especially in the United States.

General Appearance: The Dalmatian should be a well balanced, strong, muscular and active dog, free from coarseness and lumber: capable of great endurance and speed compatible to its purpose.

Temperament: A lively, active dog of good demeanour.

Size: Over-all balance is of prime importance and the height of dogs ideally is 22−24 in. (56−61 cm), bitches 21−23 in. (53−58 cm).

Coat and Colour: The coat should be short, dense and fine, slightly glossy, neither woolly nor silky. The colour and markings are most important. There are two acceptable colours: white with black spots and white with liver spots. The ground colour should be pure white. Black spots should be as deep and rich as possible. Liver spots should be of a colour closer to chocolate than to tan or yellow. The spots should not intermingle, but be as round and well defined as possible, the more distinct the better, in size they should be from that of a dime to half a dollar. The spots on the face, head, ears, legs, tail and extremities should be smaller than those on the body.

Head: Should be of a fair length exhibiting a moderate amount of stop, and not in one straight line from the nose to the occiput bone. *Skull:* flat, rather broad between the ears and moderately well defined at the temple. It should be entirely free from permanent wrinkle. *Muzzle* should be long and powerful, never snipey; the lips clean, fitting the jaws moderately close. *Nose* in the black spotted dogs, should always be black: in the liver-spotted dogs always brown. *Mouth:* the teeth should meet in a scissors bite. The incisors of the lower jaw touch very lightly the bottom of the inner surface of the upper incisors. *Eyes* should be set moderately well apart, and of medium size, round, bright and sparkling, with an intelligent expression, their colour greatly depends on the markings of the dog. In the black-spotted dogs, the eyes should be dark (black or brown) in the liver-spotted dogs they should be lighter (amber or brown). Blue or partly blue eyes are undesirable and should be penalized. The rims around the eyes in the black-spotted dogs should be black; brown in the liver-spotted dogs. No dog should have flesh-coloured eye rims. *Ears* should be set on rather high, of moderate size, rather wide at the base and gradually tapering to a rounded point. They should be carried close to the head, be thin and fine in texture, and always spotted, the more profusely the better. Solid black or liver is undesirable.

Neck: The neck should be fairly long, nicely arched, light and tapering and entirely free from throatiness.

Forequarters: Shoulder should be well laid, not straight, and should be clean and muscular denoting speed. It should be laid flat against the body. Leg: the forelegs should be perfectly straight, strong and heavy in bone; elbows close to the body. Pasterns should be straight. Feet: forefeet should be compact, with well arched toes, and tough elastic pads. Nails in the black-spotted dogs should be black or white: or a nail may be both black and white; in the liver-spotted dogs, brown or white, or a nail may be both brown and white.

Body: Topline should be level and may arch slightly over the loin. Chest should not be too wide, but very deep and capacious, ribs moderately well sprung, never rounded like barrel hoops (which would indicate want of speed). Loin should be strong and muscular.

Hindquarters: Upper thigh and lower thigh muscles should be clean, powerful and well defined. Hocks should be well let down. Stifle should be moderately well bent. Feet: as for the forefeet.

Tail: The tail should reach the hock, being strong at the base and gradually tapering towards the end, free from coarseness; it should not be set on too low down and should be carried with a slight upward curve but never curled. It should preferably be spotted.

Gait: The Dalmatian should have great freedom of movement; a smooth, powerful, rhythmic stride and action with good reach and drive. Viewed from behind the hind legs should track the fore with no indication of the body moving at an angle to the point of direction. A short stride and/or a paddling action are incorrect.

Faults: Partly flesh-coloured nose. Cowhocks. Flat feet. Incompletely coloured eye rims. Any eye colour other than black, brown, or amber.

Disqualifications: *Patches; a patch is defined as a solid sharply defined mass of black or liver that is appreciably larger than any other of the markings on the dog. Several spots that are so adjacent that they actually touch one another at their edges do not constitute a patch. Tricolours. Any colour other than liver and white or black and white. Undershot or more than ⅛ inch (.3 cm) overshot bite.*

Scale of Points:

Head and eyes	10
Ears	5
Neck and shoulders	10
Body, back, chest, and loins	10
Legs and feet	10
Gait	10
Coat	5
Colour and markings	25
Tail	5
Size, symmetry, etc.	10
TOTAL	100

French Bulldog

AUTHORITIES SEEM TO AGREE that the British Bulldog was the breeding stock from which the Miniature or Toy Bulldog was developed. It took further crosses to various breeds before the French Bulldog, as we know it today, came into being. What these breeds might have been remains a mystery, but the facts are that during the mid-nineteenth century, the tiny Bulldog was much favoured as a family pet, and that the dogs were the most numerous in the English Midlands, where lace-making flourished as a local industry. Attracted by the prospects of better jobs many of these English laceworkers emigrated to France taking their toy Bulldogs with them. It was there that the crosses to other breeds took place, and the resultant offspring completely charmed the French, especially those specimens with erect, bat ears. Prior to this the ear had been the typical Bulldog "rose ear."

Returning from a visit to France an American brought two of these little dogs with him to the United States where, once again, the breed attracted a following of admirers. It is the American fanciers who are credited with "fixing" the bat ear which has become the hallmark of the breed. A few imports found their way back to England as well as others from the continent. It is these imports that are credited with strengthening the British-bred type.

Defying opposition from the Miniature Bulldog faction, "Frenchie" enthusiasts formed their own specialty club in 1902, gained official recognition of the breed from The Kennel Club (England) and three years later held the first championship show for French Bulldogs. Although it was some time before the breed name was Anglicized, being first known in Britain as the "Bouldogue Français," some die-hard Britons were horrified that a continental breed presumed to use the bulldog appellation which to them had become the symbol of the British Empire.

While the Frenchie has never attained extreme popularity, it does have a following around the world and an almost universally accepted breed standard except in the matter of colour. The

French Bulldog

fawns and creams, which are highly favoured in Britain, the United States, and Canada, are still unacceptable colours in Europe. While show entries seem to be on the increase in the United States, especially at the larger shows, only the occasional French Bulldog appears in the show ring in Canada.

Official Breed Standard for the French Bulldog

General Appearance: The French Bulldog should have the appearance of an active, intelligent, muscular dog, of heavy bone, smooth coat, compactly built, and of medium or small structure.

The points should be well distributed and bear good relation one to the other, no feature being in such prominence from either excess or lack of quality that the animal appears deformed or poorly proportioned.

In comparison to specimens of different sex, due allowance should be made in favour of the bitches, which do not bear the characteristics of the breed to the same marked degree as do the dogs.

Size: A lightweight class under 22 lb. (10 kg); heavyweight class, 22 lb. and not over 28 lb. (10–13 kg).

Coat and Colour: Acceptable colours are: all brindle, fawn, white, brindle and white, and any colour except those which constitute disqualification. The skin should be soft and loose, especially at head and shoulders, forming wrinkles. Coat moderately fine, brilliant, short and smooth.

Head: The head should be large and square. The top of the *skull* should be flat between the ears; the forehead should not be flat but slightly rounded. The stop should be well defined, causing a hollow or groove between the eyes. The *muzzle* should be broad, deep, and well laid back; the muscles of the cheeks well developed. The *nose* should be extremely short; nostrils broad with well defined line between them. The nose and flews should be black, except in the case of the lighter-coloured dogs, where a lighter colour of nose is acceptable. The flews should be thick and broad, hanging over the lower jaw at the sides, meeting the underlip in front and covering the teeth which should not be seen when the mouth is closed. The underjaw should be deep, square, broad, undershot, and well turned up.

The *eyes* should be wide apart, set low down in the skull, as far from the ears as possible, round in form, of moderate size, neither sunken nor bulging, and in colour dark. No haw and no white of the eye showing when looking forward. The **ears** shall hereafter be known as the bat ear, broad at the base, elongated, with round top, set high in the head, but not too close together, and carried erect with the orifice to the front. The leather of the ear, fine and soft.

Neck: The neck should be thick and well arched, with loose skin at throat.

Forequarters: The forelegs should be short, stout, straight and muscular, set wide apart.

Body: The body should be short and well rounded. The back should be a roach back, with a slight fall close behind the shoulders. It should be strong and short, broad at the shoulders and narrowing at the loins. The chest, broad, deep and full, well ribbed with the belly tucked up.

Hindquarters: The hind legs should be strong and muscular, longer than the forelegs, so as to elevate the loins above the shoulders. Hocks well let down. The feet should be moderate in size, compact and firmly set. Toes compact, well split up, with high knuckles and short, stubby nails; hind feet slightly longer than forefeet.

Tail: The tail should be either straight or screwed (but not curly), short, hung low, thick root and fine tip; carried low in repose.

Disqualifications: *Other than bat ears; black and white, black and tan, liver, mouse or solid black (black means without any trace of brindle); eyes of different colour; nose other than black except in the case of the lighter-coloured dogs, where a lighter colour of nose is acceptable; hare lip; any mutilation; over 28 lb. (13 kg) in weight.*

Scale of Points:

GENERAL PROPERTIES

Proportion and symmetry	5	
Expression	5	
Gait	4	
Colour	4	
Coat	2	20

HEAD

Skull	6	
Cheeks and chops	2	
Stop	5	
Ears	8	
Eyes	4	
Wrinkles	4	
Nose	3	
Jaws	6	
Teeth	2	40

BODY, LEGS, ETC.

Shoulders	5	
Back	5	
Neck	4	
Chest	3	
Ribs	4	
Brisket	3	
Belly	2	
Forelegs	4	
Hind legs	3	
Feet	3	
Tail	4	40
TOTAL		100

Keeshond

THE **KEESHOND IS A MEMBER OF** the Spitz family (or northern dogs), believed to be descended from the German Wolfspitz, and therefore a close relative to the Pomeranian. The breed has been known throughout the Netherlands since the mid-18th century, where it was a popular "dog of the people." The breed was most numerous in the villages and on the farms, where it was used as watchdog, herder, for draught work and hunting. It was also often to be seen on barges where the dogs were valued as guards and companions. Thus it came to be commonly known as the Barge Dog.

The most accepted explanation of the breed's present name goes back to a period of unrest in Holland, when the symbol of the Orangists was the Pug and that of the Patriot party, the little dog of the people named for the nickname of the leader which was *Kees*. Thus "Keeshond" or "the dog of Kees," pronounced "kayshond."

The breed was exhibited at Dutch shows as early as 1891, but it was not until 1905 that the breed was introduced to England. A Mrs. Wingfield-Digby, on a visit to the Netherlands, saw the barge dogs, and was so taken with them she brought a pair of pups back to England with her. A breeding programme was commenced, and in 1923 the Keeshond made its ring debut at the Birmingham National Show. Two years later Mrs. Wingfield-Digby founded the first breed club under the title of "The Dutch Barge Dog Club." A name that was later changed to Keeshond. The first imports began arriving in the United States and Canada within the next five years, and the breed has enjoyed a steady, devoted following ever since.

In the early days it is reported that solid black and solid white dogs would occasionally appear in litters. Today the only accepted colour of the body coat is shaded grey with black tipping. A unique characteristic of the Keeshond is its head markings, which give the appearance of spectacles and impart a look of great intelligence.

The Keeshond was first registered in Canada in the years 1928–1929.

Keeshond

Official Breed Standard for the Keeshond

General Appearance: The Keeshond is a handsome dog, well balanced and short-coupled in body, attracting attention not only by his alert carriage and intelligent expression, but also by his luxurious coat, his richly plumed tail, well curled over his back, and by his fox-like face and head with small pointed ears. His coat is very thick round the neck, forepart of the shoulders and chest, forming a lion-like mane. His rump and hind legs, down to the hocks, are thickly coated forming the characteristic "trousers." His head, ears and lower legs are covered with thick short hair.

Size: The ideal height of fully matured dogs (over 2 years old), measured from top of withers to the ground is: for males, 18 in. (46 cm); bitches, 17 in. (43 cm). However, size consideration should not outweigh that of type. When dogs are judged equal in type, the dog nearest the ideal height is to be preferred. Length of back from withers to rump should equal height as measured above.

Coat and Colour: The body should be abundantly covered with long, straight, harsh hair; standing well out from a thick, downy undercoat. The hair on the legs should be smooth and short, except for a feathering on the front legs and "trousers," as previously described, on the hind legs. The hair on the tail should be profuse, forming a rich plume. Head, including muzzle, skull, and ears, should be covered with smooth, soft, short hair—velvety in texture on the ears. Coat must not part down the back.

The colour should be a mixture of grey and black. The undercoat should be very pale grey or cream (not tawny). The hair of the outer coat is black tipped, the length of the black tips producing the characteristic shading of colour. The colour may vary from light to dark, but any pronounced deviation from the grey colour is not permissible. The plume of the tail should be very light grey when curled on back, and the tip of the tail should be black. Legs and feet should be cream. Ears should be very dark—almost black.

Shoulder line markings (light grey) should be well defined. The colour of the ruff and "trousers" is generally lighter than that of the body. "Spectacles" and shadings, as later described, are characteristic of the breed and must be present to some degree. There should be no pronounced white markings.

Faults: Silky, wavy or curly coats. Part in coat down the back. Entirely black or white or any other solid colour; any pronounced deviation from the grey colour.

Head: Expression is largely dependent on the distinctive characteristic called "spectacles"—a delicately pencilled line slanting slightly upward from the outer corner of each eye to the lower corner of the ear, coupled with distinct markings and shadings forming short but expressive eyebrows. Markings (or shadings) on face and head must present a pleasing appearance, imparting to the dog an alert and intelligent expression. *Skull:* the head should be well proportioned to the body, wedge-shaped when viewed from above. Not only in muzzle, but the whole head should give this impression when the ears are drawn back by covering the nape of the neck and the ears with one hand. Head in profile should exhibit a definite stop.

The *muzzle* should be dark in colour and of medium length, neither coarse nor snipey, and well proportioned to the skull. The *mouth* should be neither overshot nor undershot. Lips should be black and closely meeting, not thick, coarse or sagging; and with no wrinkle at the corner of the mouth. The teeth should be white, sound and strong (but discolouration from distemper not to penalize severely); upper teeth should just overlap the lower teeth. *Eyes* should be dark brown in colour, of medium size, rather oblique in shape and not set too wide apart. *Ears* should be small, triangular in shape, mounted high on the head and carried erect; dark in colour and covered with thick, velvety, short hair. Size should be proprotionate to the head—length approximating the distance from outer corner of the eye to the nearest edge of the ear.

Faults: Absence of "spectacles." Apple head, or absence of stop. Overshot or undershot. Protruding round eyes or eyes light in colour. Ears not carried erect when at attention.

Neck: The neck should be moderately long, well shaped and well set on shoulders; covered with a profuse mane, sweeping from under the jaw and covering the whole of the front part of the shoulders and chest, as well as the top part of the shoulders.

Forequarters: Forelegs should be straight seen from any angle, and well feathered. Faults: Black markings below the knee, pencilling excepted.

Body: The body should be compact with a short straight back sloping slightly downward towards the hindquarters; deep and strong of chest, well ribbed, barrel well rounded, belly moderately tucked up.

Hindquarters: Hind legs should be profusely feathered down to the hocks—not below, with hocks only slightly bent. Legs must be of good bone and cream in colour. The feet should be compact, well rounded, cat-like, and cream in colour. Toes are nicely arched, with black nails. Faults: White foot or feet.

Tail: The tail should be set on high, moderately long, and well feathered, tightly curled over back. It should lie flat and close to the body with a very light grey plume on top where curled, but the tip of the tail should be black. The tail should form a part of the "silhouette" of the dog's body, rather than give the appearance of an appendage. Faults: Tail not lying close to the back.

Gait: Dogs should show boldly and keep tails curled over the back. They should move cleanly and briskly; and the movement should be straight and sharp (not a lope like a German Shepherd Dog). Faults: Tail not carried over back when moving.

Faults: Silky, wavy or curly coats. Part in coat down the back. Absence of "spectacles." Apple head, or absence of stop. Overshot or undershot. Protruding round eyes or eyes light of colour. Ears not carried erect when at attention. Black markings below the knee, pencilling excepted. White foot or feet. Tail not lying close to the back. Tail not carried over back when moving. *Very serious faults*—Entirely black or white or any other solid colour; any pronounced deviation from the grey colour.

(Breed Standard continued)

Scale of Points:

GENERAL CONFORMATION AND APPEARANCE 20   20

HEAD

Shape   6
Eyes   5
Ears   5
Teeth   4   20

BODY

Chest, back, and loin   10
Tail   10
Neck and shoulders   8
Legs   4
Feet   3   35

COAT   15   15
COLOUR AND MARKINGS   10   10

TOTAL   100

Lhasa Apso

THE LHASA APSO HAS BEEN bred in Tibetan monasteries for 2000 years. In its country of origin the breed was esteemed as companion and watch dog, as it still is in all parts of the world. It is said that the Tibetan Mastiff stood guard outside the homes and monasteries while the little Lhasa gave warning of any intruder that might have slipped indoors.

Opinion is divided on the origin of the breed name. Some claim it is derived from *Rapso*, meaning goat-like, because when the dog's coat is long and unkempt he resembles a small Tibetan goat. The other opinion holds that the name comes from *Abso Seng Kye*, which means Barking Lion Sentinel Dog, and that the breed symbolizes the lion, the protector of Buddha. Legend has it that lamas who failed to reached Nirvana were reincarnated as Lhasa Apsos.

The dogs were regarded as good luck talismans that kept evil away, and were never sold but given as gifts to those the lamas held in high esteem. As recently as 1948, Tenzing, the Sherpa guide, who was one of the men who climbed Mt. Everest, was presented with two Lhasas from the Tibetan monastery in Ghanghar. Tenzing became so interested in Lhasas that he subsequently bred them.

Similarly in 1921, a member of the Indian Medical Service was given two Lhasas by a grateful patient. These dogs were later given to the wife of a British officer serving in Tibet, who brought them with her when she returned to Britain. Other imports followed, and by 1933 the breed had become established and was granted official status by The Kennel Club (England).

First called the Lhasa Terrier, the breed name was changed to Lhasa Apso after the formation of the Tibetan Breeds Association in Britain in 1934.

In that same year breeding on this continent got off to a good start with stock imported from the Dalai Lama. First Canadian registrations were recorded in 1934 under the breed name Lhassa Terrier and classified in the Terrier Group. Subsequently the name was changed to the present one, and in January 1974, the Lhasa Apso was reclassified, and is now regarded as a member of the Non-Sporting Group in Canada (as it is in the United States).

G. STENHOUSE

Lhasa Apso

Official Breed Standard for the Lhasa Apso

Origin and Purpose: Beyond the northern boundary of India, where Mt. Everest stands like a guardian sentinel, is the land of Tibet. A country of huge mountains, deep valleys, wind-swept plateaus, warm summers and cold winters, it is the home of the Lhasa Apso. It is an ancient breed and genealogical tables show them to be in existence as far back as 800 B.C. Having been bred for centuries as a special indoor sentinel, the Lhasa Apso has never lost this characteristic of keen watchfulness.

General Appearance: The Lhasa Apso is a medium small, exotic, very hardy breed with a well-developed body, strong loins, good quarters and thighs. The long, straight, hard, dense coat enhances the beauty of the breed and completely covers the dog.

Temperament: Gay and assertive but chary of strangers.

Size: Ideal size for dogs is between 10–11 in. (25–28 cm) with up to 11½ in. (30 cm) permissible. Bitches should be slightly smaller. Lhasa Apsos over 11½ in. (30 cm) are to be disqualified. Body length from the point of the shoulder to the point of the buttocks should be slightly longer than the height at the withers. A well-balanced type is to be preferred.

Coat and Colour:
a) The adult coat is heavy, straight, hard, not woolly or silky, of good length and dense. The coat should be parted from the nose to the root of the tail.
b) The head should have heavy furnishings with a good fall over the eyes. Good whiskers and beard. In Obedience the hair may be tied back from the eyes.
c) Ears should be heavily furnished.
d) Legs should be well furnished.
e) Tail should be well furnished.
f) Feet should be surrounded with hair. The pads have hair between them which may be trimmed.
g) Forequarters, hindquarters and neck are heavily furnished.
h) All colours and mixtures of colours considered equal.

Head: *Skull* narrow, falling away from behind the eyebrow ridges to a marked degree. Cranium almost flat, not domed or apple-shaped. Viewed from the front, the top of the cranium is narrower than the width at the level of the eyes. The foreface is straight.

Muzzle: The length from the tip of the nose to the inside corner of the eye to be roughly 1 ½ in. (4 cm) or the length from the tip of the nose to the inside corner of the eye to be roughly one-third of the total length from the tip of the nose to the back of the skull. A square muzzle is objectionable. *Nose* black. The tip of the nose is level with or very slightly below the lower eye rim when viewed from the front.

Mouth: Bite—reverse scissors (upper incisors just touching the inner face of the lower incisors). Full dentition. Incisors (6) to be in a straight line. Acceptable bite—level (the front incisors of the upper and lower jaw meeting edge to edge). Undesirable bite—overshot. Excessively undershot (more than ⅛ in. (.3 cm)). The teeth must not show when the mouth is closed. Lips black.

Eyes dark brown. Not large and full or small or sunken. The iris should be of reasonable size, no white showing at the base or top of the eye. The eyes are frontally placed in an oval-shaped black rim. *Ears* pendant. The ears should be well set back on the skull at eye level (not level with the topline of the skull). The leather should hang close to the head and in an adult dog should reach the level of the lower jaw.

Neck: Well set on to the shoulders. Long enough to carry the head well creating an impression of elegance. Slightly arched.

Forequarters: Shoulders strong, muscular, well laid back. The upper arm should not be "Terrier straight," allowing for the desired width and depth of the chest. Lower Arm: the forelegs should not be bowed. From the front when the dog is standing, the legs should be straight parallel, elbows well under the body. The forelimbs support a good share of the body weight when the dog is standing or when moving at a slow pace. The pasterns should be straight and firm when viewed from the front. Slight deviation from the perpendicular when viewed from the side. Feet: short, round and compact with good pads turning neither in nor out. Nails: ideally black. In particoloured or light-coloured coats, light nails and pads are permitted. Dewclaws permissible.

Body: Topline level. Chest well ribbed up, *i.e.,* the ribs should extend well back along the body. The slightly curved ribs should not extend below the elbows. Loin: too long a loin adds excess length to the back and results in a loss of strength to the fore-part of the body. If the loin is too short there will be a loss of flexibility. The loin should be firmly muscled. Croup: the angle formed by the pelvis and the backbone should not be more than 30 degrees from the horizontal. This angulation gives power for the forward propulsion. Abdomen: tucked up to a shallower depth at the loin.

Hindquarters: Strongly muscled and in balance with the fore-quarters. Hocks, when viewed from the rear at a stance, should be strong, straight, and parallel, turning neither in nor out. When viewed from the side, they should be perpendicular to the ground and not stretched out beyond the rump of the dog. Stifle bend: the stifle is moderately bent. Feet: same as in forequarters.

Tail: Set high. Carried forward close to the back with the tip draped on either side of the body. The tail should not rise vertically. A kink in the end is permissible. A low carriage of the tail is a serious fault.

Gait: An easy moving free-flowing trot is the normal pace of the Lhasa Apso. This trot shows the character of his movement at its best and is what should be aimed for. The pads should be seen as the dog moves away indicating a strong hind drive which is balanced by a good reach of the forelegs. Moving too quickly in the ring throws the dog off gait and should be avoided.

Disqualifications: *Lhasa Apsos over 11½ in. (30 cm) are to be disqualified.*

Poodle (Standard and Miniature)

UNTIL ABOUT 1930 the Poodle was commonly called the "French Poodle," an appellation that is seldom heard nowadays. The name implied French origin, but while France deserves credit for popularizing the breed and perfecting the Poodle's stylized trim, the breed belongs to a family of water dogs and has been known in Russia and Germany since the early 16th century. The breed is closely related to the Portuguese Water Dog and the Irish Water Spaniel and takes its name from the German word *puddeln* which means "to splash in water."

An efficient retriever of waterfowl, the Poodle's characteristic trim was devised to aid his progress in the water and, at the same time, protect the dog's vital organs and joints from the cold.

By the early 19th century the breed had become popular in France where it was known as the *caniche* or "duck dog." The breed was a favourite family pet and, because of its excellent scenting ability, was also used as a truffle dog. The truffle is a fungus that grows underground and is found in particular districts in France. Considered a great delicacy, truffles are searched out during the winter months. The animal most often used to scent them out is the pig. But, as a truffle finder, the Poodle is considered superior, being satisfied just to paw the ground. The pig, it is said, will more than likely root out the truffle and start to eat it.

The Poodle's sense of fun and trainability made him a natural choice for a performing circus dog, and by the end of the 18th century every travelling circus is said to have had a performing Poodle act.

After the defeat of Napoleon at the Battle of Waterloo (1815), soldiers returning from France and Germany brought numbers of the breed home with them to England as family pets. Within a few years the Poodle became established in Britain and was being exhibited at dog shows by 1880.

The Standard (over fifteen inches) Poodle was the "original," and was shown in both corded and brushed coat. While both

Poodle (Standard and Miniature)

coat types are still acceptable in the show ring, the corded coat is rarely seen. Originally only three colours, black, brown, and white, were permissible. Today Poodles are bred in a wide range of solid colours but particolours are considered as mismarks, and are disqualified from competition.

A gradual increase of interest in the smaller size Poodle encouraged breeders to develop the under fifteen-inch Miniature, which was granted separate breed status by The Kennel Club (England) in 1910. Poodles were first registered in Canada in 1916.

Official Breed Standard for the Poodle (Standard and Miniature)

FOR SHOW PURPOSES, THERE ARE THREE VARIETIES OF THE POODLE BREED—STANDARD, MINIATURE, AND TOY.

Origin and Purpose: The breed probably dates back to the late Roman period but certainly the variety we know as the Standard Poodle was well established across the whole of Europe by the 16th century. The Miniature and Toy varieties developed in the next two hundred or so years. The Poodle is the world's oldest water retriever, circus performer, and truffle hunter. The ubiquitous Poodle is such a versatile dog he can be all things to all people.

General Appearance, Carriage and Condition: That of a very active, gay, intelligent, smart and elegant-looking dog, squarely built, well proportioned and carrying himself proudly. Properly clipped in the traditional fashion and carefully groomed, the Poodle has about him an air of distinction and dignity peculiar to himself.

Size: The Standard Poodle is over 15 in. (38.1 cm) at the highest point at the shoulder. Any Poodle 15 in. or less in height shall be disqualified from competition as a Standard Poodle. The Miniature Poodle is 15 in. (38.1 cm) or under at the highest point at the shoulder, with a minimum height in excess of 10 in. (25.4 cm). Any Poodle which is over 15 in. or 10 in. or under at the highest point at the shoulder shall be disqualified from competition as a Miniature Poodle. The Toy Poodle is 10 in. (25.4 cm) or under at the shoulder. Any Poodle which is more than 10 in.

at the highest point at the shoulder shall be disqualified from competition as a Toy Poodle.

Coat: Quality—Curly Poodles—dense, naturally harsh texture, even length, frizzy or curly. Corded Poodles—all hair hanging in tight even cords of varying lengths.

Clip—A Poodle under 12 months may be shown in the "Puppy Clip." In all regular classes, Poodles 12 months or over must be shown in the "English Saddle" or "Continental" Clip. A Poodle shown in competitive classes in any other clip shall be disqualified. However, the Brood Bitch and Stud Dog may be shown in any clip.

a) Puppy Clip: A Poodle under a year old may be shown in the Puppy Clip with the coat long. The face, throat, feet, and base of the tail are shaved. The entire shaven foot is visible. There is a pompon on the end of the tail. In order to give a neat appearance and a smooth unbroken line, shaping of the coat is permissible.

b) English Saddle Clip: In the English Saddle Clip, the face, throat, feet, forelegs, and base of tail are shaved, leaving bracelets on the forelegs and a pompon on the end of the tail. The hindquarters are covered with a short blanket of hair except for a curved shaved area on each flank and two shaved bands on each hind leg at the stifle and hock joints. The entire shaven foot and a portion of the shaven foreleg above the bracelets are visible. The rest of the body is left in full coat but may be shaped in order to ensure over-all balance.

c) Continental Clip: In the Continental Clip, the face, throat, feet and base of the tail are shaved. The hindquarters are shaved with pompons (optional) on the hips. The legs are shaved leaving bracelets on the forelegs and rear legs. There is a pompon on the end of the tail. The entire shaven foot and a portion of the shaven foreleg above the bracelets are visible. The rest of the body is left in full coat but may be shaped to ensure over-all balance.

In all three clips the hair of the topknot may be left free, or shaped, or held in place by not more than three elastic bands.

Colour: Any solid colour. The coat is an even solid colour at the skin. In the blues, greys, silvers, browns, café-au-laits, apricots and creams, the coat may show varying shades of the same colour. This is frequently present in the somewhat darker feathering of the ears and in the tipping of the ruff. While clear colours are definitely preferred, such natural variations in the shading of the coat are not to be considered faults. Brown and café-au-lait Poodles may have brown-coloured noses, eye rims and lips, dark toenails and dark amber eyes. Black, blue, grey, silver, cream, and white Poodles have black noses, eye rims and lips, and black or self-coloured toenails, and very dark eyes. In the apricots, while the foregoing colour is preferred, brown noses, eye rims and lips and dark amber eyes are permitted but not desirable. Particoloured Poodles shall be disqualified. Particolour is at least two definite colours appearing in clearly defined markings at the skin.

Head and Expression: *Skull* should be slightly full and moderately peaked with a slight but definite stop. Cheekbones and muscles flat. Length from occiput to stop about the same as the length of muzzle. Viewed from the side, the plane of the top of the skull should extend parallel to the plane of the top of the muzzle. *Muzzle* long straight and fine, but strong without lippiness. Moderate chiselling under the eyes. The chin definite enough to preclude snipiness. Teeth (42) white and strong. Tight scissors or level bite. Nose sharp with well-defined nostrils. *Eyes* oval shaped, very dark. Happy, alert and full of fire and intelligence. *Ears* hanging close to the head, set at or slightly below eye level. The ear leather is long, wide and thickly feathered, and when drawn forward almost reaches the nose.

Neck: Well proportioned, strong and long enough to admit of the head being carried high and with dignity. Skin snug at the throat.

Shoulders: Strong and smoothly muscled. The shoulder blade (scapula) is well laid back and is about the same length as the forearm (humerus).

Body: The chest deep and moderately wide. The ribs well sprung and braced up. To ensure the desirable squarely built appearance, the length of the body measured from the breastbone (sternum) to the pinbone (ischiatic tuberosity) approximates the height from the highest point at the shoulders to the ground. The back short and strong and very slightly hollowed immediately behind the withers. The loins short, broad and muscular. Bone in proportion to the size of the dog.

Legs: Forelegs—straight, parallel when viewed from the front. When viewed from the side, the perpendicular line falls through the fourth thoracic vertebra, the rear point of the scapula, the elbow at the deepest point of the brisket, and the back of the pastern. The pasterns are strong.

Hind legs—straight and parallel when viewed from the rear. When viewed from the side, muscular with width in the region of the stifles, which are well bent. Pelvis and femur are about equal in length; pad to heel short and perpendicular to the ground. When standing, the rear toes are only slightly behind the point of the rump. The angulation of the hindquarters balances that of the forequarters.

Feet: Rather small and oval in shape. Toes well arched and close with webbing. Pads thick and firm. Nails short. The feet turn neither in nor out. Dewclaws may be removed.

Tail: Set on high, docked and carried up. Never curled nor carried over the back.

Gait: A straight, smooth, forward trot, verging on the single track, showing balanced reach and drive; pasterns, hocks and feet showing light springing action. Head and tail carried high. It is imperative that all three varieties be moved in the ring fully and decidedly to show correct gait.

Major Faults: Any distinct deviation from the desired characteristics described in the breed standard with particular attention to the following:

Temperament:	Shyness or viciousness
Bad mouth:	Undershot, overshot, wry mouth, missing teeth
Eyes:	Round protruding, large or very light
Muzzle:	Down-faced, dish-faced, Roman nose, snipiness
Tail:	Set low, curled or carried over the back
Hindquarters:	Cowhocks or sicklehocks
Feet:	Flat or spread, thin pads, no webbing

Disqualifications: *Particolours, unorthodox clip, size—a Poodle over or under the height limits specified.*

Scale of Points:

General appearance, temperament, carriage, and
  condition 25
Head and expression 15
Neck and shoulders 10
Body, tail, and hindquarters 10
Legs and feet 10
Coat, colour, and texture 10
Gait 20

        TOTAL 100

Schipperke

THERE ARE THREE OPINIONS regarding the ancestry of the Schipperke. One is that this is a miniature version of an ancient breed of black Belgian Sheepdog. Another is that the Schipperke descends from the northern race of dogs called the Spitz family, while the third claims that the breed is a cross between the German Pomeranian and some breed of terrier. Whichever, the little dog has been known for about 200 years in Flanders, where it was used as a canal barge dog as both sentry and ratter. It was also said to perform the same duties as a carriage dog.

A Belgian by the name of Reussens, who operated a fleet of barges, is known as the father of the breed and is credited with getting the breed recognized in Belgium. The breed became very fashionable in that country after Queen Marie Henrietta of Belgium bought a winning dog that she saw at a Brussels show in 1885. Three years later a specialty club was organized in Brussels and the breed named the Schipperke. As with its ancestry, there are several interpretations of the name. The most credible is that it comes from the Flemish word for "boat" which is *schip*. Hence Schipperke means "little boatman."

Within a very few years the little dog had been imported to Britain, the United States, and Australia where, as in its homeland, the Schipperke became a popular house pet. In Britain in 1890, a breed standard was adopted and shortly afterwards the Schipperke was granted full breed status. It is said that for a few years in Britain breeders disagreed on the desired points of conformation and, as a result, breed popularity waned. But once these differences of opinion were resolved the breed returned to public favour.

One fallacy seems to persist in regard to the Schipperke. This is that puppies are born tailless. Some may be, but the majority are not. Their tails are docked when they are a few days old.

Overseas a variety of coat colours are acceptable but not preferred. These include chocolate, sable, and cream. In Canada and the United States black is the only permissible colour.

The Schipperke was first registered in Canada in the years 1908–1909.

Schipperke

Official Breed Standard for the Schipperke

Origin and Purpose: The Schipperke is thought to have originated in the Flemish province of Belgium from the native black sheepdogs now believed to be extinct, the Leauvenaar, from which the Groenendael Belgian Sheepdog has also probably evolved. The Schipperke may lay claim to being one of the oldest pure-breds in Europe, for in 1690 a show for the Schipperkes of the Guild workmen was held in the Grand Place of Brussels. The Schipperke is an excellent and faithful little watchdog, a hunter of moles and other vermin. He seeks the company of horses, can be used to hunt, and is a good rabbit dog.

General Appearance: The Schipperke should have a short, thickset cobby body with hindquarters slightly lighter than the foreparts. The head is fox-like and the expression is questioning, sharp and lively, not mean or wild. The distinctive black coat, ruff, and tailless rump give a unique silhouette to this small dog.

Temperament: The Schipperke is active, agile, indefatigable and continually occupied with what is going on around him, careful of things that are given him to guard, very kind with children, and suspicious of strangers. He knows the ways of the household, is always curious to what is going on behind closed doors, or about any object that has been moved, betraying his impressions by his sharp bark and upstanding ruff.

Size: 12–18 lb. (5.5–8 kg).

Coat and Colour: The coat must be black, abundant, and slightly harsh to the touch, short on the ears, front of the legs and on the hocks, fairly short on the body, but longer around the neck, beginning back of the ears and forming a ruff and cape which give the appearance of the withers being higher than the hindquarters, and a jabot extending down between the front legs. The coat is longer on the rear where it forms a culotte, the points turning inward. The undercoat is dense and short on the body, very dense around the neck making the ruff stand out. The culotte should be as long as the ruff.

Head: *Skull* fairly wide, narrowing at the eyes, when the ears are up in the alert position, the correct skull in profile will appear flat. *Muzzle* tapering, not too much stop. The length of the muzzle from tip to stop is equal to the length of the skull from the stop to the occiput. *Nose* small and black. *Mouth:* teeth strong and even, a level or scissors bite is acceptable. *Eyes* very dark brown, small, oval rather than round, neither sunken nor prominent. *Ears* very erect, small, triangular, placed high, strong enough not to be capable of being lowered except in line with the body.

Neck: Strong and full, slightly arched.

Forequarters: Shoulder muscular and sloping. Legs straight, well under the body, with bone in proportion to the body. Pasterns straight.

Body: Back strong, short, straight, and level. Chest broad and deep in the brisket, ribs well sprung, broad behind the shoulders. Loin muscular and well drawn up from the brisket but not to such an extent as to cause a weak and leggy appearance of the hindquarters. Croup slightly sloping, rump well rounded.

Hindquarters: Lighter than the foreparts but muscular and powerful. Thighs muscular and powerful. Hocks well defined. Metatarsus short. Feet small, round, and tight (not splayed), nails straight, strong, and short.

Tail: Docked to no more than 1 inch (3 cm) in length.

Gait: Unrestricted, free, and vigorous. The Schipperke is tireless and quick to move in any direction. In a correctly proportioned and angulated Schipperke at a trot, the feet and legs converge as seen from the front or the rear, and each hind foot falls on or ahead of the print of the forefoot.

Faults: Any deviation from the standard is considered a fault.

Disqualifications: *Any colour other than solid black, drop or semi-erect ears, overshot or undershot mouth.*

Scale of points:

Head, nose, eyes, and teeth 20
Ears 10
Neck, shoulders, and chest 10
Back and loins 5
Forelegs 5
Hind legs 5
Feet 5
Hindquarters 10
Coat and colour 20
General appearance 10

TOTAL 100

Shih Tzu

ALTHOUGH THE SHIH TZU (pronounced shid-zoo) is generally regarded as a Chinese breed, it was developed from Tibetan temple dogs which had been bred in Tibet for some 2000 years. At one time there was considerable contact between the rulers of Tibet and China, and the temple dogs were presented to the Chinese as gifts of high esteem. The last of these tribute gifts was presented by the Dalai Lama to the Dowager Empress when he visited China in 1908.

It is generally agreed that the gift dogs (which were similar to the present-day Lhasa Apso), were crossed with the Pekingese to produce the Shih Tzu, whose name in Chinese means lion dog. The Shih Tzu lived a life of luxury as a palace dog and was seldom seen outside the confines of the court until after China became a republic in 1912. It was during a visit to China in 1920 that General Sir Douglas and Lady Brownrigg first saw a Shih Tzu, and later brought the first pair home with them to England. Further imports followed, and fortunately for the breed, the Shih Tzu became well established in Britain and on the continent before the Communists took over China.

In the 1930s breeding began in Britain and Norway, and in 1935 the breed was officially named the Shih Tzu, but not elevated to championship status in Britain until 1949. It is reported that in 1952 an English breeder crossed some Shih Tzu with the Pekingese. The resultant improvement in coat and structure was so marked as to bring the breed almost instant popularity.

Since its introduction to this continent the Shih Tzu has enjoyed enormous success. First officially recognized by the American Kennel Club in 1969, the very first time the breed was shown a Shih Tzu went all the way to win Best in Show.

In the United States the breed is classified in the Toy Group; in Canada it is in the Non-Sporting Group and a somewhat larger dog is specified in the Canadian breed standard.

Shih Tzu

Official Breed Standard for the Shih Tzu

General Appearance: Very active, lively and alert, with a distinctly arrogant carriage. The Shih Tzu is not a toy dog.

Size: About 11 in. (28 cm) at the withers, but considerable variation from this standard is permissible, provided other proportions are correct and true to type.

Coat and Colour: Coat long and dense, but not curly; looks harsher than it feels to the touch. All colours; but a white blaze on the forehead and white tip to tail are highly prized. Dogs with liver markings may have liver noses and lighter eyes.

Head: Head broad, round, and wide between the eyes, shock headed, with hair falling well over the eyes; good beard and whiskers; the hair growing upwards on the nose gives a distinctly chrysanthemum-like effect. *Muzzle* square, short, but not wrinkled like a Pekingese, flat and hairy. *Mouth* level or slightly underhung—overshot jaws undesirable. *Eyes* large, dark and round but not prominent. *Ears* large and carried drooping, so heavily coated that they appear to blend with the hair of the neck.

Forequarters: Legs short, straight, and muscular. The legs should look massive on account of the wealth of hair.

Body: Body between withers and root of tail should be considerably longer than the height of withers; well ribbed up.

Hindquarters: Legs short, straight, and muscular. The legs should look massive on account of the wealth of hair. Feet should be big with hair between the pads. The feet should look massive on account of the wealth of hair.

Tail: Heavily coated and curled well over back; set on high.

Tibetan Spaniel

ALTHOUGH A COMPARATIVE NEWCOMER to the Western world, the Tibetan Spaniel is said to be of ancient lineage, and as evidenced by archaeological findings, dates back to prehistoric times.

Originally bred in Tibetan monasteries, the dog has also been called the Tibetan Prayer Dog because one of its duties is said to have been working the prayer wheel. The breed also served as watchdog and was thought to bring good luck.

At one time China and Tibet were closely linked politically, and because of this dog historians are of two minds concerning the Tibetan Spaniel's development. They believe that Tibetan Spaniels may have been presented to Chinese noblemen as tribute gifts. These dogs then were crossed with the Oriental Pug to create the Pekingese. Or the development may have been the other way around. That is, the Chinese gave Pekingese, also as tribute gifts, to the Tibetans, and the progeny of these dogs developed along quite different lines from the Pekingese of the Imperial palace. There is some evidence to support the latter opinion. Paintings dating from the 15th century depict the Pekingese of China as strongly resembling the present-day Tibetan Spaniel. It is also said that photographs of many of the early Pekingese imports into the United States look more like the Tibetan Spaniel than they do the modern Pekingese.

Of one point dog authorities are certain: the breed is not a spaniel in the true sense of the word. The name was selected to distinguish this breed from the Tibetan Terrier, and because of the ear placement and carriage, "spaniel" seemed appropriate.

First imports to Britain were brought there in 1920 by Dr. Greig, a medical missionary. But the breed did not become established until after the close of World War II. Since then the Tibetan Spaniel has achieved great popularity in England both as a show dog and family pet. First imports arrived on this continent in the mid-1960s. By 1979 there was sufficient interest in the breed in Canada to warrant its inclusion on The Canadian Kennel Club's registry of recognized breeds, and the present breed standard for the Tibetan Spaniel was adopted.

Tibetan Spaniel

Official Breed Standard for the Tibetan Spaniel

Origin and Purpose: The Tibetan Spaniel is a little companion dog related to the Pekingese, the Pug, and the Japanese Spaniel. His origins cannot be traced.

General Appearance: Should be small, active and alert. The outline should give a well-balanced appearance, slightly longer in body than the height at withers.

Temperament: Gay and assertive, highly intelligent, aloof with strangers.

Size: Weight 9—15 lb. (4—7 kg) being ideal. Height about 10 in. (25 cm).

Coat and Colour: Double coat, silky in texture, smooth on face and front of legs, of moderate length on body, but lying rather flat. Ears and back of forelegs nicely feathered, tail and buttocks well furnished with longer hair. Should not be overcoated and bitches tend to carry less coat and mane than dogs. All colours, and mixture of colours allowed.

Head: Small in proportion to body and proudly carried, giving an impression of quality. Masculine in dogs but free from coarseness. *Skull* slightly domed, moderate width and length. Stop slight, but defined. Medium length of *muzzle,* blunt with cushioning, free from wrinkle. The chin should show some depth and width. Black *nose* preferred. Ideally slightly undershot, the upper incisors fitting neatly inside and touching the lower incisors. Teeth should be evenly placed and the lower jaw wide between the canine tusks. Full dentition desired. A level *mouth* is permissible, providing there is sufficient width and depth of chin to preserve the blunt appearance of the muzzle. Teeth must not show when mouth is closed. *Eyes* dark brown in colour, oval in shape, bright and expressive, of medium size set fairly well apart but forward looking, giving an ape-like expression. Eye rims black. *Ears* medium size, pendant, well feathered in the adult and set fairly high. They may have a slight lift from the skull, but should not fly. Large, heavy, low set ears are not typical.

Neck: Moderately short, strong and well set on. Covered with a mane or "shawl" of longer hair which is more pronounced in dogs than bitches.

Forequarters: Shoulder well placed. The bones of the fore-legs slightly bowed but firm at shoulder. Moderate bone.

Body: Level back. Slightly longer from the point of shoulder to root of tail than the height at withers. Well ribbed with good depth.

Hindquarters: Well made and strong, hocks well let down and straight when viewed from behind. Stifle well developed, showing moderate angulation. Hare-footed, small and neat with feathering between toes often extending beyond the feet. White markings allowed.

Tail: Set high, richly plumed and carried in a gay curl over the back when moving. Should not be penalized for dropping tail when standing.

Gait: Quick moving, straight, free, positive.

Faults: Large full eyes; broad flat muzzle; very domed or flat wide skull; accentuated stop; pointed, weak or wrinkled muzzle; overshot mouth; long, plain down face, without stop; very bowed or loose front; straight stifle; cowhocks; nervousness; cat feet; coarseness of type; mean expression; liver or putty-coloured pigmentation; light eyes; protruding tongue.

   NOTE: Male animals should have two apparently normal testicles fully descended into the scrotum.

Tibetan Terrier

"Terrier" is something of a misnomer for this breed, for it has no terrier characteristics; it does not go to ground for its quarry. Originating in the Lost Valley of Tibet, the breed was used to guard the monasteries and was regarded as a "holy dog" and a "bringer of good luck."

While some authorities do not agree, others claim that the Tibetan Terrier was also used as a shepherd dog in the mountains of Tibet. Some credence should be given to this, because it is generally acknowledged that Tibetan Terriers were stolen by nomadic tribes which eventually migrated to Hungary. There the Tibetan Terrier became the progenitor of the Hungarian Puli, a sheepherding breed. While the Puli is somewhat larger than the Tibetan Terrier and has a corded coat, the similarities between the two breeds are apparent.

It is said that Tibetan Terriers were never sold but given to visiting dignitaries as "luck bringers" which would guide them safely out of the Lost Valley, and as gifts in appreciation for favours. It was as such a gift that Dr. A.R.H. Greig of Essex, England, received her first Tibetan Terrier while she was practising medicine in India. Later Dr. Greig obtained a mate for this dog and commenced her breeding programme. It was Dr. Greig who was responsible for having the Tibetan Terrier admitted to the Stud Book of The Kennel Club of India in the 1920s.

After her return to England, Dr. Greig established her Lamleh Kennels and in the 1930s succeeded in obtaining official breed status for the Tibetan Terrier from The Kennel Club (England).

The breed was first imported to this continent in 1956 but it was not officially recognized in the United States until 1973 and in Canada in 1974.

G. STENHOUSE

Tibetan Terrier

Official Breed Standard for the Tibetan Terrier

Origin and Purpose: The Tibetan Terrier was bred for centuries in the monasteries in the high Himalayas where they were loved and used by the Monks and Lamas as mascots, good luck charms and watchdogs. The dense coat allowed survival in the extreme climatic conditions. The compact size and unique foot structure permitted movement over snow and terrain inaccessible to man.

General Appearance: A profusely coated dog of sturdy build, square in proportion with the tail curled over the back. The facial hair covers the eyes and muzzle providing protection from the elements. The large round feet, with no discernible arch, produce a snowshoe effect while providing traction for traversing and climbing in extreme terrain.

Temperament: The Tibetan Terrier is reserved without evidence of shyness or viciousness, but capable of acquitting himself adequately when the situation demands.

Size: Height—14–16 in. (35–41 cm).
Weight—18–30 lb. (8–14 kg). The weight must be proportionate to the height, maintaining a sturdy, compact build.

Coat and Colour: Double coated. The undercoat fine wool. The topcoat profuse, fine, but not silky or woolly, long, either straight or waved. Any colour or colours including white.

Head: *Skull* of medium length and width, not coarse, slightly domed, narrowing slightly from ear to eye, there shall be a distinct but not exaggerated stop. The cheek bones curved but not overdeveloped so as to bulge. The length from the eye to tip of the nose should be equal to that from the eye to the occiput.
   Muzzle: the jaws between the canines should form a distinct curve. The lower jaw should carry a small but not over-exaggerated amount of beard. The head should be well furnished with long hair falling forward over the eyes. *Nose* black, *any other colour to be disqualified. Mouth:* level bite preferred, overshot more than 1/16 inch (.15 cm) or undershot by more than 1/4 inch (.6 cm) or wry mouth to be severely penalized. *Eyes* large, dark, neither

prominent nor sunken; should be set fairly wide apart. Eyelids dark. *Ears* pendant, not too close to the head. V-shaped, not too large; heavily feathered.

Neck.   The neck is well set on the shoulders, slightly arched, and carried erect.

Forequarters: Shoulders sloping, strongly muscled, flat and well laid back. The forelegs should be straight when viewed from front or side. In motion the elbows should move close to the body and parallel to the line of travel. Pasterns are short and slightly sloping. Feet should turn neither in nor out and must be large, round and heavily furnished with hair between the toes and pads. The dog should stand well down on his pads, the foot has no arch.

Body: Compact and powerful. Length from point of shoulder to root of tail equal to height at withers. Well ribbed up. Loin slightly arched.

Hindquarters: Strongly muscled, in balance with the fore-quarters. Thighs broad with well-bent stifles. Hocks well let down, turning neither in nor out. Both front and hind feet are structurally the same.

Tail: Medium in length, set on fairly high and carried in a gay curl over the back. Very well feathered. There is often a kink near the tip.

Gait: When in motion the legs and feet should move parallel to the line of travel with the hind legs tracking the fore. A dog with the correct foot moves with elasticity and drive indicating great agility and endurance.

Faults: Poor coat; mouth overshot by more than $^{1}/_{16}$ inch (.15 cm) or undershot more than $^{1}/_{4}$ inch (.6 cm); weak, snipey foreface; wry mouth.

Disqualifications: *Nose any other colour than black.*

A Short History of Canadians and Their Dogs

DOGS HAVE BEEN used and cared for in Canada longer than can be traced. From what can be surmised from Indian legend, gleaned from settlers' accounts, and is established in modern records, it is apparent that dogs have had important roles as servants and companions. As conditions, needs, and outlooks have varied for men, so have the roles played by dogs varied to meet new challenges.

I Amerindian

The attitude of Indian tribes to the dog have varied across North America, so the beliefs of and attitudes to the dog of individual tribes must be examined.

In Labrador, the Montagnais used the dog for tracking game and sledding, but it held no importance in their religion. Indeed, the dog who transgressed by chewing the bones of game animals like the caribou was speedily sacrificed to appease the spirit of the dead animal, and thus stave off possible famine should the spirit hide his living brethren from the hunters. Unlike the Algonquins, the Montagnais never ate their dogs during famine.

Some Indians were good to their dogs; some were not. The following tale from the New Brunswick area makes the point.

An Indian hunter owned two dogs, one of which he liked and fed well; the other he neglected. A stranger and his dog arrived in camp one day, intending to hunt in the same area. The stranger's dog began to play with the first hunter's favourite, and was told that the hunting in the area was not good. The stranger, who understood the language of dogs, listened well when the neglected dog spoke up to say that if well treated and fed, he could find plenty of game. As he was leaving, the stranger offered the hunter a beaver skin for the neglected dog. Although protesting that the price was too generous, the hunter finally sold his poor dog.

After a few weeks of good food and care, that same dog took his new master in a short time to a bear's den and then to a beaver pond. He proved a far more successful hunter than either of the other two dogs. After a while, his former owner came up, astonished at his skill, and attempted to buy him back. But the Indian who understood the language of dogs said: "He gets all my game for me. If you had treated him decently and fed him well he would have done the same for you. Now I will not sell him for any price."

One of our finest sources of information on early Canada is the Jesuit "Relations." These men of God were trained observers and, like the Venetian ambassadors, were required to send their observations back to headquarters.

Their travels covered eastern Canada, and here and there in the reports they refer to dogs. In 1653 the Jesuit Bressani observed that the native domestic dog differed from European ones in having an undercoat during winter. Another Jesuit missionary, Le Jeune, between 1634 and 1638, said that the Indians' dogs were as dear to them as their children, and shared their beds, plates, and food. Inside the communal house, he could not decide which was worse—the smoke, the fleas, or the dogs!

In the worst of the cold weather the dogs crowded inside, and as Le Jeune had only one blanket, he was not averse to accepting their company for warmth. However, he relates, "As they were large and numerous, they occasionally crowded and annoyed me so much, that in giving me a little heat they robbed me of my sleep, so that I very often drove them away... a savage having thrown himself upon me while asleep, I thought it was a dog, and finding a club at hand, I hit him, crying out, 'Aché, aché,' the words they use to drive away the dogs. My man woke up greatly astonished, thinking that all was lost. He protested his treatment saying, 'It is not a dog; it is I'."

During the winter there would be very little to eat. The dogs, inside from the cold, would chew on anything and scramble all over. When food was served, the dogs had no hesitation in stealing from the plates, as Le Jeune observed:

If any one happened to throw them a bone, there was straightway a race for it, upsetting all whom they encountered sitting, unless they held themselves firmly. They have often upset for me my bark dish, all it contained, in my gown. I was amused whenever there was a quarrel among them at our dinner table, for there was not one of us who did not hold his plate down with both hands on the ground, which serves as table, seat, and bed both to men and dogs.

According to Le Jeune, the Indians valued their hunting dogs highly, especially those who could take on bear, or who could scent and kill beaver after they were driven from the lodges. A valued dog lost while hunting might be mourned as much as a fellow man.

The Jesuits noted that dogs were used by the Indians to pull travois, and similarly French Canadians used them to pull sledges. An interesting anecdote from New France recorded by a Jesuit in 1647–48 during a war with the Iroquois, tells of a bitch in Montreal who used to do guard duty, taking her pups with her on her rounds of the boundaries. Normally she hunted squirrels, but that winter she would patrol every day to look for Iroquois, and she often warned the settlement that enemies were near.

One native practice which the Jesuits constantly tried to stop was the sacrifice of dogs. They were killed to appease the spirits of the dead, or were buried with the dead, or in some cases were killed in order to restore a young man to sanity. Some tribes ate these sacrifices as part of the ceremony.

Among the Eastern Woodland Indians, the White Dog Festival was important, for which a special breed of white dog was kept for sacrifice. The Ojibway had two festivals, one to inspire courage in their warriors, and a second to encourage endurance among their people during famine. Norval Morrisseau describes such a festival, probably the one for warriors, in his *Legends of My People*. The most famous white dog festival, however, was that of the Iroquois. It was held in February and was the climax of a week-long New Year's celebration to restore life after the long death of winter, and to renew man's ties to a fruitful nature. Should the ceremony fail, game would not return north in the spring, hibernating animals would not wake, crops would not grow and man would perish in famine.

The last recorded white dog sacrifice was described in *Harper's Weekly*, February 1872. Thereafter the festival died out, partly because of the weakening of tribal religion, partly because Europeans objected to dog sacrifice. As a result, the breed of white dog also became extinct.

The Dogrib Indians along the Athepasca believed they were descended from a woman who married a dog. She was driven from her tribe into the region of the Coppermine River, and there gave birth to a litter of pups which turned into human children under the sun's rays. Four of these children became the ancestors of the Dogrib. That tribe was known to take greater care of their dogs than other tribes.

The Assiniboine have a legend of how the dog entered heaven. Grey Wolf, a chief, was rewarded for his valour by being called to the hunting ground of the gods. He set out towards the setting sun with his wife, his two sons, and his little dog who carried his moccasins. The day was very hot, and the trail difficult. One by one his sons grew tired and dropped back. The next day his wife fell, gave up, and returned to look for her children. But the little dog, whose tongue was panting to the ground, kept on. When he arrived at the hunting grounds of the gods, Grey Wolf was asked by the Great Spirit where his family was.

"They grew tired and fell asleep on the way," Grey Wolf said.
"And the little shadow who's been following you?"
"That's my dog. He has never left my side."
"Let him enter, then," said the Great Spirit. *"He has earned his place, and a place for all his tribe, in the Land of Shadows."*

On the West Coast attitudes towards, and uses of, the dog varied widely. Among the Tsimshian Indians, there was a secret society which used to tear apart and eat live dogs. This practice horrified not only European explorers, but also other Indian tribes. In contrast, the Kwatkiutl tribe never ate dogs, but kept them as pets, treating them well and allowing them total run of the house. Dogs were believed to protect the family and home against sickness and invisible spirits as well as prowlers. This tribe believed that earthquakes (which were caused by malign spirits) were the result of mistreating dogs.

Another tribe which valued their dogs was the Coast Salish. Not only were dogs used to drive mountain goats into hunting range, but a very special breed of white woolly dog was the source of highly-prized wool for blankets. Paul Kane portrayed this dog in his painting "Clal-lum Women Weaving" in 1847. The introduction of European trading blankets doomed this breed and they were extinct by 1860. Captain Vancouver described the breed as similar to but larger than the dogs of Pomerania:

They were all shorn as close to the skin as sheep are in England; and so compact were their fleeces, that large portions could be lifted up by a corner without causing any separation. They were composed of a mixture of a coarse kind of wool, with a very fine, long hair, capable of being spun into yarn.

In recent years there has been some scholarly investigation into the specific wolf species which were used as foundation for certain groups of dogs. Only the Tibetan wolf has a woolly coat, and it has been suggested as an ancestor of those European dogs such as the Poodle, who displays this characteristic. Is it possible that this Salish breed is another descendant, brought across the Bering land bridge during the remote migration of the Indian tribes into North America?

Most west coast tribes used their dogs to hunt bear. One indigenous breed which survived European incursion over two gold rushes and lasted into the 20th century was recognized by the CKC but now seems to be extinct—the Tahl-tan Bear dog. It was a small fox-like dog, very alert, quick moving, with an unusual erect tail, characteristic of the breed. The dogs usually had a black head, with bodies either black, or black and white, white, or slate grey.

Besides bear, the dog was used to hunt lynx and porcupine. Two dogs were usually carried within sight of the bear, released, and so harried and distracted the bear that the Indian hunter was able to sneak up and kill the bear. This method worked best when they were able to "crust"—that is, chase the bear over snow crust which would hold the dogs yet hinder the bear. Although the breed resembles Spitz-type dogs, the tail is described as unique— five to eight inches, erect, and covered with a wiry bristle.

Transplantation of the dog to outside areas did not work. The dog was a finicky eater, susceptible to distemper and other diseases and subject to heat prostration. There were some exceptions to this sad ending, but not enough to prevent the dog from becoming extinct in the 1950s.

II Inuit

If the dog were more or less valuable to the Indian, in the Arctic, among the Inuit, the dog was essential. "The Eskimo knows that his own comfort, if not his very existence, depends on his dogs, and the better he uses them the more faithful will be their service." The dog provided transportation; he provided help in hunting polar bear, seal, and musk ox; in times of starvation, he provided food. Just how essential the dog was to Eskimo life is illustrated by a "massaging" ceremony performed on the newborn pup. First the legs would be pulled out to make the pup grow big and strong, and the tail twisted over its back to make it beautiful and healthy; then the nostrils were expanded so that it would become keen-scented, able to follow a trail, or discover seal holes (*agloos*) under the snow; the body was stretched to make it grow big; a tiny harness was fastened around it, and the traces pulled to ensure the pup would be a willing worker; a loaded pack was placed on its back and the pup was supported in a "walk" to make sure it would be able to pack loads in the summer; an arrow was rubbed along the belly to make it swift in pursuit; head, body, and feet were bitten to make it aggressive and fierce; finally its mouth was applied to sealskin so that the pup would be quick to pounce on seals. All the time the Inuit would exhort the pup to become a perfect Inuit dog.

Only a couple of pups might be kept from a litter, and these were given as an honour to the new owner for life. The new owner had to care for the pup—carrying it, keeping it warm and fostering it if necessary until it could fend for itself. Ties between owner and dog could become so close that the dog would not accept or work for anyone else, or accept strange team-mates. If the owner died, some dogs might have to be forced to leave the grave.

The dogs were as well treated as circumstances permitted, because an Inuit's life might depend upon the willing help of his dog. They had the status of servants or children, and were named for dead relatives. In winter, the pups were kept inside in special nooks in the snow house, but the adult dogs were allowed in only to have a special tidbit after meals. They slept either in the passage to the house or outside. Training for sled work started at about four months of age. Traditionally, an Inuit family's prosperity and success could be estimated by the number of dogs owned.

A five to eight-dog team could cover ground quickly but required a high number of seals to keep fed. In the Central Arctic areas where food was not abundant, the teams might be from three to five in number, and family members shared in pulling the sled. The dogs were almost never struck, but if discipline had to be enforced, then punishment could be severe. A troublesome dog might, however, be hobbled to "cool it down," rather than be beaten.

The winter was the best time for the sled dog. Travel was light, and the dog's food contained plenty of seal blubber. During the summer the diet changed to fish entrails and scraps, hauling work was much harder, trips longer and more frequent, and the dogs were kept permanently in harness and muzzled to keep them away from the meat drying in the camp. They became scrawny and thin. Nevertheless, the Inuit sled dog was still capable of working, whether fed or not. Traditionally, the Inuit counted on getting ten days' work out of a good team after the food ran out.

In hunting, the dogs were used to locate hidden seal holes in the winter. They would also attack a musk-ox herd, forcing it to form a defensive circle until the hunter could catch up. They were used to harry a polar bear so that the hunter could approach and kill it.

Today in the arctic the snowmobile and rifle have replaced dog sled and spear. Still, in more remote areas, dog sleds are still preferred. From these remote Inuit, biologist Bill Carpenter obtained foundation stock for his efforts to preserve the magnificent Eskimo Dog. (See breed history). Carpenter's efforts at recreating the Canadian Eskimo Dog, as it is now called, have involved placing foundation stock with breeders, and reintroducing pure stock to work with the Inuit. As part of his programme, in 1977 several remote outpost camps were sent specimens of the breed. In view of the isolation of the groups involved, it is likely that the breed will remain pure at those locations. This magnificent breed is at the point where the CKC will be taking over registrations, and the success story has been the subject of a 1982 National Film Board documentary.

As has happened time and time again, the introduction of modern technology has meant that the native breed of dog has lost its importance. As well, European dogs have made their way into the Arctic and have cross-bred with the native breeds. The changeover to modern ways is not total, or totally desired. An Inuit working for the government might live in a house, but he keeps his dogs in case he is fired, and lends them to a relative to be worked in the winter.

I used to like my dog teams... All my dogs have names like Tuksalik, "Double Eyes," with two spots over the eyes, and Shenunugok, which means "grey." We make little sealskin boots for the dogs, and cut two holes for the middle claws to get a grip on the ice so it don't cut their feet,

*but every time you stop, you have to take off the boots, or the dogs would
eat them.*

If not used for sledding, sled dogs today are used to warn of
polar bears at mining sites. Considering the harsh demands of
the Arctic climate, there will probably always be a place for the
Inuit's sled dog.

III   Dogs of European Origin

Whether that gentle giant, the Newfoundland, arrived with the
Vikings, or came with the Portuguese and Basque fisherman
to the Banks, or was native to the Indians, is not known, but
the breed has existed in the eastern Maritimes since the time
of the first European settlers. (See breed history.) It appears in
French Canadian folklore, and a Newfoundland-type draught
dog is shown again and again in the paintings of Cornelius
Kreighoff. The eastern coast of Canada has produced two other
breeds of dog, the Labrador Retriever and the Nova Scotia Duck
Toller. (See breed histories.)

However, as useful as the dog was to the Canadian pioneer,
the importation of specific European breeds seems to have
remained in the hands of the English gentry. It was the English
sportsman who bemoaned not having a proper dog with which
to hunt the plentiful game found in the Canadas.

*Let no one persuade you against bringing out your dogs as they would
be invaluable. I have not been able to use or hear of a good one in
this country.*

Major Samuel Strickland indicated that the dogs available were
of little use, not only for hunting, but also as working dogs. He
describes whole flocks of sheep lost to wolves because the
cross-bred dogs were not courageous enough to guard the flock.
He may have done something to attempt to rectify the problem,
because he mentions losing an Irish Greyhound (Irish Wolfhound)
to porcupine quills.

Besides the traditional quarry of sporting dogs—bear, deer,
birds—there was developed a new sport: raccoon hunting. The
dog for that sport could be "half lurcher and half cur," as long as
it had a good nose and a big voice. This was a far cry from the
coonhounds being developed south of the border. Yet the method
of hunting was the same. The dog found the 'coon at night, treed
him and barked until the settler came to shoot the 'coon out of

the tree. Sometimes there was no gun, then the enterprising settler's family chopped down the tree to get at the 'coon.

As settlement moved west towards the prairies, the more settled urban areas saw the importation, not only of sporting dogs, but also of pet dogs. Kreighoff in the 1840s shows a terrier, a Boston Bull, and later two toy spaniels in his paintings. English officers introduced fox hunting with imported English Foxhounds, and hunt clubs were some of the earliest social organizations founded. One of the last pictures of Peter Jones, a Mississauga Indian who had married an English gentlewoman and returned as missionary to his people, shows him with an old spaniel. By the 1880s, southern Ontario was producing some of the best Setters and Pointers in North America. A founding member of the CKC, T.G. Davey, wrote training books under the pseudonym "Chipmunk."

By the 1860s news of gold started a rush westward. The diaries and letters of that period give a picture of western forts. Fort Edmonton was the jumping-off point for the hardest part of the overland journey—across the Rockies. There were so many dogs at the Fort that travellers had to sleep on top of their food supply to prevent it from being stolen. One particular artist-diarist eventually wrote on the back of one sketch, "I hate dogs!" Photographs of the settlers on the prairies, who came after the Overlanders, show their dogs, inevitably a large-farm collie type. There is seldom mention of these dogs in the diaries. They were there, kept outside, used in farm work, but not important enough to be talked about.

It took the gold rush into the Klondike to bring any numbers of pure-bred dogs into the west. The demand for dog teams was so great that any pet of appropriate size in the cities of the American west coast was in grave danger of being stolen and sent north. There is a relatively clear photograph of a Pointer at Edmonton in the late 1890s. Although humane societies had been formed in Canada (Ontario Humane Society in 1873), public opinion was not really roused by animal suffering and pack horses and dog teams were very badly treated. However, some incidents were so extreme that they made an impression. One greyhound in a team was left outside during a bad night, and was found the next morning, hunched over, frozen solid. The fate of another badly abused spaniel was better. A blacksmith's wife on the White Pass Trail acquired the dog as a companion and pet for her daughter, and it lived to a ripe old age.

IV   Dogs in the Dominion of Canada

The last quarter of the nineteenth century saw the establishment of kennel clubs in eastern and central Canada. A Canadian owned Setter, "Leicester," won second prize at a Chicago dog show in 1876. A Clumber Spaniel took a first prize at the Nova Scotia Kennel Club in 1881. In 1888, a nucleus of members from the London Canine Association in Ontario formed The Canadian Kennel Club. Even after the founding of a national kennel club in Canada, dog shows and registrations were handled by the American Kennel Club. The first dog show in western Canada was held at Victoria in 1889. The same period saw the rise of the humane movement in Canada. The Ontario Society for the Prevention of Cruelty to Animals was founded in 1873, the Canadian SPCA of Montreal and the Toronto Humane Society followed in 1887. Horses and children, not dogs, were the chief concerns of these societies. Most dogs, even pure-breds, at that time were working outdoor dogs whose lifespan depended on their usefulness. The retired, arthritic hound who was allowed a corner by the stove was probably only 8 or 9 years old.

The attitude of the predominantly agricultural population of that time towards their dogs is well illustrated in Morley Callaghan's short story, "The Little Business Man." The boy in the story, Luke, has made a pet of his uncle's old farm collie, but the dog is too old to work, and the uncle decides to drown the dog. Luke risks his life to prevent the drowning, and with the help of a kindly neighbour convinces his uncle that the dog can still pay for his keep. The contrast between these two attitudes to the dog—the dog as tool to be discarded when worn out, and the dog as companion and pet—is evident at all stages of the social history of twentieth-century Canada.

Foxhunting, because of its association with the English gentry, had early become organized as a sport. The Toronto Hunt Club was founded in 1843, and regularly met within the city boundaries. In the 1890s, Cannington Manor in Alberta was the site of an attempt to transfer the whole English gentry system to the Prairies. Along with horse racing, a local foxhound pack was established with dogs imported from England. The Hunt Ball was an opportunity for the ladies to acquire new gowns and for the community to reaffirm its membership in the British Empire. The future of this thriving community was cut short, as were so many others, by the fact that the railroad passed it by.

Just a few years later came the exploration of the Banff and

Jasper area mountains, by the early outfitters and guides. One guide named Yates was accompanied by his pet "bulldog," Hoodoo. A photograph shows a large, long-tailed dog, possibly what we would call a Bullmastiff. This amazing dog accompanied his owner on all his travels. On one particular climb, they reached a steep cliff at a point near the summit. The dog could not bear to be left behind and had to be hauled bodily up the final ascent by rope. Yates named the peak Mt. Hoodoo in his dog's honour.

V Between the Wars

This period saw the real establishment of pure-bred dog sports in Canada. While field trials for Pointers and Setters were going strong during the 1890s, the next major expansion of field sports was into Beagle pack trials in the 1920s. Retriever trials and Spaniel field trials followed in the 1930s. The late 1930s saw the introduction of obedience training, although the sport was not really sure of its rules and procedures for another decade. Trials were very informal, as were the dog shows of the day. Judges and competitors could be forgiven for not knowing the rules. One obedience trial was rained out and moved indoors to an armoury—with the army vehicles still parked inside. It was a true test of the "retrieve," since no human could reach the dumbbell under the tanks. Although Whippets were first raced in 1911, the sport of racing dogs always had to contend with the vexing gambling problem and so has not developed in Canada to the extent that it has in the United States and England. Interest in sled dog racing was sparked after a dramatic race against time by Leonhard Seppala and his dog team to bring serum to stop a diphtheria epidemic in Nome, Alaska in 1925.

The rising number of dog fanciers, and the start of the migration from farm to city, resulted in an increasing number of dogs who were valued as pets. The dog as pet and companion deserved far better than table scraps and a short life, so there came a change in the treatment of dogs. Commercial dog food, promising a balanced diet, was used more and more. Perhaps the greatest changes in the treatment of the dog were the development of the small animal practitioner and the small animal clinic. The refinement of canine distemper vaccine and its implementation in the 1930s was just the first of many improvements in the health care of dogs. At the same time, one of the great achievements in human medicine in Canada, Banting's and Best's discovery of insulin, depended on their dogs. Since there is always the question of how much suffering is morally justified with experimental animals, Banting's biographer emphasizes that to Banting and Best the dogs were pets and companions as well as experimental subjects.

VI   The Postwar Period

Two more sporting activities, sheepdog trials and lure coursing, appeared. Foxhound field trials were added to The Canadian Kennel Club's list. The pet market boomed. As a result, the need for education of pet owners to their responsibilities became acute. Many kennel and obedience clubs took on the job of educating the public through obedience courses and talks on general pet care. Some efforts were made to introduce "kindness" training to elementary school children. Grooming salons proliferated, especially after the rising popularity of such long-coated breeds as the Poodle. At a number of colleges and universities, formal courses to train breeders in genetics, parasitology, nutrition, and anatomical structure were offered. More popular were club-sponsored seminars, usually on such health problems as PRA (progressive retinal atrophy) and hip dysplasia. Large numbers of dogs in the cities has meant health problems, especially in parks, and the conflicting needs of children and dogs have led to "leash" laws, and in some cases, an outright ban on dogs. In addition, it has become more and more difficult to obtain a kennel licence near urban areas.

Another major problem, especially with closer contact between owner and pet, has been the spread of rabies from the wild animal population. Although rabies has always been evident in domestic canines, (indeed, one governor-general of the Canadas, Charles Lennox, Duke of Richmond, died of rabies in 1819) it was controllable after rabies vaccine was developed. In 1947, however, a reservoir of the disease was found among the arctic foxes of Baker Lake, and from there serious epidemics spread the infection to the northern prairies and into Ontario and Quebec. Today, it is not uncommon to find rabid skunk or fox in the heart of cities. Governments have attempted to counter this menace by holding free rabies clinics in afflicted areas, and through public education. The most promising counterattack is the attempt to develop an oral vaccine which can be given to the wild fox population through bait.

One of the most fascinating developments in the long history of dog and man is the discovery of new ways in which dogs can help man. Seeing Eye, Hearing Ear, and therapy dogs for psychiatric patients have all made their appearance in Canada. Many police departments have added canine members for crowd control, locating lost children, and for search and rescue.

Dogs have been very effective in locating drugs for Canada Customs and for border patrols. One professional dog trainer used to describe his two types of clients—the daytime police types whom he taught to search for smugglers, and the night-time clients, whom he taught to avoid customs patrols. The banning of poison baits to control predators has resulted in the use of Komondorok in the West and the Yugoslavian Shar Planinatz in the East. Dogs can be used to locate pipeline leaks, either of chemicals or oil and gas. Their senses are still more effective than any electronic or chemical detection means developed to date. These same abilities have allowed dogs to be trained to prospect for ore-bearing rocks.

The position of the dog in modern life is assured, despite the disappearance of his traditional working role. New jobs have been found, and we have come to realize that human beings need the dog as companion.

History of
Dogs in Canada *Magazine*

*F*OR OVER NINETY-TWO YEARS, The Canadian Kennel Club has been involved in the publication of an "official organ." It has taken many forms and weathered a variety of "handlers"—editors, publishers, and numerous CKC Boards of Directors. Through the long years it has been the subject of controversy—it's been called a "rag" but it has also won international acclaim (*not* simultaneously). Regardless, it has lasted, providing a fascinating record not only of the activities of The Canadian Kennel Club and its members, but of pure-bred dogs in Canada.

The Earliest Years: For a glimpse of the publication's "whelping," one can turn to a summary written by James D. Strachan in the August 1936 issue of *Kennel and Bench,* forerunner of *Dogs in Canada.* Strachan, Secretary-Treasurer of the CKC, had edited the publication since 1919; he recounted its past history in a form of "swan song" because in the fall of 1936 Bert Swann took over the editor's chair. Wrote Strachan:

Almost immediately after The Canadian Kennel Club had been organized in 1888, it became instantly expedient that the new government for canines in this country should have a convenient mouthpiece that could be recognized as being representative of Canadian fanciers. Through the kind offices of Mr. H. B. Donovan, of the Canadian Poultry Review, *Toronto, the* Kennel Gazette *made its appearance for the first time at the beginning of February 1889.*

The Kennel Gazette, *being supplementary to the* Canadian Poultry Review, *had a subscription list of 8,000 to start with, and that was a much larger circulation than our journal has ever enjoyed since that time. Number 1 of Volume 1 of the* Kennel Gazette *contained five pages of reading matter, one page of advertising matter, and one full-page illustration featuring the black Field Spaniel, Moonstone, who was bred by the late Theo Marples,* FZS, *the founder of our English contemporary,* Our Dogs, *and was described at the time as being "probably the longest, the lowest, the flattest-coated, and heaviest boned Field Spaniel on the bench.*

In January, 1890 Number 1 of Volume 2 appeared in a fine heavy blue cover, bearing the title Canadian Kennel Review. *The issue was one of*

Cover of January 1891 *Canadian Kennel Gazette*

eleven reading pages, three advertising pages, two of which appeared on the front outside and inside covers, the back inside and outside covers being blank and indicating the fact that Canadian breeders and exhibitors had not taken too much advantage of the available advertising space.

To scan the early illustrations is to visualize the tremendous changes— for the better, no doubt—of nearly all the breeds which were being bred nearly fifty years ago. The illustration showing the Irish Terrier, Breadenhill, for instance, is outstanding in this respect. Here is a genuine hard bitten terrier, crop eared and all ready for the fray.

James Strachan's observations about the changes in breeds are even truer today. For instance, in the issues of the early 1920s, Boston Terriers and Bulldogs seemed to dominate. Other breeds mentioned then included the Russian Wolfhound, Prince Charles and Blenheim, Black and Tan Terrier, and Scotch Terrier.

In January 1901, the *Canadian Kennel Gazette* appeared in a smaller size: 5 by 8 inches. However, there were 40 pages plus the cover. Editor and Secretary of the CKC from 1891 to 1912 was H.B. Donovan, whom Strachan praises as someone who "pushed a vigorously constructive pen."

In October 1912, the official organ became *Kennel and Bench*, returning to its original 7 by 10 inch page size. It was published and edited by Dr. Alfred Boultbee, then Secretary of the CKC. In declaring his paper's policy, Dr. Boultbee, who owned the publication outright, said *"Kennel and Bench* distinctly wishes it to be understood that the whole responsibility of its success or failure financially is separate from The Canadian Kennel Club, but in spirit the two are bound together. We intend to maintain our independence in every way, even to criticizing The Canadian Kennel Club, where we deem such a course to be of advantage to the club; no other course would be of any value." Nonetheless, the first issue of this Volume (24 pages including the cover) was almost wholly given over to the official end of the Club's business.

After Boultbee's death in 1916, says Strachan, the paper marked time—"at the mercy of those who were kindly disposed towards it." Then, in April 1919, James D. Strachan took over the helm, both as editor of the paper and as Secretary of the CKC.

Inside *Kennel and Bench:* It is perhaps easiest to get a feel for the publication of those days by examining the November 1919 issue. At that time, a subscription cost $1.00 a year (10¢ an issue). There were 32 pages, printed on a kind of "upgraded" newsprint. No colour was used and it was actually referred to as a "paper," not a magazine (although it was of magazine size).

Breeder advertising rates in that 1919 issue were $13.50 for a page, $6.75 for a half page, $4.50 for a third, and 50¢ for a column inch. The front cover sold for $8, but the space allowed was about a sixth of a page (for a black and white photo).

News items emerging from that issue included the fact that Toronto's Canadian National Exhibition was considering replacing its Dog Show Building. Now, of course, there isn't even a CNE dog *show*, let alone a building. It was also reported that "Jas. Whitham, Cornwall, Ontario, had a terrible scourge visit his kennel, which he believes was the 'flu,' but being a 'sticker,' he has kept going and is still a contender at the shows..." Could the "scourge" have been parvovirus?

Show results were presented under the heading "Our Recent Dog Shows" and occupied just over eleven pages. Winners were not listed by group or even alphabetically. News of people and events appeared in a column entitled "Short Barks from Everywhere," which a later editor changed to "Snappy Barks." Stud dog services were advertised for $10 to $20—one ad read "to approved matrons only." An eight-month-old Bulldog puppy was offered for $90, while a two year old had a $200 price tag.

That particular issue contained only two commercial advertisers—a dog food called Mixco, from Battle Creek, Michigan (100 lb. for $6, "for sale at all druggists"), and Spratt's Dog Cakes and Puppy Biscuits. The latter supported the publication for several years; its red colour on the outside back cover led to a red front cover for a considerable time.

In 1936 Bert Swann took over from James Strachan. The Board of Directors had decided that in order to make the magazine more educational, interesting, and profitable, the editorship should be a full-time position and not paired with the major responsibility of secretary, which had been the case from the beginning. Different colours were now being used on the cover— still with small photos—and a full-page ad cost $30. Inclusion in the Breeder's Register was $4 a year, while classified notices cost 5¢ per word or letter.

The publication made a big splash in September 1938 to mark The Canadian Kennel Club's Golden Jubilee year. This issue featured the first four-colour cover and began a 13-part series on the history of the CKC. For the occasion, 200 CKC members and friends assembled at the King Edward Hotel for a jubilee dinner. Apparently, however, the celebratory year was not entirely smooth. Signs of conflict include Swann's departure (circumstances unknown) and the appointment of Dallas E. Jones as the new editor. Issues under Jones' guidance did appear professional; however, at the end of one year he voluntarily resigned to take up a position elsewhere. The editorship of the magazine passed back into the hands of James Strachan.

A New Name: Perhaps it's fitting that the man who guided the publication for so many years was on hand for the name change which has lasted over 40 years now. As of March 1940, the CKC's publication became *Dogs in Canada,* with *Kennel and Bench* in brackets for two years following to ease transition.

At the Annual General Meeting of the CKC held in February 1941, the members decided that henceforth, the Club's official organ would be restricted to official business of the Club and would no longer contain any editorial matter or news. The magazine became a shell of its former self and it is safe to say that no one was more disappointed over this development than James Strachan who had laboured so hard to make the publication one which the members would enjoy. In June of 1941 he submitted his resignation and he was succeeded by Mr. Norman F. Brown. But the decision to eliminate all editorial and news matter was short-lived. Within a year the members clamoured for the publication to resume its status as a magazine with something more than official business. The Board of Directors responded to that demand and it fell to Norman Brown, as Secretary-Treasurer, to re-establish the magazine. During his tenure as editor, the publication began to look more like a magazine as Brown directed a new design, improved the stock, and added new departments.

In November 1942, Mr. Brown enlisted in the RCAF and the services of Phyllis Robson, editor of *Dog World* in England, were engaged. Mrs. Robson was visiting on this side of the Atlantic and served as acting editor during Mr. Brown's absence. Over the following ten years, the editorship changed hands on at least five occasions. In between each change, it fell to Mr. Brown to ensure the magazine continued its monthly publication. The last editor appointed by the Board left the Club's employ in October 1954. The Board of Directors decided that a bold new move was timely and placed the magazine in the hands of independent publishers.

Under New Management: Elizabeth Dunn and her associate, Kaye Peer, had started *Key to Toronto,* a publication for visitors to the city, in 1953. Because of their love of the subject matter, they were instantly intrigued when hearing that the CKC was looking for someone to manage their publication. Misses Dunn and Peer held discussions with the CKC and negotiated the formation of a separate company to publish *Dogs in Canada.* Called Apex Publishers and Publicity Ltd., it is jointly owned by Misses Dunn and Peer and The Canadian Kennel Club (with the CKC as minority shareholder).

The aims of the new company were stated in their first issue in 1955. It was said that the "publishers are making every effort to make *Dogs in Canada* a magazine in which an exchange of ideas keeps interest fresh and keen, a publication to which all dog owners may turn for pleasure and information, and through which the breeders may best merchandise their kennel stock."

The scope of the magazine was to be broadened beyond a club newsletter—and it was to be run in a businesslike manner. The primary purpose was to communicate to breeders, but it was felt from the beginning that circulation could be enlarged by reaching non-CKC subscribers and that percentage of the dog-owning public who had a deep interest in dogs. In 1955, circulation was about 3500. Now it is 18,000 (of which, 6000 readers are not CKC members).

From the start, the tone of *Dogs in Canada* was lightened, adding more general articles, larger photographs, and touches of humour. A great deal of work was spent to increase the amount of advertising, from both breeders and commercial companies so that the magazine could, in turn, afford more editorial space. Long, hard work was the order for the first five years or so. The magazine had been a losing proposition; therefore no money was available to hire staff. Laudatory letters and comments in those early days indicated that the changes implemented were appreciated. In four years, a half dozen "departments" were added, articles introduced on genetics, rabies, and other educational topics, and circulation doubled.

A Few Highlights from the Past:
—In February '56 the Honour Roll was instituted, now published annually in the March issue
—in '57 a "provincial" series was started, profiling the people, dogs, and events of each province

—in November '57 the first annual Kennel Directory appeared (all of 16 pages)

—in January '58 the CKC official news and show results were published in a separate section on green paper

—in October '58 the first annual stud register ran, now an annual February feature (the Gallery of Stud Dogs and Brood Bitches)

—in March '60, a "Dogs in Competition" insert appeared, with statistics on leading shows and breeds

—for the 75th Anniversary of the CKC, an 84-page souvenir issue was published in February '63, with a silver cover and the history of the club

—July '63 was the first "standards" issue (132 pages plus CKC news, for a total of 180)

—in October '65, the CKC pages switched from green to their familiar yellow.

One highlight stands out. In June of 1964, *Dogs in Canada* inaugurated the Top Dog Point System. There had been nothing like it. The system encouraged people to continue exhibiting, striving for the Top Dog title instead of retiring their dogs upon completion of their championships. It provided (and still does) an overall, unifying goal—one which carries a tremendous amount of emotion and prestige. A year later, a point system was developed and introduced to recognize top obedience dogs.

A hitch in the magazine's upward development occurred in 1969−70 when the CKC attempted to set up its own computerized registration records in Toronto. The failure of this computer system caused extreme financial hardship for the Club and publication of show and trial results was suspended for three months. In order to help resume publication of this vital material, and save money, two issues were combined (December '70 and January '71), and a tabloid newspaper format was adopted. This move saved thousands of dollars for the CKC in the first year alone, but wasn't generally popular with readers. Since copies of *Dogs in Canada* are kept for years as reference and record, the tabloid format was not suited to this; the larger size was awkward, the paper tore easily, and it yellowed with age.

During the next few years the coffers were somewhat replenished and with the January '79 issue a new and improved standard magazine format was adopted. The magazine is sent to all major kennel clubs in the world, and the magazine constantly gets requests from dog magazines and club newsletters in other countries for reprint permission. *Dogs in Canada* is proud that its reputation enhances the international standing of the CKC, Canadian breeders, and Canadian dogs.

Dogs Annual: When the *Dogs Annual* was first introduced in 1975, the dream of really reaching out to the general public was realized. Pet owners could be informed and educated about the responsibilities of dog ownership. Breeders could rely on the magazine to sell their puppies to a discerning public, and the publication's commercial success has allowed the improvement and expansion of the monthly magazine, which appeals more to the "hard-core" dog lovers.

Dogs in Canada has always invited and welcomed input from its readers. By sharing their views and news with other dog lovers across the country, it serves to unite a caring a very special "community." May it always continue to do so.

THE VETERINARY SECTION

by John A. Reeve-Newson D.V.M.
and Martin E. DeForest D.V.M.

*I*T IS HOPED that this section will be of guidance to both the novice pet owner and the experienced breeder. Topics discussed include canine reproduction and puppy rearing, and the care of the adult dog; a special section is devoted to the care and needs of the geriatric patient. The principles of first aid are also included, which will hopefully enable the dog owner to be of assistance to his pet in times of illness or emergency, until veterinary care can be sought.

Reproduction in the Female Dog

The Oestrous Cycle: The oestrous, or reproductive, cycle in the female dog is dependent on the ovary and its hormones. Although many of the factors which control the function of the ovaries are still not understood completely, much knowlege has been gained in recent years concerning events which control the reproductive cycle in the bitch.

Bitches usually begin to cycle at about eight months of age (with a range of six to nine months). At this time, the bitch is said to be "in season," "in heat," or "in oestrus." This recurs every six to eight months. The oestrous cycle can be divided into four phases: proestrus, oestrus, dioestrus and anoestrus.

Proestrus, the first phase of the cycle, generally lasts six to nine days. Although the bitch will begin to attract males during this period, she will not be receptive to mating. The vulva will take on a swollen, turgid appearance and a red discharge will be present. This discharge contains high numbers of red blood cells, which migrate from tiny uterine blood vessels (capillaries) in response to increasing oestrogen (hormone) levels. This hormone also stimulates the vaginal epithelium (the tissue lining the vagina) to proliferate, and causes enlargement of the cervix. As a result, vaginal smears taken at this time contain many red blood cells and vaginal epithelial cells.

Oestrus is the period during which the female will accept the male. This phase lasts six to twelve days. When in the presence of the male, the bitch will usually lift her tail to one side of the perineum (flagging) and will stand to be bred. During the days most favourable to mating, the vulva appears softer and flabbier. This facilitates penetration by the stud. Vaginal discharge at this time is usually straw-coloured. Vaginal smears during oestrus contain superficial epithelial cells and some cellular debris. However, no neutrophils (white blood cells) are seen yet, even if bacteria are present. During proestrus, mature ova grow towards the surface of the ovary and protrude as fluid-filled follicles. Ultimately, during oestrus, follicles burst and release ova which travel down the reproductive tract to await fertilization.

Dioestrus is the period that extends from the last acceptance of the male until the corpus luteum, a hormone-secreting structure on the ovary, regresses. On average, dioestrus lasts from 60 to 90 days. Vaginal swabs taken during this phase contain noncornified epithelial cells (parabasal cells), partially cornified epithelial cells and white blood cells (neutrophils).

The anoestrus period, characterized by the sexual inactivity of the bitch, generally lasts from two to ten months. The variability in duration of anoestrus accounts for the variable length of time between periods of sexual receptivity. Levels of the ovarian hormones progesterone and oestrogen are low during anoestrus.

Control of the canine oestrous cycle is possible if the length of anoestrus can be controlled. Shortening anoestrus and thereby inducing a "heat" is desirable to people who want puppies from a bitch at a specific time. This can be achieved by injecting follicle stimulating hormone (FSH) or pregnant mare's serum (PMS). When contemplating this in cases of delayed oestrus, it is most important to evaluate the bitch's general health as several systemic disease states can cause delayed oestrus. Hypothyroidism, hypoadrenocorticism, and hyperadrenocorticism are examples of diseases which can alter the pattern of the reproductive cycle.

While hormones can be used to induce oestrus, one should be aware of possible adverse side effects. For example, repeated treatments with luteinizing hormone can render a sub-fertile bitch infertile. Since many such hormones are glycoproteins, they have the ability to stimulate the immune system to produce antibodies against these exogenous (injected) hormones. These antibodies may cross-react with natural hormones, neutralizing them.

Anoestrus can be lengthened both surgically and with drugs. Ovariohysterectomy (spaying) is an effective means of lengthening anoestrus in the bitch. The effects are permanent and, if done properly, the procedure is safe. It also eliminates the possibility of uterine disease and, if performed in the young bitch, it will significantly lower the incidence of mammary tumours in later life. Obviously, because of its permanence, it is not an acceptable means of contraception in breeding animals whose owners desire only a temporary means of oestrus control, with a return of fertility at some future date. For this reason, canine oral contraceptives have some advantages over ovariohysterectomy in selected cases. In recent years these drugs have received considerable publicity and have gained much public acceptance. Currently available canine contraceptives include megestrol acetate and mibolerone. Research in this field is continuing and the future promises many new products of this general type which will be both effective and safe, and will be associated with few or no adverse side effects.

Breeding

The age at which a bitch can be mated for the first time can vary with the breed and depends largely upon the rate of maturity. A good rule of thumb is to breed after the second heat cycle. Most members of the larger breeds experience their first heat cycle later than do the small, early-maturing breeds.

The decision to breed should be considered carefully and rationally. The merits of both the sire and dam must be viewed with a mind to breed improvement. The marketability of the puppies is also of prime importance. The dog pounds of the nation are filled with unwanted dogs. Overpopulation and indiscriminate breeding should be of utmost concern to all members of the dog fancy.

Once the decision has been made to breed and a prospective sire for the bitch has been found, the bitch should undergo a complete physical examination. This should include a test for brucellosis, a faecal examination for internal parasites, and a urinalysis to detect possible urogenital infection. In addition, she should receive booster vaccinations for all communicable diseases. This serves to stimulate a high level (titre) of antibody production in the dam and this level of disease protection is transferred to the puppies when they nurse. Although this is of vital importance, it is often overlooked by breeders. Any external parasites, if present, should be eliminated also.

The heat cycle has been described previously. The time to first attempt a breeding can vary, but generally is between ten and fourteen days after the onset of discharge. It is advisable to bring the female to the male, as the male will feel much more confident on his home territory. This is especially true of a younger, inexperienced male. As in all relationships, time to court is important. Introduce the male to the female and allow them time to get acquainted. Conduct the breeding in a quiet room with no distractions. Provide a mat or surface with good traction. In the case of toy dogs, the breeding can be done on a table with a non-slip surface. Have someone to hold the bitch and someone to assist the male, although the latter may not be necessary with an experienced male who knows the ropes. It is a good idea to muzzle the female regardless of how calm and easily manageable she seems. She may bite when the male penetrates.

As the male enters the female, he will become "locked" in her. This is known as the "tie" and it can last for several minutes to well over an hour. During this phase, place the male so his front feet are both on the ground. Some males prefer to turn completely around, which is also acceptable. Hold the mating pair until the "tie" is broken and the dogs separate. Never attempt to separate the dogs before the "tie" is broken as this is painful and potentially injurious to both. When the "tie" is broken, check that the penis has returned to the sheath of the male and return the female to her kennel for several hours of quiet rest.

If you cannot manage a natural breeding, you may resort to artificial insemination. Follow the advice of your veterinarian in this as both collection of semen and its insertion into the bitch must be done carefully. Sometimes a breeding pair, even though both are experienced and willing, will fail to breed successfully. If this occurs, separate the pair and place them in cool, separate kennels and try again a few hours later. They will usually be successful the second time.

Following a successful breeding, record the date in your dog book. Repeat the mating two days later and once again record this date. Good records are invaluable for accurate prediction of projected whelping dates. This will help to ensure that you are fully prepared for the event. The average bitch will whelp 63 days from the date of mating. However, anywhere from 58 to 65 days is not uncommon.

Whelping

The bitch has become pregnant and, with a new family due, it is necessary to be ready. The bitch should be fed a good quality diet. Select a commercially available dog food that is complete and well balanced. Each year many thousands of dollars are spent on research in canine nutrition. It is not necessary to spend countless hours in the kitchen cooking for her. Supplements may or may not be necessary. If you do elect to supplement her diet, make sure that the supplement is balanced and given according to directions on the label. Excesses can be just as damaging as deficiencies.

In the last trimester (third) of pregnancy, increase her food intake by 50 to 100 per cent, administered in two or three feedings per day. Keep up the expectant mother's exercise also, for fit muscles are needed for delivery. A few days prior to whelping, clip her abdomen and, in long-haired, long-tailed breeds, also clip or bandage the tail. This will facilitate both the delivery and nursing. A whelping box should be prepared of adequate size for the mother and her puppies. Be certain to build a guard rail around the inside of the box to prevent the dam from accidentally squeezing a puppy between her and the side of the box. For the delivery, line the box with newspapers. After the delivery, a layer of terry towelling can be placed over fresh papers to provide the puppies with traction as they nurse. Prepare a whelping tray which contains the equipment that you may need to assist the mother. Include several terry cloth towels, scissors, disinfectant, haemostats (to seal the umbilical cords of the puppies), scales to weigh the puppies, and a thermometer.

As the time draws near, the bitch may appear restless and apprehensive and may refuse to eat. "Nesting" behaviour, such as shredding newspapers and panting, are commonly seen. In addition, her rectal temperature will fall below 100 degrees Fahrenheit about 24 hours before whelping and a mucousy vaginal discharge may appear as the cervix dilates.

With the actual birth of the first puppy, the bitch will lie down and you will notice strong contractions of the abdominal musculature. Soon, a fluid-filled sac will begin to protrude from the vulva, followed closely by a puppy. Usually, the neonate will be enveloped in foetal membranes which the bitch will tear open to permit breathing. If she fails to do so, immediately tear the membrane off the puppy. Next, clamp the umbilical cord with haemostats one inch below the abdomen, then cut below this with scissors and remove the haemostats. Vigorously dry the puppy or let mother lick it and clean up the afterbirth being certain to account for an afterbirth for each puppy.

If the bitch is in active labour for more than one hour without presenting a puppy, there may be a problem. The birth canal of the bitch may be too small to allow her to expel the puppy, the cervix may have failed to dilate, or a puppy may be in an abnormal position. Some bitches may also experience uterine inertia in which the uterus fails to contract properly. Regardless of the cause, if the delivery is not proceeding properly, call your veterinarian for advice. Time is of the essence for both the dam and the litter.

Following delivery, the bitch will probably be hungry. Offer her some milk, followed soon after by a full meal. While lactating, she will require two or three times her daily ration. This volume of food should be divided into several meals per day. Fresh drinking water should be available at all times, but not located such that a puppy may crawl into the bowl. Keep in mind that for the next three or four weeks, the dam will be providing all of the puppies' food. Considering that the birth-weight of the puppies will at least quadruple in this period, proper feeding of the bitch is essential.

It is advised that within 24 hours of the arrival of the last puppy, the bitch be taken to your veterinarian for an examination. This will ensure that no puppies or afterbirths remain, as this can lead to some very serious complications.

Your Puppy's First Year

Care of the Newborn: Following the delivery of a litter, the real work begins. At this time, those persons caring for the bitch must also become actively involved in the care of the neonates. The bitch, especially if it is her first litter, may need considerable support at this time if a healthy litter is to be raised. Initially, dry each puppy and place him on a teat to ensure that he receives a good meal. This is most important, as not only does this first feeding provide the puppy with added strength, but also confers protection against disease.

For the first 24 hours after whelping, the bitch's milk is called colostrum. This milk is rich in antibodies called gamma globulins, which provides disease protection to the puppies for their first weeks of life. Puppies are best able to absorb these special proteins through their intestine for 24 to 36 hours after birth. This "maternal antibody protection," as it is called, begins to fade after a few weeks. However, by then the puppy's own immune system will be more competent and a vaccination programme conducted under veterinary supervision should be commenced. This will provide longer-lasting immunity.

Most puppies will have little difficulty finding where dinner is being served and will instinctively attach themselves to a nipple and begin to nurse. Occasionally, some pups may require a little extra assistance until they get the idea. If such is the case, gently open the puppy's mouth and place it over a nipple, while holding him steady. Squeeze in a drop or two of milk and he will probably take to it quickly. This method will suffice for most puppies. Additional assistance may be required for weak pups, however. This may be in the form of a commercially-prepared simulated bitch's milk product or a special formula, depending on what your veterinarian feels is warranted. It might contain serum, concentrated liver extract, gamma globulins, vitamins, and minerals or may simply be warm distilled water for dehydrated puppies.

If your bitch is unable to feed all her puppies, or if the litter is orphaned, they can be raised by hand. A normal litter is quiet, with the puppies being asleep most of the time when not nursing. Constant crying or squirming may be a signal that something is wrong. This may be neglect by the dam or perhaps some illness, such as diarrhoea, an inability to nurse, weakness or a lowered body temperature (see table below). If you suspect illness in the litter, have the puppies examined by a veterinarian at once.

Puppy's Age (days)	Normal Rectal Temperature (F°)
1	92– 97
2	95– 98
7	96– 98
14	97– 98
21	98– 99
28	99–101

Puppies which are separated from their dams must be kept in a warm, draught-free environment because they have difficulty regulating their body temperature. For the first five days, they should be in a room which is between 85 and 90 degrees. From five until twenty days of age, they should be in an 80-degree environment. By the fourth week the temperature should be lowered to about 72 degrees. An excellent way to provide the proper temperature for orphan puppies is by using an electric heating pad. Hang this down one side of the box and over 25 per cent of the bottom. This will allow the puppies an opportunity to get away from the heat if necessary. This is essential, as serious thermal burns may occur if a puppy lies for long periods of time on a very warm surface. The temperature control on the pad should be adjusted to maintain a proper air temperature. Gently handle each puppy daily. Studies have shown that puppies so treated are more emotionally stable, resistant to stress, and are better socialized when the time comes for them to go to their new homes.

When feeding orphan puppies, the object is to provide a composition which most approaches normal bitch's milk. Many excellent commercial products are available through your veterinarian. To determine the amount to feed, weigh the puppy and use a table of caloric requirements. The required amount of formula can then be divided into four portions and fed at six-hour intervals.

Age (in weeks)	Calories (Kilocalories) Needed Daily/Pound
1	Approximately 60
2	Approximately 70
3	Approximately 80–90
4+	Greater than 90

If the puppy cannot ingest the required daily amount in four feedings, the number of feedings will have to be increased. At each meal the puppy should take in just enough formula to be comfortably full. Overfeeding should be avoided (the abdomen will appear tight and overly distended) as it will make the puppy uncomfortable and may create digestive upsets such as diarrhoea. Formula should be heated to body temperature (about 100 degrees F) before feeding. It can be administered by syringe, eye dropper, stomach tube, or nursing bottle. The latter is probably the easiest and safest way for the inexperienced breeder. If this method is chosen, select a nipple size that is appropriate for the puppy. If the formula does not drip freely from the nipple when the bottle is inverted, enlarge it with a heated straight pin.

When feeding from the bottle, the puppy should be held on its abdomen. Separate the lips with your fingers and insert the nipple. Once he gets a taste of milk, he will begin to suckle vigorously. Weak puppies may be held vertically, with the formula then placed slowly into their mouths. Never feed the puppy on his back or force liquid into the mouth too rapidly, as the puppy may aspirate the liquid into his lungs. This is a prelude to pneumonia.

After each feeding, it is important to stimulate the young puppy to urinate and defecate. This is easily achieved by gently massaging the anogenital area with a piece of cotton moistened with warm water. Normal stools at this time are firm in consistency and yellow in colour. If diarrhoea occurs, it may be because the formula is too rich. This may be remedied by diluting it in half with boiled water. If the condition continues, consult your veterinarian immediately.

Congenital Defects and Inherited Diseases: Congenital defects are abnormalities of structure or function present at birth. They can involve any system in the animal's body, although some body systems appear to be more frequently affected by this type of abnormality. Not all congenital abnormalities are inherited, that is, having genetic basis. Some are errors in development that stem from various environmental factors to which the pregnant bitch may have been exposed. These include such things as the toxic effects of certain chemicals or drugs, nutritional deficiencies, or systemic disease of the bitch.

When congenital malformations appear in a litter, responsible breeders attempt to determine if the problem is of an inherited nature, transmitted on the genes. If this is ascertained, the parents of the litter are usually withdrawn from the breeding programme.

Some of the more common congenital defects are discussed below, although there are many more. When contemplating the purchase of a puppy, one should inquire about any inherited problems prevalent in the breed and request that a guarantee be given should any such conditions develop, since all inherited diseases are not visible at birth. Congenital diseases that appear later in life are referred to as LATENT.

Umbilical Hernias: One of the most common hernias that occurs in puppies is the umbilical hernia. It occurs as a portion of fat, or occasionally intestine, which protrudes through an incompletely closed umbilical ring. Many umbilical hernias are present at birth, but they can be acquired if the mother chews at the umbilical cord too vigorously or if it is improperly handled in some other way. Generally, umbilical hernias are small and they tend to get smaller as the puppy ages. Large hernias, especially those that contain abdominal organs, require surgical repair. Your veterinarian can advise you on these.

Cleft Palate–Cleft Lip: This term encompasses a group of malformations affecting the roof of the mouth. As a result, there is incomplete separation of the oral and nasal cavities. Severe cases may be accompanied by a cleft lip. This condition may appear singularly as well.

The cleft palate usually represents a defect of varying width and length and generally is incompatible with life. Affected puppies frequently display an inability to nurse because they cannot create the necessary vacuum between the tongue and the palate. In less severe cases, there may be chronic irritation of the nasal passages and pharynx with regurgitation of milk through the nostrils. Animals with a cleft lip and a normal palate are capable of sustaining life. In these, the defect is primarily a cosmetic consideration.

In small domestic animals these malformations are generally believed to be genetic in nature. However, experimentally, stress, vitamin deficiencies and drug administration have been implicated as possible causes as well. Regardless, euthanasia or neutering of affected individuals is advised in order to lower the incidence of these defects. If surgical correction of these defects is attempted, it should not be before six to eight weeks of age, in order to lower the risk of anaesthesia and to provide more time for the affected tissues to develop.

Cryptorchidism: This common defect concerns the failure of one or both testes to descend into the scrotum. Most authorities agree that it is genetic in origin but the mode of inheritance is poorly understood. If the condition is bilateral, the animal is sterile. Unilateral cryptorchids (where only one testicle has failed to descend) are fertile. Apart from being a disqualification in the show ring, the defect has health significance to the affected animal, as retained testes are more subject to developing tumours in later life.

Congenital Deafness: Failure to respond to auditory stimuli may be due to disinterest, depression, distraction, pain, and other causes unrelated to deafness. Congenital deafness usually is apparent by four to six months of age. A deaf dog will be unresponsive to sound stimuli and will be difficult to arouse from sleep. Congenital deafness is most common in Dalmatians, Bull Terriers, Sealyhams, Scottish Terriers, Border Collies, Fox Terriers, Blue Merle Shelties, and Foxhounds. The external ear and ear drum appear normal but the mobility of the ears is usually less. The deaf dog relies more heavily on other senses, which become very acute.

Congenital Cataracts: A cataract is any opacity of the lens of the eye. Congenital lens opacities may occur at any period of lens development. Often these defects are inherited. Others may occur as reaction to influences within the uterus. They occur with increased incidence in Afghans, Beagles, Chesapeake Bay and Labrador Retrievers, Cocker Spaniels, English Setters, Miniature Schnauzers, Poodles, and Staffordshire Bull Terriers. The presence of a cataract is detected by veterinary examination with a slit-lamp biomicroscope. Generally, the condition progresses to blindness.

Congenital Hydrocephalus: This condition involves a malformation of the internal structure of the brain. Affected animals may have an excessively dome-shaped skull with open fontanelles. Puppies with this disorder may show signs of disorientation, blindness, seizures, and an inability to walk normally. It is most common in the toy breeds, but may occur in any breed. Generally, treatment is unrewarding.

Collie Eye Anomaly: This is a syndrome of inherited disorders affecting several structures within the eye. It is most common in the Collie and Shetland Sheepdog but also has been reported in various other breeds including the Borzoi, Dachshund, German Shepherd, and Poodle. Generally, it is non-progressive (except where retinal detachment and haemorrhage occurs) and has a limited effect on vision in most affected animals.

Congenital Heart Disease: This topic includes several separate disease entities and is very common in dogs. Some of the diseases included in this group are operable while others are not. The most common disease of this group, *Patent Ductus Arteriosis,* an inherited disease, is operable. Prior to birth, the ductus arteriosis functions as an essential shunt between the aorta and the pulmonary artery. At birth, this structure closes and blood circulates properly through the lungs to be oxygenated. However, if the ductus arteriosis remains patent, blood recirculates through the lungs. As a result, the heart is overworked, and enlarges. If the situation is not remedied, the puppy will die. Correction of the defect involves exposing and tying off the ductus arteriosis, which enables circulation to return to normal. This lesion can be inherited and produced experimentally by environmental agents.

Pulmonic stenosis is the second most common congenital heart lesion. It too is an inherited disease but the exact mechanism is poorly understood. It is an obstruction to blood flow between the right ventricle and the pulmonary artery. Various anatomic abnormalities can cause the obstruction but regardless of which one it is, the result is the same. The heart is overworked by pumping blood through a restricted passage. Surgical correction is possible in most cases.

Subaortic stenosis, another inherited abnormality, is similar to *pulmonic stenosis.* This one occurs between the left ventricle and the aorta. However, it is much more difficult to repair surgically.

Ventricular Septal Defect is an opening between the right and left ventricles. Consequently, when the ventricles contract, some of the blood from the left ventricle passes into the right ventricle, where there is lower pressure. As a result, this blood recirculates through the lungs. While a small defect of this nature may be compatible with life, larger ones produce serious consequences. Without corrective open heart surgery, a large lesion will result in death.

Persistent Right Aortic Arch is a genetic condition which has the greatest incidence in German Shepherds. Essentially, it involves abnormal development of blood vessels originating from the heart. Abnormal blood vessels eclipse the oesophagus and trachea and thereby impede swallowing, but because circulation is not impaired, congestive heart failure does not develop. The main clinical signs are those of oesophageal dysfunction. Puppies begin to regurgitate immediately when started onto solid food. Further complications include stunted growth and pneumonia which results when accumulated ingested material in the oesophagus is aspirated into the lungs. The stricture to the oesophagus can be relieved surgically. If left untreated, most puppies die before reaching maturity and the sooner that the patient is treated, the greater the chance of complete recovery.

Legg Perthes Disease: This disease affects the head and neck of the femur bone in the hind leg. Although the underlying predisposing causes are in some dispute, most authorities feel that an interruption in blood supply to these structures results in cell death. The disease is seen most commonly in the toy breeds, but it has been reported in some terriers as well. Both sexes seem to be affected equally and the peak incidence for the onset of clinical signs is six to seven months of age. The condition rapidly progresses to a severely painful lameness, often leading to complete disuse of the limb. Surgical removal of the head of the femur (excision arthroplasty) is the treatment of choice. The condition is believed to be inherited but the exact mode of inheritance is not known.

Hepatic Encephalopathy: This disease is caused by a birth defect characterized by an abnormal arrangement of blood vessels, which bypass the liver. Consequently, toxic waste products of metabolism accumulate in the bloodstream and irritate the central nervous system. Signs of a neurological disturbance are common and become evident during the first year of life. Affected puppies are generally unthrifty then, and undersized when compared to normal littermates. Clinically, puppies experience episodes of staggering, dementia and even convulsions. While surgical correction of the defect is possible in some cases, the prognosis is guarded.

Osteochondritis Dissecans: *Osteochondritis Dissecans* (OCD) of the head of the humerus is a type of localized cell death due to an impaired blood supply, the cause of which is unknown. It is a disease of large, young dogs from one to twelve months of age. Often there is a history of trauma. The clinical signs of this disease include a severe lameness which worsens with exercise. It can involve one or both forelimbs.

This disease is diagnosed by radiography of the shoulder joint. Mild cases may be treated with restriction of exercise while severe cases often require surgical treatment.

Cosmetic Surgery: Surgical removal of the dewclaws, a portion of the tail (docking) and part of the ear (cropping) are procedures performed largely for cosmetic reasons. Dewclaws, it left in place, especially those which are loosely attached, do have a tendency to become snagged and torn. Dewclaw removal and tail docking (in the appropriate breeds) is done by your veterinarian at day three or four. These procedures are relatively atraumatic at this time and anaesthesia is not required. To determine which dewclaws and how much tail to remove consult the breed standards. The optimal time for ear cropping, if elected, varies somewhat between breeds but is usually around ten weeks of age. In order to get the desired effect following cropping, one must be prepared for several weeks' work using tape and other support materials. This can be an ordeal for both you and the puppy and one should be aware of this when making the decision to crop or not to crop.

Weaning and Feeding: Provided that she has adequate milk and that the litter is not too large, the dam can supply all or most of the puppies' food for the first four weeks. At this age, or perhaps even earlier, many breeders begin the process of weaning. A primary advantage of early weaning is that it imposes less in on the bitch. This, in turn, enables her to make a faster comeback following weaning. During this period, the dam may occasionally regurgitate food in front of the puppies. This is a natural process and is no cause for alarm.

Weaning can be achieved with puréed puppy kibble mixed with warm water or milk. Offer this food to the puppies in a shallow dish. As they will begin to investigate the food, often feet first, they will teach themselves to lap. Always take the bitch away from the puppies for an hour or two before feeding to ensure that they are hungry for the food that you are providing. As the puppies become older, you can gradually make the mixture of food more solid by incorporating less liquid. At eight weeks of age, the puppies should be eating food of a consistency suitable for an adult. That is, feed puppy kibble softened with water. Cooked eggs, cottage cheese, yogurt or a little cooked meat, may be added to the diet as the pups become accustomed to eating solid food. Make any changes in the diet gradual ones to avoid creating digestive upsets.

To reduce milk production by the dam at this time, do not feed her on the first day of weaning, but allow her free access to water. The next day feed her half of her usual ration. Increase this to three-quarters of her usual ration on the third day and by the fourth day she can be back on her normal regimen. Do not remove milk from her mammary glands during this process, as this will only stimulate futher milk production.

Newly weaned puppies should be fed four times daily until four months of age at which time this may be reduced to three daily feedings. Further reduce this to two at six months of age until the puppy reaches one year. One daily feeding is all that most dogs require at that point.

Housebreaking: This usually does not present a problem. Dogs are naturally den dwellers and instinctively are very clean. During this period, it is probably best to confine your puppy to a relatively small area—his bed. By nature, he will avoid "soiling" his bed, if possible. After he eats, naps, or plays, be certain to take him outside. Always praise him when he performs appropriately. Frequent trips outdoors and lots of positive reinforcement in the form of praise should bring about the desired results.

If you are not able to make frequent trips outdoors with the puppy, it will be necessary to provide him with a "spot" indoors. Try training him to use a newspapered section of the kitchen floor. Later, transfer his "spot" by moving a soiled piece of newspaper outside. Again, the key to making it work is plenty of praise. Remember, reprimanding a puppy for his mistakes, if you don't catch him in the act, is counter-productive. It only serves to confuse and frighten him.

Infectious Diseases: For the first weeks of life, puppies are protected from several infectious diseases by antibodies derived from the dam in colostrum. This passive immunity declines after a few weeks. A vaccination programme should be initiated by a veterinarian at this time to confer longer-lasting protection to the puppy.

Within seven to ten days of contact by the animal with an infectious organism, antibodies are produced by the immune system of the animal. In addition, this contact imparts some memory to the immune system, so that later invasions by that organism are quickly brought under control before clinical disease has a chance to develop. Vaccination programmes make use of this same principle, except a relatively harmless form of the infective agent is administered as the initial stimulus to impart memory. Following this, contact with the agent results in an early and explosive production of antibody which will effectively neutralize the invading organism.

Vaccines are prepared by converting the infectious agent into a harmless form without destroying its ability to stimulate the immune system. Vaccines may be killed or live. Killed or inactivated vaccines have had their infectivity completely destroyed. Most vaccines currently available are modified live virus or attenuated preparations. They are weakened or altered to produce no clinical signs of disease but replicate within the animal to produce a prolonged stimulus to the immune system. This gives rise to a substantial level of immunity. Killed vaccines, because of their inability to replicate within the animal, produce a shorter duration of immunity than attenuated, live products.

Viral Diseases: As the heading implies, the diseases discussed in this section are caused by viruses. These agents of infectious diseases only multiply naturally in the presence of living cells. Viruses are so tiny that they cannot be observed with ordinary microscopes. Rabies is the only viral disease of dogs that affects man.

Canine Distemper Virus: Canine distemper is the most common infectious disease in dogs. The distemper virus can be transmitted from dog to dog and also can be contracted from a contaminated environment. Generally, spread of the virus is by the airborne route. Fortunately, because of the effectiveness of commercially-prepared distemper vaccines, this disease is rarely encountered today.

A vaccination programme against distemper is usually begun at seven or eight weeks of age. Your veterinarian will recommend the regimen best suited to your puppy.

Initially, distemper is difficult to differentiate from several other diseases. Clinical signs may include inappetence, depression, fever, and discharge from the eyes and nose. Profuse diarrhoea and pneumonia usually develop next, followed by neurological signs. These may include convulsions and muscle twitching as the virus gains access to the central nervous system.

Canine Adenovirus 1 (Infectious Canine Hepatitis Virus): This virus (CAV 1) primarily affects the liver and usually enters the body of a susceptible dog by way of the mouth. In the initial phase, this disease can resemble distemper. Affected animals may experience a sudden rise and fall in temperature, depression, loss of appetite, and possible discharges from the eyes and nose. Painful abdomen, vomiting, and excessive skin bruising are also common signs.

Hepatitis can be prevented by vaccination. Usually vaccines against infectious canine hepatitis are administered at the same time as those against canine distemper. This disease is not transmissible to humans.

Canine Adenovirus 2 (Infectious Canine Laryngotracheitis Virus): This virus is closely related to *Canine Adenovirus 1*. Dogs vaccinated against infectious hepatitis (CAV 1) are protected from CAV 2 infection, which is restricted to the respiratory tract. This is one of the infectious agents involved in the Kennel Cough Syndrome, the typical signs of which include a dry, hacking cough.

Canine Parainfluenza Virus: This is the primary virus in the Kennel Cough Syndrome. This viral disease is spread in the air and affects the upper respiratory tract. Clinical signs include a mild fever, nasal discharge and enlargement of the tonsils. Gagging, retching, and a harsh, dry, non-productive cough are usually present. Recently a vaccine has been produced to protect dogs from this disease.

Canine Herpesvirus: This virus is a threat to newborn puppies, where it frequently causes a sudden death syndrome. However, fatal infections of newborn puppies can be caused by a variety of viral and bacterial agents. Generally, herpes affects only puppies under one month of age. Occasionally it is responsible for mild vaginitis in young adult bitches or mild nasal discharge in older animals. In cases of neonatal infection, death follows within 24 hours of the onset of signs of illness.

Canine Parvo Virus: Since its sudden appearance in the summer of 1978, *Canine Parvo Virus* (CPV) infection has been a major concern to veterinarians, dog breeders, and pet owners. This virus attacks the lining of the intestinal tract producing signs of profuse bloody diarrhoea and occasionally, vomiting. A second form of CPV infection is *myocarditis* or inflammation of the heart muscle. This type is often seen in puppies less than three months of age and is caused by reproduction of CPV in the rapidly growing cells of the heart. This syndrome often produces sudden death.

Canine Parvo Virus is transmitted through contact with the faeces of an affected dog. Hence, thorough sanitation and disposal of all faecal waste is important to control the disease in the event of an outbreak.

Commercial vaccines against *Canine Parvo Virus* are now available through your veterinarian. He can give advice concerning the best vaccine and the optimal times for vaccination.

Rabies: This viral infection is transmitted in the saliva of an animal with the disease. It may affect many species of animals and man. The incubation period which is the time between exposure and the onset of clinical signs, may be several months. The signs are variable, but include paralysis, an inability to swallow, unprovoked aggressive behaviour, and ultimately, death.

The probability of your dog being exposed to rabies varies greatly with the geographical area in which he resides. The incidence of rabies tends to be much higher in rural regions. Because of its public health significance, suspected cases of rabies must be handled according to federal regulatory measures. Vaccination against rabies is usually given after the puppy reaches four months of age.

Bacterial Diseases: A number of bacterial diseases can cause serious illness or death. The presence of the bacteria in the body, combined with their growth products and toxins, can be especially detrimental to puppies.

Leptospirosis: This infectious disease affects man, dogs, cattle, pigs, horses, rodents, and other mammals. There are three species that have significance to dogs in North America: *L. icterohemmorrhagiae, L. pomona,* and *L. canicola.*

Spread of the disease is by direct contact between the organism and a susceptible animal. This bacteria is believed to have the ability to penetrate intact skin and mucosa (the lining of the mouth, nose, digestive tract, and genital organs). The signs of this disease are sudden in onset and include fever, vomiting, inappetence, weakness, reluctance to move, and abdominal pain. In fatal cases, death usually follows within a week of the onset of clinical signs. Because the bacteria causes extensive damage to the digestive tract, liver, and kidneys, recovery is slow. *Leptospirosis* can also follow a more chronic course which is characterized by progressive damage to the kidneys.

With early treatment, leptospiral infections will respond to intense antibiotic therapy. Vaccination of young dogs with killed leptospiral bacterins is recommended even though the duration of protection is short-lived.

Bordetella Bronchiseptica: This bacterial organism plays a major role in respiratory disease of dogs. Alone, it can cause mild respiratory disease characterized by coughing. Clinical signs are more severe when associated with viruses. There is a bacterin (vaccine) that can be administered against this disease.

Neonatal "Fading Puppy Syndrome": Bacterial infections are a major cause of mortality in puppies under three weeks of age. Often these infections gain access to the body by way of the umbilicus. Affected puppies cry intermittently and tend to isolate themselves from other puppies in the litter. Treatment must be instituted quickly if the puppies are to be saved. Antibiotics and supplemental fluids must be administered and affected puppies must be kept warm. Sanitation in the whelping area is of the utmost importance as the infection is acquired from the environment.

The Internal Parasite Problem: Many puppies acquire internal parasites from their dam or from the environment in which they are raised. Internal parasites are much more detrimental to puppies than to adult dogs, but with proper treatment worms need not be a problem. However, if neglected they can seriously reduce a dog's over-all vitality, undermine his general health, and may initiate digestive tract upsets and skin problems. A heavy worm burden may even prove fatal in very young puppies.

To determine the presence of internal parasites and to select the appropriate medication to eliminate them, consult your veterinarian. This is most important, as there are many types of worms but many drugs are designed to treat only one or two of these. Selecting over-the-counter medications without knowledge of the types of worms present is at best a hit-or-miss approach and is not very effective.

Ascarids (Roundworms):   Ascarids are the type of roundworm most commonly found in the stool of puppies. They are white in colour and are cylindrically-shaped with pointed ends. Generally, adult ascarids live in the small intestine where they obtain nourishment through the absorption of digestive juices through their cuticle or outer surface. The mature worms produce eggs which are passed out in the faeces. Within one to four weeks of this, the eggs become infective and contain the larval form of the worm. Once ingested by the proper host, the infective eggs complete their life cycle, ultimately developing into adult worms in the intestine. If the eggs are ingested by an abnormal host such as a rodent, the cycle is broken, at least temporarily, as the larva encysts in the tissues of the animal. This is a dead-end process unless the abnormal host is later ingested by a dog or some other animal thereby releasing the larvae. When dogs older than one month swallow an infective egg of the common roundworm, *Toxocara canis,* the larvae do not complete their life cycle. Instead, they become encysted in body tissues where they remain dormant in males and spayed females. However, when an intact female becomes pregnant, the larvae are activated by hormone changes and become mobilized. From their resting place in muscles, they enter the uterus and infect the developing puppies. This process is called PRENATAL INFECTION and is the means by which puppies can be born with roundworm infection. *This cannot be prevented by deworming the dam before breeding,* as drugs will eliminate only those parasites residing in the intestinal tract but will not affect those encysted in muscle.

Signs of roundworm infection are usually seen only in puppies. Ascarids seldom produce apparent disease in adult dogs. Common signs in puppies include vomiting (of worms, occasionally), diarrhoea, progressive weakness, dull, unthrifty coats, and a thin, pot-bellied appearance. Occasionally, a heavy worm burden in puppies can lead to death.

There are various drugs available to remove adult roundworms from the intestinal tract. Salts of the drug piperazine are used most commonly, as this drug is both safe and effective. Even puppies as young as two weeks of age can be dewormed with this drug. Early deworming removes the adult worms from pups before they start producing eggs, thereby preventing contamination of the environment. Deworming should be repeated at least once, two to three weeks after the initial treatment. This will rid the puppies of any adult worms which were immature and not killed by the initial treatment. Sometimes, several dewormings are necessary in the case of heavy infestation. Repeated faecal examinations by your veterinarian will ensure that the problem is eliminated. At the time the puppies are being dewormed, it is important that the dam of the litter be dewormed also. The reason for this is that, no doubt, she will have become infected also while keeping her infant puppies clean.

Rigorous sanitation procedures with prompt (daily) removal of stool helps to prevent reinfection of dogs and infection of humans. Ideally, dogs should be housed on surfaces that are easily cleaned. Rodents and cockroaches, which act as intermediate hosts for worms, should be eliminated from the immediate environment.

Human Health Hazards of Roundworms: Canine roundworms do not inhabit the digestive tract of humans. However, larval forms of the parasite can cause a disease in man known as *Visceral Larval Migrans*. This is a rare condition in which larvae migrate in the human body. Symptoms of this disease range from none to severe. Reportedly, it can even cause blindness in children who play in contaminated areas. This of course emphasizes the need for ascarid control and good sanitation procedures.

Hookworms: Hookworms produce clinical signs similar to roundworms, although often, they are much more severe. Very loose, bloody stools, anaemia, scratching at areas of the skin, weakness, and emaciation are frequently seen in puppies with hookworm infection.

The hookworm, true to its name, attaches itself to the intestinal mucous membrane to suck blood. Since the worms secrete an anticoagulant, the site of attachment often continues to bleed long after the worms have moved to a new location. This causes considerable blood loss into the stools and consequently, mortality in young, severely affected puppies can be high.

Dogs become infected with hookworms by consuming infective larval worms from the ground. Larval worms can also penetrate intact skin (usually on the feet). Prenatal infection from the dam's tissues occurs and infective larvae may even be transferred from mother to puppies shortly after birth in colostrum. As signs of hookworm infection are similar to those caused by other diseases, it is best diagnosed and treated by a veterinarian. Once again, sanitation is extremely important to the control of the disease.

Tapeworms: Tapeworms are a common internal parasite of dogs. Tapeworms are long, flat, and ribbonlike in appearance. They can be several feet in length and are made up of small segments, each of which contain hundreds of eggs. Most frequently, they affect adult dogs and can be difficult to eliminate. Dogs acquire tapeworms by ingesting infected material. This may be prey or animal parts, raw freshwater fish, or infected fleas or biting lice.

Many tapeworm infections are not evident, although heavy tapeworm infestations may be responsible for poor appetites, weight loss, poor growth or coat changes. Usually, tapeworm infections are discovered by the presence of tapeworm segments clinging to the haircoat around the anus or in fresh feces, although they are not always present. Fresh tapeworm segments are creamy-white in colour and are flat and rectangular in shape. When the segments dry, they become yellow or off-white in colour and resemble grains of rice.

Medications to rid dogs of tapeworms are available through your veterinarian.

Whipworms: These small intestinal parasites have a whiplike body, $1\frac{1}{2}$ to $2\frac{1}{2}$ inches in length and are thinner than a needle. Whipworms reside in the colon (large intestine) and the caecum, a blind pouch located between the large and small intestine.

Whipworms can be responsible for chronic diarrhoea which is frequently foul-smelling and may contain blood or mucous. There are several effective and relatively non-toxic drugs which will eliminate whipworms from dogs. Good sanitation is the key to preventing reinfestation, as dogs acquire whipworms by the ingestion of infective larvae from a contaminated environment.

Protozoal Organisms: There are several types of protozoa that may infect dogs. Some of these are quite rare, while others are not at all uncommon. There are four types of coccidia which infect dogs. These are detected by microscopic examination of the faeces. Once diagnosed, *coccidiosis* should be promptly treated, as it can lead to severe intestinal upsets, especially in puppies. It seldom causes serious upsets in adult dogs, although carrier animals can spread it to others. The organism burrows into the lining of the small and large bowel and produces signs of profuse diarrhoea, often with blood and mucous. The associated fluid loss leads to dehydration and if the condition remains untreated, puppies will develop discharges from the eyes and nose and will cough and run a fever. Death is not an uncommon sequel in young animals.

This disease is most frequently seen in puppies raised in crowded, unsanitary conditions. However, signs of the disease can be induced by stress, such as dietary changes, being suddenly placed in a cold environment, or being shipped from a kennel to a new home.

Treatment of the condition must involve a multifactorial approach. First, while treating animal with *coccidiosis*, stringent sanitation must be used. As for the animals themselves, antidiarrhoeal drugs are given to prevent further fluid and blood loss and electrolyte disturbances. Fluid therapy may be required if dehydration is marked. In addition, sulfanilamide drugs must be administered to destroy the coccidia and antibiotics are given to eliminate pathogenic bacterial organisms that are present. Acute cases of *coccidiosis* resemble canine distemper and must be differentiated from this.

Heartworms: The presence of heartworms in dogs is both serious and life threatening. Adult heartworms live in the right atrium and ventricle of the heart, as well as the pulmonary arteries and vena cava. Adults, which range in length from three to fourteen inches and are less than one-eighth of an inch in diameter, produce microscopic larvae known as microfilaria. These circulate in the bloodstream, and are detected by means of a blood test. Mosquitoes feeding on an infected dog take up larvae with a blood meal. Following this, the larvae become infective within the mosquito in about two weeks. The infective larvae are then passed on to another dog when bitten by the mosquito.

Dogs with heartworms may show signs of laboured breathing, reduced tolerance to exercise, and may appear unthrifty. Coughing is also common, and signs of liver disease or heart failure may be present. Since this is such a potentially dangerous disease, dogs that live in endemic heartworm areas should be tested twice yearly.

Once heartworm infection is diagnosed, careful treatment must be conducted by a veterinarian. This is usually carried out with the animal hospitalized since drug reactions to the toxic chemical used are not altogether uncommon. Once the adult worms are eliminated, follow-up treatment is performed to rid the dog of microfilaria.

There are two basic ways of preventing heartworm infection in dogs. One is to prevent mosquito bites by keeping dogs in screened-in enclosures. The other is to administer a drug known as diethylcarbamazine citrate, which is given daily to prevent heartworm infection. It is most important that the dog is heartworm free before placing him onto preventive medication.

External Parasites: The external parasites of dogs are hard-coated insects and insect-like animals known as arthropods. They live on the surface of the skin or just under it, obtaining nourishment from the skin itself, tissue fluids or blood.

Fleas: Fleas are the most common external parasite of dogs. They sustain themselves by sucking blood and although there are several different species of fleas they are not terribly host specific; that is, dog fleas will bite cats and humans too. Their presence in great numbers can be responsible for considerable blood loss and can even lead to death in young puppies. In addition, fleas are carriers of disease (*e.g.* tapeworms).

The female flea does not lay her eggs on the host. Since the eggs are not sticky, even if this does occur, the eggs drop off. Flea eggs are white and are about the same size as a grain of sand. They hatch into larvae from two to fourteen days after laying. Mature larvae are maggot-like in appearance and are creamy white in colour and are about one-quarter inch long. They live in bedding, carpets, in cracks between floorboards, and other similar locations where they spin cocoons in which they develop into adult fleas.

It is important to recognize that since such a small part of the flea life cycle is spent on the dog, flea control must be directed at the environment as well as the animal. Washing of bedding and thorough vacuuming are often sufficient to eliminate small numbers of fleas. But when the situation gets out of hand, houses or kennels may require spraying or fumigating by professional exterminators.

If you discover fleas on your dog, begin by giving him a good flea bath. Obtain a product from your veterinarian and follow the instructions explicitly. Once your dog is clean, routinely use either a flea spray or powder to keep him that way. Ask your veterinarian to recommend a product, and once again, carefully follow the directions on the label. The chemicals contained in these products are toxic and can make a dog extremely ill if used incorrectly.

You might consider using a flea collar or tag which the dog will wear continually during flea season. The most effective ones contain organophosphate insecticides (*e.g.* dichlorvos, naled). These substances are incorporated into a plastic base for slow release and act directly on the fleas, causing death. Flea collars can be safely used on healthy puppies as young as two months of age, but follow the directions on the package. Occasionally dogs will have an allergic reaction to the organophosphate. Generally this will be seen as a contact dermatitis, with reddening on the skin and hair loss in the area of the collar. If you see this occurring, remove the collar immediately, as the condition will progress dramatically to large raw areas with a secondary bacterial infection complicating the matter.

Ticks: Dogs are most likely to pick up ticks in woody or rural areas. Ticks attach themselves to the skin and suck blood. Adult female ticks swell up after ingesting a blood meal. The male ticks do not swell. Generally, the tick causes only an area of skin irritation around the site of attachment. However, ticks can be responsible for more serious diseases as well. These include such things as anaemia, due to marked blood loss, and tick paralysis. In some geographical areas, the ticks carry disease-causing organisms (*e.g. babesia* and *rickettsia*). Consequently, a tick infestation should never be treated lightly.

Ticks are easiest removed by hand. Grasp the tick, as close to the skin as possible, between your thumb and index finger. Exert a firm but gentle pull and you will find that the whole tick will detach. Do not worry if part of the mouth parts fail to detach. This seldom will create a problem. The inflammation surrounding the tick bite usually subsides in about two weeks.

Never employ toxic chemicals such as kerosene or attempt to burn off the tick with matches. These procedures can seriously damage a dog's skin. If you feel that you must apply something to the tick, try dabbing it with alcohol or fingernail polish remover. But apply this only to the tick, not to the surrounding skin. In problem areas, commercial tick dips are suggested. These help to rid the dog of existing ticks and prevent the attachment of new ones.

Lice: Lice are rarely seen on well-cared-for-dogs. Mature lice are off-white in colour and are generally about one-tenth of an inch in length. They tend to spend their entire life on one host. Their tiny white eggs are called nits and are attached to the hair.

Some lice live off of blood and tissue fluids while others consume exfoliated skin cells. Lice carry certain tapeworm larvae and can also create discomfort for the dog through intense itchiness, so it is necessary to rid the dog of them as soon as possible. Consult your veterinarian as to the best product to use.

Mites (Mange):   Mange is the general term for infestation with mites. The four most common types of mites which affect dogs are Demodex mites, Sarcoptes mites, Cheyletiella mites and Otodectes mites.

Sarcoptic Mange: Sarcoptic mange is caused by *Sarcoptes scabei* (*var. canis*). This microscopic mite of dogs can transiently affect humans. They burrow in the superficial layers of skin producing signs of redness, itching and hair loss. The preferred sites for inhabitation on the dog is the skin of the ears, elbows, legs and face.

The condition is diagnosed by microscopic examination of a skin scraping of the affected area. Treatment of the condition is achieved with various topical insecticides. These should be dispensed by and used under the auspices of a veterinarian.

Demodectic Mange: This type of mange of dogs is caused by *Demodex canis,* a mite that lives within the hair follicles. The mite is present on most dogs and seldom causes disease. In animals which develop signs of demodectic mange, there is believed to be a co-existent problem in the immune system, which fails to keep the mites in check.

Demodectic mange may be seen in a localized form. This occurs primarily in dogs under one year of age and causes localized areas of hair loss, without itchiness. Usually, these patches are seen on the face (especially around the eyes) and forelimbs. Most cases of this type of mange will heal spontaneously without treatment. Generalized cases of demodectic mange can appear in dogs of any age. In these, hair loss progresses to involve most areas of the body. Itchiness and secondary bacterial infections are present in these. This form is extremely difficult to treat effectively. Fatalities are not uncommon when treatment fails.

Cheyletiella Dermatitis: This skin disorder is caused by a large, red-coloured mite known as *Cheyletiella yasguri.* It most commonly affects puppies and it can create widespread problems in kennels. It is responsible for itching and severe dandruff. It is eliminated from animals by use of an insecticidal shampoo or dip. The environment must also be treated with an insecticide such as chlordane, ronnel, or malathion.

Ear Mites: *Otodectes cynotis* is the name of ear mites which live in the ear canal of dogs and cats. They feed off of skin debris and their presence is responsible for the formation of large amounts of dark brown wax in the ear canal. Most animals with ear mites show signs of vigorous ear shaking and scratching.

This condition is diagnosed by microscopic examination of a sample discharge from the ear. This is collected quite simply on a cotton swab. Although very tiny, they are visible to the naked eye, appearing as tiny white specks. Treatment includes careful and thorough cleaning of the external ear canal, followed by instilling insecticidal liquid with an eyedropper. Treatment should be initiated by a veterinarian who will provide you with an appropriate medication to be used at home. It often will require treatment twice daily for a period of several weeks to completely eliminate the mites.

Fungal Infections: Ringworm is a fungal disease of dogs and other animals and is communicable to man. It is caused by at least three species of fungi that parasitize the skin. Fungal infections appear to be more of a problem in the short-coated breeds and affect the skin, hair, and nails. Characteristic lesions appear as circular, scaly areas with associated hair loss. Pustules and small vesicles may be present at the periphery of denuded areas. The most common fungus causing ringworm in dogs is *Microsporum canis.* It is diagnosed by its characteristic fluorescence when illuminated with ultraviolet light and by laboratory tests of skin scrapings.

There are many very effective methods of treating ringworm. Veterinary advice should be sought in cases of suspected ringworm infection because of the tendency for the disease to spread to other areas of the body, to other animals, and to man.

Spaying and Neutering: Unless you intend to breed or show your dog, neutering or spaying is advisable. Generally, this surgery is more psychologically disturbing for the owner than for the dog.

Female Dog: Female dogs reach breeding age as early as five to six months. This is the time when they experience their first oestrous or heat period. Consequently, the ideal age for spaying is about five to six months, just before the puppy enters her first seasonal period.

The surgery itself is known medically as ovariohysterectomy. It involves complete removal of the ovaries and the uterus and is performed under a general anaesthesia. For the first few days after she arrives home from the hospital, the bitch should not be exercised vigorously, as she is recuperating from the surgery.

The advantage of spaying is that it eliminates the inconveniences of heat periods. This includes the attraction of male dogs, unwanted pregnancy and puppies, and it guards against the development of uterine problems in later life. The spayed bitch is also less likely to develop breast tumours as she gets older, especially if she has raised several litters.

The alternatives to having your female dog spayed are keeping a close watch on her for the entire time that she is in heat or administering oral contraceptives. Consult your veterinarian on these.

Male Dog: Neutering or castration of the male dog may be safely performed after four months of age. Ideally, however, if one can wait until at least eight or nine months, it is best, as this will allow for the development of male secondary sex characteristics. The surgery involves the removal of both testicles and is performed under general anaesthesia.

The advantages of neutering are numerous. Neutered male dogs are less apt to roam and are therefore less likely to be injured on the streets, or to become a neighbourhood nuisance. Other male behavioural traits, such as mounting, are less likely to develop in males neutered while they are young.

The Middle Years

Diseases: There are several diseases that are commonly encountered in mature dogs. Some of these are discussed below.

Hip Dysplasia: Hip dysplasia results from faulty development of the hip joint, a "ball and socket" joint. The first signs of this disorder are abnormal gait, weakness in the hindquarters and pain upon movement. Since this is an inherited disorder, most breeders of larger dogs only incorporate dogs free of hip dysplasia in their breeding programmes. Do discuss this problem with the breeder prior to buying any large breed.

Hip dysplasia is diagnosed by radiography of the pelvis. There are various surgical procedures that can be performed to relieve the discomfort. Nothing, however, can correct the basic defect in the hip joint.

There are a number of hypotheses concerning environmental factors which contribute to the development of hip dysplasia in a genetically susceptible animal. The roles of nutrition and exercise, in formation of the hip joints, have recently received particular attention. No doubt there are other factors, still unknown, which are involved in the development of the disease.

Progressive Retinal Atrophy (PRA):   This degenerative condition involves the retina of the eye and consists of two varieties— generalized and central PRA. Both types are believed to be inherited. In generalized PRA night blindness is an early clinical sign which progresses to total blindness. In the central variety, peripheral vision is usually retained. In animals where this problem is prevalent, breeding animals should be examined by a qualified ophthalmologist and certified as normal before being incorporated into a breeding programme.

Gastric Torsion: Gastric torsion involves a twisting of the stomach on its axis. The stomach enlarges as gas accumulates, giving the abdomen a distended appearance. Other clinical signs include pain, rapid respiration, pale membranes, and collapse. Death will follow soon thereafter. The problem is especially prevalent in the deep-chested dogs such as Great Danes, Irish Wolfhounds, German Shepherds, Irish Setters and other breeds with similar structures.

One major contributing factor seems to be the excessive consumption of water, especially following eating. Ensuring that the dog has constant access to fresh water may help to prevent the problem. Self-feeding, which enables the dog to ingest small amounts of food throughout the day, is suggested also.

Patella Dysplasia: Problems involving the stifle (knee joint) of dogs, especially the toy breeds, are common. Usually these problems involve congenital malformations which lead to recurrent dislocation of the knee cap (usually in the medial direction). There does not appear to be any sex predilection. Affected individuals have a bow-legged appearance, with the stifle joints turned outward and the toes pointed inward. As the affected dog matures, the deformity becomes more obvious and contracture of the stifle muscles limits the range of movement. Ultimately, a peculiar crouched posture and severe lameness become the most evident signs of the disease. Many dogs with congenital patellar luxation are not overtly lame until the anterior cruciate ligament in the knee joint ruptures. This may occur as early as four to six months of age. Surgery is the only effective treatment for patellar luxation. This condition is believed to be inherited, although the exact mode of inheritance is not clearly defined.

Pyometra: *Pyometra* is one type of uterine infection. It occurs primarily in older, unspayed female dogs and it is believed to be the result of a hormone imbalance. Often, this disease will follow a heat period. If the cervix is open (open *pyometra*) a thick, foul-smelling, reddish or yellow discharge will be present. If the cervix is closed, no discharge will be evident. Other clinical signs of *pyometra* include listlessness, decreased appetite, increased water intake and urination, fever and vomiting. Failure to recognize and promptly treat *pyometra* can result in death. Ovariohysterectomy (spaying) combined with antibiotic therapy is the treatment of choice.

Feeding: Dogs in the "middle years" (between one and seven) are considered to be in the prime of life. The larger breeds, such as Wolfhounds and Great Danes, have shorter life spans than some of the smaller ones. Proper nutrition during this period, is important as this is often the most active in terms of reproduction and exercise.

The ancestors of our present-day dogs were considered carnivores or meat-eaters. However, since they also ate the stomach, intestines, and contents, thus obtaining carbohydrates, vitamins, and other vital substances, they actually fall into the classification of omnivore. Dogs today, like their ancestors, cannot survive on a diet of total protein without supplements.

Most pet food manufacturers have expended considerable research funds to develop foods which can safely be given as the sole diet. One can identify such foods by looking for the words "balanced" or "complete" on the label. The use of these labels is controlled and is a guarantee of quality.

A good quality meal or kibble, mixed with meat, should be the basis of the diet. If you feel you must give your dog table scraps or other foods, try not to let the "extras" exceed ten per cent of the diet. Supplements are not necessary if the diet is balanced.

As with anything, you get what you pay for. As protein is expensive, it follows that most inexpensive dog foods are low in this ingredient. As a means of easy evaluation, one can assess the amount of stool produced. Faecal production should be less than twenty-five per cent of the total amount of food ingested. If the stool resembles the food, the diet is not readily digestible. Palatability to the dog is also very important.

An excellent source of information for dog owners on nutrition and feeding is *The Collins Guide to Dog Nutrition* available from the *Dogs in Canada* Book Department.

Obesity: Overfeeding is as serious an error as underfeeding and obesity is as serious a problem in dogs as it is in people. As well as being harmful to health, overweight dogs have a higher incidence of heart disease, are less resistant to infectious disease, and are also very poor anaesthetic risks. Since dieting is no easier for the dog than for you, it is best to prevent the dog from becoming obese in the first place.

Grooming and Coat Care: The often used adage, "you are what you eat," can easily be applied to coat condition in dogs. Coat quality and condition are a reflection of general body health.

The four most important factors governing coat condition are a well-balanced diet, control of internal parasites, control of external parasites, and regular grooming.

As stated above, diet is of vital importance. It must be properly balanced, with protein, fat, and carbohydrate. There are various dietary supplements that may be useful in maintaining coat quality. Generally, these products are high in fat-soluble vitamins and may be useful in producing and maintaining a healthy coat, even when the animal is under stress. This balance is especially important when a dog is engaged in a heavy campaign schedule and is being constantly bathed and groomed.

Intestinal parasites, by their debilitating effect on the dog's general health and condition, adversely affect the coat. The physical presence of the parasites interferes with uptake of nutrients from the alimentary tract. Some, such as hookworms, actually suck blood from the animal's body, causing anaemia in heavy infestations.

External parasites, particularly fleas, create obvious irritation to the skin and the animal responds to these irritants by chewing, scratching and self-excoriation. Good coats can be seriously damaged by flea infestations and subsequent scratching. This emphasizes the importance of pest control.

Clean hair is healthy hair. Keep the dog clean and groomed on a regular basis. This is especially important to long-coated dogs. Often the harsh-coated breeds do not require as much bathing as their coats seem almost weather-proof. Excess bathing can be as harmful as too little, as it may remove essential oils from the coat. If, for any reason, your dog requires frequent bathing, replace the lost oils with a cream rinse or spray. Discuss the particular coat type of your dog with an experienced breeder. He or she may be able to give you some helpful tips and may even share some trade "secrets" with you.

All dogs, with few exceptions, such as Poodles or Kerry Blue Terriers, undergo a shedding cycle. The dense winter coat is usually shed in the springtime and hair loss in heavy-coated, long-haired breeds can be very dramatic. Comb or brush out the dead hair on a daily basis. The sooner you remove it, the more quickly the healthy new hair will grow in to replace it.

A dog that is maintained in show condition or is being prepared for a show career demands extra care. Avoid excessive exercise in bright sunlight as it may alter the colour of the coat. This is especially true in darker-coloured dogs, where the sun may produce a reddish tinge in the coat. The choice of bedding is important. Select soft material such as blankets or white newsprint. Rugs, especially the stiff-fibre varieties, while affording softness, can often pull and damage coats. The size of the kenneling area is important also. It must be large enough so that the dog does not rub or abrade himself.

All dogs are born with a genetically predetermined number of hair follicles per square inch of skin. Some breeds and bloodlines within breeds have more follicles than others. While it is not possible to change this, you can, with proper care, make the most of the coat.

Grooming and Bathing: Each breed requires individual coat care. The short-coated dogs need regular brushing, terrier types should be plucked, and long-coated dogs require combing and brushing. Brushing should penetrate to the skin to stimulate circulation and remove specks of dandruff. Daily grooming is best; however, a weekly routine can often suffice if time is limited.

A dog should be bathed as often as necessary for show or hygenic purposes. Always make sure that the dog is completely matt-free before it is bathed. Plug the ears with cotton wool and place a drop of mineral oil into the eyes. The latter is very important as soap is a frequent cause of eye ulcers. Be certain to thoroughly rinse all traces of shampoo from the coat, then dry your pet completely.

Nails: Cutting the nails should be part of regular grooming. If allowed to grow too long, the dog will bear weight on his nails rather than on his pads. Not only is this uncomfortable, but eventually will cause the feet to splay (spreading of the toes). Dewclaws, if present and neglected, will grow in a circle and pierce the skin. Nails can be easily clipped with commercial nail trimmers. With clear nails, cut just outside of the pink line. The area contains a small blood vessel known as the quick, and should be avoided. When cutting black nails, merely trim off the excess curvature. If cut too short, bleeding will occur but this can be controlled with a styptic pencil or other commercially available products. Nails can also be kept at the correct length with emery grinders. Exercise, especially on hard surfaces, tends to wear down the nail, reducing the amount of required trimming.

Ears: Some breeds have an excessive amount of hair in the external ear canal. This should be gently plucked out on a regular basis. If left in, this hair can lead to wax accumulation and infection. All breeds should have the wax and dirt cleaned from the ear canal routinely. This can be accomplished using cotton-tipped applicators dampened with hydrogen peroxide.

Teeth: Care of the teeth is an often overlooked health point. Dental care in dogs is as important to the over-all health of a dog as it is to people. At the age of two or three years, dental plaque (tartar) begins to build up between the tooth and gum line. As the tartar accumulates, it causes an irritation of the gums, with subsequent infection of the gums and teeth. Ultimately, this can proceed to tooth loss and may serve as a source of infection in other parts of the body.

In the early stages, the tartar can be easily removed with a tooth scaler, either by yourself or your veterinarian. If the accumulation of tartar is substantial, a general anaesthetic may be necessary in order to clean the teeth properly. Once the teeth are cleaned, this can be maintained with brushing or by rubbing the teeth with a rough cloth. Hard foods, such as dog biscuits, also help to keep the teeth free of tartar. However, some dogs still require regular professional cleaning by a veterinarian.

Vaccinations: Some people believe that after the vaccinations in puppyhood have been completed, no further ones are required. This is, unfortunately, a very ill-founded belief. Without annual booster vaccines, the level of disease-fighting antibodies declines. Booster vaccinations ensure that this is maintained at a protective level. Prevention is still the best cure. Have your dogs vaccinated annually against *distemper, hepatitis, parainfluenza, leptospirosis, parvo virus,* and *rabies*.

Old Age

"Grow old along with me / The best is yet to be."
Robert Browning wrote this many years ago but unfortunately it does not apply to our pets because we tend to outlive them. With proper care and management, though, these older years can be relatively problem free. If you have healthy stock and have cared for your dog properly, there is no reason why you cannot expect him to live to a ripe old age.

A chart below compares the age of the dog to man. As you will see, the old axiom that one year of man's life equals seven of the dog's life is really not valid.

Dog	Man	Dog	Man
6 months	10 years	7 years	44 years
1 year	15 years	8 years	48 years
2 years	24 years	9 years	52 years
3 years	28 years	10 years	56 years
4 years	32 years	15 years	76 years
5 years	36 years	21 years	100 years
6 years	40 years		

There are many other factors involved, however. Certain breeds age at a faster rate than others. Illness, poor diet, overbreeding in females, a poor start as a puppy and obesity, all contribute to a shortened life span in dogs.

Feeding the Older Dog: In older dogs, feeding often becomes an individual matter. As dogs age, the total number of cells in the body decrease and metabolism slows down. Consequently, older dogs may gain weight more easily and thus, food intake may have to be reduced. Older dogs require protein of higher biological value and each dog may have to be fed according to his or her individual needs.

Special prescription diets with the needs of older dogs in mind, have been formulated. There are diets designed for maintenance of animals with heart disease, kidney disease, gastrointestinal disturbances, and allergic conditions.

Diseases: Good care is even more important for the older dog and there are several diseases to be on the look out for in older animals. Some of these are discussed below.

Arthritis: Stiff joints and stilted movement with marked difficulty in rising, jumping, and stair climbing may indicate a problem in the skeletal system. Arthritis is a common joint problem seen in older dogs and is diagnosed by radiography of the affected joints. Treatment usually involves administering pain relievers when indicated. Buffered aspirin is still one of the best medications to relieve the pain of arthritis. Also, with the aim of making an arthritic animal more comfortable, provide a warm, dry sleeping area with a padded mattress to lie on and reduce the amount of daily exercise.

Cancer: Tumours, or growths as they are often known, can be of two types—benign and malignant. They can involve internal organs or organ systems or may appear as masses or ulcerations on the surface of the body. Excessive weight loss, changes in toilet habits, lethargy, abdominal distension, and difficult breathing are all clinical signs which can be associated with *neoplasia*. Should your dog show any of these clinical signs, have him examined by a veterinarian at once.

Dental Problems: Infected, receding gums and loose teeth are not uncommon maladies in old dogs who have had inadequate dental care throughout their lifetime. Not only do these conditions make eating painful for the dog, gum infections, if present, can serve as a source of infection elsewhere in the body. Decayed, loose teeth should be extracted and gum infections should be treated with antibiotics and oral hygiene.

Kidney Disease: As animals grow older, many organ systems fail to maintain their former level of performance. As the kidneys lose their ability to concentrate urine, increased urination (*polyuria*) occurs. The dog, in an attempt to maintain its normal fluid balance, compensates for this lost ability of the kidneys by excessive consumption of water (*polydipsia*). This often tends to be a progressive condition but animals with chronic renal disease can survive for long periods, especially if fed a diet formulated for the kidney patient. There should be free access to fresh water at all times. As *polyuria* and *polydipsia* can be associated with other diseases, it is your veterinarian who should make the diagnosis.

Heart Disease: A condition known as mitral insufficiency is common in older dogs and is believed to be part of the aging process. The mitral valve of the heart often becomes fibrotic and is unable to close properly. Consequently, a little blood leaks back through it each time that the heart beats. Thus circulation becomes inefficient and the heart attempts to compensate for this by enlargement and by attempting to work harder. The condition progresses to the point where fluid (pulmonary oedema) accumulates in the lungs. At this point, the condition is known as congestive heart failure. Clinical signs of this disorder include coughing (especially at night), shortness of breath, fatigue, and occasional fainting (cardiac syncope). This condition is chronic and with proper management, many animals with congestive heart failure can live comfortably for considerable periods of time. Drugs to alleviate the pulmonary oedema and strengthen the force of heart contractions are often prescribed. Diets low in sodium are recommended for heart patients as sodium binds water in the body thereby increasing the workload of the heart.

Prostatic Disease: This affliction of the older male dog usually involves enlargement of the prostrate gland, which is a secondary sex organ. Often, there is co-existent infection of the gland. Clinical signs of prostatic disease are difficult or painful walking or difficulty in passing of stool and urine. Often the urine will contain blood (*haematuria*). The diagnosis is established by examination of the urine (urinalysis) under a microscope, physical examination of the dog, and radiography of the abdomen. Treatment often includes castration to reduce the size of the gland by removing hormonal influences on it, and antibiotic therapy.

Other Problems: Loss, either partial or complete, of sight and hearing is common in old dogs. Frequent causes of blindness are changes in the lens, such as cataracts or nuclear sclerosis. Most dogs with impaired vision or hearing can cope very easily in familiar surroundings.

Behavioural changes also may occur in old dogs. Crankiness, loss of patience (often with young children), sleeping more, decreased awareness of the world around them, and occasional lapses in toilet habits are other indications that your dog's days may be drawing to a close.

Euthanasia: The choice to euthanize, or to put your dog to sleep, is a very difficult one. It is an alternative to prolonging discomfort and should be regarded as a kind and humane deed. Most commonly, a concentrated barbiturate solution is injected, which is both fast and painless. The choice of staying with your pet is a personal one. Some pets are comforted by the presence of a familiar voice or touch while others may perceive your anxiety.

Your Dog After You: Many people forget to plan for their dog in the event of their own death. If you died suddenly, what would happen to your dog? Do not leave anything to chance by assuming that friends or family will come and take over. Lawyers advise that you leave complete instructions in your will and before bequeathing an animal to someone, discuss it with them to ensure that they have the interest and financial resources and time to care for this animal. Remember that if the dogs are left and no one has instructions for their care or disposal, they will be taken to the local animal control centre where an arbitrary decision will be made either for euthanasia or adoption.

First Aid

First aid should be a temporary measure to control life-threatening problems and provide some relief while veterinary care is sought.

Handling: Any injured dog may bite. Rather than risk being bitten, muzzle any injured dog prior to handling. A length of rope, a necktie, piece of gauze or anything similar can be utilized. Make a loop and place it over the dog's muzzle and tie, bring the ends down around the muzzle, cross them and bring the ends behind the ears and tie. This muzzle will not interfere with breathing. It should be tied but not so tight as to hurt or cause injury to the tissue by interfering with circulation.

If the dog cannot walk, make a stretcher out of a coat, blanket, or towel. This will facilitate easy lifting and transporting by two people.

Bandaging: Apply a piece of gauze or cloth to the wound and wrap a strip bandage around the injured area. Sufficient pressure can be applied to stop most of the bleeding. However, if the bandage is too tight or is left on for too long, the tissue will die because of impaired circulation. Loosen the bandage every fifteen minutes to allow blood to flow through the wound.

Administering Medication:

Liquids: With the head of the dog held at an angle of approximately thirty degrees, pull out the lipfold at the side of the muzzle to form a pouch and pour the liquid in slowly. As it runs through the teeth, the dog is able to swallow it. Do not pour too much, too quickly, because the dog will choke.

Pills: To administer a pill to your dog, first place one hand over the top jaw. With your thumb on one side and remaining fingers on the other, open the mouth by applying gentle pressure to the lips. With the other hand pull down the lower jaw. Now, with the mouth open, place the pill well back along the midline of the tongue. Now, close the jaws, elevate the head slightly and wait for the dog to swallow. If this fails, try disguising the medication in a small piece of meat or cheese. Feed him two or three of these tidbits to arouse his interest, then slip him one with a concealed pill.

Tourniquets: In cases of severe laceration of limbs or tail, it may be necessary to apply a tourniquet to control blood loss. Wrap a piece of cloth or bandage above the wound and tie securely.

Wrap or twist snuggly with a stick. It is advisable to loosen the tourniquet every ten to fifteen minutes to allow circulation to the area and prevent tissue death from lack of oxygen.

Heatstroke: This is truly a tragedy of the summer months and is the product of neglect. Dogs should never be left unattended in direct sunlight or in closed vehicles in hot weather. Clinical signs of heatstroke include panting, hypersalivation, fever, shock, unconsciousness, and death. Heroic measures are required to save an animal in this situation. Immediately immerse the dog in cool water to lower his body temperature. Monitoring this with a rectal thermometer, bring the temperature to within the normal range, but do not lower it below this.

Burns: For a burn, any household preparation that you have may be used. For an acid burn, use a paste of bicarbonate of soda (baking soda). Burns become infected very easily so watch closely, even superficial burns that can become quite serious.

Poisoning: If you suspect your dog has ingested a poisonous substance, attempt to induce vomiting. This can be achieved by administering hydrogen peroxide (about two tablespoonsful for each ten pounds of body weight), or by applying a teaspoon of salt on the back of his tongue. As many poisons have specific antidotes, take a sample of the substance with the dog to your veterinarian. This will facilitate prompt and effective treatment, as time is of the essence in most poisonings.

Shock: Shock can follow almost any type of severe injury. The clinical signs include shallow breathing, pale grey-coloured mucous membranes, glassy eyes, dilated pupils, and collapse. Keep the dog warm by wrapping him in a blanket and place hot water bottles around him. Immediate professional help is of the utmost importance as time can make the difference between life and death.

Bleeding:
Small wounds: A small wound may be first cleaned with soap and water, following which an antiseptic and bandage can be applied. If possible, pull the wound edges together and hold them in place with adhesive tape. This will facilitate healing.

Deep Wounds: A severed artery "spurts" in time with the heart beat and produces bright red blood. Blood escaping from a lacerated vein will be much darker in colour and will ooze. A tourniquet or a firmly applied pressure bandage will be required to control bleeding from a severed artery. A pressure bandage will usually suffice for cut veins. Clean the wound only when the bleeding has subsided, then bandage the wound and seek veterinary attention promptly.

Seizures: Seizures or convulsions can be caused by many different diseases. Most seizures last one to three minutes. When the seizure is over, keep the dog quiet and do not excite or stimulate him or another seizure may result. Never place anything in the mouth of a seizuring dog. You may get bitten and he may choke. If seizures fail to abate after a few minutes, apply a muzzle to the jaw, wrap the dog in a blanket and transport him to a veterinarian immediately.

Eye Infections: To soothe inflamed eyes, wash out any discharge present with a solution of boracic acid or warm water. Do not use salt and water. Apply an eye ointment on the advice of a veterinarian. This is important as certain eye ointments are contra-indicated in some conditions. For example, cortisone preparations should not be used where corneal ulcers are present.

Diarrhoea: This common complaint has a number of causes. These include internal parasites, infections, ingesting garbage or other substances which irritate the digestive tract, travel, and changes in water to name a few. Simple diarrhoea can be treated by feeding the dog a bland diet, such as boiled white rice mixed half and half with boiled lean meat, cottage cheese or cooked eggs. Human preparations such as Kaopectate, available at any pharmacy, may also be administered. If diarrhoea persists for more than two or three days, consult your veterinarian.

Vomiting: Vomiting, like diarrhoea, can be caused by diet changes, internal parasites and ingestion of irritants and foreign materials. It can also, however, be a sign of some very serious diseases such as gastric torsion and pyometra. Before attempting to treat a vomiting dog with a home remedy, be certain that you are certain of the cause. Withhold solid food and administer small amounts of tepid water frequently. Human preparations such as Maalox or some other soothing gastric preparation may be given.

   If vomiting has subsided after twenty-four hours, feed the dog a small amount of the bland diet discussed in the section entitled *Diarrhoea*. Should the vomiting continue for more than this period of time, seek professional advice.

GLOSSARY

Albino: Animal deficient in pigmentation.

Almond eyes: The eye set in surrounding tissue of almond shape. The eye itself is always round, its "shape" as designated in breed standards signifying the contour of the surrounding flesh.

Amble: A relaxed, easy gait in which the legs on either side move almost, but not quite, as a pair. Often seen as the transition movement between the walk and the faster gaits.

Angulation: The angles formed by a meeting of the bones, mainly the shoulder and upper arm, stifle and hock.

Apple head: Rounded skull, shaped like an apple.

Apron: The frill or long hair below the neck on long-coated dogs, such as the Collie.

Back: Variable in meaning depending upon context of the standard.

Bad mouth: Crooked or unaligned teeth; bite over or undershot in excess of standard specifications.

Balanced: A consistent whole; symmetrical, typically proportioned as a whole or as regards its separate parts; *i.e.,* balance of head, balance of body, or balance of head and body.

Bandy legs: Having a bend of leg outward.

Barrel: Rounded rib section; thorax.

Barrel hocks: Hocks that turn out, causing the feet to toe in. Also called spread hocks.

Barrel-legged: Bowed legs (front).

Barrel-ribbed: Excessively curved ribs.

Basewide: Wide footfall, resultant of "paddling" movement, causing body to rock from side to side. See *Paddling*.

Bat ear: An erect ear, rather broad at the base, rounded in outline at the top and with orifice directly to the front. (*e.g.,* French Bulldog)

Bay: The voice of a trailing hound while hunting or when the quarry is brought to a stand.

Beard: Thick, long hair growth on the underjaw.

Belton: A colour designation. An intermingling of coloured and white hairs, as blue belton, lemon, orange, or liver belton. (*e.g.,* English Setter)

Bench show: A dog show at which the dogs are kept on benches while not being shown in competition. Most shows in Canada are not benched.

Best in Show: A dog-show award to the dog adjudged best of all breeds.

Bilateral cryptorchid: See *Cryptorchid*.

Bird dog: A sporting dog trained to hunt birds.

Birdy: A dog with strong bird-hunting instincts.

Bitch: A female dog.

Bite: The relative position of the upper and lower teeth when the mouth is closed. See *Level bite, Scissors bite, Undershot, Overshot*.

Blanket: The colour of the coat on the back and upper part of the sides, between the neck and the tail.

Blaze: A white stripe running up the centre of the face usually between the eyes.

Blocky: Square or cubelike formation of the head or body.

Blooded: A dog of good breeding; pedigreed.

Bloom: The sheen of a coat in prime condition.

Blue: Colour. Dilute black due to recessives.

Blue merle: Blue and grey mixed with black; marbled.

Bobtail: A naturally tailless dog or a dog with a tail docked very short. Often used as a name for the Old English Sheepdog.

Bodied up: Mature, well developed.

Bolt: To drive or "start" an animal out of its earth or burrow.

Bone: The relative size (girth) of a dog's leg bones; substance.

Brace: Two dogs of a kind; a couple.

Breeching: The tan-coloured hair on the thighs of Manchester terriers and other breeds.

Breed: A specific strain or family of related dogs similar in type and use, usually developed under the influence of man.

Breeder: A person who breeds dogs. Under CKC rules, the breeder of a dog is the owner (or, if the dam was leased, the lessee) of the dam of the dog when the dam was bred.

Brindle: Striped coat effect caused by mixture of black hairs on lighter-coloured base.

Brisket: The forepart of the body below the chest, between the forelegs, closest to the ribs.

Broken colour: Self-colour broken by white or another colour.

Broken-haired: A rough wire coat.

Broken-up face: A receding nose, together with a deep stop, wrinkle, and undershot jaw; for example, Bulldog, Pekingese.

Brood bitch: A female used for breeding. Brood matron.

Brush: A bushy tail; a tail heavy with hair.

Brushing: A gaiting fault when parallel pasterns are so close that the legs "brush" in passing.

Bullbaiting: An ancient sport in which the dog baited or tormented the bull.

Bull neck: A heavy neck, well muscled.

Burr: The inside of the ear; *i.e.*, the irregular formation visible within the cup.

Butterfly nose: A particoloured nose; *i.e.*, dark, spotted with flesh colour.

Buttocks: The rump or hips.

Button ear: The ear flap folding forward, the tip lying close to the skull so as to cover or partly cover the orifice.

Bye: At field trials, an odd dog remaining after the dogs entered in a stake have been paired in braces by drawing.

Camel back: Arched back, like that of one-hump camel.

Canine: Classification of the group of animals to which dogs, foxes, wolves, and jackals belong.

Canines: The two upper and two lower sharp-pointed teeth next to the incisors. Fangs.

Carpals: Bones of the pastern joints.

Castrate: To remove the testicles of the male dog.

Cat-foot: The short, round compact foot like that of a cat. The foot with short third digits.

C.D. (Companion Dog): A suffix used with the name of a dog that has been recorded a Companion Dog by the CKC as a result of having won certain minimum scores in Novice Classes at a specified number of CKC-licensed obedience trials.

C.D.X. (Companion Dog Excellent): A suffix used with the name of a dog that has been recorded a Companion Dog Excellent by the CKC as a result of having won certain minimum scores in Open Classes at a specified number of CKC-licensed obedience trials.

Champion (Ch.): A prefix used with the name of a dog that has been recorded a Champion by the CKC as a result of defeating a specified number of dogs in specified competition at a series of CKC-licensed dog shows.

Character: Expression, individuality, and general appearance and deportment as considered typical of a breed.

Cheeky: Cheeks prominently rounded; thick, protruding.

Chest: The part of the body or trunk that is enclosed by the ribs.

China eye: A clear blue eye.

Chippendale front: Named after the Chippendale chair. Forelegs out at elbows, pasterns close, and feet turned out. See *Fiddle front; French front*.

Chiselled: Clean-cut in head, particularly beneath the eyes.

Choke collar: A leather fabric or chain collar fitted to the dog's neck in such a manner that the degree of tension exerted by the hand tightens or loosens it.

Chops: Jowls or pendulous flesh of the lips and jaw; for example, the Bulldog.

Chorea: A nervous jerking caused by involuntary contraction of the muscles, usually affecting the face or legs.

CKC: The Canadian Kennel Club.

Clip: The method of trimming the coat in some breeds, notably the Poodle.

Clipping: When pertaining to gait, the back foot striking the front foot.

Cloddy: Low, thickset, comparatively heavy.

Close-coupled: Comparatively short from withers to hip bones.

Coarse: Lacking refinement.

Coat: The dog's hair covering.

Cobby: Short-bodied, compact.

Collar: The marking around the neck, usually white. Also a leather or chain for restraining or leading the dog, when the leash is attached.

Companion Dog: See *C.D.*

Companion Dog Excellent: See *C.D.X.*

Condition: Health as shown by the coat, state of flesh, general appearance, and deportment.

Conformation: The form and structure, make and shape; arrangement of the parts in conformance with breed-standard demands.

Couple: Two hounds.

Coupling: Part of the body between the ribs and pelvis; the loin.

Coursing: The sport of chasing prey with sight hounds.

Covering ground: The ratio of the distance between the ground and brisket and the distance between front and rear legs. As in "covers too much ground."

Cow-hocked: When the hocks turn towards each other.

Crabbing: Dog moves with his body at an angle to the line of travel. Also referred to as "sidewinding," "sidewheeling," or "yawing."

Crank tail: A tail carried down and resembling a crank in shape.

Crest: The upper, arched portion of the neck.

Cropping: The cutting or trimming of the ear leather for the purpose of inducing the ears to stand erect.

Cross-bred: A dog whose sire and dam are representatives of two different breeds.

Crossing over: Unsound gaiting action which starts with twisting elbows and ends with criss-crossing and toeing-out. Also called "knitting and purling" and "weaving."

Croup: Section from hip bones to tail set.

Crown: The highest part of the head. The topskull.

Cry: The baying or "music" of the hounds.

Cryptorchid: The adult whose testicles are abnormally retained in the abdominal cavity. Bilateral cryptorchidism involves both sides; that is, neither testicle has descended into the scrotum. Unilateral cryptorchidism involves one side only, that is, one testicle is retained or hidden and one descended. See *Monorchid.*

Culotte: The longer hair on the back of the thighs.

Cur: A mongrel.

Cushion: Fullness or thickness of the upper lips. (*e.g.,* Pekingese)

Cynology: The study of canines.

Dam: The female parent.

Dappled: Mottled marking of different colours, no colour predominating.

Deadgrass: Tan or dull straw colour.

Derby: Field-trial competition for young, novice sporting dogs usually between one and two years of age.

Dewclaw: An extra claw or functionless digit on the inside of the leg; a rudimentary fifth toe.

Dewlap: Loose, pendulous skin under the throat.

Diagonals: Right front and left rear legs constitute the right diagonal; left front and right rear constitute the left diagonal. In the trot the diagonals move together.

Dish-faced: When the nasal bone is so formed that the nose is higher at the tip than at the stop; or, a slight concavity of line from the stop to the nose tip.

Disqualification: A decision made by a judge following a determination that a dog has a condition that makes it ineligible for any further competition under the dog show rules or under the standard for its breed.

Distemper teeth: Teeth discoloured or pitted as a result of distemper or other enervating disease or deficiency.

Dock: To shorten the tail by cutting.

Dog: A male dog; also used collectively to designate both male and female.

Dog show: A competitive exhibition for dogs at which the dogs are judged in accordance with an established standard of perfection for each breed.

Dog Show, All Breed: See *Dog Show, Conformation.*

Dog Show, Conformation (Licensed): An event held under CKC rules at which championship points are awarded. May be for all breeds, or for a single breed or group of breeds (specialty show).

Dog Show, Specialty: See *Dog Show, Conformation.*

Domed: Convex topskull.

Domino: A colour pattern in Afghan Hounds characterized by light-coloured extremities and mask.

Double coat: An outer coat resistant to weather and affording protection against brush and brambles, together with an undercoat of softer hair for warmth and waterproofing.

Double-suspension gallop: Leaping gait with a period of suspension in both the open and closed positions.

Down-faced: The plane of the muzzle inclining downwards from the plane of the backskull.

Down in pastern: Weak or faulty pastern set at a pronounced angle from the vertical.

Drag: A trail prepared by dragging along the ground a bag usually impregnated with animal scent.

Drawing: Selection by lot of dogs to be run, and in which pairs, in a field-trial stake.

Drive: A solid thrusting of the hindquarters, denoting sound locomotion.

Drop ear: The ends of the ear folded or drooping forward, as contrasted with erect or prick ears.

Dry: The skin taut, neither loose nor wrinkled.

Dual champion: A dog that has won both a bench show and a field trial championship or obedience trial championship.

Dudley nose: Flesh-coloured nose.

Elbow: The joint between the upper arm and the forearm.

Elbows out: Turning out or off from the body; not held close.

Estrus: See *Œstrus*.

Even bite: Meeting of front teeth at edges with no overlap of upper or lower teeth.

Ewe neck: Concave curvature of the top neckline. Lack of crest.

Expression: The general appearance of all features of the head as viewed from the front and as typical of the breed.

Eyeteeth: The upper canines.

Faking: To change the appearance of a dog by artificial means with the objective of deceiving the onlooker as to its real merit.

Fall: Hair overhanging the face.

Fallow: Pale cream to light fawn colour: pale; pale yellow; yellow-red.

Fancier: A person especially interested and usually active in some phase of the sport of pure-bred dogs.

Fangs: See *Canines*.

Fawn: A brown, red-yellow with hue of medium brilliance.

Feathering: Longer fringe of hair on ears, legs, tail, or body.

Feet east and west: The toes turned out.

Fetch: The retrieve of game by the dog; also the command to do so.

Fiddle front: Forelegs out at elbows, pasterns close, and feet turned out; French front; Chippendale front.

Field Champion (Field Ch.): A prefix used with the name of a dog that has been recorded a Field Champion by the CKC as a result of defeating a specified number of dogs in specified competition at a series of CKC-licensed field trials.

Field Trial: A competition for sporting dogs or hounds to test hunting ability.

Flag: A long tail carried high, usually referring to one of the Pointing Breeds.

Flank: The side of the body between the last rib and the hip.

Flare: A blaze that widens as it approaches the topskull.

Flat bone: The leg bone whose girth is elliptical rather than round.

Flat-sided: Ribs insufficiently rounded as they approach the sternum or breastbone.

Flews: Upper lips pendulous, particularly at their inner corners.

Flicking pasterns: Extremely loose movement of the lower forelegs.

Floating rib: The last, or thirteenth rib, which is unattached to other ribs.

Fluffies: A coat of extreme length with exaggerated feathering on ears, chest, legs, and feet, underparts and hindquarters. Trimming such a coat does not make it any more acceptable.

Flush: To drive birds from cover, to force them to take flight; to spring.

Flying ears: Any characteristic drop ears or semi-prick ears that stand or "fly."

Flying Trot: A fast gait in which all four feet are off the ground for a brief second during each half stride. Because of the long reach, the oncoming hind feet step beyond the imprint left by the front. Also called Suspension Trot.

Forearm: The bone of the foreleg between the elbow and the pastern.

Foreface: The front part of the head, before the eyes; muzzle.

Foul colour: A colour or marking not characteristic.

Foxy: Sharp expression; pointed nose with short foreface.

French front: See *Fiddle front*.

Frill: See *Apron*.

Fringes: See *Feathering*.

Frogface: Extending nose accompanied by a receding jaw, usually overshot.

Front: The forepart of the body as viewed head on; *i.e.*, forelegs, chest, brisket, and shoulder line; also front assembly.

Frontal bone: The skull bone over the eyes.

Furnishings: The long hair on the foreface of certain breeds; also, feathering.

Furrow: A slight indentation or median line down the centre of the skull to the stop.

Futurity Stake: A class at dog shows or field trails for young dogs which have been nominated at or before birth.

Gait: The manner in which a dog walks, trots, or runs; also movement.

Gallop: Fastest of the dog gaits, has a four-beat rhythm and often an extra period of suspension during which the body is propelled through the air with all four feet off the ground.

Game: Hunted wild birds or animals.

Gay tail: Carried above the back line. Correct in some breeds, a fault in others.

Gazehound: Greyhound or other sight-hunting hound.

Genealogy: Recorded family descent.

Goose rump: Too steep or sloping a croup.

Grizzle: Bluish grey or roan colour. Also, in some breeds, a colour pattern characterized by light-coloured extremities and mask.

Groom: To brush, comb, trim, or otherwise make a dog's coat neat.

Groups: The breeds as grouped in six divisions to facilitate judging.

Guard hairs: The longer, smoother, stiffer hairs which grow through the undercoat and normally conceal it.

Gun dog: A dog trained to work with its master in finding live game and retrieving game that has been shot.

Guns: Sportsmen who do the shooting at field trials.

Gun-shy: When the dog fears the sight or sound of a gun.

Hackles: Hair on neck and back raised involuntarily in fright or anger.

Hackney action: The high lifting of the front feet, like that of a hackney horse.

Ham: Muscular development of the hind legs just above the stifle.

Handler: A person who handles a dog in the show ring or at a field trial. See also *Professional handler*.

Hard-mouthed: The dog that bites or marks with his teeth the game he retrieves.

Hare-foot: An elongated foot like a rabbit's foot; a foot with long third digits.

Harlequin: Patched or pied colouration, usually black on white. (*e.g.,* Great Danes)

Harness: A leather strap shaped around the shoulders and chest, with a ring at its top over the withers.

Haw: A third eyelid or membrane in the inside corner of the eye.

Heat: Seasonal period of the female; œstrum.

Heel: See *Hock;* also a command to the dog to keep close beside its handler.

Height: Vertical measurement from the withers to the ground. See *Withers.*

Hie on: A command to urge the dog on; used in hunting or in field trials.

High standing: Tall and upstanding, with plenty of leg.

Hindquarters: Rear assembly of dog (pelvis, thighs, hocks, and paws).

Hock: The tarsus or collection of bones of the hind leg forming the joint between the second thigh and the metatarsus; the dog's true heel.

Hocks well let down: Hock joints close to the ground.

Hocking out: Spread hocks.

Honourable scars: Scars from injuries suffered as a result of work.

Hound: A dog commonly used for hunting by scent or sight.

Hound-marked: A colouration composed of white, tan, and black. The ground colour usually white, may be marked with tan and/or black patches on the head, back, legs, and tail. The extent and the exact location of such markings, however, differ in breeds and individuals.

Hucklebones: The top of the hip bones.

Inbreeding: The mating of very closely related dogs.

Incisors: The upper and lower front teeth between the canines.

In-shoulder: Shoulders pointing in, and not parallel with backbone, a fault found in dogs with shoulder blades too far forward on chest.

Inter-breeding: The breeding together of dogs of different varieties.

Isabella: Fawn, mouse, or light red colour, due to diluted colour recessives. (*e.g.,* Doberman Pinscher)

Jowls: Flesh of lips and jaws.

Judge: The arbiter in the dog show ring, obedience trial, field trial, or lure course.

Kennel: Building or enclosure where dogs are kept.

Kink tail: The tail sharply bent.

Kiss marks: Tan spots on the cheeks and over the eyes.

Knee joint: Stifle joint.
Knitting and purling: See *Crossing over.*
Knuckling over: Faulty structure of carpus (wrist) joint allowing it to double forward under the weight of the standing dog; double-jointed wrist, often with slight swelling of the bones.

Landseer: The black-and-white Newfoundland dog, so-called from the name of the famous painter who used such dogs as models.
Layback: The angle of the shoulder blade as compared with the vertical; also, a receding nose accompanied by an undershot jaw.
Lead: A strap, cord, or a chain attached to the collar or harness for the purpose of restraining or leading the dog; leash.
Leather: The flap of the ear.
Level bite: When the front teeth (incisors) of the upper and lower jaws meet exactly edge to edge; pincer bite; even bite.
Level gait: Dog moves without rise or fall of withers.
Line breeding: The mating of related dogs of the same breed, especially the mating of a dog to one of its ancestors, for example, a dog to his granddam or a bitch to her grandsire.
Lion colour: Tawny.
Lippy: Pendulous lips or lips that do not fit tightly.
Litter: The puppy or puppies of one whelping.
Liver: A colour, *i.e.,* deep, reddish brown.
Loaded shoulders: When the shoulder blades are shoved out from the body by over-development of the muscles.
Loin: Region of the body on either side of the vertebral column between the last ribs and the hindquarters.
Lower thigh: See *Second thigh.*
Lumber: Superfluous flesh.
Lumbering: An awkward gait.
Lurcher: A cross-bred hound.

Mad dog: A rabid dog.
Mane: Long and profuse hair on top and sides of the neck.
Mantle: Dark-shaded portion of the coat on shoulders, back, and sides. (*e.g.,* St. Bernard)
Mask: Dark shading on the foreface. (*e.g.,* Mastiff, Boxer, Pekingese)
Match show: Usually an informal dog show at which no championship points are awarded.
Mate: To breed a dog and bitch.
Median line: See *Furrow.*
Merle: A colouration, usually blue-grey with flecks of black.
Milk teeth: First teeth.

Miscellaneous Class: A class at dog shows for dogs of certain specified breeds for which no regular dog show classification is provided.

Mismarks: Coat markings which do not conform to the coat colouration as defined by the standard for that breed.

Molars: Dog has four premolars on each side of the upper and lower jaw. There are two true molars on each side of the upper jaw, and three on each side of the lower jaw. Upper molars have three roots, lower have two roots.

Molera: Incomplete, imperfect, or abnormal ossification of the skull. (*e.g.,* Chihuahua)

Mongrel: A dog whose parents are of mixed-breed origin.

Monorchid: A unilateral cryptorchid. See *Cryptorchid*.

Moving close: When the hocks turn in and pasterns drop straight to the ground and move parallel to one another, the dog is "moving close" in the rear. This action places severe strain on ligaments and muscles.

Moving straight: Term descriptive of balanced gaiting in which angle of inclination begins at the shoulder or hip joint, and limbs remain relatively straight from these points to the pads of the feet, even as the legs flex or extend in reaching or thrusting.

Music: The baying of the hounds.

Mute: To run mute, to be silent on the trail; *i.e.,* to trail without baying or barking.

Muzzle: The head in front of the eyes—nasal bone, nostrils, and jaws; foreface. Also, a strap or wire cage attached to the foreface to prevent the dog from biting or from picking up food.

Muzzle band: White marking around the muzzle. (*e.g.,* Boston Terrier)

Neck well set-on: Good neckline, merging gradually with strong withers, forming a pleasing transition into topline.

Nick: A breeding that produces desirable puppies.

Non-slip Retriever: The dog that walks at heel, marks the fall, and retrieves game on command; not expected to find or flush.

Nose: Organ of smell; also, the ability to detect by means of scent.

Obedience Trial (Licensed): An event held under CKC rules at which a "leg" towards an obedience degree can be earned.

Obedience Trial Champion (O.T.Ch.): A prefix used with the name of a dog that has been recorded an Obedience Trial Champion by the CKC as a result of having earned its Utility Degree.

Oblique shoulders: Shoulders well laid back.

Occiput: Upper, back point of the skull.

Occipital protuberance: A prominently raised occiput characteristic of some gun-dog breeds.

Oestrus: The period during which a bitch is ready to accept a dog for mating.

Open bitch: A bitch that can be bred.

Open class: A class at dog shows in which all dogs of a breed, champions, and imported dogs included may compete.

Otter tail: Thick at the root, round, and tapering, with the hair parted or divided on the underside.

Out at elbows: Elbows turning out from the body as opposed to being held close.

Out at shoulder: With shoulder blades loosely attached to the body, leaving the shoulders jutting out in relief and increasing the breadth of the front.

Outcrossing: The mating of unrelated individuals of the same breed.

Oval chest: Chest deeper than wide.

Overhang: A heavy or pronounced brow. (*e.g.,* Pekingese)

Overreaching: Fault in the trot caused by more angulation and drive from behind than in front, so that the rear feet are forced to step to one side of the forefeet to avoid interfering or clipping.

Overshot: The front teeth (incisors) of the upper jaw overlap and do not touch the front teeth of the lower jaw when the mouth is closed.

Pace: A gait at which the left foreleg and left hind leg advance in unison, then the right foreleg and right hind leg. Pacing tends to produce a rolling motion of the body.

Pack: Several hounds kept together in one kennel. Mixed pack is composed of dogs and bitches.

Padding: A compensating action to offset constant concussion when a straight front is subjected to overdrive from the rear; the front feet flip upward in a split-second delaying action to co-ordinate the stride of forelegs with a longer stride from behind.

Paddling: A gaiting fault, so named for its similarity to the swing and dip of a canoeist's paddle. Pinching in at the elbows and shoulder joints causes the front legs to swing forward on a stiff outward arc. Also referred to as "tied at the elbows."

Pads: Tough, shock-absorbing projections on the underside of the feet; soles.

Paper foot: A flat foot with thin pads.

Particolour: Variegated in patches of two or more colours.

Pastern: Leg below the knee of the front leg or below the hock of the hind leg.

Peak: See *Occiput*.

Pedigree: The written record of a dog's descent of three generations or more.

Pencilling: Black lines dividing the tan on the toes. (*e.g.*, Manchester Terrier)

Pied: Comparatively large patches of two or more colours; piebald, particoloured.

Pigeon-breast: A narrow chest with a short protruding breastbone.

Pigeon-toed: Toes pointing in.

Pig jaw: See *Overshot*.

Pile: Dense undercoat of soft hair.

Pincer bite: See *Level bite*.

Pitching: Severe rocking of the haunches as the rear legs swing forward in a wide arc rather than flexing normally at the stifle and hock.

Plume: Feathery tail carried over the back, as in the Pomeranian; also, a long fringe of hair hanging from the tail as in Setters.

Poach: When hunting, to trespass on private property.

Point: The immovable stance of the hunting dog taken to indicate the presence and position of game.

Pointer: A dog which smells out game and then points until the hunter is ready to fire.

Points: Colour on face, ears, legs, and tail when correlated—usually white, black, or tan.

Police dog: Any dog trained for police work.

Pompon: A rounded tuft of hair left on the end of the tail when the coat is clipped. (*e.g.*, Poodle)

Pounding: Gaiting fault resultant of dog's stride being shorter in front than in the rear; forefeet strike the ground hard before the rear stride is expended.

Premium list: An advance-notice brochure sent to prospective exhibitors and containing details regarding a forthcoming show.

Prick ear: Carried erect and usually pointed at the tip.

Professional handler: A person who shows dogs for a fee.

Puppy: A dog under twelve months of age.

Pure-bred: A dog whose sire and dam belong to the same breed, and are themselves of unmixed descent since recognition of the breed.

Put down: To prepare a dog for the show ring; also used to denote a dog unplaced in competition.

Quality: High degree of excellence.

Racy: Slight in build and long in legs.

Ragged: Muscles appear ragged rather than smooth. (*e.g.*, English Foxhound)

Rangy: Long-bodied, usually lacking depth in chest.

Rat tail: The root thick and covered with soft curls; at the tip devoid of hair, or having the appearance of being clipped. (*e.g.,* Irish Water Spaniel)

Reach of front: Length of forward stride taken by forelegs.

Register: To record with the CKC a dog's breeding particulars.

Retrieve: A hunting term: the act of bringing back shot game to the handler. Also, in obedience the act of bringing back any article thrown out by the handler.

Retriever: A dog specially trained to go in quest of game a sportsman has shot, or a dog that takes readily to such work.

Ribbed up: Long ribs that angle back from the spinal column (45 degrees is ideal); last rib is long.

Ringer: A substitute for; a dog closely resembling another dog.

Ring tail: Carried up and around almost in a circle.

Roach back: A convex curvature of the back towards the loin.

Roan: A fine mixture of coloured hairs with white hairs: blue roan, orange roan, lemon roan, etc. (*e.g.,* English Cocker Spaniel)

Rocking horse: Both front and rear legs extended out from body as in old-fashioned rocking horse.

Rolling gait: Swaying, ambling action of the hindquarters when moving.

Roman nose: Nasal topline that forms a convex line; ram's nose.

Rose ear: A small drop ear which folds over and back so as to reveal the burr.

Rounding: Cutting or trimming the ends of the ear leather. (*e.g.,* English Foxhounds)

Rudder: The tail.

Ruff: Thick, longer hair growth around the neck.

Sabre tail: Carried in a semi-circle.

Sable: A lacing of black hairs over a lighter ground colour. In Collies and Shetland Sheepdogs, a brown colour ranging from golden to mahogany.

Saddle: A black marking over the back, like a saddle.

Saddle back: Overlong back, with a dip behind the withers.

Scent: The odour left by an animal on the trail (ground scent), or wafted through the air (air-borne scent).

Scenthound: A dog which tracks an animal by the odour left by the animal.

Scissors bite: A bite in which the outer side of the lower incisors touches the inner side of the upper incisors.

Screw tail: A naturally short tail twisted in more or less spiral formation.

Second thigh: That part of the hindquarter from the stifle to the hock; lower thigh.

Sedge: See *Deadgrass*.

Self-colour: One colour or whole colour except for lighter shadings.

Seeing Eye dog: A dog trained by the American institution, The Seeing Eye, as guide to the blind.

Semi-prick ears: Ears carried erect with just the tips leaning forward.

Septum: The line extending vertically between the nostrils.

Setter: Any of a breed of longhaired bird dog; they are trained to find the game and point out its position by standing rigid (formerly by crouching).

Set up: Posed so as to make the most of the dog's appearance for the show ring.

Shelly: A shallow, narrow body, lacking the correct amount of bone.

Shoulder height: Height of dog's body as measured from the shoulders to the ground.

Sickle hocked: Inability to straighten the hock joint on the back reach of the hind leg. Also, hocks too bent, shaped like a sickle.

Sickle tail: Carried out and up in a semi-circle.

Sidewheeling: See *Crabbing*.

Sight hound: See *Gazehound*.

Single tracking: All footprints falling on a single line of travel. When a dog breaks into a trot, his body is supported by only two legs at a time, which move as alternating diagonal pairs. To achieve balance, his legs angle inward toward a centre line beneath his body, and the greater the speed, the closer they come to tracking on a single line.

Sire: The male parent.

Skully: Thick and coarse through skull.

Slab-sided: Flat ribs with too little spring from spinal column.

Sled dogs: Dogs worked usually in teams to draw sleds.

Slew feet: Feet turned out.

Sloping shoulder: The shoulder blade set obliquely or "laid back."

Smooth coat: Short hair, close-lying.

Snatching hocks: A gaiting fault indicated by a quick outward snatching of the hock as it passes the supporting leg and twists the rear pastern far in beneath the body. The action causes noticeable rocking in the rear quarters.

Snipey: A pointed, weak muzzle.

Soundness: Free from flaws or defects, firm and strong.

Spay: To perform a surgical operation on the bitch's reproductive organs to prevent conception. (Ovariohysterectomy)

Speak: To bark.

Spectacles: Shadings or dark markings over or around the eyes or from eyes to ears.

Spike tail: Straight short tail that tapers rapidly along its length.

Splashed: Irregularly patched, colour on white or white on colour.

Splay foot: A flat foot with toes spreading; open foot, open-toed.

Spread: Width between the forelegs when accentuated. (*e.g.,* Bulldog)

Spread hocks: Hocks pointing outward.

Spring: See *Flush.*

Spring of ribs: Curvature of ribs for heart and lung capacity.

Squirrel tail: Carried up and curving more or less forward.

Stacking: See *Set up.*

Stake: Designation of a class, used in field trial competition.

Stance: Manner of standing.

Standard: A description of the ideal dog of each recognized breed, to serve as a word pattern by which dogs are judged at shows.

Standoff coat: A long or heavy coat that stands off from the body.

Staring coat: The hair dry, harsh and sometimes curling at the tips.

Station: Comparative height from the ground, as high-stationed, low-stationed.

Stern: Tail.

Sternum: Breastbone.

Stifle: The joint of the hind leg between the thigh and the second thigh; the dog's knee.

Stilted: The choppy, up-and-down gait of the straight-hocked dog.

Stop: The step up from muzzle to skull; indentation between the eyes where the nasal bone and skull meet.

Straight-hocked: Lacking appreciable angulation at the hock joints; straight behind.

Straight shoulders: The shoulder blades rather straight up and down, as opposed to sloping or "well laid back."

Stud Book: A record of the breeding particulars of dogs of recognized breeds.

Stud dog: A male dog used for breeding purposes.

Substance: Bone.

Superciliary arches: The ridge projection, or prominence of the frontal bone of the skull over the eye; the brow.

Suspension trot: See *Flying trot.*

Sway back: Concave curvature of the back line between the withers and the hip bones.

Symmetry: Pleasing balance between all parts of the dog.

Tail-set: How the base of the tail sets on the rump.

T.D. (Tracking Dog): A suffix used with the name of a dog that has been recorded a Tracking Dog as a result of having passed a CKC-licensed or member tracking test. The title may be combined with the U.D. title and shown as U.D.T.

Team: Usually four dogs.

Terrier: A group of dogs used originally for hunting vermin.

Terrier front: Straight front, as found on Fox Terriers.

Thigh: The hindquarter from hip to stifle.

Throatiness: An excess of loose skin under the throat.

Thumb marks: Black spots on the region of the pastern.

Ticked: Small, isolated areas of black or coloured hairs on a white ground.

Tied at the elbows: See *Paddling*.

Timber: Bone, especially of the legs.

Tongue: The barking or baying of hounds on the trail, as to give tongue.

Topknot: A tuft of longer hair on top of the head.

Topline: The dog's outline from just behind the withers to the tail set.

Toy dog: One of a group of dogs characterized by very small size.

Trace: A dark stripe down the back of the Pug.

Tracking Dog: See *T.D.*

Trail: To hunt by following ground scent.

Triangular eye: The eye set in surrounding tissue of triangular shape; three-cornered eye.

Tricolour: Three distinct colours, usually black and white with tan markings. The latter are usually found over the eyes, on the cheeks, inside the ears, on the chest and under the vent. Where specific markings are required, see individual breed standards.

Trim: To groom the coat by plucking or clipping.

Trot: A rhythmic two-beat diagonal gait in which the feet at diagonally opposite ends of the body strike the ground together, *i.e.*, right hind with left front and left hind with right front.

Trumpet: The slight depression or hollow on either side of the skull just behind the orbit or eye socket, the region comparable with the temple in man.

Truncated: Cut off. (Old English standard calls for jaw that is square and truncated.)

Tuck-up: Characterized by markedly shallower body depth at the loin; small-waisted.

Tulip ear: Ears carried with a slight forward curvature.

Turn-up: An uptilted foreface.

Twisting hocks: A gaiting fault in which the hock joints twist both ways as they flex or bear weight. Also called "rubber hocks."

Type: The characteristic qualities distinguishing a breed; the embodiment of a standard's essentials.

U.D. (Utility Dog): A suffix used with the name of a dog that has been recorded a Utility Dog by the CKC as a result of having won certain minimum scores in Utility Classes at a specified number of CKC-licensed or member obedience trials. The title may be combined with the T.D. title and shown as U.D.T.

Undershot: The front teeth (incisors) of the lower jaw overlapping or projecting beyond the front teeth of the upper jaw when the mouth is closed.

Unilateral cryptorchid: See *Cryptorchid*.

Upper arm: The humerus or bone of the foreleg, between the shoulder blade and the forearm.

Utility Dog: See *U.D.*

Varminty: A keen, very bright or piercing expression.

Vent: The anal opening.

Walk: Gaiting pattern in which three legs are in support of the body at all times, each foot lifting from the ground one at a time in regular sequence.

Walleye: An eye with a whitish iris; a blue eye, fisheye, pearl eye.

Weaving: See *Crossing over*.

Weedy: An insufficient amount of bone; light-boned.

Well let down: Having hocks close to the ground.

Wet: Loose or superfluous skin; with dewlap.

Wheaten: Pale yellow or fawn colour.

Wheel back: The back line arched markedly over the loin; roached.

Whelps: Unweaned puppies.

Whip tail: Carried out stiffly straight, and pointed.

Whisker: Longer hairs on muzzle sides and underjaw.

Wind: To catch the scent of game.

Winging: A gaiting fault; one or both front feet twist outward as the limbs swing forward.

Winners: An award given at dog shows to the best dog (Winners Dog) and best bitch (Winners Bitch) competing in regular classes.

Wirehair: A coat of hard, crisp, wiry texture.

Withers: The peak of the dorsal vertebrae; the highest part of the body just behind the neck and between the shoulders.

Wrinkle: Loose, folding skin on forehead and foreface.

Wry mouth: Lower jaw does not line up with upper jaw.

INDEX